America, Sea Power, and the World

America, Sea Power, and the World

Edited by

James C. Bradford

WILEY Blackwell

This edition first published 2016

© 2016 John Wiley & Sons, Inc

Registered Office: John Wiley & Sons Ltd, The Atrium, Southern Gate, Chichester, West Sussex, PO19 8SQ, UK
Editorial Offices: 350 Main Street, Malden, MA 02148–5020, USA
9600 Garsington Road, Oxford, OX4 2DQ, UK
The Atrium, Southern Gate, Chichester, West Sussex, PO19 8SQ, UK

For details of our global editorial offices, for customer services, and for information about how to apply for permission to reuse the copyright material in this book please see our website at www.wiley.com/wiley-blackwell.

The right of James C. Bradford to be identified as the author of the editorial material in this work has been asserted in accordance with the UK Copyright, Designs and Patents Act 1988.

Library of Congress Cataloging-in-Publication Data applied for.

9781118927922 (hardback)
9781118927939 (paperback)

A catalogue record for this book is available from the British Library.

Cover image: Dean Mosher, *The Battle of Flamborough Head,* oil on canvas. © Dean Mosher

Set in 10/12pt Bembo Std by Aptara Inc., New Delhi, India

Printed by C.O.S. Printers Pte Ltd, Singapore

1   2016

To

Members of the United States Naval Academy
Class of 1957

They made and appreciate history

Contents

Contributors

1 Sea Power and the Modern State System, by James C. Bradford

James C. Bradford, Professor of History at Texas A&M University, has been a Visiting Professor at the Air War College and held the Class of 1957 Distinguished Chair in Naval Heritage at the US Naval Academy. He edited *The Papers of John Paul Jones* (1986), *The Atlas of American Military History* (2003), the *Companion to American Military History* (2009), and *The International Encyclopedia of Military History* (2006). A naval and maritime historian, he served as president of the North American Society for Oceanic History and was an inaugural recipient of the Naval Historical Foundation's Commodore Dudley W. Knox Naval History Lifetime Achievement Award in 2013.

2 The American War for Independence at Sea, by Virginia W. Lunsford

Virginia W. Lunsford, Associate Professor of History at the US Naval Academy, specializes in early-modern maritime history, especially Age of Sail naval warfare and the history of piracy. She holds a PhD from Harvard University and is the author of *Piracy and Privateering in the Golden Age Netherlands* (2005). Among other endeavors, she currently is writing *Dead Men Tell No Tales: A Cultural History of Piracy in the Modern Age* and working on a collaborative Franco-American research project exploring the French role in the naval history of the American Revolution.

3 Genesis of the US Navy, 1785–1806, by Joseph P. Slaughter

Joseph P. Slaughter is Junior Permanent Military Professor in Early American History at the US Naval Academy. His MA thesis (University of Maryland)

"A Navy in the New Republic" examines the debates over the reestablishment of the Navy in the early national period, while his PhD research investigates the intersection of early nineteenth-century religious revivals, emergent technologies, and the market revolution. He resides in Annapolis with his wife Casey, daughter Wren, and son Graydon.

4 The Naval War of 1812 and the Confirmation of Independence, 1807–1815, by Gene Allen Smith

Gene Allen Smith is Professor of History at Texas Christian University in Fort Worth. During the 2013–2014 academic year he served as the Class of 1957 Distinguished Chair in Naval Heritage at the US Naval Academy. He is the author or editor of numerous books, articles, and reviews on the War of 1812, naval and maritime history, and territorial expansion along the Gulf of Mexico, and his most recent book is *The Slaves' Gamble: Choosing Sides in the War of 1812* (2013). Since 2002 he has served as the director of the Center for Texas Studies at Texas Christian University.

5 The Squadron Navy: Agent of a Commercial Empire, 1815–1890, by John H. Schroeder

John H. Schroeder is Chancellor Emeritus and Professor Emeritus at the University of Wisconsin–Milwaukee. He served as the Class of 1957 Distinguished Professor of American Naval Heritage at the US Naval Academy in 2010–2011. He is the author of numerous articles and books including *The Shaping of a Maritime Empire: The Role of the US Navy, 1829–1861* (1985); biographies of Commodore Matthew C. Perry (2001) and Commodore John

Rodgers (2006); and *The Battle of Lake Champlain* (2015). His biography of Perry won the Theodore and Franklin D. Roosevelt Prize for American Naval History in 2002.

6 Technological Revolution at Sea, by William M. McBride

William M. McBride is Professor of History at the US Naval Academy, where he teaches courses in the history of technology, science, and engineering as well as naval and military history. He is the author of *Technological Change and the United States Navy, 1865–1945* (2000). Prior to coming to Annapolis, he was on the history faculty at James Madison University, where he was named inaugural Edna T. Shaeffer Distinguished Humanist.

7 The Civil War: Blockade and Counter-Blockade, by Craig L. Symonds

Craig L. Symonds, Professor Emeritus at the US Naval Academy, is the author of numerous works, including *Decision at Sea: Five Naval Battles that Shaped American History* (2005), *Lincoln and His Admirals* (2008), and *The Civil War at Sea* (2012). They have earned him the Theodore and Franklin D. Roosevelt Prize in Naval History (2006), the Barondess Prize (2009), the Lincoln Prize (2009), the Abraham Lincoln Book Award (2010), and other awards. Symonds returned to the Naval Academy to hold the Class of 1957 Distinguished Chair in Naval Heritage from 2011 to 2012. In 2014, the Naval Historical Foundation awarded him the Commodore Dudley W. Knox Naval History Lifetime Achievement Award.

8 The Civil War on Rivers and Coastal Waters, by Wayne Hsieh

Wayne Wei-siang Hsieh, Associate Professor of History at the US Naval Academy, is the author of *West Pointers and the Civil War: The Old Army in War and Peace* (2009), along with various academic articles. Hsieh

was detailed to the Department of State between July 2008 and June 2009 to serve as the senior civilian US government official assigned to the Tuz district of Iraq, where he worked among the area's 150,000 inhabitants on ethnic political issues.

9 The New Navy, 1865–1895, by Frederick S. Harrod

Frederick S. Harrod, Professor of History at the US Naval Academy, received a bachelor of arts from Carleton College and a doctorate from Northwestern University. He is the author of *Manning the New Navy: The Development of a Modern Naval Enlisted Force, 1899–1940* (1978) and several articles on naval history including "New Technology in the Old Navy: The United States Navy during the 1870s" (1993).

10 War with Spain and the Revolution in Naval Affairs, 1895–1910, by James C. Rentfrow

James C. "Chris" Rentfrow, US Naval Academy Class of 1989, flew the EA-6B Prowler before being selected to participate in the Permanent Military Professor program. Commander Rentfrow completed his doctoral work at the University of Maryland, College Park, graduating in 2012, and taught at the US Naval War College before joining the faculty at the US Naval Academy, where he teaches US and naval history. His book, *Home Squadron: The US Navy on the North Atlantic Station*, was published in 2014.

11 Defending Imperial Interests in Asia and the Caribbean, 1898–1941, by Aaron B. O'Connell

Aaron B. O'Connell is an Associate Professor of History at the US Naval Academy and a Lieutenant Colonel in the Marine Corps Reserve. His first book, *Underdogs: The Making of the Modern Marine Corps*, was published in 2012. He is currently writing a history of the American War in Afghanistan.

12 Naval Rivalry and World War I at Sea, 1900–1920, by Jon K. Hendrickson

Jon K. Hendrickson earned his PhD in military history from the Ohio State University in 2012 and was the first Class of 1957 Postdoctoral Fellow in Naval History at the US Naval Academy. The author of *Crisis in the Mediterranean: Naval Competition and Great Power Politics in the Mediterranean, 1904–1914* (2014), he currently teaches at Coastal Carolina University in Conway, South Carolina.

13 Finding Certainty in Uncertain Times: The Navy in the Interwar Years, by Craig C. Felker

Craig C. Felker joined the faculty of the History Department at the US Naval Academy in June 2004 and now serves as its chair. Captain Felker's publications include *Testing American Sea Power: US Navy Strategic Exercises, 1923–1940* (2007) and *New Interpretations in Naval History*, an edited collection of papers from the 2011 Naval History Symposium. In December 2011 he returned from a one-year deployment to Afghanistan, serving as the command historian and commanding officer, US Navy detachment, for NATO Training Mission Afghanistan.

14 World War II in the Atlantic and Mediterranean, by Marcus O. Jones

Marcus Jones is Professor of History at the US Naval Academy. He took his degrees from the Ohio State University and the University of Hamburg, Germany, and finished his PhD at Yale University in 2005. His publications on World War II, U-boat design and construction, and the strategic policy of Bismarckian Germany and the Kaiserreich include *Nazi Steel: Friedrich Flick and German Expansion in Western Europe, 1940–1944* (2012).

15 Defense in the Pacific, 1937–1943, by Davin O'Hora

Davin O'Hora teaches US naval history and the history of airpower at the US Naval Academy. He holds a BA in history from Florida State University

and an MA in diplomacy and military studies from Hawaii Pacific University. As a naval flight officer flying the carrier-based E-2C Hawkeye, he has made numerous deployments to the Mediterranean and Arabian Gulf and flown combat missions over Iraq. Between deployments he has served on major staffs in both the Pacific and the Middle East.

16 Offensive in the Pacific, 1943–1944, by William F. Trimble

William F. Trimble, Professor Emeritus at Auburn University in Alabama, held the Class of 1957 Distinguished Chair in Naval Heritage at the US Naval Academy from 2014 to 2015. His many books include *Wings for the Navy: A History of the Naval Aircraft Factory* (1990), *Admiral William A. Moffett: Architect of Naval Aviation* (1994), *Jerome C. Hunsaker and the Rise of American Aeronautics* (2002), *Attack from the Sea: A History of the US Navy's Seaplane Striking Force* (2005), and *Hero of the Air: Glenn Curtiss and the Birth of Naval Aviation* (2010). In 2011 he received the Admiral Arthur W. Radford Award for Excellence in Naval Aviation History and Literature from the Naval Aviation Museum Foundation.

17 The Victory of Sea Power in the Pacific, by Edward J. Marolda

Edward J. Marolda, whose 40-year career in the US government included service as the Director of Naval History (Acting) and Senior Historian of the Navy at the Naval Historical Center, Washington, DC, served as a US Army officer in Vietnam during 1969 and 1970. He earned a PhD from George Washington University in 1990 and is the author, coauthor, or editor of 15 books, including *FDR and the US Navy* (1998), *The US Navy in the Korean War* (2007), *Ready Sea Power: A History of the US Seventh Fleet* (2012), and seven works on the Vietnam War. Marolda currently teaches a course on the United States and China during the Cold War at Georgetown University

18   The Uneasy Transition, 1945–1953, by Kenneth W. Estes

Kenneth W. Estes, a 1969 Naval Academy graduate, served in a variety of command and staff assignments in the US Marine Corps until his retirement in 1993. The recipient of a doctorate in European history in 1984, he has taught at Duke University and the US Naval Academy. Estes has edited or written over a dozen books, including *Marines under Armor: The Marine Corps and the Armored Fighting Vehicle, 1916–2000* (2000), *Into the Breach at Pusan: The 1st Provisional Marine Brigade in the Korean War* (2012), and *A European Anabasis: Western European Volunteers in the German Army and SS, 1940–45* (2014), and contributed numerous chapters and essays to other compendiums, plus articles in military and academic journals. In 1992 he became an Honorary Legionnaire in the Spanish Legion, and, in 2001, garnered a Gutenberg-e Prize from the American Historical Association for a Distinguished Dissertation in History.

19   Cold War Challenges, 1953–1963, by Lori L. Bogle

Lori L. Bogle, a cultural and intellectual historian, teaches at the US Naval Academy. The author of *The Pentagon's Battle for the American Mind: The Early Cold War* (2004) and several journal articles, she is currently working on another book-length study, "Selling Sea Power: Theodore Roosevelt and Turn of the Century Naval Public Relations."

20   The Test of Vietnam, by Richard A. Ruth

Richard A. Ruth teaches Southeast Asian history at the US Naval Academy. He worked as a field agent for American non-governmental aid agencies in Vietnam, Cambodia, and Thailand from 1989 to 1995; earned his PhD in history at Cornell University in 2007, specializing in Southeast Asia during the 1960s and 1970; and is the author of *In Buddha's Company: Thai Soldiers in the Vietnam War* (2010). Currently, he is finishing a history about the origins of the Royal Thai Navy.

21   Twilight of the Cold War: Contraction, Reform, and Revival, by Joseph T. Stanik

Joseph T. Stanik, a retired US Navy surface warfare officer and former history instructor at the US Naval Academy, is the author of *"Swift and Effective Retribution": The US Sixth Fleet and the Confrontation with Qaddafi* (1996) and *El Dorado Canyon: Reagan's Undeclared War with Qaddafi* (2003). Since leaving active duty, he has served as a high school history teacher with Baltimore City Public Schools. He also teaches Middle Eastern history at Anne Arundel Community College in Maryland. A 1978 graduate of the Naval Academy, he holds advanced degrees from the Naval Postgraduate School and University of Maryland, Baltimore County.

22   Contours of Conflict: Worldwide War on Terrorism, 1990–2015, by Ernest Tucker

Ernest Tucker has been a professor of history at the US Naval Academy since 1990. He has published numerous books and articles on Middle Eastern history including *The Middle East in Modern World History* (2012). He is currently finishing a monograph on the Ottoman/Turkish Red Crescent Society (a part of the International Red Cross movement) as a window on Middle Eastern life in the late nineteenth and early twentieth centuries. In 2005–2006, he was a Fulbright Senior Scholar in Istanbul, Turkey.

23   Quo Vadis? by Mark R. Hagerott

Mark R. Hagerott, Captain USN(ret.), former Deputy Director and Distinguished Professor of the US Naval Academy Center for Cyber Studies, is Chancellor of the North Dakota University System. A member of the Defense Science Board study of autonomy, his book chapters and articles have been published by the National Academy of Sciences, *Naval War College Review, Foreign Policy, Journal of Military History, Joint Forces Quarterly, Naval Institute Proceedings, Combat Studies Institute*, and, in Europe, by École Spéciale Militaire de Saint-Cyr. A former ship captain, he served on five ships including duty on both nuclear-powered ships and Aegis cruisers. He is an Afghan war veteran and Rhodes Scholar.

Maps

Tracy Ellen Smith, Cartographer

Figures

Tables

Tables

Vignettes

Preface

On Pennsylvania Avenue, midway between the White House and the Capitol Building, stands the Navy Memorial with its iconic statue, the Lone Sailor. That sailor faces, across the street, the researchers' entrance to the National Archives Building, where statues atop pedestals bear the inscriptions "What is Past is Prologue" and "Study the Past." This study accepts the challenge to "study the past" of the US Navy knowing that the Navy's history is "prologue" to its present and future and to that of the United States.

The history and development of the United States are inextricably linked to the sea. Maritime industries and commerce are vital components of the American economy and for over two centuries the Atlantic and Pacific Oceans played vital roles in protecting the United States from foreign enemies as the burgeoning American people spread across the North American continent. Conversely, in the past century, the oceans have supported the projection of American military power far beyond its shores. Though strategically an island, the United States, for a century and a half, was a component part of the Great Power System that developed during the seventeenth century. At times the system benefited the young republic, such as during its War for Independence, when Britain faced multiple enemies as a result of the balance of power among the major powers having been upset by treaties ending the Seven Years' War in 1763. During the quarter-century following the outbreak of the Wars of the French Revolution, the system had an adverse effect on the United States as belligerents sought to limit American commerce with their enemies.

The world wars of the twentieth century shattered that system and the European-dominated imperialism that accompanied it. During the late 1940s and the 1950s, the United States led the development of a new system based on fiscal stability, ever widening free trade, and increasingly democratic institutions, all sheltered by the American nuclear umbrella. The ability to navigate and trade freely in the Atlantic Ocean, a fundamental national interest of the United States since its inception, had during the twentieth century expanded to include all the oceans of the world. By the dawn of the twenty-first century that new order, the "Free World," had triumphed over its rival based upon communism and championed by the Soviet Union and the People's Republic of China. American influence, once limited to the Western Hemisphere, expanded to include such disparate areas as the Balkan Peninsula, the Indian Ocean, and the Middle East. The twenty-first century, like the seventeenth, promises to be an era of transition in world politics, one in which the United States, currently the primary defender of maritime commerce and enforced stability, must come to terms with distant but powerful continental powers and blocs in order to maintain its position of leadership in world affairs.

It is within this context of world affairs and the application of naval forces to achieve political and economic objectives that this volume offers an analytical history of American naval power. This project developed over four decades of teaching American naval history first at the US Naval Academy, then at Texas A&M University followed by a return to Annapolis to hold the Class of 1957 Distinguished Chair in Naval Heritage in 2012–2013. As is the case each year, instructors of the naval history course met regularly to discuss teaching. Conversations about the utility of various naval histories confirmed a long-held belief that a new survey of American sea power was needed. This book is the product of those conversations. It has been a joint venture of all the authors, all of whom have professional links to the Naval Academy History Department, the earliest being those of Kenneth Estes, a member of the Class of 1969 who returned to teach there during the mid-1970s; the most recent being those of William Trimble, the current Class of 1957 Distinguished Professor of Naval Heritage.

The editor outlined the chapter structure and suggested threads to develop—debates concerning the interests of the nation, the size and type of navy needed to protect those interests, and an assessment of the Navy's success in fulfilling its derived missions; during periods of conflict, the wars' aims and the strategies and campaigns devised and executed in pursuit of those aims; and the evolution of the Navy as an institution over the course of its history. No attempt was made to impose a single thesis on the contributors—all were encouraged to reach their own interpretive conclusions—but the emerging discussions found a unity that spans American naval history from the Age of Sail through the present and parallels the rise of the United States to its preeminent position in the twenty-first century. There are discernable several patterns and traditions ranging from technological innovation in ship design and weapon systems to offensive-based aggressive strategies, and a tendency toward an elitism (usually based on merit) that mirrors American society.

Any navy relies heavily on ships and weapon systems. Thus, each chapter is accompanied by a brief vignette that discusses a technological development of the era. Equally, or perhaps more important, are personnel. "Without officers what can be expected from a navy?" Captain Thomas Truxtun wrote Secretary of War James McHenry, civilian head of the Navy in 1797. "The ships cannot maneuver themselves."[1] Nearly two centuries later, Admiral James Calvert echoed this point: "Important as ships are, naval history is made by men."[2] Thus, each chapter also includes a vignette about an individual who shaped the Navy or reflected the naval service of that era. Thus, this is a story of men, machines, and missions, punctuated by the combat operations executed by the Navy in support of American national interests over the course of its existence.

The opening chapter of this study sketches naval developments leading to the mid-eighteenth century and outlines the geopolitical system of the era that gave rise to the United States and its Continental Navy, precursor of the US Navy. Succeeding chapters, with three exceptions, analyze periods of American naval history in chronological order. Chapters on the defense of American lives and property overseas during the nineteenth and early twentieth centuries and on the technological transition from the Age of Sail to the Modern Age span time periods covered in multiple chronological chapters. Other histories of the US Navy often have a chapter on naval technology between 1820 and 1860 followed by chapters on the Civil War then a section on naval technology in the late nineteenth century. Such an organization masks the fact that naval technological was constantly evolving. Wartimes speed experimentation and change rather than interrupt the process. A final chapter explores the future of naval developments. This work is neither comprehensive nor encyclopedic. Rather, it is presented to students of naval history at all levels and of all kinds—and to readers in general—as a tool with which to learn about the past and gain perspective in viewing the present and future.

Notes

1. Truxtun to McHenry, March 3, 1797, James McHenry Papers, Huntington Library, San Marino, California.

2. Calvert, *The Naval Profession* (1965), 6.

Acknowledgments

Historical scholarship is a blend of individual and collaborative endeavor and many contributed to this volume. I first discussed the concept behind the project with Richard P. Abels, chair of the Naval Academy History Department; Captain C. C. Felker, the senior naval officer in the department; and Professor Aaron B. O'Connell, Course Coordinator for the naval history core course, and, receiving their enthusiastic approval, began planning. The contributing authors bore my pleas for concise writing and my sometimes heavy-handed editing with patience. To them goes my greatest debt of gratitude.

The volume is dedicated to the Naval Academy Class of 1957 in recognition of its establishing the program that brought me and four other contributors to Annapolis. Without that program, this book would not exist. Class president Captain William H. Peerenboom offered welcome support and encouragement over the past two years. Craig Symonds and C. C. Felker provided valuable advice on topics ranging from potential contributors to content and design, and Kenneth Estes and William Peerenboom read portions of the manuscript. Charles Todorich, Naval Academy Class of 1970 and former colleague in the History Department, applied his keen eye to the page proofs.

It was a pleasure to work with cartographer Tracy Ellen Smith, whose maps complement the text. At Wiley Blackwell, Peter Coveney, who first recruited me for another project, welcomed this one; Julia Kirk, our senior project editor, guided the manuscript through publication; and Hazel Bird expertly copyedited the text. At my home institution, Texas A&M University, Kelly Cook cheerfully provided assistance whenever asked.

Judy, my wife of over 50 years, has been a constant source of support. Without her this book, and my life, would not be complete.

CHAPTER 1

Sea Power and the Modern State System

Sea Power played a major, often decisive, role in the wars that led to the rise and fall of ancient empires. Once rivers and seas became avenues rather than barriers to communication and commerce, conflict followed in the form of rivalry between traders, pirates who preyed on shipping, and governments that formed navies to protect their own commerce and seize that of others. The latter gave rise to the first warships, most of which were galleys (i.e., long vessels, propelled by oarsmen).

Sea Power in the Ancient World

Bronze-Age Minoa (c. 2000–1420 BCE) was the first thalassocracy (i.e., civilization dependent on the sea) and the first sea power. Located on the island of Crete at the nexus of trade routes between the Aegean, Adriatic, and eastern Mediterranean Seas, Minoan civilization relied largely on coastal fortifications for defense until its conquest by Mycenaeans from mainland Greece (c. 1470–1420 BCE), who operated the western world's first navy.

Sea power saved the Greek city-states from Persian domination when an Athenian-led flotilla of galleys defeated the Persian navy at the Battle of Salamis (480 BCE) and destroyed the remainder of their galleys at Mycale (479 BCE). Later during the same century Athens' fleet provided the city and its allies with their main defensive bulwark during the Peloponnesian Wars with rival Sparta. Those wars decimated Greece and led to the region's decline at the same time that Rome was rising to power in the central Mediterranean. Though best known for its infantry legions, it was the Roman navy that brought Rome victory over its rival Carthage in the Punic Wars (264–146 BCE) by allowing Rome to isolate Carthage from its colonies, cut Hannibal's army off from support from home when it invaded the Italian Peninsula, and, finally, to invade and defeat Carthage itself. Roman control of the Mediterranean facilitated commerce, including the grain trade vital to support of a city the size of Rome, and the movement of army legions to trouble spots in the empire.

Transition to the feudal system of medieval Europe brought with it myriad small states—none, except Venice, large or wealthy enough to support a significant navy—and a decline in overseas commerce. When Vikings reached North America (c.1100) and established L'Anse aux Meadows on Newfoundland, there was no political entity capable of sustaining the settlement and there were no ships with the capacity to conduct transoceanic commerce. Four centuries later, when Columbus visited the West Indies, this had changed. Poised on the brink of the modern era, Europe was developing the technology needed for overseas trade and the political and economic institutions to maintain overseas empires.

America, Sea Power, and the World, First Edition. Edited by James C. Bradford.
© 2016 John Wiley & Sons, Inc. Published 2016 by John Wiley & Sons, Inc.

The Modern World and the Great Power System

The transition from the medieval to the modern world was marked by technological advances in metallurgy, chemistry, and navigation, and by the replacement of oar-powered galleys by sailing ships of a much greater size that, by tacking, could sail against the wind. Equally important was the rise of nation states—that is, political units (states) composed of a common people (nations). These new unified entities could and often did support trade, establish overseas colonies, and construct navies.

The first nation states developed on the Iberian Peninsula; Portugal dates its emergence as a nation state from the reign of John I (1385–1433), who initiated European exploration of the Atlantic coast of Africa, and Spain became a nation state following either the 1475 marriage of Ferdinand of Aragon and Isabella of Castile or newly unified Spain's expulsion of the Moors from the whole of the peninsula except Gibraltar in 1492. That year coincided with Christopher Columbus' first voyage to the Americas. Over the next century, Portugal and Spain established the first great oceanic empires before England and France formed nation states: England after the Wars of the Roses (1455–1487) and France after the War of the Three Henrys (1587–1589). These civil wars had kept England and France from developing the characteristics of a strong nation state—that is, one with a central government (in that era a monarch) that had the allegiance of the political classes, a bureaucracy that administered an efficient tax system, and a standing army (though in England's case its Royal Navy was more important than its army).

The seventeenth century proved a transitional era during which emerged the Great Power System, which would continue for three hundred years. By 1600 Iberian power was eroding. Seven northern Netherlands provinces declared their independence from Spanish Hapsburg rule, formed the Dutch Republic, fought the Dutch War of Independence (1568–1648), and challenged the Iberians by establishing settlements on the Cape of Good Hope, the north coast of South America, Java, and elsewhere. England and France also began forming overseas empires while Prussia, Russia, and Austria rose to prominence in central and eastern Europe.

The Thirty Years' War swept Europe between 1618 and 1648. While virtually every nation was involved, the main fighting occurred in central Europe, where it decimated populations and devastated large sections of land. Following its settlement in the Treaty of Westphalia there emerged an enduring Great Power System in which five nation states—Russia, Austria, Prussia (Germany after 1870), France, and England (Great Britain after 1707)—played dominant roles. The goal was to maintain a "balance of power" that would prevent total wars such as the Thirty Years' War in the future.

Though never formally enunciated in a single document, five core tenets underlay the Great Power System: 1) five is the correct number of powers to maintain a healthy balance; 2) no great power should ever be destroyed or reduced to a position that prevented it from playing an independent role in the system; 3) no single nation should ever be allowed to grow powerful enough to threaten the continued existence of any other great power; 4) no nation has permanent friends, just permanent interests, so alliances should shift to preserve the balance; and 5) wars are acceptable tools for upholding the system. Within the system, a great (first-rate) power was one that possessed sufficient political, economic, and/or military strength that every other nation had to consider the great power's interest and possible reaction to any diplomatic or military action it might take. A great power possessed total sovereignty in its internal affairs and would consider any interference in its domestic business a *casus belli*.

Lesser nations played roles in the system based on their relative power. Second-rate, or regional, powers could pursue independent foreign policies and control their internal affairs. Great powers had to consider the interests of second-rate powers when operating in the sphere of influence of such a power. Third-rate powers controlled their foreign policy and, in a major conflict, could chose, if not to remain neutral, at least which side to join as an ally. A fourth-rate power did not have such a choice and was basically a client or satellite of a more powerful state, usually a neighbor. Fifth-rate, even weaker, powers rarely controlled even their internal affairs.

During the eighteenth and nineteenth centuries, Spain, the Ottoman Empire, Switzerland, and Sweden maintained regional-power status. The Netherlands and several lesser German states were third-rate powers, while Portugal and Denmark became third-rate powers by the eighteenth century. The United States began as a third-rate power that benefited from the system during its War for Independence and grew to be a regional power by the late nineteenth century.

During the eighteenth century Britain participated in a series of wars with various allies to counter France, which repeatedly upset the balance of power. With the defeat of Napoleon in 1814, France was finally contained, but not reduced from great power status. Instead, the other great powers forced France to accept a king who promised to not again challenge the balance of the Great Power System. The first significant blow to the system came at the end of World War I when Austria-Hungary was destroyed as a great power. Germany was temporarily reduced in power but able to begin rebuilding by the 1930s. By 1900 Italy sought great power status, as did Japan a quarter-century later. By World War I the United States had achieved virtual great power status but chose not to participate actively in world affairs until World War II, the conflict that finally destroyed the system.

Competition for Empire

During the 300 years that the system functioned, the three eastern powers competed for advantage on the Eurasian continent while Britain and France vied for economic, political, and military power not only in Europe but also in their empires in America, Asia, and Africa.

Their competition was guided by mercantilism, an economic theory that held sway in Europe from the sixteenth through the early nineteenth centuries. Mercantilists believed there was a finite amount of wealth in the world, that national wealth was measured in specie (gold and silver) reserves, and that it was the role of government to promote policies, particularly a positive balance of trade, that would build the nation's wealth and therefore its power at the expense of rival nations. Those policies included: 1) protective tariffs to stimulate internal production and limit imports that would lead to the outflow of specie; 2) establishment of colonies to produce commodities, such as sugar and tobacco, not producible at home so they would not have to be purchased from foreigners; 3) prohibiting colonies from trading with other nations so that they would purchase manufactures from the mother country, which could also profit by re-exporting colonial products to other parts of Europe; and 4) forbidding trade in foreign ships. The goal of mercantilist policy was to strengthen a nation's economy and, thereby, increase its military power.

While mercantilism is most closely identified with Jean Baptiste Colbert, French minister of finance (1662–1683), it was also the philosophical foundation for England's Navigation Acts. The first such act, passed in 1651, banned the importing of goods from outside Europe into England and its colonies in foreign ships and limited the import of goods from Europe to English ships or those of the nation that produced the goods. The Navigation Act of 1660 added a requirement that, in addition to being English-built and owned, "English ships" had to be commanded by an Englishman and have a crew that was three-quarters English. The act also included a list of "enumerated articles," including tobacco, cotton, sugar, dyewoods, and naval stores, that could only be sold by England's colonies to England, from which many were re-exported to Europe. The Navigation Act of 1663 stipulated that all European goods had to pass through England before going anywhere in the empire.

Anglo-Dutch Wars

The 1651 restriction on foreign ships was aimed directly at the Dutch, who had replaced the Portuguese as the dominant traders in Asian, Baltic, and north European waters and was a major cause of the first of three Anglo-Dutch Wars. All were largely economic conflicts.

At the start of the First Anglo-Dutch War (1652–1654), the Dutch navy had 76 warships in commission and 150 under construction or conversion from merchantmen. England could not deploy more than 123 warships so adopted the strategy commonly employed by the weaker naval power, that of *guerre de course* (i.e., commerce raiding) to force the Dutch to the negotiating table. The more powerful Dutch sought to engage and destroy the English navy— that is, they adopted a *guerre d'escadre* (i.e., combat between fleets) strategy of fleet engagements and blockades, usually employed by the stronger naval power. Despite the English capture of 1,200–1,500 Dutch merchantmen, and naval victories at Portland, the Gabbard, and Scheveningen in 1653, there was no clear victor in the war, so, with both sides nearly exhausted, a peace was signed in 1654 that settled few outstanding issues.

In 1660 Charles II, restored as king of England after nearly a decade of parliamentary rule, sought to strengthen his position by expanding English trade and settlement in America. In addition to supporting the Navigation Act of 1660, Charles granted proprietorships to supporters who would establish colonies in America that would produce taxable commodities such as sugar, rice, and indigo. With an eye to expelling Dutch shippers from the Chesapeake tobacco trade and gaining control of the lucrative fur trade, Charles ordered the capture of New Netherland, and gave the Dutch colony to his brother, James, Duke of York and Lord High Admiral of the Royal Navy. In 1664 James sent four frigates to capture the colony and renamed it New York. When England seized several Dutch trading posts in West Africa, the Dutch dispatched a fleet that took back the posts and evicted the English from their own posts in the region. The result was the Second Anglo-Dutch War (1665–1667), a conflict between evenly matched opponents. The Royal Navy defeated that of the Netherlands at the Battle of Lowestoft (1665) but lost the Four Days' Battle (1666) and was humiliated when a Dutch raid up the Thames River destroyed several English warships. By 1667, both belligerents wanted peace, so they signed the Treaty of Breda. By its terms England retained New York, the Dutch kept English settlements they had captured in Suriname, and minor changes were made to the Navigations Acts to favor Dutch traders.

The Third Anglo-Dutch War (1672–1674), part of a larger Franco-Dutch War (1672–1678), was the product of the secret Treaty of Dover, in which Charles II conspired with Louis XIV to annex parts of the Netherlands. When the Royal Navy was defeated at the Battle of Texel (1673) and forced to abandon its blockade of Dutch ports, Parliament compelled Charles to end the war. French pressure on Dutch land borders forced the Netherlands to invest less in its navy and more in its army. The mid-sixteenth century proved to be the height of Dutch imperial expansion and oceanic trade. The Netherlands simply had too small a population and borders that were too difficult to defend to be a great power.

Development of Modern Navies

Modern navies with their purpose-built warships and permanent administrative bureaucracies first developed during the late seventeenth century. Prior to this era navies were ad hoc in nature as governments cobbled together fleets largely composed of converted merchantmen.

During the Anglo-Dutch Wars, commanders on both sides sought to bring order to naval engagements. Instead of their warships individually attacking any target that presented itself, commanders began organizing their ships in formations designed to place them in mutually supportive positions as they attacked the enemy. The line-ahead formation, in which warships formed a single column and remained together as they maneuvered and engaged the enemy, soon became the preferred tactic (see Figure 1.1). Victory usually went to the fleet that could bring the most firepower to bear on its opponent. Converted merchantmen of various sizes and sailing characteristics carrying varying numbers of cannon that fired differing sized shot for variable distances simply could not effectively execute line-ahead tactics. Successful execution of such tactics required purpose-built warships of common design, armed with standardized cannon, and sailed by trained crewmen led by experienced officers. To design, construct, and maintain such warships required a permanent shore staff. The development of modern navies with these characteristics was spurred by the Anglo-French wars that began in 1688.

Figure 1.1 Battle of the Virginia Capes, 1781. British and French ships-of-the-line in parallel line-ahead columns exchange broadsides. French victory in the battle led to the British loss at Yorktown and to the Treaty of Paris, which recognized the independence of the United States. *Source:* Courtesy of the US Navy Art Collection, Washington, DC. US Naval History and Heritage Command Photograph.

War of the Grand Alliance (1688–1697)

France emerged from the Franco-Dutch War as the most powerful nation in Europe, yet Louis XIV sought to extend French territory further to the north and east. His aggression precipitated the War of the Grand Alliance, in which the Anglo-Dutch leader, William of Orange, formed the Grand Alliance, which included England, to contain France. Military operations centered in the Rhineland but spread to Asia and the Caribbean, where the English and Dutch navies gave them an advantage. In North America, where the conflict was called King William's War, France and its Algonquin Indian allies dominated in the interior, but in 1690 New Englanders captured Port Royal in Acadia and launched an unsuccessful attack on Quebec via the St. Lawrence River. In 1697 most of the belligerents neared financial exhaustion so signed the Treaty of Ryswick, which, except for

French retention of Lorraine, was a *status quo antebellum* treaty—that is, one that brought peace by returning to prewar conditions, including borders.

The French and Allied navies were roughly equal in numbers when the war began in 1688, but, unable to match Allied construction—during the last four years of the war, France completed 19 major warships, the Dutch 22, and England 58—France adopted a *guerre de course* strategy and relied largely on privateers to attack English and Dutch merchant ships.

Privateering

Privateering provided a means for a government to enlist private enterprise in maritime warfare. The goal was to seize enemy merchantmen and their cargoes and thereby to damage the enemy's economy and drive up insurance rates until merchants pressured their government to make peace. A legal system had developed by the mid-seventeenth century under which a government could issue a letter of marque (i.e., a license) to investors who would obtain, arm, and fit out a ship to attack enemy vessels during wartime. Regulations required that the capture of a vessel be reviewed by a prize court, and, if the captured ship was proved to be enemy-owned or carrying enemy-owned cargo, that the ship and its cargo be sold at auction. The government that issued the letter of marque would receive a portion of the proceeds from the sale and the rest would be divided between the investors, officers, and crew of the privateer that made the capture. Weaker naval powers, including the young United States, often used privateering to bring economic pressure on their opponents and to force those opponents to deploy naval assets to protect their merchant shipping. A vessel engaged in privateering was itself referred to as a "privateer," defined by an eighteenth-century maritime dictionary as a privately owned ship sent in wartime "to cruise against and among the enemy, taking, sinking or burning their shipping" in exchange for shares of any captured prizes.[1]

War of the Spanish Succession, 1701–1714

When Charles II of Spain died childless in 1700, Leopold I of the Austrian Hapsburgs claimed the Spanish throne for an heir as did Louis XIV of France. To prevent upsetting the balance of power through a union between France (the strongest military power in Europe) and Spain (with its huge empire), a coalition led by Austria, England, and Prussia declared war on France (called Queen Anne's War in North America). The bulk of the fighting again took place in Europe, though it spread to the English, French, and Spanish empires, where England's Royal Navy and troops from New England again captured Port Royal and launched assaults on Quebec, which, like the one in 1690, failed.

Allied victory at Blenheim led to the Treaty of Utrecht (1713), which banned union of the French and Spanish thrones, gave Gibraltar to Britain (formed by the union of England and Scotland in 1707), and attempted to extend the balance of power from Europe to North America by transferring Acadia (renamed Nova Scotia), Newfoundland, and Hudson's Bay to Britain. The result was three and a half decades of peace among the great powers of Europe.

By war's end the Royal Navy's transition to a modern, professional force with a mature administration, career officer corps, and purpose-built warships was complete.

Sailing Warships

By the eighteenth century purpose-built warships had become the norm in all major navies, though a few minor navies, such as the Continental Navy of Britain's rebelling North American colonies, continued to employ converted merchantmen. Warships were divided into three broad groupings identified by their function and number of guns carried.

Ships-of-the-line took their name from their ability to stand in the line of battle formation employed to engage enemy squadrons and fleets. The largest, first-rate warships had three continuous decks and carried 90 or more guns. Few in number, these usually served as flagships. By the mid-eighteenth century the standard ship-of-the-line was a third-rate that had 74 guns mounted on two continuous decks plus a forecastle and quarterdeck. Fourth-rate warships were usually classified as ships-of-the-line because they had two continuous gun decks, but they were often used like frigates because of their limited firepower (see Table 1.1).

Frigates, with their single continuous gundeck, came next in size. Even the largest never stood in the battle line but supported it by scouting, carrying dispatches, and conveying signals during engagements. Frigates also operated independently of the fleet, convoying merchantmen, patrolling empires, and countering piracy.

Unrated warships, including sloops, brigs, and pinnaces, carried fewer than 20 guns. These shallower-draft, faster sailing vessels filled a variety of functions including carrying dispatches and patrolling

---

[1] William Falconer, *A New Universal Dictionary of the Marine* 1830 [1769], 353.

Table 1.1 Royal Navy warship classes in 1800.

Class	Rate	Guns[a] (size built[b])	Through gun decks	Number of crewmen	Number in commission
Ships-of-the-line	First rate	100–120 (100, 110)[c]	3	850–950	11
	Second rate	90–99 (90, 98)[d]	3	700–750	21
	Third rate	60–89 (64, 74, 80)[e]	2	600–700	148
	Fourth rate	50–60 (50)[f]	2	350–450	20
Frigates	Fifth rate	30–50 (36, 38, 40, 44)	1	200–350	162
	Sixth rate	20–30	1	150–200	51
Sloops and brigs	Not rated	10–20 (16, 18)	1	100–120	134
Bomb ketches	Not rated	8	1	>120	127

[a] "Guns" designates the range of the number of guns a warship was designed to carry; actual armaments varied.
[b] "Size built" identifies the size (as designated in terms of guns designed to carry) of warship built for the Royal Navy.
[c] The Royal Navy's last 100-gun ship, *Queen Charlotte*, was launched in 1800; its first 110-gun ship, *Ville de Paris*, was completed in 1795.
[d] The last 90-gun ships were launched in 1767; the first 98-gun ship was launched in 1772.
[e] Very few 64s were constructed after 1780, because 74s could better carry 32-pound guns.
[f] The last fourth-rate ship-of-the-line was launched in 1759.

off enemy harbors to alert the ships-of-the-line on blockade duty when enemy ships put to sea. Bomb ketches were armed with mortars that fired explosive "bombs" in high trajectories used to attack coastal fortifications.

Wars of the Mid-Eighteenth Century

War returned to the Atlantic world in 1739 when conflicts over English trading in Spanish America led to the War of Jenkins' Ear, so named for an incident in which the captain of a Spanish revenue cutter ordered the cutting off of the left ear of Robert Jenkins, an English merchant captain whom he accused of smuggling. Added to other cases of "Spanish Depredations upon the British Subjects," the incident led Britain's Parliament to declare war on Spain in 1739.[2] Within a year the Royal Navy captured Porto Bello in Panama but failed in attempts to take Cartagena on the Caribbean coast of South America, as did an attempt by forces from Georgia to capture St. Augustine in Spanish Florida.

In 1740 this Anglo–Spanish war merged with the War of Austrian Succession, a conflict pitting France and Prussia—which contested the right of Maria Theresa of Austria to succeed her father, Charles VI, as ruler of the Hapsburg family lands—against Austria, Britain, and Russia. Each side was joined by lesser powers in a series of inconclusive wars that lasted until 1748. Operations were equally indecisive in King George's War, the North American phase of the war, except for the capture of Louisbourg on Cape Breton Island by Massachusetts militia with the support of the Royal Navy in 1745. That fortress, the "Gibraltar of America," was returned to France by *status quo ante bellum* provisions of the 1748 Treaty of Aix-la-Chapelle.

[2] *The History and Proceedings of the House of Commons*, vol. 10: *1737–1739* (1742), 159–182.

Ships-of-the-Line

At the Battle of the Gabbard in 1653, the British abandoned single-ship actions and boarding tactics, formed their ships in a single column, and engaged the Dutch broadside-to-broadside. The new strategy required stout warships able to "stand in the line," absorb fire from the enemy, and return effective fire. In the beginning, typical ships-of-the-line carried 30 guns, a number that had risen to 50 by 1700, 64 by 1750, 74 by 1800, and 80 by 1840. Ships-of-the-line were usually 160 to 200 feet long and had two or three gun decks. The lowest gun deck carried the largest cannon, usually 42-pounders (42 pounds being the weight of the cannon balls it fired) or 32-pounders. The middle deck mounted 24-pounders and the upper deck 12-pounders. Long-range nine-pounders were often mounted on the forecastle and quarterdeck. The fire power of a warship was expressed in "weight of broadside," meaning the total weight of shot that could be fired in a single volley by all the guns on one side of a warship. A third-rate 74, the standard ship-of-the-line in Britain's Royal Navy during the late eighteenth century, could deliver a broadside weight of approximately 1,750 pounds. With 140 guns, the *Pennsylvania* was the largest US Navy sailing ship. Ships-of-the-line were so expensive that only a few nations could afford to construct, maintain, and man a significant number. Ships-of-the-line soon became symbols of national prestige, as did their descendants, during the early twentieth century.

USS *Pennsylvania*. The largest sailing ship ever built by the US Navy, the 140-gun ship-of-the-line was authorized in 1816, laid down in 1821, and commissioned in 1837. Lithograph by Currier & Ives, 1848. *Source:* Currier & Ives: A catalogue raisonné / compiled by Gale Research. Detroit, MI : Gale Research, ca. 1983, no. 6850. Library of Congress Prints and Photographs Division.

William Pitt

William Pitt (1708–1778) was one of Britain's great wartime prime ministers. He believed that Britain's future lay in its overseas empire rather than as a continental power. As the dominant member of the British government between 1756 and 1761, he made North America and India the focus of British operations during the Seven Years' War and adopted a "peripheral strategy" in which Britain would not commit a major army to Europe but would instead support a continental ally by blockading their common enemy and conducting diversionary attacks on the coasts of enemy-held territory that would force that enemy to dissipate its resources by stationing troops in port cities and responding to British conjunct operations. Subsequent British leaders followed these policies for over two centuries. Pitt resigned from the government when it refused to declare war on Spain in 1761, and criticized the 1763 peace treaty with France as too lenient. Pitt remained a member of the House of Commons, where he opposed the Stamp Act. He argued that, while Parliament had the power to enact legislation, including external taxes for Britain's colonies, it did not have the power to levy internal taxes, such as the Stamp Act. In 1766 Pitt moved to the House of Lords as Earl of Chatham. Consistently focusing on France as Britain's archenemy, he sought first compromise then reconciliation with the Americans before his death in 1778.

William Pitt, after a portrait by Richard Brompton, 1771. *Source:* © National Portrait Gallery, London.

Nothing having been settled between the British and French empires, colonists from both continued to jockey for position, and the next war between the antagonists was the first to begin in America and spread to Europe. The immediate point of contention was control of the forks of the Ohio River (site of modern-day Pittsburgh), which brought with it domination of the Ohio River Valley. In 1754 Virginians began establishing a trading post at the site but were forced by the French to abandon the area. Receiving reports that the French were erecting a fort there, Virginia's governor, Lord Dunmore, sent Colonel George Washington and a party of militiamen to scout the area. When they were ambushed by French troops and their Indian allies, Dunmore sought troops from England, which dispatched General Edward Braddock to evict the French. Braddock's expedition was soundly defeated in 1755.

In 1756 the French and Indian War in America merged with the Seven Years' War in Europe to form the Great War for Empire (1756–1763), a name that reflects operations after William Pitt formed a coalition with the Duke of Newcastle and took strategic control of British conduct of the war in August 1757. Prior to that time the war had gone badly for Britain both in Europe and its empire. In Europe Britain and its ally Prussia faced a coalition of Austria, France, Russia, Spain, and Sweden—a major shift in alliances since the previous war. The coalition overran George II's Hanover and Minorca was lost to France. Meanwhile, in America, French forces pressed colonial outposts in an arc from Nova Scotia to western Pennsylvania.

Upon taking office, Pitt fundamentally altered British national strategy—henceforth, he announced, Britain would abandon territorial ambitions on the continent of Europe and seek its future in its empire. In pursuit of this policy, Pitt adopted a "peripheral strategy" for conducting the war in Europe, one in which Britain would subsidize its allies, in this case

Prussia, but not commit a major army to the continent. Instead it would use the Royal Navy to blockade enemy ports cutting off trade and support from the outside and launch a series of raids and conjunct operations to tie down enemy forces away from the main theater of operations. Forces would also be dispatched to the empire to protect and expand Britain's colonial possessions. These principles characterized British military strategy and foreign policy for the next two centuries. The military strategy underlay the Duke of Wellington's Iberian Campaign during the Napoleonic Wars, the Gallipoli Campaign of World War I, and British preference for the North Africa–Italy Campaigns versus a cross-channel line of attack during World War II. The 1973 abandonment of preferential trading agreements with members of the British Commonwealth of Nations, successor to the pre-World War II British Empire, and entry into the European Economic Community signified a shift in national or grand strategy.

During the Seven Years' War the new strategy led to British raids on Rochefort and the Isle d'Aix in 1757 and St. Malo and Cherbourg in 1758. Royal Navy victories at the Battles of Lagos and Quiberon Bay in 1759 ended French plans to invade Britain that year and prevented France from sending significant support to its empire where British and colonial forces had captured French Forts Frontenac on Lake Ontario, Duquesne at the forks of the Ohio River, and Louisbourg on Cape Breton Island in 1758. This set the stage for the British occupation of French forts on Lake Champlain and the capture of Quebec on the St. Lawrence River in 1759 followed by Montreal in 1760. British forces were equally successful in the West Indies, where they captured the French islands of Guadeloupe (1759) and Martinique (1762) and Spanish Havana (1762). On the other side of the world British forces seized Senegal in Africa (1758) and Karikal (1760) and Pondicherry (1761) in India from the French, and Manila in the Philippines (1762) from Spain.

In February 1763, the *status quo ante bellum* Treaty of Hubertusburg brought peace to Europe and the Treaty of Paris ended the war outside Europe. In the latter, France transferred ownership of Canada (except the tiny islands of St. Pierre and Miquelon in the Gulf of St. Lawrence), most of Louisiana east of the Mississippi River, and the islands of Dominica, Grenada, St. Vincent, and Tobago to Britain and the bulk of Louisiana to Spain. Britain returned Guadeloupe and Martinique to France. In the Eastern Hemisphere, Britain abandoned Manila to Spain and France ceded Senegal to Britain in exchange for the return of only five trading posts in southern India, a settlement that left Britain dominant in India.

The war marked a triumph for Pitt's peripheral strategy and for Britain as an empire, but, in the euphoria of victory few understood that the achievements of the past five years contained the seeds of problems that would plague the British Empire for two decades. Britain emerged from the war with a huge national debt, vast new lands to govern, and demands by West Indian planters for assistance in recovering from French depredations suffered during the war. The policies developed by the administrations of George Grenville (including the Sugar and Stamp Acts), Charles Townshend (duties on paint, lead, glass, and tea), and Lord North (the Tea and Coercive/Intolerable Acts) to deal with these problems alienated 13 of Britain's North American colonies and in only a dozen years drove them to rebellion. The removal of France from Canada freed the Americans from any dependence on Britain for defense. During that same time the use of the Royal Navy to enforce revenue laws changed its image in America from that of a guardian into one of an oppressor. Internationally, an unintended outcome of the Treaty of Paris was the upsetting of the balance of power so that, when its colonies rebelled, France assisted those colonies in their war for independence with the goal of reducing British power to reset the balance of power. France was joined in the War for American Independence by Spain and the Netherlands, Britain faced opposition from the Armed Neutrality formed by Russia, and, for the only time between 1689 and 1980, Britain was without a continental ally. Thus the stage was set for American rebellion and the emergence of the new United States.

CHAPTER 2

The American War for Independence at Sea

The American Revolution conjures up images of Paul Revere, George Washington, battles with British "Redcoats," and the Declaration of Independence. In contrast, the naval aspects of the American Revolution are not widely known or recognized. Naval warfare, however, played a crucial role in the colonists' attainment of independence from Britain. Britain's Royal Navy, the most powerful in the world, was a formidable foe, but somehow the Americans, however desperate and penurious, managed to assemble an amalgam of naval forces and use them effectively in a variety of ways. These naval forces included the units formed as part of the Army, privateers, state navies, and the Continental Navy. After 1778 and the sealing of an alliance with France, the French navy entered the mix. Ultimately, the array of naval forces deployed on the American side of the Revolutionary War contributed significantly to the Americans' victory.

The immediate roots of American rebellion lay in the French and Indian War (known as the Seven Years' War in Britain), which took place from 1754 to 1763. Although Britain ultimately achieved victory against its perennial rival, France, in this fateful struggle that spanned five continents, triumph came at a high cost. By the end of the war in 1763, Britain was seriously in debt and indeed close to bankruptcy. Consequently, in an attempt to raise revenues, Britain imposed new taxes on the American colonists. The colonials found these measures, including the Sugar Act (1764), the Stamp Act (1765), the Townshend Duties (1767), and the Tea Act (1773), to be onerous and the methods used to enforce them, especially the Coercive Acts (1774), to be repressive. By 1774, in a show of political resistance, the colonists established the Continental Congress to express their grievances. Britain remained unmoved, and in 1775 open war between Britain and the Thirteen Colonies erupted at Lexington and Concord in Massachusetts.

Royal Navy Operations to 1778

At the onset of war, the opponents appeared to be far from evenly matched. The mother country's most formidable asset was its 270-ship navy (including 131 ships-of-the-line and 98 frigates). Over the course of the war, the fleet increased in size dramatically, reaching a total of 478 ships (including 174 ships-of-the-line and 198 frigates) by 1783. Control of the sea gave British strategists great flexibility. It allowed them to evacuate Boston in 1776 and make New York City their center of operations, to approach and capture Philadelphia from a less defended route in 1777, and to shift to a southern strategy—occupy Savannah, Georgia—in December 1779 and from there to capture Charleston in April 1780 (see Map 2.2). Despite its obvious naval strength, however, Britain's great navy was experiencing some temporary weaknesses at the start of the American Revolution.

America, Sea Power, and the World, First Edition. Edited by James C. Bradford.
© 2016 John Wiley & Sons, Inc. Published 2016 by John Wiley & Sons, Inc.

The Royal Navy of 1775 was underfunded, lacked trained personnel, contained a number of poorly constructed ships, and suffered from administrative inefficiency and corruption. Moreover, in 1775, Royal Navy warships assigned to the colonies—the North American Squadron—included only 24 vessels. Fortunately for the Americans, it would take the Royal Navy several years to correct these weaknesses.

Before 1778, the Royal Navy served primarily to support British Army operations in what was for Britain a challenging expeditionary war. British warships transported soldiers and supplies across the Atlantic and moved them around the colonies as military strategy and exigency demanded. British operations before 1778 focused on the northern and middle colonies (a 1776 attempt to link up with Loyalists in North Carolina and a subsequent attack on Charleston had failed). When the British decided to abandon Boston in March 1776, the Royal Navy evacuated approximately 10,000 British soldiers without a casualty. Four months later, the Royal Navy conveyed some 32,000 troops to New York from Europe and Nova Scotia and supported their operations in the lower Hudson River Valley. The British capture of New York City sent George Washington's Continental Army into retreat across New Jersey to Pennsylvania.

The following year, when Britain adopted a dual strategy of subdividing America along the Hudson River–Lake Champlain–Richelieu River corridor and capturing the rebel capital at Philadelphia, the Royal Navy transported troops from New York to the head of Chesapeake Bay, from which they marched on Philadelphia, occupying the city from September 1777 until British strategy changed and its troops returned to New York the following spring (see Map 2.2).

In addition to transporting soldiers and supplies, the Royal Navy also contributed to the British war effort in other significant ways. It attacked and bombarded several American ports, with mixed success; for example, it shelled then put ashore landing parties to burn Falmouth (now Portland), Maine, on October 18, 1775, and Norfolk, Virginia, on January 1, 1776. However, the attack on Charleston, South Carolina, failed in June 1776. Royal Navy ships also escorted convoys of British merchantmen. Finally, while the Royal Navy initially endeavored to blockade the

coastline of New England in the early months of the war, so as to prevent the Americans from receiving crucial supplies, this policy could not be sustained over the long term, due to the higher priority placed on supporting the Army and the meager size of the North American Squadron.

America's Naval Response

When the Revolution erupted, the American colonists possessed no naval militiamen or units of naval militia like those that provided the structure and experience upon which the Continental Army was built. Professional navies were (and are) expensive institutions to create and maintain, for ships are costly to acquire, the recruitment of and training of personnel takes time, and development of an effective officer corps takes even longer.

What, then, could the Americans do to confront the British at sea, especially considering the intimidating size and capabilities of the Royal Navy? The traditional way for a weaker naval power to challenge an enemy with a larger navy was to adopt a *guerre de course* strategy—that is, make war on the enemy's maritime commerce. This is exactly what the American colonists did. Over the course of the Revolutionary War and using an array of different forces, the Americans harassed British trade in the Caribbean, the Atlantic, and the waters surrounding Britain itself.

American naval forces—including units organized by the Continental Army, privateers, state navies, and the Continental Navy—also contributed to the Patriot cause in a variety of ways other than commerce raiding. They were also called upon to assist in the defense of American ports and coasts, ferry diplomats across the Atlantic, protect American merchant shipping, transport supplies, and execute amphibious landings. Given the meager resources allotted to them and the size and power of their opposition, the Royal Navy, they compiled a remarkable record.

Washington's Navy

The first "national" naval force was formed by General George Washington while his Continental Army laid siege to British forces occupying Boston. When Washington took command of the

15,000–18,000 militiamen surrounding Boston in July 1775, they were desperately short of gunpowder, firearms, cannon, and shot. Meanwhile, the British garrison within Boston continued to receive supplies courtesy of the Royal Navy and British control of the seas. Inspired by the suggestion of a fellow officer, Washington began to create a "navy" in September 1775 when he leased the schooner *Hannah*. Ultimately, the squadron of 11 ships comprising "Washington's Navy" captured some 55 prizes, applying pressure to the British and providing essential military equipment to the Continental Army before that "navy" disbanded when the British evacuated Boston in March 1776.

Battle of Valcour Island

At virtually the same time, Brigadier General Benedict Arnold began constructing a variety of armed vessels with which to challenge the British invasion of northern New York from Canada. In an area with few roads, the most important one of which ran along the western shore of Lake Champlain, control of the lake was vital to the movement of troops and transport of supplies. In the summer of 1776, Quebec Governor Guy Carleton, intent on invading New York and New England, began assembling a flotilla of 25 heterogeneous vessels to ferry his army of 11,000 soldiers

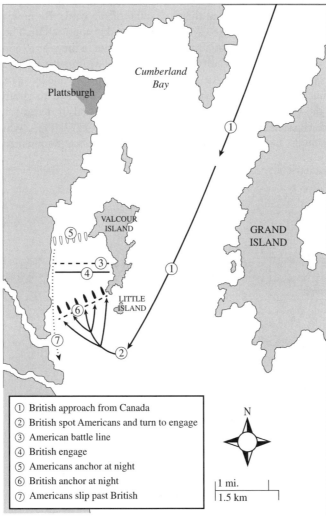

Map 2.1 Battle of Valcour Island, October 11–12, 1776.

southward across Lake Champlain. Benedict Arnold, a commander of American forces in the area, hired shipwrights, blacksmiths, carpenters, and sailmakers and put them to work in the lakeside village of Skenesboro, New York. Over the course of the summer, the workmen constructed 16 "gundalows" and "galleys." At the end of August, Arnold and his men launched this fleet of hastily constructed craft and sallied northward to engage the British, who were reported to be on the move from Canada. When Arnold reached a bay near the village of Plattsburgh, New York, he anchored his ships in a line between Valcour Island and the shore so that his outnumbered, out-skilled—few had nautical experience—and more weakly armed crewmen could focus on firing their cannon when the British engaged them (see Map 2.1). On October 11 the British arrived, spotted the Americans, and turned to engage them. Carleton's gunboats could row into position to fire on Arnold's gundalows and galleys, but his sailing vessels had to laboriously beat against the wind to get in position. Once they did, the British engaged and inflicted serious damage on Arnold's flotilla before the approach

of darkness led both sides to withdraw and anchor. During the night, Arnold and his "navy," fearing total ruination, slipped single file past the British and fled southward. The British pursued them, captured a galley and a cutter, and watched as the Americans ran the rest of their vessels aground and burned several to keep the British from capturing them (see Figure 2.1).

Indisputably, the contest ended in a tactical defeat for the Americans. The British could now reassert control over all of Lake Champlain and began transiting soldiers across the lake. They faced one irrefutable challenge, however, and that was the passage of time. The British had spent the summer constructing ships, fighting Arnold, and then searching for him in the wake of the battle. By now, in mid-October, winter was quickly approaching. The British soon decided it was too late in the year to continue their invasion and withdrew to Canada. They reopened their campaign the next spring, but by then the Continental Army was better prepared to confront them in operations that culminated in defeat for the British at Saratoga in October 1777. Thus, while the naval action on Lake Champlain represented a tactical victory for

Figure 2.1 Battle of Valcour Island, 1776. "A Sketch of the New England Armed Vessels, in Valcure Bay on Lake Champlain as seen in the morning of 11 October 1776 ..." by C. Randle, c. 1777. *Source:* Library and Archives Canada, Acc. No. 1996-82-2.

the British, it proved to be a critical strategic victory for the Americans because it bought them time to prepare for and win one of the most decisive campaigns of the war. Indeed, the American victory at Saratoga was consequential not only because a major British army surrendered. More importantly, France, impressed by the Americans' victory, entered into a formal alliance with the United States, a development that proved critical to the eventual defeat of Britain.

State Navies

Beginning in 1775, the American colonies began to establish their own naval forces. It is not surprising that the New England colonies, with their deep maritime traditions and needs, led the way. The impulse spread southward, and soon every state except Delaware and New Jersey had some sort of navy. It is difficult to assess the success of state navies in defending commerce (a major role) or even in executing their complementary, but secondary, role of attacking British merchant shipping. In their other main role, that of operating in conjunction with state militia troops to defend coastal areas, state navies enjoyed little success. Virginia's, the largest state navy, had little success in countering British operations in Chesapeake Bay and the British raiders destroyed all but one of its vessels in April 1781. The South Carolina Navy, the next largest of the state navies, lost most of its ships trying to defend Charleston in 1780. Pennsylvania's navy was more successful. It stopped two British frigates from attacking the Continental Army as Washington retreated across the Delaware River after evacuating New York City in 1776. The next year it joined in the defense of the Delaware south of Philadelphia, leading Admiral Richard Howe to bypass that route and take the longer one via Chesapeake Bay to land his brother's army for its march on the capital. The British captured the city in September but, for two months, until November, were prevented from receiving supplies via the Delaware.

Ultimately, states' navies achieved little while they competed with the Continental Navy for personnel, arms, and other resources. Moreover, their utility for larger military and naval purposes was limited. The Penobscot Campaign, the largest American naval expedition of the Revolutionary War, proved disastrous. In July 1779, a combined armada of six warships (two from Massachusetts, one from New Hampshire, and four from the Continental Navy), 16 vessels leased and armed by the government of Massachusetts, and 18 transports carrying a thousand Massachusetts troops sailed to Penobscot Bay in Maine to evict British troops who were constructing a fort in the area. The British defenders kept the Americans at bay until a relief expedition arrived from New York and forced the Americans to destroy their ships and flee southward by land. The fiasco led to the dismissal of the armada's naval commander, Dudley Saltonstall, from the Continental Navy and to the court martial of artillery commander Paul Revere, and nearly bankrupted Massachusetts.

Privateers

Privateering allowed governments to harness private enterprise in service of the state. Both the Continental Congress and state governments commissioned privateers, with those of maritime New England leading the way in 1775. The commerce raiders were active along the Atlantic seaboard, in the Caribbean, and around the British Isles. Evidence is fragmentary with estimates for Continental commissions alone varying from 1697 to 1809, those for Massachusetts ranging from 307 to 998, those for Pennsylvania from 83 to 448, and so on. The number of commissions issued by Continental authorities rose steadily from 1776 to a peak in 1781, then declined in 1782 and 1783 (see Figure 2.2).

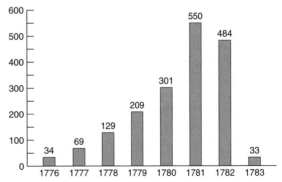

Figure 2.2   Privateering commissions issued by the Continental Congress.

All told, American privateers seized at least 600—and possibly as many as 2,000—prizes and insurance rates rose 30 percent for ships sailing in convoys and 50 percent for ships sailing alone. Whatever the correct totals, the number of privateers was far greater than the fewer than 75 ships of the Continental Navy, and the privateers inflicted substantially more damage on British shipping. However, the Continental Navy was America's force at sea—a symbol of nationhood—and charged with wider responsibilities than the commerce raiding engaged in by privateers.

The Continental Navy

The Continental Navy embodied the first manifestation of the US Navy. Established by the Continental Congress on October 13, 1775, the Continental Navy acquired its first ships by refitting existing merchantmen while it awaited delivery of purpose-built warships, the first of which, 13 frigates, were ordered by the Continental Congress in December 1775. In the end, only eight of these frigates made it to sea and, by 1781, the British had sunk or captured nearly all of them. The size and composition of the Continental Navy fleet fluctuated dramatically over time due to erratic political support and funding, the vagaries of war, and the challenges of creating a professional navy and all that entailed—from establishing regulations and an administrative structure to acquiring a fleet, hiring personnel, and commissioning officers—and all from scratch and under duress. Over the course of the war, some 65 vessels served in the Continental Navy, the greatest number (34) operating in 1777.

The Continental Navy's existence was not universally applauded by members of Congress, and there was considerable disagreement concerning its utility. Although supporters of the Continental Navy, such as John Adams, ultimately prevailed, sectionalist opposition was robust. Maryland's Samuel Chase said it was "the maddest idea in the world to think of building an American fleet."[1] Indeed, southerners in general remained deeply skeptical about the need for a national navy, what form it should take, and the expense it promised. They questioned why state navies were not sufficient, and they also feared that the northern colonies would monopolize the Continental Navy to protect northern colonies' maritime interests.

In January 1776, partially in an attempt to mollify southern opposition, Congress ordered Esek Hopkins, commander of the new Continental Navy, to sail to Chesapeake Bay and capture or drive off Loyalist forces that were raiding towns and plantations in Virginia and Maryland, and then to proceed to the Carolinas and do the same thing there. But Hopkins, exploiting a loophole in his orders, sailed instead to New Providence Island in the Bahamas. Arriving in March 1776, Hopkins landed 250 sailors and marines who captured 88 cannon and 15 mortars but failed to secure the powder so badly needed by Washington's army. When Hopkins returned to the United States, narrowly escaping capture by the Royal Navy sloop-of-war *Glasgow* (20 guns) en route, he turned many of the captured munitions over to state authorities in Rhode Island and Connecticut rather than to Continental authorities under whose direction he served. Although often glorified as the first amphibious expedition by American forces, Hopkins' failure to follow orders and his giving the captured munitions to New England states confirmed the anti-navy suspicions of many southerners.

Much less controversial and problematic was the Continental Navy's *guerre de course* campaign. Indeed, Continental Navy captains such as John Barry, Nicholas Biddle, Gustavus Conyngham, John Paul Jones, Abraham Whipple, and Lambert Wickes were very successful commerce raiders, both in home waters and abroad. Unofficially operating out of French ports with tacit French consent despite France's stated position of neutrality before 1778, Continental Navy raiders attacked and captured British merchant shipping in Britain's own backyard. *Guerre de course* operations, especially those in European waters, only intensified after the American alliance with France in 1778.

---

[1] John Adams, [Notes on Debates in Congress, October 7, 1775], *John Adams' Diary*, quoted in William Bell Clark et al., eds., *The Naval Documents of the American Revolution* (1964–), 2:341.

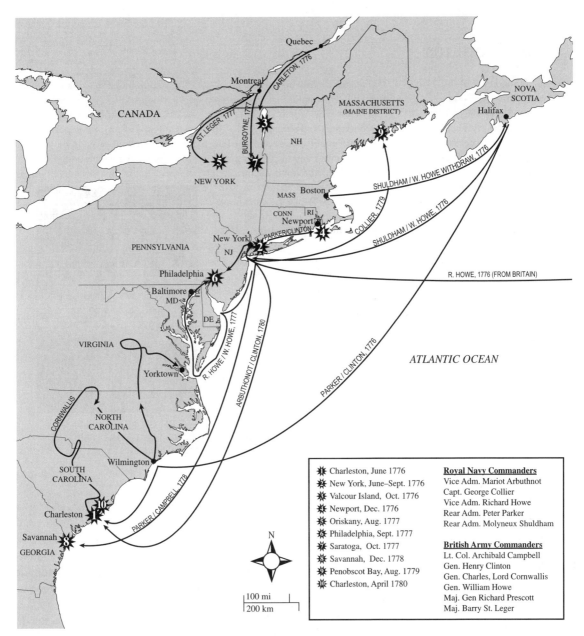

Map 2.2 British operations in America, 1776–1780.

Esek Hopkins

Esek Hopkins (1718–1802) was the first commodore (i.e., commander-in-chief) of the Continental Navy. The brother of an influential member of the Continental Congress' Naval Committee, Hopkins had an extensive background as a merchant captain and privateer. A native of Rhode Island, he had also served as a delegate in the Rhode Island General Assembly and, in fall 1775, was selected as the general in charge of all military forces in Rhode Island. A few months later, in December 1775, Congress designated him the commodore of the Continental Navy. Immediately after appointing Hopkins, Congress ordered him to proceed with his squadron to Chesapeake Bay to stop British raiding and thereafter to the Carolina Capes for the same reason. However, Hopkins took advantage of a loophole in his orders and

sailed to the Bahamas, where he led the first amphibious landing performed by American sailors and marines and returned with 103 pieces of captured artillery. En route home, Hopkins, his flagship, the 24-gun *Alfred*, and its consorts were roughly handled by the 20-gun *Glasgow*. While the expedition was a success from a matériel perspective, Hopkins' neglect of his responsibilities in the Chesapeake and Carolinas deeply alienated southerners in the Continental Congress and reinforced their reservations and even antipathy toward a "national" professional navy. Hopkins never again put to sea as an officer in the Continental Navy. After languishing in port unable to recruit sufficient seamen to fill his crew, and with his leadership criticized by several of his officers, Hopkins was censored by Congress in August 1776, relieved of command in January

1778, and dismissed from the service on July 30, 1778, despite the staunch support of navalists such as John Adams. Still popular at home, Hopkins served in the Rhode Island legislature until 1786.

Esek Hopkins. Mezzotint published by Thomas Hart, London, 1776. *Source:* National Archives.

The French Alliance

Both the elite and the general public in France viewed the American Revolution favorably, considering it a concrete manifestation of Enlightenment ideals. Benjamin Franklin received an enthusiastic welcome when he arrived in Paris in December 1776 to cultivate diplomatic support for the cause. France had begun providing covert aid to the Americans in 1776, but the victory at the Battle of Saratoga (1777) convinced the French of the Americans' seriousness and capability to combat the British. Seeing an opportunity to reset the European balance of power and reclaim honor after France's loss in the Seven Years' War, France signed the Treaty of Alliance with

the Continental Congress on February 6, 1778. By its terms France formally recognized America's independence from Britain and promised military support for the war. Shortly thereafter, Britain declared war against France.

The alliance with France was momentous for the Americans in myriad ways. The Continental Army immediately received badly needed supplies of French weapons and uniforms. France also provided economic aid, troops, ships, and military expertise. American privateers and Continental Navy warships could now use French ports openly and were able to adjudicate their captures through French prize courts. The alliance also brought the French navy into the war. That service—unlike the Continental Navy—could and did engage Britain's Royal Navy in fleet actions, and one such engagement—that off the Virginia Capes in 1781—proved a decisive element in American victory in the war.

French entry into the war transformed it from a rebellion within the British Empire into an international conflict. In 1779, Spain, which had covertly provided aid to the American rebels, cemented a formal alliance with France, and, with hopes of recovering Gibraltar, which it had lost to the British in 1704, declared war against Britain. Henceforth the Spanish fleet cooperated operationally with the French navy, and, when combined, the Franco-Spanish fleet was larger than that of Britain. Moreover, Franco-Spanish naval operations in the Atlantic and Mediterranean forced Britain to allocate naval assets to protect British trade and prevent an invasion of the British Isles. This diffusion of British naval resources could only benefit the Americans. Later, in 1780, the Netherlands (which had already sheltered Continental Navy commerce raiders in 1779) declared war against Britain as well. This conflict (the Fourth Anglo-Dutch War) was a direct result of British suppression of Dutch trade with the Americans and posed yet another naval threat for Britain. That same year Catherine II of Russia joined several minor naval powers in a League of Armed Neutrality designed to defend neutral commerce from British interference. Thus Britain found itself diplomatically and militarily isolated without a major-power ally for the first time in a century.

The Continental Navy and *Guerre de Course*

American commerce raiders targeted British shipping in the Caribbean, North Atlantic, and North Sea. Lambert Wickes, who carried Benjamin Franklin to France, and Gustavus Conyngham commanded the first Continental Navy warships to operate in British home waters, but the most famous American to do so was John Paul Jones (see Map 2.3).

Jones arrived in France in early 1778. After refitting the *Ranger* (18), Jones sailed from France in April, entered the Irish Sea, and led a landing party into Whitehaven, England, where his men

spiked the guns of a British fort and set fire to ships in the harbor. The following morning, Jones crossed the Solway Firth to St. Mary's Isle, Scotland, where he attempted to kidnap the Earl of Selkirk (who turned out to be away from home) to hold captive and exchange for American seamen held prisoner by Britain. Undeterred by this failure, Jones crossed the Irish Sea to Belfast Lough, where he and the *Ranger* defeated the sloop-of-war *Drake* (20) and returned to France with the British warship as a prize. Several months later, Jones received command of a former French East Indiaman courtesy of the French government. Jones converted it into a warship, renamed it the *Bonhomme Richard* (40) (i.e., the "Goodman Richard," in homage to Benjamin Franklin and his *Poor Richard's Almanac*), and put to sea on August 14, 1779. Five weeks later, after circumnavigating the British Isles, Jones lay in wait off Flamborough Head for a convoy carrying naval stores from the Baltic. When it arrived on September 23, Jones and the *Bonhomme Richard* defeated and captured its escort, the *Serapis* (50), in one of the deadliest single-ship actions of the Age of Sail (see Figure 2.3). When asked during the battle by Captain Richard Pearson whether he had surrendered, Jones is reputed to have responded, "I have not yet begun to fight!" Soon Pearson was forced to surrender. The next day Jones had to abandon the sinking *Bonhomme Richard* and shift his flag and crew to the captured British frigate. Victory in the Battle of Flamborough Head made Jones a hero in France and lifted morale in America at a time when the war did not appear to be going well for the allies.

Changes in Strategy, 1778–1780

The Franco-American alliance led to shifts in both American and British strategy. Since virtually the beginning of the war, George Washington had desired such a partnership and anticipated that it would lead France to send a fleet to operate with his army. The ease with which British forces captured both New York City and Philadelphia convinced Washington that, lacking the support of a naval ally, his strategy had to be to conduct a war of attrition until the enemy tired of the conflict, withdrew, and recognized American independence, or France

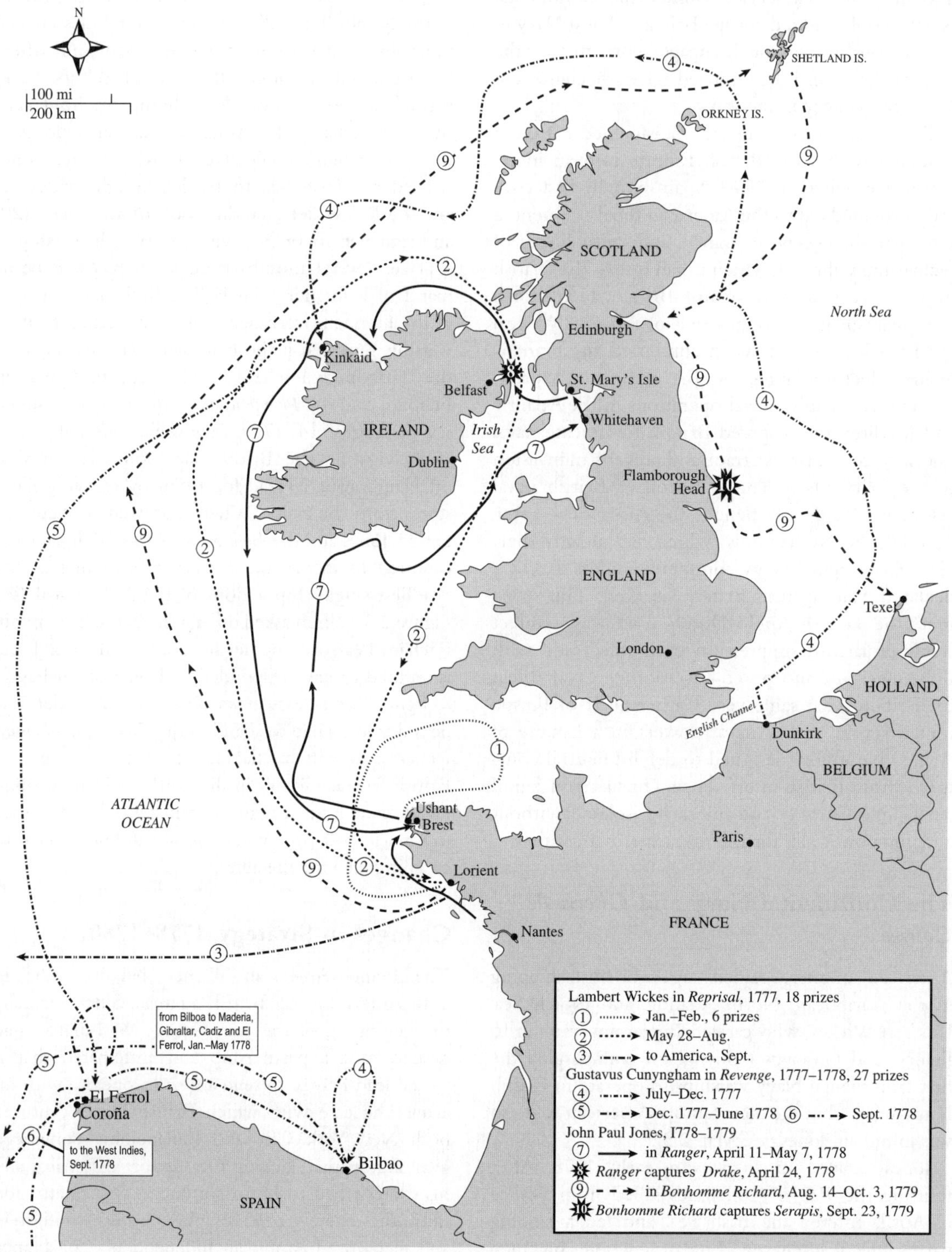
N
100 mi
200 km
SHETLAND IS.
ORKNEY IS.
SCOTLAND
North Sea
Edinburgh
Kinkaid
Belfast
St. Mary's Isle
Whitehaven
IRELAND
Irish Sea
Dublin
Flamborough Head
ENGLAND
Texel
London
HOLLAND
English Channel
Dunkirk
BELGIUM
ATLANTIC OCEAN
Ushant
Brest
Paris
Lorient
Nantes
FRANCE
from Bilboa to Maderia, Gibraltar, Cadiz and El Ferrol, Jan.–May 1778
El Ferrol
Coroña
to the West Indies, Sept. 1778
Bilbao
SPAIN
Lambert Wickes in *Reprisal*, 1777, 18 prizes
1 Jan.–Feb., 6 prizes
2 May 28–Aug.
3 to America, Sept.
Gustavus Cunyngham in *Revenge*, 1777–1778, 27 prizes
4 July–Dec. 1777
5 Dec. 1777–June 1778
6 Sept. 1778
John Paul Jones, 1778–1779
7 in *Ranger*, April 11–May 7, 1778
8 *Ranger* captures *Drake*, April 24, 1778
9 in *Bonhomme Richard*, Aug. 14–Oct. 3, 1779
10 *Bonhomme Richard* captures *Serapis*, Sept. 23, 1779

Map 2.3 American operations in European waters, 1777–1780.

Figure 2.3 Battle of Flamborough Head, 1779. Contemporary painting by William Elliot, R.N. *Source:* The Granger Collection/Topfoto.

joined the war and a joint campaign by a French fleet and his Continental Army could evict the British from the 13 states. In July 1778, Washington believed that time was at hand when Vice Admiral Charles Hector, Comte d'Estaing, arrived off New York with 12 ships-of-the-line, but was disappointed when the French commander, fearing his ships would ground, refused to attempt to enter the harbor to engage the British. Instead, d'Estaing proposed attacking Newport. Washington sent troops to Rhode Island to work with the French, but, after suffering damage in a storm, d'Estaing went to Boston for repairs, then sailed to the West Indies in November. This set a pattern for French operations: France would send a fleet to North America during hurricane season, July

to October, but the rest of the year the fleet would operate in the sugar-rich West Indies, the center of French economic and strategic interests.

French entry into the war changed British priorities and strategy. General Henry Clinton was ordered to send 8,000 of the 10,000 troops he had in Philadelphia to the West Indies and to return with the rest to New York by sea. Clinton sent his heavy equipment by sea, but, fearing being caught at sea by a French fleet, he marched his troops overland in June 1778 and entered the city just prior to the arrival of d'Estaing. Meanwhile officials in England decided to refocus their military efforts on the American South. In December 1778, a British expeditionary force seized Savannah, Georgia, and shortly thereafter captured Augusta as well. D'Estaing returned to North America in August 1779 to join Major General Benjamin Lincoln's Southern Continental Army in a siege of Savannah. In mid-October d'Estaing insisted on a premature assault on the city that was repulsed with great losses, following which, with hurricane season over, he returned to the West Indies.

The British next moved against Charleston, South Carolina, using the Royal Navy to blockade the harbor and besiege the city with some 10,000 troops in March and April 1780. By May 1780, the American army of 5,000, along with three ships of the Continental Navy (another was scuttled to prevent its capture), surrendered. In perhaps their greatest victory of the war, the British captured the South's largest city and busiest seaport.

The Yorktown Campaign

From summer 1780 through winter 1781, per his orders and using Charleston as a base, Lord Charles Cornwallis endeavored to rid the Carolinas of Patriot partisans and the Continental Army alike. Gradually, he worked his way north, eventually ending up in Yorktown, Virginia, where he encamped and waited for the Royal Navy to arrive with supplies and reinforcements. The Marquis de Lafayette and a small force of Continental troops was shadowing Cornwallis and reporting his movements to George Washington. On August 14 Washington received word that a French fleet commanded by Admiral François -Joseph Paul, Comte de Grasse had left the West Indies and would arrive at the Chesapeake by the end of the month. Washington could see the stars finally aligning for a combined Franco-American sea- and land-based attack on a major British army. Anticipating such a scenario, Washington had convinced French General Jean Baptiste, Comte de Rochambeau, to move his army from Newport to New York in July and Rear Admiral Jacques-Melchoir Saint-Laurent, Comte de Barras, to load Rochambeau's artillery and be ready to set sail. On August 21, Washington left his camp on the Hudson River with his 3,000 and Rochambeau's 4,000 troops and marched southward.

The British, too, were aware that de Grasse's fleet was on the move. They discerned that he had left the Caribbean, but they were unsure of his destina-

tion. Consequently, Rear Admiral Sir Samuel Hood was ordered to sail from the Caribbean and find de Grasse and his fleet (see Map 2.4). Hood looked first at the mouth of the Chesapeake, where he arrived on August 25. Not finding de Grasse in Virginia, Hood and his 14 ships-of-the-line proceeded to New York, arriving on there on August 28.

Meanwhile, departing from the French colony of Saint-Domingue (present-day Haiti), de Grasse and 29 ships-of-the-line sailed up the North American seaboard, arrived at the mouth of the Chesapeake on August 29, and dropped anchor off Norfolk the next day. Wasting no time, de Grasse quickly blockaded the British in the York River, landed his 3,300 French soldiers to reinforce the Marquis de Lafayette's army, then ferried another 1,600 American soldiers from Virginia's James River to the York to further strengthen Lafayette. Cornwallis' prospects began to look dim.

When Hood reached New York and found no French fleet there, he realized his mistake and implored Rear Admiral Thomas Graves, the commanding officer in New York, to send warships back to the Chesapeake to find and engage de Grasse. Graves joined five of his eight ships-of-the-line to Hood's 14 and put to sea on September 1. Four days later Graves and Hood reached the Virginia Capes, and de Grasse, with his 24 ships-of-the-line, came out to engage them.

French morale was high and de Grasse's men were well disciplined. Plus, de Grasse understood the strategic setting: he did not need to destroy the enemy, just prevent him from entering the Chesapeake and lifting the siege of Yorktown. During the ensuing four-hour battle both fleets suffered significant damage, but neither gained the upper hand (see Figure 1.1). Graves was cautious and did not seize the tactical initiative when he could have done so. At the same time, de Grasse was happy to maintain his position at the mouth of the Bay and keep Graves' fleet at arm's length. The two fleets watched one another warily for another two days.

The noose was now tightening inexorably around Cornwallis; Washington's and Rochambeau's forces arrived, as well as Comte de Barras bringing siege artillery and adding his six ships-of-the-line to de Grasse's 28. Recognizing that a naval victory was

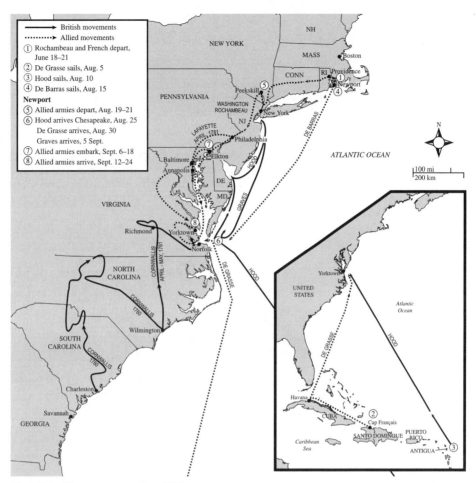

Map 2.4 Yorktown campaign, 1781.

now impossible, Graves returned to New York, and Cornwallis was doomed. Surrounded by the Franco-American army on land and de Grasse's fleet at sea, Cornwallis knew he had no option but to surrender. The Battle of the Virginia Capes was the decisive event of the war in North America. During the next two years, Britain sent additional ships and troops to the Caribbean but did not reinforce its army in New York.

The End of the War

The dispatch of forces to the West Indies was made necessary by the French seizure of St. Kitts and of several smaller islands from the British. At the same time, the Franco-Spanish Siege of Gibraltar continued in Europe. These events, coupled with Cornwallis' 1781 defeat at Yorktown, put overwhelming pressure on the British government. In April 1782, the British House of Commons voted to end the war in America and the various parties began to negotiate a peace settlement.

The Royal Navy did end the war on a high note. During the spring of 1782, French and Spanish naval forces planned to invade Jamaica, but a British fleet commanded by Admiral George Rodney achieved a dramatic victory in the Battle of the Saintes (April 9–12, 1782), which shifted the balance of naval power in the Caribbean in Britain's favor. In the waning days of the war, then, the Royal Navy had again asserted its power and proficiency. Despite this naval achievement, however, the war was over for Britain.

The *Turtle*

In 1776, in an effort to defend New York City harbor from British incursion, General George Washington approved and funded an innovative naval weapon: a submarine. Connecticut native and inventor David Bushnell had designed and built a radically new sort of vessel: a submersible that he named the *Turtle*. Bushnell was not the first to design a submersible—others had been experimenting with this notion for several centuries. However, Bushnell's vessel was the first submarine ever used to wage war. It possessed a watertight, oak hull whose cross-section resembled the shape of a turtle shell (hence its name); a hand-powered crank propeller; a lever-operated ballast pump; a tiller rudder; and only enough air to last its solo operator 30 minutes. Bushnell's plan was to use the *Turtle* to place underwater explosives on British ships without detection. To accomplish this task, the craft would submerge, maneuver beneath a British ship, and plant an explosive device (a watertight oak cask filled with gunpowder) by driving a long screw into the enemy ship's hull. After the *Turtle* had safely escaped, a timed fuse would ignite the explosion. In theory, the plan appeared feasible; in reality, however, the undertaking proved to be more problematic. On September 6, 1776, the *Turtle*'s operator, Army Sergeant Ezra Lee, successfully piloted the submersible beneath the British warship *Eagle* in New York Harbor. However, the *Turtle*'s screw hit an iron plate and thus could not puncture the *Eagle*'s hull.

After several unsuccessful attempts to attach the explosives, Lee began to run out of air and had to abort the mission. Despite the *Turtle*'s failure, David Bushnell indeed had pioneered an entirely new approach to naval warfare with his visionary approach and invention.

The *Turtle*. Drawing by Lieutenant Commander F. M. Barber, 1885. *Source:* Courtesy of the US Navy.

In September 1783, Britain signed a series of treaties with its opponents collectively known as the Peace of Paris. In the Treaty of Paris with the United States, Britain recognized American independence, and, to provide the new nation with a sense of security and prevent it from becoming a French satellite dependent on that enemy of Britain for its defense, Britain granted its former colonies generous borders stretching from the Atlantic Ocean to the Mississippi River and from the Great Lakes to Florida. In three other treaties, Britain returned Florida and Minorca to Spain but kept Gibraltar, which Spain had entered the war to recover, and Britain, France, and the Netherlands returned various islands in the West Indies and posts in India and Africa that each had captured from another during the war. Thus the United States and, to a lesser degree, Spain achieved their goals. Britain soon recovered from the financial costs of the conflict, but France did not and its debt contributed significantly to the coming of the French Revolution.

In 1785, the government of the new United States of America sold the last ship of the Continental Navy. The current political framework, the Articles of Confederation, did not provide for a national government with the power to tax, and without such power the Continental Congress could not support a navy. Moreover, a national, standing, professional navy was ideologically controversial, and many Americans did not believe that the benefits to be derived from a navy were great enough to justify the costs.

Conclusion

Few Americans appreciated the role of naval forces in the war just concluded. They failed to see that the Royal Navy was an integral component in Britain's conduct of expeditionary warfare. The Royal Navy moved troops and supplies around as military strategy and demand dictated, protected British maritime commerce, blockaded and bombarded American coasts when needed, and maintained control of the seas.

In comparison, American naval forces were meager and their operations fragmented. The only "national" force, the Continental Navy, was small, erratic in its performance, and politically controversial. Despite this, naval operations proved to be essential to the eventual American victory in the Revolutionary War. The Americans cobbled together an amalgam of naval forces including privateers, Washington's and Arnold's squadrons, and state navies, which were joined in 1778 by the French Navy. Certainly, American naval performance was uneven and there were unqualified naval disasters, such as at Penobscot Bay (1779). More typically, however, naval activities such as *guerre de course* commerce raiding by privateers and Continental Navy warships operated quietly in the background, steadily chipping away at British trade, forcing the British to allocate naval assets to defend its merchant shipping, and injecting needed resources into American coffers. There were crucial strategic victories at Valcour Island in 1776 and off the Virginia Capes in 1781. There were even moments of radical innovation, such as the case of the *Turtle* (1776), and individuals, such as Continental Navy Captain John Paul Jones, who attained renown as naval heroes. Ultimately, then, as heterogeneous and complicated as the American naval effort was in the American Revolution, it played a significant (if often underappreciated) role in the victorious outcome.

CHAPTER 3

Genesis of the US Navy, 1785–1806

Samuel Smith slowly rose from his seat in Congress. The respected Revolutionary War veteran could remain silent no longer. Reminding his colleagues that Algerine raiders had captured at least 11 American merchant ships and imprisoned their sailors, he pled surely "the defenceless state" of America "was contrary to the maxims of the Republics of all former ages."[1] It was February 1794, and the frustrated Smith was participating in a much broader debate than what should be done about the depredations of Barbary corsairs. Should the United States have a navy or not? If so, what kind of a navy should it be? One limited to coastal defense, one able to protect commerce in foreign seas, or a capital-ship navy to rival those of Europe? The Founders were in uncharted waters.

The years following the 1783 Treaty of Paris were a time of severe unrest in American society. The decentralized government provided for by the Articles of Confederation proved incapable of alleviating the postwar depression; quelling political unrest, such as Shays' Rebellion in Massachusetts; or dealing effectively with foreign powers. As the new government under the Constitution confronted these challenges during the early 1790s, two political parties emerged with radically different visions of America's future. Federalists championed a strong central government—including a Federal navy—that could shape a balanced economy based on agriculture, manufacturing, and trade while their opponents, the Republicans,[2] feared that over-commercialization would corrupt American society and pressed instead for a limited central government and an agrarian economy. To many Republicans, a navy would serve commercial interests while promising heavy taxation to support never-ending shipbuilding programs. In reality, neither party was totally united; for example, Republicans from commercial areas, such as Samuel Smith, were often ardent supporters of naval expansion, while Federalists representing agrarian areas often opposed naval measures.

The new republic had been without a navy since 1785. Indeed, few Americans then saw the need for a navy; they naively believed that the Treaty of Paris would lead to a resumption of trade with Britain and new trade with other nations. In fact, France,

---

[1] US Congress, *Annals of the Congress of the United States*, 42 vols. (1834–1856), 3rd congress, 1st sess., 447. Hereafter cited as *Annals of Congress*.

[2] As the first political parties formed, opponents of the Federalists were referred to as Republicans or Democratic Republicans and should not be confused with the modern Republican Party, which emerged during the 1850s.

America, Sea Power, and the World, First Edition. Edited by James C. Bradford.
© 2016 John Wiley & Sons, Inc. Published 2016 by John Wiley & Sons, Inc.

Spain, and other colonial powers did not open their empires to American commerce, and Britain treated its former colonies like any other foreign nation. Independence also deprived American shipping of the protection previously afforded it by Britain's Royal Navy. A year prior to the disbanding of the Continental Navy, Sultan Sidi Muhammad of Morocco ordered American merchant ships seized after the United States ignored his demand that it pay tribute in return for their safe passage. In 1785, Algiers joined Morocco in attacking American trade. The American merchant marine received temporary relief when Portugal blockaded the Strait of Gibraltar, preventing corsairs from entering the Atlantic, and American ships unofficially joined Portuguese convoys entering the Mediterranean. When Portugal and Algiers reached a peace settlement in 1793, American ships again fell prey to the North African corsairs. That same year, France declared war on Britain and each began seizing American merchantmen found trading with the other nation.

The Constitution endowed the new government with power to tax, which provided the wherewithal to support a navy, but there was little consensus on naval policy. During long and often acrimonious debates, groups favoring four differing types of navies emerged:

1. *coastal navy* to defend American territorial waters;
2. *regional navy* to operate in the Atlantic off North America and in the Caribbean;
3. *commerce navy* to defend American trade worldwide; and
4. *capital-ship navy* able to influence the international balance of power as an instrument of foreign policy, and perhaps, in the future, to compete with the navies of the great powers.

Advocates of each policy held sway at times during the next two decades. Those in favor of a commerce navy dominated policy from 1794 to 1796; proponents of a regional navy set policy from 1797 to 1800 (with a strong push toward a capital-ship navy in 1799 and 1800); commerce navy supporters regained the ascendancy from 1801 to 1805; and backers of a coastal navy held sway from 1806 to the War of 1812.

Commerce Navy, 1794–1796: The Humphreys Frigates

Prior to the Revolution, the colonies rarely worried about the protection of their commerce, thanks to the Royal Navy. After the Revolution, American merchants saw their ships seized, sailors impressed (forced into service with the Royal Navy, on the grounds that they were British citizens evading their service duty), insurance rates skyrocket, and markets constricted with the closure of the British West Indies to imports and shipping from the United States. The change seriously impacted American shipbuilding. An investigation by Britain's Committee on Trade and Plantations determined that 182 ships were under construction in the United States in 1772, but only 31 in 1789. Consequently, during the 1780s, American merchants began to seek new markets worldwide, a move that exposed their ships to the dangers posed by pirates and privateers, most notably those of Morocco, Algiers, Tunis, and Tripoli.

A domino effect of events in 1793 increased American problems. France declared war on Britain in February and opened its West Indian trade to Americans, whose trade skyrocketed (see Figure 3.1). But this economic boom proved short lived as Britain soon invoked the Rule of 1756 ("trade that is illegal in time of peace is illegal in time of war") and began seizing American vessels caught trading with France or its colonies. Britain also widened the commonly accepted list of contraband (war goods that could not be sold to belligerents) to include foodstuffs, making one of America's most lucrative exports subject to seizure.

Renewed Anglo-French warfare also quickly led to an increase in impressment. The expansion of the Royal Navy from 135 ships requiring 36,000 personnel in 1793 to 596 needing 114,000 seamen in 1805 forced British commanders to seek crewmen by whatever method was necessary. The American merchant marine offered higher pay, better living conditions, and shorter terms of service than the Royal Navy, plus only rarely did merchant mariners have to fight. It is estimated that these factors induced as many as 500 sailors to desert the Royal Navy each month, thereby contributing to a manpower shortage created by expansion of the fleet. In theory, only

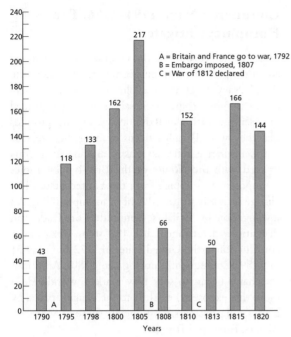

A = Britain and France go to war, 1792
B = Embargo imposed, 1807
C = War of 1812 declared

Figure 3.1 Value of waterborne imports and exports (in millions of dollars), 1790–1820.

British citizens could be impressed, but, in practice, naval officers put their need for seamen above legal distinctions. Americans maintained that a person could change citizenship and that a neutral nation's flag protected its sailors, views rejected by the British, who maintained that a British sailor remained subject to British law, including impressment, wherever he served. It is estimated that the British impressed as many as 15,835 American mariners during their wars with France.

To avoid war with Britain, President George Washington sent Supreme Court Chief Justice John Jay to London to negotiate a treaty to settle these and other issues. Public reaction was far from positive. While the British agreed to evacuate posts south of the Great Lakes, the Jay Treaty recognized the Rule of 1756, accepted Britain's expansive view of contraband, and granted Britain "most favored nation" trading status (meaning it received as low tariffs and port

fees as any of America's trading partners). The last particularly angered Republicans because it nullified the use of economic coercion, the foreign policy tool that they preferred to military force. In addition, the treaty also ignored impressment, the issue most important to many Americans because it involved not just property but the lives of US citizens.

In December 1793, conditions grew even more precarious for the republic's commerce as news reached America that Portugal had signed a treaty with Algiers. Without the Portuguese navy patrolling the Strait of Gibraltar, Algerine corsairs poured into the Atlantic and within days captured several American ships.

Congress responded by debating whether "a naval force, adequate to the protection of the commerce of the United Sates against the Algerine corsairs, ought to be provided."[3] While many policymakers agreed on the importance of securing the nation's commerce, they disagreed concerning how to protect it. Some congressmen proposed building small sloops, brigs, and a few powerful frigates to protect American merchantmen by forming convoys, hunting down enemy commerce raiders, and retaliating by attacking the merchant ships of countries that violated American maritime rights. A few congressmen hoped this would provide a foundation for a larger force capable of countering the British and French navies, while others preferred instead the arming of merchant vessels and the issuing of letters of marque authorizing retaliatory attacks on enemy merchantmen by American privateers. Ultimately, the "Act to provide a Naval Armament" that passed Congress on March 27, 1794, authorized the construction of four 44-gun frigates and two 36-gun frigates with the provision that work would cease on the vessels should peace be reached with Algiers. When such a settlement was negotiated in 1796 (one that provided for an immediate American payment of $600,000 in tribute plus additional annual gifts), construction should have ceased on the frigates. Instead, President Washington asked Congress to finish the three frigates nearest completion and to place them "in ordinary" (i.e., to hold the vessels in "reserve") rather than lose the money spent

---

[3] *Annals of Congress*, 3rd congress, 1st sess., 153–154.

Humphreys Frigates

Designed by Philadelphia Quaker shipwright Joshua Humphreys, the frigates of the Act of 1794 were larger, more heavily armed, and carried more sail than British *Minerva*-class and French *Pomone*-class frigates. In effect, Humphreys' ships were a hybrid of a ship-of-the-line and a cruising frigate, and, consequently, before they proved themselves during the Quasi-War, were somewhat controversial among traditional shipwrights. Longer and narrower than standard frigate designs, Humphreys' designs used diagonal ribs to prevent the hogging (when stress causes the center of the keel to bend upwards) that slowed a ship. Carrying as many as 50 guns, mostly 24-pounders, Humphreys' frigates were able to fire twice the broadside of a typical British frigate. President Washington directed that they be built in six different shipyards to spread the investment throughout the states. One of Humphreys' stipulations was that all the shipyards must use *Quercus virens* (or southern live oak), a variant of oak found along the US coast (to about 20 miles inland) between southern Virginia and eastern Texas. Its trunks grow to nearly 20 feet in diameter and are extremely dense on account of their thick, gum-like sap, making them resistant to the two banes of shipbuilders, rot and saltwater—although this made it particularly hard for craftsmen to work with, quickly dulling sharp tools and requiring extra muscle to cut and shape its pieces.

The Humphrey Frigates were foundational to the early US Navy, forming the backbone of the service in the Quasi-War, Barbary Wars, and War of 1812. The *Constitution* remains in commission today as a symbol of the Navy in the Age of Sail.

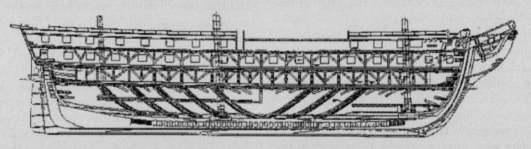

USS *Constitution*. Profile of hull showing diagonal riders on the orlop deck.

on them to date. Washington would have preferred to put some of the warships in service—in his final address to Congress he stated that, "To an active external commerce the protection of a naval force is indispensable"—but he knew Congress would not agree.[4] Federalists argued that the threat posed by the building of the ships had driven Algiers to the peace table and Congress accepted Washington's recommendation for a "reserve fleet."

While the importance of securing commerce would remain a significant goal of congressional naval strategists throughout the late 1790s, John Adams introduced a more expansive naval strategic vision when he assumed office in 1797.

---

[4] "Washington's Eighth Annual Address to Congress," December 7, 1796, in the Papers of George Washington, http://gwpapers.virginia.edu/documents/washingtons-eighth-annual-address-to-congress.

Regional Navy, 1797–1800: The Quasi-War

When citizens of Paris stormed the Bastille on July 14, 1789, many Americans thought the event a natural successor to 1776 and celebrated by erecting liberty poles, flying revolutionary Tricolors, and addressing one another by the French term "citizen." In April 1793, Edmond-Charles Genet, the new envoy of France, landed in Charleston. Intent on capitalizing on this revolutionary fervor, Citizen Genet commissioned four privateers and raised an army to invade Spanish Florida. When Washington denounced Genet's actions, the diplomat appealed to the American people over the head of the president (who responded by requesting that France recall Genet).

Most Americans shared Washington's disdain for Genet and the increasing radicalization of the French Revolution in 1793 began to tip public sentiment in their favor. The execution of Louis XVI and Marie Antoinette shocked many Americans while the frenzied work of the guillotine during the Reign of Terror (September 1793–November 1794) precipitated an even stronger backlash. The French Revolution's project of de-Christianization (killing priests, seizing church lands, and banning church holidays) alienated those not already alarmed by the escalating violence.

The actions of the French revolutionary government on the high seas only reinforced the growing animosity toward France. Viewing the Jay Treaty as establishing a virtual maritime and economic alliance between the United States and Britain, French officials ordered the seizure of American ships trading with the British Empire. French privateers captured 316 American merchant ships in 1795 alone, while over the next two years the French government increased its restrictions on American trade and French privateers expanded their operations from the Caribbean to include the coast of North America.

Despite these developments, President John Adams endeavored to keep America out of war with France, even as he made preparations for conflict. On May 16, 1797, Adams asked Congress to equip the three Humphreys frigates still under construction under the Naval Act of 1794—*United States* (44 guns), *Constitution* (44), and *Constellation* (36)—to build an unspecified additional number of sloops of war, to arm merchantmen, and to authorize convoying American commerce. Congress responded by funding the fitting out of the three frigates.

Hoping to avert open war, Adams sent diplomats Charles Cotesworth Pinckney, Elbridge Gerry, and John Marshall to negotiate with France. Shortly after its arrival in Paris, the delegation received demands for bribes (most prominently £50,000 to Minster of Foreign Affairs Charles Maurice de Talleyrand-Périgord) before even opening negotiations. Americans were outraged when newspapers publicized these demands by French agents (dubbed X, Y, and Z in the diplomatic correspondence). Public support for the Federalists' war preparations, especially naval expansion, soared.

On April 27, 1798, Congress authorized procurement of up to twelve 22-gun vessels, and three days later it established the cabinet-level Department of the Navy. On May 3 and 4, acts were passed to provide for coastal defense, including harbor fortifications and ten galleys. Congress stopped short of declaring war on France, but, in four separate acts during the summer of 1798, it escalated the conflict: first, by authorizing capture of any foreign armed vessel "found hovering on the coasts of the United States, for the purpose of committing depredations" upon American commerce (May 28); next, by allowing American merchant vessels to defend themselves from French search and seizure (June 25); third, by authorizing privateering and the seizure of French vessels operating anywhere on the high seas (July 9); and, finally, by funding completion of the final three 1794 Humphreys frigates, *President* (44), *Congress* (36), and *Chesapeake* (36) (July 16). Congress also declared all treaties with France void (June 27), and Adams signed the act "for the Establishing and Organizing a Marine Corps" (July 11). Eight months later, Congress decreed that the cutters of the Revenue Service (the forerunner of the Coast Guard) "shall, whenever the President of the United States shall so direct, cooperate with the Navy of the United States, during which time they shall be under the direction of the Secretary of the Navy" (March 2, 1799), setting a precedent that continues today.

Congress was not the only body concerned with warship construction in the late 1790s. By the summer of 1798, notices such as the one appearing in the

June 1 edition of Philadelphia's *Aurora* were increasingly common.

The patriotic citizens of this town, determined to show their attachment to their own government, and to vindicate its commercial rights, have opened a subscription for the purpose of building a 20-gun ship; and loaning her to government. The sum proposed for building her, is 20,000 dollars.

Citizens from Newburyport, Massachusetts, to Charleston, South Carolina, followed suit and between 1798 and 1800 financed eight warships ranging in size from the *Philadelphia* (36) to the *Richmond* (16). The quality of these ships varied greatly. Some were built from the bottom up according to the latest trends in naval architecture (e.g., *Philadelphia*) while others were converted merchant vessels (e.g., *Baltimore*, armed with 20 guns after its deck was strengthened).

Averaging 28 guns, these "subscription ships" fit well into President Adams' concept of a regional navy. Being neither capital ships meant to impress Europe nor coastal defense gunboats, they were designed to convoy merchantmen and patrol the waters of the United States and Caribbean. Accordingly, this vision incorporated elements of both the commerce and coastal navy strategic visions by making dual priorities of the security of the American coastline and the defense of American commerce, both of which distinguished the vision of John Adams from leaders who focused exclusively on protecting either commerce or the American coast, but not both. Adams knew from experience during the American Revolution that the United States could not defeat the navy of a great power, but he hoped to keep the navies of France or Britain off balance by exploiting geographic advantages and diplomacy. At the same time, he would field a naval force consisting of frigates, brigs, and sloops in order to allow American trade to continue under the banner of neutrality. While all of this sounded good in theory, it was up to Secretary of the Navy Benjamin Stoddert and the small American navy to execute the strategy.

Constellation under the command of Thomas Truxtun was the first frigate to put to sea. Truxtun had served as a privateer in the American Revolution and authored books on navigation and signaling, but despite his experience Truxtun, like other American captains, was learning on the fly. No Americans had commanded such large vessels, and the handling qualities of these new frigates were a mystery. Truxtun, for example, initially over-armed and misrigged *Constellation* so that it excessively heeled, rendering the lee broadside unusable in battle. The over-arming—he selected twelve 24-pound cannon versus the planned 18-pounders—may have been a product of the scramble for cannons during the spring of 1798 as American foundries struggled to meet the demand of coastal fortifications, frigate construction, and merchant ship conversions.

Initial deployments reflected Adams' vision: *United States* and *Delaware* (20) under Commodore John Barry were dispatched to the Caribbean, Truxton's *Constellation* to the southern US coast, Richard Dale and *Ganges* (a converted 24-gun merchant ship that was distinctive as the first American warship to put to sea since the disestablishment of the Continental Navy in 1785) to the central US coast, and Samuel Nicholson and the *Constitution* were sent to patrol off New England. Secretary Stoddert did not share Adams' regional navy vision and pressed the president to redeploy all the ships in the Caribbean, abandoning the coastal defense mission and focusing exclusively on the French privateers and cruisers that frequented the West Indies. Stoddert and the American captains could rest assured they would likely not find a French fleet in the region thanks to Britain's blockade of France's European ports. Stoddert's desire to concentrate on the Caribbean meant that by the end of the year there were 13 Navy warships and eight revenue cutters operating in that region (see Map 3.1).

On Truxton's advice, Stoddert situated a small squadron (Stephen Decatur Sr.'s *Delaware* and two revenue cutters) off the windward coast of Cuba to deal with privateers operating between Cuba and the Bahamas, and stationed Thomas Tingey and the *Ganges* (24) in the Windward Passage between Cuba and Santo Domingo. Stoddert sent 15 ships to the Lesser Antilles, dividing his forces into northern and southern squadrons somewhat awkwardly. Truxton and *Constellation* headed the northern squadron of five vessels, while the larger frigates, *United States* and *Constitution*, were combined with eight smaller vessels to the south. Lack of confidence in the commander

Benjamin Stoddert

Revolutionary War veteran Benjamin Stoddert (1744–1813) was 47 years old when President John Adams appointed him the nation's first secretary of the navy in May 1798. As one of the young republic's foremost advocates of a capital-ship navy, Stoddert administered a navy comprising 55 warships and numerous revenue cutters, and federal naval expenditures that by 1800 totaled $3,448,716.03 and consumed 29 percent of the US budget. Incredibly, the Baltimore merchant managed the complicated logistics of naval expansion and conduct of the Quasi-War with a staff of just six. He repeatedly pushed for the construction of 74-gun ships and the establishment of a navy possessing all the trappings of a large European navy, including ships-of-the-line and flag officers. While acknowledging that commissioning admirals in a navy whose largest warships were frigates would expose him to "ridicule," Stoddert was convinced that "by a Navy alone we can secure respect to our rights as a Sovereign Nation," and recommended the designation of two full admirals, two vice admirals, and two rear admirals.[5] Even after his Federalist Party lost power to the Jeffersonian Republicans in 1801, Stoddert clung to his capital-ship navy vision for America and maintained that 12 ships-of-the-line and "double the number strong frigates" would be the minimum deterrent necessary for the nation "to avoid those wars in which we have no interest."[6] Stoddert's argument highlighted one of the key arguments of the supporters of the capital-ship navy, that a strong maritime force in peacetime would ensure both the security of commerce and the nation's coastline. Ultimately, his structuring of the new Navy Department laid the foundation for the naval service vital to its survival and continued success.

Benjamin Stoddert. Painting by E. F. Andrews.

of the *United States* drove this imbalanced arrangement—Stoddert, with good reason, had little faith in Samuel Nicholson, who had twice failed to distinguish between French and British warships, nearly causing an international incident when he erroneously seized HMS *Niger* (24) in 1798. Determined to avoid making him a commodore, Stoddert paired him with John Barry, the only captain senior to Nicholson.

It was Truxton, in the smaller squadron, who became the hero of the Quasi-War. Sighting an unknown ship off Nevis on February 9, Truxton raised all available sail (despite the onset of a fierce rain squall). The ship sighted proved to be the *Insurgente* (36), a French frigate that had, with another French frigate, captured *Retaliation* (12) the previous November. Michel Barreaut, captain of *Insurgente*, did not flee, but, mistaking the Humphreys frigate for a smaller British corvette, turned to meet it. While Truxton survived the squall with little damage, *Insurgente*'s topmast was severed, limiting its maneuverability before the battle even began. Approaching from the weather gauge, Truxton crossed the stern of *Insurgente* and inflicted great damage, firing his 24-pounders into the hull of the French ship. *Insurgente* returned fire in French fashion—aiming at the *Constellation*'s rigging—causing significant damage, but not before Truxton crossed the bow

---

[5] Benjamin Stoddert to Josiah Parker, March 10, 1800, in Dudley Knox, ed., *Naval Documents Related to the Quasi War between the United States and France* (Washington, DC: 1935-38), 5:287-288.

[6] [US Congress], *American State Papers … Naval Affairs*, 4 vols. (1839), 1:75.

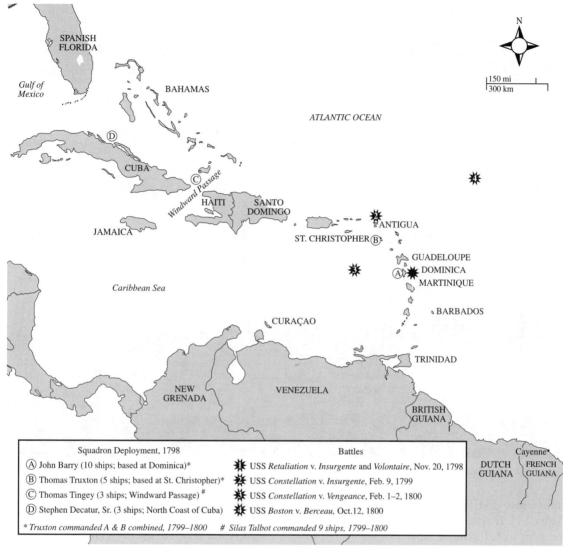

Map 3.1 Quasi-War with France, 1798–1800.

Figure 3.2   *Constellation* vs. *Insurgente*, 1799. Painting by John William Schmidt, 1799.

of *Insurgente* and fired with devastating effect (see
Figure 3.2). Truxton next maneuvered alongside, and
the ships traded multiple broadsides before Truxton
prepared to cross *Insurgente*'s stern for yet another raking broadside. At this point Barreaut struck his colors,
barely an hour since the engagement began, having
only inflicted three casualties on *Constellation*.

The spring and summer of 1799 witnessed a lull
in American operations as ships refitted in a disorganized manner, leaving the Caribbean largely unpat-
rolled while Stoddert and Adams fumed at the failure
of the officers in command to coordinate the rotation of ships on station. This was especially problematic since the reopening of trade with the ex-slaves
of Santo Domingo in the summer of 1799 meant a
certain increase in Franco-Spanish privateering in the

Windward Passage. Fortunately, five additional smaller
frigates were nearing operational status as the summer
ended, which, added to the three Humphreys frigates,
brought the total number of operational frigates to
eight. This freed up *Constitution* and *United States* to
pursue Stoddert's mission of "showing the flag" in
European waters, reflective of the capital-ship naval
vision that Stoddert shared with "High Federalists"
Alexander Hamilton and Secretary of State Timothy Pickering. That vision also led Stoddert to advocate building six 74-gun ships-of-the-line, a class of
ships synonymous with late eighteenth-century capital-ship navies. Such ships could enhance respect for
America abroad, the importance of which was a common thread in the discourse of those who supported
a capital-ship navy. To them, as to navalists a century

later, "respect" equated to securing America's place in the international political culture. In an age when the traditional European powers expected the American republican experiment to fail, the formation of a strong naval force would demonstrate the strength of the new United States.

Unlike many of his fellow Federalists, Adams was never a proponent of a capital-ship navy and in an 1808 letter to Massachusetts Republican J. B. Varnum he expressed regret over his decision to support Stoddert's push for a capital-ship navy by recommending to Congress the construction of ships-of-the-line in February 1799. Rather, Adams reiterated that his desire was always "to have fast-sailing frigates to scour the seas and make [an impression] on the enemy's commerce." He was certainly opposed to the navalist philosophy of fleet engagements, countering that "our policy is not to fight squadrons at sea."[7] Additionally, many High Federalists advocated forming an Anglo-American alliance. Perhaps as many as 300–400 cannons and carronades were purchased from Britain to make up for domestic production shortfalls, and copper sheathing was purchased for the bottoms of American warships. Stoddert additionally allowed his officers to share intelligence with British captains in the West Indies, an informal cooperation that was aided by a set of maritime recognition signals devised by the Royal Navy's Vice Admiral George Vandeput and Stoddert himself. Such collaboration ran counter to Adams' firm belief that Britain's global maritime dominance needed balancing. There is no evidence that Adams condoned any of the steps taken by Stoddert and Pickering toward cooperation with Britain.

While Stoddert struggled through the summer and fall of 1799 to establish his capital-ship navy (*Insurgent* and *United States* made voyages to Europe, the latter carrying a peace envoy to France), the French Directory organized an expedition to secure colonies in Cayenne, Guadeloupe, and Saint-Domingue. Several warships, including *Vengeance* (44), were included. On the morning of February 1, 1800, Truxton sighted *Vengeance* and gave chase. Captain F. M. Pitot wished to avert an engagement because *Vengeance* was carrying numerous French soldiers, a cache of money,

and 36 American prisoners. When *Constellation* finally closed with *Vengeance*, the French frigate commenced the firing, aiming as usual for the American ship's rigging. Truxton maneuvered for the weather gauge before ordering his gunners to open fire. The battle was brutal as the ships pounded each other with successive broadsides before finally approaching boarding distance an hour before midnight. With the French sailors waiting to leap, *Constellation* poured grapeshot into the main deck, decimating the boarding party. Only battle lanterns and the flash of guns and muskets lit the fight as the ships drifted apart again until an hour after midnight, when Pitot struck his colors. Unfortunately for Truxton, just as he made preparations to take control of *Vengeance*, his mainmast gave way, allowing the French frigate to escape. *Vengeance* had seven feet of water in its hold, 28 dead, and 40 wounded, although some reports put the number considerably higher. Pitot was convinced that his adversary, which he believed was a 60-gun ship-of-the-line boasting 500 men, had sunk. Although the *Constellation* was in fact outgunned by as much as 50 percent, Truxton's crew fired 1,229 rounds to *Vengeance*'s 742 rounds. Ultimately, *Constellation* owed its survival not to any superior design qualities or slightly larger tonnage but to the proficiency of its crew.

By November 1799, unbeknownst to these mariners, their governments were on the way toward peace as the Consulate (a three-headed executive led by Napoleon Bonaparte that overthrew the Directory) moved to isolate Britain by improving relations with neutral nations such as the United States. The Treaty of Mortefontaine, signed September 1800, accepted the American view that the Treaty of 1778 did not obligate the United States to support France in its war with England and included a French pledge to stop seizing American commerce. Thus, as in its War for Independence, the United States benefited from the European balance-of-power system. Unaware of the peace treaty, *Boston* (28) captured the smaller *Berceau* (24) on October 12, 1800, 500 miles northeast of Guadalupe in what was the final engagement of the war.

Adams' decision to seek peace with France split the Federalist Party and contributed to his loss in the

---

[7] John Adams to J. B. Varnum, December 26, 1808, in Charles Francis Adams, ed., *The Works of John Adams*, 10 vols. (1856), 9:607.

election of 1800 to Thomas Jefferson and the Republicans, who argued the Quasi-War had achieved nothing that could not have been obtained far more cheaply through economic coercion. Peace with France also dealt a serious blow to proponents of a capital-ship navy. On his last day in office, Adams signed the "Act providing for a Naval peace establishment" in an effort to preserve some semblance of a navy. This legislation mandated the selling off of all the ships of the US Navy except for 13 frigates, six of which were to be retained on active duty (the rest "in ordinary"), but even such a small fleet was more than the Jeffersonian Republicans would ultimately accept.

When the Federalists fell from power in 1801, their naval legacy included the purchase of land for six navy yards; stockpiles of masts, timbers, and other naval stores; nascent cordage, copper sheathing, and canvas- and sail-manufacturing industries; and an independent naval service with a functioning administration headed by a cabinet-level secretary. Under the leadership of President Adams and Secretary Stoddert, the young service had performed well in its first conflict, capturing or destroying three French warships, 86 privateers, and over 300 enemy merchantmen while recovering 70 American merchant ships, all at the cost of only one US warship lost.

Commerce Navy, 1801–1805: The Tripolitan War

Thomas Jefferson had two primary goals when he took office: first, to unite the American people by ending political parties, and, second, to pay off the national debt, a goal that required cutting the national budget, the largest portion of which went to the Navy during the Quasi-War. During that war Jefferson made clear his vision for the Navy, writing that he favored

such a naval force only as may protect our coasts and harbors from such depredations as we have experienced [and that he was not for] a navy, which, by its own expenses and eternal wars in which it will implicate us, grind us with public burdens & sink us under them.[8]

The new president planned to retire virtually the entire Navy as soon as sheds of his personal design could be constructed in the Washington Navy Yard to preserve the hulls of the reserve ships.

However, a week before Jefferson assumed the presidency, Basha Yusuf Karamanli of Tripoli declared war on the United States and set a one-time payment of $225,000 plus annual installments of $25,000 as the price of peace. After consulting with his cabinet on May 15, Jefferson ordered the US frigates still in service to the Mediterranean to protect American commerce. Only Congress could declare war, and, although it did not formally do so, Congress passed the "Act for the protection of the Commerce and Seamen of the United States, against the Tripolitan Cruisers" on February 6, 1802. This act was followed by another ordering the building or purchasing of four 16-gun sloops to protect American shipping.

Jefferson was confronting a way of life in the Mediterranean with a long history. What Europeans and Americans deemed piracy (and the Barbary States believed was legitimate maritime privateering) developed during the sixteenth-century wars between the Ottoman Empire and the Holy Roman Empire that upset commerce in the Mediterranean and eventually brought Algiers, Tripoli, and Tunis under Ottoman rule. Over the next two centuries, this system of commerce raiding formalized: investors provided the ships and crews while government officials ensured that North African rulers received a portion of the proceeds (and in turn paid tribute to the Ottoman Empire, their nominal sovereign).

By the late eighteenth century, Barbary rulers made commercial warfare a national policy, and Europeans accepted payment of tribute as a cost of doing business in the Mediterranean. For example, when Portugal made peace with Algiers in 1793, Algerian raiders immediately began seizing American merchant ships, leading to a 1796 treaty providing US payment of $600,000 and four American-built warships in tribute/ransom plus additional annual tribute in gold. After Karamanli took power in Tripoli in a 1795 coup, he immediately began expanding his fleet in an effort

---

[8] Jefferson to Elbridge Gerry, January 26, 1799, in Paul Leicester Ford, ed., *The Works of Thomas Jefferson,* 12 vols. (1904–05), http://oll .libertyfund.org/titles/jefferson-the-works-vol-9-1799-1803.

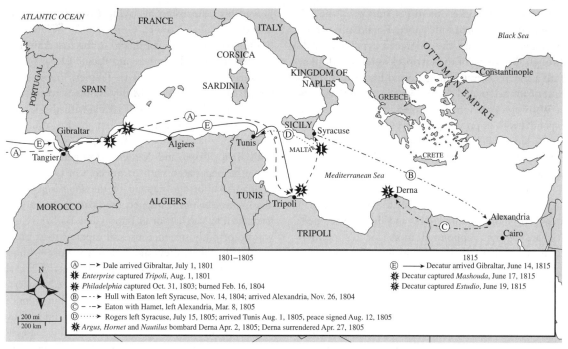

Map 3.2   The Barbary Wars.

to reestablish lapsed tribute payments. Tripolitan raiders soon captured American merchant ships *Betsy* and *Sophia* (enslaving the crew of the former) and negotiated a tribute of over $40,000 in cash and presents in November 1796. It took another $180,000 to buy peace with Tunis in 1797.

While the US Navy focused on France in the late 1790s, Barbary tribute demands increased every year—up to $140,000 to Algiers and $150,000 each to Tunis and Tripoli by 1799. To make matters worse, when the American warship *George Washington* (32) arrived in Algiers with a cargo of delinquent tribute in 1800, the dey (ruler) forced the ship to fly the Algerian flag and transport his tribute to the Ottoman sultan in Constantinople (now Istanbul). Given the trend of escalating tribute payments, it was clear to Jefferson that continuing to pay tribute was incompatible with his desire to trim the government's budget.

Since the Constitution granted Congress the power to declare war, Jefferson authorized force only toward vessels that attacked American merchant ships. The squadron commanded by Richard Dale arrived at Gibraltar on July 1, 1801 (see Map 3.2), composed of the frigate *President*; the Quasi-War subscription ships *Philadelphia* and *Essex* (32); and the schooner *Enterprise* (12). Only a month after its arrival *Enterprise* captured the Tripolitan raider *Tripoli* (14). The three-hour firefight was notable for the superior gunnery of *Enterprise* and the actions of the Tripolitan captain, who three times lowered his colors in surrender, each time raising them and resuming the battle in an attempt to catch *Enterprise* in a compromising position as it attempted to accept *Tripoli*'s surrender. Amazingly, *Enterprise* did not suffer a single casualty, while 60 of *Tripoli*'s 80 sailors were killed or wounded. Given the orders that governed his operations, Captain Andrew Sterrett of *Enterprise* had to release *Tripoli*, but before doing so he followed Dale's orders to "heave his guns overboard, cut away his masts and rigging and [set him free] in a situation

that he can just make out to get into some port."[9]
When *Tripoli* limped into port, Karamanli vented
his anger by forcing the disgraced captain to ride
through the streets of the city backward on a donkey
with a sheep's entrails hung around his neck. Even as
Americans celebrated the news of *Enterprise*'s victory,
in Washington Jefferson pleaded with Congress to
expand his war power authority—which Congress
finally did on February 6, 1802, when it authorized
the Mediterranean squadron to use all available force
against the Barbary States.

The capture of *Tripoli* was one of the few notable
moments of the first two years of the Mediterranean
squadron. Commodore Dale and his replacement
Richard Morris (appointed more for his political
connections than naval pedigree) struggled to implement an effective blockade of the Tripolitan harbor.
The drafts of the American warships forced them to
patrol far enough offshore that smaller corsairs could
evade them by hugging the coastline. When his pleas
for gunboats or other such littoral craft were ignored,
Morris decided convoying American merchant ships
made more sense than a blockade, an action that violated his orders from Navy Secretary Robert Smith.
This action, combined with his lack of consistent
communication with Washington and the growing
frustration in the Republican-dominated Congress
with the mission's high expense and low yield, earned
him dismissal from the Navy.

American fortunes changed dramatically with
the arrival of Commodore Edward Preble in
September 1803 at the head of a squadron consisting
of the frigates *Constitution* and *Philadelphia* (36); the
sloops *Argus* (16), *Nautilus* (16), *Siren* (16), and *Vixen*
(14); and the schooner *Enterprise* (12). Preble had been
a lad of 14 when the first shots were fired at Lexington and Concord, but by the end of the American Revolution he was a seasoned veteran having
served as a privateer before entering the Massachusetts State Navy as a midshipman. Taken prisoner, he
nearly died of typhoid in the prison ship *Jersey* before
being paroled and promoted to lieutenant on board
the sloop *Winthrop* (12). During the Quasi-War, he

proved his seamanship by saving *Essex* during a gale
that dismasted its cohort, *Congress* (36), before continuing on mission in command of the first American
warship to enter the Indian and Pacific Oceans.

During a brief port call in Tangier, Preble compelled Moroccan Sultan Muley Soliman to re-ratify
his father's 1786 commercial treaty with the United
States before proceeding to Tripoli. En route he
learned of the disaster of *Philadelphia*, which along
with *Argus*, *Vixen*, and *Nautilus* had been sent ahead
while he negotiated with Morocco. On October 31,
William Bainbridge, captain of the *Philadelphia*, was
chasing a xebec as it hugged the coast in an attempt
to make it to safe harbor in Tripoli. The Barbary Coast
was notoriously treacherous, and captains took enormous risks when they sailed close to shore without
a seasoned pilot on board. As the minarets of Tripoli
came into view, some of the crew murmured concerns
over *Philadelphia*'s speed and course. Within minutes
the ship ran aground on the Kaliusa Reef. Four hours
of jettisoning cannons, anchors, and even a mast did
nothing to dislodge the ship from the sandbar, as Tripolitan ships stood off Bainbridge's quarter (where his
guns could not be brought to bear) and poured fire
into the immobile *Philadelphia*. Bainbridge surrendered rather than subject his crew of 307 to almost
certain death. Humiliated, Bainbridge wrote a report
to Preble admitting his mistakes, but, through hidden
writing in the margins (using diluted lemon juice visible when heated by a flame), he encouraged Preble
to send a squad of men to set fire to *Philadelphia*,
now riding at anchor under the guns of the city fort,
thanks to a storm that had lifted it clear of the reef a
few weeks earlier.

Arriving off Tripoli in December 1803, Preble
learned that Stephen Decatur's *Enterprise* had captured a Tripolitan ketch. Preble renamed it *Intrepid*
and formulated a plan: Decatur would sail *Intrepid*,
along with 62 volunteers (including eight marines)
and a pilot who spoke Arabic into Tripoli Harbor and
destroy *Philadelphia*. Arriving off Tripoli on February
16, Decatur and *Intrepid* quietly approached *Philadelphia*, clearly silhouetted against the lights of the city.

[9] Richard Dale to Andrew Sterrett, July 30, 1801, in Dudley Knox, ed., *Naval Documents Related to the United States Wars with the Barbary Powers*, 6 vols. (1939–1944), 1:535.

BURNING of the FRIGATE PHILADELPHIA in the HARBOUR of TRIPOLI. 16.Feb.1804.
by ye Gallant Tars of Columbia commanded by Lieut. Decatur.

Figure 3.3 Destruction of the *Philadelphia*, 1804. Engraving by J. B. Guerazzi, 1805. *Source:* © Collection of the New-York Historical Society, USA.

Lookouts on the frigate quickly grew suspicious of *Intrepid*, even though most of the boarding party lay hidden. *Intrepid*'s Arabic-speaking pilot told the lookouts that the ketch had lost its anchor in a recent storm and needed to tie up to the frigate for the night. It was not until the two ships came within a few feet that the Tripolitans detected the ruse and shouted "Americani!" By then the two ships were alongside, and, rushing on board the larger ship, the Americans overpowered the frigate's crew. Within 10 minutes, they placed and ignited incendiary charges that turned the ship into an inferno. Quickly returning to the *Intrepid*, Decatur and his men escaped the harbor just as the fire on *Philadelphia* reached the powder magazines, creating a sight few of the men on *Intrepid* ever forgot (see Figure 3.3). It was an incredibly

audacious and successful mission, one that earned Decatur a captaincy at only 25 years of age and the acclaim of Admiral Horatio Nelson, who reputedly called it "the most bold and daring act of the age."

The *Philadelphia* dealt with, Preble hastily turned to offensive operations with the goal of bringing Karamanli to the bargaining table. Pressure was mounting back in Washington. Many Republicans were annoyed at the expense of the Mediterranean squadron, especially in light of the cost of the recent Louisiana Purchase and the continued ineffectiveness of the squadron itself. Consequently, throughout August 1804, Preble tasked his small fleet (now augmented with eight gunboats and two bomb ketches secured from the sympathetic Kingdom of the Two Sicilies) with shelling the city and fortress at Tripoli. On August 3,

Preble opened with a duel between his ships and the Tripolitan shore batteries, then launched an attack against Tripolitan gunboats that led to fierce hand-to-hand combat before the Americans withdrew, but not before capturing three enemy gunboats, sinking another three, and inflicting over 120 casualties while suffering only 14 casualties of their own. Preble followed this attack with an offer to exchange prisoners, and, since the American prisoners greatly outnumbered the Tripolitans, he offered $50,000 in ransom.

When Karamanli rejected his proposal, Preble again attacked the city, causing modest damage while losing a gunboat and nine men to shore fire. Again, his ransom proposal (this time for $80,000) was refused. In the meantime, learning that he was about to be relieved by Commodore Samuel Barron, Preble launched another three attacks, causing more damage but still failing to gain a favorable response from Karamanli. His final operation before relief on September 9 was an ill-fated plot to send the gunpowder-laden *Intrepid*, under the command of Lieutenant Richard Somers, into Tripoli Harbor in an attempt to blow it up amid the Tripolitan fleet anchored under the walls of the fort. *Intrepid* barely made it into the harbor before exploding in a tremendous fireball that killed the entire crew without inflicting any damage on the enemy. (A monument erected in 1808 to memorialize *Intrepid* now resides at the US Naval Academy.)

William Eaton, US consul at Tunis, spearheaded the final phase of the Tripolitan War, one that produced one of the more colorful affairs in American military history, memorialized today in the "Marines' Hymn" and the Mameluke sword carried by Marine Corps officers. A veteran of the Revolution and Ohio Indian wars, Eaton planned to help Hamet Karamanli replace his elder brother as ruler of Tripoli. Congressmen and naval officers had discussed such a solution to the Tripolitan problem for nearly a decade, and, while initially opposed, Commodore Barron eventually agreed to provide limited naval support to the coup, while Jefferson authorized expending $40,000 to finance the operation.

In late November, Eaton went to Alexandria, Egypt, where he linked up with Hamet and set about raising an army. He was joined by Marine Lieutenant Presley O'Bannon, a sergeant, six enlisted marines, and midshipman Paoli Peck—all from *Argus*. Eaton quickly spent in excess of $100,000—two and a half times the authorized amount—to raise and provision his mercenary army, an eclectic hodge-podge of Muslims and Christians drawn from a dozen nations.

On March 8, 1804, the ragtag force of 400–600 set out by foot for Derna, to rendezvous with *Argus*, *Nautilus*, and *Hornet* for an assault on the city. Eaton employed promises and intimidation to cajole the motley band as it crossed nearly 600 miles of desert and steppe to reach Derna on April 25. Two days later, *Argus*, *Hornet*, and *Nautilus* initiated the assault on the city by shelling the harbor fort and city proper. Meanwhile, a timely charge by Lieutenant O'Bannon and 60 mercenaries attacked the city's numerically superior defenders while a flanking maneuver by Hamet and hundreds of Bedouin horsemen captured the city's palace. Two marines died, one was injured, and Eaton himself had his wrist broken by a stray bullet, but he had his prize, the city of Derna. Days later (May 11), Yusuf Karamanli's army arrived and, after an unsuccessful counterattack, settled down for a siege.

The capture of Derna drove Yusuf into serious negotiations with Tobias Lear, US consul at Algiers, on May 26. Yusuf agreed to release *Philadelphia*'s crew in return for $60,000 and to waive claims to future tribute in exchange for the return of Derna. Eaton reluctantly evacuated Derna, bitter that he was forced to forgo the march on Tripoli. Finally, in a moment important to Marine Corps mythology, Hamet, though abandoned by the United States, presented his prized Mameluke sword to Lieutenant O'Bannon.

Despite missteps and growing pains, the young US Navy emerged from the Quasi- and Tripolitan Wars with a sense of pride and accomplishment, its men gaining valuable operational experience and its traditions beginning to take shape.

Coastal Navy, 1806–1812

On April 17, 1806, the Senate ratified the treaty with Tripoli, bringing Jefferson the peace he sought and, he thought, an opportunity to downsize the expensive Navy. Soon, though, he would face renewed maritime problems, of a much graver proportion. Britain and France were still at war and violating American maritime rights. In an incident that captured public opinion, HMS *Leander* (50), a frigate searching American merchant vessels for contraband and deserting sailors off New York Harbor, fired a warning shot that crossed the bow of a merchant ship and decapitated John Pierce, a sailor on board a coastal sloop on the other side of the intended target. Outraged New Yorkers rioted, burned a British flag, and waylaid a shore party from *Leander*.

The *Leander* incident helped to push the debate over the Navy from one about protecting commerce to one primarily concerned with securing America's coastline. Many policymakers abandoned the old argument that the United States did not need a coastal navy because Europe was "3,000 miles away." With peace in the Mediterranean, support for a coastal force rose rapidly.

Conclusion

The first 20 years of America's naval strategy and operations were shaped by international events, domestic politics, economic pressures, and Americans' ideas of what a republic should be. From 1785 to 1793 anti-navy policymakers held sway as the poor state of America's finances and lack of strong external pressures provided little justification for a peacetime naval force. The last ships of the Continental Navy were sold and the Articles of Confederation severely limited the ability of Congress to support a new naval force. The Constitution of 1787 granted this power to the central government, but it was not until Portugal made peace with Algiers that advocates of a commerce navy were able to pass an act to construct six frigates for the purpose of protecting overseas commerce.

A treaty with Algiers interrupted this building plan and the vision of a commerce navy gave way to John Adams' regional navy vision. From 1797 to 1800 the US Navy met the threat to America posed by French privateers and warships by building frigates and sloops and deploying them along the American coastline and in the Caribbean. During the Quasi-War, President John Adams' plans for a regional navy faced competition from Benjamin Stoddert and other Federalists who envisioned a capital-ship navy, and in 1799 their strategic vision began to predominate as Congress authorized the construction of six ships-of-the-line.

This philosophical switch to a capital-ship navy was short lived. Instead, the new century saw the United States return to the strategic vision of a commerce navy when President Thomas Jefferson ordered the Navy's warships to the Mediterranean to subdue the corsairs of Tripoli. Their success and an increasing violation of America's territorial waters, highlighted by the *Leander* affair, led to a refocus on a coastal defense by a gunboat navy—a naval strategy with significant implications for the War of 1812.

CHAPTER 4

The Naval War of 1812 and the Confirmation of Independence, 1807–1815

On June 22, 1807, Captain James Barron and the USS *Chesapeake* (36 guns) departed Hampton Roads, Virginia, for the Mediterranean. The decks stood cluttered with supplies and equipment, while the ship's guns had been secured for heavy weather. Captain Salusbury Pryce Humphreys of HMS *Leopard* (50) hailed the US frigate and demanded that Barron surrender four seamen who he alleged had deserted from the Royal Navy. When Barron refused to stop, the British ship fired two devastating broadsides directly into the *Chesapeake*. Before Barron's sailors could fire a single shot or surrender, a third British broadside ripped through the *Chesapeake*, inflicting even more damage. After 15 minutes Barron surrendered his ship; British officers boarded the *Chesapeake*, examined its crew, then returned to the *Leopard* with the four alleged deserters, leaving *Chesapeake* to limp back to Norfolk with three dead and 18 wounded.

Plight of a Neutral

The incident was the most serious in a string of events that involved the neutral United States since the wars between Britain and Revolutionary France began in 1793. At the outset American merchants and shipowners had prospered by expanding trade with both countries, but they soon began to suffer as Britain and France each began seizing ships caught trading with their enemy. The enforcement of British Admiralty laws—especially the Rule of 1756, which maintained that any trade illegal in peacetime was illegal during war—led neutrals to seek creative ways to evade such restrictions. Americans argued that stopping in an American port converted a vessel's cargo into neutral American goods. During the Quasi-War, a British Admiralty court issued the *Polly* decision, which upheld the legality of this "Doctrine of the Broken Voyage." Four years later, with the United States at peace with France, the British High Court of Admiralty reversed the *Polly* decision by rendering the *Essex* decision, which ruled that the point of origin determined the nationality of goods, which upheld the "Doctrine of the Continuous Voyage." During the same period British Orders in Council—regulations issued by the monarch with approval of the Privy Council—also limited trade by expanding the list of goods illegal to sell a belligerent to include arms, ammunition, naval stores, or other military items ("absolute contraband") and any item, including food, that could be used to support military operations ("conditional contraband").

On October 21, 1805, Admiral Horatio Nelson defeated a combined Franco-Spanish fleet off Cape Trafalgar in a victory that made the Royal Navy mistress of the seas for the remainder of the war. Five weeks later, on December 5, Napoleon's victory at Austerlitz made France master of the European

America, Sea Power, and the World, First Edition. Edited by James C. Bradford.
© 2016 John Wiley & Sons, Inc. Published 2016 by John Wiley & Sons, Inc.

continent, and the war devolved into a conflict between "Tiger and Shark."

Since Britain and France could not engage one another directly, the two countries waged economic warfare. In mid-May 1806 British Orders in Council required that any ship bound for a French-controlled port must first stop at a British port and allow itself to be searched for contraband. Napoleon responded with his "Continental System," a plan designed to paralyze British commerce. His Berlin Decree (November 1806) forbade British ships to enter European ports, while the Milan Decree (December 1807) permitted French seizure and confiscation of any neutral ship that complied with British rules by stopping in Britain before landing in Europe. Thus, American ships that complied with British regulations risked seizure by the French, while those ships that ignored British rules risked seizure by the Royal Navy.

Despite these hazards, and an upsurge in the impressment of American sailors between 1805 and 1811, US commerce flourished as American merchantmen carried more than 90 percent of the country's growing trade between 1800 and 1812.

A new crisis arose in June 1807 when HMS *Leopard* fired on the USS *Chesapeake* and removed four suspected Royal Navy deserters from the US warship. Under international law warships—unlike merchant ships—enjoy a sovereign status similar to embassy grounds in a foreign nation. Americans were outraged by this violation of American honor and demanded war. President Thomas Jefferson realized the country was ill-prepared for such a conflict and delayed calling Congress into session, hoping tempers would cool. Meanwhile, he instructed state governors to make preparations for defense, and quietly took measures to enlarge the Army and Navy, train militia units, and repair fortifications.

Path to War

Jefferson believed that a coastal defense navy—backed by a militia system—offered the most effective and economical method to defend the nation and preserve its honor. He understood that a limited number of larger warships were needed "to prevent the blockading [of] our ports" and defend overseas commerce, but Congress overwhelmingly defeated legislation for building such ships, making Congress rather than Jefferson responsible for the seagoing navy's being unprepared for war in 1812.[1]

When Congress convened, Jefferson proposed and Republicans in Congress passed an Embargo Act forbidding all foreign trade. Both remembered how effective non-importation/non-exportation had been when employed against the Stamp Act and Townshend Duties during the 1760s and 1770s and hoped that the loss of American trade would convince the British and French to respect American neutral rights. Instead, from December 1807 to March 1809, American ships deteriorated at the wharves, agricultural harvests went unsold, and government revenues declined by $9 million. Many Americans violated the Embargo Act and traded illegally, especially with Canada. Neither the Navy nor the Revenue Service could effectively enforce the despised embargo. The policy hurt Americans more than either Britain or France, and, in doing so, it gave new life to the Federalist Party.

Recognizing this, congressional Republicans repealed the embargo during the final days of Jefferson's presidency and replaced it with the Non-Intercourse Act of March 1809, which lifted all embargoes on American shipping except for those vessels bound for British or French ports. Not surprising, this restrictive measure also failed because once ships departed US ports there was no way to control where they went. In May 1810, in a further retreat from the embargo, Congress replaced the Non-Intercourse Act with Macon's Bill Number 2, which forbade British and French warships from entering US waters and provided that, if either Britain or France ceased attacks upon American shipping, the United States would end trade with the other, unless that country also agreed to recognize America's neutral rights. Napoleon quickly announced that France would respect American neutral rights. The French emperor did not intend to follow through on his promise, but Madison accepted his word at face value and threatened to stop trade with Britain if it did not follow the French lead.

---

[1] Jefferson to Jacob Crowninshield, May 13, 1806, in Paul Leicester Ford, ed., *The Writings of Thomas Jefferson* (1904), 10:267.

Relations between the United States and Britain deteriorated throughout the spring of 1811. In early May, HMS *Guerrière* (38) stopped the merchant brig *Spitfire* off New York Harbor and impressed an American passenger. Learning of the outrage, Captain John Rodgers and the *President* (44) set sail from Annapolis hoping to recover the American. On May 16, Rogers closed on a ship that he believed to be *Guerrière*. As darkness descended and fog enveloped the two ships, both Rodgers and Captain Arthur Bingham of HMS *Little Belt* (22) loudly demanded that the other ship identity itself; neither captain responded. Shortly after 2215 both ships opened fire. Within 15 minutes, British guns fell silent. Badly damaged in the exchange, *Little Belt* suffered 13 killed and 19 wounded. *President* had only one man wounded. On the following morning Rodgers offered assistance to the British ship, but Bingham staunchly refused and sailed off toward Halifax. The Royal Navy was outraged, but many Americans believed the events just retribution for the *Chesapeake* incident four years earlier.

Meanwhile, on the Northwest frontier, Shawnee chieftain Tecumseh and his shaman brother Tenskwatawa (known as the Prophet) were forming a coalition of Indian tribes to resist the expansion of white settlement. In early November 1811, Governor William Henry Harrison advanced with 1,000 regulars and volunteer militia into the heart of Indian country to meet the challenge. Making camp in an elevated defensive position close to Prophet's Town (near present-day Lafayette, Indiana), Harrison instructed his men to sleep with their guns. When the Prophet's warriors attacked during the predawn hours of November 7, 1811, Harrison's men held their position, and, despite suffering almost 200 casualties, drove the attackers back, then counterattacked against the Indians' flanks. Suddenly the Indians broke and ran. Following the conflict, which became known as the Battle of Tippecanoe, Harrison's men burned Prophet's Town, reducing it to ashes. British weapons found at the site convinced many Americans that the British had backed Tecumseh and were responsible for the violence in the northwest.

President James Madison's 1811 annual address to Congress cited the need to bolster the country's defenses, and Congress responded by increasing the Army by 25,000 recruits, adding 50,000 militiamen and appropriating $2 million for ordnance. Congress did not expand the Navy because many Republicans believed it would be resources wasted given the size of Britain's navy. War Hawks—predominantly southern and western congressmen who supported territorial expansion and resented British economic policies and impressments—noted that the Halifax Squadron of the Royal Navy alone numbered 111 ships, including seven ships-of-the-line and 31 frigates, while the US Navy had only 17 frigates, sloops, and brigs plus some 170 gunboats. Thus anti-navy Republicans defeated a proposal to build 10 new frigates. Navy supporters then proposed bills to build six, then four, and finally three frigates; all the bills were rejected by the Republicans, many of whom believed that American troops could easily capture Canada and force Britain to the peace table without a naval campaign.

In May 1812, news reached the United States that the British had not softened their position on neutral trade or on impressment. Seeing no acceptable alternative, Madison sent a message to Congress on June 1 citing four reasons for declaring war against Britain: 1) impressment; 2) illegal blockades; 3) the Orders in Council; and 4) British support for the Indians of the Northwest Territory. Expansionist-minded southern and western War Hawks pushed the vote for war through the House (79–49), while it passed the Senate by a mere three votes (19–13). Congressmen, and Americans alike, anticipated a quick victory. Thomas Jefferson predicted that the conquest of Canada would be "a mere matter of marching."[2] Unfortunately, the Sage of Monticello's prophecy proved unfounded.

On June 16, a day before the Senate opted for war, Britain's foreign secretary announced a suspension of the Orders in Council. Once news of the British repeal reached the United States, many anticipated the two sides would find common ground, but American fervor for war destroyed any possibility of peace.

---

[2] Jefferson to William Duane, August 2, 1812, in J. Jefferson Looney, ed., *The Papers of Thomas Jefferson: Retirement Series*, vol. 5: *1 May 1812 to 10 March 1813* (2008), 293–294.

Gunboats

The Jeffersonian gunboats were one- or two-mast shallow-draft vessels designed to defend American bays and harbors. Generally 40–80 feet long, 15–20 feet abeam, and four to seven feet in the hold, they usually carried one or two long 24- or 32-pound cannon, plus assorted smaller guns. Because of their limited sailing abilities, they became the focus of the navalist "blue-water" versus anti-navalist "white-water" coastal defense debate of the early national period.

During that time Republican theories of defense held that the United States only needed ships-of-the-line or frigates if the country intended to protect its trade or project offensive power overseas. Jefferson, an astute, economy-minded politician, viewed the gunboats as part of a political–military policy rather than a naval program in itself. Gunboats served as an economic and politically sound alternative to the financial burdens of a blue-water navy. Their initial costs would be small; when not in use they could be hauled up and protected under cover, eliminating costly maintenance; manning them with a naval militia would avoid the costs of a standing navy; and, as a defensive weapon, they were unlikely to cause incidents at sea that might provoke war. Gunboats could also be used to enforce revenue laws, suppress piracy along the coastal frontier, and check the illegal slave trade. Finally, gunboat construction provided a unique political opportunity—gunboats could be built throughout the country, allowing the distribution of contracts beyond the regular centers of naval activity.

Jefferson never intended gunboats to replace blue-water vessels, but, when Congress chose to build only gunboats, they became stereotyped as the Jeffersonian alternative to a blue-water navy. Their failure during the War of 1812 represented congressional myopia rather than the inadequacy of Jefferson or his naval policy.

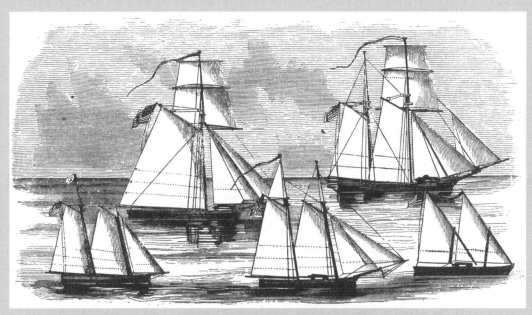

US Navy gunboats. *Source:* Benson J. Lossing, *Pictorial Field-Book of the War of 1812* (1869).

1812: Strategy and Opening Operations

The American strategy of conquering Canada offered the chance to win the war quickly but soon proved unrealistic. During mid-July General William Hull crossed from Detroit into Canada, but, fearing attacks by Indians following the fall of Fort Michilimackinac at the head of Lake Huron, retreated to Detroit and surrendered to General Isaac Brock on August 17 (see Map 4.1). Hull's cowardly submission of Detroit gave the British control of the western Great Lakes. In mid-October General Stephen van Rensselaer crossed the Niagara River with regular Army forces, but was soon defeated at the Battle of Queenston Heights, in part because New York militiamen refused to cross into Canada and support him—they argued that their contractual obligation was limited to defense of their state and did not include offensive operations in another country. A month later General Henry Dear-

born led a militia-based invasion force north along the Lake Champlain corridor toward Montreal, but again the militia refused to enter Canada, resulting in another fruitless campaign. Thus, by the end of 1812, all three invasion attempts—and the strategy of invading Canada—had failed.

Ten days before Madison sent Congress his annual message, Secretary of the Navy Paul Hamilton asked Commodores John Rodgers and Stephen Decatur for "a plan of operation, which … will enable our little navy to annoy in the utmost extent the Trade of Great Britain while it least exposes it"[3] to the Royal Navy, a question that presupposed a *guerre de course* (i.e., commerce warfare) strategy. Rodgers suggested sending two squadrons to sea: one to protect the American coastline, the other to attack shipping in the waters around Britain. Decatur countered saying that US ships should sail singularly or in pairs to engage single enemy warships and attack British trade. Hamilton initially chose Rodgers' plan and divided the US

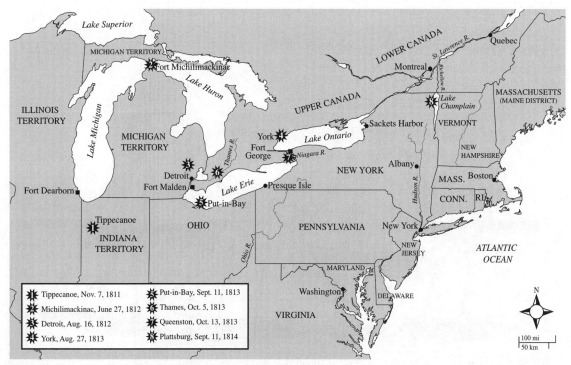

Map 4.1   Operations in the North, 1811–1814.

---

[3] Hamilton to Rodgers and to Decatur, May 21, 1812, in William S. Dudley, eds., *The Naval War of 1812: A Documentary History*, 3 vols. (1985–2002), 1:118–119.

USS *Constitution* sinks HMS *Guerriere*, Aug. 1812
USS *Essex* captures HMS *Alert*, Aug. 1812
USS *United States* captures HMS *Macedonian*, Oct. 1812
USS *Wasp* captures HMS *Frolic*; HMS *Poictiers* captures *Wasp*, Oct. 1812
USS *Constitution* sinks HMS *Java*, Dec. 1812
USS *Hornet* sinks HMS *Peacock*, Feb. 1813
HMS *Shannon* captures USS *Chesapeake*, June 1813
HMS *Pelican* captures USS *Argus*, Aug. 1813
USS *Enterprise* captures HMS *Boxer*, Sept. 1813
HMS *Phoebe* & HMS *Cherub* capture USS *Essex*, Mar. 1814
HMS *Orpheus* & HMS *Shelburne* capture USS *Frolic*, Apr. 1814
USS *Peacock* captures HMS *Epervier*, Apr. 1814
USS *Wasp* (II) sinks HMS *Reindeer*, June 1814, & HMS *Avon*, Sept. 1814
HMS *Endymion* captures USS *President*, Jan. 1815
USS *Hornet* captures HMS *Penguin*, Mar. 1815
- - - British blockaders focused on these ports, 1812–1814

Map 4.2   The War of 1812 at sea.

Fleet into two squadrons, one to be commanded by Rodgers and the other by Decatur, ordering both to target British trade away from American waters.

Upon learning of the declaration of war, Rodgers immediately put his squadron—frigates *President* (44) and *Congress* (36) and sloops *Hornet* (18) and *Argus* (16)—to sea in the hope of catching the British Jamaica convoy that had recently departed the Caribbean. Only two days out of New York, Rodgers spied the frigate *Belvidera* (32) and immediately pursued. After a day-long chase, Rodgers opened fire with a bow gun that soon found its target, slamming round

shot into the *Belvidera*'s stern and killing and wounding several sailors. When the British ship returned fire, a terrifying explosion ripped through the American ship. A gun had exploded, setting off nearby powder and spewing fire through the bow—16 lay dead or wounded, nearby cannon were badly damaged, and *Belvidera* slipped away. The first shots of the War of 1812 at sea had not brought the result sought by Rodgers and Secretary Hamilton (see Map 4.2).

Instead of returning to New York, Rodgers continued searching for the elusive convoy for nearly three weeks, sailing to within 300 miles of the British coast, then south toward the Canary and Azores Islands, finally returning to the United States in late July. This squadron, the largest US naval force to sail since the Barbary War, although unproductive, influenced both British and American operations. Its lack of tangible victories led US Navy leaders to adopt Decatur's plan of deploying frigates individually, and forced the British to divert ships from the coast of the United States to search for Rodgers.

Meanwhile, Isaac Hull and the *Constitution* (44) scoured the area between Chesapeake Bay, Nova Scotia, and Bermuda before encountering HMS *Guerrière* (38) 700 miles east of Boston on August 19. Captain James Dacres of the *Guerrière* initiated battle by twice crossing the bow of the *Constitution*, firing broadsides with each pass. As he did so American sailors could read "NOT THE LITTLE BELT" painted across the foretopsail (top sail on the foremast of the ship) of *Guerrière*. After the second British pass and broadside, Hull closed quickly on the *Guerrière*'s port quarter. For 20 minutes the two ships exchanged fire. Then suddenly the British frigate's mizzenmast gave way, crashing across the deck and into the sea. This proved the turning point in the battle, because the mast, now acting as an anchor, impaired the *Guerrière*'s sailing ability. Hull soon crossed its bow and the *Constitution*'s guns slowly dismantled the British frigate, forcing Dacres to surrender. The following morning, Hull recovered the British wounded, burned the shattered *Guerrière*, and sailed toward Boston, where he received a hero's welcome. Hull's victory, when combined with Rodger's lack of productivity, further convinced Secretary Hamilton of the merit of single-ship or tandem cruises.

Six weeks later Stephen Decatur departed Boston in the *United States* (44). Just after sunrise on October 25, his lookouts and those on board HMS *Macedonian* (38) each spotted the other ship. As Decatur and British Captain John Carden maneuvered to engage, Decatur maintained the windward advantage and prevented the British ship from bringing its carronades in range. Forced to rely on its 18-pound main deck guns, *Macedonian* could inflict little damage on the *United States* while broadsides from the American frigate's longer-range 24-pound cannon ripped into the *Macedonian*, inflicting damage that toppled the British frigate's mizzenmast, leaving it immobile and

forcing Carden to strike his colors rather than suffer certain death. In early December, Decatur landed his slow-sailing prize in New York, where he, like Hull, received a hero's welcome.

When Hull had returned to Boston in late August, William Bainbridge relieved him as commander of the *Constitution*. Putting to sea on October 27, Bainbridge planned to rendezvous with the frigates *Chesapeake*, *Constellation* (36), and *Essex* (32) near the Cape Verde Islands, but, not finding them there, he made for Rio de Janeiro to resupply. At 0900 on December 29, Bainbridge's lookouts spotted two strange sails, which separated almost at once. The larger of the two ships was HMS *Java* (38), commanded by Captain Henry Lambert. Upon seeing the strange sail, Lambert cast off his prize and tried to close on the American frigate. Bainbridge kept his distance until he had determined *Java* was not a ship-of-the-line, then closed and fired two larboard broadsides that damaged the British frigate's rigging and sails. *Java* jockeyed to cross astern of the *Constitution*, delivering a raking broadside that wounded Bainbridge, destroyed the ship's wheel, and killed several sailors. "Old Ironsides" began to drift before the wind, and the lack of maneuverability permitted Lambert to bring *Java* around its stern again, with each British gun hitting its mark. The wounded Bainbridge instructed his sailors to steer using the ship's tiller, and within minutes the *Constitution* regained the windward position. American heavy guns damaged the *Java*'s bowsprit, greatly slowing the frigate and permitting Bainbridge to fire another damaging broadside into the British ship's stern. As musket shot swept the deck of the British ship, *Java*'s foremast crashed into the sea. Bainbridge then took up a position first on *Java*'s stern then off its bow and hammered *Java* into submission. Heavy American guns had won a third frigate victory, yet this had been the bloodiest battle of the naval war—Americans had suffered 36 casualties and the British 124.

American victories in the summer and fall of 1812 forced the British to alter their strategies. While no British naval commander had struck his colors in nearly a decade, by the end of 1812 the Royal Navy had lost six ship-to-ship engagements, which surprised and exasperated British citizens, political leaders, and naval commanders. To prevent additional

Table 4.1 Royal Navy vessels on blockade duty, 1812–1815.

Date	Number of vessels
July 1812	19
July 1813	57
Dec 1813	72
Nov 1814	121
Jan 1815	136

losses the Admiralty ordered frigate captains to avoid single-ship engagements with American super-frigates and tightened the blockade to prevent US warships from getting to sea (see Table 4.1).

Despite these naval victories, the United States had performed woefully in 1812, leading Republican congressmen to call for the replacement of Secretary of War William Eustis and Navy Secretary Paul Hamilton. President Madison yielded to the pressure and requested their resignations. Eustis quickly complied yet Hamilton resisted until December, when he begrudgingly stepped aside, and Madison replaced him with Philadelphia merchant William Jones. The new secretary stressed a new shipbuilding program and made the inland lakes a priority by sending additional resources to upstate New York and western Pennsylvania.

1813: The Naval War Expands

Britain's tightening of the blockade came too late to stop David Porter, commander of the *Essex*, from departing Delaware Bay in September 1812. His orders were to join Bainbridge's squadron but, failing to find Bainbridge at any of the four designated places of rendezvous, Porter rounded Cape Horn to attack British vessels in the Pacific. After a brief stop in Peru, he proceeded to the whaling grounds near the Galápagos Islands. There he took 12 prizes between April and July 1813. The largest of these he armed with 20 guns and renamed *Essex, Junior*. Learning that the British were sending three warships to apprehend him, Porter sailed further west to the Marquesas Islands, where sailors and natives scraped and recoppered *Essex*'s bottom, fumigated its interior

to kill rats, and refit its sails and rigging. Porter's sailors enjoyed the seven-week respite on the island, spending free time with the scantily clad native women. By mid-December Porter departed for Valparaiso, Chile, which he reached in early February 1814. Five days later two British warships, *Phoebe* (36) and *Cherub* (28), entered the harbor. Porter met ashore with Captain James Hillyar and challenged the British officer to a ship-to-ship duel between the *Essex* and *Phoebe*. Hillyar declined and the four ships remained in harbor for almost two months.

On March 28, 1814, a heavy storm hit Valparaiso harbor and *Essex* lost its anchor. As his ship drifted, Porter noticed the enemy ships were out of position, so he decided to make a run for the open sea. While *Essex* departed the harbor, a squall struck the frigate, taking away its main top mast. Unable to outrun the British ships or to return to Valparaiso harbor, Porter took his frigate to a small, shallow harbor south of Valparaiso and anchored as close to shore as possible. Porter hoped that British officers would respect Chile's neutrality and not fire on his vessel, but he was not surprised when Hillyar anchored off the *Essex*'s stern and repeatedly blasted the American frigate. Unable to return fire, Porter tried to close on and board the *Phoebe* and, when unable to, sought to get even closer to shore, out of range of the British guns. When this failed to stop the carnage, Porter ordered his men to swim for land while he remained on board *Essex* with the 58 dead and 66 wounded and struck his flag. He later blamed his loss on the short-range carronades of the *Essex*, whose shot could not reach the *Phoebe* as its long guns pounded his ship. Others, including David Farragut, who, during the Civil War, became the first admiral in the US Navy, blamed Porter's bravado in returning to Valparaiso when he knew that superior Royal Navy ships were in the area. Porter's cruise further validated the strategy of deploying single ships to destroy enemy commerce. Moreover, his actions tied down disproportionate enemy resources by forcing the British to dispatch multiple ships in his pursuit.

Back in the North Atlantic the Royal Navy extended its blockade from Long Island Sound to New Orleans (see Map 4.1). By mid-1813, the *Constellation* was bottled up in Norfolk, and the *United States* and *Macedonian* in New London. Captain James Lawrence, commanding the hard-luck frigate

Chesapeake, waited in Boston for the opportunity to run to sea as two British frigates stood offshore. Philip Broke, commander of HMS *Shannon* (38), was confident that he could defeat the Americans, so he ordered his companion frigate to leave the area and challenged Lawrence to a ship-to-ship duel. Lawrence could not resist this bold challenge despite his untrained crew and *Shannon's* reputation for having the most skilled seamen in the British fleet. Lawrence foolishly accepted Broke's challenge, raised a flag that bore the slogan "Free Trade and Sailors' Rights," and put out to sea. To neutralize the British superiority in long guns, Lawrence planned to fight at close range where his cannonades could carry the day. The artillery exchange between the two frigates began about 1700 and, within an hour, as Lawrence had wished, the two warships closed to 50 yards. The sustained, disciplined, and precise British cannon barrage broke the morale of Lawrence's crew. Soon the *Chesapeake* floundered, drifting uncontrollably into the range of British snipers, who began picking off American officers. When *Shannon* closed to boarding distance, panic spread through the *Chesapeake*. A sniper's bullet felled Lawrence, who was carried below, repeatedly uttering "don't give up the ship." Meanwhile Broke and a British boarding party drove the American crew below deck, pulled down the American flag, and raised the Union Jack, signifying that the ship had been taken. The brutal hand-to-hand engagement cost 70 lives, 100 wounded, and the loss of the *Chesapeake*.

On inland lakes, the US Navy performed better. Following the failed campaigns of 1812, Navy Secretary Hamilton ordered Isaac Chauncey to Lake Ontario with instructions to build a fleet and gain control over the strategic waterways. In early October 1812, Chauncey established his headquarters at Sackett's Harbor, New York, and sent Lieutenant Jesse Elliott to Presque Isle to take command of a squadron then being constructed on Lake Erie (see Map 4.2). During late April 1813, Chauncey supported General Zebulon Pike's raid on York (near Toronto). While still flying the Union Jack above the fort, the British detonated the bastion's ammunition magazine. Pike was struck and killed by flying stone. Already angered by this, American soldiers became even more enraged by reports of soldiers finding a white scalp. Once York had been taken, American soldiers and sailors set fire

to public buildings and looted unattended homes on the pretense that their owners were fighting against the Americans. These actions hardened Canadian attitudes toward the Americans.

Chauncey next sailed westward, to support Colonel Winfield Scott's capture of Fort George, at the mouth of the Niagara River. British Commodore Sir James Yeo took advantage of Chauncey being at the opposite end of Lake Ontario to attack Sackets Harbor, where he burned two vessels and destroyed stores valued at $500,000. Convinced the British would not have attacked had his squadron been there, Chauncey vowed not to leave Sackets Harbor again until he had gained unquestioned naval superiority over his British opponents. As a result, the struggle on Lake Ontario devolved into a war of the adz, ax, and hammer—a naval building race in which neither side ever gained a clear advantage over the other.

When Oliver Hazard Perry succeeded Elliott in command at Presque Isle during the spring of 1813, he found 11 vessels at varying stages of completion. Somehow Perry overcame shortages in cannon, construction materials, and equipment to complete most of the ships by August. Taking advantage of a storm that drove a blockading British squadron off station, Perry redeployed to Put-in-Bay at South Bass Island, a position from which he could threaten British–Canadian lines of communication through Lake Erie.

Perry's move forced British Captain Robert H. Barclay to try to dislodge the Americans. Early in the morning of September 10, he approached Put-in-Bay, and Perry sortied to meet him. Flying above Perry's flagship, the *Lawrence* (20), was a dark flag emblazoned with white letters: "Don't Give Up the Ship"—the dying words of Perry's friend James Lawrence.

Perry's fleet—led by *Lawrence* and *Niagara* (20)—carried short-range carronades, meaning that Perry would need to close in on his opponent. The British ships *Queen Charlotte* (16) and *Detroit* (12) carried long guns, which permitted them to fight at long range. Perry told his officers that he would pair his larger ships against those of the British, leaving commanders of his smaller ships to fire on other targets. Perry then approached the British fleet at an acute angle, which minimized the damage of long-range British raking fire. While closing on the British, a large gap opened between Perry's *Lawrence* and Elliott's *Niagara*. For two hours, the *Lawrence* endured the brunt of three British ships while fighting alone. When the *Lawrence* could no longer fight—75–80 percent of its crew were killed or wounded—Perry left the national ensign on the mast, lowered his commodore's pennant and battle flag, boarded a small rowboat, and departed for the *Niagara*.

Taking command from Elliott, Perry sailed the *Niagara* across the bow of the *Detroit* and delivered a damaging broadside. As the *Detroit* wore around to bring a fresh broadside into action, it collided with the *Queen Charlotte*, leaving both ships immobile. Perry positioned *Niagara* so it could fire on both British warships and raked the helpless vessels into surrender. Perry then took an old letter from his jacket and scribbled a note to General Harrison: "We have met the enemy and they are ours: Two Ships, two Brigs, one Schooner, & one Sloop."[4]

For a victory of such importance, the casualties were relatively light: 123 for the Americans (with two-thirds from the *Lawrence*) and 135 for the British. Despite these low numbers, Perry's victory on Lake Erie profoundly altered the war in the Northwest. By the end of the month, Perry had repaired his fleet and transported Harrison's army across Lake Erie, forcing the British to evacuate Detroit and Malden. Harrison pursued the British and their Indian allies, catching and defeating them at the Battle of the Thames on October 5, 1813. During the battle, the Indian leader Tecumseh was killed and with his death the Indian confederation died as well. The British defeat and Tecumseh's death restored the Northwest Territory to American control.

1814: Tragedy and Triumph

On March 31, 1814, Allied Coalition armies entered Paris, and four days later the French army surrendered, forcing Napoleon to abdicate. With France subdued, Britain turned the full force of its military against the United States. During the spring the Admiralty and War Offices devised a four-prong strategy to break the American will to continue fighting: 1) tighten the blockade and extend it to include New England; 2)

increase operations in Chesapeake Bay to hold American troops in the region to prevent their transfer northward; 3) launch an invasion southward from Canada down the Lake Champlain corridor to sever the New England states from the remainder of the Union and drive Americans to accept a peace settlement; and 4) attack New Orleans to close the Mississippi River to American exports and obtain a bargaining chip for use in future negotiations. British leaders believed if these operations succeeded the United States would fall apart and the American experiment would fail.

British Rear Admiral George Cockburn had spent much of 1813 reconnoitering Chesapeake Bay. In 1814, he expanded his operations, destroying trade, raiding plantations, and liberating slaves. On May 3, British troops ransacked and burned 40 of the 60 houses at Havre de Grace, and, in early June, Cockburn neutralized the Chesapeake Bay Flotilla commanded by Joshua Barney by driving its gunboats and barges into St. Leonard's Creek, off the Patuxent River (see Map 4.3). Leaving a few vessels to blockade Barney, Cockburn sailed down the Bay, and, after failing to take Norfolk, sacked nearby Hampton, where British troops perpetrated untold atrocities.

In mid-April, Vice Admiral Alexander Cochrane arrived in the Chesapeake. With the summer arrival of 2,500 veteran troops from Wellington's army commanded by General Robert Ross, Cochrane wanted to attack Baltimore or Philadelphia. Instead, Cockburn recommended Washington, because it would be easier to attack and "the greater political effect [was] likely to result" from striking the nation's capital.[5] By mid-August, British forces started moving up the Patuxent. They landed troops at Benedict and began marching north along the river while barges closed in on Barney's gunboat flotilla. On August 23 Barney scuttled his vessels (except for one captured by the British) and retreated with his sailors and marines to the Washington Navy Yard. There he gathered cannon and moved them to a defensive position on the western side of the Anacostia River, where they were joined by General William Winder's 7,000 militiamen and regular troops, the only defenders of Washington.

---

[4] Dudley, *Naval War of 1812*, 2:553.

[5] Cockburn to Alexander Cochrane, July 17, 1814, in Dudley, *Naval War of 1812*, 3:156–157.

George Roberts

George Roberts' (1766–1861) story reveals the full gambit of Atlantic world experiences that African Americans endured during the War of 1812. Born a freeman in 1766, Roberts signed on board the privateer *Sarah Ann* (1) and sailed from Baltimore in July 1812. While cruising off the Bahamas during September 1812, HMS *Statira* (38) captured the *Sarah Ann*. Forced to muster on deck, Roberts and five others were singled out as British deserters and taken in irons to Jamaica, where, as deserters, all could be executed. Knowing that Roberts and at least some of the others were undoubtedly Americans, the owners of the *Sarah Ann* retaliated by holding 12 British sailors hostage in Charleston until they were freed in return for Roberts and his fellow prisoners.

In July 1814 Roberts returned to sea as a gunner on board the *Chasseur* (16), a privateer that slipped by the British blockading squadron at New York City and sailed toward the British Isles. There Captain Thomas Boyle preyed on merchant shipping and, in late August, boldly proclaimed the entire British Isles to be under the blockade of a single ship—the *Chasseur*, which had taken 17 prizes, causing the British to send several ships in its pursuit. Roberts and the *Chasseur* returned to Baltimore and a hero's welcome on April 8, 1815.

During the years that followed, Roberts marched in uniform on each September 12 at the annual Defenders' Day commemoration, "never appear[ing] on parade except in uniform."[6] Until his death, Roberts maintained that he would gladly volunteer again, if necessary, to defend Baltimore.

George Roberts. *Source:* Courtesy of the Maryland Historical Society.

The next day, British forces faced a withering fire from Barney's artillery as they approached the bridge at Bladensburg. Other British soldiers stepped into the gap made by each falling man and pressed forward, and, as the determined British crossed the river, the American militia broke and ran. Only Barney's flotillamen stood their ground, but, when their commander fell wounded, they, too, retreated. That evening British troops marched into Washington and torched public buildings, including the Capitol and Executive Mansion, in retaliation for the American burning of York. Captain Thomas Tingey set fire to the Washington Navy Yard and two half-built warships to prevent them from falling into British hands. In the early morning of August 26, British forces evacuated the city and returned to their fleet.

After their easy victory at Washington, the British advanced against Baltimore. On September 12, Admiral Cochrane landed General Ross and troops at North Point to march on the city. Almost immediately Ross fell, mortally wounded by sniper fire. The next morning his successor, Colonel Arthur Brooke, pressed on toward Baltimore but retreated when entrenched defenders blocked his advance. That same morning, September 13, British ships began shelling Fort McHenry. Throughout the day and night,

---

[6] "Another Old Defender Gone," *Baltimore Sun*, January 16, 1861, as quoted in "Star-Spangled History: George Roberts," *Star-Spangled 200*, http://starspangled200.org/History/Pages/Roberts.aspx.

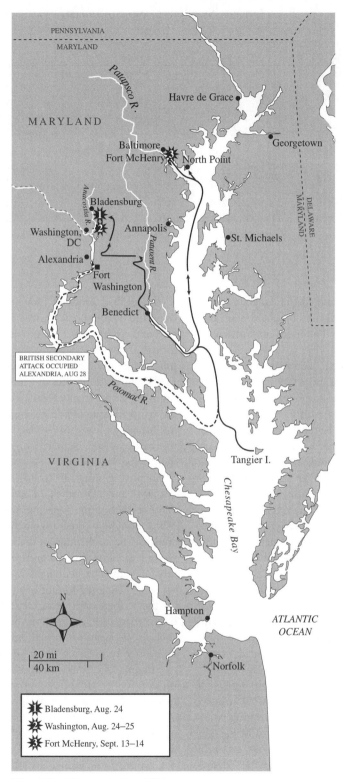

Map 4.3   Chesapeake Bay, 1814.

Figure 4.1   Battle of Plattsburg, 1814. Painting by Dean Mosher. *Source:* Courtesy of Dean Mosher.

cannon fire and rockets battered the American fort, but, after 25 hours of ineffective bombardment, the British withdrew, leaving Baltimore in American hands (see Map 4.3).

Meanwhile, in the north, Governor-General of Canada Sir George Prevost and 8,000 men launched what was expected to be the war-winning invasion of New York. Again, as in the American Revolution, control of Lake Champlain held the key to success (see Map 4.1). Master Commandant Thomas Macdonough had spent months carving a fleet from the New York and Vermont wilderness to counter the flotilla being constructed by British Captain George Downie. In a remarkable achievement, American craftsmen completed the *Saratoga* (26) in 35 days and the *Eagle* (20) in only 19 days. The American squadron ultimately consisted of four ships, six row galleys, and four gunboats.

When news arrived that the British were moving southward, Macdonough, lacking enough sailors to fully man his vessels, begged the Army for any man with naval or artillery experience. He knew that, with short-range guns and inexperienced crewmen, his only hope to defeat Downie lay in forcing a close action. Thus, Macdonough deployed his ships bow to stern off the town of Plattsburg and skillfully prepared for battle by running lines to kedge anchors fore and aft. This would permit him to wind his ships (i.e., turn each one around) to bring a fresh broadside to bear on the enemy should that be necessary.

Prevost had prodded Downie to move his four ships and 12 gunboats against the American squadron in a joint attack as quickly as possible, even though Downie's flagship, the *Confiance* (37), was still being fitted out and manned. On September 11, Downie acquiesced and moved to attack. As he rounded Cumberland Head, the peninsula blocked the wind, making Downie's ships drift slowly toward the American line. Just as Macdonough had wanted, the battle would be determined by gunfire rather than by sailing ability.

Anchoring some 300 yards apart, Macdonough's *Saratoga* and Downie's *Confiance* pounded one another with both suffering severe damage. Then, Macdonough ordered his anchor line cut and his crew to haul in the lines of the kedge anchors, which wound the ship around and presented a fresh battery of guns. The lieutenant in charge on the British ship—Downey having been killed near the start of the engagement—tried to duplicate Macdonough's maneuver, but without having prepared kedge anchors the *Confiance* turned only half way, leaving its vulnerable bow facing the fresh guns of the *Saratoga* (see Figure 4.1). American cannon fire raked the British ship fore to aft and within minutes *Confiance* surrendered. The other British ships followed suit while a pair of gunboats withdrew unmolested. Seeing the naval disaster, Prevost broke off his land attack and retreated to Canada.

Coming in the immediate aftermath of the British burning of Washington, the American victories at

Lake Champlain and Baltimore provided significant boosts to American morale and conversely weakened British resolve to continue the war. By early October British negotiators in Belgium had softened their demands. Diplomats soon negotiated a *status quo ante bellum* treaty (i.e., one that returned to the state of affairs that had existed before the war). Several controversial issues remained unresolved, including the maritime issues that had helped to cause the war, but both sides acknowledged that the treaty ended the war without sacrificing honor, territory, or rights. The Treaty of Ghent was signed on December 24, but news of it did not reach America for over a month.

War in the Southwest

Meanwhile, operations continued in the Gulf of Mexico (see Map 4.4). In early December Admiral Cochrane and a British fleet approached Louisiana carrying 7,500 troops. General Edward Pakenham planned to land his army at Lake Borgne and follow Bayou Bienvenue to the Mississippi River, a 70-mile line of supply and communication from the British

fleet anchored in the Gulf to the river below New Orleans.

When warned of the British approach, Lieutenant Thomas ap Catesby Jones moved his five gunboats to the shallows where Lake Borgne met the Gulf of Mexico and anchored them in a line-abreast formation. As the enemy approached, Jones counted 42 barges armed with light carronades and three gigs altogether carrying more than 1,200 men, whereas Jones had but 204. Two bloody assaults against *No. 156* failed before British barges finally overwhelmed both it and *No. 163* (see Figure 4.2). The remaining American defenders then succumbed one by one to the numerically superior British. The Battle of Lake Borgne had been a costly tactical defeat for the United States but played a key role in the defense of New Orleans.

Americans had previously constructed forts and positioned small seagoing vessels, as well as stationary, moveable, and floating artillery, all along the Mississippi River to guard the most obvious avenues of attack. By delaying the British, the gunboats robbed the enemy of the element of surprise and bought

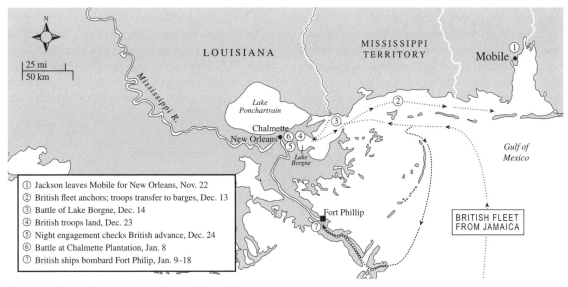

Map 4.4 Operations in the southwest, 1814–1815.

Figure 4.2   Battle of Lake Borgne, 1814. Painting by T. L. Hornbrook, 1815.

Major General Andrew Jackson time to reposition his defenses before the Redcoats could launch an assault against the city. It took the British forces a week to cross Lake Borgne and hack their way through swamps and cane fields to reach the Mississippi River before they could launch the two-week land campaign for New Orleans that culminated with the January 8, 1815, engagement on the Plains of Chalmette. Commodore Daniel Todd Patterson's sloop *Louisiana* (16) and schooner *Carolina* (14) contributed greatly to Jackson's success in that decisive battle. Both vessels sailed down the Mississippi River to fire on the British left flank while Jackson's army attacked the British center and right on December 23. Four days later, the British destroyed the becalmed *Carolina*, but on December 28 well-directed fire from *Louisiana* broke the attacking columns of British troops when they probed Jackson's defensive line at Chalmette. During the climactic attack on January 8, 1815, the *Louisiana*, still anchored in the Mississippi River to the right of

the American position, poured devastating fire into the Redcoats, contributing to the more than 2,000 casualties, including General Pakenham.

The British campaign against New Orleans failed for a number of reasons including Britain's inability to use its naval forces in the engagement at New Orleans. News of the Treaty of Ghent reached the Gulf Coast on February 13, and, the war over, the British sailed away.

Rhetoric and Reality

The War of 1812 settled very little. The Americans had not captured Canada, but they had not lost any territory either. The United States did break the power of the Indian confederations in the north and south, and the British in Canada walked away from their native allies once and for all. Americans had fought for "free trade and sailors' rights" but the peace settlement ignored impressment. In the end, each side shaped its view of the peace to support its national message: Britain had defeated Napoleon and saved the world; the United States had stood up to the victors against Napoleon. Both sides could claim a victory of sorts while neither side thought it had lost.

The US Navy benefited greatly from the 1812 frigate victories against the British. These encounters, combined with the exploits of Oliver Hazard Perry and Thomas Macdonough, fed American pride. Yet the rhetoric masked a truly different reality. During the war, the US Navy won 13 of the engagements at sea and Britain's navy 12. Heavier firepower rather than innate American talent as sea warriors determined all but two of these victories. Indeed, the US Navy's ability to match the Royal Navy ship for ship had little impact on the war at sea, given Britain's numerical superiority. Once the British blockaded the American coastline, US warships found it difficult to get to sea. Ultimately, Republican reliance on militia and gunboats failed the country during the war because neither the militia nor gunboats prevented the British from landing and operating wherever they wanted.

The War of 1812 exposed serious weaknesses in American defense policy. The militia and Army had both performed poorly, so Congress voted to create a reorganized peacetime army of 10,000, or three times the size of the Jeffersonian standing army. Secretary of War William Crawford demobilized the wartime Army by removing incompetents and initiated a coastal fortification program that would build some 40 bastions stretching from Maine to Louisiana. Within a few years, his successor, John C. Calhoun, further reorganized the Army, reducing it to a skeleton force of 6,000 men but doing so in such a way that the Army could be quickly "expanded" to 19,000 men if needed.

In early February 1815, Congress created a three-member Board of Naval Commissioners to relieve the navy secretary of logistical matters such as supply and ship construction; personnel matters and operations stayed under the secretary's authority. In 1816, via an "Act for the Gradual Increase of the Navy," Congress authorized construction of nine 80- to 100-gun ships-of-the-line, 12 heavily armed frigates carrying 40 to 60 guns, and three steam batteries. This represented the largest peacetime naval expansion program in American history until that time.

The Treaty of Ghent had settled few disagreements between the United States and Britain, but within three years tensions between the two were reduced by the Rush–Bagot Treaty, which demilitarized the Canadian–American border and ended the Anglo-American shipbuilding race that had resumed on the Great Lakes after the war. Similarly, the Convention of 1818 settled the US–Canadian border, fishing rights off Newfoundland and Labrador, and American claims for compensation for slaves that the British had liberated during the war. A year later, the United States and Spain signed the Transcontinental Treaty of 1819, transferring ownership of Florida to the United States and delineating the border between Spanish America and the United States.

In 1816, the Navy had begun to prepare for the last war it fought, but these agreements with Britain and Spain reduced threats to the continental United States and work on ships-of-the-line was suspended. What the Navy needed now were nimble, quick, and shallow-draft warships able to protect merchant shipping. A new era was at hand.

CHAPTER 5

The Squadron Navy

Agent of a Commercial Empire, 1815–1890

Shortly after the War of 1812 ended, Commodore John Rodgers observed that the "navy will never again I fear present such a field for the acquirement of glory as it has done."[1] A distinguished senior officer and combat veteran of the Quasi-War, the Barbary Wars, and the War of 1812, Rodgers presciently foresaw that the glorious Age of Fighting Sail had ended. The nations of Europe did not fight another major war for a century. For the United States, this meant that its navy would not be required to protect American neutral rights and commerce from attacks by European powers. As a result, the role of the US Navy changed dramatically. In the next eight decades, the United States fought two conventional wars lasting a total of only six years. Both the Mexican–American War and the Civil War were continental affairs confined almost exclusively to North America. Although the Navy played an active role in each conflict, neither war required the use of frigates or ships-of-the-line. The Navy also fought in several unconventional wars including the Second Seminole War in Florida, from 1835 to 1842.

Between 1815 and 1890, naval advocates pressed periodically for the nation to create a large European-style navy, but they failed to redefine the nation's traditional defense and naval policies. Accordingly, the wartime Navy would be expected to defend the nation's coastline while its fast cruisers would attack the enemy's merchant ships on the high seas. In the decades after 1815, the key naval question, then, was what role or mission the nation wanted its peacetime Navy to perform. Although public officials and naval officers periodically debated this issue, the Navy's primary mission was shaped by the nation's dramatic geographic and economic expansion in the nineteenth century. Most importantly, the exponential growth of American foreign trade and the sharp increase in the size of the American merchant marine required naval support and protection. While the greatest percentage of American foreign trade continued to be with Britain, Europe, and the Caribbean, the geographic scope of American trade expanded as new markets opened to American trade in Latin America, China, the Pacific, and other parts of Asia. In addition, one of the nation's most important industries prior to the Civil War, whaling, required naval support as it spread across the vast reaches of the Pacific. The need for an expanded naval presence further accelerated after the United States became a two-ocean power with the acquisition of Oregon in 1846 and Upper California in 1848, then with the discovery of gold, which brought tens of thousands of settlers to northern California by 1850.

---

[1] Rodgers to Minerva Rodgers, February 14, 1815, Rodgers Family Papers, Manuscript Division, Library of Congress.

America, Sea Power, and the World, First Edition. Edited by James C. Bradford.
© 2016 John Wiley & Sons, Inc. Published 2016 by John Wiley & Sons, Inc.

John T. McLaughlin

John T. McLaughlin (1812–1847) entered the Navy as a midshipman in 1827. Nine years later the Navy was ordered to prevent shipments of arms from Cuba and the Bahamas to the Seminole Indians, who were resisting efforts to remove them from Florida. McLaughlin, still a midshipman, was shot in the chest during an Indian attack in February 1837. A year later, the War Department purchased two schooners and several barges to be operated by the Navy in support of operations against the Seminoles. Recovered from his wound, McLaughlin, now a lieutenant, took command of this "Mosquito Fleet," a division of the West India Squadron, in December 1839 with orders from Secretary of the Navy James K. Paulding to "furnish yourself with a sufficient number of flat bottomed boats and in addition to these procure a like sufficiency of long plantation canoes [and to use these] to penetrate the Everglades, [to] surprise and capture the Indian women and children and thus end the war which has cost so many millions."[2]

Acting on these orders, McLaughlin increased his command until it included as many as seven small warships, two barges, 140 canoes, 68 officers, several hundred sailors, and 130 marines. Parties of these men soon began pursuing Seminoles into the interior of Florida. Between December 31, 1840, and January 19, 1841, McLaughlin personally led a force of 90 sailors and 60 marines from Fort Dallas on the Atlantic across the Everglades to the Gulf of Mexico. Similar operations followed until an end to the war was declared in May 1842. McLaughlin and his "Swamp Sailors" encountered few Seminoles but burned many of the Indians' crops and dwellings in what proved to be a futile effort to capture them and send them west of the Mississippi River. Five years later, in July 1847, McLaughlin died from diseases contracted during his naval service.

John T. McLaughlin.

The term repeatedly used to describe this nineteenth-century peacetime naval mission was the "protection of commerce," which was never precisely defined by Congress, the president, or the Navy Department. Rather, the operational definition of the term evolved and expanded in response to domestic political pressures and external demands that the nation's foreign trade and commercial diplomacy placed on the Navy. In the United States, interest groups such as the sealing and whaling industries, merchants and shipping companies, and supporters of a transpacific steamship line demanded active protection and support from the Navy. In addition, American activities in remote areas inevitably produced instances in which the Navy needed to protect American lives and property, conduct diplomacy, fight pirates, and sometimes retaliate against attacks on American merchant ships.

For the peacetime Navy, the years from 1815 to 1890 do not constitute a single, coherent chronological period but are best divided into three periods broken respectively by the Mexican–American War (1846–1848) and the Civil War (1861–1865); that is, separate periods of activity from 1815 to 1846, from 1848 to 1861, and from 1865 to 1890.

---

[2] Pauling to McLaughlin, December 2, 1839, as quoted in Nathan D. Shappee, "Fort Dallas and the Naval Depot on Key Biscayne, 1836–1926," *Tequesta*, 21 (1961), 23.

Distant Stations

Between 1815 and 1846, the Navy's peacetime role expanded unevenly as most Americans remained preoccupied with expansion across the continent. Since American overseas trade increased steadily but slowly, demands on the Navy for the protection of that commerce also grew slowly. Immediately after the War of 1812, postwar nationalism and the popularity of the Navy led Congress to authorize construction of nine ships-of-the-line, 12 heavily armed frigates, and three steam batteries in 1816. However, work was halted when treaties were signed that settled US borders with British and Spanish colonies to the north and west, and the Panic of 1819 ushered in a national depression that made it impossible for the federal government to afford a large navy. By 1820, it was also clear that the Navy's primary peacetime role would be the defense of the nation's overseas commerce.

The most immediate threat to that commerce came from Algiers, whose ruler had begun seizing American merchant ships during the War of 1812. Eight days after the Senate ratified the Treaty of Ghent (ending war with Britain), President Madison asked Congress to declare war on Algiers. Congress refused to pass a formal declaration of war but authorized deployment of naval forces on March 3, 1815. Secretary of the Navy Benjamin Crowninshield immediately ordered squadrons commanded by William Bainbridge and Stephen Decatur to the Mediterranean. Decatur departed first and reached Gibraltar before Bainbridge even set sail. On June 17 his squadron captured the Algerian flagship *Mashouda* (46 guns) and by month's end Decatur had forced the dey (ruler) of Algiers to release the American seamen he held prisoner, to pay America $10,000 in reparations, and to relinquish payment of all tribute by the United States. Decatur proceeded on to Tunis and Tripoli, where he obtained indemnity for American prizes turned over to the British during the war and release from payment of future tribute. His goals achieved, Decatur departed for home but left behind a "squadron of observation" to ensure compliance to the treaties signed. Those ships formed the nucleus of the Mediterranean Squadron, the first of six squadrons established to protect American lives and property around the world (see Map 5.1).

The most persistent problem was piracy in the Caribbean. One newspaper estimated that there were more than 3,000 pirate attacks between 1816 and 1823. Some pirates operated as privateers with authorization from Latin American loyalist or revolutionary governments but most simply preyed on ships, crews, and passengers sailing in the Caribbean. Most operated small, shallow-draft ships from the innumerable shallow inlets, bays, and stream entrances of the Caribbean's many islands. They struck suddenly, outmaneuvered pursuers, and disappeared quickly. Ships-of-the-line and heavy frigates were useless in combating them. Instead, the United States needed to build smaller warships, sloops, and schooners, which were fast and could operate in shoal waters.

Congress responded to the piracy problem by building or purchasing dozens of sloops and schooners and establishing the West India Squadron in 1821. Its mission, the destruction of piracy, proved tedious and dangerous. Caribbean pirates were elusive. Their lairs on foreign soil were widely scattered, hard to locate, and difficult to attack. Disease, particularly yellow fever, posed a threat that forced the Navy to suspend operations on a number of occasions.

Exacerbating the challenge was the reluctance of some foreign officials to cooperate with the Navy. Their shielding of pirates produced some sensitive political situations. The most serious occurred in 1824 when Commodore David Porter learned that American naval officers (in civilian clothes) had been temporarily jailed while on shore to confer with the mayor of Fajardo on Spanish Puerto Rico. Porter responded by landing 200 men, demanding an apology, and threatening to destroy the town. Porter received his apology but his overreaction displeased American officials, who feared diplomatic repercussions with Spain. As a result, Porter was recalled to the United States, court martialed, and sentenced to a six-month suspension from the Navy. Although his penalty was light, Porter resigned angrily from the Navy. Not until the end of the 1820s did American and British efforts largely eliminate piracy from the Caribbean.

The breakup of the Spanish Empire in Latin America after 1815 also posed threats to US commerce as neutral ships, including American, were caught in the struggle between Spanish loyalist and revolutionary

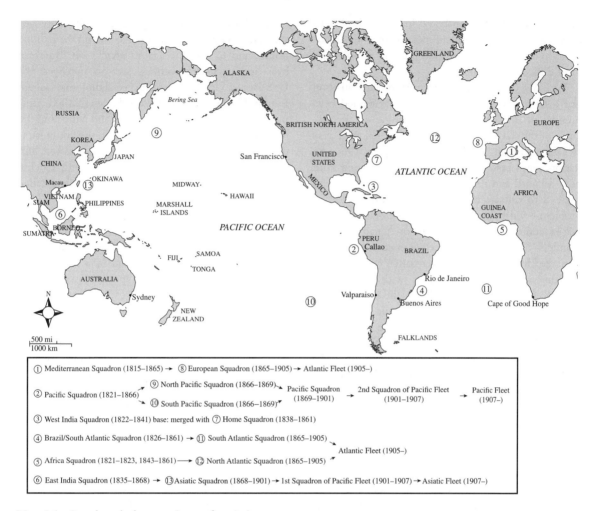

Map 5.1 Squadron deployment (years of service).

governments, both of whom commissioned privateers, established blockades, seized neutral ships, and harassed American citizens in various ways. In response, the United States dispatched naval forces with instructions to protect American property and preserve American neutrality. Although both royalist officials and rebel leaders violated American neutral rights in various ways, commanders of the Pacific Squadron (established 1821) and Brazil Squadron (established 1825) only rarely intervened forcefully. Instead they protected American rights and commerce in less dramatic but substantive ways, such as by furnishing convoys and escorts between ports that had been illegally blockaded. In various ports, the presence of naval ships helped to minimize harassments of American citizens and sailors. Naval crews also furnished supplies and equipment for merchant ships and whalers. And naval ships acted as safe depositories for money and specie collected by American merchant ships and transported that specie back to the United States.

Although direct naval intervention was rarely needed to protect American interests overseas, a constant naval presence was required. Deployment of the Mediterranean, Pacific, and Brazil Squadrons was followed, in 1821, by the creation of the Africa Squadron to protect American interests on the coast of North Africa and police the international slave trade, which the United States had outlawed in 1808. The Mediterranean was the largest and most prestigious squadron while the Africa station was the least popular and most difficult assignment.

Typically, the flagship of each American squadron was a frigate or ship-of-the-line accompanied by a number of smaller warships. Depending on the distance of the station from the United States, the cruise of each squadron lasted two or three years. Once on station, naval vessels showed the flag by sailing from port to port, and American commanders paid their respects to officials and helped Americans who had problems with local authorities. Distant stations placed additional responsibilities on squadron commanders. In the era before telegraphic communication, squadron commanders were often weeks or even months out of communication with government officials in Washington. In addition, the United States maintained a minimal or no diplomatic presence in many countries around the world. As a result, naval officers stood in to perform routine diplomacy, sign basic commercial agreements, and sometimes make decisions that defined American policy. Although they occasionally exceeded their authority, commanding officers on overseas stations tended to be both deliberate and cautious in their diplomatic behavior.

Andrew Jackson, Navalist

The peacetime role of the Navy continued to grow under the unlikely leadership of President Andrew Jackson. An agrarian Democrat and former militia general, Jackson believed in a limited federal government, fiscal retrenchment, and a small, professional military establishment. After he assumed office in 1829, Jackson announced that the Navy required "no more ships of war than are requisite to the protection of our commerce."[3] However, Jackson pursued an aggressive diplomacy to defend the nation's honor and to expand American trade abroad. He took pride in his ability to resolve commercial disputes with European nations, to sign commercial treaties with Russia and Turkey, and to restore direct trade between the United States and British ports in the Caribbean.

To achieve his objectives, Jackson readily employed the Navy to open new markets, to defend the nation's honor, and to retaliate against attacks on American lives and property overseas. Jackson deployed the USS *Peacock* (18) to transport special diplomatic agent Edmund Roberts on a mission that established commercial relations with Siam in Asia and Muscat in the Middle East in 1833. Two years later, the administration dispatched Roberts on a second mission, this time to establish commercial relations with Cochin China (Vietnam) and Japan, but the project failed when Roberts died in Macao in 1836.

When American merchantmen were attacked, Jackson readily deployed the Navy to retaliate. In 1831, he sent the Navy to the Falkland Islands after three American ships were seized in a seal-hunting dispute. A year later, Jackson supported Josiah Tattnall, commander of the *Grampus* (12), when Tattnall seized a Mexican ship for alleged piracy. The most serious incident, however, occurred in Asian waters in 1831. When the captain of the *Friendship* went ashore at Kuala Batu (Quallah Batoo), Sumatra, to buy pepper, armed locals seized the American ship. The captain and the several crewmen managed to escape, enlist the support of three nearby merchant ships, and recapture the *Friendship* three days later. But three Americans had been killed in the attack, the ship had been plundered, and an estimated $41,000 in specie, opium, and other cargo had been stolen.

After learning of the attack, Jackson dispatched Captain John Downes in the frigate *Potomac* (50) to demand restitution of the lost property and punish the men responsible for the attack. When he reached Kuala Batu in February 1832, Downes did not investigate or confer with local officials, but instead, based on information he had gathered en route, simply attacked the village. In the ensuing battle, the American force destroyed forts, burned the village, and killed 100 natives including some women and children. In talks with villagers, Downes emphasized that any future attacks would bring similar American reprisals. The *Potomac* then sailed along the nearby coast, where Downes received rajahs from other villages and accepted their assurances of friendship.

---

[3] Jackson, "First Annual Message [to Congress]," December 8, 1829, in *The Addresses and Messages of the Presidents of the United States, from Washington to Harrison* (1841), 369.

Word of the attack on Kuala Batu reached Washington in July 1832 with partisan feelings running high during the campaign to re-elect Jackson. When it became apparent that Downes had acted precipitously, without investigating the situation, and had secured neither an indemnity nor restitution of the lost property, Jackson's opponents castigated Downes for not negotiating prior to his assault and denounced Jackson for waging war without congressional authority. A political controversy followed but it passed quickly when it became clear that Downes had disobeyed his orders. Although the administration did not publicly criticize Downes or subject him to a court martial, it was clearly displeased with his conduct. The long-term effect of Downes' actions also proved questionable because subsequent attacks on Americans occurred in the area.

The Jackson administration also supported an unprecedented role for the Navy in overseas exploration. The idea of a government exploration expedition to the southern and central Pacific (or South Seas) dated back to the Madison administration but it did not generate strong support until the early 1830s. Then—driven by dreams and supported by a disparate group of scientists, whaling captains, politicians, and young, progressive-minded naval officers such as Matthew F. Maury, Thomas ap Catesby Jones, and Charles Wilkes—the project gained momentum. The proposed naval expedition would enhance American stature by exploring Antarctica, conducting scientific research, compiling geographic and commercial information, and surveying the waters of islands of the vast region. According to the writer Jeremiah Reynolds, who had served as Downes' secretary on board the *Potomac*, American "commerce, science, [and] patriotism" demanded such an expedition. In atypical fashion, in 1836, large, bipartisan majorities in Congress quickly approved funding for the US Exploring Expedition. Even Jackson, an agrarian Democrat from Tennessee, wrote of his "lively interest" in the project. By the last two years of his administration, Jackson's use of the Navy had converted him into a proponent of naval expansion. Operating with a federal surplus for one of the few times in American history, Congress responded to the president's requests for naval expansion by increasing naval expenditures by 50 percent in 1836 and an additional 113 percent in 1837.

In those years, naval expenditures represented almost 20 percent of total federal expenditures.

None of Jackson's presidential successors in the late 1830s and 1840s took an active interest in the Navy or used it aggressively as an arm of American foreign or commercial policy. For example, President Martin Van Buren took little interest in the US Exploring Expedition, and disagreements between naval officers and the Secretary of the Navy over the size and goals of the project resulted in long delays. The first commander resigned in frustration. Then, after several senior officers declined the command, the appointment of Lieutenant Charles Wilkes produced a hail of criticism because of his junior rank. Finally, after more than two years of delays, the expedition sailed from Norfolk in August 1838 on what became a nearly four-year cruise that circumnavigated the globe.

China and the East India Squadron

Nevertheless, in spite of official indifference, the peacetime role and importance of the Navy continued to grow. In China, a few Americans had engaged in a small but very lucrative trade for years as they exchanged furs, sandalwood, cotton goods, and some opium for Chinese silks and tea. Without a formal trade treaty, Americans and other foreigners operated at the pleasure of Chinese officials under tight restrictions from a small compound at Canton (present-day Guangzhou). The East India Squadron was created inadvertently in 1835 when the Navy Department dispatched Captain Edmund Kennedy to Asia with two ships and authorized him to fly the broad pennant of a squadron commander (or commodore). Although Washington paid little attention to the new squadron, President Van Buren acknowledged its permanent status in 1840.

Tension and differences between the Chinese and foreigners grew during the 1830s and eventually resulted in the First Opium War (1839–1842) between China and Britain. The British prevailed and in 1842 imposed a treaty that expanded its rights and opened five ports for trade. Since the United States had no diplomatic presence in China, the small two-ship squadron played an important role in protecting American trade in that country. After the First Opium War, Commodore Lawrence Kearny secured from Chinese officials the unofficial right for Americans to trade at the five ports in China on an equal basis with the British. Then in 1844, with the assistance of the East India Squadron, American diplomat Caleb Cushing negotiated the Treaty of Wanghia, which formally extended commercial privileges and granted "most favored nation" status to the United States. Since Chinese officials interpreted the treaty as a means of restricting (not expanding) trade and contact with the Western "barbarians," the Navy's primary responsibility in China during the 1840s and 1850s was to ensure that the terms of the treaty were being observed by regularly visiting and occasionally intervening at the treaty ports.

Reform and Exploration

In the early 1840s, the Navy enjoyed a brief period of reform and rejuvenation under the leadership of Secretary of the Navy Abel P. Upshur. Although a lawyer and Virginia planter, Upshur had personal ties to the Navy and vigorously sought to reshape the service. The result was an increased budget that produced new ships, introduced new steam and ordnance technologies, and implemented administrative reforms that saw the ineffective Board of Navy Commissioners replaced by a more efficient bureau system. Congress had established the Board after the War of 1812 exposed administrative weaknesses in the Navy. The three senior Navy captains who formed the board were charged with studying and making recommendations to the Secretary of the Navy concerning the location of yards, the proper armament and equipment of ships, rations to be issued to seamen, and other logistical and material matters. They had no power over personnel or operations. Though helpful at first, the Board became extremely conservative and retarded technological innovation until Congress abolished it, replacing it with the bureau system, in which the captain heading each of five new bureaus—Yards and Docks, Construction and Repair, Provisions and Clothing, Ordnance and Hydrography, and Medicine and Surgery—had administrative responsibility and could be held accountable in his particular field.

Upshur also used the Navy aggressively when he chose Captain Thomas ap Catesby Jones to command the Pacific Squadron and instructed Jones to protect American interests in politically unstable Upper California. Unfortunately, Jones misinterpreted conditions there to mean that the United States was at war with Mexico. In October 1842, Jones seized Monterey and claimed it for the United States. Embarrassed officials in Washington disavowed this action and recalled Jones but their aggressive intentions were unmistakable. However, the momentum begun by Upshur did not persist. As a member of the politically beleaguered Tyler administration, Upshur's influence with Congress was limited and he was killed in 1844 by an explosion on the new steam warship *Princeton* after he left the Navy Department to become secretary of state.

Ironically, one of the Navy's major achievements in the early 1840s became embroiled in controversy and did not receive the recognition that it had rightfully earned. The US Exploring Expedition consisted of six ships and an initial complement of 346 officers and men. During its four-year absence, little news of the expedition's progress reached the United States because the expedition spent much of its time in remote parts of the Pacific from which communication was primitive. Moreover, some of the reports that did reach the United States revealed problems with the expedition, particularly with its commander, Charles Wilkes.

After departing from Norfolk in 1838, the expedition sailed south to Cape Horn, where it surveyed the straits and islands near Terra del Fuego and explored the ice shelf to the southeast. In 1839, the squadron proceeded north along the coast of South America and then west to extensively survey three of the Tuamotu Islands: Fiji, Samoa, and Tonga. The expedition proceeded next to Sydney, Australia, before heading south to survey 1,500 miles of the coast of Antarctica (see Figure 5.1). In 1840, the expedition sailed north to Tonga and Fiji en route to Hawaii. In the Fijis, islanders killed two Americans. In response, Wilkes burned the village of the offenders, killing 87 natives in the process. He also forced the survivors to beg forgiveness by crawling to him on their hands and knees. During the winter of 1840–1841, the expedition used Hawaii as a base from which to explore Samoa, Tahiti, and the Marshall Islands. In 1841, the expedition visited the Pacific Northwest before heading for home by sailing further west across the Pacific. After touching in the

Figure 5.1 US Exploring Expedition party ashore on Antarctica, 1840. *Source:* US Naval History and Heritage Command # NH 51495.

Philippines, Borneo, Singapore, and the Cape of Good Hope, the remaining three ships of the expedition reached the United States in June 1842.

By any measure, the accomplishments of the expedition were impressive. It had lost two ships and 28 officers and men. (Another ship had returned to the United States after the first phase of the voyage.) Its ships had logged more than 87,000 miles, surveyed 280 Pacific islands, and produced 180 charts. It had confirmed the existence of the continent of Antarctica and mapped 1,500 miles of its coastline. The expedition also charted 800 miles of coastline in the Pacific Northwest including Puget Sound, the lower Columbia and Willamette Rivers, and San Francisco Bay. The information contained in these charts and surveys would prove invaluable to whaling and sealing ships as well as to merchant ships involved in the

China trade. Along the way, the expedition's civilian and naval scientists had collected thousands of scientific specimens of plant, animal, and marine life as well as numerous other artifacts. Plus, Wilkes signed a number of commercial agreements with island kingdoms.

However, from the moment it arrived home, controversy engulfed the expedition. Launched by a Democratic administration, it returned to a tense partisan atmosphere in Washington in which the Whig Party was in power and President John Tyler politically beleaguered. Moreover, Wilkes was a controversial and divisive figure. Although he was an intelligent and capable officer, Wilkes was also vain, conceited, insecure, and overbearing. As a result, he ended up alienating many of the officers who should have been his strongest supporters. Once back in the United

States, Wilkes was the object of sharp criticism. Navy secretary Uphsur subjected Wilkes to a court martial. The subsequent trial exonerated Wilkes on most charges but he was nevertheless humiliated by a public reprimand from Upshur. In the controversy, which continued for months, the important achievements of the US Exploring Expedition were largely overshadowed, but, in fact, the expedition had set an important precedent for other naval exploring expeditions that followed in the 1850s.

War with Mexico

The dominant historical theme of the 1840s for the United States was continental expansion as the nation aggressively spread westward. The United States annexed the Republic of Texas in 1845 and acquired

the Oregon Country in a treaty with Britain in 1846. That same year Mexican troops attacked an American patrol in disputed border territory, and the two countries went to war in a conflict in which the United States conquered and acquired a huge area in the southwest including the Mexican provinces of Upper California and New Mexico. During the war, the US Navy played an active role in the Gulf of Mexico (see Map 5.2). Commodore David Connor commanded the Home Squadron, blockading the coast of Mexico. His second-in-command, Captain Matthew C. Perry, directed attacks on Mexican ports, and together they executed the landing of General Winfield Scott's 8,600-man army in the largest amphibious operation in history prior to the one at Gallipoli during World War I (see Figure 5.2). Scott's army, including a battalion of 357 marines, then marched from Veracruz to

Figure 5.2 "Landing of American Forces ... at Vera Cruz," 1847. Lithograph by N. Currier, 1847. *Source:* Anne S. K. Brown Military Collection, Brown University.

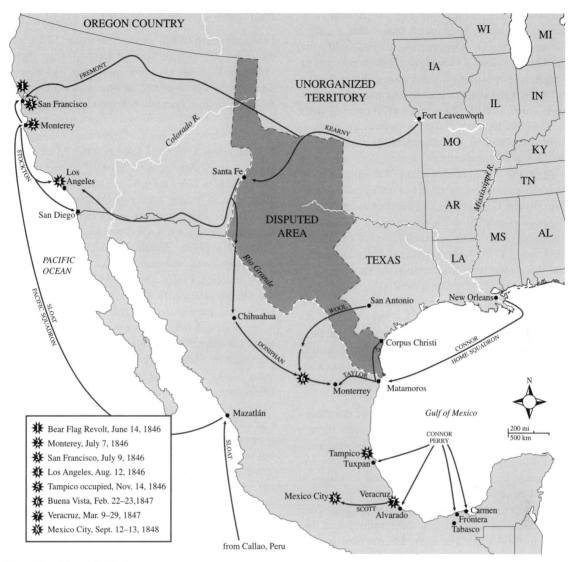

Map 5.2 War with Mexico.

"the halls of Montezuma" (i.e., Mexico City), which surrendered in September 1848.

Military operations were much smaller in lightly populated California. With the embarrassing seizure of Monterey by Commodore Jones fresh in his mind, Commodore John Sloat, commander of the Pacific Squadron, acted cautiously. He waited until he received definitive news that war had started before he sailed for northern California and occupied

Monterey and San Francisco in early July 1846. Sloat's scheduled replacement, Commodore Robert Stockton, proved to be much more aggressive. Acting with American soldiers already in California under Colonel John C. Fremont, American naval forces occupied San Diego and then captured Los Angeles in August. A local uprising compelled US troops to withdraw, but American forces recaptured Los Angeles in January with the assistance of the small army of General Lawrence Kearny, who had arrived after a long march from Santa Fe. With the acquisition of Oregon and Upper California, the United States emerged as a two-ocean power. American population in the region grew as American settlers flocked overland to Oregon, and then to northern California after gold was discovered there in 1848. Within two years, the population of California exceeded 80,000 and it had been admitted to the Union as a new state.

After the Mexican–American War ended, many Americans confidently expected additional acquisitions. In the Caribbean, Cuba loomed as an obvious target. In Central America, a route across either Nicaragua or Panama was needed for a canal or railroad. However, the 1850s were dominated not by continued American territorial expansion but instead by the rising sectional crisis that divided the nation over the slavery issue and eventually led to the Civil War in 1861. During this decade, the Navy occasionally intervened in Cuba and Central America but these actions were intended to preserve American neutrality and to prevent the illegal actions by American-based filibusters who sought to overthrow regimes in Cuba, Nicaragua, and Panama.

Nevertheless, between 1848 and 1861, the Navy's peacetime mission grew dramatically even though it was not employed as a strong arm of American expansion. The Navy assumed additional commercial, scientific, and diplomatic duties as it sought to expand American economic opportunities overseas. The acquisition of Oregon and California had added 1,300 miles of coastline and three magnificent harbors on the Pacific. The United States now seemed poised on the verge of a "new commercial era" in which it would extend its influence and trade into the relatively untapped markets in China and the East Indies. In the Pacific, Americans already dominated the valuable whaling industry. Trade with the Hawaiian Islands flourished. While American trade with Asia did not come close in volume or value to trade with traditional markets in Europe, the Mediterranean, or the Caribbean, an article of faith among many Americans held that commerce with Asia and particularly the China trade would in the not too distant future surpass the value of trade with these traditional markets.

Matthew Fontaine Maury

In the vanguard of this expected commercial advance into Latin America and the far reaches of the Pacific stood whalers, entrepreneurs, merchants, and clipper-ship captains who expected support from the US Navy. Among the least dramatic but most important forms of this support was the work of Lieutenant Matthew Fontaine Maury, the head of the Naval Observatory in Washington, DC, from 1844 to 1861. Maury envisioned a global American commercial empire that the Navy would to help create. Maury attracted and trained a number of young officers who shared his vision of using the Navy to promote a commercial empire through scientific activity and overseas exploration.

Maury collected hundreds of logs and observations from naval and merchant captains to produce maps and charts of prevailing winds and currents in the Atlantic and Pacific. These changed existing sailing routes and dramatically reduced sailing times on many routes, thereby decreasing costs for American merchant ships. For example, on the important New York to San Francisco run in the early 1850s, ships using Maury's charts averaged a passage of 144 days while those that did not use them averaged 187 days. Maury also convinced whaling captains to share their logs and reports with him. He then created charts that showed the reported locations of whales during various seasons of the year in the Pacific.

Maury believed that the exploration of major river systems and remote parts of Latin America would promote American economic interests in these areas. He promoted expeditions to descend the Amazon River (1851–52), to explore the La Plata River Basin (1853–56), and to examine a potential canal route across Panama (1854). One of Maury protégés, Lieutenant William Herndon, led a small party that descended the Amazon from Peru to its mouth and collected a vast amount of geographic information pertinent to the navigation and commercial development of the vast river basin.

The "Opening" of Japan

In the Pacific, various forces produced the Navy's most important expedition of the 1850s. The Expedition to Japan was particularly noteworthy for American naval history for two reasons. First, it was the largest

American peacetime naval operation of the nineteenth century when it reached its full strength of 10 warships. Second, it was primarily a diplomatic expedition that was led not by a civilian American diplomat but by a senior American naval officer, Matthew C. Perry.

By 1850, Japan had been closed to the western or occidental world for more than two centuries. Its only contact with the outside world was through a small Dutch settlement on Dejima Island, near Nagasaki. There the Japanese acquired the few items and their only information from abroad. In the United States, the idea of an expedition to Japan dated back to 1815 but it was not until the early 1850s that President Millard Fillmore and Secretary of State Daniel Webster focused seriously on Japan. As commerce-minded Whigs, both leaders were responsive to groups—including China merchants, whaling captains, naval officers, and promoters of a transpacific steamship line between California and China—that wanted to expand American commerce in Asia. Japan was of particular interest to whalers and the promoters of the steamship line. Having pressed into the dangerous waters of the northwest Pacific, American whalers sought authority to use the coast of Japan as an inclement weather refuge for their ships and to recover shipwrecked sailors held in Japan. Supporters of a proposed transoceanic steamship line needed to locate a source of and a place to refuel with coal on the great-circle route between San Francisco and Shanghai.

After several failed attempts and false starts, the Fillmore administration settled on Perry to command the expedition. Intelligent, resourceful, ambitious, and progressive, Perry came from a distinguished naval family that included his older brother Oliver Hazard Perry, the hero of the Battle of Lake Erie. Commodore Perry's nickname "Old Bruin" well captured his serious, overbearing manner, but his ships were highly disciplined and his crews respected him as a tough but fair commander.

Perry had a clear vision of the character and purpose of the mission. Upon accepting command of the East India Squadron, Perry insisted that his primary duty be the expedition to Japan not the routine duties of a squadron commander. Moreover, Perry demanded that he control a large enough squadron to both impress and intimidate the Japanese. Since the

Japanese had never seen a steamship, the steam frigates *Mississippi* and *Susquehanna* were chosen in part to awe Japanese observers. Perry prepared himself thoroughly. In addition to reading extensively about Japan, Perry also met with naval officers, whaling captains, and merchants who knew about Japan. As a result, Perry became exceptionally well prepared to deal with the Japanese because of his detailed knowledge of the history, culture, and customs of that mysterious empire.

Perry also had a direct hand in preparing his own instructions and describing the objectives of the expedition. He was to deliver a letter from President Fillmore to the Emperor of Japan and to establish formal contact with high-ranking Japanese officials. He was to negotiate a treaty that would protect shipwrecked American mariners on Japanese soil and provide refuge for American ships driven into Japanese ports by bad weather. The treaty would also allow American ships to obtain provisions, water, wood, and coal while in port. In addition, the treaty would open selected Japanese ports to American ships, which could sell or trade their cargoes there. Finally, the expedition had a scientific and geographic component. In addition to surveying the ports it visited, it included civilian scientists who were to collect information and artifacts on the geography, people, and customs of Japan. Although Perry commanded a powerful force that could overwhelm Japan coastal defenses, this was to be a peaceful operation. Perry was authorized to use force only under extreme circumstances of self-defense or to retaliate against an attack on any of his men.

Sailing from the United States in late 1852, the *Mississippi* reached China in April 1853. From here, Perry intended for the expedition to have four phases. First, he would establish a base on Okinawa, close to Japan. Second, in the summer of 1853, he would sail to Tokyo (Edo) Bay to establish initial contact and deliver the president's letter to Japanese officials. Third, the squadron would return to Okinawa and China to allow the Japanese time to deliberate. Fourth, in the spring of 1854, Perry would return to Japan with a much enlarged naval squadron to negotiate a treaty.

Although there were minor setbacks, the expedition proceeded largely as Perry had planned. In spite of local resistance, he established a base in Okinawa, then proceeded to Tokyo Bay with four warships including

US Naval Academy: Ex Scientia Tridens

Few antebellum events held more portent for the transition of the Old Navy to the New than the founding of the Naval Academy. Old Navy midshipmen learned their trade as shipboard apprentices, some receiving basic tutelage in mathematics, navigation, and languages from shipboard chaplains or schoolmasters. The first official proposal for a naval academy, by Navy Secretary William Jones in 1814, failed, as did attempts by reformers over the next three decades. Opponents feared that training ashore would produce "effeminate" officers lacking the seamanship skills, daring, and dash of frigate captains of old. The adoption in the late 1830s of steam propulsion, which demanded technically trained officers, tipped the balance to the reformers, but the instigating event was the infamous 1842 Somers Mutiny, which saw the hanging at sea of Midshipman Philip Spencer (son of the Secretary of War) for alleged mutiny. The ensuing uproar focused national attention on naval education, a situation exploited in 1845 by Navy Secretary George Bancroft,

who, by shrewd maneuver, acquired old Fort Severn from the Army at no cost, gathered funds to operate a shore-based school by discharging most of the Navy's sea-going schoolmasters, convinced an influential group of senior officers that such a school should be located in Annapolis, and assembled a three-man board of middle-grade officers, including Marylander Commander Franklin Buchanan, who backed the plan. On October 10, 1845, the Naval School at Annapolis opened its doors with Buchanan as its first superintendent.

The antebellum years were among the most interesting—and significant—in Academy history. Most of what was *interesting* stemmed from the fractious behavior of the midshipmen. With no requirement for uniforms, formation, or drill, it was not spit and polish but, rather, duels, drunkenness, and "over-the-wall" forays that characterized these early years. Most *significant* were the reorganizations of 1850–1851, which initiated the class system, demerits, marching, and drill; outlawed civilian clothes;

restricted liberty; forbade marriage; established the continuous four-year program with summer cruises; and renamed the school the Naval Academy. When an 1852 act of Congress established the system of congressional appointments, the mold for the modern Naval Academy was complete.

Under threat from secessionists, the Academy moved to Newport, Rhode Island, during the Civil War. During that conflict, Academy graduates distinguished themselves in scores of battles. Physical courage was still a trademark of the American naval officer. Half a century later, when America became a great power with a navy to match, the three naval officers who contributed most to that development were Naval War College founder Stephen B. Luce, historian–navalist Alfred Thayer Mahan, and Spanish–American War hero George Dewey, all antebellum graduates. Appropriately, when in 1898 the Academy adopted its coat of arms, it was emblazoned with the words "Ex Scientia Tridens"—From Knowledge, Sea Power—a motto befitting the school of the sea.

US Naval Academy, 1853. *Source:* Courtesy of Beverley R. Robinson Collection, US Naval Academy Museum.

the steam frigates *Mississippi* and *Susquehanna*. Once in Japanese waters, he refused to allow small Japanese boats to harass or board his ships. He also insisted on meeting only with high-ranking officials of the Imperial Empire rather than local officials. On the historically dramatic day of July 14, 1853, Perry led a delegation of Americans who delivered the president's letter to Japanese officials in a brief formal ceremony at Uraga. During his two-week stay, Perry's ships continually charted and surveyed Japanese waters.

Perry then retired to Okinawa and China before returning to Japan in February 1854 (see Figure 5.3). The American squadron now consisted of eight warships with two more en route. Fortunately, Perry had selected a propitious moment to approach the Japanese. Facing troubles at home and dangers from abroad, the Japanese regime felt vulnerable and decided to grant limited concessions to the Americans. More than a month of negotiations finally produced the Treaty of Kanagawa on March 31, 1854. The accord established formal relations, provided restricted commercial privileges, and guaranteed favorable treatment of shipwrecked Americans and refuge for American ships in distress. It also designated two ports (Hakodate and Shimoda) where American ships could purchase wood, water, and provisions at a fair price and trade for Japanese goods; included a "most favored nation" clause; and permitted the United States to send a consul to reside at Shimoda. In spite of its very modest concessions, the treaty represented a landmark achievement for Perry and the Navy. Most importantly, Perry had achieved his objectives without resorting to force. He had compelled Japan to deal with the United States as an equal, not as an inferior, "barbarian" power, yet

Figure 5.3 Perry meeting Japanese officials at Yokohama, 1854. Lithograph by Saxony and Major.

he departed with American–Japanese relations on a friendly basis. The treaty was not without its short-comings. First, American assumptions about Japan as a source of coal proved wrong, and the selection of Shimoda as one of the two ports was a poor choice because the harbor was small and relatively unpro-tected. Nevertheless the treaty proved important in the long term because it provided the foundation for strong relations after the 1868 Meiji Restoration in Japan signified a new direction in which Japan would embrace modern industry and western technology.

In 1854–1855, another naval expedition, com-manded by Lieutenant John Rodgers, supplemented the work of the Perry Expedition and tested the Treaty of Kanagawa. The three naval vessels of the North Pacific Expedition charted the ports of Hakodate and Shimoda, surveyed hundreds of miles of Japan's coast-line, and collected a wealth of valuable scientific, geo-graphic, and commercial information. The expedition also explored the Bering Sea. In the process, it created nautical charts that, because of the difficulty and dan-ger of navigating in this region, proved invaluable to mariners for decades.

Late Nineteenth-Century Naval Retrenchment

The outbreak of the Civil War in 1861 abruptly ended most of the Navy's overseas activities because all but a few ships were called home from all but the African Squadron (whose maintenance was required by the Webster–Ashburton Treaty with Britain). After the war, the United States reorganized and reestab-lished its prewar squadrons (see Map 5.1). In 1868 it acquired Alaska and Midway Island but this brief postwar expansion movement quickly stalled. It was not until the 1880s that the United States acquired the right to build naval bases at Pearl Harbor in Hawaii and Pago Pago in Samoa, yet rejected a treaty offering a site for a base in the Dominican Repub-lic. With the nation's attention focused on domestic affairs, Congress rejected creation of a large Euro-pean-style navy, instead insisting on the maintenance of a navy sufficient only to protect America's coasts and its commercial interests abroad. As a result, the postwar Navy declined steadily until it ranked among those of a third- or even fourth-rate naval power. By

1875, the Navy totaled only 147 ships, many of which were small, technologically backward, and inactive.

This decline mirrored an era of profound maritime eclipse for the United States between 1860 and 1900. The tonnage of American merchant ships engaged in foreign trade fell steadily from 2,546,000 tons in 1860 to just 827,000 tons at the end of the century. In the 1850s, about 70 percent of the value of American imports and exports had been carried in American ships, but that figure had dropped to below 10 percent by 1900. The American whaling industry also suffered a catastrophic decline, ceasing to be a major American industry by the 1870s.

At home the American economy industrialized and grew dramatically after 1865. The gross national prod-uct, the manufacturing index, and agricultural pro-duction grew greatly in this period. So too did Amer-ican foreign trade. However, most goods were carried in foreign ships and trade was mainly conducted with Canada, European countries, or the Caribbean, all regions that tended to be politically stable and peace-ful and did not require active naval protection. In the Pacific, American trade grew but still constituted only a small fraction of the nation's total.

During this period, the United States largely failed to open new markets in undeveloped areas. During 1877–1878, Admiral Robert W. Shufeldt circumnavi-gated the globe in the screw sloop-of-war *Ticonderoga* but failed in his effort to expand American commer-cial opportunities in the ports he visited in Africa, the Indian Ocean, and Asia. Shufeldt's one success came in Korea, where he laid the groundwork for a formal treaty. After Shufeldt returned to the United States, he convinced the State Department to appoint him as a "naval attaché" to Korea. Shufeldt then returned to Asia, where, with the assistance of the Chinese, he concluded a formal treaty with Korea in 1882.

These economic and political factors combined to diminish the need for a large and active peacetime navy between 1865 and 1890. Ironically, although the Navy declined in force and prestige, it still performed its primary peacetime mission of supporting and pro-tecting American commerce in an effective if undra-matic manner. During the 1850s, the "protection of commerce" had required an expanded mission for the Navy. In the 1870s and 1880s, the range of duties sta-bilized and even declined. With few exceptions, the

Navy was not asked to "open" new markets, to explore remote areas, or to conduct diplomacy. And, while there were occasional diplomatic confrontations and "war scares" with nations whose navies might have embarrassed the US Navy if hostilities had occurred, all of those confrontations were averted peacefully. In 1873, in the aftermath of the *Virginius* Affair in Cuba, effective diplomacy avoided hostilities with Spain. In 1879–1880, during the War of the Pacific between Chile and Peru, the skill of American naval officers and good fortune averted hostilities.

The most serious threat arose in Samoa in 1889 when three American warships, three German warships, and a British warship confronted one another. During the 1870s, Samoa had maintained a tenuous and shaky sovereignty. Although the island kingdom sought American protection, the United States negotiated only the right to create a naval depot at Pago Pago while refusing to accept Samoa as an American protectorate. Meanwhile, Germany sought to add the islands to its empire or to partition them between Germany, the United States, and England. When diplomatic efforts failed to resolve the situation in 1889, it appeared that hostilities were imminent as the German, Amer-ican, and British forces squared off. However, the threat was literally shattered by a hurricane that effectively destroyed the German and American squadrons. The two countries then agreed to a joint protectorate over the island kingdom.

Conclusion

By the late 1880s, new international, domestic, and technological developments combined to produce a naval revolution that would create a modern American navy. A new and aggressive age of European imperialism threatened to close overseas markets previously open to Americans. In the United States, various economic and political conditions joined to produce the rise of a "new expansionism" that stressed the importance of overseas colonies and naval stations as well as the building of a large, modern, European-style navy. One factor was the influence of a group of naval historians led by Alfred Thayer Mahan, who emphasized that a large navy was indispensable for any nation that hoped to be secure during war and prosperous in peace. With these developments, the end of the "Old Navy" and its long-standing mission to "protect American commerce" was at hand.

CHAPTER 6

Technological Revolution at Sea

By their very nature, navies are technological institutions. American naval technology, like that of other maritime countries, was an expression of national policy, the prevailing strategy, material and engineering cultures, national capital, manufacturing (and later industrial) capability, geostrategic factors, and the overarching maritime environment. The sail-powered ship-of-the-line, whose basic attributes had changed little in 200 years, defined first-rate naval power in 1800. By mid-century, technological change had resulted in a shift from a purely quantitative measure of perceived naval greatness—typically the number of ships-of-the-line a country possessed—to a nascent qualitative measure of naval power based on significant technological differences. These included steam propulsion, armor for hulls, iron and then steel hulls, the use of propellers instead of paddlewheels, and advances in naval ordnance such as rifled barrels, turrets, and exploding projectiles. By the 1890s the rapid, disparate, and often confusing evolution of naval technology focused upon a new measure of naval power: the battleship, armed with modern, large-caliber guns and possessing relatively efficient triple-expansion, reciprocating steam engines and metallurgically advanced steel armor.

During the 200 years before 1840, the technology of warships changed little. Wood limited the size of ships. A ship's hull is structurally similar to a box girder and endures greatly varying loads from waves, wind, and the weight of its own structure. By the early seventeenth century, square-rigged, three-masted ships-of-the-line, typified by England's 102-gun *Sovereign of the Seas* (1637), were arguably the most sophisticated engineering and manufacturing endeavors of their time. The term "capital ship" reflected the enormous expense these ships entailed. The cost of *Sovereign of the Seas* exacerbated the financial crisis under Charles I that contributed to the English Civil War. By 1692, the financial burden of maintaining this type of fleet also became too much for Louis XIV, and France scaled back its naval expenditures after losing 12 ships run aground at La Hogue during the Nine Years' War (1688–1697).

Attempts to build wooden ships appreciably longer than 200 feet resulted in hull failure. Until eclipsed by France's mammoth 5,000-ton, 116-gun, three-decker *Océan* (1788), the largest warship was the Spanish 4,950-ton, four-decker *Nuestra Señora de la Santísima Trinidad* (1769), which carried 130 guns and a crew of a little over 1,000 on a hull just 201 feet long. The preeminent British Royal Navy preferred ships-of-the-line, with the largest typically rated at 98 guns. Britain had 144 ships-of-the-line (ranging from 74-gun two-deckers to the larger three-deckers) in commission in December 1799. Within this expensive and competitive environment, the United States was not a naval power during most of the

America, Sea Power, and the World, First Edition. Edited by James C. Bradford.
© 2016 John Wiley & Sons, Inc. Published 2016 by John Wiley & Sons, Inc.

nineteenth century. The US Navy had no ships-of-the-line before 1816 and, for most of the nineteenth century, had an average of only 40 ships of all sizes in commission at any one time. However, from the very beginning, the American navy embraced a design philosophy in which its warships would exceed the capabilities of foreign warships of a similar type. American warships would be structurally stronger (later that would also mean more heavily armored), would be faster, and would carry superior weapons. In addition to the material limits of wood, the Navy was also limited by the lack of political consensus for a large navy, the country's small population, and the absence of wealth. If the Americans could not have quantity, they made a conscious decision to have qualitative, technological superiority in each type of warship built.

Technology in the Early Navy

When the Americans rebelled against British rule in 1776, there was an established maritime tradition, especially in the northern and middle colonies. From the very first warships designed and built in America during the Revolutionary War, American naval architects tended to build larger ships, within particular ship classes, than did European, especially British, designers. This trend continued with the 44-gun frigates designed by the Philadelphia constructor Joshua Humphreys, which formed the cadre of the six frigates authorized by the 1794 Naval Act to deal with Algerian corsairs. These 44s were longer and faster than British frigates and employed American live oak, a very dense wood of 55 to 75 pounds per cubic foot. The heavier scantlings of the Humphreys frigates enabled them to carry larger guns (typically 24-pounders) and more of them—sometimes up to 60—and the nickname earned by *Constitution*—"Old Ironsides"—was based on the material superiority of the live oak. After three American frigate victories over the Royal Navy in 1812, the Admiralty forbade its frigate captains from engaging the large 44-gun American frigates, *Constitution*, *United States*, and *President*, in single-ship combat.

The exceptional design qualities of the Humphreys frigates continued in the 74-gun ships-of-the-line authorized in 1813 and 1816. For example,

the *Ohio*, laid down in 1817, typified the American criterion of giving its ships the heaviest armament possible within a ship type. In contrast to European practice, the Americans equipped ships with long and medium guns and carronades of the same caliber to prevent the inability to use any part of the battery due to a lack of shot. The post-1815 ships-of-the-line and larger frigates carried 32-pound guns and the ships-of-the-line later were upgraded to 42-pounders. While rated at 74 guns, American ships-of-the-line such as *Ohio* sometimes carried up to 102 guns and their weight of broadside equaled British 120-gun ships. The three American ships-of-the-line laid down in 1817–1818 were fast and popular with their crews once they finally entered service. The largest American ship-of-the-line, *Pennsylvania*, authorized in 1816 but not completed until 1837, was a 3,105-ton, four-decked, 140-gun ship similar to *Santísima Trinidad*.

These ships-of-the-line were a technology that had some difficulty fitting into national defense. President James Monroe's most pressing maritime concern was the lack of smaller warships to protect American trade, especially in the Caribbean. Monroe favored completing the ships-of-the-line and large frigates but laying them up "in ordinary" (i.e., in reserve), from where they could be crewed and readied in response to a crisis. The economic panic of 1819 had a chilling effect on the Navy's building program. The 1820 congressional debate focused on fiscal responsibility and the need for smaller warships to protect commerce. By 1821 the navalist view of a peacetime force of ships-of-the-line as an expression of American power had been eclipsed by a militia concept in which the Navy and coastal fortifications would be fully activated only in the case of an invasion.

The renunciation of a large peacetime fleet was finalized by the 1827 Act for the Gradual Improvement of the Navy. The Navy received $3 million over the next six years with $2 million of it to procure timber for future wartime construction. The large warships already built were housed and kept ready to fit out in case of hostilities, a prospect that seemed less and less likely since America's expansionist focus lay not with a high-seas challenge to Britain but rather westward across the continent.

Technology in the "Old Navy"

While pursuing qualitatively superior ships in terms of weapons and hull strength, the US Navy was the first to operate a steam-propelled warship, *Demologos* (1815). The fact that the first steam warship was built in America was as much a by-product of Robert Fulton's earlier rejection by the French as any prescient vision within the American government. Designed as a floating steam battery for harbor defense, *Demologos* had a centerline paddlewheel and a speed under steam of four knots. The important need to protect American port cities from attack and ransom by the blockading Royal Navy was underscored by the $320,000 cost of the vessel, which exceeded that of the heavy frigate *Constitution*, built for $302,719 in 1797.

The novelty of steam propulsion, along with its inefficiency and unreliability, worked against its acceptance. The perceived weakness in *Demologos'* steam propulsion made it the first of many nineteenth-century American warships modified to conform better to the prevailing professional preference of sail over steam. Captain David Porter, given command of *Demologos* after losing the frigate *Essex* (32 guns) to the British in 1814 off Valparaiso, balked at *Demologos'* mode of propulsion. He forced the addition of two masts and two bowsprits to carry sails and the war ended before these modifications were complete.

The Navy purchased and put into service a second steamship, the shallow-draft galliot *Sea Gull*, in 1822 for use in David Porter's efforts to suppress piracy in the Caribbean, but laid the vessel up in 1825 and sold it in 1840. There was no consensus among American naval officers that these early forays into steam propulsion were in any way successful. Their early and inefficient steam engines were incapable of supporting the Navy's primary mission of commerce protection in far oceans. Meanwhile, in contrast to the US Navy's cautious forays into steam propulsion, almost 700 commercial steam vessels were in use in American waters by the 1830s while the Navy had none.

The US Navy's flirtation with steam propulsion lay dormant until 1835, when Secretary of the Navy Mahlon Dickerson directed the three captains on the Board of Navy Commissioners to begin construction of a steam vessel. This order caught Board members off balance and they were forced to admit, writing in the third person, that "they are incompetent themselves, and have no person under their direction who could furnish them with the necessary information to form a contract for steam engines that may secure the United States from imposition, disappointment, and loss."[1] In February 1836 the Navy hired its first engineer, Charles Haswell, to assist the Board. Haswell was appointed chief engineer of the steam warship *Fulton (the Second)*, a harbor-defense vessel then under construction.

While steam propulsion was effective enough to use within a harbor, the general inefficiency of marine steam engines offered no advantages to a navy operating commerce-protection squadrons as far away as the East Indies. Some naval officers objected to steam propulsion on grounds ranging from aesthetic to military. Steam engines were large and noisy and their lubricating oil and coal fuel were intrusions into the clean and orderly world of a sailing man-of-war characterized so well by Herman Melville in his autobiographical novel *White-Jacket* in 1844. Side-mounted paddlewheels also had significant military disadvantages: they were vulnerable to gunfire and displaced many broadside guns.

By 1842 the Navy had two paddlewheel frigates, *Missouri* and *Mississippi*. The attraction of steam propulsion for naval officers—independence from natural forces—was similar to that felt by early users of water-wheels and windmills. The weaknesses of the engines—the inefficient transmission of engine power and the engines' voracious appetites for coal or wood—limited the potential of these early steam-propulsion systems to providing added speed during pursuit, evasion, or battle.

For naval officers, the ultimate validation of technology was its performance at sea and in war. Perhaps more surprising than the opponents to technological change were the seagoing officers of the line, such as Matthew C. Perry, who championed steam

---

[1] John Rodgers, Board of Navy Commissioners to Secretary of the Navy, December 30, 1835, as quoted in Frank M. Bennett, *The Steam Navy of the United States* (1896), 18.

Table 6.1 Naval steam plant efficiency, 1820s–1880s.

	Pressure (PSI)[a]	Range (nm/ton)[b]	Range per 500 tons of coal	Cost of machinery (dollars/ton)
1820s	5	2.5	1,500	10.0
1840s	15	5–72	500	8.0
1870s	75	10–12	5,000	5.0
1880s	155	15–20	7,500	3.5

[a] PSI: pounds per square inch.
[b] Range nautical miles per ton of steam machinery.

propulsion. Perry made good use of steam propulsion when he commanded US naval forces in the Gulf of Mexico during the Mexican–American War, just as the British had done a few years earlier during the First Opium War with China. However, keeping ships coaled in Mexico, more than 800 miles from the nearest US naval base, was a significant logistical problem. The inefficiency of steam engines on even more distant operations was demonstrated in the maiden voyage of the side-wheel steamer *Susquehanna* in 1851. The 2,450-ton ship departed Norfolk for duty as flagship of the East India Squadron. The eight-month trip covered 18,500 miles and the ship consumed its weight in coal and 1,100 sticks of wood. Twenty-five percent of the voyage was spent coaling the ship.

By the mid-1850s paddlewheel steamers had given way to new classes of propeller-driven ships with improved steaming and sailing qualities, but the problem of coal was far from resolved. Without overseas bases, and improvements in the power and efficiency of steam engines, especially in the Pacific, the US Navy would continue to rely on sail power (see Table 6.1).

The Civil War brought about many ad hoc warships, especially in the area of harbor defense for the Confederacy and the river campaigns for both sides. The nature of US naval operations during the Civil War—maintaining a close blockade of the Confederacy and fighting in the rivers and coastal waters against shore fortifications—forced the Navy to rely increasingly on steam propulsion. Some Civil War ships, such as the Confederate submarine *Hunley*, were truly revolutionary. In terms of traditional, oceangoing warships, the one that embodied the most exceptional technology was the purpose-built commerce raider *Wampanoag*. Unable to challenge British sea power directly, the United States reverted to its traditional strategy for dealing with a larger navy and built a group of fast commerce raiders for use against Britain should it enter the war to support the Confederacy. Of these ships, it was Engineer-in-Chief Benjamin Isherwood's geared-drive propulsion plant that made *Wampanoag* unique and a true expression of American *guerre de course* (i.e., commerce warfare). *Wampanoag* made almost 18 knots on trials in rough seas, a speed unmatched by the Royal Navy for 11 years. The response in British engineering circles was disbelief.

However, *Wampanoag* concerned the Royal Navy's chief constructor, Sir Edward Reed, who designed HMS *Inconstant* to counter the "prospect of a fifteen-knot commerce destroyer rampaging over the lanes of British commerce." As Reed observed, "We could not afford, in this country, to wait and see whether they ['a powerful class of American vessels'] were to be successful or not; we had to produce a ship which would compete with them."[2] HMS *Inconstant* reached 16.5 knots during its 1869 trial but stability issues forced the addition of 300 tons of ballast, which reduced its speed by one knot.

Britain had little to fear from *Wampanoag* since Admiral David Dixon Porter rendered it impotent. When Engineer-in-Chief Isherwood claimed he was entitled to the rank of rear admiral as head of a bureau, even though he was a member of the Engineering Corps, Porter told a friend that "to punish

[2] E. R. Reed, "Remarks" [on T. Brassey, "On Unarmoured Vessels"], in Royal Institution of Naval Architects, *Transactions* [henceforth INA *Transactions*], 17 (1876), 21.

him [Isherwood] for his folly we intend not only to strip him and the engineers of all honors, but to make them the most inferior corps in the Navy."[3] In 1869 Porter and his senior line-officer colleagues, under the guise of the Board on Steam Machinery Afloat, rejected the ship, as built, for naval service. Porter ordered half of *Wampanoag*'s propulsion plant removed as well as two of the four blades of its propeller in order to make it a better sailing ship with the endurance to defend American commerce across the Pacific. The future director of naval construction for the Royal Navy, William White, ignorant of the internecine crippling of *Wampanoag*, attributed its failure to its wooden hull, which he deemed "not suited for the great engine power" installed. He observed that "American shipbuilders are, at length, devoting themselves energetically to the development of iron ship construction."[4]

The shift to metal warships removed Americans from their familiar wooden material culture and forced them, initially, to rely upon ideas and construction methods from Britain. Similarly, the rise of science-influenced naval architecture rooted in a formal educational—rather than artisanal—setting forced American naval constructors to pursue British and French education in naval architecture. However, by the century's end, America's pursuit of a modern navy and the industrial base it required would foster innovation in metal ship construction that would rebound to Europe and change shipbuilding methods there.

While the Navy pursued high-speed commerce raiders to deter British intervention, the war at hand with the Confederacy needed new ships and new technology. The US Navy burgeoned to 671 ships in commission in 1864. However, most of the newly constructed warships were not oriented toward high-seas naval power but served very narrow purposes— examples include the ironclad monitors employed in the western river campaigns. The bulk of the Navy's "warships" were converted merchant ships includ-

ing New York City's Staten Island ferries and the original racing yacht *America*. While suitable for the blockade of the Confederacy, such ships hardly made the United States a great naval power. The Civil War forced the US and Confederate navies to pursue technological innovations. The efforts of both navies paled in comparison to the technological change ongoing in Europe, especially within the preeminent Royal Navy.

For much of the two decades after the end of the Civil War in 1865, the US Navy was largely a technological backwater as developments in metallurgy, steam propulsion, and science-influenced naval architecture ushered in an uncertain and highly competitive period for the leading naval powers. In studying the few examples of war at sea, naval officers worldwide struggled to find portents of the proper technological basis of naval power. The 1866 Battle of Lissa resurrected ramming and the 1879 maritime component of the War of the Pacific seemed instructive regarding turreted ironclads. In the United States, Admiral Porter presided over a terribly weak US Navy. Even after the 1873 war scare with Spain over the *Virginius* Affair and the subsequent failed Key West maneuvers, Porter defended the status quo strategy of *guerre de course*.[5]

Porter was a complex figure and had definite views regarding the role of steam engineering in the Navy. Historically, he is considered either a naval Luddite regarding modernizing the Navy or a realist who understood the geostrategic realities of the Pacific and the challenges it offered to American naval power and, as a result, appreciated which technologies were appropriate for the country's worldwide commerce-protection mission. Porter established a steam-engineering course at the Naval Academy in 1865 but also worked hard to "break" the Navy's officer corps of steam engineers. He designed the futuristic *Alarm*, a harbor-defense ram, but he also eviscerated the most exceptional American warship design to emerge from the war, *Wampanoag*. Porter and his seagoing colleagues generated a short-sighted and prejudicial

---

[3] Porter as quoted in Peter D. Karsten, *The Naval Aristocracy* (1972), 66.

[4] W. H. White, *A Manual for Naval Architecture for the Use of Officers of the Royal Navy...* (1877), 367.

[5] "Report of Admiral D. D. Porter to the Secretary of the Navy, November 7, 1874," in *Annual Report of the Secretary of the Navy for the year 1874* [henceforth *SecNav Annual Report*] (1875), 198–222.

Benjamin Franklin Isherwood and George W. Melville

Two noteworthy American naval engineers contributed significantly to the rise of the new, mechanical navy. Benjamin Franklin Isherwood (1822–1915; engineer-in-chief, 1862–1869) designed and oversaw the acquisition and installation of the propulsion and auxiliary machinery of the expanding US Navy during the Civil War. George W. Melville (1841–1912) served several terms as engineer-in-chief (1888–1903) during the design and construction of the "New Navy." Each had wartime sea duty as shipboard engineer officers but came from different educational engineering traditions.

Isherwood came from the American artisanal engineering tradition of the 1840s. After his sea service during the Mexican–American War, he wrote over 50 articles on steam engineering and ship propulsion for the well-regarded *Journal of the Franklin Institute*. He also published a theoretical work on thermodynamics in two volumes that was translated into six languages.

Melville graduated from the Brooklyn Collegiate and Polytechnic Institute. He enlisted in the Navy in July 1861 and was commissioned in the Engineering Corps. Melville served as an engineer officer in four ships during the war, including USS *Wachusett* when it rammed and captured the Confederate commerce raider *Florida* in Bahia, Brazil, in 1864. Melville also served in several Arctic explorations and was the senior surviving officer of the ill-fated 1879 *Jeanette* expedition, for which he was awarded a Congressional Gold Medal in 1890. As engineer-in-chief, Melville supervised the design and construction of the machinery for the ships of the "New Navy," which included the water-tube boiler, vertical reciprocating engines, and the triple-screw propulsion system. He also served as president of the American Society of Mechanical Engineers (1899–1900).

While Isherwood bridged the gap between artisanal and shop-culture engineering in America, Melville was rooted in the later, dominant mechanical school culture. Both of these officers were influential in refining the technological paradigm for American naval engineering that lasted into the early twentieth century.

Benjamin Franklin Isherwood.

George W. Melville.

cultural backlash at the growing importance of steam propulsion and engineers to the Navy. This resulted in technological stagnation for the Navy and the temporary eradication of the engineering curriculum at the US Naval Academy in 1882—a curriculum that had received the Diplôme de Medaille d'Or at the 1878 Paris Universal Exposition.

Technology in the "New Navy"

While the US Navy stagnated during the 1870s, other navies were constructing ships based upon the most advanced technology that modern industry and emerging science-influenced engineering could produce. Aware of the growing gap between the outdated

ABCD Ships

In the period of rapid technological change after 1860, there was no consensus on what the ideal warship should be. By 1880 it was increasingly clear to many Americans that their expanding maritime commerce could not be protected by the 21 antiquated ships in commission (mostly coastal defense monitors and a few sailing ships with auxiliary steam engines). In 1881 Secretary of the Navy William H. Hunt created a Naval Advisory Board to develop a plan to revitalize the Navy. This board, led by Rear Admiral John Rodgers, called for 68 new warships. Supporting the traditional American desire for strong ships, the Board asked for every ship to be made of steel. The reticence of some of the naval constructors on the Board as to whether American shipyards, still trying to shift from a wooden to an iron material culture, could produce proper steel ships resulted in a four-month investigation of steel-ship construction by the Naval Affairs Committee of the House of Representatives. The Committee deemed steel construction feasible. When Chester Arthur assumed the presidency after James Garfield's assassination, Navy Secretary

William Chandler convened another advisory board under Commodore Robert Shufeldt. The Shufeldt Board called for five ships and Congress approved four steel-hulled ships in the 1883 Naval Act. Three—*Atlanta*, *Boston*, and *Chicago*—were hybrid sail–steam oceangoing protected cruisers while the fourth, *Dolphin*, was a dispatch vessel. These white-hulled, fully rigged "ABCD ships" formed the so-called "Squadron of Evolution" that deployed to

Europe in 1889 and are considered the first ships of the "New Navy." John Roach's Delaware River Iron Ship Building and Engine Works received the contracts to build the vessels but was forced into receivership, after which the Navy completed and launched the ships. Their steel double hulls with watertight compartments and full electrification made them harbingers of the future, and their completion proved that the United States could now build steel ships.

USS *Atlanta*, c. 1891. *Source:* US National Archives and Records Administration, 512894.

ships of the Porter era and those of major naval powers such as Britain and France, a preference grew among American naval officers for technologically sophisticated ships so the Navy could again become a viable force. The initial step came in 1883 when Congress authorized the first four ships constituting the New Steel Navy (cruisers *Atlanta*, *Boston*, and *Chicago* and the dispatch ship *Dolphin*—the "ABCD" ships).

The ABCD ships marked the beginning of the "New Navy" but not an abandonment of the traditional American naval strategy based upon commerce raiding. The sail-heavy ABCD ships seemed archaic compared to foreign warship designs. However, no international consensus had yet emerged as to the optimum warship in this period of rapid technological change. The picture was clouded further by the differing strategies

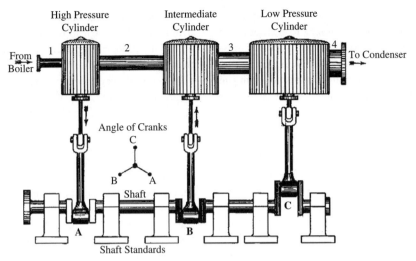

Figure 6.1   Three-cylinder, vertical, triple-expansion engines, first used on ships in the 1880s, were more efficient than their predecessors because the same steam was employed to drive three pistons, the first a high-pressure cylinder from which the steam was exhausted to enter a larger cylinder with equal stroke but under lower pressure, a process repeated in a third cylinder. *Source:* Diagram from Archibald Williams, *How It Works* (1911).

pursued by maritime countries ranging from France's *Jeune École* to Britain's defense plans based on the strategy of *guerre d'escadre* (i.e., combat between fleets) and expressed in the Two-Power Standard and embodied in the National Defence Act of 1889.

Operating within the new, and unfamiliar, metal material culture meant that, for the two armored cruisers that followed the ABCD ships, Secretary of the Navy William C. Whitney looked to Britain. The Navy obtained plans for the cruiser *Charleston* from Armstrong Mitchell Company, Ltd. The design was similar to the Imperial Japanese Navy's cruiser *Naniwa* but contained a mélange of machinery including less efficient double-expansion steam engines at a time when three-cylinder, vertical, triple-expansion steam engines were the norm (see Figure 6.1). The choice of such a retrograde propulsion plant was ironic given the history of *Wampanoag*, but Isherwood had long since been removed from power and banished to the Mare Island Navy Yard in California. Whitney turned to Armstrong Mitchell again for the cruiser *Baltimore* (similar to a cruiser built for Spain, *Reina Regente*); however, the third cruiser, *Newark*, was a domestic design.

At the same time the Navy was prying funding for a few new warships from Congress and trying to steer amid the confusing sea of contemporary naval technology, naval officers were pursuing professional status within contemporary American society. The US Naval Institute (founded 1873) with its *Proceedings*, the American Society of Naval Engineers (1888), and the Society of Naval Architects and Marine Engineers (1893) all worked to professionalize, and internationalize, American naval officers and their perceptions of technology, among other things. The Naval War College (1884) was created to prevent creeping technicism from dominating naval officers' lives and to encourage the broader study of warfare at sea.

The increasing professionalism of American naval officers, naval constructors, and naval engineers resulted in a growing cross-pollination of ideas and practices between the US Navy and its European counterparts, especially Britain, with whom intellectual interaction was facilitated by the common language. The supremacy of the Royal Navy meant that any technology it selected, to a point, was evaluated by other maritime nations.

The shift to steel construction in the ABCD ships was part of the technological trajectory from a wooden to a metal material culture in American warship design. Initially, American shipbuilders, used to working solely with wood, had to rely on techniques and artisans of European origin, especially from Britain. Yet it was not long before US shipbuild-ers developed pneumatic machinery to revolutionize the process to the point that by 1900 American ship-building tools and techniques were being copied by European shipbuilders. For a short period of time, the production of steel armor offered a similar tale.

Armor and Metallurgy

Warship armor was initially made during the 1850s by applying wrought iron over wood. By the mid-1880s, the dominant protection for armored ships was com-pound armor composed of a layer of brittle, high-carbon steel backed by a more elastic, low-carbon wrought-iron backing plate. These plates were welded together by molten steel poured between them. The harder face-plate was to break up an incoming shell while the more elastic, wrought-iron plate absorbed the energy and kept pieces of the shell from penetrat-ing the ship. The disadvantage of compound armor was the tendency of the plates to separate when struck and of splinters to then penetrate the rear plate and enter the ship.

In 1889, an American engineer, Hayward A. Har-vey, developed a process in which a single steel plate could emulate the best protective properties of com-pound armor without the failures. In his process, one side of a steel plate was covered with charcoal and heated at a very high temperature for several weeks. This increased the carbon content at the face and pro-vided the same resistance of compound armor while using thinner plate.

Harvey's method was part of an international effort to develop improved armor technology. During the late 1880s, the French company of Schneider-Creusot added nickel to steel, producing even stronger armor plate. Nickel was in short supply and Secretary of the Navy Benjamin Tracy worked hard to stockpile it. In 1890, at Annapolis, the Navy conducted point-blank tests using eight-inch shells. The compound-armor plates were destroyed and the all-steel plates cracked while nickel-steel plates, treated using the Harvey pro-cess, stopped all test shells. Some considered ships of the Royal Navy, which was using all-steel plate, to be

vulnerable. The clear superiority of the Harveyized armor caused the British to adopt it under license. As with many modern engineering processes, incremental changes often brought notable improvements. Within a few years, Harveyized armor was surpassed by Krupp armor, in which the layer of coal used to carbonize the face of the armor was replaced by heating the face of the plate with carbon-rich gases as well as the addition of chromium to the steel during manufacture.

Even with the construction of battleships in 1890 and a shift toward a *guerre d'escadre* strategy, commerce raiding remained important and was manifested in the new commerce raiders *Columbia* (1890) and *Min-neapolis* (1891). The Columbias were designed for high speed (22 knots) to overtake passenger liners, and their novel and economical triple-screw drive, a product of Engineer-in-Chief George Melville, was projected to allow them to cruise for 103 days at 10 knots and to circle the earth without need for refue-ling or bases. Their designs reflected the unique engi-neering culture and collective memory that contin-ued to guide American naval technology. In his 1890 annual report, Secretary of the Navy Tracy wrote that these cruisers "would exterminate the commerce of any country under the present conditions of com-merce protection and would thus, under these con-ditions, also preclude an attack from a commercial state, however threatening in its demands, powerful in its armored fleet, or aggressive in its foreign policy."[6] American construction of these two long-range and high-speed *Columbia*-class commerce raiders quickly garnered the attention of the British Admiralty, where the design was known as "the pirate."

The Columbias embodied traditional technologi-cal expressions of American warship design: focus on strength, speed, and endurance. An important tacti-cal advantage for *Columbia* and *Minneapolis* involved the geometry and lesser amount of armor, for the same thickness, required to protect the propulsion machinery. The higher horsepower required a larger armored volume, and more weight in armor, to pro-tect the propulsion machinery. Melville's design was well outside the norm for contemporary warships. He divided the required horsepower among three

---

[6] *SecNav Annual Report* (1890), as quoted in Norman Friedman, *US Cruisers* (1984), 40.

engines and propellers in the Columbias rather than the international norm of two. As a result, less height was required under the protected deck.[7] Less height translated into less armor, which resulted in a ship with less displacement and a higher speed for the same horsepower. A ship with three engine compartments and three propeller shafts would also be stronger, as in the Humphreys frigates of the Early Republic, and less susceptible to immobilizing battle damage if struck by an enemy.

Melville also believed that the American triple-screwed protected cruisers were the answer to the long-standing critical American design criterion: economy of operation across the broad Pacific, which translated into range with a ready option to go to high speed if warranted by the tactical situation.

Naval Ordnance

Heavy, broadside cannons had been the mainstay of warship armament since the sixteenth century. They changed little save for the addition of a gunlock firing mechanism first used in the Royal Navy in 1745. While gunlocks allowed more precise aiming and

firing, they could not easily be retrofitted to existing cannon. Exploding shells, which were dangerous to handle and to load, were used on land and fired at high trajectories at fairly low velocities. In 1823 a French general, Henri-Joseph Paixhans, developed a delayed fuse so that shells could be fired safely in the flat trajectory typical of naval combat.

The most famous American naval ordnance expert was John Dahlgren, who developed a series of soda-bottle-shaped naval guns (mostly smooth-bored) that were used widely during the Civil War. A significant drawback of the Paixhans gun was its inability to fire the solid shot so essential to breaking the protective plates of ironclads. Dahlgren's aim was to design effective, large cannon capable of delivering the solid shot necessary to defeat enemy ironclads (see Figure 6.2). Dahlgren was one of several Army and Navy officers developing new ordnance. The effort to develop an effective breech-loading gun was international. The advantages of breech loaders included ease of loading and higher projectile velocities due to the longer barrels possible since the guns did not have to be withdrawn into the hull for reloading. In Britain, in 1855, William Armstrong developed a breech-loading,

Figure 6.2 Dahlgren gun. A nine-inch Dahlgren smooth-bore gun on a Navy gunboat, c. 1862–1865. *Source:* US National Archives and Records Administration, 524794.

---

[7] Ibid., 33.

rifled gun that augured in modern artillery. It was the invention of the interrupted screw obturator in 1872 by a French artillery officer, Charles de Bange, that made large-caliber naval guns possible. As part of the traditional American emphasis on gun power (which included increasing rates of firing), US Navy Lieutenant Robert B. Dashiell developed a simpler, single-motion breech mechanism around 1890 that could be operated more quickly and efficiently and that was used in the Battle of Manila Bay in 1898. In 1889 the British development of smokeless gunpowder, called cordite, cleared much of the dense gunnery smoke from naval battles. By 1896, the US Navy had developed its own smokeless propellant using nitrocellulose.

Technology in the Early Battleship Period

In armored ships such as the modern battleships of the 1890s, guns had to be protected in armored turrets. In 1895 Congress authorized a third round of battleships, the *Kearsarge*-class battleships number 5 and 6 (*Kentucky*), to follow the three Indianas (1890) and one Iowa (1892). The *Kearsarge* class included a unique design feature to bolster the ships' armored strength: superposed gun turrets. Reflecting the historical American emphasis on gun power and resistance to damage, Congress specified that these ships "carry the heaviest armor and most powerful ordnance upon a displacement of about ten thousand tons."[8] The desire to mount eight-inch guns and to maximize their arcs of fire while staying at 10,000 tons' displacement resulted in an eight-inch twin-gunned turret atop each of the two twin 13-inch main gun turrets. The barbette armor for the main guns simultaneously protected the ammunition hoists for the eight-inch guns, simplifying the overall design while maximizing protection with thicker armor. The subsequent five battleships of the *Illinois* and *Maine* classes did not

employ the superposed turrets, since they carried no eight-inch guns. The eight-inch guns returned with the *Virginia* class (authorized 1899) because they had inflicted the majority of damage on Admiral Pascual Cervera's squadron at Santiago de Cuba. During the pursuit of the Spanish ships, 319 eight-inch shells had been fired and achieved 13 hits (4.07 percent) whereas only one battleship main-battery gun had found its mark. For the *Virginia*s, Congress specified the "heaviest armor and most powerful ordnance" that would fit in a displacement of 13,500 tons while also having "the highest practicable speed and great radius of action."[9]

The superposed turrets were distinctly American and exceptionalist in their intent to satisfy the traditional American desire dating back to the Humphreys super-frigates of 1794: great resistance to shot. In fact, the chief constructor, Rear Admiral Philip Hichborn, referred to the turret mountings for the eight-inch guns as "the American system."[10]

Prior to the commissioning of the five Virginias in 1906–1907, service opinion had turned decidedly against the superposed turret. In his annual report for 1907, Rear Admiral Washington L. Capps, chief of the Bureau of Construction and Repair, wrote, "At the present writing there is certainly no well-informed officer of the seagoing or construction branch who would advocate a system of gun mounting which, only a few years ago, was urgently recommended."[11]

Any value of the "American style" of turret was overtaken by the launch of HMS *Dreadnought*. The push for an all-big-gun battleship, consonant with the historical American design philosophy, had been well underway in the US Navy. In an article in 1900 in the US Naval Institute's *Proceedings*, the professional journal of the naval officer corps, Captain Asa Walker called for the construction of larger battleships to protect American imperial responsibilities in the Far East. To achieve a desirable level of "all-around efficiency," Walker argued that armament and armor should take

---

[8] *SecNav Annual Report* (1890), as quoted in Friedman, *US Cruisers* (1984), 40.

[9] Act of Congress, as quoted in ibid., 137.

[10] Philip Hichborn, "Recent Designs of Battleships and Cruisers for the United States Navy," *Transactions of the Society of Naval Architects and Marine Engineers*, 8 (1900), 263.

[11] Capps as quoted in John C. Reilly and Robert L. Scheina, *American Battleships*, 140–141.

precedence over speed. Walker wanted battleships with moderate speed (not to exceed 17 knots) and coal capacity to provide for 7,000 miles of steaming.[12] His emphasis upon invulnerable armor designs and maximum gun power was in line with Civil War experience that emphasized armor strength and gun power and harkened back to the same features in the 44-gun Humphreys frigates. Far East operations, on the other hand, required warships with the capability for long-range, economical steaming, which could only be had at the expense of speed, armor, or number or size of guns. Thus the US Navy faced the same technological tensions in its warship designs at the dawn of the century as it had since the inception of the Navy: reconciling the competing design factors of speed, endurance, strength, and power.

Americans also carved a unique niche within marine engineering in their pursuit of the newly introduced steam-turbine propulsion. Steam turbines offered the possibility for more compact propulsion machinery, which, in armored ships, could be protected more efficiently. Unfortunately, the lack of any effective transmission system between steam turbines, which operated at high speeds for optimum efficiency, and the slower rotative speed required for efficient propeller operation meant that steam turbines were connected directly to the propeller shaft with adverse efficiency effects on the overall propulsive system. In is initial response to the Royal Navy's interest in turbines, the US Navy signed contracts for the construction of three cruisers in 1905, one to be equipped with British Parsons turbines, one with American Curtis turbines, and the third with traditional reciprocating steam engines, in order to compare their relative economies.

Based upon these 1905 cruiser trials, the US Navy decided to accept the steam turbine as the prime mover in its capital ships. Attracted by the compact size of the turbine, and undoubtedly copying Fisher's turbine-propelled HMS *Dreadnought*, the Navy selected US-built Curtis impulse turbines for its first dreadnought battleship, *North Dakota*, in 1907. Parsons turbines were rejected since they required an engine room 24 feet longer than the Curtis installation. Unfortunately, deterioration of the turbine

steam nozzles adversely affected the performance of the Curtis turbines and resulted in the use of Parsons turbines in the next four US battleships. The Parsons turbines did not deteriorate during use, but their relative inefficiency reduced the battleships' steaming range and came up against the primary geostrategic design criterion for American warships. This led to a reversion to the more economical, and strategically consonant, reciprocating engines in the two *Texas*-class dreadnoughts of the 1910 program.

The ideal solution was to equip battleships with turbines, but with a speed-reduction device that would allow the steam turbine and propeller to operate at their respective efficient rotative speeds. The British pursued a traditional industrial solution: close-tolerance, large, mechanical reduction gears that were difficult to manufacture in the sizes need to transmit such a large amount of power. The US Navy considered reduction gearing, offered by a consortium led by George Westinghouse and that included former Engineer-in-Chief George Melville. However, the Navy's trials of the turbo-electric drive, designed by the General Electric Company, proved it to be a phenomenal 20 percent more efficient at cruising speeds (where most of a ship's life was spent) than the direct-drive turbine and 6 percent more efficient than the Westinghouse–Melville reduction gear. In the turbo-electric drive, steam turbines powered generators that produced electricity (just like a shore-based electric-power-generating station), which was then used to power large electric motors connected to each propeller shaft. The turbo-electric drive was elegantly simple and robust, and satisfied that primary US Navy design criterion of propulsive efficiency required by the vastness of the Pacific Ocean. This was a distinctly American approach and the Navy chose the turbo-electric drive to power the 10 super-dreadnoughts and six battle cruisers of the massive 1916 program.

"The Americans Are Very Clever"

In the wake of the Two-Power Standard, the British were very interested in the US Navy and any technological challenge it might pose to British dominance. In 1901 John Harvard Biles, professor of naval

---

[12] Asa Walker, "With Reference to the Size of Fighting Ships," US Naval Institute *Proceedings*, 26 (1900), 515–522.

architecture at the University of Glasgow, delivered a paper before the Institution of Naval Architects on the previous decade of naval construction in the United States. As part of the discussion, Admiral Sir John Hopkins, former commander-in-chief of the British Mediterranean Fleet (1896–1899), offered "an officer's point of view" on the differences between the American and British battleships. Hopkins was favorably impressed by the strength and gun power of the American designs and thought that "the Americans are very clever."[13]

The question that lingers is whether Admiral Hopkins was correct. Were the Americans "very clever"? In terms of success the record is mixed. By 1907 American naval officers judged the "American system" of superposed turrets a failure and it was not repeated after the *Virginia* class. The US Navy never again constructed a major warship with three screws. The Columbias, however, were good enough. Their actual (as opposed to design) 7,000-nautical-mile range was more than enough to reach the Philippines. The speedy commerce raider USS *Wampanoag* was destroyed by petty jealousy and competing cultures within the officer corps.

Conclusion

Overall, the US Navy—through the collective memory and culture of its seagoing officers, naval constructors, and naval engineers and mindful of the geostrategic constraints posed by the vast Pacific Ocean—pursued technologies that reflected a distinctly American engineering culture and shipbuilding capabilities, prevailing material cultures, and geostrategic factors to emphasize structurally strong ships that were resistant to damage and capable of long-range, economical operations, and incorporated as many of the most powerful guns that could be carried.

From the first ships of the Navy authorized in 1794 through the nineteenth century, American warships were often quite different from those of other navies. In seeking to assess Admiral Hopkins' judgment as to whether the Americans were indeed clever, Professor Biles offered this answer over a century ago: "US Naval Constructors have produced ships which should give them satisfaction in their results."[14]

---

[13] Comments of Admiral Sir John Hopkins, GCB, LLD (Associate), "Discussion on 'Ten Years' Naval Construction in the United States,'" INA *Transactions*, 43 (1901), 19–20.

[14] John Harvard Biles, "Ten Years' Naval Construction in the United States," INA *Transactions*, 43 (1901), 12.

CHAPTER 7

The Civil War

Blockade and Counter-Blockade

On November 6, 1860, Abraham Lincoln was elected president of the United States. Though he got no votes at all from most of the southern states, and won only 39.6 percent of the popular vote nationwide in a four-man race, his margin of victory in the Electoral College was decisive. Lincoln had campaigned on a platform of preventing slavery from expanding into the western territories, and southerners from slave-holding states feared that such a policy would cripple their "peculiar institution." News of his election therefore triggered long-threatened efforts to dissolve the union.

South Carolina was the state with the most to lose since black slaves made up 58 percent of its population. Within days of the election, South Carolina leaders called a convention, and on December 20 the delegates to that convention voted to secede. Six other states soon followed, so that, by the time Lincoln took office on March 4, 1861, seven states had formed the Confederate States of America and named Jefferson Davis of Mississippi their provisional president.

Lincoln was determined to keep the union intact, reminding listeners at his inauguration that his presidential oath required him to "preserve, protect, and defend" the Constitution, a pledge that, in his view, included the unity of the nation itself. He embarked on a policy of non-confrontational firmness, insisting that secession was not a legal recourse to losing an election but at the same time pledging that he would not interfere with the southern states unless they provoked a confrontation. He did, however, authorize an expedition to carry supplies to the Federal garrison in beleaguered Fort Sumter in Charleston Harbor. Perceiving that as a challenge to Confederate sovereignty, Jefferson Davis ordered forces in Charleston to open fire on the fort, which after holding out for two days surrendered on April 14. The next day, Lincoln called for 75,000 volunteers "to cause the laws to be duly executed."[1]

The southern states interpreted that a threat to coerce them back into the union, and four more states, including Virginia and North Carolina, cast their lot with the Confederacy. As Lincoln put it later: "Both parties deprecated war, but one of them would *make* war rather than let the nation survive, and the other would *accept* war rather than let it perish."[2]

Portions of Chapter 7 are based on Craig L. Symonds, *The Civil War at Sea* (2008).

[1] Lincoln, "Proclamation Calling the Militia and Convening Congress," April 15, 1861, in Stephen B. Smith, ed., *The Writings of Abraham Lincoln* (2012), 333. Lincoln was invoking the words of section 2 of the 1795 Militia Act.

[2] Lincoln, "Second Inaugural Address," March 3, 1865, in Roy P. Basler, ed., *Abraham Lincoln: His Speeches and Writings* (1946), 336.

America, Sea Power, and the World, First Edition. Edited by James C. Bradford.
© 2016 John Wiley & Sons, Inc. Published 2016 by John Wiley & Sons, Inc.

War Aims and Strategy

Northern war aims—the preservation of the Union—dictated an offensive strategy for the North to reassert its authority in the South. US Army General-in-Chief Winfield Scott advised the establishment of a "complete blockade" of southern ports and launching a "powerful movement down the Mississippi to the ocean … so as to envelop the insurgent states" while keeping pressure on Confederate forces in Virginia.[3] Though never officially adopted, this strategy, which sought to capitalize on the South's weak industrial base and slowly crush it, was dubbed the "Anaconda Plan" (after the snake that squeezes its prey to death) and came to guide Union operations through the four years of war.

Union Blockade

The first strategic decision Lincoln made in that war was to announce a naval blockade of the seceded states, which he did on April 19, five days after the surrender of Fort Sumter. Because blockades were an act of war, his proclamation seemed to concede that the Confederacy was a foreign power, though that ran counter to his official position that the conflict was simply a rebellion by large numbers of men in the southern states. Given that, some in the Lincoln administration thought Lincoln should have avoided the word "blockade," but, whatever the merit of their concerns, those reflections soon gave way to more pragmatic considerations of how to make the blockade a reality.

It would not be easy. Once Virginia and North Carolina joined the Confederacy, the self-proclaimed new nation boasted a coastline more than 3,500 miles long that included 189 harbors, inlets, and navigable rivers. To blockade so vast an area would be daunting even for the greatest naval power on earth, and the US Navy in 1861 was far from that. Officially, the Navy carried 90 vessels on its register of warships, though only 42 of them were actually in commission, and most of those were serving on distant stations off Africa, Brazil, and the China coast and in the Mediterranean. When Lincoln asked his Navy secretary, Gideon Welles, how many ships the Navy could "at once" put into service, Welles answered 12. Clearly the US Navy could not blockade 3,500 miles of coastline with a dozen ships.

Moreover, the blockade Lincoln declared was significantly different from blockades in previous wars. During the Napoleonic Wars, Britain's Royal Navy had blockaded the French coast (and, after 1812, the American coast as well). In that conflict, however, the objective had been to keep French and American warships from getting to sea. The goal in this new war was, in Lincoln's words, to "prevent entrance and exit of vessels from the ports" in all of the seceded states. This was a hugely ambitious goal, so much so that it provoked mockery and ridicule both in the South and in Europe. No navy in history had ever attempted to assert such complete control over so vast a coastline.[4]

According to the Paris Declaration Respecting Maritime Law (1856), a naval blockade was not binding on neutral nations unless the nation imposing the blockade stationed "a competent force" off every harbor within the area blockaded. In other words, Lincoln could not simply *say* that the southern coast was under blockade; he had to station warships off the entrance to each of those 189 harbors and inlets. To do that, the obvious first step was to expand the existing US Navy to five, 10, or even 20 times its size, and that would have to be done at the same time as the Union was attempting to mobilize an army of unprecedented size. Navy Secretary Gideon Welles did what he could, dispatching the handful of warships that were immediately available to patrol the waters off the South's principal seaports, ordering home the vessels on distant stations, and authorizing construction of two dozen new propeller-driven steamers despite the fact that with Congress out of session there was no appropriation to pay for the vessels. Welles assumed (correctly as it proved) that Congress would authorize the expenditure after the fact when it came back into session in July, but his willingness to bend the rules demonstrated the sense of urgency in Washington.

[3] Winfield Scott to George McClellan, May 3, 1861, in George B. McClellan Papers, Library of Congress.

[4] Lincoln, "A [Blockade] Proclamation," April 19, 1861, in Roy P. Basler, ed., *Collected Works of Abraham Lincoln* (1953), 4:339.

These first steps gave the US Navy a total of over 100 warships, most of them steamers. The decision made in the 1850s to modernize the fleet by building six new *Merrimack*-class steam frigates plus a dozen more new steam sloops gave the Navy a core of modern, steam-powered warships, but that was only a fraction of the hundreds that would be needed to make the blockade effective. To obtain them, the North began a program of converting merchant steamers into wartime use. During the Age of Sail, such a transformation had been relatively easy; all that was necessary was to place a few guns on board an existing ship and increase the size of the crew. The technological revolution of the 1850s, however, had changed that. The introduction of steam propulsion plus the dramatic changes in metallurgy and the much larger and heavier naval ordnance made such transformations more difficult (see Chapter 6). On the other hand, ships destined for service on the blockade did not need to confront modern warships; they only needed to overpower unarmed merchant vessels, and for that converted merchantmen proved quite adequate.

Shipyards in the North were soon filled with vessels in various stages of transformation. Their decks were strengthened with timbers to support the weight of the new naval guns, magazines were constructed below the waterline, crews' quarters were greatly expanded, and, often in a matter of weeks, they received a captain, crew, and commissioning pennant, and were sent to join the growing blockade force off the southern coast (see Table 7.1). One thing that nearly all the blockading vessels had in common was that, with very few exceptions, they were all steamships. From the very start of the war, it was clear that the tactical advantages that derived from steam propulsion had made sailing warships all but obsolete.

Table 7.1 US Navy warships in service, 1861–1865.

Date	Number of warships
July 1861	82
Dec 1861	264
Dec 1862	427
Dec 1863	588
Dec 1864	671

Having procured the ships—or at least having made a start in that direction—questions remained about how to organize them. Simply sending ships down the coast to anchor off southern ports would not do; some overall organization had to be imposed on the growing armada and, to accomplish that, the Union authorized what became known as the Blockade or Strategy Board in June 1861. To head this board, Welles picked Captain Samuel Francis Du Pont, a career officer who emerged as the first Union naval hero of the war. His report recommended the establishment of different squadrons for the Gulf of Mexico and Atlantic coasts, and eventually these were subdivided into the East and West Gulf Squadrons and the North and South Atlantic Squadrons (see Map 7.1).

Port Royal

One of the most difficult issues Du Pont dealt with concerned logistics. Coal-burning steamships had to be continually supplied with fuel as well as provisions, and, since the Union lacked any coaling stations between Hampton Roads in Virginia and Key West in Florida, a major recommendation of Du Pont's Strategy Board was to seize and develop several bases along the southern coast.

Port Royal became the Navy's first major target for three reasons. The first was its location almost exactly halfway between Charleston and Savannah, which would afford the blockading squadrons at both of those cities a convenient base for supply and repair. Second, Port Royal was an enormous roadstead, large enough to accommodate the entire Union Navy, and the swampy marshes that separated the offshore islands from the mainland would protect occupying Union forces from attack by Confederate armies. Finally, Port Royal and the Broad River estuary provided navigable access to the interior of South Carolina.

Du Pont's plan of attack at Port Royal was straightforward. His fleet of eight warships, led by the propeller-driven steam frigate *Wabash* and the sidewheeler *Susquehanna*, would escort a flotilla of Army transports crammed with troops and supplies to the South Carolina coast. With 78 vessels in all, it was the largest accumulation of American maritime power ever assembled. Du Pont's warships would batter the Confederate forts into submission, and then the

Figure 7.1 South Atlantic Blockading Squadron bombarding Port Royal, 1861. *Source:* US Naval History and Heritage Command # NH 59256.

troops would land to secure the base as a depot for the blockading squadron.

Du Pont led his warships into Port Royal Sound on November 7, 1861. They passed up the middle of the channel between the two forts, and then turned to port, still in a line-ahead formation, to pass Fort Walker on the southern headland at a range of 800 yards. As they passed, each ship unleashed a full broadside with its heavy naval guns, which significantly outranged anything the Confederates had (see Figure 7.1). Du Pont then led his ships around in an elliptical circle and passed the fort again, this time at 600 yards. From that range, the fire of the Union warships was devastating. The navigator on the *Wabash* wrote that "the air over the fort was filled with clouds of sand, splinters, and fragments of gun carriages and timbers."[5] The side-wheel steamer USS *Pocahontas* joined the Union squadron for the third pass. Its captain, as fate would have it, was Commander Percival Drayton, the brother of the fort's Confederate commander, Brigadier General Thomas Drayton. After the third pass, many of the fort's guns had been disabled, and the defenders were down to only 500 pounds of powder. Accepting the inevitable, General Drayton hauled down the flag.

The Federal victory at Port Royal had several important consequences. Psychologically, the news was extremely welcome in the North, which was still mourning the Union defeat at Bull Run that summer. Strategically, it provided the South Atlantic Blockading Squadron with the base it needed to maintain the blockades of Charleston and Savannah. Indeed, it is hard to imagine how the North could have maintained its blockade of the South Atlantic coast at all without the possession of Port Royal. Elsewhere along the Confederate coast, the North Atlantic Squadron used Hampton Roads, Virginia; the East Gulf Squadron was based out of Key West, Florida; and the West Gulf Squadron was staged out of Ship Island off Biloxi, Mississippi. Collectively, these bases allowed the blockaders to maintain a constant presence off the rebel coast.

Blockade Duty

Service on the blockade was tedious. The Union sailors who kept the watch, fed the engines, and manned the guns on the blockading ships from Virginia to Texas spent interminable days with eyes focused intently on the horizon, or peering into the blockaded

[5] John D. Hayes, ed., "The Battle of Port Royal, S.C. from the Journal of John Sanford Barnes, October 8 to November 9, 1861," *New-York Historical Society Quarterly*, 45 (1961), 391.

harbors hoping to catch a trace of black smoke that might indicate that a ship was getting under way. Alas, day after day—often week after week—passed with no sign of a blockade runner trying to enter or leave a port. On most such days, the familiar routines of shipboard life measured the passage of time: at 0600 orders to turn to and lash up sounded throughout the ship; the decks were swabbed and sanded; watches changed at 0800, noon, and 1600; dinner was piped; then, late in the day, the sky turned to pink and then to indigo, and finally to full dark as another day ended and night set in.

Night was the most dangerous time, for that was when blockade runners were most likely to challenge the blockaders. In the middle of a moonless night, perhaps in a misting rain, a lookout on a blockade vessel might perceive a slightly darker shadow moving amid the blackness. Wary of firing into a friend, the officer of the deck might order the night signal for "friend or foe," and the signals officer put up the required combination of red or white flares. If the appropriate response was not forthcoming, a rocket would be fired into the dark sky, alerting the squadron. Feet pounded on the ladders and decks as men tumbled up from below to cast loose the big guns and train them out into the darkness toward the shadowy outline of the blockade runner, going past now at 10, 12, or even 14 knots. The blockading ships opened fire, the muzzle flashes lighting up the night and temporarily blinding the gunners. Some of the blockading ships slipped their anchors and set out in pursuit. And then, as suddenly as it began, it was over, more often than not with the runner escaping, the men angry about their missed opportunity, and the officers frustrated.

A typical encounter took place off Charleston on June 23, 1862. At 0300 in the pitch black of the predawn darkness, the deck watch on the USS *Keystone State* spotted an unidentified steamer coming out of Charleston. The watch officer fired a gun, slipped the anchor cable, and set out in pursuit. Thus alerted, two more ships joined the chase. All three Union warships set out at full speed after the illicit vessel. After three hours and more than 40 miles, two of the Union ships gave up the chase to the swifter *Keystone State*, which had a reputation as the fastest ship in the squadron. When the sun rose, the commander of the *Keystone State*, William LeRoy, identified the fleeing vessel as the *Nashville*, a notorious

blockade runner that had already made several successful passes through the blockade. LeRoy ordered the coal heavers to redouble their efforts. To lighten ship and gain speed, he had the ship's drinking water pumped over the side and jettisoned several lengths of anchor chain. When the *Keystone State* began to gain on its quarry, the officers and crew on board the *Nashville* grew so desperate that they threw their million-dollar cargo of cotton overboard then began tearing apart the deck cabins to burn the wood to raise more steam.

For more than 300 miles, the two ships raced across the ocean. Finally, after a day-long chase, the *Nashville* slipped into a squall and disappeared. Eventually it reached Abaco in the Bahamas. Statistically this went into the books as a successful escape, though of course the loss of the *Nashville*'s cargo meant that it brought no benefit to either the ship's owners or the Confederacy.

Running the Blockade

For the Confederates, blockade runners constituted a logistical lifeline. Early in the war, when the number of blockading ships was still very small, blockade runners made tremendous profits, bringing in cargoes of both munitions of war and consumer goods. Some southerners argued that, to ensure a reliable flow of supplies, blockade running should be managed by the government. That, however, ran contrary to the laissez faire values of southern society, and both Confederate War Secretary James Seddon and Navy Secretary Stephen Mallory, burdened as they were with fighting a war for survival, decided to leave blockade running to private entrepreneurs. That proved a mistake, for, instead of bringing in the kinds of materials the Confederacy desperately needed, the profit-driven blockade runners often brought in what was most lucrative and drained gold and silver from the South to pay for the imports. Not until the last year of the war did the Confederate government attempt to exert control over the blockade-running effort, and by then it was too late.

Another error was the South's perverse decision to halt exporting its cotton. During the first year of the war, when the blockade was very weak, the South might have sent millions of pounds of cotton overseas to establish credit in European markets. Instead, convinced that "cotton was king," the South withheld its cotton in the belief that the British would be

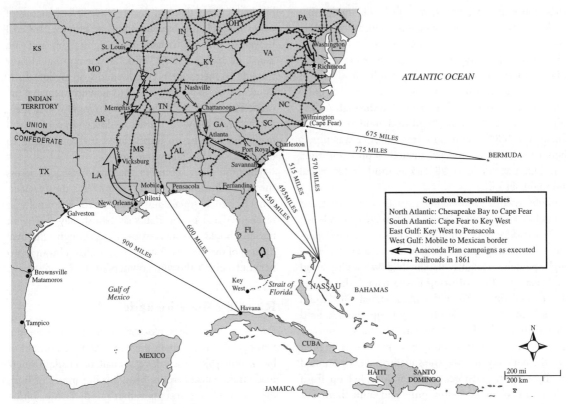

Map 7.1   Blockade and blockade running.

so desperate for it they would join the South in its war for independence. By the time southerners abandoned this gambit, the blockade had become much more efficient.

Blockade-running traffic operated in two stages. Goods intended for the Confederacy were purchased in England or France and shipped in neutral vessels to another port nearer to the United States, the most popular being St. George's in Bermuda, Nassau in the Bahamas, and Havana in Cuba. The US Navy could not interfere with this trade because it was proceeding quite legally from one neutral port to another. At these intermediary ports, the cargoes were transferred into ships that were specially designed to run the blockade: low, fast steamers with their masts stripped down to reduce their profile. Their skippers also sought to time their voyages so that they would arrive off the Confederate coast just at dusk in order to make the final run into port in the dark.

Though every voyage was different, a representative example of what it was like to run the blockade comes from the memoir of Thomas E. Taylor, who was the supercargo (owner's agent) on the English-built, steel-hulled *Banshee*. The *Banshee* made its first attempt to run through the blockade in May of 1863, departing Nassau for Wilmington, North Carolina. The *Banshee* managed to avoid seeing any ships during the transit, but the danger grew as it approached the North Carolina coast, for now the ship and its crew would have to thread through (in Taylor's words) "a swarm of blockaders … without lights and with a coast-line so low and featureless that as a rule the first intimation we had of its nearness was the dim white line of the surf." The *Banshee*'s captain, Jonathon Steele, ordered absolute silence and that no lights be shown. "We steamed on in silence," Taylor remembered, "except for the stroke of the engines and the

Figure 7.2 USS *Kanawha* cutting out a blockade runner under the guns of Fort Morgan at the mouth of Mobile Bay. *Source:* US Naval History and Heritage Command # NH 1855.

beat of the paddle-floats, which in the calm of the night seemed distressingly loud."[6]

The Yankee blocking ships were blacked out as well, but, suddenly, the pilot grabbed Taylor's arm: "There's one of them," he said, pointing. Straining to peer through the blackness, Taylor saw "a long black object on [our] starboard side lying perfectly still." A moment later the pilot whispered again—"Steamer on the port bow"—and there was another one dead ahead. "Stop," Steele whispered urgently to the helmsman. Taylor all but held his breath as the *Banshee* lay dead in the water with ships of the Yankee blockading squadron all about them until finally the ship ahead of them slowly moved off. The *Banshee* restarted and crept on toward the shore. The sky was beginning to show a little gray in anticipation of dawn when Taylor made out "six or seven gunboats" nearby. In the growing light, the lookouts in those gunboats spotted the

Banshee and they opened fire (see Figure 7.2). Now the *Banshee* made a run for it, steaming for the Cape Fear River as shell splashes erupted close around it. It was, Taylor, recalled, "an unpleasant sensation," especially considering that much of the *Banshee*'s cargo consisted of gunpowder. The Yankee warships were getting closer, and their shots were increasingly accurate, when suddenly the big guns from Fort Fisher guarding the entrance to the river boomed out and huge shell splashes erupted just ahead of the pursuing blockade vessels. It was "music to our ears," Taylor recalled. Unwilling to challenge the big guns of the fort, the blockaders "steamed sulkily out of range," and the crew of the *Banshee* cheered as the blockade runner rounded the headland and entered the safety of the river.[7]

The *Banshee*'s experience is a kind of metaphor for Confederate blockade running generally. It made four

[6] Thomas E. Taylor, *Running the Blockade: A Personal Narrative...* (1896), 50.
[7] Ibid., 52, 54.

successful and quite profitable runs (which was the average for blockade runners), but in the end was captured and ended up a prize of the Yankees. Even with its loss, however, the profits generated in those four voyages were so great that it made a substantial profit for its owners.

The success of the *Banshee* and scores of other blockade runners led some in the North to wonder whether the effort and expense of the blockade were worth it. Every time a vessel made it through the blockade, critical northern newspapers assailed the inefficiency (or, in the words of one, the "imbecility") of the Navy Department for failing to stop them.[8] While it seemed inefficient to these critics, by the end of 1863, the blockade was having a clear impact on the overall health of the southern economy. Though the South managed to import enough materials of war to supply its armies, the blockade had a constant wearing effect on the rest of the southern economy. Cotton exports, which were at the heart of the South's cash-crop economy, declined from three million bales in 1860 to fewer than 50,000 bales in 1861, and the numbers continued to fall as the blockade became increasingly effective. During the whole four years of the war, the South exported a total of only 350,000 bales of cotton, which was about one-ninth of what had been shipped in a single year before the war. Despite a dramatic increase in the price of cotton, net revenues from cotton exports dropped by 90 percent, from over $130 million a year to less than $12 million. An important and often overlooked factor was the powerful deterrent effect of the blockading squadrons. While many of the ships that tried to run through the blockade did so successfully, hundreds more never tried it because they were deterred by the presence of those blockading warships.

The dramatic drop in trade led to shortages of a wide variety of consumer goods across the South, and to hoarding, speculation, and inflation. Coffee and tea became nearly as prized as gold or silver. Some of the shortages were caused by a collapsing internal transportation system, but that, too, was affected by the blockade. Coastal traffic, a critical aspect of prewar

commerce in Virginia and the Carolinas, could no longer make use of the offshore sounds, now patrolled by Union gunboats, and that put increased pressure on the weak and overburdened southern railroad system. Moreover, railroads were unable to obtain replacement rails and engine parts to keep the trains running. By 1864, the cumulative impact of all this led to a weakening of civilian morale, depressed not only by disappointing news from the battlefield but also by the constricting influence of the blockade.

New Technology

Unable to break the blockade, the Confederacy relied on two quite different efforts to overcome Union naval superiority. First, it experimented with cutting-edge technology. Aware that they could not match the North in the number of ships it built, Confederate leaders sought to produce a few revolutionary weapons with extraordinary capabilities: ironclads, mines, and even a submarine. Second, the South employed commerce-raiding ships, sending them out to assail the Union's maritime trade in much the same way that Americans had targeted British merchant shipping during both the American Revolution and the War of 1812. Each of these Confederate efforts was partially successful, but in the end neither was decisive, largely because the South simply lacked the maritime infrastructure necessary to build ironclads in large numbers, or to sustain a large enough fleet of commerce raiders.

From the very start, Confederate Secretary of the Navy Stephen Mallory recognized the central importance of an ironclad warship. Only three weeks into the war, he wrote to the chairman of the Confederate Committee on Naval Affairs declaring that "the possession of an iron-armored ship" was "of the first necessity." One such ship, he argued, could neutralize a whole fleet of conventional wooden warships.[9] His initial notion was to purchase an armored ship from France, which had commissioned the ironclad *Gloire* in 1859. The French were unwilling to sell, however, both because they did not want to part with such a powerful

---

[8] The critic was James Gordon Bennett, in the *New York Herald*, October 9, 1863.

[9] Mallory to C. M. Conrad, May 10, 1861, in *Official Records of the Union and Confederate Navies in the War of the Rebellion (1894–1922)*, series II, 2:69.

USS *Monitor*

The iconic warship of the Civil War era was so revolutionary that most officers of the day hardly recognized it as a ship at all. The engine, crew's quarters, and officers' staterooms were all under the waterline, and the only portholes were in the overhead. Officers in their staterooms could glance upward to see fish swimming past over their heads.

The design of this remarkable vessel came from the inventive mind of the Swedish immigrant John Ericsson, but it might not have been built at all but for a man named Cornelius Bushnell. In 1861, Bushnell went to Ericsson's Brooklyn home to seek his advice about an entirely different vessel. While he was there, Ericsson showed him the model he had made of the "Ironclad Battery" he had designed, and Bushnell took it to Washington, where he showed it to President Lincoln. Lincoln was interested in practical inventions, and he was intrigued by the novel design. The president attended the meeting of the Ironclad Board where the *Monitor*

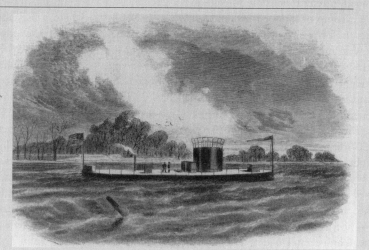

USS *Monitor*. *Source:* Courtesy of the US Navy Art Collection, Washington, DC. US Naval Historical Center Photograph # NH 76324-KN.

was proposed, and offered his views in a characteristic way by declaring, "It reminds me of what the girl said when she put her foot in the stocking. It strikes me there's something in it."[10]

Following its famous duel with the *Virginia* on March 9, 1862, the Navy Department sent the *Monitor* southward to participate in the assault on Charleston. En route

there under tow, the *Monitor* sank in a fierce storm off Cape Hatteras on the last day of the year. It lay on the bottom for more than a hundred years, until a team of US Navy divers brought up significant elements of it in 2002, including the iconic turret, which is on display at the USS *Monitor* Center, part of the Mariners' Museum, in Newport News, Virginia.

vessel and also because it would be a violation of the neutrality laws. Mallory next hoped to build an iron-armored warship from the keel up, but that proved to be beyond the capability of the South's marine industry. In the end he accepted the proposal of John Mercer Brooke and John L. Porter that the wooden steam frigate USS *Merrimack*, abandoned when the US Navy evacuated the Portsmouth Navy Yard near Norfolk, should be converted into an ironclad.

The Confederacy raised the sunken and partially burned hull of the *Merrimack* from the bottom of the Elizabeth River, put it into the Portsmouth dry dock, and began to convert it into something quite different. Though the frigate *Merrimack* had carried 40 guns, the reconstructed version, christened the *Virginia*, carried only 10. Its key feature was a casemate superstructure constructed of angled wooden walls two feet thick, over which workers affixed two

---

[10] As quoted in Robert Schneller, *Quest for Victory* (1996), 189.

layers of two-inch-thick iron plate—800 tons of it altogether. The completed vessel was rechristened the CSS *Virginia*, though both then and later many continued to refer to it as the *Merrimack*.

Learning of these efforts, Gideon Welles in Washington formed an ironclad committee to consider how to respond to this threat. Of the many plans for armored vessels that were submitted to the board, three received approval, including one from John Ericsson for a vessel that would eventually be christened the USS *Monitor*. Not everyone was enthusiastic about Ericsson's "floating battery," which boasted a 120-ton rotating cylindrical turret, 22 feet across and eight feet high, that rested on a perfectly flat deck. Ericsson's design called for only two guns, though they were 11-inch Dahlgren guns capable of firing shot that weighed 165 pounds each, a far cry from the 24- and 32-pounders of the Age of Sail. Aware that the Confederates had a head start in this miniature naval arms race, the Ironclad Board gave Ericsson only 100 days to build his strange little craft. He did it with seven days to spare, and even then it was very nearly too late.

The CSS *Virginia* (*Merrimack*) sortied from the Elizabeth River into Hampton Roads, the principal base of the North Atlantic Blockading Squadron, on March 8, 1862, and in just a few hours it inflicted on the US Navy its worst defeat in history until the Japanese attack at Pearl Harbor 80 years later. The *Virginia* was under the command of former US Navy Captain Franklin Buchanan, who had been the founding superintendent of the Naval Academy back in 1845. An aggressive and determined officer, Buchanan steered his ungainly ironclad directly toward two US Navy warships: the 24-gun USS *Cumberland* and the 44-gun USS *Congress*. The two Union warships opened fire on the curious vessel, but their shot and shells bounced off its iron casemate without inflicting any apparent damage. The *Virginia* smashed its iron prow into the side of the *Cumberland*, a mortal blow that sent the wooden ship to the bottom so swiftly that it very nearly took the *Virginia* down with it. Extracting his ship from the side of the *Cumberland*, Buchanan next targeted the *Congress*, which soon surrendered, though Buchanan was unable to take possession of it because US Army soldiers on shore continued to fire across its deck. Buchanan therefore

ordered the use of hot shot, which set the *Congress* aflame. In one day, the *Virginia* had sunk two warships and taken the lives of more than 240 US sailors.

To the Confederates it seemed only the beginning. Mallory had visions of the *Virginia* lifting the blockade of the entire Confederate coast, perhaps even steaming northward to threaten cities from Baltimore to Boston. Union leaders in Washington had similar visions. Secretary of War Edwin Stanton feared that the *Virginia/Merrimack* might steam up the Potomac to destroy the White House and other government buildings. In fact, both Confederate hopes and Union fears were wildly unrealistic. The *Virginia* was too slow, was too unwieldy, and drew too much water to leave Hampton Roads. It did, however, threaten to drive the rest of the Union fleet from the roadstead. It did not do so because of the arrival, that very night, of Ericsson's little *Monitor*, commanded by Navy Lieutenant John L. Worden, for whom the drill field at Annapolis was subsequently named.

On March 9, 1862, the CSS *Virginia* and USS *Monitor* engaged in the first ever battle between armored vessels. The engagement proved that, temporarily at least, armor had outpaced ordnance, for neither ship was able to deliver a mortal blow against the other. For four hours they blasted away at each other from point-blank range, but neither ship was seriously injured, and no one, on either side, was killed. While the battle was a tactical draw, it was a strategic victory for the smaller *Monitor* because its arrival effectively neutralized the offensive dominance of the *Virginia* and allowed the US Navy to remain in Hampton Roads, a base that it kept for the rest of the war.

The *Virginia*'s service lasted barely two months. When the Union Army captured Norfolk, it lost its base, and, in order to prevent the ship falling into the hands of the Yankees, its own crew destroyed it. Mallory sought to duplicate the success of the *Virginia* elsewhere, and, before the war was over, the South began construction on no fewer than 50 ironclads. The effort was slowed by the scarcity of resources—especially iron armor and marine engines—and also by the vulnerability of the building sites, many of which fell to advancing northern armies. Despite that, the South managed to complete 22 ironclads, one of which—the CSS *Albemarle*—was constructed in a cornfield on the Neuse River, a circumstance that underscores the weakness of the southern maritime industry. The *Albemarle* succeeded in sinking the USS *Southfield* in Albemarle Sound, though it was itself later destroyed in one of the most daring acts of the war by a group of volunteers led by US Navy Lieutenant William B. Cushing.

By late 1863 the South had assembled modest but meaningful ironclad squadrons at several sites including Charleston, Mobile, Richmond, Savannah, and Wilmington. These ironclads helped to keep the blockading squadrons at arm's length, and occasionally they went on the offensive, but in the end there were simply too few of them to change the strategic balance of power.

Meanwhile, the Union had built more than 60 ironclad warships, most of them larger clones of the original *Monitor*, with thicker armor and bigger guns. But, revolutionary as the *Monitor* was, it proved a dead-end technology after all. As the penetrating power of rifled guns became greater, the thickness of the armor had to be increased until its weight threatened to sink the ship. Though the idea of a revolving turret survived into the next century, the notion of producing vessels that were completely impervious to shot became unsustainable. Iron (and, soon, steel alloy) replaced wood in the construction of warships, but those ships were not fully armored like either the *Monitor* or the *Merrimack/Virginia*.

Confederate Raiders

The second element of Confederate naval strategy was a reliance on commerce raiders in an effort to weaken the enemy's overall economy, just as the blockade weakened the economy of the Confederacy. As noted in Chapter 2 and Chapter 4, the United States had relied heavily on commerce raiding in its wars with Britain, which, as an island power, was particularly vulnerable to this kind of *guerre de course* (i.e., commerce warfare).

During the nineteenth century, there were two ways to conduct *guerre de course*. One was by relying on privateers to capture or destroy enemy shipping. Privateering had been declared illegal in the 1856 Declaration of Paris, but the United States had declined to sign the protocol, no doubt thinking that privateering might be a useful weapon in a possible

future war with Britain. As a result, on April 17, 1861, two days before Lincoln announced the blockade, Jefferson Davis declared that the Confederacy would soon begin issuing letters of marque. Confederate privateering did not last long, however. The principal motivation for privateers was the possibility of earning prize money, but, to get it, any ship they captured had to be sent into a port where it could be condemned by a prize court judge and sold at auction along with its cargo. The presence of the blockade squadrons made it all but impossible to send prizes into Confederate ports, and the neutrality of the European powers meant they could not use those ports either. Absent the opportunity to make money, Confederate privateering died out only a few months into the war, and potential privateersmen turned to blockade running as more profitable. The task of raiding Union commerce became the job of Confederate Navy warships.

To acquire ships that could destroy Union commerce, the Confederacy turned to Europe, and particularly to Britain. Jefferson Davis sent James D. Bulloch as a special agent to England to supervise a ship-acquisition program, and Bulloch found a sympathetic partner in the firm of Fraser, Trenholm and Company in Liverpool. It was an open violation of both international and British laws to produce warships for a belligerent, but Bulloch conducted an elaborate campaign of subterfuge to disguise the ships under construction there as intended for other clients, such as Italy or the Ottoman Empire. Though the Confederates eventually commissioned more than a score of commerce raiders, much of the damage to Union shipping was inflicted by three ships, all of which came out of British shipyards: the *Florida*, the *Alabama*, and the *Shenandoah*.

The *Florida* was the first such vessel to be commissioned. Initially named the *Oreto* (to encourage the belief that it was intended for Italy), it put to sea from Liverpool in March 1862, then steamed to the Bahamas, where it took on its naval guns and wardroom of Confederate officers. After running successfully into Mobile Bay to refit and recruit a crew, it steamed out again in December 1862 to begin a two-year campaign of destruction. The protocol was simple: espying a ship on the horizon, *Florida* would chase it down, fire a shot across its bow to stop it, and then demand to see its papers. If it proved to be an American ship,

Raphael Semmes

Though he was born in Maryland, Navy Commander Raphael Semmes lived for some time in Alabama, and, when that state seceded, he resigned his US Navy commission and "went South." Semmes commanded one of the Confederacy's first warships, the CSS *Sumter*, on a cruise through the Caribbean and across the Atlantic to Gibraltar, burning a dozen American merchant ships en route. Trapped in Gibraltar by two US Navy warships, Semmes paid off the crew, sold the ship, and made his way to England.

Semmes made his reputation in command of the CSS *Alabama*, conducting a two-year campaign of destruction across three oceans. Though Semmes and his officers were all from the Confederacy, his crew was an international one composed of Dutch, English, French, Irish, Italians, and Spaniards. To convince them to serve, Semmes promised them double wages and prize money at the end of the war, but keeping such a heterogeneous crew to the task was a delicate balancing act.

After devastating American shipping off the east coast of North America and in the Caribbean and sinking the USS *Hatteras* in the Gulf of Mexico, Semmes headed southward for the coast of Brazil, then east to the Cape of Good Hope, and across the Indian Ocean to the South China Sea, taking 64 prizes in all. Inevitably, his ship began to wear down, and he decided to return to European waters for a refit.

After the *Kearsarge* sunk the *Alabama* off Cherbourg, Semmes made his way back to the Confederacy, doing so in time to participate in the evacuation of Richmond, Virginia. Robert E. Lee appointed him an acting brigadier general with the result that for the rest of his life Semmes could sign his letters "Raphael Semmes, Admiral and General."

Raphael Semmes on the deck of the CSN *Alabama*, 1863. *Source:* US Naval History and Heritage Command # NH 57256.

the crew was removed, along with any stores of special value, and then the ship was set afire.

The most famous and successful of the Confederate commerce raiders was the CSS *Alabama*, commanded by Raphael Semmes. It, too, was a product of the Birkenhead shipyard on the Mersey River near Liverpool, and it was specially designed for long cruises. About the length of a *Hartford*-class US Navy steam sloop, *Alabama* was 12 feet narrower, which gave it rakish lines, less displacement, and a remarkable turn of speed. Its 300-horsepower engines made *Alabama* a swift steamer, but it also had a full suite of

sails so that it could remain at sea for long periods. Unlike the *Florida*, which had been able to recruit its crew in Mobile, the crew of the *Alabama* was a polyglot mixture of Dutch, English, French, Irish, Italians, and Spaniards.

Semmes first attacked the American whaling ships near the Azores and then embarked on a meandering course that led him to New England, the Gulf of Mexico, the bight of Brazil, the Cape of Good Hope, the Indian Ocean, and the South China Sea (see Map 7.2). Altogether, the *Alabama* burned 64 American ships. Periodically, Semmes used one of the

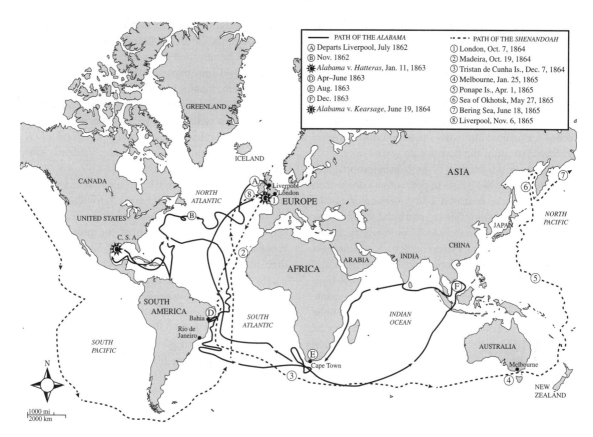

Map 7.2 Confederate cruisers.

captured ships as a cartel to rid himself of his accumulated prisoners. In the Gulf of Mexico, Semmes sank the Union blockading ship USS *Hatteras* in a single-ship action, the first time in history that a steam warship sank another steam warship in battle.

After a voyage of nearly two years and many thousands of miles, the *Alabama* arrived in Cherbourg Harbor in northern France in July 1864 for a refit, and soon afterward the USS *Kearsarge*, under the command of Captain John A. Winslow, appeared offshore. Though Semmes knew his ship was in need of repair, and that much of his gunpowder was questionable, he nevertheless decided to engage the *Kearsarge*. Very likely his sense of chivalry prevented him from refusing combat on near-equal terms. The battle took place on June 19, 1864, and stands alongside the duel between the *Monitor* and *Virginia* as the iconic naval duel of the Civil War. The two ships circled around

a central point, firing at each other as fast as possible. One of the *Alabama*'s shells struck the sternpost of the *Kearsarge* and, had it exploded, it might well have sent the ship to the bottom. Instead it was a dud, and soon the steady fire of the *Kearsarge* overwhelmed the *Alabama*. As the *Alabama* took on water, Semmes struck his colors and told his men to save themselves. Semmes himself escaped in an English yacht, and afterward he complained that Winslow had effectively cheated by hanging anchor chain over the side of his ship to give it extra protection. That Semmes would consider such preparations unfair is a window into his pre-modern worldview.

The fate of the *Florida* was less dramatic, though it was, and remains, controversial. After a long search Commander Napoleon Collins, of the USS *Wachusett*, found the *Florida* in the neutral harbor of Bahia, Brazil. Though Brazil's neutrality should have prevented both ships from engaging in any hostile action, Collins was determined that the *Florida* should not escape. He waited until the middle of the night on October 6–7, when most of the *Florida*'s crew was ashore, and then, getting up a full head of steam, he rammed the raider, fully expecting to send it to the bottom. Instead, *Florida* remained stubbornly afloat. Collins sent a boarding party onto the crippled vessel and towed it out of the harbor into open water.

It was a gross violation of both international and Brazilian law, and the Brazilian government demanded that the *Florida* be returned. The Americans reported that it would be impossible to return the ship because it had sunk under mysterious circumstances in the crowded anchorage of Hampton Roads. Collins' act was too flagrant to overlook, and he was tried and found guilty by a court martial and suspended from the service. During his trial, he argued that, while illegal, his action was nevertheless "for the public good."[11] His suspension from the service had to be confirmed by the president, but Lincoln's assassination a few days later postponed that. Finally, in the fall of 1866, Collins was quietly restored to duty.

The third Confederate commerce raider with a disproportionate impact on the war was the CSS *Shenandoah*, whose remarkable history is a classic sea tale. The iron-ribbed, wood-hulled, fully rigged ship did not become a Confederate raider until the fall of 1864, when it was purchased by the Confederacy, and Bulloch assigned it to the North Pacific with instructions to wreak havoc among the American whaling ships that operated there. Under the command of James I. Waddell, the *Shenandoah* steamed around the Cape of Good Hope and across the Indian Ocean to Melbourne, Australia, where it underwent a refit (see Map 7.2). Next it steamed northwestward through Micronesia to the North Pacific whaling grounds, where it destroyed a total of 23 American whaling ships. What Waddell did not know was that, back home, the war was coming to an end. In April

of 1865, as Robert E. Lee met with Ulysses S. Grant at Appomattox Court House, Waddell continued his rampage. Though men on board some of the ships he captured told him that the war was over, he did not believe them. Finally in early August of 1865, nearly four months after the end of the war, he encountered a British ship with recent newspapers and he knew that it was true: Lee had surrendered, Jefferson Davis was a prisoner, and the South was, in Waddell's word, "subjugated."

His concern now was that all his actions since May might well be construed as piracy. Unwilling to bring his ship into a southern port where he feared arrest and prosecution, he dismounted his guns and sailed the *Shenandoah* southward, around Cape Horn, and then up through the Atlantic and back to England, where the voyage had begun. After a 58,000-mile around-the-world cruise, Waddell hauled down his flag in Liverpool on November 6, 1865.

Four years later the US government sought damages from the British government for losses sustained by American shipping from Confederate commerce raiders built in England. In 1872 an international tribunal endorsed the American position and Britain paid $15.5 million in reparations.

Conclusion

In retrospect, it is clear that the blockade contributed to Union victory by weakening the Confederacy's economy and preventing it from obtaining critical war materials from abroad. On balance, given the Confederacy's weak industrial and maritime assets, technological experimentation and commerce raiding were perhaps the best naval strategies available. In the end, however, the experiments could not be reproduced in numbers large enough to tilt the naval balance of power, and the raiders failed to injure the Union's economy enough to change the outcome of the war.

---

[11] Collins as quoted in Louis M. Goldsborough to the Navy Department, March 23, 1865, in ibid., series I, 3:268.

CHAPTER 8

The Civil War on Rivers and Coastal Waters

Military historians of the American Civil War have seen the sectional conflict as a war fought primary on dry land, with naval power playing only a subordinate role in the Union's military efforts. Nevertheless, subordinate need not mean insignificant, and naval power played an important and necessary part in securing Union victory. Indeed, General-in-Chief Winfield Scott, the Union's most seasoned commander of land forces, incorporated naval power into his early strategic planning for Union victory. In a proposal later dubbed the "Anaconda Plan" by contemporary observers, Scott suggested that, in addition to a naval blockade of the Confederate coast, a powerful Union military expedition should advance down the Mississippi River, "the object being to clear out and keep open this great line of communication in connection with the strict blockade of the seaboard, so as to envelop the insurgent States and bring them to terms with less bloodshed than by any other plan."[1] Scott unsurprisingly proved prescient in his expectation that such an expedition would require both gunboats and steamers acting as troop transports moving downstream, even as Union forces assaulted and then occupied New Orleans near the Mississippi's mouth.

The importance of close cooperation between ground and naval forces holds obvious relevance for Scott's planned expedition down the Mississippi, but enforcement of the blockade also required well-coordinated joint operations. Not only did the Union blockading squadrons require bases on the southern coastline to refuel and refit their vessels but also the vast expanse of the Confederacy's 3,500 miles of coastline with its 189 harbors and coves made it impossible to maintain a truly leak-proof blockade without capturing Confederate port cities. Even as the Union Navy rapidly expanded and acquired vital bases on the Confederate coast to supply and maintain its blockading squadrons, specialized Confederate blockade runners could take advantage of the cover of darkness, stealth, and speed to evade Union patrols. The capture and subsequent closure, however, of Confederate ports provided a solution to the insuperable logistical and technological problems of maintaining an offshore blockade. But the capture of Confederate port cities usually required joint cooperation between ground and naval sources—cooperation that was not necessarily forthcoming due to inter-service rivalries between the Union Army and Navy. Such rivalries, combined with and exacerbated by the inattention of senior Union military and naval leaders, resulted in missed Union opportunities to close Confederate ports during the war's early years. In short,

---

[1] United States War Department, *The War of the Rebellion: A Compilation of the Official Records of the Union and Confederate* Armies, 128 vols. (1880–1901), ser. 1, vol. 51, pt. 1, p. 369.

America, Sea Power, and the World, First Edition. Edited by James C. Bradford.
© 2016 John Wiley & Sons, Inc. Published 2016 by John Wiley & Sons, Inc.

Scott's mooted plans for a riverine expedition down the Mississippi and for a naval blockade of the Confederacy's ports required military *and* naval forces to act together in concert, but such coordinated action was not always present.

Whether or not the failure to close all the Confederacy's ports earlier in the war substantially hindered Union military efforts remains controversial among historians. As a mostly agricultural society, the Confederacy did not in principle require overseas imports to procure foodstuffs, but the new nation's miniscule industrial base compared to the North made arms imports vital at the start of the war. Fortunately for the Confederacy, the relatively weak initial blockade made possible the arming of its troops, and herculean efforts by Josiah Gorgas, the Confederate Ordnance Chief, provided the Confederacy with sufficient arms and ammunition to keep its armies in the field. What Gorgas could not improvise, and speedy but cramped Confederate blockade runners could not import, was the heavy industrial plant and materials needed to maintain the Confederacy's over-taxed and vulnerable rail network. Furthermore, recent scholarship by economic historians has argued that the blockade's largest effect came not from restricting the Confederacy's overseas commerce but from its destruction of the South's coastal shipping network. This forced even more Confederate commerce onto the South's already overburdened rail network, further exacerbating its problems with internal transportation.

Finally, the Union blockade had an important demoralizing effect on the Confederacy's civilian population. From the perspective of our own era, the Confederacy appears a doomed relic of the past, fighting to keep alive an archaic institution (human slavery) on the verge of extinction. In contrast, Confederates believed their national project to be a righteous and modern cause. While the Republican Party called for a protective tariff, Confederates called for an international regime of free trade that would benefit the new nation's cotton exports—a crucial component of British industrial might centered in the textile mills of Lancashire. Although Confederates vastly overestimated their own importance to a larger economic system dominated by the British Empire, British liberals for a time found the Confederacy an eminently respectable cause. A crucial component of antebellum white southerners' self-conception as a "modern" and forward-thinking people was their connection to a larger transatlantic print culture of arts and letters. The Union blockade fractured those links and, in conjunction with the Confederacy's diplomatic reverses, it fed into a growing sense of isolation and doom on the Confederate home front.

While the Union blockade clearly contributed to Confederate defeat, albeit in a somewhat ambiguous and indirect fashion, historians do not dispute the importance of Union control of inland waterways. The Union's dominance of the Confederacy's rivers was a necessary, although by no means the decisive, factor in northern victory. The Union faced the dilemma of sustaining armies and campaigns across a continent bereft of the population density and road network that had helped to support European armies during the Napoleonic Wars. Union armies of invasion thus sought control of coastal and inland waterways due to the unparalleled efficiency of waterborne transportation, which remained far superior to even the best rail transportation. The Confederacy hoped to defend important geographical choke points on waterborne lines of communication in order to deny the Union such advantages, and the fall of Vicksburg represented the last crushing blow to the Confederacy's defensive riverine strategy. Nevertheless, the Confederacy fought on, because important inland objectives (i.e., Atlanta and Richmond) remained out of the reach of the rivers that the Union's naval power dominated. Furthermore, as with coastal operations to close Confederate ports, Union success in river operations generally required close coordination between Army and Navy assets.

Piercing the Northwest Barrier

Scott's early strategic planning not only sought to use the logistical efficiencies of water transport as a line of communication to support an invading Federal army but also hoped to use the Mississippi as a means of maneuver to reduce the war's level of violence and thus facilitate postwar reconciliation between the sections. By using its mobility on the river to outflank its opponents, Scott argued that the Federal expeditionary force would be able to avoid hard fighting and heavy casualties on both sides. Americans since the Revolutionary War had understood the political and symbolic importance of controlling rivers that unified or divided large sections of new nations. During that previous conflict, the Lake Champlain and Hudson River corridor had been the crucial contested waterway between the Middle Colonials and New England. Indeed, most Union and Confederate generals had received their initial training at West Point, a military installation originally emplaced to protect the Hudson River.

Scott's plans went for naught in the short term, however, as a *rage militaire* gripped the North and demanded aggressive Federal military operations to crush the Confederacy in a climactic Napoleonic battle. Nevertheless, western military commanders on both sides intuitively realized the importance of riverine transport and acted accordingly. However, the Union also benefited from the influence and innovative mind of James B. Eads, a native Indianan who had settled in St. Louis as a salvage expert for Mississippi River traffic. Despite his strictly civilian background, Eads recognized very early on the importance of controlling the Mississippi, and, with the support of US Attorney General Edward Bates (another Missourian,

whose only military experience was serving as a sergeant in the Virginia militia during the War of 1812), Eads persuaded the War Department early in the war to fund the acquisition of steam-driven, shallow-draft river gunboats with iron plate armor.

The Union Navy's leaders at the outset of the war saw the river war as the Army's and the War Department's financial and operational responsibility, but Secretary of the Navy Gideon Welles sent Commander John Rodgers west to provide advice to the Army on gunboat acquisition. Fortunately for the Union, Rodgers proved flexible in his conception of naval warfare, and he exceeded his instructions in order to purchase and convert three so-called "timberclads," which used five-inch oak backing as armor instead of iron plates. After some wrangling, the Army and Navy would find a compromise where the sea service would provide and pay river gunboats' officers, while the Army would provide its enlisted personnel. In addition to purchasing Rodgers' timberclads, the Army would also purchase seven new gunboats designed by Eads and modified by both Rodgers and naval architect Samuel Pook.

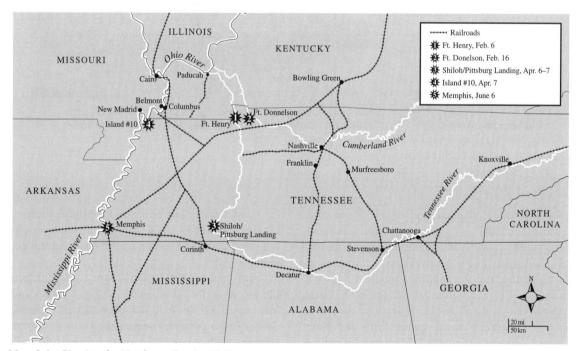

Map 8.1 Piercing the Northwest Barrier, 1862.

Ironclad River Gunboats

At the outbreak of the Civil War the largely self-educated but talented salvage expert James B. Eads was contracted to construct ironclad gunboats for the Army's Western Gunboat Flotilla. After consulting with Commander John Rogers to determine operational requirements with Samuel Pook to design the vessels while he, Eads, built a shipyard to construct the vessels. Eads delivered seven *City*-class gunboats in five months.

Instead of vulnerable sidewheels, the gunboats used a single recessed sternwheel for propulsion. Guns, machinery, and wheel were enclosed in a protective wooden casemate, while iron plate provided additional protection for the boilers, the engines, and the forward casemate. Both Rodgers and Eads rightly realized that the gunboats would not use the broadsides of the blue-water navy but would attack with or against the current—hence the additional armor to protect the gunboats' prows. The world's first ironclads to do battle, the *St. Louis* (14) and *Essex* (5), engaged three

Confederate cotton-clad warships at Lucas Bend on the Mississippi River on January 11, 1862, forcing them to retreat to Columbus, Kentucky, with the floating battery they were towing. Four Eads-built gunboats led the attack on Fort Henry a month later, four bombarded Fort Donelson, and two fought at Island No. 10 before the Western Gunboat Flotilla was transferred to the Navy and became the Mississippi River

Squadron in October 1862. By war's end Eads would build more than 30 ironclad gunboats, some so seaworthy that they would participate in Admiral Farragut's attack on Mobile Bay in 1864. After the war Eads would design and construct a steel road and rail bridge across the Mississippi River at St. Louis. The longest arch bridge in the world when it opened in 1874, the Eads Bridge remains in service today.

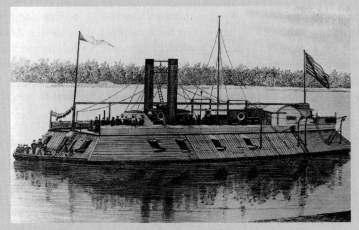

USS *St. Louis*, launched in 1861, was renamed USS *Baron de Kalb* in 1862. Engraving by George Perine & Co., c. 1865. *Source:* US Naval History and Heritage Command # NH 78178.

In September, Captain Andrew H. Foote took command of this new fleet of Union gunboats. Faced with all sorts of administrative and logistical challenges, Foote nevertheless persevered in the equipping and manning of a gunboat fleet that proved vital to the Union war effort in the West. Federal law and institutional practice prevented unity of command among Union Army and Navy commanders, since neither could impose his will on the other. Such an arrangement could lead to dis-

cord and disaster, but Foote and Brigadier General Ulysses S. Grant forged a close and productive relationship that would yield fantastic dividends for the Union cause.

Grant commanded Union troops based in Cairo, Illinois, near the confluence of the Cumberland, Mississippi, Ohio, and Tennessee Rivers. During Grant's first significant engagement, Foote's gunboats provided both water transport and supporting artillery fire to Grant's disembarked ground troops, which assaulted a Confederate position at Belmont, Missouri, downstream from Cairo and located across the Mississippi from the powerful Confederate fortifications at Columbus, Kentucky. After an initial success, Grant's green and overconfident troops met a fierce Confederate counterattack and escaped via the transports they had arrived in, supported by covering fire provided by two of the timberclads Rodgers had had the foresight to purchase. Grant had intended his initial foray at Belmont to be part of a larger campaign to take the powerful Confederate position at Columbus, defended by works mounting 140 guns. Columbus was the linchpin of a larger system of fortifications at strategic and defensible points that the Confederacy had established to anchor a "Northwest Barrier" running westward from the Allegheny Mountains along the Cumberland and Tennessee Rivers to the Mississippi River and to block Union invasion of the South (see Map 8.1). Although the Confederacy also

embarked on a program of obtaining and building river gunboats, its limited industrial base required it to focus on a network of fixed fortifications to defend its river network.

Fortunately for the Union, the timberclad *Conestoga* (4) commanded by Lieutenant Seth L. Phelps had conducted aggressive scouting operations on the Tennessee and Cumberland Rivers, which revealed the relative weakness of Forts Henry and Donelson, the Confederate fortifications guarding those rivers. Despite his inherent caution, Grant's superior, Major General Henry Halleck, recognized the potential benefits of seizing control of the Cumberland and Tennessee Rivers to outflank the Confederate garrisons at Columbus and Bowling Green, Kentucky. As William T. Sherman recalled in his memoirs, Halleck had in his presence drawn the Confederate line on a map and outlined the Tennessee River breaking the line in the center, declaring, "That's the true line of

Figure 8.1 Attack on Fort Henry, 1862. *Source:* Library of Virginia.

operations."[2] Halleck authorized the ever-aggressive Grant to begin his planned offensive on February 1, 1862; it would be supported by three timberclads and four ironclads from Foote's gunboat fleet.

On February 4 and 5, Grant landed his troops near Fort Henry for a planned joint Army–Navy assault on the Confederate position protecting the Tennessee River. Grant's troops found themselves trapped by mud-clogged roads produced by torrential rainstorms, and on February 6 Foote's gunboats made a purely naval assault on the poorly constructed Confederate fortification. Fort Henry had not benefited from competent engineering advice in its construction, and the same storms that trapped Grant's troops in mud partially flooded its works, while its guns had not been situated on high ground. Its commander, Confederate Brigadier General Lloyd Tilghman, had such little confidence in his position that he had already evacuated most of the garrison. He commanded only enough troops to man Fort Henry's 12 guns covering the river. Foote's ironclads comprised the first line of an assault that closed to within 300 yards of the Confederate works, which surrendered after most of its guns had been disabled by the Union bombardment (see Figure 8.1). After Henry's fall, Foote's timberclads traveled 175 miles upriver (i.e., southward) and wreaked havoc on limited Confederate shipbuilding resources, but, most importantly, they destroyed the railroad bridge over the Tennessee River that linked the Confederate garrisons at Bowling Green and Columbus.

Displaying the aggressiveness that would later become one of the calling cards of his generalship, Grant then planned an immediate assault on Fort Donelson, where Federal forces faced a much more formidable set of fortifications than the feeble works at Fort Henry (see Map 8.1). Foote took his damaged but victorious ships to Cairo for repairs, where he fretted over the high ground occupied by Confederate batteries at Donelson. Nevertheless, he assented to Grant's request for a naval assault on February 14, to coincide with a ground movement by troops to encircle the Confederate garrison from its landward side. Foote's concerns proved justified, and the same tactics

that had been so successful at Fort Henry failed at Donelson. Plunging fire from guns emplaced 40 feet above the river badly damaged Foote's ironclads, all four of which were disabled, while the Confederates did not lose a single artillery piece to the Federal bombardment. Eleven of Foote's sailors perished, and another 41 were wounded, including Foote, who suffered a painful ankle wound.

However, because Foot had not made his attack in isolation, the Union still emerged triumphant from the campaign. Despite the Navy's repulse, the Confederate garrison still found itself trapped in its works, with Foote's battered fleet still controlling access to the Confederate garrison via the river and Grant's army cutting off its communications by land. After a failed breakout attempt on the 15th, Grant counterattacked and the weakly led Confederate garrison surrendered its 12,500 troops the following day. Grant and Foote had erred in too aggressively attacking Donelson with Union naval forces, but their coordinated operations still obtained a tremendous Union victory.

The fall of Donelson resulted in the fall of Nashville, since Union naval forces could now steam to that important Confederate city unimpeded. With their Northwest Barrier pierced and Union forces now penetrating deep into central and western Tennessee, the Confederates abandoned their formidable fortifications at Columbus, ceded Kentucky to the Union for the moment, and fell back down to Corinth, in northeast Mississippi. On the Mississippi River, a Confederate garrison remained at Island No. 10, whose powerful fortifications overlooked a reverse-S curve in the Mississippi. Once again, however, Union Army and Navy forces showed how much the two forces could accomplish when they worked in concert with one another.

With Grant massing his troops at Pittsburg Landing on the Tennessee River in preparation for a drive against the key Confederate railroad junction at Corinth, Foote now conducted operations in conjunction with Brigadier General John Pope, who commanded the 18,000 men of the Army of the Mississippi. A physically and mentally ailing Foote had lost his prior aggressiveness, and on March 17 he

---

[2] William Tecumseh Sherman, *Memoirs of William T. Sherman* (1990), 238.

conducted a cautious bombardment of Island No. 10 with both his ironclads and mortars emplaced on specially designed rafts. The Federal assault proved ineffective, but Foote had ample reason not to repeat the aggressive tactics he had used at Donelson. Where he had less justification was in only reluctantly assenting to Pope's request that Union gunboats run past the Confederate works to link up with Union ground forces holding New Madrid downstream from Island No. 10. With naval support, Pope planned to cross the river and cut Island No. 10's line of communications to the south. After much prodding, and with the cooperation of one of Foote's more aggressive subordinates, Commander Henry Walke, Pope finally succeeded in persuading Foote to allow Walke's USS *Caronde-let* (14) to run the Confederate batteries under cover of darkness during a thunderstorm on April 4. Walke prepared the *Carondelet* for the attempt by lashing a coal barge to its side and applying improvised armor to its decks and pilot house to provide extra protection against Confederate fire. The attempt succeeded, and Foote reluctantly allowed the USS *Pittsburgh* (14) to perform the same feat on April 6–7. With the support of these two powerful gunboats, Pope crossed the Mississippi on April 8 and cut off Island No. 10's line of communications to the south, forcing the surrender of the garrison and most of its personnel. Once again, when Union naval and ground forces worked in harmony with one another, they could cut off even well-emplaced Confederate fortifications.

On April 6, shortly before the USS *Pittsburgh* ran the batteries of Island No. 10, the timberclads *Lexington* (6) and *Tyler* (7) provided naval gunfire support for Grant's army at Pittsburg Landing (also known as Shiloh), helping to blunt the Confederate assault on the battle's first day. The Federal gunboats continued to shell the Confederates overnight, and they protected the arrival by river of reinforcements from Major General Don Carlos Buell's command on the battle's second day. If Grant had lost his nerve after the shock of the first day of Shiloh, as George B. McClellan did during the Seven Days Campaign, his advantages in freedom of movement and naval artillery support would not have prevented a Union disaster. But Grant was not McClellan and his famed equanimity, combined with naval support, converted a near disaster into a narrow tactical victory for Union arms.

Near victory or not, Shiloh ruined Halleck's confidence in Grant's generalship, and the senior officer concentrated troops throughout the western theater, including Pope's army, at Pittsburg Landing under his own direct command to support an advance on Corinth followed by a campaign down the Mobile and Ohio Railroad to Meridian, Mississippi, and on to Mobile, Alabama. Pope's departure caused the Federal advance down the Mississippi to pause at Fort Pillow, where Captain Charles H. Davis replaced the wounded and exhausted Foote as commander of the Union's riverine squadron.

During the Union gunboats' cautious bombardment of the Confederate position, a small force of Confederate rams originally built to defend New Orleans but transferred upriver surprised the gunboat flotilla on May 10 and disabled two Union gunboats. However, this rare victory for Confederate naval power on inland rivers could not prevent the eventual forced evacuation of Fort Pillow after the Union capture of Corinth on May 30 threatened to cut off the Confederate garrison. The Union's gunboat flotilla continued its advance down the river to Memphis, where a combined force of ironclads and rams—the latter designed and commanded by Charles Ellet, another civil engineer turned naval architect—crushed the same small force of Confederate rams that sought to defend the city in the absence of any fixed fortifications on June 6, 1862. After Memphis' fall, Vicksburg became the next logical target for fulfilling Scott's plan for the Union to seize control of the Mississippi, and it was at that city that the gunboat flotilla advancing down the Mississippi linked up with Captain David Glasgow Farragut's fleet moving up the river after its victory at New Orleans.

New Orleans

New Orleans, the Confederacy's most important port city, was where the riverine and blockade aspects of Scott's Anaconda Plan merged. Scott had aimed to take the city early in the war, in part because the plethora of access points between the city and the Gulf of Mexico made it impossible to blockade at a distance. On April 18, 1862, a fleet of mortar boats under Commander David Dixon Porter, in support of a larger naval force under Farragut, began

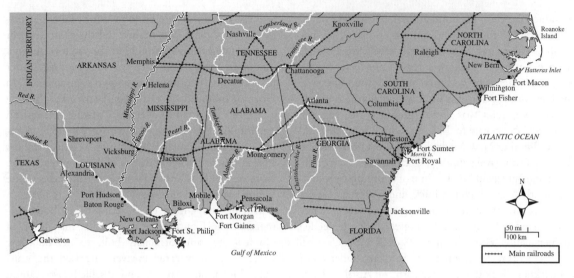

Map 8.2   Conjunct operations.

a sustained bombardment of Forts Jackson and St. Philip, which stood between the Federals and New Orleans 70 miles upstream of the forts. The mortars caused some damage to the Confederates but could not by themselves obtain a decisive decision. Farragut thus ordered his fleet to run past the Confederate forts to cut them off from the city and facilitate their capture by 15,000 Army troops under the command of Major General Benjamin Butler. Not only did Farragut's forces face the emplaced artillery of the Confederate fortifications but they also had to fight off a small force of Confederate gunboats and fire ships, an immobile ironclad used as a floating battery, and the ironclad ram *Manassas*. Getting underway during the early morning hours of April 24, the Union naval assault suffered serious casualties in a fierce and sharply fought battle during which Farragut himself had a few close calls with mortality.

The following day, April 25, Farragut arrived off New Orleans, where his ships easily brushed aside the weak fortifications guarding the city as its remaining militia defenders fled (the city's regular garrison had been sent north to Tennessee after Fort Donelson's fall to Grant). The city descended into virtual anarchy as Farragut attempted to negotiate a formal surrender; on the 29th, he ordered marines to take the city by force. Meanwhile, to the south, Forts Jackson

and St. Phillips, isolated by the Union Navy, surrendered as Butler's troops then moved on to reach New Orleans on May 1. While the Navy had borne the brunt of the fighting to take the city, Butler's 15,000 soldiers were indispensable for the campaign's success. The absence of a sizable supporting force of Army troops would, in contrast, doom Farragut's attempt at capturing Vicksburg later that summer.

The Peninsula Campaign

While their geographic position as lines of invasion made western rivers obvious objectives for the Union to seize and for the Confederacy to obstruct, rivers formed geographic obstacles to a Union advance in the crucial Virginia theater located between the two contending national capitals of Washington and Richmond. The Rappahannock and Rapidan rivers flowed west to east, forming natural defensive lines for Confederate forces protecting Richmond. However, Richmond's relatively close geographic position to the coast offered an enterprising Federal commander the possibility of using sea power to outflank those rivers and approach Richmond from the southeast via the Peninsula between the James and York Rivers. The drawback of such a move, however, would be that it would potentially leave Washington vulnerable to a

Confederate army marching overland. Nevertheless, if the Federal capital could be adequately secured from such a Confederate *coup de main*, an amphibious move against the Confederate capital had obvious advantages. It would allow a Federal army attacking Richmond to supply itself in large part by water, as opposed to a frail land-bound supply line awash in a sea of pro-Confederate guerrillas. In January 1862, Union General-in-Chief George B. McClellan planned to outflank Confederate forces facing Washington by having the Navy land his army at Urbanna on the Rappahannock River, but had to abandon that plan when Confederate General Joseph E. Johnston repositioned his army south of that river.

McClellan reacted by changing his landing point to Fort Monroe, on the tip of the peninsula between the James and York Rivers. In mid-March the Navy embarked the first of the over 120,000 troops it would transport to the area. Ever cautious, McClellan refused either to support the Union Navy's attempt to replicate its success at New Orleans by sailing up the James River or to begin his army's advance up the Peninsula toward Richmond. The delay gave the Confederates time to concentrate forces from elsewhere in Virginia and to erect three lines of defense between McClellan and Richmond. At Drewry's Bluff, they built a powerful fortification 200 feet above the water and placed obstructions in the river that made simply running past the batteries impossible. An attack led by Commander John Rodgers on May 15 failed to reduce the Confederate works with naval gunfire alone, and McClellan did not recognize the possibilities of using ground troops to support the Navy's efforts. In short, while sea power could facilitate McClellan's campaign to take Richmond, it could not ensure the Confederate capital's fall, and its potency could only be fully exploited if ground troops acted in close collaboration with naval forces (see Map 8.3).

Combined with Confederate countermoves and the anxieties of senior Union political leaders, McClellan's excessive caution robbed his campaign of its intended objectives. In May 1862, Thomas "Stonewall" Jackson's Valley Campaign eviscerated Federal forces in the Shenandoah Valley, allowing Jackson to make threatening moves on Washington. The brusque and arrogant McClellan had never bothered to gain Lincoln's confidence, and Jackson's victories in the

Valley raised alarms about the Union capital's physical security. As a consequence, Lincoln withheld from McClellan the 35,000-man First Corps, which would have improved McClellan's position considerably when General Robert E. Lee took over the Confederate army defending Richmond and launched what became known as the Seven Days Campaign.

Starting at the battle of Mechanicsville on June 26, Lee's army suffered grievous casualties before McClellan fell back, thinking his own army badly outnumbered. McClellan did not realize that Lee had stripped bare the lines defending Richmond to free up the mobile reserves necessary for the Confederate counteroffensive, and Lee's aggressiveness seemed to confirm McClellan's assumptions about overwhelming Confederate superiority in numbers. McClellan's amphibious cast of mind directed his gaze to the James River, where he sought to reestablish a new base of operations for his army under the watchful eye of Federal gunboats' heavy guns. Unfortunately, McClellan had confused operational dexterity with strategic logic, and his unrealistic demands on Washington for reinforcements and influence on political matters such as emancipation policy exasperated Lincoln, who withdrew most of his Union forces in August.

The near collapse of the Union's eastern field armies at Second Bull Run in late August forced Lincoln to return McClellan to command, but Lincoln ended the general's career as a Civil War field commander for his passivity after McClellan's close-run victory at Antietam on September 17. The dubious demise of McClellan's military career also tarnished the whole operational concept of using Union sea power to sustain and support a march on Richmond from the southeast. The Union's political leaders, including Lincoln, would now always associate the Peninsula with McClellan's tactical passivity, as opposed to the more imaginative and even innovative aspects of his military mind.

Various joint Army–Navy operations on the eastern seaboard had shown the promise of joint operations in the war's first year, and McClellan had helped to midwife those operations as General-in-Chief. However, McClellan himself lost interest in these operations as he became increasingly preoccupied with his own campaign against Richmond. While the short-lived and inter-service Blockade

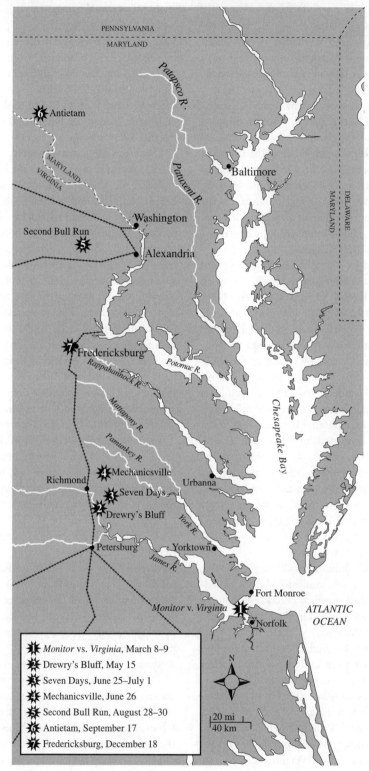

Map 8.3 Operations in Virginia, 1862.

Board in the summer of 1861 had helped to plan these early operations, Army–Navy cooperation for even coastal operations never acquired much institutional support in Washington. Furthermore, even the first year's successful campaigns already exhibited warning signs of how inter-service and inter-personal rivalry could later stall Federal efforts to capture and close Confederate port cities. Arch-navalists such as Assistant Secretary of the Navy Gustavus Fox believed that the early examples of naval gunfire reducing Confederate fortifications (the battle of Hatteras Inlet in North Carolina's Outer Banks in August 1861 and the capture of Port Royal off South Carolina's coast that November) without significant assistance from ground troops could be replicated on a wider scale, due to the increasing power of naval ordnance and the ability of steam-ships to direct their fire without being completely bound to wind and current. In contrast, truly joint operations conducted by Brigadier General Ambrose Burnside and Captain Louis M. Goldsborough (later replaced by Commander Stephen C. Rowan) off the North Carolina coast showed the promise of joint Army–Navy cooperation. This joint force closed all North Carolina ports with the important exception of Wilmington during the spring of 1862. Unfortunately, Union naval power could not directly support a planned movement on Goldsboro (with its vital rail junction) before Burnside's recall along with half of his troops to Virginia in July after the Seven Days Campaign.

Every one of McClellan's successors in the eastern theater—the aforementioned John Pope transferred from the West, Ambrose Burnside, and Major General George Meade—would approach Richmond by land, keeping their own armies in between the Confederates and Washington. As McClellan loyalists, Burnside and Meade might be sympathetic to the Peninsula as a line of operations, but they would bow to Lincoln's demand that the Union capital be completely secure. Even Grant, who by the time he moved east in 1864 enjoyed Lincoln's confidence far more than any other Union commander, would choose the direct overland route, although he would pair his own advance with a secondary campaign under Butler, attacking Richmond from the old Peninsula line of operations.

Mississippi River Operations

With any coherent plan for joint operations on the eastern seaboard fated to become another casualty of McClellan's tactical failures and subsequent departure from command, the western theater's inland rivers became the primary arena of Federal joint operations by geographic necessity, as opposed to strategic design. On the Mississippi, after the Union's impressive run of riverine successes in the spring of 1862, attention shifted to Vicksburg after the fall of Memphis (see Map 8.3). Unfortunately, even after the Union's western flotilla of gunboats linked up with Farragut's ships sailing upstream from New Orleans, their combined combat power proved unequal to the task of reducing Vicksburg's powerful fortifications, sited 200 feet above the river near a sharp curve. Without a significant army acting in cooperation, a naval force could not dislodge the Confederate batteries or fend off attacks by 15,000 nearby Confederate infantry under Confederate Major General Earl Van Dorn. With more ground forces acting in cooperation, Farragut might have been able to take the city that summer and gain Union control of the entire Mississippi, but Halleck refused to recognize the opportunity before him and sent no ground troops. After some desultory shelling of the city and a sharp skirmish with the Confederate ironclad *Arkansas* (10), which sustained enough engine damage fighting Federal gunboats that it eventually had to be scuttled, Farragut, the Union's greatest fighting admiral, sailed down the Mississippi to his beloved blue water before the river's falling water level trapped his deep-draft salt-water naval vessels. Thus the absence of coordinated and inter-service planning contributed to the Union's failure to take Vicksburg in the summer of 1862, before the Confederacy massed even more troops to defend the city.

After Farragut's withdrawal, the Union gunboat fleet retreated to Helena, Arkansas. In December Grant took charge of the Federal effort to secure Vicksburg, a task now considerably more difficult due to further reinforcement of the city's formidable defenses. Grant attempted various lines of operation to take the Confederate position in close coordination with the new commander of the Union's riverine fleet, Captain Porter. Grant first attempted to use an overland route

David Glasgow Farragut

Born James Glasgow Farragut (1801–1870) in Tennessee, Farragut moved to New Orleans with his family in 1804. When his mother died of yellow fever, he was sent to live with a friend of his father, David Porter, who took the young boy to sea as a midshipman. Farragut sailed to the Pacific in the *Essex* (36) during the War of 1812, and, when only 12 years old, took command of a prize taken by the *Essex* and sailed it into port. Farragut, who changed his first name to David in honor of Porter, was given his first warship command, USS *Ferret* (3), in 1824. When David Porter left the US Navy and joined the Mexican Navy following the Fajardo Incident, he took with him his son David Dixon Porter, but his adopted son, Farragut, remained in the US Navy.

Farragut settled in Norfolk, Virginia, in 1823, and some officials questioned both his loyalty and that of David Dixon Porter to the Union at the outbreak of the Civil War. Nevertheless, Secretary of the Navy Gideon Welles, trusting both officers, made his most inspired personnel choices of the war and gave Porter command of a gunboat flotilla on the Mississippi and assigned Farragut command of the West Gulf Blockading Squadron.

Farragut's capture of New Orleans led to his being named the US Navy's first rear admiral in July 1862. Returning to blockade duty, Farragut suffered a series of setbacks including the fall of Galveston to Confederate forces in October 1862 and the escape of the CSS *Florida* from Mobile Bay in January 1863.

Farragut's operations on the Mississippi River later that year and victory at Mobile Bay brought him promotion to vice admiral in December 1864. The preeminent naval hero of the Civil War, Farragut was advanced to the rank of admiral in 1866 and died on active duty in 1870, ending an illustrious career of 57 years.

David Glasgow Farragut at Mobile Bay. Painting by Dean Mosher. *Source: Courtesy of Dean Mosher.*

from Memphis with his main body, in conjunction with a subordinate attack on the Chickasaw Bluffs, north of the city, by a detachment transported by the Navy via the Yazoo River. Confederate raiders destroyed Grant's overland supply line, however, dooming the secondary assault to failure and illustrating the tenuous nature of land-based communications. After various failed joint Army–Navy attempts to create a navigable waterway to transport Grant's troops to the east side of the river, where they could attack Vicksburg from the dry land to its southeast, the Union general requested that Porter support a risky venture to run gunboats and transports past Vicksburg while Grant's army marched down the river's western bank. They would then cross the river with support from the gunboats, separating Grant from his base of supply but placing his army on dry ground, where he could fight and maneuver outside the swamps, waterways, and bluffs that protected Vicksburg to the north and west. Porter remained skeptical of the plan, but, after some prodding from Secretary Welles, he agreed to do his part, and, on the night of April 16–17, 1863, he successfully ran his fleet past Vicksburg's batteries. Grant crossed the Mississippi with his army on April 30 and then proceeded to defeat the hapless Confederates in detail in five separate engagements, culminating in the siege of Vicksburg and its eventual surrender with its 30,000-man garrison on July 4.

Five days later, the garrison at Port Hudson, the last Confederate stronghold on the Mississippi River, surrendered after a 48-day siege.

Conjunct Operations, 1863–1865

While the Vicksburg campaign showed how local army and navy commanders could overcome the Federal failure to plan joint operations at the same strategic level as Scott's original Anaconda Plan, the Union's frustrating operations in the vicinity of Charleston showed the costs of allowing inter-service and inter-personal rivalries to hinder what should always be truly joint operations. Due in large part to Fox's animus against the Army, Union naval commander Samuel F. Du Pont attempted a purely naval assault on the powerful fortifications guarding Charleston Harbor on April 7, 1863 (see Map 8.2). The attack failed miserably, and the Union only managed to close Charleston to blockade running when the Union Army and Navy cooperated in capturing the strategically positioned Morris Island in September 1863. Even then, while new Union commanders Rear Admiral John A. Dahlgren and Brigadier General Quincy A. Gillmore for the most part worked well with one another, their relationship collapsed after an acrimonious dispute over two uncoordinated Army and Navy attempts to capture Fort Sumter later that month resulted in a first-rate fiasco. Charleston finally fell to an overland expedition from Savannah in February 1865.

Grant's promotion to Union general-in-chief after his triumph at Missionary Ridge in November 1863 did not fully resolve the Union's systemic problems coordinating joint operations, but it did put a first-rate strategic mind at the head of the Union Army. Grant's planning in the winter of 1863–1864 for the following spring's campaigns by necessity focused on ground operations, but it incorporated naval elements in a manner even more sophisticated than Scott's and McClellan's early explorations of joint operations. Grant planned multiple campaigns to inflict simultaneous pressure across the entire Confederacy. Three of those campaigns involved exclusively land-based operations: the Army of Potomac would use the now-traditional overland route against the Army of Northern Virginia to take Richmond; Sherman's army in the west would move on Atlanta; and Major General

Franz Sigel's army would advance into the Confederate-held Shenandoah Valley. However, Grant's two remaining campaigns involved maritime components. Grant hoped to close the Confederate port at Mobile with a strong ground-based expedition led by Major General Nathaniel Banks, and, most importantly, he planned for a subordinate field army under Butler to advance on Richmond via the old Peninsula line of operations in conjunction with the Army of the Potomac's main effort along the overland route.

Grant's desire for Banks to close the Confederate port of Mobile represented a useful return of substantive Army participation in the naval blockade originally proposed by Scott's Anaconda Plan. Unfortunately, Grant's proposed Mobile expedition fell victim to the Lincoln administration's desire for Banks to embark on an expedition (March 10–May 22, 1864) up the Red River in Louisiana. Not only did the administration want to move Union forces into Texas via the Red River in response to French machinations in Mexico that violated the Monroe Doctrine but it also hoped to support Lincoln's early experiments with Reconstruction in Louisiana by putting more of the state's territory in Union hands. With support from Porter's Mississippi flotilla, composed of vessels lacking the seaworthiness to accompany Farragut's force to Mobile, Union troops got to within 70 miles of Shreveport before being forced to abandon the campaign. Falling water on the Red River then nearly stranded Porter's fleet, but an Army officer with civil engineering experience improvised a dam that raised the water levels at the falls at Alexandria enough to save the flotilla.

While troublesome and inefficient, Banks' distraction from Mobile was more a nuisance than a strategic disaster, especially since a primarily naval expedition led by Farragut would close the port later that August. In contrast, Butler's failure to provide appreciable support to the Army of the Potomac's campaign against Lee proved far more significant and nearly cost Lincoln reelection, and perhaps even victory for the Union. Grant's hard-fought Overland Campaign during the summer of 1864 led to 55,000 combat casualties—a fearsome toll that crushed northern morale. For all that bloodshed, the Union could not claim a decisive battlefield victory against Lee, but instead the start of a grinding and difficult siege of Confederate forces defending Richmond and the crucial railroad hub of Petersburg south of the Confederate capital. That siege would eventually culminate in the collapse of Lee's military position in the spring of 1865—a fate Lee himself foretold—but the fearsome and unprecedented losses Grant suffered had a crushing effect on Union morale less than a half year before the 1864 presidential canvass.

A whole host of factors fed into Grant's inability to achieve a decisive victory over Lee during the war's climactic campaign between its two greatest field commanders: Lee's operational dexterity, the overly cautious command culture of the Army of the Potomac, the failure of Sigel's expedition to threaten Virginians' share of the Shenandoah Valley, and some plain bad luck for a Union field army plagued by more than its fair share of ill fortune. However, one important factor was Butler's inability to take advantage of McClellan's old line of operations to draw significant forces away from Lee's army north of Richmond. While Grant took fearsome losses during the Overland Campaign, so did Lee, and the reinforcements he received from Richmond and Petersburg proved crucial to his ability to stalemate Grant's advance. Like McClellan, Butler had a secure line of communications via Union naval power, but he proved even less tactically capable than his more well-known predecessor and allowed his forces to hunker down in unproductive static positions well south of the Confederate capital.

Closing Confederate Ports

Fortunately for the Union, good news arrived from Mobile Bay in August. In order to breach the Confederate port's defenses, Farragut's fleet overcame Confederate torpedoes (mines), a small defensive fleet that included the ironclad CSS *Tennessee* (6), and fixed fortifications (see Map 8.2). When a torpedo sank the USS *Tecumseh* (2), Farragut fearlessly commanded his fleet to continue its advance (see Figure 8.2), and he may or may not have exclaimed, "Damn the torpedoes! Full speed ahead!" Whatever the historical veracity of this most famous of Civil War naval utterances, Farragut and the Navy deserved the lion's share of the credit for this Union victory, but Army troops under Major General Gordon Granger played valuable supporting roles, including the occupation of Forts Morgan and Gaines at the mouth of Mobile Bay. In conjunction with Sherman's capture of Atlanta in September, the fall of Mobile Bay provided the morale boost Lincoln needed to ensure his reelection—although the former had far greater significance since it involved the defeat of the Confederacy's primary western field army.

From a historian's perspective, Confederate prospects rapidly dimmed after Atlanta's fall, since Sherman's triumph ensured Lincoln's reelection. Nevertheless, the Confederacy stubbornly fought on, and the Union still had to finish the job. After Mobile Bay's closure to blockade runners, only Wilmington,

Figure 8.2   Battle of Mobile Bay, 1864. Painting by Dean Mosher. *Source:* Courtesy of Dean Mosher.

Figure 8.3 Bombardment of Fort Fisher, 1865. Engraving by T. Shussler. *Source:* US Naval History and Heritage Command # NH 52051.

North Carolina, remained as the Confederacy's last viable outlet to the sea. Union authorities now shifted their attention to Fort Fisher, a crucial Confederate position that protected its last port (see Map 8.2). Porter would command the naval half of the expedition while Butler would try to make himself useful as the Army commander for the campaign. Unfortunately, bad blood between Butler and Porter originated in their prior service in New Orleans, and neither man properly coordinated the assault on the fort in late December, which included a failed attempt to use a ship filled with powder as a giant mine to breach the walls of the Confederate position. While Porter was hardly blameless, he, unlike Butler, had a distinguished combat record and productive relationship with Grant. Thus Butler was replaced by Brigadier General Alfred Terry, who worked well with Porter. After a preparatory bombardment, a joint coordinated assault by soldiers, sailors, and marines attacked Fort Fisher on January 15, 1865 (see Figure 8.3). The Navy's own assault force failed, but it distracted attention from the successful Army-led attack, which benefited from well-coordinated naval gunfire support that bombarded each successive Confederate traverse as Union soldiers came upon them.

As great a triumph as it was, Fort Fisher's fall still raises questions about the momentum Union arms lost in 1862 due to the neglect of joint operations both on the Confederate coast and in its inland arteries. What if Burnside's North Carolina expedition had been reinforced, instead of withdrawn, or if Halleck had sent a field army to operate in conjunction with Farragut at Vicksburg? These failures highlighted the absence of professional staffs to guide the larger Union war effort and coordinate such inter-service issues. Nevertheless, through improvisation and sagacious conduct by local commanders such as Grant and Porter, the Union still found a path to victory in the margins where earth and water met.

Conclusion

Conjunct operations on western waters, coastal operations that tied down a significant proportion of Confederate state and national forces, and the naval blockade contributed to victory in the war of attrition envisioned in Scott's Anaconda Plan in 1861. Without them the war would certainly have lasted longer and its cost might have surpassed the price the loyal states were willing to pay to preserve the Union.

CHAPTER 9

The New Navy, 1865–1895

After the Civil War, the Navy resumed the duties and strategy of the antebellum years. By the Spanish–American War it had acquired new technology, embraced new strategy, and participated in the nation's more outward-looking role in world affairs. Technology constantly evolved, and the new strategy altered the uses of the fleet. Eventually modern ships forced fundamental shifts in personnel policies. The result of these evolutionary changes was a New Navy that was recognizably different from that of previous years.

Return to Peacetime Missions

After Robert E. Lee's surrender at Appomattox, the Navy turned to the realities of peacetime. It sold or scrapped ships and closed bases. The number of officers and men plummeted from over 58,000 in 1865 to slightly more than 10,500 by 1870. Concentrating on internal growth, the nation imposed limited demands on the Navy. Comfortable behind tariff walls, American businesses catered to the domestic market—a market expanding with the westward movement of railroads and settlers. Periodic depressions meant that economic growth was uneven, but, by the Spanish–American War, the United States ranked as a world power in essentially every measure except military strength.

In this situation, the Navy returned to its antebellum strategy and activities. Within a year, half of its active-duty warships returned to squadron duty protecting American lives and property around the world (see Map 5.1). In case of war with a major naval power, the Navy would engage in commerce raiding, protect American commerce, and participate in coastal defense. Coastal defense and commerce raiding would be the Navy's fundamental roles, and the experience of the war had reinforced belief in the strategy's soundness. The well-known exploits of the *Alabama* became shorthand for referring to all Confederate raiders. In 1874, for example, Admiral David D. Porter asserted that in war with "a great nation … one vessel, like the Alabama, roaming the ocean, sinking and destroying, would do more to bring about peace than a dozen unwieldy iron-clads cruising in search of an enemy of like character."[1] For a strategy of commerce raiding, the Navy required ships independently traversing vast oceans. For harassment of an enemy in coastal waters, monitors and torpedo boats met the Navy's needs.

As the century wore on, improving communications reduced the independence of commanding

---

[1] "Report of Admiral D. D. Porter," in *Annual Report of the Secretary of the Navy* (1874), 209 [henceforth *SecNav* (year)].

America, Sea Power, and the World, First Edition. Edited by James C. Bradford.
© 2016 John Wiley & Sons, Inc. Published 2016 by John Wiley & Sons, Inc.

officers on distant stations. A growing worldwide network of undersea telegraph cables permitted timely instructions from home that had previously been impossible. As a newspaper noted in 1882, the "time was when a flag officer really commanded his fleet" but now "the movement of the vessels nominally under his command is practically dictated by the Navy Department."[2]

Naval responsibilities determined the ships the Navy acquired. During the 1870s it built 14 cruising vessels designed to sail independently in peace and war. Yet, the ships did incorporate new ideas. The *Trenton*, the largest of the ships at 3,800 tons, brought a number of innovations into its live-oak hull. It had compound engines, electric signaling bells, and electric thermostats with remote alarms to warn when the temperature rose above 140 degrees Fahrenheit. The vessel also sported a ram. While the ram was probably not all that useful, rams were in vogue in foreign navies.

Construction also addressed coastal defense needs. During the 1870s, the department began five new monitors under the guise of repairing scrapped vessels. Although these ironclads were not completed until the 1890s, the effort reflected the Navy's conception of the armored ships it needed. Harbor defense also stimulated interest in spar-torpedo boats. In the 1870s Admiral Porter secured funding for the *Alarm*, which incorporated both a ram and spar torpedoes. Although not a success, the *Alarm*, like the monitors, underscored the commitment to coastal defense.

A few new ships could not, however, conceal an increasingly outdated force. Rapid technological change overseas left the United States increasingly behind the navies of other nations. On November 11, 1879, Rear Admiral Christopher R. P. Rodgers, writing from Callao, Peru, carefully listed the modern foreign warships present. After observing that "all these ships are full-powered steamships, very fast, and armed with modern guns," he lamented that "there is not a smooth bore gun upon any ship-of-war on this station, except the ships of the United States."[3]

Professional Development

Within the constraints of a small and increasingly obsolete force, naval officers worked at professional development. In the generation after the Civil War, four such developments stand out: the creation of the Torpedo Station at Newport in 1869; the formation of the US Naval Institute in 1873; the establishment of the Office of Naval Intelligence in 1882; and the opening of the Naval War College in 1884.

Convinced by the war of the value of torpedoes, the Navy established the Torpedo Station at Newport, Rhode Island, in 1869. Begun for training, the facility expanded its duties to include manufacturing and research. In its research capacity, Newport first sought ways to improve torpedoes but soon expanded into related fields. When the Navy in 1874 showed interest in electric lights, Newport conducted the first tests. Because of its interest in explosives for warheads, it also experimented with gun cotton—an explosive made with nitric acid and cellulose. Within limits dictated by its size and multiple functions, the Torpedo Station encouraged involvement in new technologies even while US warships incorporated few innovations.

Founded at Annapolis, Maryland, in 1873, the Naval Institute encouraged the "advancement of professional and scientific knowledge in the Navy" by sponsoring seminars and circulating papers on naval topics.[4] Unlike the other three organizations, the Institute was nominally private. Closely tied to the officer corps, it nevertheless had an outsider's flexibility in analyzing and even challenging official policy. In 1874 the Institute began publishing its *Proceedings*.

The Office of Naval Intelligence (ONI) arose from the Navy's need to compile information from around the world. Although the department encouraged shipboard officers to report on foreign developments, there was no agency to arrange and analyze this material. In 1882 the Navy created ONI to gather "such naval information as may be useful to

---

[2] "Distribution of Ships in Commission," *Army and Navy Journal*, 19 (July 15, 1882), 1166.

[3] Rogers to Secretary of the Navy R. W. Thompson, November 11, 1879, in *Letters Received by the Secretary of the Navy from Commanding Officers of Squadrons, 1841–1886*, National Archives and Record Service [henceforth NARA], microfilm publication M-89, roll 40.

[4] "Constitution," US Naval Institute *Proceedings* [henceforth *USNIP*], 1 (1874), 11.

the Department."[5] ONI would publish much of the material collected. Beyond helping the department itself, these publications helped to foster public support for the New Navy. In November 1882, ONI stationed its first attaché abroad, Lieutenant French Ensor Chadwick in London. By the turn of the century naval attachés were stationed in Britain, France (also accredited to Russia), Germany (with additional responsibility for Italy and Austria-Hungary), and Japan (also serving China).

Initially European governments regarded Americans more as potential customers than as possible rivals and shared information freely. As the 1890s progressed, attachés faced increasing difficulties. In part, this development reflected a general trend of the European powers toward increasing secrecy, but there was also an altered perception of the United States. The crisis and ultimate war with Spain provided further changes. Attachés expanded their operations and these efforts fostered additional foreign reticence. Intelligence gathering no longer enjoyed its earlier easy access to facilities and information.

Ultimately the value of information disseminated by ONI or the Naval Institute or of new technology from the Torpedo Station depended upon the officers who would use it. None of these organizations prepared officers to apply knowledge to naval strategy. Education after the Naval Academy was necessary. The Naval War College addressed that need. The leading advocate for the school was Commodore Stephen B. Luce. Luce traced his own interest to an 1865 meeting with General William T. Sherman. Commanding a Union gunboat, Luce met with Sherman before an impending operation. The general pointed at a map and declared, "You navy fellows have been hammering away at Charleston for the past three years. But just wait till I get into South Carolina; I will cut her communications and Charleston will fall into your hands like a ripe pear."[6] Luce then realized that the Navy's futile attempts to take the city with ships alone showed a lack of understanding of the basic principles of war.

A school of the kind Luce sought did not come until 1884, when the Navy Department established the Naval War College at Newport with orders to provide "an advanced course of professional study for naval officers."[7] Appointed the first president of the War College, Luce developed a curriculum that included coursework on strategy and international law. He also stressed the study of history and recruited Commander Alfred Thayer Mahan to develop naval history lectures. Although founded, the college's existence was not secure. Some officers challenged the need for education in history and strategy and preferred postgraduate education in technical matters. Not until the late 1890s was the War College an accepted part of the Navy.

Rebuilding the Navy

Although new institutions kept the service abreast of changes in naval warfare, during the 1870s the American fleet lagged behind potential rivals. As its condition became increasingly apparent, legislation in the 1880s began a process of rebuilding the service. The result was known virtually from its start as the New Navy.

In 1873, the *Virginius* Affair, a short-lived crisis with Spain, highlighted the unsatisfactory condition of the Navy. When the Navy Department ordered its ships to gather at Key West to conduct maneuvers, the result was embarrassing, as several ships broke down and others could barely make headway. A peaceful settlement was reached, which was lucky because, as Admiral Porter wrote, "the fleet showed itself very unsuitable for war purposes, either to contend against the improved class of vessels now being constructed by all foreign powers, or to cut up an enemy's commerce."[8]

Reacting to growing misgivings about the Navy, Congress launched its own investigations. From these hearings, a picture emerged of mismanagement and the use of navy yards for political patronage.

[5] "General Order 292," March 23, 1882, *Navy Department General Orders, 1863–1948*, NARA microfilm publication M984, roll 1.

[6] Stephen B. Luce, "Naval Administration, III," *USNIP*, 29 (1903), 820.

[7] "General Order 325," October 6, 1884, *Navy Department General Orders, 1863–1948*, NARA microfilm publication M984, roll 1.

[8] "Report of Admiral D. D. Porter," *SecNav* (1874), 198.

Stephen B. Luce

Stephen B. Luce (1827–1917) was a skillful shiphandler, a respected author, an important force in the revival of the apprentice system, and the founder of the Naval War College. After his death in 1917 a prominent officer characterized Luce as the man who "taught the navy to think."[9] The thought involved training and strategic doctrine to ensure the Navy was prepared for war.

Commissioned a midshipman in 1841, Luce served first at sea and then, in 1848, went to the Naval School in Annapolis. While there, Luce participated in a protest over the superintendent's refusal to let midshipmen march in the presidential inaugural parade. As a result of disciplinary action, he was dropped 72 places on the Navy list.

During the 1850s, Luce served on board a variety of vessels and in 1860 he returned to the Naval Academy as an instructor, where he wrote *Seamanship*, a textbook for the midshipmen that went

through nine editions. During the Civil War, Luce commanded monitors on blockade duty then returned to the Academy as the Commandant of Midshipmen (1865–1866). After service at sea and at the Boston Navy Yard, Luce took command of the training ship *Minnesota* (1878–1881), became involved in the apprentice system, and worked to make the revived program successful. Believing that singing could build camaraderie, he published *Naval Songs* (1883).

Luce played a key role in the establishment of the Naval War College in 1884 and served as the institution's first president. In 1886 he took command of the North Atlantic Squadron. Luce wanted the squadron to conduct exercises in conjunction with the Naval War College to combine tactical and strategic education, but it proved difficult to implement the idea fully.

Following retirement in 1889, Luce remained active in naval affairs and returned to the Naval

War College from 1901 to 1910. Luce was an early and vocal supporter of establishing a position for a senior officer who would be empowered to coordinate various parts of the service.

Stephen B. Luce, c. 1888. *Source:* US Naval History and Heritage Command # NH 2323.

Responding to evidence of excessive work on obsolete ships, in 1882 Congress restricted repairs, prohibiting the spending of more than 30 percent of the cost of a similar new vessel to repair a wooden ship. In 1883 the proportion was cut to 20 percent. Under these constraints, the wooden fleet dwindled.

In 1881 Secretary of the Navy William H. Hunt appointed a board of officers under Rear Admiral John Rodgers to assess the Navy's need for new warships. Its recommendations were not modest. It sought 68 vessels estimated to cost $29,607,000—almost twice

the Navy Department's total expenditure that year ($15.7 million). The board specified "full sail power" to meet the anticipated missions for the Navy.[10]

Congress balked at the ambitious program. It authorized two steel cruisers but did not appropriate money for construction. It also mandated a Naval Advisory Board to make new recommendations. Working from the Advisory Board's report, in 1883 Congress funded construction of three cruisers and a dispatch boat—subsequently named *Atlanta*, *Boston*, *Chicago*, and *Dolphin* (the ABCD ships). With steel

[9] Bradley A. Fiske, "Stephen B. Luce: An Appreciation," *USNIP*, 43 (1917), 1936.

[10] "Report of the Board," *SecNav* (1881), 33.

hulls, breech-loading guns, and electric lighting, the ABCD ships incorporated new technology, but they, like existing oceangoing American warships, were designed for commerce raiding and protection. They were a rebuilding of the Navy rather than a redirecting of its strategy. As befit vessels to fulfill the traditional mission of extended cruising, they still carried sail, albeit not the full sail power the 1881 board had sought.

After the ABCD ships Congress moved cautiously. It waited two years before authorizing two cruisers and two gunboats. In 1886, it authorized two more cruisers (one equipped with a dynamite gun). It also acknowledged the need for other types of ships to provide coastal defense and funded construction of a torpedo boat and two armored vessels—the *Maine* and *Texas*.

Traditionally the nation preferred using American plans and materials for its ships. The New Navy, however, incorporated unfamiliar technology, and the service had to seek foreign sources. It went overseas for plans for some of the cruisers and for the *Texas*. American steelmakers, furthermore, could not supply the required armor. To secure domestic armor the Navy eventually entered into generous long-term agreements with American steelmakers.

As it moved toward modern warships, the Navy retained a fondness for monitors for coastal defense. Throughout the 1880s work continued sporadically on five monitors begun in the 1870s. When the *Miantonomoh*, one of these ships, was commissioned in 1891, a popular magazine bragged with greater pride than accuracy that the ship was "more than a match for the first-rates of the great maritime powers of the world."[11]

In the late 1880s, Congress engaged in a flurry of activity. From 1887 to 1889 it authorized a total of 17 ships. It funded six more in 1890, including "three seagoing coast-line battle ships."[12] The word "coast-line" represented a gesture to a strategy of coastal defense, but these *Indiana*-class battleships had sufficient range,

armor, and firepower to cross the Atlantic Ocean and compete with foreign warships.

The New Navy also confronted issues concerning managing the department. The investigations of the 1870s had revealed problems of inefficiency and possible corruption. In 1885, newly appointed secretary William C. Whitney attempted to reform the bureau system. Since their creation in 1842, the bureaus had become independent fiefdoms. The system fostered duplication in purchases and stymied coordination among the bureaus. Whitney offered the *Omaha* to highlight his concerns. After four years of repairs, the Navy had spent as much as the cost of a new vessel but had produced a ship that could "neither fight nor run away."[13] Solutions to organizational problems proved difficult. Sweeping reforms were unattainable, but in 1889 Secretary Benjamin Tracy shifted responsibilities among bureaus and carefully defined their duties.

Reorganization of the bureaus improved efficiency but fell short of the desires of many reformers. Luce, among others, desired to have an officer as the "professional head in our naval administration to govern its purely military operations."[14] Advocates for this idea argued that the officer would provide professional knowledge and free the secretary from responsibility in areas about which he knew little. In the nineteenth century, such proposals died in the face of concerns that they would undermine the tradition of civilian control over the military.

Alfred Thayer Mahan and a New Strategy

Creation of the New Navy began in an era committed to commerce raiding. Over the 1880s, however, many officers considered alternative uses of naval power. There emerged an increasing belief in the importance of forming battleships into fleets to engage a similar enemy. The new strategy would come to be associated with Alfred Thayer Mahan and his book *The Influence of Sea Power upon History, 1660–1783*, which brought

[11] W. Nephew King, Jr., "Our First Battle Ship," *Harper's Weekly*, 35 (November 7, 1891), 874.

[12] Act of June 30, 1890, in *Navy Yearbook* (1916), 64.

[13] Report of the Secretary of the Navy, *SecNav* (1885), xxxix.

[14] Luce, "Administration, Naval," in *Naval Encyclopedia* (1881), 19.

the ideas into a single work and popularized the concept throughout the world.

The son of a US Military Academy professor, Mahan spent his first 12 years at West Point before attending boarding school in Maryland and then enrolling in Columbia College in New York. In 1856, against his father's wishes, he entered the Naval Academy. Because of his work at Columbia, he skipped the fourth class (freshman) year and graduated second in the Class of 1859. Until the publication of his book, Mahan was not a distinguished officer. He spent most of the Civil War on monotonous blockade duty. Afterward, he had generally uneventful service in the peacetime navy. Mahan's 1883 publication of *The Gulf and Inland Waters* as part of a multi-volume series of Civil War naval histories led Luce to invite him to join the faculty of the newly established War College the following year. Luce believed that the study of history would reveal broad principles and asked Mahan to prepare lectures on naval history. Mahan began reading and concluded that control of the sea had influenced even such apparently land-based campaigns as the third century BCE Roman defeat of Hannibal's invading Carthaginian army. With the discovery of the idea of the superiority of sea power over land power, Mahan scoured history for further examples supporting his thesis. He presented his conclusions first in lectures at the War College and then in *The Influence of Sea Power upon History, 1660–1783* (1890).

Mahan believed the past could "afford lessons of present application and value" independent of the state of technology. He dismissed those who from "a vague feeling of contempt for the past" ignored the "permanent strategic lessons which lie close to the surface of naval history." The oceans, Mahan asserted, provided "a great highway" or "a wide common" for maritime trade. At its heart, the idea of sea power was that a nation should gain control of the sea through its naval fleet. Although being a sea power would benefit any nation, Mahan noted six "principal conditions affecting the sea power of nations" that would influence countries' ability to achieve the goal. The conditions were geographical position, physical conformation,

extent of territory, number of population, character of the people, and character of the government.[15]

Mahan primarily analyzed the historic rivalry between Britain and France, but he also noted America's unfulfilled potential as a sea power. Developing the interior of the country had encouraged the "neglect of that great instrument" of sea power. As a nation without sea power, the United States faced the prospect of disastrous blockades by possible enemies. What the nation needed was a fleet capable of keeping an enemy far from the American coast. Mahan argued that this use of the Navy would still be within the traditional defensive strategy of the nation. He distinguished between "passive defence," which "strengthens itself and awaits attack," and an "offensive defence," which "is best secured by attacking the enemy." The first type belonged to the Army and fixed fortifications and the second to the Navy, which would "not wait for attack, but go to meet the enemy's fleet, whether it be but for a few miles, or whether to his own shores." Such a strategy was still defensive because the object was the enemy's fleet and not the enemy's country.[16]

Mahan's book reflected principles that were already part of professional discussions. Its strength was marshaling historical examples and suggesting their timeless applicability. The book was enthusiastically received abroad. It achieved an early success in Britain and was translated into foreign languages including German and Japanese. In the United States, Mahan's book was not immediately popular, but it won praise from navalists such as Luce and Theodore Roosevelt. Public awareness soon increased, and by 1895 Mahan's ideas were routinely cited in congressional naval debates. His new status as a writer encouraged him to retire from the Navy in 1896 to concentrate on publishing.

In many of his writings, Mahan linked geopolitical affairs and naval strategy and addressed the strategic position of the United States in what he predicted would be the Pacific-oriented world of the future. In an 1890 article in *Atlantic Monthly*, he argued that "Americans must now begin to look outward"

---

[15] Alfred T. Mahan, *The Influence of Sea Power upon History, 1660–1783* (1890), 2, 11, 25, 28.

[16] Ibid., 39, 87 n.1.

to obtain markets for "the growing production of the country." The United States enjoyed a position "between the two Old Worlds [of Europe and Asia] and the two great oceans." The prospect of a Central American canal, however, "in our present state of unpreparedness ... will be a military disaster to the United States." It speeded the ability of European nations to dispatch warships to the lightly defended Pacific coast of the United States. The canal also increased European interest in existing or new bases in the Caribbean, and these bases potentially threatened American security. To protect its interests, the nation needed "to have its sea frontier ... defended" and a navy "as shall suffice ... to weigh seriously when inevitable discussions arise."[17]

As the US fleet moved further from American shores, Mahan foresaw requirements for coaling stations. The United States did not need a worldwide system but should focus on areas of particular concern such as the Caribbean and eastern Pacific. The anticipated building of a canal across Central America would only increase their importance. Although the United States had ports near those regions, Mahan stressed that the fleet still required coaling stations to protect a canal. He defined America's defensive perimeter in the Pacific as running from Alaska to Hawaii and Panama, thereby linking a canal to the acquisition of Hawaii. A canal would increase trade in the Pacific and, without Hawaii as a coaling station, any potential enemy would face insurmountable problems in attacking the Pacific coast of America.

From his study of history, Mahan drew lessons that challenged both America's traditional strategy of commerce warfare and its dividing of its warships into squadrons deployed on distant stations. The goal of sea power should be to gain "command of the sea."[18] Commerce raiding could not accomplish this control and was thus a secondary role for navies. Sea control demanded that war "be waged offensively" and the enemy "smitten down." For this purpose, "the backbone and real power of any navy" was a vessel

"capable of taking and giving hard knocks." Under sail, ships-of-the-line had fulfilled that role but battleships had since taken on the task. Mahan stressed that "offensive action—not defensive—determines the issues of war," and successful action required battleships concentrated in a fleet. Because battleships "are meant to act together, in fleets; not singly, as mere cruisers," Mahan repeatedly stressed the importance of keeping the fleet together and not dispersing it to secondary operations. The primary objective of the fleet would be the enemy fleet. A victory deprived the enemy of free use of the sea and was the most important naval contribution to winning a war.[19]

As the doctrine of sea power boosted the importance of a concentrated battle fleet, it became desirable to practice maneuvering as a single unit. Yet normal peacetime duties required ships responding individually to worldwide demands, frustrating early training efforts. An early attempt at fleet training came in 1889 when the Navy formed the Squadron of Evolution to emulate similar foreign organizations. It dispatched the cruisers *Atlanta*, *Boston*, and *Chicago* and the gunboat *Yorktown* to the Mediterranean. Once there, the squadron practiced basic maneuvers and landing sailors and marines. If fleet maneuvers represented a new strategy, landing drills reflected the continuing relevance of past duties, which entailed sending forces ashore to protect American lives and property. Although continuing in existence until 1892, the squadron subsequently largely limited its cruising to US waters, where it combined maneuvering with displaying the new ships to the American public.

A commitment to a fleet-based wartime strategy would eventually place a premium on peacetime planning for possible conflicts. In the 1890s, the Navy made occasional rudimentary efforts. Both ONI and the War College at various times produced plans, but unfortunately the two organizations sometimes regarded each other as rivals to be shut out. In these years the Navy failed to develop a coherent method for planning.

---

[17] Mahan, "The United States Looking Outward," *Atlantic Monthly*, 66 (December 1890), 820, 822.

[18] Mahan, "The Importance of Command of the Sea," *Scientific American*, 105:24 (December 9, 1911), 512.

[19] Mahan, *The Influence of Sea Power on History*, 138. Mahan, *The Interest of America in Sea Power* (1918), 193, 198. Mahan, *Lessons of the War with Spain* (1899), 267, 39.

The New Navy and America's Role in the World

The world did not cooperate with officials' hopes to keep the New Navy together for training. Demands from foreign stations continually pulled ships to scattered duties. In the early 1890s, for example, disputes between the United States and Britain over hunting seals in the Bering Sea required warships in Arctic waters to enforce American rights. Another sudden need for a naval presence came when the outbreak of the Sino-Japanese War (1894–1895) compelled the department to deploy ships to protect American missionary and commercial interests in the Far East.

In many ways, the activities of the New Navy were similar to naval duties throughout the nineteenth century. Yet, by the 1890s the Navy was being used in ways that reflected a growing American assertiveness in world affairs. Actions in Samoa in 1889, Chile in 1891, and Hawaii in 1893 suggest this pattern.

Samoa's location and harbor made it an ideal site for a coaling station, and in 1878 the United States secured rights to establish one at Apia. A decade later ships from the United States, Britain, and Germany faced off in a confrontation for influence within the islands. The warships tensely monitored one another until a hurricane smashed into the islands, wrecked the three US and three German warships, and provided time for diplomats to reach a peaceful distribution of Western power in the islands.

America's willingness (displayed at Samoa) to assert its policies was demonstrated more forcefully during a confrontation with Chile in 1891 after two sailors from the cruiser *Baltimore* were killed and 16 injured during a brawl outside the True Blue Saloon in Valparaiso. The United States demanded an apology and that reparations be paid for the killed and wounded. Commander Robley D. Evans and the gunboat *Yorktown* joined the *Baltimore* on November 30. Evans dismissed efforts to prove the men sober, believing them "probably drunk ... properly drunk; they went ashore ... for the purpose of getting drunk, which they did on Chilean rum paid for with good United States money" and that ashore "in this condition they were more entitled to protection than if they had been sober." Chile had a respectable navy, and an authoritative British writer suspected that the American navy "would have been very much embarrassed if a rupture had taken place with Chili." Evans, however, believed that "the Baltimore and Yorktown would give their navy a drubbing in two hours."[20] European nations sympathized with the Chilean interpretation of events and regarded American motives with suspicion, but none wished to confront the United States directly. Chile soon moved to avoid a war it could not win and agreed to terms.

Part of this confrontation stemmed from Chile and the United States contesting issues of dominance in the Pacific. Chile had recently defeated Peru and Bolivia in the War of the Pacific (1879–1883) and annexed Easter Island in 1888. Some Americans feared a similar takeover of the independent Hawaiian Islands by Britain, Germany, or Japan. Hawaii stood at a crossroads for Pacific trade (see Figure 9.1). As 1893 opened, the Hawaiian government was a monarchy under Queen Lili'uokalani. A substantial portion of the economically important sugar industry was under American control. Those interests grew increasingly restive under the queen's rule. Sugar plantations also suffered when an 1890 American tariff law ended the advantageous position Hawaiian sugar had enjoyed in the American market. In January 1893 a group of residents, dominated by those with ties to the United States, revolted and declared a republic. The US minister to Hawaii immediately requested that the *Boston*, anchored in Honolulu Harbor, land men to protect the legation and American lives and property. On January 16, the *Boston* landed 162 sailors and marines. The queen's government interpreted the action as American support for the rebellion and concluded that her forces could not prevail.

---

[20] Robley D. Evans, *A Sailor's Log* (1901), 259–260, 262. E. F. Weyl, "Progress of Foreign Navies, 1891–92," in T. A. Brassey, ed., *Naval Annual 1892* (1892), 32.

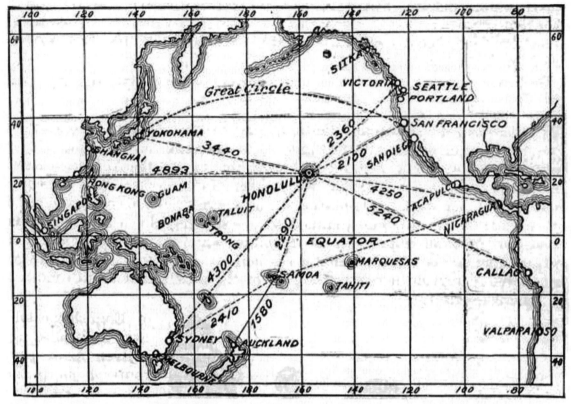

Figure 9.1 Hawaii: Crossroads of the North Pacific, 1893. Supporters of Hawaiian annexation stressed the value of its location for naval and commercial activities in the Pacific. *Source: Review of Reviews*, 7 (March 1893), 181.

The new government quickly dispatched representatives to Washington seeking US annexation. In its last weeks in office, the Benjamin Harrison administration negotiated a treaty and forwarded it to the Senate. Supporters rejoiced that the nation now had the "opportunity for gaining control of the Hawaiian group—the Gibraltar of the Pacific."[21] Opponents of annexation decried a "shamelessly dishonest" and "utterly unrepublican" action and sided with newly elected President Grover Cleveland, who withdrew the treaty from Senate consideration.[22] The American nation was not yet united on the issue of acquiring overseas possessions—even one as desirable as Hawaii.

Although Cleveland pulled back from Hawaii, he aggressively asserted US influence in Latin America. At the end of 1895 he threatened war over a long-running boundary dispute between Venezuela and British Guiana. He determined that the Venezuelans were being deprived of their territory and that as a result it was the duty of the United States to intervene on their behalf. When diplomatic communications with Britain failed to get a satisfactory reply, Cleveland, on December 17, sent Congress a

---

[21] "The Rebellion in Hawaii," *Army and Navy Journal*, 30 (February 4, 1893), 399.

[22] N. A., "The Policy of Justice," *Harper's Weekly*, 37 (November 25, 1893), 1118.

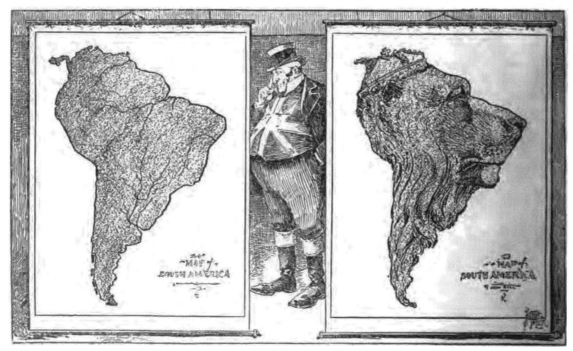

Figure 9.2   British threat to South America. This cartoon, showing South America changing into the British lion, reflects American concerns about British intentions in locating a border between British Guiana and Venezuela.

strongly worded message in which he declared that the Monroe Doctrine was "important to our peace and safety as a nation" and that it was "fully applicable to our present conditions." He demanded that Britain accept arbitration on the issue (as Venezuela had previously indicated it would) and threatened that, in the absence of such an outcome, the United States would appoint its own commission, draw the boundary itself, and "resist by every means in its power" any attempt by Britain to occupy lands given to Venezuela (see Figure 9.2).[23]

Cleveland's message caught Britain unprepared. London had interpreted earlier American statements as unimportant rhetoric. Discovering that Cleveland was serious, the British moved quickly to defuse the situation. Eventually Britain and the United States agreed to arbitration under rules acceptable to Britain.

Venezuela was not a participant in these negotiations, but it had little choice other than to accept the plan. The readiness of the British to placate the United States underscores that national strength involves more than just naval power—international trade, industrial development, and balance-of-power politics all played a role. Clearly, in the Venezuelan Boundary Controversy, these factors motivated the British more than any fear of the US Navy.

Publicizing the New Navy

In addition to becoming more active in world affairs, the Navy in the 1890s became more visible to the public. Increasingly, people viewed the new vessels as symbols of the American nation. The Navy for its part welcomed this attention.

---

[23] James D. Richardson, *Messages and Papers of the Presidents, 1789–1897* (1898), 9:656–658.

Figure 9.3   The concrete "battleship" *Illinois*, built on pilings in Lake Michigan at the 1893 Chicago World's Fair. The brick and cement "battleship" copied warships then under construction. Housing the Navy's display, it offered citizens from the interior a glimpse of the New Navy. *Source:* Illustration from *The Century World's Fair Book for Boys and Girls* by Tudor Jenks, 1893. https://openlibrary.org/books/OL7248990M/The_Century_World's_fair_book_for_boys_and_girls.

The Columbian Exposition of 1893 and the accompanying naval review gave a particularly prominent opportunity to generate favorable publicity for the New Navy. As a part of the celebration of the 400th anniversary of Columbus' landing in the New World, the US Navy hosted a naval review of ships from foreign navies. In April 12 US and 17 foreign ships assembled at Hampton Roads and steamed to New York.

This naval parade, of course, was not visible to citizens of the interior, so, at the fair in Chicago, the Navy Department built a novel and successful exhibit. It constructed a model battleship "of brick, iron, and cement … on piles in Lake Michigan, off the Fair Grounds." Named the *Illinois*, the exhibit's main deck and superstructure replicated those of the *Oregon* (see Figure 9.3). The weight of the actual 13-inch and 8-inch guns prohibited mounting them, and the exhibit's guns were made from wood, wire, and cement, though the 6-inch guns and other smaller arms, signaling equipment, and searchlights were naval issue. Sailors drilled and explained the ship to visitors. The display was "thronged with visitors from morning to night," as over 3 million fairgoers visited the "ship."[24]

Personnel

It soon became clear that the New Navy required a different kind of personnel to operate it. Officers were concerned with issues of promotion and the place of engineers within the officer corps. In the case of the enlisted force, traditional policies failed to meet the needs of the New Navy. Consequently, enlisted policies underwent sweeping changes that altered where and how the Navy recruited, who joined, and how the men were trained.

During this period, the service relied on the Naval Academy for new officers. During the Civil War the

[24] "Report of the Secretary of the Navy," *SecNav* (1893), 58. [No Title], *Army and Navy Journal*, 30 (July 22, 1893), 801. "Report of the Representative of the Navy Department at the World's Columbian Exposition at Chicago," *SecNav* (1894), 116.

academy had moved to Newport, Rhode Island. On its return to Annapolis, the active and opinionated Vice Admiral Porter, as superintendent, improved its physical plant and reformed its curriculum. Porter directed a clean-up of the yard and secured funding for additional buildings—including a steam engineering building. He instituted an honor system, intermural athletics, and dances to prepare graduates socially. A staunch advocate of keeping engineers subservient, Porter limited instruction in technical subjects to what was "actually requisite for an officer to know," because he believed that "the construction and planning of engines belongs to another branch of the service."[25]

After Porter left, the academy endured the navy-wide problem of reduced budgets. By the eve of the Spanish–American War, many buildings were in such terrible condition that one classroom building was condemned as unsafe (in 1897). This general decay precipitated plans for a major reconstruction. Construction began in 1899, and the resulting buildings still set the basic character for the Academy grounds. By the early twentieth century, the new academy provided a fitting entry for officers into the New Navy.

For a generation after the Civil War, midshipmen entered a navy in which promotion was glacially slow as officers waited for their seniors to retire or die. While senior officers at least enjoyed the salaries and status of their rank, junior officers confronted years stuck in positions traditionally filled by younger men. To address the problem, in 1882 Congress limited the number of commissions available for those completing the six-year course (four in Annapolis and two at sea). The same law permitted Academy graduates to apply for commissions in the Marine Corps.

Officers in the post-Civil War period struggled with relations between line and staff. The Civil War had established that steam was vital but had not decided issues of rank and status for those in charge of it. At the end of the war, engineers sought legislation to increase their numbers and grant them ranks equivalent to line officers. Led by Porter, line officers rallied and defeated the attempt. Finally, in 1899 legislation transferred engineers to the line, the Corps of Engineers disappeared, and all officers would serve both on deck and in the engine room.

Ultimately, training for officers caught up with the expanded duties, but there were a rough few years. Engineers had to learn basic ship handling, and the line entered the foreign world of the engine room. A stark example of the inherent dangers came on July 21, 1905, when the boiler of the gunboat *Bennington* exploded with the loss of one officer and 65 enlisted men. At the time an untrained ensign was serving as chief engineer of the ship.

The real solution for the problem of the rate of promotion came as new vessels entered the fleet. In the first years of the twentieth century, the commissioning of new ships finally created a need for junior officers, and the service expanded enrollment at Annapolis. Entering at the lowest ranks, Academy-produced officers would not clog promotions for officers already commissioned.

Because of the stagnation in promotions, officers reached high ranks and significant commands much later than did officers in foreign navies. Critics condemned this result as wasting the talents of younger men and filling the most responsible positions with men whose age made them unfit for the rigors of their duties. Not everyone agreed that aged senior officers represented a crisis. These individuals countered that the nation had done well in the Civil War with a 60-year-old David Farragut and in the Spanish–American War with a 61-year-old George Dewey. Nor did admirals themselves willingly concede unfitness for duty. A rear admiral who had graduated in 1865 contended in 1905 that he had witnessed "on the part of a number of officers a want of experience and knowledge of their profession" and suggested that "promotion in the lower grades is now too rapid."[26]

Regardless of positions on age, commenters agreed on the need to reestablish the ranks vice admiral and admiral. The Navy had first bestowed the ranks in the Civil War, but vice admiral perished in 1890 and admiral in 1891 with the deaths of the incumbents.

---

[25] "Report of the Superintendent," *SecNav* (1867), 74.

[26] R.B. Bradford to commander-in-chief, North Atlantic Fleet, July 1, 1905, in "Report of the Chief of the Bureau of Navigation," *SecNav* (1905), 473.

For services in the Spanish–American War, George Dewey became Admiral of the Navy in 1900, the only individual ever to hold that title. Repeatedly requesting resumed appointments for additional admirals, the Navy stressed that the new fleets required officers of advanced rank for overall command. Furthermore, it reported that American officers were usually outranked when in the presence of foreign fleets. Nevertheless, not until 1915 did Congress re-authorize the two ranks of admiral and vice admiral.

Between the Civil War and the turn of the century, the Navy largely retained its earlier personnel policies concerning enlisted men, but after the Spanish–American War a rapid series of changes meant that by 1910 the key elements of the new enlisted force were in place.

The Old Navy recruited sailors from the seafaring population. It found them in the ports of the world and sent them immediately to cruising vessels. Here their existing knowledge permitted men to fit directly into shipboard routine. The nineteenth-century Navy was never totally satisfied with its enlisted force. One problem was high turnover, as large numbers deserted each year. The Navy was also displeased with the composition of the force. The crews were both multinational and multiracial. About half the men in the late nineteenth century were foreign born and about one-tenth were African Americans. Officers denounced this force as being the "dregs of all countries."[27]

The service chaffed particularly at the multinational composition. Communication with men uncomfortable with English was one problem. The service also feared that "mongrel crews" would not fight in the case of war.[28] Furthermore, as the New Navy became a national symbol, having American crews became a matter of pride.

After the Civil War, the Navy sought improvement through an apprentice system. Modeled on apprentice training for civilian trades, the program accepted boys in their mid-teens to serve until age 21. The Navy

had established an apprentice program in 1837 and revamped it in 1855 and 1864, but the system still had shortcomings. The apprentice program emerged yet again in 1875 with its goal "solely to make the boys good and intelligent sailors for the Navy."[29] Originally the apprentices lived on board a ship at New York, but in 1880 the department established a training station at Newport. Here the boys first stayed on board a station ship and then trained on board cruising vessels of a training squadron. Finally, they served until age 21 on board regular Navy vessels. The Navy hoped to obtain a force of "*bona fide* American citizens," but few apprentices stayed in the Navy.[30] The apprentice system was very much a reform within Old Navy personnel policies. Unfortunately it did not even meet the needs of the nineteenth century: the system produced too few career, American-born men, and it stressed training under sail.

By the late 1890s, commissioning new ships forced the Navy to alter fundamentally its personnel policy governing enlisted men. Changing technology demanded men to run it, and traditional sources failed to provide the skills needed. Established methods also could not supply enough men. In the years after the Spanish–American War the enlisted force grew dramatically. From the 1830s until 1897, with the exceptions of war years, the authorized strength of the enlisted force had ranged between 7,500 and 10,000. It then surged dramatically upward. By 1900, the authorized strength was 20,000, by 1905 it was 34,000, and by 1910 it was 44,500. Between 1896 and 1910, the enlisted force nearly quintupled. Figure 9.4 offers a longer perspective and shows the total numbers of officer and enlisted personnel on active duty over the half-century after 1870.

To meet its needs, the Navy had to increase its pool of applicants. The solution was to recruit from inland areas, and, after the Spanish–American War, the Navy moved enthusiastically to the interior. Forced to recruit men without seafaring backgrounds, in 1899

---

[27] N. H. Farquhar, "Inducements for Retaining Trained Seamen in the Navy, and Best System of Rewards for Long and Faithful Service," *USNIP*, 11 (1885), 2:176.

[28] *SecNav* (1889), 1:24.

[29] "Report of the Secretary of the Navy," *SecNav* (1875), 18.

[30] "Report of Admiral D. D. Porter," *SecNav* (1875), 296.

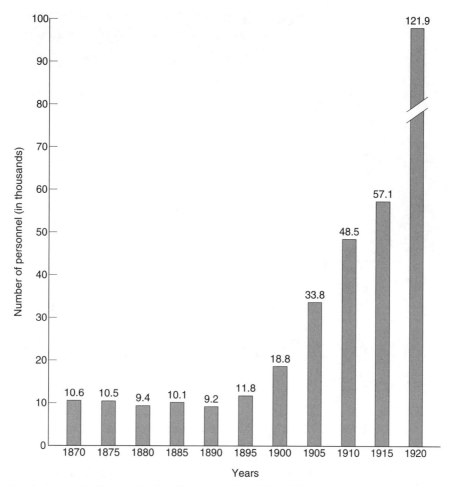

Figure 9.4 Naval personnel (officers and enlisted) on active duty, 1870–1920. *Source:* Bureau of the Census, *Historical Statistics of the United States, Colonial Times to 1957* (1960), 736.

the department began identifying these men as "landsmen for training" to designate recruits who were to receive training rather than unskilled men for immediate assignment. In 1904 the name was changed to "apprentice seamen" and that was shifted in 1948 to "seaman recruit."

To attract inland recruits, the Navy developed new recruiting practices designed to capture men's interest and explain the nature of service life. Recruiters now fanned out far from existing facilities, and recruiting stations opened in cities with no other naval presence. The department developed advertising to attract young men to the recruiter (see Figure 9.5). Even advertising posters underwent a significant change.

Nineteenth-century posters tended to contain mostly text describing pay and benefits. Twentieth-century posters increasingly provided less information but instead featured a dramatic picture or slogan. Some of these changes reflected general trends in advertising, but many of them came from the shift from an audience of seamen to one of landsmen.

In addition to adapting the traditional medium of posters, the twentieth-century Navy embraced a range of other options. It advertised in newspapers and magazines, sent direct mail solicitations to high school students, and made very early use of motion pictures. All of these efforts helped to explain just what the Navy looked like. Advertising also sought

Figure 9.5 Joy riding in China. With the shift to enlisting men without seafaring experience, the Navy began to appeal to young men's desire for travel and adventure by producing glass slides such as this for use by recruiters. *Source:* National Archives.

to overcome reluctance of parents to let their sons enlist.

Inland recruiting changed the recruits. Most obviously, few enlistees came from seafaring backgrounds. In addition, they were increasingly citizens, and in 1907 the Navy limited first enlistments to citizens, though it permitted reenlistment by aliens already serving in the Navy. In the multiracial force of the late nineteenth century, non-whites served in all ratings, though disproportionally as servants. Because men ate and slept in the company of those performing similar duties, ships had integrated crews. After 1900 most recruits were white. As the number of white sailors

increased, the Navy limited opportunities for blacks and in 1919 stopped all first enlistments of African Americans. Such enlistments would not resume until 1932. The Navy's actions coincided with the passage of Jim Crow laws, when segregation was prevalent in much of the nation.

Recruits without experience compelled the Navy to provide initial training before transfer to naval vessels. There was a brief debate over whether the training should be on board ship or at shore stations. The first preference was for ships—training men in the environment in which they would serve—but the department soon favored instruction ashore. The men

Steam or Sail for Training

Even while embracing new technology, the Navy debated whether to use sail or steam vessels for the initial training of personnel. Advocates of sail stressed that sailors were more than technicians operating machinery snugly isolated from the elements. Sailors needed to appreciate the sea, and service under sail provided this understanding. Sail-based training—particularly going aloft in all weather—also developed character and helped men gain confidence. Critics of these views countered that initial training should reflect a navy in which "smokestacks have replaced topsails."[31]

For future officers, the New Navy supplied first a steamship and then a sail-powered vessel. In 1888, Congress authorized an 800-ton steel practice ship. Named *Bancroft*, the gunboat was steam powered with auxiliary sail and possessed modern machinery and armament. Unfortunately, it proved too small for Academy cruises and soon moved to other duties. As a replacement, Congress in 1897 authorized a sail-powered training ship. The ship reflected the recommendation of the Academy's superintendent, who asserted that "it is entirely useless to argue that sufficiently good seamen can be made on board steamers."[32] Commissioned in 1900 as the *Chesapeake*, the ship soon acquired a new name. The frigate *Chesapeake* had suffered a lopsided loss in 1813, and historically minded officers

insisted it was not the best sort of example for midshipmen. In 1905 the ship became *Severn*. Too small to accommodate the expanded number of midshipmen, the *Severn* was not totally satisfactory.

For "landsmen for training," the Navy first emulated the practices of the apprentice system and assigned ships for training. In 1903 the department secured funding for three sail-powered training vessels. None of these ships were commissioned before the navy abolished the Training Squadron itself in 1905.

Naval apprentices reefing the top sail. The apprentice system trained boys aboard sailing ships in an attempt to secure a native-born, career enlisted force for the Old Navy. *Source:* University of Florida George A. Smathers Libraries.

---

[31] "Report of the Chief of the Bureau of Steam Engineering," *SecNav* (1900), 829.

[32] "Report of the Superintendent of the Naval Academy," *SecNav* (1896), 246.

needed basic information that could be conveyed more efficiently on land. Training occurred ashore at Newport, Norfolk, and San Francisco. Expectations were limited. Indoctrination sought "to teach the recruit how to keep himself and his clothes clean, to imbue him with the spirit of military discipline, and to provide him with an elementary knowledge of the duties of a man-of-war's man."[33] Needing additional training facilities, the department turned inland. In 1911 it opened the Great Lakes Naval Training Station north of Chicago, Illinois. Located far from other naval installations, Great Lakes existed only for enlisted training.

Recruit training did not produce skilled ratings. The Old Navy had relied on either "strikers"—men learning on board ship from those already performing the job—or on enlisting trained civilians. Neither method met the needs of the New Navy. The department, therefore, began to offer its own advanced training. It had made limited efforts in the nineteenth century with the formation of gunnery schools in Washington in 1883 and in Newport in 1885. After the Spanish–American War, the Navy steadily expanded its advanced training. In 1899 it opened electricity classes in Boston and New York, in 1901 a petty officers' school at Newport, and in 1902 an artificers' school at Norfolk for blacksmiths, painters, plumbers, shipfitters, and woodworkers. The Navy would continue to add courses as needed.

With an eye to increasing the number of reenlistments, the Navy improved living conditions on board warships. Although not undertaken as a systematic program, over the first part of the twentieth century changes occurred in many important areas. One change was opening limited possibilities for commissions. Legislation in 1901 permitted chief warrant officers to take examinations and become ensigns. In 1914, Secretary Josephus Daniels secured legislation for appointments to the Naval Academy from the enlisted force. To help men study for the entrance examination, in 1919 the Navy established preparatory schools at Norfolk and San Diego. A number of improvements also took place in general ship habitability. The Navy replaced hammocks with bunks and shifted from having ships' crews store clothes in sea bags to providing lockers.

Conclusion

Changes in personnel policies were a natural continuation of the events in the Navy from before the Spanish–American War. On the eve of the conflict, the Navy was already substantially different from what it had been at the end of the Civil War in 1865. By the 1890s it had incorporated new technology, had embraced a new strategy, and was serving a nation becoming more actively engaged in the world. Once the enlisted force also changed, the Old Navy was gone.

---

[33] "Report of the Chief of the Bureau of Navigation," *SecNav* (1905), 377.

CHAPTER 10

War with Spain and the Revolution in Naval Affairs, 1895–1910

In November of 1895, the first of a new class of battleships, *Indiana*, was commissioned. Authorized by Congress in 1890, the *Indiana*-class ships reflected a transformation that had slowly been taking place both in the nation as a whole and in the Navy in particular. As the United States emerged onto the international stage as a world power, two new missions—defense of America's new possessions in the Pacific and developing the capability to engage a major European power in fleet-to-fleet combat—were added to its traditional peacetime mission of defending American lives and property and wartime roles of coastal defense and the conduct of commerce warfare. Yet, even while the US Navy was adapting to new roles and strategies, developments in technology would change forever the established thinking about naval warfare, requiring new capabilities, tactics, and organization.

Revolution in Naval Affairs

Indiana's launch was significant because, unlike the previous vessels authorized by Congress, the ship had a range that gave it the ability to project power against modern warships beyond the Western Hemisphere. While cruisers can be used for a variety of missions, a battleship is built for one purpose: to engage and destroy enemy warships. How to do so, though, was a question in the 1890s.

With the introduction of armor, the methods of defeating enemy warships in combat changed. Naval warfare in the Age of Sail emphasized killing as many of the opposing crew as possible while leaving the ship itself (mostly) in one piece and able to be claimed as a prize. With the crew, magazines, and machinery protected by armor and with the ranges of the new rifled guns such that boarding was no longer a viable option, the goal of modern naval warfare shifted to simply sinking one's opponent outright. This was easier said than done. Advances in armor technology had, for the moment, eclipsed those in armament. Furthermore, as ranges increased, fire-control technology had not yet solved the problem of accurately firing a shell from a moving platform at a moving target that was miles away. Naval tacticians looked for ways to compensate for these limitations.

One solution was simply to gouge a large hole in any unarmored portion of a ship, usually that below the waterline. In the Battle of Lissa in 1866, the first between fleets of ironclad steam-powered warships, Austrian Admiral Wilhelm von Tegetthoff deployed his ships in three V-shaped line-abreast formations designed to facilitate ramming. Italian Admiral Carlo di Persano deployed his warships in a line-ahead column designed to bring broadsides of guns to bear on the advancing Austrians. In the resulting melee, Tegetthoff's flagship, *Ferdinand Maximilian*, rammed

America, Sea Power, and the World, First Edition. Edited by James C. Bradford.
© 2016 John Wiley & Sons, Inc. Published 2016 by John Wiley & Sons, Inc.

Indiana-Class Battleships

The decision for the United States to possess a navy with the capability to take the offensive against a peer naval competitor on the high seas received the status of law on June 3, 1890, when Congress authorized the construction of three "sea-going coast-line battleships." The carefully worded legislation and the limited capacity of the warships' coal bunkers reflected a desire by lawmakers to maintain, at least in public discourse, that the vessels were defensive in nature. Nonetheless, the three *Indiana*-class battleships represented a fundamental change in the mission of the US Navy. The emphasis on *guerre de course* (i.e.,

commerce warfare) and the ability to sweep an opponent's merchant shipping from the sea lines of communication was now replaced by a focus on *guerre d'escadre*, or the ability to fight against an enemy's battle line.

At 10,288 tons, the *Indiana* was smaller than many of its European contemporaries, and its top speed of 15.5 knots was slightly slower, but these limitations were more than made up for by a main battery of four 13-inch rifles mounted in turrets fore and aft, eight 8-inch rifles mounted in four intermediate turrets, and four 6-inch rifles— giving the *Indiana* a weight of broadside unequaled by any other ship in the world. These impressive

weapons, as well as six torpedo tubes, were protected by over 2,700 tons of steel armor, most of which was forged using the latest methods for hardening and strengthening. All told, *Indiana* was widely considered to be the most powerful battleship afloat when it was commissioned on November 20, 1895.

The *Indiana* class eventually consisted of three battleships: *Indiana*, *Massachusetts*, and *Oregon*. All three were assigned to the North Atlantic Squadron during the War with Spain and performed admirably in combat at the Battle of Santiago de Cuba, on July 3, 1898.

USS *Indiana. Source:* Courtesy of the Naval Historical Foundation. US Naval History and Heritage Command # NH 73975.

and sank the new Italian steam frigate *Re d'Italia*, thereby bringing the engagement to an end. This sinking by ramming combined with that of the USS *Cumberland*, rammed by CSS *Virginia*, led naval officers and ship designers to debate whether the ram would replace the gun in naval warfare. There were no other engagements pitting guns against rams for over a quarter-century, but the British inadvertently provided proof of the efficacy of rams when HMS *Camperdown* accidentally rammed HMS *Victoria*, the flagship of the Mediterranean Fleet, during a complicated fleet maneuver in 1893, sinking it in a matter of minutes with massive loss of life. The possibility of using ramming as a tactic during battle gave rise to one of the most distinctive visual features of ships during this time period, the ram bow, which was internally reinforced against collision and curved forward and downward (in the opposite direction to a modern warship's bow), with a ram attached to the bow below the waterline.

The parallel development of torpedoes contributed to the debate over the efficacy of weapons systems and tactics based on guns. The idea of sinking a warship with an underwater explosion was nothing new. The "torpedoes" that Farragut "damned" at Mobile Bay in 1864 were moored underwater mines. The self-propelled torpedo was first developed by a British mechanic, Robert Whitehead, in 1866. Navies around the world raced to embrace the technology. The US Navy founded the Torpedo School at Newport, Rhode Island, in 1869, largely to experiment with stationary torpedoes and electric detonating systems, but by 1891 the Torpedo School was actively experimenting with the self-propelled variant of the torpedo. The great danger of the torpedo was not just the massive explosion that it could cause under a warship's hull. From a strategic point of view, the torpedo could be constructed relatively cheaply and carried by a small, inexpensive vessel. The fact that such a vessel and weapon could potentially destroy a far more expensive capital ship created nightmares for naval planners. As an early example of asymmetric warfare, the torpedo could conceivably give a second-rate nation without a large naval budget the capability

to threaten a battle line that cost exponentially more to build and deploy.

The self-propelled torpedo posed a significant danger to a fleet, which in combat would be massed in formation to achieve maximum effectiveness of its broadsides—thus making it an easy target. This danger made even more urgent the ability to order maneuvers for an entire fleet, quickly and efficiently, thereby enabling a commander to avoid a spread of torpedoes while maintaining the integrity of his fighting formation. The only way to become proficient at fleet tactical formations was through rigorous practice at sea. By the end of the nineteenth century, the patterns of deployment in the US Navy were such that the squadrons on each station spent substantially more time together, as a coherent combat unit, than split up to visit ports independently. Secretary of the Navy Hilary A. Herbert alluded to this in his annual report for 1894, when he announced a policy of assigning enough vessels to each station to "allow frequent fleet and squadron evolutions, which are absolutely necessary for the instruction of officers and men."[1] Under the new policy, the North Atlantic Squadron cruised the Caribbean in a single unit in 1895, rather than sending its ships to cruise independently throughout the region, as had been prior practice.

The large, relatively cumbersome battleships were still vulnerable to attack by smaller vessels, running in at high speed under the guns of a fleet to launch their torpedoes. To combat these "torpedo boats," navies developed "torpedo boat destroyers" that carried small-caliber "quick-firing" guns to confront torpedo boats before they could come within range to launch their deadly weapons. By the end of the century these two ship types were combined in a single vessel, the "destroyer." The US Navy launched its first destroyer, the *Bainbridge*, in 1899.

The command and control of these multiple formations of large and small warships became increasingly difficult. Since the days of Nelson, fleet commanders had directed the movements of their ships through the use of complicated flag signals. Modern naval warfare demanded a faster and more efficient long-range method of directing large numbers of

---

[1] *Annual Report of the Secretary of the Navy* (1894), 23.

ships in combat. The US Navy began to experiment with the Marconi wireless radio in 1895. In 1903, construction began on large transmitters on both coasts, while wireless receivers and transmitters were installed in Navy ships. These transmitters were not effective enough for tactical control, but they allowed greater coordination between ships at sea and shore stations, and kept ships at sea abreast of developments in the rest of the world.

Revolution in American Foreign Affairs

Increasingly, these developments in the rest of the world concerned a United States that had, until recently, endeavored to steer clear of global entanglements. During the quarter-century following the Civil War, the attention of the American people was focused on Reconstruction, continued westward settlement, and the rise of industry, cities, and immigration. As the nineteenth century came to a close, however, Americans were beginning to look for opportunities beyond their own borders. By 1890, Alfred Thayer Mahan could confidently claim in an *Atlantic* magazine article that the United States was "Looking Outward."[2]

Prior to the 1890s American foreign policy had been guided by leaders with limited achievable goals that could be easily measured. The revolution in American foreign affairs had three components. The most striking, and the one that resonated with the most Americans, was war with Spain in 1898. It was a different sort of war, declared out of humanitarian desires to help the Cuban people. Whether that was the United States' only goal remains a matter of historical debate, but the fact remains that the war prefigured goals of US warfare in the twentieth century. President Woodrow Wilson called World War I the "war to end all wars" and told Americans that it would "make the world safe for democracy." In World War II, Franklin D. Roosevelt made war in the name of his "Four Freedoms." While the proclamation of such unachievable or at least immeasurable goals may have rallied public support during a war, it could lead

to a backlash when people concluded, as they did after World War I, that the goal had not been achieved.

The second component of the revolution, the acquisition of the Philippine Islands, came as a result of the war with Spain and gave America its first possession outside the Western Hemisphere. This thrust the United States, willing or not, into the role of a true imperial power. Annexation of the Philippines had immense implications for the US Navy, which now had the responsibility for protecting US territory not isolated geographically by the Atlantic and Pacific Oceans.

The third component of the revolution was the issuance of the 1899–1900 Open Door Notes. These diplomatic communications by Secretary of State John Hay committed the United States to the preservation of equal access for all nations to trade and investment in China, as well as to defense of the administrative and territorial integrity of that nation. These were policies clearly beyond the ability of the United States to enforce, but ones that would lead to a constant US Navy presence in the Asiatic theater for the next 40 years.

Spanish–American–Philippine–Cuban War of 1898

What Americans typically refer to as the "Spanish–American War" is unfortunately named, as the title does not recognize the Cuban and Filipino people, who had been fighting for their independence from Spain long before the United States entered the conflict.

In Cuba, a long-simmering independence movement grew increasingly violent in the mid-1890s. The crumbling empire of Spain was equally unable to quell the rebellion or to part with the island, which was the most important remnant of its once-great empire. In an effort to prevail, both sides committed atrocities that provided exciting copy for the high-speed presses of the increasingly competitive newspaper market. The so-called "yellow journalism" fueled public cries for US intervention. In February of 1898, the battleship *Maine* was sent to Havana, ostensibly to protect US

---

[2] Alfred T. Mahan, "The United States Looking Outward," *Atlantic Monthly*, 66 (December 1890), 816–824.

citizens and their property in the city but more importantly to convey to Spanish authorities the keen US interest in the deteriorating situation in their colony.

At 2140 on February 15, 1898, a terrific explosion ripped through the *Maine*, causing the ship to sink within minutes, carrying 266 of its 345-man crew to the bottom. The disaster, which as a tactical side note showed yet again the terrible efficiency of putting a large hole below the waterline of an armored capital warship, horrified the American public and caused immediate demands for action. The press, already reporting extensively on the civil war in Cuba, erupted with accusations against the Spanish government and clamors for war. Although President William McKinley did not want war with Spain, by April he saw no other political alternative. Under pressure from the public, as well as his own party, McKinley went before Congress to ask for a declaration of war, which was passed on April 25, 1898, retroactive to April 21.

Immediately after the sinking of the *Maine*, Assistant Secretary of the Navy Theodore Roosevelt took advantage of Secretary John D. Long's absence from the Navy Department one afternoon to send out a flurry of messages that essentially put the US Navy on a war footing. Among the messages Roosevelt directed to be sent out that afternoon was one to Commodore George Dewey, commander of the Asiatic Squadron, ordering him to "keep full of coal. In the event of declaration of war Spain, your duty will be to see that the Spanish squadron does not leave the Asiatic coast and then offensive operations in Philippine Islands."[3]

Immediately upon receipt of this cable, Dewey brought his ships together and prepared them for battle. Dewey's little squadron consisted of the cruisers *Olympia* (flag), *Baltimore*, *Boston*, and *Raleigh*; the gunboats *Concord* and *Petrel*; and the revenue cutter *McCulloch*. While today Dewey is largely remembered for his victory in battle at Manila Bay, his most important work probably took place prior to the battle, which itself was largely anti-climactic. In an era in which the New Steel Navy had no established doctrine to prepare for battle—having never done

it before—Dewey acted quickly and efficiently. He had his ships painted gray instead of the buff, white, and red scheme common in that era. Bottoms were cleaned, if needed, and all unnecessary equipment was thrown overboard, including the ornate paneling and wooden furniture common to ships of the era. Naval observers at the Battle of the Yellow Sea during the Sino-Japanese War (1894–1895) had noted that the wood created a fire and shrapnel hazard. When war was formally declared on April 25, Dewey moved his squadron from British Hong Kong eastward to a pre-selected anchorage at Mirs Bay. There, final preparations for combat were completed before the squadron departed for the Philippines.

Awaiting Dewey was Rear Admiral Don Patricio Montojo. With a small force consisting of two cruisers, one of which was unable to get underway on its own power, and an assortment of smaller ships, Montojo knew that his squadron was no match for Dewey's Asiatic Squadron in a battle at sea. Thus he decided to fight at anchor. This tactic can work well for a defender who knows that the commander on the offensive must come to him to seek action, a case in point being Commodore Thomas Macdonough's success at the Battle of Lake Champlain (1814). Montojo, however, in wanting to spare the city of Manila from errant shells from the American ships, did not anchor under the guns of the city fortress, where they could have supported him, but instead chose to anchor off Cavite, effectively removing the shore artillery from the battle.

Shortly before dawn on May 1, Dewey formed his squadron into a column. There was reason to be concerned about Spanish mines in the narrow waters around Corregidor. Dewey, who always attributed his inspiration as a commander to his service under Admiral David Farragut ("Damn the torpedoes! Full speed ahead!"), pressed on resolutely. Once inside Manila Bay, Dewey directed the movements of his column as it steamed in a racetrack pattern and took the anchored Spanish warships under fire. At about 1100, Dewey withdrew momentarily to assess the situation, then resumed the attack. The outcome of the battle was never in question, with Montojo's

---

[3] Roosevelt to Dewey, February 25, 1898, Theodore Roosevelt, *Theodore Roosevelt: An Autobiography* (1913), 214.

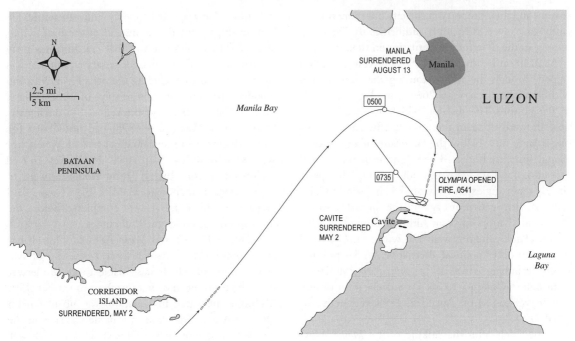

Map 10.1   Manila Bay, 1898.

little squadron completely destroyed by noon (see Map 10.1). The naval battle itself, which resembled nothing so much as a squadron target practice, was probably less important, strategically, than the steps Dewey took afterward.

Unable to attack Manila itself without infantry support, Dewey took up position in the bay and waited for the Army to arrive. During this lull in the action, one of the more peculiar incidents of the war took place when a German squadron arrived off Manila and began conducting landing exercises. The implication was that, if the United States was not going to take the Philippines, Germany would be happy to. This only ceased when Dewey sent the commander of the German squadron a note telling him to cease and desist or face action against the American squadron.

Meanwhile, Dewey sent a ship to Hong Kong to bring back Emilio Aguinaldo, the exiled leader of the Philippine rebellion against Spain. The Filipinos had initial hopes that the Americans would assist them in their struggle to liberate the Philippines from the Spanish, but it was not to be. With the arrival of 11,000 US Army troops, a surrender was hastily arranged between the Spanish garrison in Manila and the Americans, with Aguinaldo and his Filipino soldiers conspicuously not invited to the ceremony. The US Army and Marine Corps would spend the next three years fighting Aguinaldo's forces, who, not surprisingly, were not interested in exchanging one colonial power for another. The Philippine–American War did not end until 1902 and was an early example for the United States of the difficulties encountered when trying to impose one's will on other peoples, even with the best of intentions. For better or for worse, the United States was now formally an imperial power.

On the other side of the world, Navy leaders decided to form two combat squadrons and one patrol squadron with all assets available. In addition to the North Atlantic Squadron, dispatched to the Caribbean under the command of Commodore William T. Sampson, the so-called Flying Squadron was formed at Hampton Roads and placed under the command of Commodore William S. Schley. Here, it was believed that Schley would be close enough to Key West to reinforce the North Atlantic Squadron

George Dewey

Admiral of the Navy George Dewey (1837–1917) occupies a special place in the pantheon of US naval officers. His career, equally effective in combat as well as administration, spanned the naval revolution of the late nineteenth century and he was instrumental in creating the modern US Navy. Dewey graduated from the US Naval Academy in 1858, standing fifth in his class of 14 midshipmen. Dewey distinguished himself in combat during the Civil War, including participation in Farragut's attack on New Orleans and the assault on Fort Fisher late in the war. He later attributed his success as a naval commander to the fearless example set by Farragut.

After the war, Dewey held a number of assignments before taking command of the Asiatic Squadron. War clouds were already on the horizon when Commodore Dewey broke his broad pennant in Hong Kong in December of 1897. While most historians focus on Dewey's combat leadership at the Battle of Manila Bay, his true achievement was arguably the methodical way he prepared his squadron for combat in the weeks prior to the engagement. Early in the morning of May 1, 1898, Dewey led his little squadron of seven well-prepared vessels into Manila Bay. The ensuring battle, over before noon, was a decisive victory against the Spanish navy.

Dewey's triumph captured the imagination of the American population. In 1903 Congress awarded him the special rank of Admiral of the Navy, equivalent to a five- or six-star admiral today. His immense public popularity led him to make an ultimately unsuccessful bid for the Democratic presidential nomination in the 1900 election. After withdrawing from the race and endorsing McKinley, Dewey served on active duty as president of the General Board of the Navy until his death at age 79 in 1917.

Commodore George Dewey on the bridge of his flagship, *Olympia*, May 1, 1898. *Source:* US Naval History and Heritage Command # NH 84510-KN.

if needed yet close enough to protect the coast from New York southward, if necessary. The battleships *Iowa*, *Massachusetts*, and *Texas* formed its nucleus, with the armored cruiser *Brooklyn* as Schley's flagship. Further north, the Northern Patrol Squadron, commanded by Rear Admiral John Adams Howell, was formed to patrol between Maine and Delaware. It drew upon assets of the various state naval militias and was built around a core of four converted Morgan Line steamships, renamed *Dixie*, *Prairie*, *Yankee*, and *Yosemite*. These ships were scattered up and down the East Coast, ostensibly to provide early warning of the approach of the unlocated Spanish squadron. The real purpose of the vessels was to assuage the fears of the public, which were greatly magnified by the constant alarmist reporting of newspapers.

On March 26, William T. Sampson (now a rear admiral) and the third, and largest, force, the North Atlantic Squadron, were dispatched to Key West, there to await orders from the Naval War Board being formed in Washington. Chaired by Theodore Roosevelt until he resigned on April 25, the Board first advised Secretary Long to follow war plans developed at the Naval War College over the past 16 months that called for a naval blockade of Cuba. Early on the morning of April 22, Sampson's flagship *New York* departed Key West, followed by the battleship *Indiana*; the cruisers *Castine*, *Cincinnati*, *Helena*, *Machias*, *Nashville*, and *Wilmington*; seven torpedo boats; and three monitors. The challenge facing Sampson was to mount a blockade that would deprive Spanish troops centered in Havana of the supplies necessary to continue fighting while

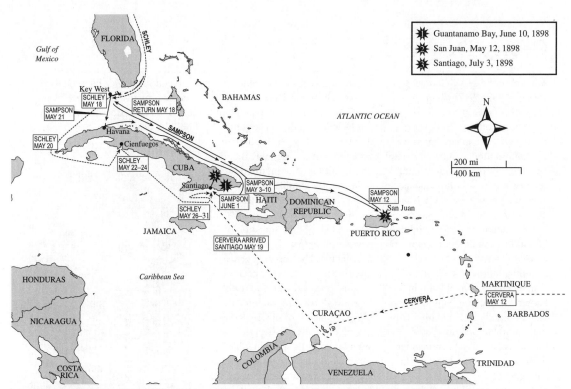

Map 10.2   Caribbean operations, 1898.

keeping prepared to engage the Spanish squadron that was forming in Spain under the command of Admiral Pascual Cervera once its location was known. When news arrived that Cervera had left Spain, Sampson, believing that the Spanish warships would need to refit and refuel after their transatlantic voyage, moved to Puerto Rico to intercept the enemy. While waiting for Cervera, Sampson bombarded San Juan.

Eventually, Sampson received intelligence that the Spanish had been sighted first at Martinique, in the Lesser Antilles, then at Curaçao, off Venezuela. With proof that Cervera did not, therefore, pose a threat to the East Coast of the United States, Schley's Flying Squadron was ordered to leave Hampton Roads and report to Sampson at Key West. The squadrons met at the naval station on May 18.

Sampson augmented the Flying Squadron with *Iowa* and sent Schley to blockade the harbor of Cienfuegos on the south coast of Cuba while he took the remainder of the North Atlantic Squadron to blockade Havana (see Map 10.2). After learning that Cervera had been sighted at Santiago, on the southeastern coast of Cuba, Sampson sent a dispatch vessel after Schley with orders for him to proceed to Santiago at once and confirm the Spanish presence there. On the evening of May 28, after some delay and concern about the coal levels of his squadron, Schley verified that the Spanish squadron was in the harbor of Santiago and reported its presence there to Sampson and the Navy Department.

Sampson brought the North Atlantic Squadron around Cuba immediately, and, with the two forces finally unified, established a close blockade of the long, narrow harbor at Santiago. On June 10 he ordered a battalion of marines ashore at nearby Guantanamo Bay to establish a coaling and resupply station. The successful operation validated the many landing exercises the North Atlantic Squadron had carried out over the previous years. When 16,000 US Army troops landed at Daiquiri, 20 miles east of Santiago,

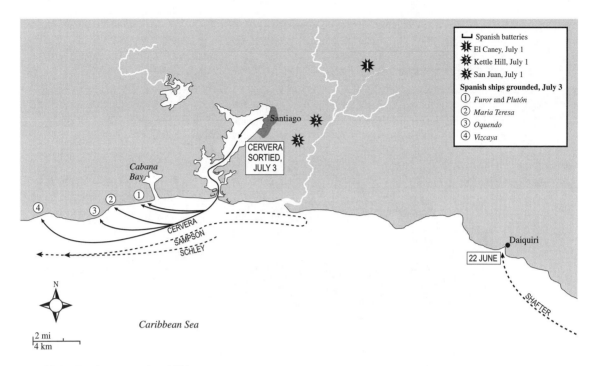

Map 10.3   Santiago campaign, 1898.

Sampson called upon their commander, Major General William R. Shafter, to capture Santiago's fortifications so that he could attack the Spanish warships in the harbor without exposing his capital ships to fire from Spanish coastal batteries

General Shafter first responded that he could not attack the city until Sampson and the Navy had destroyed the Spanish squadron to ensure that the warships could not fire on his troops. After Sampson met personally with Shafter on June 20, the general agreed to attack Santiago's outer defenses but not the city itself. On July 1 the Army attacked and occupied El Caney and San Juan Hill, but over 1,500 men were killed or wounded in the battles. Shafter was concerned that he would have to withdraw and sent a message to Sampson begging him to attack the harbor to relieve pressure on the Army forces.

This, of course, was impossible, due to the mines and the guns of the still-uncaptured Spanish fortifications. On the morning of July 3, Sampson set out in *New York* to meet with Shafter and tell him so. Schley was left in charge of the blockade. At 0930 the Spanish squadron sortied from Santiago. Every US ship that could get up enough steam took off in pursuit of the Spanish ships, firing wildly (see Map 10.3). *New York*, with Sampson on board, turned around and frantically raced toward the scene of battle, only to find the action largely over by the time the ship got within gun range of the Spanish. The final outcome of the engagement was never really in question. After a frenzied three-hour chase along the Cuban coast, the hapless Spanish squadron was annihilated by the somewhat disorganized but materially superior North Atlantic Squadron (see Figure 10.1).

In the battle's aftermath, controversy erupted over which admiral deserved credit for the victory. Sampson, although he had left the area for his meeting with General Shafter, had devised the plan used to blockade and engage the Spanish when they emerged from harbor and had remained in overall command of the victorious fleet; by not mentioning Schley in his initial telegrams to Washington, he left no doubt that he considered himself the victor. However, Schley, as the acting commander-in-chief in Sampson's

Figure 10.1   Spanish cruiser *Vizcaya* aground after the Battle of Santiago, 1898. *Source:* Murat Halstead, *Our Country in War* (1898).

absence, was in command during the battle itself. Newspaper reporters, with whom Schley was popular, ensured that accounts of the battle in the popular press acknowledged Schley as the victor. The uneasy relationship between the two admirals erupted into open controversy over the next three years. In 1901 Schley demanded, and received, a court of inquiry into his conduct. Alerted in advance that the board's findings were largely unfavorable to him, he retired quietly before it could issue its report.

New Responsibilities for the Navy

During the war with Spain, the US Congress annexed Hawaii and, by the terms of the Treaty of Paris (which ended the war), Guam, the Philippine Islands, and Puerto Rico became US posses-

sions. The Navy became partially responsible for the defense of these islands, as well as the Panama Canal, whose construction was triggered in large part by naval defense requirements. Thus, by the turn of the century, the battle-tested US Navy had new, major commitments on both coasts and beyond. These commitments fueled a renewed building program, overseen by the energetic Theodore Roosevelt, who was elevated to the presidency in 1901 after the assassination of William McKinley.

Under Roosevelt, the Navy grew to a total of 20 battleships by 1907. Mindful of Mahan's dictum that a fleet should remain concentrated for maximum battle effectiveness, these new battleships were not sent out on cruises to "show the flag," as had been the custom. Instead, they were organized into two fleets, one for each ocean. By 1906, the European and South

Atlantic Squadrons had been incorporated into the new Atlantic Fleet, homeported in Hampton Roads. In the Pacific, three battleships made up the nucleus of the Pacific Fleet, created in 1907 by combining the Asiatic and Pacific Squadrons. In keeping with his infamous "Big Stick" policy, Roosevelt did not hesitate to use his capital ships liberally to represent US interests, sending eight of them to the Mediterranean in 1906, during the First Moroccan Crisis and subsequent Algeciras Conference.

While Mediterranean concerns and continual unrest in the Caribbean kept the Atlantic Fleet busy, defense of the Philippine Islands and enforcement of Hay's Open Door policies was made difficult in the Pacific by the rising power of Japan. Leaders of that island nation read with great interest the writings of Alfred Thayer Mahan, who preached the importance of controlling sea lines of communication. They soon concluded that Japan should seek a dominant position in China and that Japan's national security required control of the island of Sakhalin, north of the Home Islands; the Korean Peninsula, to their east; and the island of Taiwan, to the south. Since Korea and Taiwan were dominated by China and Sakhalin was controlled by Russia, this new strategy meant inevitable conflict between Japan and its neighbors.

War with China came in 1894, with Japan eventually winning terms that included the recognition of Korea as a sovereign nation not under Chinese control and the cession of Taiwan to Japan. A key factor in the Japanese victory was the Imperial Japanese Navy's besting of a slightly larger Chinese fleet in the Battle of the Yalu River, in 1894.

A decade later, news of Russian plans to construct a railroad across Manchuria to Vladivostok alarmed Japanese leaders, who sought US support in their opposition to this violation of the principle of the Open Door. When American diplomats declined to join Japan in protesting the Russian plans, Japan acted to block the threat to its interests in Manchuria and Korea by launching a surprise attack on Port Arthur and the Russian Pacific Squadron based there on February 4, 1904. After Japanese forces landed near Incheon, Korea, and laid siege to Port Arthur, Tsar Nicholas II dispatched Russia's Baltic Fleet, led by Vice Admiral Zinovi Petro-

vich Rozhestvenski, to the Pacific. Over the next seven months, the Baltic Fleet underwent a grueling journey to the Pacific, made more grueling and much longer by Britain—acting in accord with the Anglo-Japanese Alliance of 1902—closing its coaling stations to the Russians and denying them transit of the Suez Canal. With their destination of Vladivostok almost in sight, the Russian fleet was met by Admiral Tōgō Heihachirō and the Imperial Japanese Navy. Taking advantage of their much shorter lines of communication and the superior state of their ships and men, the Japanese dealt the Russians a crushing defeat at the Battle of Tsushima on May 27–28, 1905 (see Map 10.4).

Defeat at Tsushima rendered Russia's position on land untenable, eventually forcing the Russians to sue for peace. The peace negotiations were carried out at Portsmouth Naval Station, hosted by US President Theodore Roosevelt. Although clearly the victor, both on land as well as the sea, Japan did not get everything it desired in the 1905 Treaty of Portsmouth. While Russia abandoned plans for a railroad in Manchuria, recognized Korea as a Japanese sphere of influence, and ceded Port Arthur and the southern half of Sakhalin Island to Japan, the Japanese did not receive the war reparations they expected, a result for which they blamed Roosevelt.

A year later US–Japanese relations became openly hostile after the school board of San Francisco, succumbing to a wave of anti-immigrant sentiment, forced the children of Japanese immigrants to attend the Oriental Public School previously established for Chinese students. Officials in Japan viewed this as an insult and a violation of the Treaty of 1894, which had guaranteed Japanese immigrants rights equal to those of American citizens. A compromise, the "Gentlemen's Agreement," was reached in 1907; according to its terms, Japanese students would not be forced to attend segregated schools and in return Japan's government would severely limit the immigration of its citizens to the United States.

From the standpoint of naval tactics, the Battle of Tsushima answered many of the questions that had been bothering naval tacticians for the previous 30 years. Neither rams nor torpedoes played a significant role in the battle, the outcome of which was determined by gunfire from the main batteries of the engaged warships.

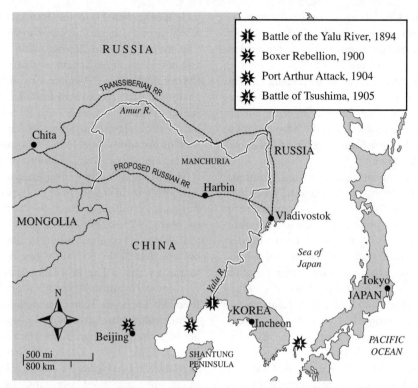

Map 10.4   Northeast Asia, 1894–1905.

This indicated that the main battery of long-range guns would be the primary weapon on battleships used to fight other warships, a tenet that held true until the advent of naval aviation. Admiral Tōgō had deployed his warships in a column and used his superior speed to repeatedly "cross the T" to bring his guns to bear on the enemy. This put to rest, once and for all, debates about which weapon system and formation would most suit the needs of modern steel warships.

The ascendancy of Japan and the necessity of protecting US possessions in the Philippines brought renewed interest in a canal across Central America. Such a canal would offer a solution to the problem of shifting the battle fleet from one ocean to the other rapidly. During the 1880s, a company headed by Ferdinand de Lesseps, builder of the Suez Canal, failed in an attempt to cut a sea-level canal through the isthmus, as did another French company a decade later. By 1904, US officials, notably President Roosevelt, were ready to try. After purchasing the rights from the French company and recognizing a new Panamanian government that had conveniently chosen that moment to rebel against its Colombian masters, the US effort got underway. After 10 years and almost $400 million (in 1914 dollars), the Panama Canal opened. It was an amazing advance for commercial interests, but, more importantly, it paved the way for the US Navy's ability to redeploy warships from one ocean to the other relatively swiftly.

Reform in the New Steel Navy: Organization and Tactics

New responsibilities and rapid changes in technology led to much-needed organizational changes in the Navy. The spectacular victories at Manila Bay and Santiago made the service popular with the American people and created an environment of broad public and congressional support for expansion, modernization, and reform of the Navy.

The division of naval officers into the line and engineering corps had caused unhealthy friction for decades. After much debate, the Naval Personnel Act of 1899 amalgamated the line and engineering corps. Henceforth, and to this day, all line officers would be engineers and all ships' engineers would be line officers. Enrollment at the Naval Academy was increased to provide the technically educated officers required by the growing fleet, and the larger enrollments led Congress to appropriate funds for construction of Bancroft Hall, the Mahan–Maury–Sampson Hall academic complex, and the Naval Academy Chapel, structures that define the modern institution.

Navy shore installations were easy to deal with compared to other shortcomings made manifest by the war. These organizational weaknesses would have to be corrected in order for the Navy to carry out its new, increased responsibilities. The preparations for war in 1898 highlighted the lack of a staff to coordinate strategic and operational planning and to provide resources to the on-scene commanders. An ad hoc Navy War Board that included Alfred Thayer Mahan performed some basic planning functions during the war, but there was no institutional way to coordinate efforts between bureaus, save through the office of the Secretary of the Navy, or to settle disputes between Army and Navy commanders such as those between Sampson and Shafter, save by the president.

In March 1900, Secretary of the Navy Long issued General Order 544, which established the General Board of the Navy. Composed of admirals near the end of their careers, as well as members from the Naval War College, the Office of Naval Intelligence, and the Bureau of Navigation, the new organization had no command authority. However, it served as a central source of advice and policy coordination. The General Board was a step in the right direction, but it would be another 15 years before the creation of the office of the chief of naval operations led the Navy closer to having a true staff. In 1903 the Joint Army–Navy Board was formed to coordinate war planning, to recommend locations for military bases, and to foster inter-service cooperation. Admiral George Dewey headed both boards until his death in 1917. The greatest success of the Joint Board came in war planning, particularly the "color plans" for war with various foreign powers. Of these, "War Plan Orange," the contingency planning for war with Japan, would occupy US Navy strategic thinking for the next four decades. Although these organizations represented important advances in organization, the power of both was limited by their inability to officially do much more than make recommendations. Executive authority remained vested in the Secretary of the Navy and the chiefs of the various bureaus.

Operationally, the Battles of Manila Bay and Santiago exposed dangerous weaknesses in American naval gunnery. Naval tacticians already knew that, while improvements made in propellants and in the construction of high-caliber naval weapons had produced main-battery guns that could fire large rounds out to a distance of several miles, there was no effective way to deliver this ordnance accurately. Naval gunfire is, of course, a problem that must be worked out in several dimensions. The target is moving, and, as the shell is in the air for several seconds, the shell must be aimed at where the target will be, not where it is when the gun is fired. At the same time, the platform carrying the gun itself is moving in three dimensions, as the ship moves on a given course and speed while it pitches and rolls with the ocean waves. At the Battle of Manila Bay, when the targets were not moving, Commodore Dewey's squadron fired 1,257 6- and 8-inch shells, only 28 of which actually hit enemy warships. Fortunately for the Asiatic Squadron, the Spanish managed to do even worse. It was evident that advances in fire control were crucial to the continued development of naval power.

Bradley Fiske, a 1874 Naval Academy graduate, was something of an inventor, with an interest in improving gun accuracy. During the Battle of Manila Bay, Fiske was aloft on the mainmast of the gunboat *Petrel* using a stadimeter—a device he had invented—to estimate the range to the enemy warships. Eventually, Fiske's optical range-finding devices would become standard throughout the fleet.

Being able to measure the range to a target with reasonable accuracy was important, but it still did not account for the pitching and rolling of one's own ship. The British experimented with a system called "continuous aim," whereby the gunner, rather than simply training the gun and then firing it, would continuously work the controls to keep the gun trained on a point up to the very moment of firing. Royal Navy

Figure 10.2   The Great White Fleet steaming in line-ahead formation with USS *Kansas* in the lead, 1907.
Source: Collection of Roy D. France. US Naval History and Heritage Command # NH 92091.

Captain Percy Scott pioneered the method of continuous-aim gunfire in the British navy. While a member of the staff of the commander of the Asiatic Fleet in 1901, US Navy Lieutenant William Sowden Sims met Scott, who taught him these methods and helped Sims to modify the elevation gear on one of the guns of the USS *Kentucky*. Soon that ship was performing remarkable feats at gunnery practice. It seemed that the new methods would be adopted immediately, but that was not the case.

Skeptical naval officials attempted to re-create Sims' results. Unfortunately, they carried out these tests at the Washington Navy Yard, using guns mounted on land. Continuous aim does not work under these conditions, as the method depends on the momentum of the roll of the ship to assist in training (i.e., aiming) the gun rapidly. When officials in the Bureau of Ordinance wrote Lieutenant Sims to thank him for his ideas but tell him that the Navy had no future use for them, Sims, in a move that would be impos-

sible today but that was still feasible in 1901, wrote President Theodore Roosevelt a letter explaining the success of continuous-aim gunfire and asking his assistance in convincing the Navy to adopt it.[4] Rather than referring Sims' letter back to naval officials, Roosevelt had Sims recalled to Washington and appointed him Inspector of Naval Gunnery in November 1902. By 1905 continuous-aim firing had become standard in the US Fleet.

While Sims' gunnery methods and Fiske's work on optical and range-finding systems continued to improve the battleship's offensive potency, other innovators worked to exploit weaknesses of the great warships. The submarine was originally developed as a way to press home an attack against the unarmored hull of a warship, hidden beneath the waterline. The US Navy purchased its first submarine, *Holland*, in 1900. By 1914, advances in underwater navigation and diesel propulsion gave submarines a true ocean-going capability. Once this capability was harnessed to

---

[4] Sims to Roosevelt, November 16, 1901, as quoted in Kenneth Wimmel, *Theodore Roosevelt and the Great White Fleet* (1998), 163.

threaten sea lines of communication and vital supplies, strategic thinkers were forced to reconsider Mahan's dismissal of the effectiveness of commerce raiding.

Voyage of the Great White Fleet (1907–1909)

The crowning achievement of Theodore Roosevelt's naval policies came at the end of his second term: the worldwide tour of the Great White Fleet. Ostensibly, the combined fleet of 16 US battleships left Hampton Roads, Virginia, in December 1907 to cruise from the East Coast of the United States to the West Coast. Only a few of Roosevelt's closest advisors knew that his real intention was to send them around the world. One of the earliest presidents to fully grasp the power of modern public relations, Roosevelt had several

purposes in mind for this global display of US combat power. He clearly intended the voyage to build public support for continued generous naval appropriations. This was in line with other initiatives by Roosevelt, such as the return of the body of John Paul Jones to a specially prepared crypt in the newly constructed chapel of the US Naval Academy. The crypt closely resembled Nelson's tomb in London, and the implications were not lost on anyone. The globe-circling voyage was also designed to reassure Americans on the West Coast that the fleet could be transferred there rapidly should it be needed for their defense (see Figure 10.2). Meanwhile, such a long voyage would both test the ability of US warships to operate at distances from their bases without suffering debilitating mechanical problems and provide opportunities for training and the practice of tactics and maneuvering.

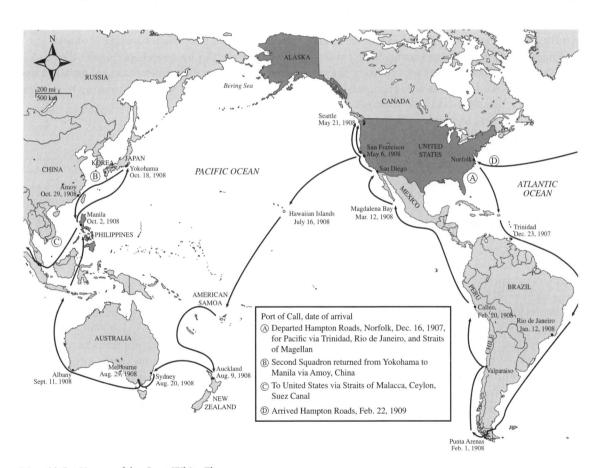

Map 10.5   Voyage of the Great White Fleet.

Geopolitically, Britain had, in 1905, expanded its 1902 naval alliance with Japan to allow the Royal Navy to move its capital ships closer to home to focus on the rising German threat in the North Sea. Roosevelt hoped, by the expanded cruise, to demonstrate to Britain and to its Australian and New Zealand dominions (who like Canada were alarmed by the Anglo-Japanese Alliance) the operational reach of US naval power. The transpacific voyage was also intended to demonstrate to Japan that the United States had the capability to project power over great distances, specifically to the Philippines.

The 14-month, 43,000-nautical-mile voyage of the Great White Fleet proved a great success (see Map 10.5). The 14,000 sailors and marines and their ships were received with much fanfare at every port of call as the cruise progressed from Hampton Roads to Trinidad and Rio de Janeiro; through the Straits of Magellan and up the coast to Callao, Peru, and Magdalena Bay, Mexico, and to several cities in California and the Puget Sound; then west to Hawaii, New Zealand, Australia, Japan, and the Philippines; and from there to Ceylon, Egypt, Gibraltar, and back to Hampton Roads. Along the way the ships faced and overcame logistical challenges relating to keeping a fleet of battleships and their accompanying destroyers and auxiliaries fueled and provisioned at great distances from their home base. The invited comparison to the spectacular Russian failure three years earlier was obvious.

HMS *Dreadnought* (1906)

Impressive as it was, however, the Great White Fleet was largely obsolete when it sailed. This shocking development was the result of the launch of a Royal Navy warship that would create such a sensation in the shipbuilding world that, henceforth, all battleships would be rated as either "pre-dreadnoughts" or "dreadnoughts."

Naval architects designing the armored warships of the new steel navies were faced with a choice. The three important components of any battleship were guns, armor, and speed. Generally speaking, a ship could be designed to be superior in any two of those three categories. In other words, a warship could have large, heavy guns and thick armor, but it would be comparatively slow. This was the usual

design model followed for battleships. Cruisers had large guns as well but were faster, sacrificing some weight in armor protection in order to have more powerful engines.

Dreadnought shattered the mold by mounting an all-big-gun main battery while maintaining superior armor protection as well as the speed that the Battle of Tsushima proved was so vital to gaining the upper edge in an engagement. This was done primarily by using the newly developed turbine technology for the ship's engines. Turbines were substantially lighter than the old reciprocating-arm triple-expansion steam engines, yet they produced greater horsepower. The result was a capital warship that led all potential adversaries in weight of broadside, armor protection, and speed.

Faced with the obsolescence of their battleships, the other major navies of the world, including the United States, immediately began to modify their building plans. The decades leading to World War I would be marked by a race—not unlike the nuclear arms race later in the century—to field modern capital warships. This race would continue up to the outbreak of World War I.

Conclusion

The decade and a half between 1895 and 1910 was marked by rapid change and modernization, as new technologies dramatically altered the conduct of naval warfare. The revolution in American foreign affairs—entry into the Spanish–American War, America's acquisition of its first non-Western-Hemisphere possessions, and the issuance of the "Open Door" notes—fundamentally changed the mission of the US Navy from its traditional emphasis on coastal defense, commerce warfare, and protecting American lives and property to new requirements concerning power projection and the engagement of enemy fleets thousands of miles from North America. During the following decade the United States, on the verge of great-power status, flexed its power from the Atlantic and Caribbean to the Far East. During the same era, the US Navy was transformed by changes and reforms in technology, strategy, and tactics; the recruitment and training of enlisted personnel; and administration.

CHAPTER 11

Defending Imperial Interests in Asia and the Caribbean, 1898–1941

In 1898, the United States became an empire and started acting like one. It annexed colonies and territories in Asia and the Caribbean, continuously deployed naval power to newly acquired bases in the Caribbean and the Pacific, and soon conducted long, unpopular military occupations. It fought insurgencies in four countries, killing tens of thousands of combatants and noncombatants. It trained foreign police forces throughout the Caribbean and kept thousands of troops in China to defend businessmen and missionaries. All of these operations—plus World War I—caused the Navy and Marine Corps to grow. In 1898, the Navy had 160 ships in active service. By 1935, it had 320. The Marine Corps' active-duty personnel tripled in the same period and the Navy's quadrupled.

This larger role for the Navy in foreign affairs was both a continuation of earlier trends and a departure from them. America has *always* been an experiment in expansion: since the first settlement at Jamestown in 1607, white settlers had consistently expanded westward, settling new territory at the expense of Indians and, later, Mexicans. The nation's hemispheric ambitions can be dated to 1823, when the Monroe Doctrine proclaimed the Western Hemisphere closed to European colonial expansion and banned the transfer of colonies from one outside power to another (even though the United States lacked the military force to enforce such a policy). Given these earlier patterns, it is no surprise that at the start of the twentieth century, with the economy booming and no frontier left

to settle, Americans began going abroad in search of markets and missions alike.

But the expansionist foreign policy of the early twentieth century also represented a departure from earlier patterns. For its first hundred years, the United States believed itself to be fundamentally different from the European powers and used the rhetoric of anticolonialism as the proof of that difference. And yet, after 1898, the United States took colonies and territories and fought "Banana Wars" that were virtually indistinguishable from the European colonial wars Americans had become so fond of disdaining. Somehow, the fact that the United States had to traverse water to take the new territories made a difference: conquering the North American continent through Indian removal and the Mexican War could be called something other than colonialism; taking Guam, Hawaii, the Philippines, and Puerto Rico could not. An American Anti-Imperialist League emerged to oppose the new foreign policy in 1898, but, even with such prominent members as Jane Addams, Andrew Carnegie, John Dewey, and Mark Twain, it had little effect.

Despite their limited influence, the anti-imperialists were right to protest because this was not national defense. In most cases, the goal was to increase America's sphere of influence by keeping larger European navies at bay. Other times, the operations were motivated less by strategy and more by economics, as well as by an idealistic vision of spreading democracy and good governance. None of the

America, Sea Power, and the World, First Edition. Edited by James C. Bradford.
© 2016 John Wiley & Sons, Inc. Published 2016 by John Wiley & Sons, Inc.

countries the United States invaded or occupied presented any significant threat to US national security.

In the end, the efforts to contain European influence mostly succeeded. So too did the efforts to protect American business interests, though the record here is more mixed. The attempts at uplift through occupation were almost all complete failures.

The Philippine–American War and Cuban Occupations

Most Americans think of the Spanish–American War as both "splendid" and "little" because they focus only on the six-month conflict between the United States and Spain. But, after that war concluded, an anticolonial insurgency continued in the Philippines for several years. Just 379 Americans were killed taking the Philippines from Spain. Another 4,000 died trying to convince the new colonial subjects to accept American rule.

The Americans' problems with the Filipinos began before the war even ended. Despite having destroyed Spain's fleet, Admiral Dewey had no forces to occupy the colony and, in June, Filipino guerillas surrounded the Spanish garrison in Manila. At first, Dewey thought he could cooperate with the Filipinos and sent a cruiser to Hong Kong to bring in their commander, a 29-year-old former provincial mayor named Emilio Aguinaldo. Urging Aguinaldo to "go ashore and start your army,"[1] Dewey and other American officials either hinted or proclaimed outright that the United States had no plans to keep the Philippines. Aguinaldo hastily declared himself the supreme chief of the nation, read a declaration of independence, and persuaded an American businessman named Colonel L. M. Johnson (retired) to sign it. (Despite his previous military experience, Colonel Johnson had no official role in the Philippines; he was in Asia to exhibit a new invention—the cinematograph.) Admiral Dewey refused to attend the ceremony or give any recognition to Aguinaldo's government.

After Aguinaldo went ashore, the Spanish in Manila were even more helpless than before, but still they would not surrender. They feared they would be slaughtered en masse by the Filipinos if they did; moreover, as they explained to the Americans, they could be court

martialed for cowardice if they surrendered without a fight. The two sides arrived at a bizarre solution: a phony battle. Admiral Dewey ordered his ships to fire on Manila—but to hit nothing of consequence—and the Spanish were supposed to fire wide of the mark as well. Unfortunately, well-meaning sailors adjusted the gun coordinates to hit the defenders. The Spanish panicked and shot to kill. Six Americans and almost 50 Spaniards died before the charade ended and the garrison surrendered. The Americans occupied Manila alone and prohibited Aguinaldo from participating in the surrender ceremonies or stationing any of his troops in the city.

President William McKinley had not ordered the occupation of Manila, but, unwilling to turn its residents over to Aguinaldo and nervous about the European warships lurking in the harbor, he decided to keep the Philippines. His greatest concern was keeping them out of the hands of other colonizers—Germany in particular—but the islands' close proximity to China convinced him they would be useful for opening markets in Asia as well. Despite loud and frequent cries from anti-imperial voices in Congress, McKinley insisted it was America's duty "to educate the Filipinos, and uplift and Christianize them," a justification that ignored the fact that most of the Philippines had been Catholic for more than 200 years.[2]

Aguinaldo and his *insurrectos* vowed to fight. Once the insurgency began, it quickly degenerated into the type of brutality that irregular wars always entail. The US Army provided the bulk of the troops, but 300 marines participated as well under the command of a hard-fighting, hard-drinking commander, Major Littleton W. T. Waller. The Americans encountered few constraints on warfare in the "boondocks" (an Americanism stemming from a Tagalog word meaning "mountain") and responded in kind. American soldiers and marines shot prisoners, used torture in interrogations, burned whole villages, and set up camps that killed thousands through disease. One marine wrote home that his men "were hiking all the time killing all we come across." After a surprise attack on the Americans at Balangiga, Samar, in 1901, the Army general in charge, Brigadier General Jacob "Hell-Roaring Jake" Smith, told Waller, "I want no prisoners. I wish you to kill and burn. The more you kill and burn, the better you will please me." Anyone over the age of 10

---

[1] "Hearings on Philippine Affairs," *Senate Document 331*, part 3, 57th congress, 1st sess., 1901–2 (1902), 2928.

[2] James Rusling, "Interview with President William McKinley," *The Christian Advocate* (January 22, 1903), 17.

was to be considered a combatant. Waller reminded his men that "we are not making war on women and children" but, in fact, few Americans made firm distinctions between suspected and confirmed insurgents.[3] After Waller executed 11 of his own Filipino guides without a trial, he was court martialed for murder but acquitted. Brigadier General Smith also went to trial and was forced into retirement after being convicted of undermining good order and discipline. By 1902, the insurgency had mostly ended, but not because of the brutal tactics on Samar. The principal reason for the victory was the eventual capture of Emilio Aguinaldo, which led to an amnesty for all fighters. Efforts to couple carrots with sticks also helped. In addition to battling the *insurrectos*, the Americans built schools, established hospitals, and administered vaccines. Along the way, they killed between 16,000 and 50,000 Filipinos in combat and another 200,000 civilians died, mostly of disease and famine. And, while most of the insurgents gave up in 1902, the Muslims of Mindanao fought the Americans intermittently for years thereafter. The Filipino government continues to fight them to this day with the help of American special forces.

Operations in Cuba were far less bloody but had similarly long-lasting effects. When US forces landed in 1898, most Americans expected their troops to stay just long enough to wrest the island from Spain. Much of the public support for war with Spain had come from a desire to liberate the Cubans from colonial rule, and Congress had already forbidden the annexation of the island. In the end, the initial occupying force stayed for four years and only left after Congress passed the Platt Amendment, which asserted the United States' unilateral rights to take naval bases and to intervene politically and militarily in Cuba's internal affairs in perpetuity. With Cuba under US protection and influence, teams of American lawyers swept in to snap up titles to the arable lands and, by 1905, 13,000 Americans held land titles in Cuba.

American troops left Cuba in 1902, but in 1906 Cuba's government faced an armed revolt from its own veterans of the 1898 war. The Navy and Marine Corps returned to impose order and established a provisional government that ruled the island for three years.

During that time the military-dominated government protected the now considerable amounts of American property, dispensed more contracts to American firms, and expanded the national police force into an army, which every political faction in the country worried would be used to target political opponents. American forces landed again in 1912 and garrisoned forces in Cuba from 1917 to 1922. In the 1930s, the United States helped a young military officer named Fulgencio Batista to establish what became a military dictatorship. With Batista's strong connections to the American business community (and the American mafia), Havana flourished while the rural poor suffered. By 1959, US companies owned 90 percent of the mines, 80 percent of the utilities, 40 percent of the sugar companies, and almost all of the oil in Cuba. That same year, Batista was ousted by Fidel Castro, who proceeded to rule the country as a dictator for five decades.

The Panama Canal and the American Lake

Economic interests were one of the reasons for the many naval landings and occupations in the Caribbean, but they were not the primary one, particularly during the presidency of Theodore Roosevelt (1901–1909). Impressed by the time it took the *Oregon* to steam from the West Coast to the Caribbean during the Spanish–American War, Roosevelt was far more concerned with the need for a trans-Central American canal and with incorporating the surrounding countries into America's sphere of influence. If European powers could be persuaded that the entire Caribbean Sea was a de facto American lake, the United States could both build the canal and hold it in the event of a major war.

American diplomats first sought permission to construct a canal across Nicaragua. Once rebuffed, they turned their attention to Panama, a rebellious province of Columbia. The United States already had a long tradition of using military force in Panama (in fact, it had landed forces more than a dozen times since the 1850s to protect American lives and property), but it had never challenged Columbia's claim to

---

[3] As quoted in Brian McAllister Linn, "We Will Go Heavily Armed: The Marines' Small War on Samar, 1901–1902," in W. R. Roberts and Jack Sweetman, eds., *New Interpretations in Naval History: Selected Papers from the Ninth Naval History Symposium* (1991), 273–292.

the province. That changed in 1903 when President Roosevelt actively conspired with a French business-man and a group of Panamanian rebels to launch a rebellion. When fighting broke out on the isthmus in November 1903, President Roosevelt sent in 10 war-ships and landed a battalion of marines, preventing Columbia from quelling the revolution. Roosevelt's gunboat diplomacy worked. The United States rec-ognized Panama as an independent nation and its first ambassador to the United States immediately signed a treaty that gave Panama $10 million and rent of $25,000 a year in exchange for rights to construct and own a canal. The treaty also gave the United States a strip of land five miles wide on either side of the canal—the Canal Zone—which became an unincor-porated US territory with its own courts and police

force. The United States remained in Panama until the 1990s, and in 2000 it voluntarily turned operation of the canal over to the Panamanian government.

Having a canal meant defending it, and here President Roosevelt's biggest concern was the small and fragile states nearby that owed millions to European banks. After Britain, Germany, and Italy imposed a naval blockade on Venezuela in 1902 to force it to repay its debts, Roosevelt decided to act. His Roosevelt Corollary to the Monroe Doctrine announced to Europe that, when disputes needed set-tling in the Caribbean, the United States—and only the United States—would intercede as "an interna-tional police power." Thereafter, the United States found itself using military force in the Caribbean nearly continuously until 1934 (see Figure 11.1).

THE BIG STICK IN THE CARIBBEAN SEA

Figure 11.1   Roosevelt Corollary to the Monroe Doctrine and "big stick" diplomacy. *Source:* The Granger Collection/ Topfoto.

The first application of the Roosevelt Corollary came in the Dominican Republic. Concerned about the nation's ballooning debt and political instability, the United States negotiated a treaty with the country's dictator in 1905. Thereafter, American naval officers managed the Republic's finances through a customs receivership and steadily repaid its debts to Europe and the United States. Keeping the Dominicans' revenues away from corrupt politicians, it was hoped, would both stabilize the country and remove the threat of European intervention. But the new system inevitably angered the Dominican elite, who had grown accustomed to receiving portions of the customs taxes. Instability increased and the Navy found itself perpetually in Dominican waters. In 1913, President Woodrow Wilson proposed a solution that went far beyond controlling the customs houses. The so-called "Wilson Plan" proclaimed that the United States would no longer support any government that came to power by force. Democratic elections would be held, even if the US president had to land marines to conduct them. Once a legitimate government was in place, the United States would stabilize it by building an army or police force and working to improve sanitation, transportation, and education systems. In the president's own words, this combination of carrots and sticks would "teach the South American Republics to elect good men."[4] Much like the president's later attempts to bring peace to Europe after World War I, it did not work. Wilson's plan would form the basic framework for the long occupations of the Dominican Republic, Haiti, and Nicaragua, none of which resulted in a smooth transition to peace or representative government.

The Dominicans took little notice of the Wilson Plan. In 1914, the Dominican secretary of war, General Desiderio Arias, broke with the government and took much of the army with him. The country again descended into violence, and the US Navy returned and bombarded the coast on four separate occasions. American sailors and marines went ashore and supervised an election that brought General Arias' principal rival to power. In May 1916, the new president fled, and Arias' army seized portions of the capital. Three days later, two battalions of marines began

going ashore and soon 14 naval vessels policed the coasts. In November, the Americans declared martial law, and Admiral Harry S. Knapp became the military governor of the country.

Wilson's goal was to "teach" good government to willing citizens; unfortunately, Admiral Knapp could not find many willing Dominican students. When elites refused to serve in the government, he appointed American military officers, some of whom held more portfolios than any one man could possibly manage. Marine Colonel Joseph H. Pendleton served as minister of war, the interior, the navy, and the police—all while commanding the US Marine Brigade. Another colonel served as minister of foreign relations, justice, and public instruction. These officers and their district commanders overruled local elites and enforced strict censorship of the press and mail, thus denying the Dominicans the very constitutional rights Wilson had trumpeted in his initial call for reform.

Admiral Knapp's military government had some successes. By mid-summer, Arias had surrendered and organized violence had subsided except for banditry. The US Navy built 400 primary schools and made substantial improvements to the roads, ports, public buildings, and infrastructure. The marines patrolled regularly, confiscated thousands of weapons, and raised a small national police force—the Guardia Nacional—that was composed, ironically enough, of a number of former bandits. Violence declined. After the first year of the occupation, the Marines had suffered just four killed and 15 wounded and the total number of Dominican deaths was probably below 100.

But the peace did not last. Worried that the occupation would go on indefinitely, Dominican elites began to protest. The American military governor responded by tightening censorship laws, which generated more resentment. World War I absorbed the bulk of American attention and military manpower, which meant occupation forces both were under-resourced and suffered from poor morale. As violence ticked upwards, the marines relied increasingly on the Guardia, which often abused civilians and in at least one instance executed a dozen defenseless prisoners. Some marines began resorting to the same brutal practices seen in the Philippines, including murder

---

[4] Wilson's statement to British envoy William Tyrrell (November 1913) as quoted in Lester D. Langley, *The Banana Wars* (1983), 81.

Map 11.1   Caribbean interventions, 1900–1935.

and mutilation. By 1919, there were 3,000 marines engaged in pacification operations—three times the number that had landed in 1916—and still the violence continued.

In 1921, the US Senate held hearings on the occupation and concluded that American operations were ineffective but that the Dominicans were not ready to govern themselves. A new military governor, Marine Brigadier General Harry Lee, embarked on a series of reforms to professionalize the Guardia and rein in the excesses of the enlisted marines. These improvements brought another temporary peace and, in 1924, the Marines left the Dominican Republic. All told, the Marines lost about 100 men during the occupation and killed or wounded more than a thousand Dominicans. In 1930, the commander of the American-trained Guardia, Raphael Trujillo, seized power and ruled the country until 1961. After his assassination, the United States invaded again in 1965 and stayed for another five months.

The occupation next door in Haiti (1915–1934) lasted longer and provoked more controversy than the one in the Dominican Republic (see Map 11.1). Although Haiti freed itself from French colonial rule in 1804, it had been chronically poor and unstable ever since. Before the American occupation began, 17 of Haiti's 24 presidents were overthrown by revolution and 11 held office for less than a year. At the start of the twentieth century, a small group of corrupt elites controlled politics and maintained their power by doling out money, most of which was drawn from government coffers. The country was badly in debt, both because of corruption and because American, French, and German investors had loaned the government enormous sums at high rates to develop railroads and agricultural interests. By 1911, the New York-based National City Bank (today's CitiBank) had muscled out French and German investors and obtained a controlling interest in the Haitian national bank.

Economic motives soon combined with—or were disguised as—strategic ones. The American secretary of state received most of his advice on Haiti from Roger L. Farnham, who was simultaneously the vice president of the National City Bank, president of the Haitian national railway, and vice president of the Haitian national bank. Farnham consistently exaggerated the threat of European interference in Haiti order to encourage an American military intervention, which would help to protect his investments. Aware of the president's concern about rival naval bases in Haiti, he warned the secretary that the German and French ministers were cooperating in the Caribbean and that "their plans include taking advantage of [a potential base site] at Môle St. Nicholas."[5] This was patently absurd, since by 1915 the French and Germans were busy slaughtering each other on the battlefields of World War I.

Farnham also withheld funds from the Haitian government in order to further destabilize the country, which caused the Office of Naval Intelligence to report that Farnham's bank was "the chief contributor to the present financial stagnation of Haitian commerce" and "directly responsible for the present political conditions in Haiti." When the country descended into revolution yet again in the summer of 1915, a mob in Port-au-Prince captured the Haitian president and dismembered him with machetes. President Wilson reluctantly ordered another landing.[6]

The Navy had already landed in Haiti over a dozen times in the previous decades, but this time it stayed for 19 years. In July 1915, Rear Admiral William Caperton sent 2,000 marines ashore under the command of Colonel Littleton W. T. Waller (the same officer who had been acquitted of murder in the Philippines), who began buying the rebels' weapons and attacking those who refused to surrender. The rebels numbered around 1,500 and usually scattered when confronted by the marines' firepower. During the first year, the Marines lost three men and had 18 wounded. The Haitians lost about 200, 51 of whom died in a single battle at Fort Rivière.

The United States did not immediately declare martial law as it had done in the Dominican Republic.

Instead, Admiral Caperton called on the Haitian legislature to elect a president, but not before informing the most popular candidate—a Paris-educated, multilingual lawyer and doctor who had long opposed American interference—that he would not be a candidate. The admiral next approached three other potential candidates, but all refused to stand for election. In the end, he settled on Senate President Philippe Sudre Dartiguenave, who agreed to take the job provided that the Navy would defend him from his own people. Marines with bayonets fixed to their rifles watched from the aisles of the National Assembly as the Haitians "elected" the American puppet. A month after the election, Caperton declared martial law, rendering Dartiguenave the president in name only. A US-authored treaty and a new constitution followed that authorized the Americans to raise and train a police force, collect customs, own Haitian land, control Haiti's finances, and intervene militarily in whatever way they saw fit. When Haitian parliamentarians protested the Constitution—principally because of the foreign landowning provision—the Americans disbanded the legislature.

Admiral Caperton departed in early 1916 and Colonel Waller became the senior officer in Haiti. Under him was Major Smedley Butler, a highly decorated officer who would eventually be awarded the Medal of Honor twice before becoming an outspoken critic of American small wars. Waller and Butler were brave, battle-hardened officers, but they were not well suited to working with the Haitians. Waller was openly hostile to President Dartiguenave, whom he claimed was "as big a crook as any of the others." He hated "bowing and scraping to these coons" and once reminded Butler that "you can never trust a nigger with a gun." Butler was no better. He called the Haitians "bad niggers," "savage monkeys," and, after he took over the Gendarmerie, "my little chocolate soldiers." In 1951, an American official in Haiti recalled that Butler was entirely ill-suited for the post and that "for years, some of us had the job of trying to heal up the scars which that gentleman left."[7]

Racism was also endemic in the enlisted ranks, which had the most direct contact with the Haitians who

---

[5] As quoted in Hans Schmidt, *The Occupation of Haiti* (1971), 53.

[6] As quoted in Schmidt, *Maverick Marine* (1987), 82.

[7] As quoted in Schmidt, *Maverick Marine*, 75, 82–84, and Schmidt, *Occupation of Haiti*, 79–81.

Smedley D. Butler

Born into a wealthy, political, Quaker family from Philadelphia, Smedley Butler (1881–1940) was both a decorated Marine hero and a fiery critic of American militarism. His career closely paralleled the age of American imperialism. In 1898, he lied about his age to join the Marines and went to Cuba in the Spanish–American War. Next followed service in the Philippines, where he fought well, was temporarily demoted for drunkenness, and got an enormous eagle, globe, and anchor tattoo that covered his entire chest. Over the ensuing three decades, Butler served in China and every one of the Banana Wars: Honduras, the Dominican Republic, Haiti, and Nicaragua. He received the Medal of Honor twice for actions in Mexico (1914) and Haiti (1915)—awards that were helped along by his father, a prominent US congressman. He contracted malaria repeatedly, had one nervous breakdown, and was wounded twice. (The second time was the most disappointing to him, because the bullet that hit his chest gouged out the Latin American portion of his Marine Corps tattoo.) After being passed over for the position of commandant of the Marine Corps, Butler retired in 1931 and became an outspoken critic of American imperialism. In a 1935 article for the Socialist political magazine *Common Sense*, he claimed:

Smedley D. Butler reviewing Marine guards in Shanghai, 1927. *Source:* US Marine Corps Archives.

I spent 33 years and four months in active military service and during that period I spent most of my time as a high class muscle man for Big Business, for Wall Street and the bankers. In short, I was a racketeer, a gangster for capitalism. I helped make Mexico and especially Tampico safe for American oil interests in 1914. I helped make Haiti and Cuba a decent place for the National City Bank boys to collect revenues in. I helped in the raping of half a dozen Central American republics for the benefit of Wall Street.

would eventually turn against them. Here, the greatest friction came from Butler's Gendarmerie, which took privates and corporals (Lewis B. "Chesty" Puller was one of them) and made them lieutenants in the Haitian constabulary. Unable to speak French or Creole, most of the white "officers" were unable to communicate with their Haitian troops except by gesturing or through translators. None knew anything of Haitian history or culture. Decorated Marine officers such as Medal of Honor recipient Lieutenant Louis Cukela contributed to a culture of lawlessness by executing unarmed prisoners.

Things got worse when Butler authorized the return of an obscure French law—the *corvée*—that forced Haitians to provide free labor in lieu of paying taxes. Armed with this law, the Gendarmerie made the rural poor build roads, often at gunpoint, and sometimes roped or chained them together. Butler championed his accomplishments in letters to Washington but cautioned that "it would not do to ask too many questions as to how we accomplish this work." Rumors spread throughout Haiti that the Marines were reintroducing slavery. Resistance grew into "a massive revolt" that eventually killed 16 marines and 3,250 Haitians. Butler discontinued the *corvée* in 1918, but the Marine in charge of one of the most restive provinces refused to comply and continued what a later investigation called "a reign of terror" that depopulated the countryside.[8]

The revolt died down after 1919, when Marines infiltrated the insurgency and killed its most prominent leader, Charlemagne Peralte. The 1920s were mostly peaceful, but Haiti never approached President Wilson's democratic dream. The Haitian president

---

[8] As quoted in Schmidt, *Occupation of Haiti*, 100–103.

was still a leader in name only; the Marine high commissioner called the shots and continued to ignore requests to reconvene the legislature or to loosen censorship laws. A new president replaced Dartiguenave in 1922, but, when he balked at holding elections in 1929, a general strike ensued. The high commissioner reimposed martial law, but the 800 marines remaining in the country were ill-equipped to stop the riots. Officers' homes were firebombed and a Marine detachment near Cayes fired on a crowd of protesters, killing and wounding more than 50 Haitians. When free elections were finally held in Haiti in 1930, every pro-American and moderate candidate was defeated. The occupation ended in 1934 and two decades later a coup brought to power the Duvalier family, who terrorized the country until 1986.

The two occupations in Nicaragua followed similar trends. After the country descended into civil war in 1909, Marines landed and helped rebels to overthrow the government. After installing Adolfo Diaz (a conservative, pro-business 36-year-old who had once worked for an American-owned gold mine) as president, the United States secured a treaty to build another canal. For the next 15 years a variety of economic interests—gold, rubber, and bananas, among others—kept a small Marine contingent in the country, where it managed the customs house, trained the Nicaraguan Guardia, and protected the American business community in Bluefields. The marines' presence was stabilizing to a degree, but it also helped American businessmen to extract sweetheart deals from the Nicaraguan government and to seize financial control of the national bank and railroads. The sight of foreign troops in the capital also generated conflict with locals, and anti-United States editorials ran in Nicaraguan newspapers. The marines responded by trashing the offices of one newspaper and destroying the press. Later that same year, marines brawled with the Managua police and killed four of them. After a US-supervised election in 1925 that pushed Diaz out of power, the marines departed.

Unfortunately, fighting broke out again almost immediately, and by 1926 Diaz was back in power and the marines returned to Nicaragua. In six months, they had brokered a peace between the warring factions, but one rebel leader, Augusto Sandino, refused to accept it. The marines battled the Sandinistas for five years. Using Thompson sub-machine guns, mortars, and even close air support, the Americans always outgunned their opponents but could not compel them to surrender. Patrols up the Coco River by Major Harold H. Utley and Captain Merritt A. Edson resulted in some innovations that would later be codified in the *Small Wars Manual*—the Marines' first attempt to author counterinsurgency doctrine. As in Haiti and the Dominican Republic, the marine-trained Guardia was of limited value, and would sometimes mutiny, mistreat their countrymen, or ally themselves with anti-American factions. By 1929, the Marines even had to station their own troops in Managua to protect the government from the Guardia.

Sandino's forces grew stronger, partially because they received regular support from Mexico (Mexico had good reason to oppose American interests in Nicaragua because the United States had occupied Veracruz in 1914 and US troops invaded northern Mexico in pursuit of Poncho Villa in 1916 and 1917). By 1931, Sandino was sending his guerillas against the foreign-owned mines and sawmills and had occupied a series of towns along the Coco River. After a relatively peaceful election in 1932, the Americans left in 1933. The new Guardia director, Anastasio Samoza, brokered a peace with Sandino then assassinated him in February 1934 and hunted down the remaining Sandinistas. In 1936 Samoza overthrew the newly elected president and established a dictatorship that lasted for four decades.

These were the largest, but not the only, military operations of the so-called "Banana Wars." The United States also intervened in Honduras seven times between 1903 and 1929, conducted shows of force in Costa Rican waters, and crossed into Mexico on nine different occasions to chase bandits and battle Mexican troops (see Map 11.1). In 1914, nearly 4,000 marines and bluejackets occupied the port city of Vera Cruz, Mexico, after Mexican authorities mistakenly arrested some American sailors and then refused to issue a 21-gun salute as an apology. During the seven-month occupation naval aviators conducted their first reconnaissance flights in a combat environment. In these and other naval landings, the threats to the US security were minimal or nonexistent, but considerable economic interests were at stake. By 1921, the United States had intervened militarily in virtually every independent nation in the Caribbean littoral.

The Marines in China, 1900–1941

No occupation lasted longer or involved as many military assets as the one in China (see Map 11.2). What began as a company-sized guard force in 1900 had grown by the 1920s to a force of 5,000 soldiers and marines reinforced by over 50 American warships in Chinese waters. Five hundred mounted "Horse Marines" guarded the Legation Quarter (a walled neighborhood for foreign residents) in Peking (now Beijing) and another 1,000 army troops guarded Americans living in the city of Tientsin. The shallow-draft gunboats of the Yangtze River Patrol steamed up and down China's longest river, and destroyers of the Asiatic Fleet patrolled the coasts. By 1928, an entire Marine regiment guarded the International Settlement in Shanghai, reinforced by a full artillery battalion, an engineer company, tanks, and an aviation element with 18 aircraft. The stated purpose of the American forces was to protect the territorial integrity of China from European and Japanese colonizers, but the bulk of the work was protecting American businesses and Protestant missionaries.

Trade with China is as old as the United States itself: the first American ship visited China in 1784 and earned a profit of 25 percent by exchanging fur pelts for porcelain, silk, and tea. The myth of the fabled "China market" quickly took hold. The long coastline and cities along the rivers were ideal for maritime trade and all the major powers—Britain, France, Portugal, and later Belgium, Germany, Italy, Japan, and Russia—vied for exclusive trading zones, called "concessions." The British acted first and most aggressively by forcing opium on the Chinese and then fighting two "Opium Wars" to preserve their right to trade drugs for tea and porcelain. The treaties (appropriately called "unequal treaties") gave the British the island of Hong Kong, ports for trading, and "extraterritoriality" status, which exempted British citizens from Chinese laws. In 1844, the wily American diplomat Caleb Cushing negotiated the Treaty of Wanghia, which gave the United States "most favored nation" status and all the same trade protections conferred to the Europeans in their treaties. For the rest of the nineteenth century, Americans engaged in "hitchhiking imperialism": enjoying the advantages of the unequal treaties without stationing any serious military power

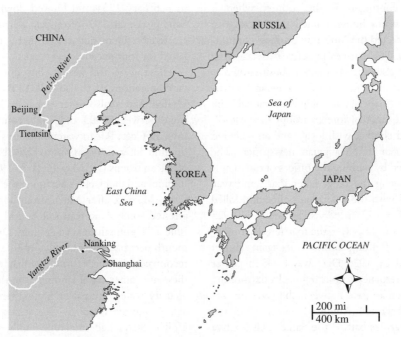

Map 11.2   The United States in China, 1900–1941.

in the country. Missionaries flowed in, as did Standard Oil, a steamship company, tobacco interests, and investors seeking to build railroads.

The presence of so many foreigners in China seriously weakened the government, and in 1899 an anti-foreign insurgency began when the Society of Righteous and Harmonious Fists (the "Boxers") attacked railway and telegraph stations and called for the expulsion of all non-Chinese. As the Boxers grew in number and began slaughtering Chinese Christian converts, the Chinese government debated whether to fight or join with the insurgents. Inside Peking, 1,000 American, European, and Japanese businessmen and diplomats huddled together in the Legation Quarter protected by an entirely insufficient force of 300 international soldiers and 50 US marines.

In July 1900, the Chinese government sided with the Boxers and declared war on the foreigners. As the westerners organized a rescue force, those inside the Legation Quarter subsisted on horsemeat and endured 55 days of artillery shelling, sniping, and fires started by the Boxers. But the real fighting happened outside Peking as a combined force of 20,000 American, English, German, Japanese, and Russian troops landed at the mouth of the Pei-ho River and fought their way through Tientsin to Peking. Accompanying them were 500 marines, including the ubiquitous Littleton W. T. Waller and Smedley Butler. Butler was shot in the chest and survived; Waller led his battalion on a costly attack, after which he called for more troops and more whiskey (see Figure 11.2). When the civilians were finally rescued in August, the Marines had suffered few battle

Figure 11.2 US Marines in a relief party in Beijing during the Boxer Rebellion, 1900.

casualties, but almost half of their numbers had been rendered ineffective by heat exhaustion. Two hundred foreigners had been killed, as had several thousand Chinese Christian converts and unknown numbers of Boxers and innocent civilians.

In the aftermath of the rebellion, the foreign powers forced the Chinese to sign the "Boxer Protocol," which was perhaps the most unequal of all of the unequal treaties. The agreement forced China to accept permanent foreign troops in the country and to pay an indemnity of over $300 million—more than twice the entire annual income of the Chinese government. Concerned that the Europeans would turn their concessions into formal colonies, the United States issued a series of "Open Door" notes to European governments urging them to respect the territorial and administrative integrity of China and to allow equality of opportunity in trade and investment in all of China. This was only partially altruistic, for, as one of the smallest commercial powers in China, the United States wanted to ensure its own access to markets.

For four decades after the Boxer Rebellion, marines guarded the Legation Quarter in Peking and the International Settlement in Shanghai. The International Settlement was, in effect, a city within a city: immune from Chinese laws, the 70,000 foreign residents had their own courts, police forces, and even a volunteer militia. Life was far different here from that in the stateside Marine Corps: Officers had two or three Chinese servants each, and most enlisted marines hired a cook and a "boy" to do laundry and rode into town on man-pulled rickshaws for liberty. The commander of the Legation Guard and his wife had 15 servants. Except for the occasional parade or marksmanship exercise, most of the "China Marines" spent their time in athletics, at dances, and or in the bars and brothels in town.

Life for the Navy was more rustic. The sailors of the Yangtze Patrol had the job of ensuring free access for American-flagged merchant vessels along the river and protecting the lives and property of American missionaries and businessmen in the area. Standard Oil, the American Tobacco Company, and the National City Bank were eager for the protection, but most of the rural Chinese were suspicious of the foreigners who had brought guns and opium up their river since the 1830s. It was an open secret that the American-owned Yangtze Rapid Steamboat Company illegally ran opium up the river in the 1920s, often with a US Navy escort. After the Chinese (Xinhai) Revolution began in 1911, free navigation was regularly threatened as Chinese troops fired on passing vessels and local commanders tried to tax cargo or commandeer American ships. The Navy responded by stationing guards on board the civilian steamers and escorting vessels with both gunboats and destroyers. Sailors also landed on occasion to disperse mobs, protect infrastructure, and rescue American missionaries, who, by the 1920s, comprised half of the 6,636 Protestant evangelizers then in China.

After Japan invaded China in 1937, starting the war that would directly lead to Pearl Harbor, the Navy and Marine Corps' mission in China grew more complicated. The Americans' job was both to protect lives and property and to guarantee the territorial integrity of China against colonizers; the Japanese invasion threatened both. Tientsin, Peking, and Shanghai all fell in the first year of the war while the Americans watched from their walled enclaves. By the end of 1937, the Japanese controlled the lower Yangtze with a force of 20,000 men and commercial traffic on the river slowed and then stopped. The day before Japanese forces began the Rape of Nanking, Japanese airplanes attacked and sank the *Panay*, a US Navy gunboat floating peacefully nearby. A testy diplomatic standoff with Japan ensued, but neither side wanted war with the other yet and the Japanese apologized. From 1938 to 1941, the United States continued to assert its treaty rights in the International Settlement, but the Japanese challenged them regularly, particularly as Americans continued to provide rhetorical support to Chang-Kai-Shek's forces as they fought the Japanese. American dependents left in 1940, the Yangtze Patrol abandoned the river, and the Fourth Marines decamped in November 1941. When the Japanese attacked Pearl Harbor on December 7, 1941, just one vessel of the Yangtze Patrol remained in Shanghai, the gunboat *Wake*, and the Japanese took it without firing a shot.

Legacies of the "Banana Wars"

What to make of these various operations and occupations? It is clear that some of the efforts were successful, particularly in regard to the larger European powers. A principal goal of the Caribbean interventions was to contain European imperial expansion and, in this

USS *Panay*

The *Panay* was one of six river gunboats commissioned in 1925 for the Yangtze River Patrol, which performed most of the riverine duties of the tiny US Asiatic Fleet. All named for American colonial possessions (Panay is an island in the Philippines), these shallow-drafted, lightly armed vessels spent most of their time escorting American-flagged merchant vessels along the Yangtze River and responding to attacks with their two 3-inch guns and eight .30-caliber machine guns. Standard Oil's barges and the commercial steamers of the Robert Dollar line were usually the most in need of escorts, but Yangtze gunboats also occasionally rescued missionaries from riots and sent landing parties to guard shore facilities. After the Chinese Civil War broke out in 1911, gunboats also found themselves preventing rebel factions from commandeering US vessels for troop transport. For the crew of roughly 60, gunboat life was at times boring but was made pleasant by Chinese shipboard

USS *Panay* underway off Woosung, China, 1928.

servants and regular stops along the treaty ports. Life on the Yangtze Patrol was romanticized in Richard McKenna's 1962 novel *The Sand Pebbles*, which later became a popular film.

In 1937, Japan invaded China, seized Shanghai, and terrorized the capital, Nanking. The "Rape of Nanking" has been enshrined in memory as one of the largest, most vicious war crimes of World War II, but, for the United States, it also involved a diplomatic standoff and a war scare with Japan. After

evacuating American citizens from Nanking, the *Panay* anchored off shore alongside three Standard Oil barges. Even though the *Panay* displayed several large American flags marking it as a neutral ship, Japanese aircraft attacked and sank the gunboat and the barges, killing three Americans and wounding three dozen others. Japan later apologized and paid reparations to the survivors, but the incident was an early indication of Japan's plans to evict all westerners from Asia and to colonize it themselves.

success, the Navy and Marine Corps played major roles. No rivals established new bases in the Caribbean; American control over the Panama Canal went uncontested; and, under American supervision, the republics repaid most of their debts. Naval power and forceful diplomacy turned the Caribbean into an American sphere of influence—an American lake.

Except for this strategic victory, however, the Banana Wars' legacies are mostly negative. In terms of national security, the operations in Cuba probably made the United States less secure in the long run. It was American support that kept Colonel Batista in

power for so long, and, once Fidel Castro took power in 1959, he made the reasonable choice to side with America's archenemy, the Soviet Union. That decision led directly to the CIA-orchestrated Bay of Pigs invasion and the Cuban Missile Crisis—the single most dangerous moment in the history of the world.

Operations in China had less immediate, but still concerning, long-term effects. The attempts to prevent competitors from dominating parts of China did not work, though it is hard to see how they could have, given Japan's belligerence. Moreover, despite the rhetoric of the "Open Door," the United States took advantage of the unequal treaties and stationed ships in Chinese waters and thousands of troops in China's cities. This helped to push China into civil war and, later, into a Cold War alliance with the Soviet Union. Chinese resentment at the West's role in its "Century of Humiliation" persists to this day, and with good reason. To the Chinese, the Americans' use of military power to advance economic interests was not only ineffective; it was immoral.

Relations with Latin America were also harmed by the many interventions and occupations. Anti-US sentiment lingers throughout Latin America to this day, even as most governments want stronger political and economic relations with the United States. People do not easily forget when foreign soldiers arrive on their shores or provide military equipment to autocratic regimes, as the United States did throughout the region for decades. American corporations also extracted much but gave little back, with help from the Navy and Marines (see Figure 11.3). This may be acceptable in business but is less appropriate for representatives of a government that claimed to be better than the European colonizers. America's influence has always stemmed from the power of its example, and here it is fair to say that, in the Banana Wars, the United States sacrificed the moral high ground for temporary profit.

Finally, the United States never accomplished the most idealistic goals of the many small wars—to use military occupations to stabilize governments, install democratic regimes, and uplift societies through development. While marines and sailors did build schools, roads, hospitals, and wells, most of those fell into disrepair almost immediately upon the Americans' departure. Each of the major insurgencies the United States faced in Latin America grew larger over time, and, because of the problems of identifying combatants, Marine tactics became more brutal. In Nicaragua and the Dominican Republic, the police forces the United States created to support democratic governments became the principal tools for overthrowing them. In all of the countries in which America intervened, the norm was either chronic instability or the iron grip of dictatorship—both before and after the Americans intervened. As a distinguished historian of the Marine Corps and its role in US interventions has put it, "the greatest lesson" learned by the United States in the Banana Wars "was that American interests in the Caribbean could not be secured by any military occupation of acceptable duration and cost," a lesson being relearned in twenty-first-century Iraq and Afghanistan.[9]

Figure 11.3   Marine veterans of American interventions and recipients of the Medal of Honor. From left: Sergeant Major John H. Quick, Major General Wendell C. Neville, Lieutenant General John A. Lejune, and Major General Smedley D. Butler.

---

[9] Allan R. Millett, *Semper Fidelis* (1991), 211.

CHAPTER 12

Naval Rivalry and World War I at Sea, 1900–1920

At the turn of the twentieth century, the great powers dominated international affairs. A great power possessed the military, naval, diplomatic, and economic clout to demand that its government's opinion on any question of war or diplomacy must count in the calculations of others. Generally speaking, great powers considered themselves wholly sovereign in their internal affairs, and any effort by a foreign government to interfere in their politics, spheres of influence, or territories would almost certainly lead to war. However, great powers did not extend this courtesy to lesser powers. Great powers considered it their prerogative to interfere in various ways with the governments within their sphere of influence, and often administrated large empires that completely absorbed foreign nations under their control. In 1900, most counted five counties in the ranks of the great powers: Austria-Hungary, Britain, France, Germany, and Russia. Italy was approaching such status, and both Japan and the United States sought to join this exclusive club.

In this era, contemporary observers judged the relative positions of great powers by their overseas possessions, the size of their armies and, thanks to the contributions of Alfred Thayer Mahan, the strength of their navies. While the US Army remained small, particularly in comparison to the armies of other great powers, the Spanish–American War brought the United States new overseas possessions, and the US Navy gained prestige from its victories at Manila Bay and Santiago. Even with these successes, however, the United States was not a leading naval power in 1900. Prior to 1900, several great powers, suspicious of the motives of the others, had begun the steady construction of new warships. As the United States looked to enter the ranks of the great powers—a move that would certainly affect the balance of power in Europe—the United States pursued naval construction and modernization of the naval bureaucracy to meet the demands of the sort of large, industrial navy that would befit a great power of the early twentieth century. This effort created the navy that the United States would use to fight World War I, and helped to create the atmosphere that led to the Washington Naval Treaties in the 1920s.

Naval Races

In many ways, the naval races that contributed so greatly to the diplomatic tension in the years before World War I began in 1890. That year, Kaiser Wilhelm II of Germany decided to assert his position in the German government and dismissed his chancellor, Otto von Bismarck. Bismarck, who had been instrumental in unifying Germany under the Prussian Crown, had long pursued a policy that avoided entangling Germany in the race for overseas colonies, and thus avoided building the warships needed to support them. However, Wilhelm believed in the

America, Sea Power, and the World, First Edition. Edited by James C. Bradford.
© 2016 John Wiley & Sons, Inc. Published 2016 by John Wiley & Sons, Inc.

theories of Alfred Thayer Mahan, and that a powerful navy and overseas colonies would bring Germany to its rightful place as the world's leading great power. Thus Wilhelm became a strong supporter of naval construction. Wilhelm also reversed Bismarck's long-standing diplomatic policy of courting Russia to an extent that kept it from allying with France. Lacking German support, Russia decided to kill two birds with one stone: the Russian government needed a strong ally in European politics and also needed investment in its industrializing economy. France needed a friend and had capital to invest in Russia. This relationship led to a formal alliance in 1894.

The Franco-Russian Alliance set off alarm bells in Britain. Despite assurances that the alliance was generally directed at Germany and Austria-Hungary, the British saw not only the alignment of their two main colonial rivals but also the alliance of the second and third most powerful navies in the world. While Britain had the largest navy, it was not clear that the Royal Navy could defeat the next two strongest navies allied against it. This concern led to the creation of the Two-Power Standard, which committed the British government to maintaining a navy that would be larger than the next two combined. To meet that standard, the British began a period of intense naval construction, adding 37 new battleships to the Royal Navy between 1894 and 1904, compared to 17 in the previous decade.

Even as British fears of a combined French–Russian fleet began to cool around the turn of the century, Britain faced a much more serious threat to its naval dominance: Germany. In 1898, the Reichstag authorized the construction of 16 new battleships over the next three years. This bill alone did not overly concern the British, as the planned German building did not substantially alter the calculations that went into the Two-Power Standard.

In the late 1890s, the Boer War stoked tensions between Germany and Britain. In 1896, British forces in South Africa attacked the Transvaal Republic, an independent nation in South Africa founded by the Boers, the descendants of Dutch settlers from previous centuries. The Boers repulsed this attack by British forces, and Kaiser Wilhelm congratulated them on their success. The British viewed Wilhelm's telegram both as an offer of German support for

the Boers and as German interference in a British sphere of influence. The British soon suspected that the Germans were supplying the Boers with arms and began stopping German freighters and searching them for contraband. Helpless to prevent this, Admiral Alfred von Tirpitz, Secretary of State of the German Imperial Naval Office and head of the German navy, returned to the Reichstag in 1900 and won approval for 38 battleships, and enough cruisers and destroyers to support them. This got the attention of the British government, not only because a hostile fleet of that size would annihilate the Two-Power Standard but also because this program seemed to target Britain directly.

The British responded by making Admiral Sir John "Jackie" Fisher First Sea Lord. Fisher quickly launched a massive effort to meet the German threat. In order to provide the sailors required to man the large number of modern ships he wanted built, he began decommissioning older ships at a rapid pace. He also began redeploying the Royal Navy to face Germany. He recalled ships from overseas stations to reinforce the Home Fleet. In 1902 diplomats signed the Anglo-Japanese Naval Alliance, which allowed the Royal Navy to transfer capital ships home from the Pacific. Three years later, the Royal Navy closed its dockyard in Jamaica, called home the ships stationed there, and, in doing so, left the US Navy dominant in the Caribbean.

The British grew increasingly concerned with the rise of German power at sea, on land, and economically. Since the Napoleonic Wars, the British had pursued a diplomatic policy of avoiding long-term entanglements with other great powers, particularly on the European continent, and had formed alliances with other powers only when immediately useful. During that time, Britain also grew to control a worldwide empire, largely defended by the Royal Navy. In 1904, when war broke out between Japan (an ally of Britain) and Russia (an ally of France), there was a chance that the war would force Britain and France to fight against each other, which would only work in Germany's favor. To avoid this possibility, Britain and France negotiated what became known as the Entente Cordiale, a series of agreements between the two powers that both greatly reduced friction between them and saw them promise to support each

Table 12.1   Naval arms race, 1900–1914.

	Capital ships			
Nation	1900	1905	1910	1914
Britain	37	56	58(7)	70(24)
France	10	12	14(0)	22(4)
Russia	12	11	6(0)	12(2)
Italy	3	7	11(0)	11(3)
Germany	6	18	27(4)	40(17)
Austria-Hungary	0	3	7(0)	12(3)
United States	7	10	27(4)	33(10)
Japan	6	6	13(0)	18(4)

Figures in parentheses are dreadnoughts. These are included in the totals.

other's anti-German diplomatic efforts. While the British never formally agreed to a military alliance, the Entente did bring them closer to the Franco-Russian Alliance, arraying it more strongly against Germany. Over the years before World War I, the British and the French also entered into a number of tentative military agreements that defined how British and French forces would cooperate if Germany invaded France and Britain agreed to join the war.

The Anglo-German naval race took a major turn in 1905–1906, when, in the course of 14 months, the British laid down, constructed, and commissioned HMS *Dreadnought*. *Dreadnought* was the first battleship completed (though not the first battleship started) with a battery primarily composed of heavy guns. Before *Dreadnought*, battleships had carried a main battery consisting of four 12-inch guns. *Dreadnought* carried ten, though only eight guns could actually fire on either broadside. This gave *Dreadnought* twice the firepower of any older battleship. These guns were laid using a more advanced fire-control system, designed to outrange ships currently in service. In addition, *Dreadnought* was slightly larger than earlier battleships, more heavily armored, and equipped with more efficient turbine engines, making it faster and more fuel efficient than its predecessors. Considered an experimental ship while under construction, it was such a complete success that subsequent battleships built on its design were called "dreadnoughts." Jackie Fisher

also ordered several large cruisers, called battle cruisers, built on *Dreadnought's* pattern but with less armor, making them faster.

Dreadnought's arrival completely upset the naval races in Europe (see Table 12.1). Britain had built up a massive lead in battleships since the 1880s, but, with dreadnought battleships entering service rapidly after 1906, that lead became increasingly less important until, by 1910 or so, it had virtually disappeared. The race now concentrated on the number of dreadnoughts the great powers could put into service. The Germans responded to *Dreadnought's* commissioning with two new Naval Laws. The first, in 1906, ordered four new battle cruisers, to match those the Germans believed Britain intended to build. The most significant, however, came in 1908, when the German government committed itself to laying down 12 new battleships over the next three years. This matched the rate of British construction, which would only give Britain a very narrow lead in battleships if Germany continued to keep pace. Britain responded with a series of measures. In 1909, the Royal Navy ordered eight new battleships the next year instead of four, and later began commissioning battleships with 13.5-inch guns, to give British ships a firepower advantage over German designs. After 1909, the two sides settled into a steady state of competition in which the Germans tried to match British technical advances while the British attempted to build three battleships for every two the Germans constructed.

Nor were Britain and Germany the only nations building up their navies during the years leading up to World War I. In the Mediterranean, Austria-Hungary's navy, under the leadership of Archduke Franz Ferdinand, transitioned from a traditional coastal defense fleet to a blue-water navy, with ambitions to be a major player in Mediterranean power politics. Austria-Hungary's sudden naval growth, combined with Britain's retreat from the Mediterranean to face Germany, forced both France and Italy to revive long-stagnant naval building programs, as the three powers jockeyed for naval and diplomatic supremacy in the region. Fresh off major victories against the Russian navy, the Japanese navy used its newfound prestige to obtain more and more naval construction. And, of course, the United States, freshly on the scene after the Spanish–American War, had to keep up.

USS *South Carolina*

While HMS *Dreadnought* was the first all-big-gun battleship commissioned, it was not the first one ordered. That honor belongs to USS *South Carolina* and its sister ship, USS *Michigan*. These ships not only abandoned previous, less effective gunnery designs but also adopted a turret layout that included super-firing fore and aft turrets, which allowed all guns on board the ships to fire to either broadside. Other navies eventually adopted this design after experimenting with less effective designs. The only thing these ships lacked, technologically speaking, was turbine engines. Instead, they used older, less effective triple-expansion engines, which limited their speed. Because of their slow speed, they generally sailed with older battleships rather than ships of later construction. *South Carolina* was laid down in 1906 in Cramp and Sons Shipyard in Philadelphia and finally entered service in 1910. From 1911 to 1913 it made diplomatic visits to a number of European and Caribbean ports, and in 1913–1914 it supported US operations in Veracruz and Tampico, Mexico, and delivered marines to Port-au-Prince, Haiti. Once World War I began in Europe, *South Carolina* returned to the United States and began engaging in training exercises as part of the Atlantic Fleet. Upon US entry into the war, *South Carolina* escorted American Expeditionary Force troopships across the Atlantic and continued training new officers and sailors off the Atlantic coast. Once the war ended, it made four trips carrying veterans back to the United States through 1919, and in 1920–1921 it resumed its training duties. *South Carolina* left service and was scrapped in 1924, in accordance with the Washington Naval Treaty.

USS *South Carolina*, c. 1910–1914. *Source:* US Naval History and Heritage Command # NH 61225.

Theodore Roosevelt and Naval Expansion

On September 5, 1901, Leon Czolgosz, an anarchist, shot President William McKinley twice in the stomach, and, despite the best efforts of McKinley doctors, the president died nine days later. This thrust McKinley's vice president, Theodore "Teddy" Roosevelt, into the presidency. Roosevelt, a disciple of Mahan, backed the continued growth of the US Navy. An Anglophile, the former assistant secretary of the navy believed that Britain and the United States shared common interests in the world. Thus he adopted Germany as his yardstick for determining the size of the US Navy.

In 1903, the General Board of the Navy issued a report that called for 48 battleships to be built by 1920, with 32 to be stationed in the Atlantic and 16 in the Pacific. The report also called for a more balanced fleet—for every two battleships, it called for one armored cruiser, seven protected cruisers, three destroyers, two colliers, two other auxiliaries, and a transport. Roosevelt personally did not like the idea of a long-term naval plan, which he did not expect Congress to fund anyway. Still, he managed to convince Congress to increase the Navy's yearly budget from $81 million to $118 million over the course of his first term, though appropriations slowed as Congress became more focused on the economy. In 1905, Roosevelt and Admiral George Dewey, head of the General Board, agreed—over the public advice of Mahan—that the Navy would begin construction of all-big-gun battleships. These both preceded the commencement of *Dreadnought*'s construction and forced Britain's hand in building ships to the new pattern.

While a great many debates revolved around battleships, the Navy also experimented with a number of new technologies during Roosevelt's administration. The first submarine entered service at the turn of the century, and another 18 were commissioned by 1910. These boats were small and were designed for coastal and harbor defense, but were the first submarines that entered regular naval service in any nation. Over the decade, the Navy improved submarine designs, making them larger, increasing the number of torpedoes they carried, and improved their cruising and underwater range. And, of course, the Navy took great interest in the Wright brothers' 1903 flight at Kitty Hawk, though it did not purchase its first aircraft until 1911.

William Taft and Naval Reform

The Great White Fleet returned from its circumnavigation of the world on February 22, 1909. Two weeks later, Theodore Roosevelt's hand-picked successor, William Howard Taft, was sworn in as president of the United States. While overall a great success, the voyage did bring to light some weaknesses in the Navy, which Taft and his Secretary of the Navy, George von Lengerke Meyer, moved to correct by making a number of reforms based on the lessons of the cruise—some immediate, some longer term. Immediately, Meyer directed modifications to existing ships to improve their seakeeping (i.e., their ability to operate in all conditions) and to support new fire-control equipment. He established committees and prizes to promote more efficient steaming and navigation. Meyer also made efforts to improve conditions for enlisted sailors. He established the Great Lakes Training Center, which modernized basic training for sailors, and improved the training system for sailors in the fleet in order to bring enlisted men up to speed in their increasingly technical profession. He also ordered improvements in recreational facilities ashore and afloat for sailors and made it a policy to, when possible, give sailors Sunday off, improving their lives and morale. Additionally, Meyer made a number of improvements in accounting and personnel practices, making naval spending more efficient and helping to move officers out of positions they were no longer physically capable of performing.

Long term, the General Board, with Meyer's support, undertook to modernize the US battleship fleet in accordance with the lessons of the Great White Fleet. In particular, the Great White Fleet showed the importance of a tactically homogeneous fleet—that is, it would be a major advantage in a naval engagement if US ships had similar designs, speeds, and maneuverability. When the Great White Fleet undertook maneuvers and cruising, the disparity in speeds, turning radii, and other design factors had hampered operations. To solve this problem, the Board called for all future warship designs, no matter their size or armament, to meet certain criteria: a top speed of 21 knots, a 700-yard turning radius, and a cruising range of 8,000 nautical miles. In addition, all battleships would carry four main turrets, two fore and two aft, and an armor scheme that concentrated armor over the areas of the ship vital to its ability to maneuver and fight. In 1911, the Navy laid down the first ships designed to meet these specifications, and it continued producing ships to this standard into the early 1920s with few changes other than the caliber of the main guns.

Woodrow Wilson and a Navy Second to None

In 1912, Theodore Roosevelt decided to stand for election once again, against William Taft and Woodrow Wilson. Roosevelt and Taft effectively split the Republican vote, allowing Woodrow Wilson to win the presidency. Wilson selected Josephus Daniels as his Secretary of the Navy. Daniels, generally speaking, was less effective a secretary than Meyer. However, he did have an able lieutenant in Assistant Secretary of the Navy Franklin Roosevelt, who supervised naval installations. While Daniels' most famous act as secretary was banning alcohol for officers (sailors had been prohibited from having alcohol on board ship in 1899), Daniels continued much of the program laid down by the Roosevelt and Taft administrations, supporting the construction of more battleships without improving the number or quality of cruisers and destroyers in the fleet. During his administration, the Navy moved from experimenting with aviation to formally adopting it into service. In 1910 and 1911, the Navy experimented with flying planes off ships and developing floatplanes. In 1913, Daniels appointed a board, headed by Captain Washington Irving Chambers, to study the aeronautical needs of the Navy. That board established a training program at the Pensacola Navy Yard, establishing the first naval air station.

While Wilson seemed content to allow the Navy to coast along on the momentum generated by his predecessors, the outbreak of World War I in 1914 forced a reexamination of American naval and military priorities. While the United States declared its neutrality at the outbreak of the war and while Wilson hoped to keep the United States out of the war, the possibility

that the Navy would need to fight compelled certain changes. With the growth of the Navy in previous years, it seemed likely that it would need to coordinate the activity of several fleets and squadrons across the globe. This effort would have to be overseen by an officer with a position superior to that of the fleet commanders, and this led to the creation of the position of the chief of naval operations. Admiral William S. Benson, the first man to hold this office, helped to define its role through the coordination of Navy and Marine Corps forces in the Caribbean and Central America, before leading the Navy into World War I.

In 1916, as the war continued, Wilson came to believe that, in order to secure the place of the United States among the great powers, America needed a Navy "second to none"—that is, one superior to all others, including that of Britain. To this end, he helped to pass the Naval Appropriations Act of 1916. While the act fell short of Wilson's ambitions, it still funded the largest expansion of the US Navy in history. In three years, the "Big Navy Act" spent $500 million and called for the construction of 10 new battleships, six new battle cruisers, 30 submarines, and 50 destroyers, as well as expanding port facilities and investing in industry and other projects. If this construction ran to completion, it would catapult the US Navy past the Royal Navy in the number of dreadnoughts afloat and in total tonnage of battleships. However, many of these ships would not be ready by 1917, when the US Navy entered World War I.

World War I

On June 28, 1914, Gavrilo Princip assassinated Austrian Archduke Franz Ferdinand and his wife, Sophie. The investigation that followed quickly linked Princip to a group with connections to the government of Serbia. The Austrians wanted a war to destroy Serbia, but Serbia was allied with Russia. Austrian leaders asked for German support against Russia, and Germany promised to back them to the hilt. On July 23, 1914, Austria presented an ultimatum to Serbia that, in effect, demanded that Serbia surrender much of its sovereignty to Austria or face a war. Serbia called on Russia, and Russia was unwilling to betray Serbia for the second time in a decade. To do so would effectively end Russians ambitions to place the Balkan kingdoms in its sphere of influence. Once it became clear that Russia would back Serbia, Germany prepared to support Austria against Russia. For Germany, this meant carrying out plans for a war with Russia, which called for invading France, Russia's chief ally in Europe. Germany hoped to knock France out of the resulting war before Russia could mobilize its vast army. So, when Austria declared war on Serbia and Russia declared war on Austria, Germany declared war on France and invaded Belgium en route to France. Germany's invasion of Belgium triggered an 80-year-old agreement between Belgium and Britain, and brought Britain into the war on the side of France and Russia. Italy decided to stay neutral until 1915, when it joined the Franco–British–Russian alliance.

At the start of the war in August 1914, Germany attacked through Belgium into northern France, bypassing the heavily wooded Ardennes region and the hills of the Vosges Mountains, along with most of France's fortresses. The French army redeployed to meet the German attack, and, in early September, the last French reserves met the final German push on the banks of the Marne to the northeast of Paris and halted the Germans. Falling back on their supply lines, the Germans began to dig in. By the end of October, both sides had largely run out of ammunition and artillery shells, and began constructing opposing trench lines that ran from the Alps to the English Channel.

From 1915 to 1918, much of the history of the Western Front consists of efforts to break out of the defensive trench lines, where infantry in protective trenches, with supportive fire from machine guns and artillery backed by efficient and untouchable rail reinforcement, made it impossible to launch the standard assaults all combatants understood as the proper way to do things. In 1915, the Allies turned to firepower, assembling thousands of artillery pieces to fire hundreds of thousands of shells into the German trenches in order to clear them ahead of a massive assault. This failed, as the Germans simply withdrew their men from the target area, then, since the Allies had tipped their hand, packed the attack areas with reserves that cut the Allied attacks to ribbons.

That same year, Britain launched the Gallipoli Campaign, which was designed to break the deadlock on the Western Front, knock the Ottoman Empire out of the war, draw Greece and Bulgaria into the war on the side of the Allies, and open a line of supply to Russia through the Black Sea. Such an attack was in keeping with the "peripheral strategy," followed by Britain since the time of William Pitt. First Lord of the Admiralty Winston Churchill planned to use obsolete battleships to break through defenses guarding the Dardanelles and capture the Ottoman capital, Constantinople. When that attack failed in April, what grew into a 78,000-man Mediterranean Expeditionary Force landed on the Gallipoli Peninsula only to be pinned down by Ottoman forces and compelled to withdraw in January 1916. The campaign was a stunning defeat for Britain.

All attempts to break the deadlock on the Western Front failed in 1916, and, as 1917 approached, both Russia and Germany began to grow desperate. With failure at the front, and economic depression at home, massive demonstrations in Russian cities forced Tsar Nicholas II to abdicate in favor of a democratic–socialist government in February 1917. This government tried to continue the war but faced famine, disintegrating rail networks, and an army nearly in open revolt. In November 1917, the radical Bolsheviks overthrew the interim government and started the Russian Civil War. The fighting on this front came to a formal end in March 1918, with the Treaty of Brest–Litovsk.

However, while the Central Powers were winning on the Eastern Front, they faced their own problems at home. The Allied blockade soon began to take its toll. Germany lacked sufficient domestic production to feed its population, and imports from Austria began to slow in 1915. During the winter of 1916–1917, the German populace suffered from a lack of food and coal for heat, and industrial production slowed as a result. In January 1917, German leaders decided they had little choice but to resume unrestricted attacks on merchant shipping near Britain. This strategy had proven very successful in 1915 but had drawn severe criticism from neutral parties, especially the United States, since the Germans did not make a serious effort to avoid attacking neutral ships. Eventually, pressure from the United States forced Germany to issue the Sussex Pledge in May 1916, in which the Germans agreed to end submarine attacks against passenger liners and merchant shipping before providing for the safety of crewmen. However, in early 1917, Germany had to put more military and economic pressure on Britain, and decided to resume unrestricted submarine warfare. Knowing that reneging on the Sussex Pledge might bring the United States into the war against Germany, German Foreign Minister Arthur Zimmerman hatched a plan to distract the United States. He sent a telegram asking Mexico to ally with Germany and declare war on the United States, as well as asking it to convince the Japanese to switch sides in the war. In return, Germany would support Mexican claims for lands lost in the Mexican–American War. This ploy quickly backfired: first, Mexico was in the midst of a civil war and in no shape to launch an invasion of the United States, and, second, Zimmerman sent the telegram via a wire monitored by British intelligence. The British had broken German diplomatic codes and passed the Zimmerman telegram to the United States in February, just as the Germans resumed unrestricted submarine warfare. On April 2, 1917, Wilson asked Congress to declare war against Germany, which Congress did four days later.

The War against Shipping

When the Italians decided to support the Allies, they delivered a preponderance of naval force to that group of belligerents. This allowed the Allies to blockade the Central Powers, preventing their access to the markets of the world, particularly food markets. However, unlike the blockades of the past, which required close surveillance of enemy harbors, these blockades were carried out at a distance: either in the waters between Norway and Scotland or in the Otranto Straits, at the mouth of the Adriatic Sea. This distant blockade did allow the Central Powers the opportunity of some maneuver. This space allowed the Germans, and to a lesser extent the Austrians, to pursue a *Riskflotte* strategy. In this strategy, a smaller navy conducts operations with the hope of catching a portion of the opposing fleet away from support and destroying it. This allows the smaller fleet to weaken the larger while avoiding battles with a superior force. The combination of Allied and German strategies led to only a few major naval engagements. Most were skirmishes, such as the Austrian cruiser raid at the Battle of the Otranto Straits and the clash of British and German

battle cruisers in the Battle of Dogger Bank. The only major fleet engagement of the war occurred when the Germans attempted to catch the British by surprise in the Battle of Jutland, only to be effectively ambushed by nearly the entire Royal Navy. The fast German retreat limited German losses, but the determined refusal of the British to split apart the Grand Fleet over four years of war prevented any German successes in the North Sea.

While the surface fleets spent most of World War I avoiding each other, submarines took a toll (see Map 12.1). The Allies generally used their submarines as scouts for their surface fleets and to defend ports and harbors, but the Central Powers used submarines as commerce raiders, attempting to cut Britain off from the trade that fueled the British economy and fed the inhabitants of the British Isles. In 1914, most U-boat patrols targeted British warships, but in 1915 the Germans declared open season on British commerce. Declaring the waters around Britain and in the Mediterranean Sea to be combat zones, the Austrians and Germans proceeded to attack merchant ships without warning in those areas. While highly effective in sinking merchant ships, these attacks without warning also struck neutral shipping—mostly American—and killed many sailors and passengers on liners. This, in turn, led to protests by the United States, leading to the Germans suspending these attacks in 1916. However, the economy in Germany began to falter over the course of that year, leading the German high command to look for a way to end the war. On February 1, 1917, in violation of assurances made to the United States, the Germans announced the resumption of unrestricted submarine warfare. They knew they were taking a calculated risk but reasoned that, if they could sink 250,000 tons of shipping a month, Britain would be forced to surrender by July, long before the period of a year the Germans believed it would take the United States to mobilize and transfer sufficient forces to Europe to have an impact on the war.

The estimate of a year was essentially correct for the US Army, but the Navy was ready for action at the very start of the war. Three days after the formal declaration of war, Admiral William Sims arrived in London to establish contact with the Royal Navy and prepare the way for support from the US Navy. That support began

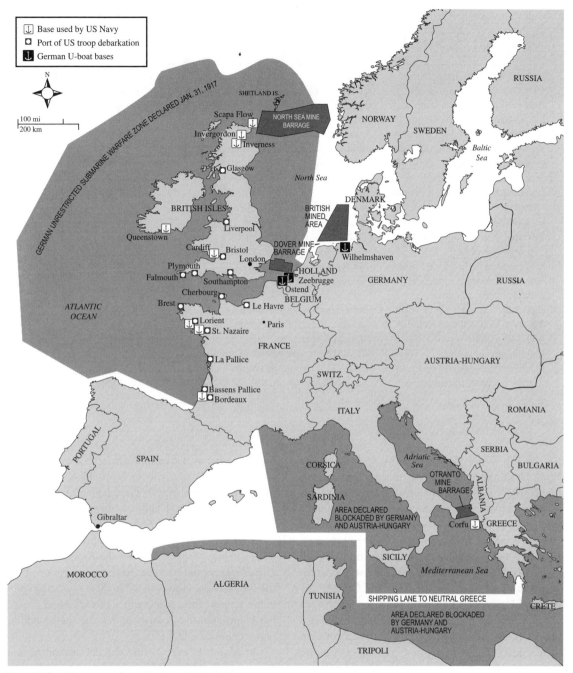

Map 12.1 The war against shipping, 1914–1917.

William S. Sims

Admiral William S. Sims (1858–1936) was born in Canada to American parents. Following his graduation from the Naval Academy in 1880, he became interested in naval reform. Appalled by the poor gunnery at Manila Bay, Sims pushed for more and better target practice. When his superiors rejected his recommendations, he appealed directly to President Theodore Roosevelt, who made him Inspector of Target Practice for the Navy and backed his reforms. Sims also supported reforms in both tactics and administration, eventually becoming president of the Naval War College. During World War I, Sims served as the London-based liaison to the Royal Navy, in which capacity he argued that the US Navy should follow Britain's lead in fighting the U-boat menace. This, combined with his Canadian birth and statements made earlier in his career, led to a widespread belief that Sims was too pro-British, which in turn led to suspicion of his proposals in Washington. After the war, Sims returned to the Naval War College and published his Pulitzer Prize-winning memoir of the war, *The Victory at Sea* (1920). As much as possible within naval regulations, this account heavily criticized Woodrow Wilson, Chief of Naval Operations Admiral William S. Benson, and Secretary of the Navy Josephus Daniels for their conduct of various operations during the war and their opposition to Sims' efforts. The account provoked a Senate investigation, but this died down as the United States attempted to move past the war. Sims retired from service in 1922.

William S. Sims
Source: Charles Carlisle Taylor, *The Life of Admiral Mahan* (1920).

to arrive less than a month after the declaration. On May 4, Destroyer Squadron 8 arrived in Queenstown (now Cobh), Ireland. When Commander Joseph Taussig was asked when his six destroyers would be ready for operations, he responded—to the surprise of Royal Navy Admiral Lewis Bayly—that "we are ready now, sir," a fact made possible by reforms completed in response to lessons learned about underway maintenance and repair from the voyage of the Great White Fleet (see Figure 12.1). In early June, the US Navy's First Aeronautical Detachment arrived in the French ports of Bordeaux and St. Nazaire. As the American Expeditionary Force began to form up and move across the Atlantic to France, it fell to the Cruiser and Transport Force under Rear Admiral Albert Gleaves to ferry them across, starting as early as May 29. The 24 cruisers and 45 transports of the Force transported 911,047 men, about half of the total personnel transported to Europe. In December 1917, the five dreadnoughts of Battleship Division 9 survived a brutal Atlantic gale to arrive in Scapa Flow. There, they joined the Royal Navy's Grand Fleet, operating in the North Sea. British officers were impressed by the machine shops and other facilities on board the US ships, which allowed them to make most repairs without entering a repair yard, and the Americans gained valuable experience in modern naval operations from the Royal Navy. However, while these operations provided support for a larger effort, the US Navy would, most importantly, contribute to the never-ending effort against the U-boat.

On March 9, even before the declaration of war, Wilson ordered Navy gun crews to man deck guns on ships heading into the war zone. When merchant ship losses rose and the US Army prepared to send the Expeditionary Force to Europe, the need for a more comprehensive U-boat strategy became clear. Sims supported British proposals for fighting the U-boats.

Figure 12.1 USS *Caldwell*, 1918. Based at Queenstown, Ireland, *Caldwell*, shown here in dazzle camouflage, served on escort duty. *Source:* US Naval History and Heritage Command # NH 55001.

He called for the United States to focus on building antisubmarine ships at the expense of large capital ships, and further called for the placement of those ships under British command for better coordination. Wilson preferred not to sacrifice American naval strength for British interests, and pushed the British to attack the U-boats at their bases. Given that the main German naval base at Wilhelmshaven was too heavily defended for any attack, the attacks would have to come against the German-held Belgian ports of Ostend and Zeebrugge. Disregarding protests from the Belgian government, the British planned raids against these ports. To succeed, the raids required the right combination of weather, wind, and tide. The first attempts, in May and June 1917, failed when the wind proved uncooperative, and later efforts in 1918 were only partially successful.

Given the difficulty of destroying the U-boats at their bases—a strategy supported by President Wilson—protecting the merchant ships became a top priority. Sims and the British Admiralty proposed switching from the independent sailing system, in which merchantmen made their way individually through U-boat-infested waters while destroyers and cruisers patrolled to hunt down and kill appearing U-boats, to an escorted convoy system. Proponents of the convoy system argued that convoys would keep merchant ships under constant surveillance, making it difficult for U-boats to approach and offering an opportunity to attack those that did, rather than hoping to stumble across one on the open ocean. The plan met opposition in Washington, where opponents protested placing merchant ships under British control and argued that convoys made ships easier for the U-boats to spot and presented fatter targets for U-boats. Opponents also calculated that convoys would slow the flow of supplies to Europe by increasing turn-around time in port as ships stood idle waiting for others to be loaded or unloaded by workers, who would be overburdened when a convoy arrived but would stand idle between convoys. Naval officers worried that merchant captains would

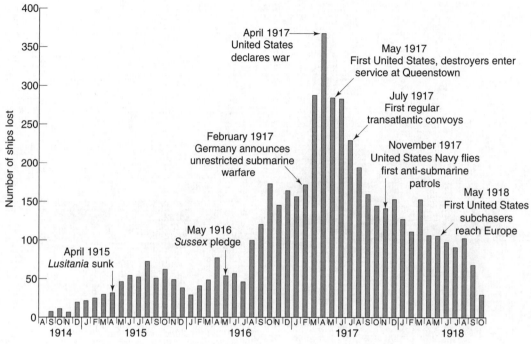

Figure 12.2   Allied shipping losses, 1914–1918. *Source:* © Cynthia Parzych Publishing, Inc.

not be able to sail in tight convoy formations without causing collisions. After more than 350,000 tons of shipping were lost in April, convoys were experimented with in May 1917. Full implementation began by July, the standard convoy consisting of 20 to 25 merchantmen with six to eight escorts. The introduction of the convoy system proved very effective in slowing the number of merchant ships sunk. In September, the number of merchant vessels lost to U-boat attacks was half of that posted in April (see Figure 12.2).

The arrival of the US Navy and American industrial might allowed the Allies to open an entirely new effort against the U-boats: the construction of a minefield that would block exits from the North Sea. While the British had constructed a number of minefields in the English Channel, they lacked the resources to manufacture and deploy enough mines to cover the 240-mile-by-15-mile area that had to be sown with mines in order to block passage between Norway and Scotland. American scientists and engineers solved the problem by inventing the antenna

mine. Ships had to strike earlier mines before the mines would detonate, but antenna mines, so named for the wires that ran from the mine to its anchor and to a float, would go off if a vessel passed near these "antennae." With their larger lethal radius, the antennae mines significantly reduced the number of mines needed to form an effective barrier. The United States had the resources to produce the nearly 75,000 mines needed, as well as provide the minelayers and escorts to lay what became the North Sea Mine Barrage. Starting in the summer of 1918, the minelayers moved in, laying mines at depths of 45, 160, and 240 feet, making it nearly impossible for U-boats to get into the Atlantic. American minelayers laid the bulk of these mines (56,000); the British laid the remaining 16,300. While these mines did not sink many submarines, since the minefield was finished as the war ended, it did drive U-boats to take the longer route through neutral, and thus unmined, Norwegian waters, thereby consuming fuel and shortening the time the U-boats could remain on station in the Atlantic.

While these efforts eventually brought German submarines to heel, they came at a cost. At a loss of 187 U-boats, the Germans sank 5,234 merchant ships, 20 destroyers, 10 battleships, and nine submarines.

Naval Aviation

The hunt for U-boats and the effort to protect the convoys encouraged the growth of naval aviation. Aircraft proved to be excellent weapons against submarines. Their altitude gave their crewmen the ability to see long distances, and their speed allowed them to cover a lot of sea in a short time. This allowed them to spot U-boats away from convoys, giving warning of any impending attack. The threat of attack by air also caused many U-boats to dive to avoid air attack, slowing their speed and thereby helping nearby merchant ships to escape. Not only did aircraft help to defend convoys and hunt U-boats; they also scouted for surface ships and executed bombing raids. The entire war effort proved the efficacy of aircraft in a naval environment while at the same time pointing the way to a number of improvements.

The need for aircraft brought about a major expansion of aviation programs in the US Navy. When the United States entered the war, the Navy had but a single air station, 109 airplanes, two balloons, and one dirigible, plus 48 officers and 239 enlisted men assigned to aviation billets. By the armistice, the Navy was operating from 43 bases—12 in the United States, two in Canada, 27 in Europe, and one each in the Azores and Panama (see Map 12.2). The Navy had over 2,000 fixed-wing aircraft, 400 of which were in the war zone, and 200 lighter-than-air ships, 53 of which were stationed in Europe (see Figure 12.3). More than 1,150 officers (almost all reservists) and 16,000 enlisted sailors crossed the Atlantic to support operations against U-boats and scout for ships at sea. Naval and Marine Corps aviators also patrolled over the front lines, engaged in dog fights with German fighters, and bombed German troops on the ground in France and Germany during both the German Peace Offensive and the Allied counterattack that followed.

This rapid, massive buildup of aviation added to American logistical requirements in Europe as men and aircraft moved to the British Isles and France.

Expansion of aviation also led to the establishment of the Naval Aircraft Factory in the Philadelphia Navy Yard to support aircraft production, particularly flying boats. A year later, the Factory completed its first delivery. The Navy also expanded pilot training from one station at Pensacola, Florida, to several across the country.

Marines on the Western Front

World War I cemented the Marine Corps' transition from the fighting tops on board ships to a body of assault infantry. The United States deployed a brigade of Marines to France, which required a massive increase in the size of the Marine Corps. This, in turn, required a substantial expansion of training facilities for the Marine Corps, and the modernization of those facilities to accept large numbers of men. In June 1917 the Fifth Marine Regiment set sail for France with the first ground-combat units of the American Expeditionary Force.

The German high command viewed the arrival of US troops in France with alarm. Following its defeat of Russia in the east, Germany began shifting troops to the Western Front. Its leaders knew that the tide was turning against them. The Allied blockade was taking a toll: Germany's people were slowly starving. Austria-Hungary, while able to grow enough food to feed its citizens, was suffering from severe inflation and the collapse of its internal infrastructure. Because of this, the Central Powers had to win the war before a large number of American troops got to France (see Figure 12.4). To that end, the Germans launched a great Peace Offensive in March 1918. Unleashing new tactics (e.g., using storm troopers to infiltrate and break through Allied trenches), the offensive reopened the road to Paris and advanced toward the French capital until May 27, when the combined efforts of French and fresh American units stopped it along the Marne River. Near Belleau Wood, the Marines made a sharp defense against a series of German flanking attacks from June 4 to June 5, holding the line and inflicting heavy casualties on the attackers. On June 6, the Marines began their counterattack against German forces in Belleau Wood and the hills around it. From June 6 to June 11, the Germans and Marines traded attacks across the wooded area,

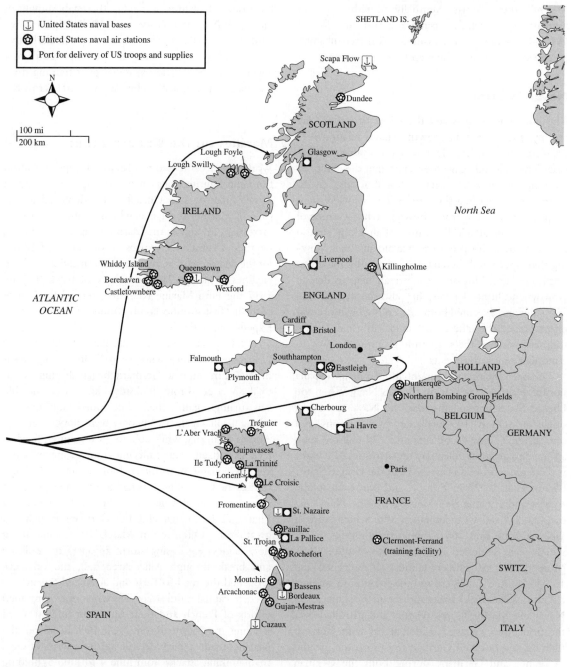

Map 12.2 The US Navy in Europe, 1917–1918.

Figure 12.3 Curtiss H-16 seaplane at NAS Wexford, Ireland, 1919.

Figure 12.4 Semaphore signaling station at Brest, France, in 1918. Brest was a major port of disembarkation for US troops arriving in France. *Source:* US Naval History and Heritage Command # NH 2443.

fighting at very close range and often struggling hand to hand. Ultimately, the sheer tenacity and fighting spirit of the Marines— rallied by Gunnery Sergeant Dan Daly's cry of "Come on you sons of bitches! Do you want to live forever?"—prevailed over the numbers the Germans brought to bear in the fighting. The struggle over Belleau Wood proved a pivotal part of the Second Battle of the Marne.

With the Peace Offensive stopped, the Allies launched the Hundred Days Offensive on the Western Front, which was a general attack all along the front. Out of Salonika, the British and French smashed through Bulgaria's defenses in the south, forcing Bulgaria from the war. Next the British and French prepared for an invasion of Hungary. Threatened with collapse, both Austria-Hungary and Turkey sued for peace. With their Allies out of the war, the army in retreat, and a hungry populace, mass demonstrations began in Germany, calling for Wilhelm's abdication. Forced to step down, Wilhelm turned Germany over to the leading opposition party. With the Germans suing for peace, the sides reached an armistice on November 11, 1918.

No war more clearly demonstrates the importance of sea power than World War I. The conflict began on land and the belligerents devoted the vast majority of their manpower and resources to land warfare, but it was the war at sea that proved decisive. When the war on land reached a deadlock, Germany—growing desperate as the Allied naval blockade strangled the Central Powers by starving them of resources of all types—adopted unrestricted submarine warfare, a strategy that led the United States to join the Allies, thereby tipping the balance conclusively against Germany and Austria. Victory at sea brought victory everywhere.

Conclusion

The American victory in the Spanish–American War vaulted the United States into the ranks of the world's great powers. In the decade that followed, those great powers measured their security and status in great part by the ability of their navies to protect their overseas empires. President Theodore Roosevelt instituted an aggressive foreign policy, and he and his successor, William Taft, supported building a navy that would give the United States great power status. In addition to constructing warships, Roosevelt and Taft reformed naval administration; improved recruitment, education, and training of sailors and officers; and invested in the development of naval technology, such as the dreadnought-pattern battleship, submarines, and aviation. Roosevelt's naval plans culminated with the world tour of the Great White Fleet, demonstrating the power and ability of the Navy. Based on the lessons learned during the circumnavigation, his successor, Taft, oversaw a variety of naval reforms. While Wilson was not initially as enthusiastic a supporter of the Navy as his predecessors, the outbreak of World War I forced the United States to move into the ranks of the great powers. To this end, in 1916, Wilson and Congress authorized naval construction to make the US Navy the most powerful in the world, and in 1917 the US Navy went to war. While there were no major naval engagements during the remainder of the war, the Navy played a major role in combating the threat posed by German submarines to commerce and troopships. These efforts included deploying escorted convoys and a large-scale mine barrage. By war's end, the United States and Britain stood head and shoulders above the rest of the world in naval power and ability.

CHAPTER 13

Finding Certainty in Uncertain Times

The Navy in the Interwar Years

Speaking at the US Naval Academy in 1922, General Board member Captain Frank Schofield offered his assessment of American foreign policy. He listed a litany of responsibilities: defense of the continental United States and its outlying possessions, such as Guam and the Philippines; enforcement of the Monroe Doctrine and the Open Door in China; and control of immigration (to include the "exclusion of Asiatics"). What connected all these obligations, in Schofield's mind, was a strong navy. Unfortunately, the policy Schofield envisioned had no political sanction. Schofield admitted that no "official statement of the national external policies of the United States" was to be found. But that did not stop the captain, nor in his opinion should it stop the US Navy, from making "its own estimate of national policies."[1]

In one sense it is easy to understand Schofield's remarks. The Navy was losing a significant part of its battle fleet. Diplomats had assembled the previous fall and by the winter of 1922 had signed treaties to defang the major powers. So, while Schofield was preaching to the choir, his message was meant to resonate beyond Annapolis to his political masters. The problem was, Schofield failed to recognize a navy had other uses to civilian leaders than simply fighting.

In fact, one of the themes of the period between 1919 and 1941 is that American presidents found the US Navy extremely useful, just not in the ways that Schofield listed but also as a diplomatic bargaining chip. Postwar administrations sought peace through naval disarmament. But those same presidents also left the service to its own devices. And so the Navy of the interwar years was weakened, but also free to figure out how to fight a modern war with not only the forces at hand but also new technologies. The Navy's ability to adapt to changing political and technological forces is the second theme of the period. As war clouds emerged on the horizon in the late 1930s, the service found itself prepared, albeit imperfectly, to fight a modern naval war.

While Schofield's remarks were implicitly directed to civilian leaders, he was also explicitly "righting the ship" from the confusing lessons of World War I. Having witnessed the transformation of the Navy in the late nineteenth and early twentieth centuries, Schofield and most of his shipmates were disciples of Alfred Thayer Mahan. To them, the world was composed of nation states all vying for overseas markets that, according to the Mahanian canon, would inevitably lead to a war that could only be won with a battleship-centered navy. Or, to a president hoping to

---

[1] Frank H. Schofield, "The General Board and the Building Programs," lecture at the Postgraduate School of the US Naval Academy, October 14, 1922, Naval War College Archives, Record Group 8.

America, Sea Power, and the World, First Edition. Edited by James C. Bradford.
© 2016 John Wiley & Sons, Inc. Published 2016 by John Wiley & Sons, Inc.

prevent entanglement in the war in Europe, the battleship might have a deterrent effect. Woodrow Wilson promised a "navy second to none" in his 1916 construction plan, which included 10 battleships and six battle cruisers. But events undermined both Wilson's and the Navy's vision. America went to war in 1917. And the threat was not the German battle fleet but German U-boats. Navy Secretary Josephus Daniels consequently scrapped capital-ship construction and instead built destroyers and other ships capable of protecting convoys of American solders heading to France.

World War I turned sea control on its head—but perhaps only temporarily. In the aftermath of the German surrender, Wilson threatened his British allies with resuming capital-ship construction should they not join the United States in the new world order the president offered. Ironically, though, while the British gave in and joined the League of Nations, Wilson's domestic enemies undermined his grand vision. As it turned out, Congress had little stomach to what amounted to an entangling alliance. But it was also not interested in pressing ahead with continued construction of battleships.

The Washington Naval Conference

The Navy thought that the failure of Wilson's diplomacy and his subsequent election defeat meant that the seas were calming, but in fact larger storms loomed on the horizon. President Warren G. Harding may have been no fan of the League, but that did not mean he was not looking for a way to prevent another great war. When his secretary of state, Charles Evans Hughes, declared at the first plenary session of the Washington Naval Conference on November 12, 1921, that "preparation for offensive naval war will stop now," the president's aspirations were aimed primarily at the Navy.[2]

Harding's peace calculus was uncomplicated. The German menace to Europe was over. The rest of the continent was financially incapable of fighting another war. That left only those nation states with the ability to project power overseas as possible belligerents in a future war. To Harding, all one had to do was remove the ability of those counties to fight offensively far from their shores. And, as battleships were the only weapons capable of projecting power abroad, reducing their numbers would curb any appetite a country might have to fight.

Consequently, in the spring of 1922, diplomats signed the Five Power Pact to reduce the number of capital ships in service, apply tonnage ratios to existing battleships, and prohibit battleship construction entirely for 10 years. Signed by Britain, France, Italy, Japan, and the United States, the treaty essentially relegated each to regional-power status. The diplomats established similar tonnage ratios for aircraft carriers (see Table 13.1).

Table 13.1 Washington Treaty naval arms limitations.

	Capital ships				Aircraft carriers	
	Ratio	Tonnage	To be retained	To be scrapped[a]	Ratio	Tonnage
United States	5	525,000	18	26	1.35	135,000
Britain	5	525,000	22/20[b]	24	1.35	135,000
Japan	3	315,000	10	16	0.8	81,000
France	1.75	175,000	10	0	0.6	60,000
Italy	1.75	175,000	10	0	0.6	60,000

[a] Includes ships under construction.

[b] When two under construction were completed, Britain would retire four pre-dreadnoughts.

---

[2] *Conference on the Limitation of Armaments, Washington, November 12, 1921–February 6, 1922* (1922), 66.

In the Four Power Pact, Britain, France, Japan, and the United States agreed to respect each other's holdings in the western Pacific and that they would not fortify any of those islands, an agreement reached to render obsolete the Anglo-Japanese Naval Alliance of 1902 (see Map 13.1). The Washington Naval Conference began a period known as the "Treaty System," which linked naval disarmament and arms control to peace. At a subsequent conference in Geneva in 1927, the British attempted to extend the Washington Naval Treaty restrictions on battleships to cruisers. With an extensive empire to defend, Britain argued for higher numbers of light cruisers armed with six-inch guns. The US Navy, on the other hand, wanted fewer but heavier cruisers armed with eight-inch guns that could endure a transpacific campaign. As line officers dominated the discussions in Geneva, the conference failed to come to an agreement. The diplomats subsequently took over and compromised on the cruiser issue in 1930. The London Naval Conference

established overall cruiser tonnage of 326,000 tons between Britain and the United States. The British government agreed to reduce the number of cruisers it would build from 70 to 50, most of which would be light. In return, the United States reduced the number of heavy cruisers it would build to a maximum of 18, making up the tonnage difference in light cruisers. The Japanese were permitted to build up their cruiser strength to 70 percent of that of Britain and the United States and were given parity in submarine and destroyer tonnage.

For US naval officers, diplomats created an environment that bedeviled a service whose traditional arguments for preparedness centered on a large, offensively oriented battle fleet. Consequently, the Navy would operate for much of the 1920s and 1930s with ships built prior to World War I or authorized by Woodrow Wilson's Navy Act of 1916. Yet, even though administrations appeared bent on reducing the Navy's role in national defense, the fleet remained intact. Ship

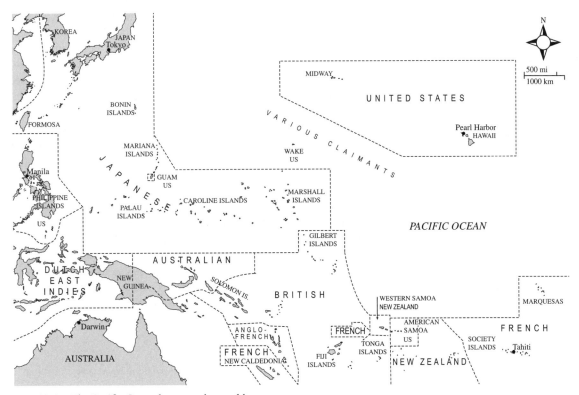

Map 13.1 The Pacific Ocean between the world wars.

construction slowed, but the ships that were built began to shift the Navy toward a more balanced fleet concept. There was another important advantage to being ignored. Comfortable with the restrictions imposed on the fleet's size and growth, postwar administrations essentially left the Navy to its own devices. The lack of formal and specific policy guidance provided planners with the opportunity to refine their own visions of war. They were forced, but at the same time free, to think and plan without interference.

Naval Aviation

The message sent by civilian policy makers in the 1920s and 1930s was that major-power war had run its course. The ensuing Treaty System succeeded in diminishing the power projection capability of the US Navy. But it did not prevent the service from adapting to the loss of battleships, nor stop it from thinking about war. One area of naval warfare that received increased attention was aviation. In hearings begun in January 1919, the General Board agreed that aviation's future lay principally in scouting for the fleet, a mission that would be best supported by placing aircraft on ships rather than relying on seaplanes or land-based aircraft. After five months of deliberations, the board agreed that aircraft had become "an essential arm of the fleet," recommended that the collier *Jupiter* be converted into an experimental aircraft carrier, and advised that the fleet's battleships be equipped with planes.[3] Aviators courted a sympathetic General Board with practical demonstrations of the capabilities of aviation. In February 1919, an aircraft provided spotting support for the battleship *Texas* during gunnery exercises off Guantanamo. With a smoke screen thrown in front of the target to obscure the ship's spotters, aircraft spotting increased *Texas'* accuracy twofold. Several months later, an attempt by four Navy Curtiss flying boats led by John Towers to cross the Atlantic was both a publicity stunt and an operational demonstration of aircraft capabilities. Only one of the four aircraft actually reached the European continent.

But, even with limited success, the flight provided important practice in the use of aircraft flight instruments such as the gyrocompass, celestial navigation procedures, and wireless radio operation. Towers and his group showed fellow officers that airplanes could extend the eyes of the fleet.

As naval aviators worked to prove themselves to a skeptical service, a serious threat loomed from outside. Brigadier General William ("Billy") Mitchell's wartime experience as commander of the largest aggregation of allied air forces (at St. Mihiel, France, in September 1918) had propelled him to the forefront of America's airpower advocates. Following the armistice, he was convinced that America's future lay in the exploitation of the sky. In Mitchell's mind, the conservative pace of aircraft development by the Army and Navy was a "wasteful trial and error process" that inhibited aviation's full potential. Should America shift its reliance for continental defense from the "obsolescent theory" of battleships to an independent force of bombing and pursuit aircraft, war would be quick, decisive, and cost-effective.[4]

In 1920, Mitchell convinced congressmen allied to his cause to attach a rider to the House Army Appropriations Bill, giving the Army complete control over all military air operations conducted from land. Recognizing the consequences to Navy shore-based aircraft, Josephus Daniels used his own political connections to have the legislation amended to ensure that the Navy could continue to fly from its own air stations. Undeterred, in testimony to the House Military Affairs Committee, Mitchell claimed that he could prove that ships were vulnerable to aircraft attack and asked Congress to press the Navy to provide a target for the demonstration.

The resulting bombing trials were held off the Virginia Capes in the summer of 1921. Over a period of several days Army, Navy, and Marine aviators bombed captured German naval vessels, ranging in size from a submarine to a cruiser. The *coup de grace*, however, was the test on the German battleship *Ostfriesland*, veteran of the Battle of Jutland. For two days, pilots dropped

---

[3] "Future Policy Governing Development of Air Service for the United States Navy," US Navy General Board report, June 23, 1919, as quoted in Archibald D. Turnbull, *History of United States Naval Aviation* (1949), 161.
[4] William Mitchell, *Winged Defense* (1988 [1925]), xv, 121.

William A. Moffett

Born in Charleston, South Carolina, William A. Moffett (1869–1933) graduated from the US Naval Academy in 1890. He served most of his seagoing career in battleships and was awarded the Medal of Honor for actions during the Veracruz Occupation in 1914. Moffett's formal relationship with naval aviation began in 1917 as commander of the Great Lakes Training Station, where he lobbied the Navy to add aviation training facilities. At Great Lakes he met William Wrigley and made him an ally of naval aviation. As commanding officer of the *Mississippi* following World War I, Moffett oversaw installation of its flight deck.

Moffett's experience and seniority made him the right officer to direct the newly established Bureau of Aeronautics (BUAER). While not a fully qualified aviator, his appreciation of aviation convinced junior aviators that they had a voice in senior Navy circles. To skeptics in the service, Moffett offered a policy that even the most salty battleship sailor would approve: naval aviators were naval officers first. The airplane was a naval weapon that would "go to sea on the back of the fleet" and serve its ships.[5]

Under Moffett's stewardship, BUAER became the clearinghouse for all matters pertaining to aviation.

He oversaw conversion of the *Langley* and construction of the fleet carriers *Lexington* and *Saratoga*. Moffett was also an enthusiastic advocate for airships. Dirigibles and blimps appeared a solution to the fleet's reconnaissance problem in a future Pacific war. Moffett believed, as well, that the impressive appearance of the airships, with a huge "US NAVY" painted on their sides, would, when flown around the country, rally public support for naval aviation.

In a moment of tragic irony, both Moffett and his dream died when in April 1933 the airship *Akron* flew into storms off the coast of New Jersey and crashed into the sea. Admiral Moffett was among the 73 sailors killed. Soon thereafter Rear Admiral Ernest King, Moffett's successor at BUAER, ended the rigid airship program.

William A. Moffett *Source:* US Naval History and Heritage Command Photograph # NH 81154.

bombs ranging in size from 200 to 2,000 pounds, making 19 direct hits before sinking the ship.

Mitchell proclaimed that the tests had proven the ascendancy of air power over navies. It appears, though, that the Navy was on to Mitchell's strategy even before the *Ostfriesland* test. Following hearings held in April 1921, National Advisory Committee on Aeronautics Chairman Charles Walcott recommended that each service retain its aviation component and that the Navy establish a Bureau of Aeronautics with

---

[5] William A. Moffett, "Some Aviation Fundamentals," US Naval Institute *Proceedings*, 51:10 (October 1925), 1877.

responsibilities consonant with the Navy's other powerful bureaus. The service responded by assisting sympathetic members of Congress in drafting the legislation. President Harding signed the bill establishing the
Bureau of Aeronautics in July 1921, effectively ending
the external threat to naval aviation.

With Mitchell thwarted, naval aviators continued
to hone their trade. *Jupiter* had been transformed into
the aircraft carrier *Langley*. Aviators experimented
with improved arresting gear and catapults, crash barriers, and landing signal officers. Flight deck operations became efficient, expeditious, and relatively safe.
Yet this early testing also revealed important tactical
limitations. *Langley* was not designed as a fighting carrier. Its maximum speed of 15 knots limited both its
ability to launch and recover heavier aircraft and its
ability to outrun hostile warships. Its initial complement of 14 aircraft was another important limitation.
Without a carrier capable of carrying more aircraft,
aviators could not reasonably expect to expand their
operational capabilities beyond defending the fleet
from an opposing air force.

Langley's shortcomings aside, naval aviators enjoyed
favorable political and policy support. In September
1924, Navy Secretary Curtis Wilbur convened a Special Policy Board on aviation matters. Many of the
board's recommendations, such as expanding the aircraft production program, expediting completion of
the fleet carriers *Lexington* and *Saratoga*, and the construction of a new 23,000-ton aircraft carrier, pointed
to the Navy's commitment to aviation. But the Board
also concluded from testimony by civilian and military experts that the trend of aviation technological
improvement would not require radical changes in
the Navy's force structure. The battleship could be
modified to retain its central position.

The prospects of aviators brightened significantly
toward the end of the 1920s. President Calvin Coolidge convened a committee to examine the state
of military and naval aviation. Headed by Dwight
Morrow, a distinguished financier and personal friend
of Coolidge, the Morrow Board proposed legislation
to create a top civilian aviation position within the
Navy secretary's office and recommended that commanding officers of the Navy's aircraft carriers and
naval air stations be restricted to aviators. By the time
Coolidge signed the recommendations, making them

law in June 1926, a five-year aircraft production program had been added that would give the Navy 1,000
operational aircraft by 1931.

The Morrow Board also laid a foundation for
naval aviation by addressing the personnel, administrative, and material needs of naval aviation. Important
technological developments and tactical initiatives
soon pushed aviation further beyond the experimental realm. By 1928 the fleet carriers *Lexington*
and *Saratoga* were available for operational missions.
Each ship carried over five times the number of aircraft and steamed at over twice the speed of *Langley*.
Naval aviators also looked with great interest at the
dive-bombing tactics used by Marine aviators in Nicaragua in 1927. The Bureau of Aeronautics' desire to
expand the mission of carrier aviation led to the purchase of the F8C-2 Helldiver. Though the aircraft's
deficiencies in speed and rate of climb in flight tests
demonstrated its unsuitability in the attack role, by
1928 the Bureau of Aeronautics had submitted design
proposals for an aircraft capable of delivering a 1,000-
pound bomb.

In January 1929 the Navy put the fleet carriers to
their first operational test. As part of annual exercises,
senior commanders were given the opportunity to
exercise their respective fleets in strategic exercises
known as fleet problems. Opposing fleets would be
assigned a notional color (black, blue, gray, etc.), each
fleet commander would be given a strategic problem
to solve, then their solutions would be played out at
sea. Fleet Problem IX was the first strategic exercise
in which the opposing American fleets both had carriers. On January 26, Black Fleet commander Admiral
William V. Pratt detached *Saratoga* and heavy cruiser
Omaha from his battleships and staged a dawn air
attack on the Panama Canal. While 32 fighters provided overhead protection, 34 bombers initiated dives
from 9,000 feet, released their simulated bombs on the
Miraflores locks and spillways, and pulled out from
their dives at 500 feet. Fleet Problem IX has often
been considered as something of a watershed for naval
aviation. Pratt's strategy to separate his carrier beyond
the protection of his battleships challenged the Mahanian maxim of concentration. *Saratoga*'s dash from the
main body of the fleet to its launch position, 140 miles
off the canal, was also a clear demonstration of the
strategic value of the fast carrier. Pratt's plan, however,

USS *Lexington*

The US Navy faced a quandary in 1921. The service had bought into aviation, and the General Board had authorized the conversion of the collier *Jupiter* to the experimental carrier *Langley*, but any plans to build a carrier from the keel up seemed destined for failure. Congress showed no inclination to fund naval construction in peacetime.

Despite the service's despair at losing battleships at the ensuing Washington Naval Conference, the treaty ironically opened the door for naval aviators. The opportunity came in the form of two battle cruiser hulls that were set to be scrapped. Naval officers convinced Secretary of State Charles Evan Hughes to pursue an agreement to permit construction of two 33,000-ton aircraft carriers.

Congress agreed, and the hulls became USS *Lexington* and USS *Saratoga*. Commissioned in December 1927, *Lexington* was the first operational fleet carrier. Measuring 1,888 feet in length and driven by a four-shaft turbo-electric drive, the carrier could carry 78 aircraft and steam at 32 knots.

Participating in fleet exercises beginning in 1929, *Lexington* was a critical factor in the development of naval aviation's offensive capabilities. When Japan attacked Pearl Harbor in December 1941, *Lexington* was away delivering aircraft to Wake Island. In early 1942, it conducted hit-and-run raids in the southwest Pacific, and in May the ship fought the first carrier engagement of the war at the Battle of the Coral Sea. *Lexington* aircraft helped to sink the light carrier *Shoho* and damaged the fleet carriers *Shokaku* and *Zuikaku* before Japanese aircraft inflicted sufficient damage to force the scuttling of *Lexington*, the first US aircraft carrier lost in World War II.

USS *Lexington* under construction using the hull of a cruiser cancelled under the terms of the Washington Naval Treaties.
Source: National Archives.

Figure 13.1   O2U Corsair scout plane approaching USS *Saratoga*, c. 1930. *Source:* US Naval History and Heritage Command # NH 94899.

came with a heavy price. The Blue cruiser *Detroit*, which had made contact with *Saratoga* on January 25, trailed the carrier throughout the night. Soon after the carrier launched its aircraft, it was engaged by battleships from the Blue Fleet, and soon thereafter by planes from the Blue carrier *Lexington*.

Perhaps Pratt had let his confidence obscure an important shortcoming of naval aviation. Only the day before, his own battleships had emerged out of rainsqualls within gun range of *Lexington* and attacked the carrier before an air attack could be launched. During the post-exercise assessment, Pratt acknowledged that his plan had placed *Saratoga* in jeopardy but insisted that the strategic mission of destroying the canal justified the potential loss of the carrier. Rear Admiral Joseph Mason Reeves, Pratt's air commander, further argued that *Saratoga* was actually safer when acting independently. Being tied to a slower main

body, he believed, made the carrier more vulnerable to attack. Fleet Problem IX demonstrated the potential of aviation as an offensive weapon (see Figure 13.1). But one exercise alone was not going to change the status quo. US Fleet Commander-in-Chief (CINCUS) Admiral Henry Wiley reflected Navy attitudes when he observed following the exercise that, while naval aviation had "found a place in the fleet," the exercise pointed to the "battleship as the final arbiter of Naval destiny."[6] The comment was a practical reminder to aviators of the limitations in their trade.

Conservatism, though, did not prevent the Navy from further refining doctrine. Fleet commanders became increasingly comfortable with independent carrier operations in subsequent exercises. Carrier aircraft continued to be used to attack warships, including battleships. Change was also afoot in the composition of the carrier air wing.

---

[6] "United States Fleet Problem IX—Report of the Commander-in-Chief, United States Fleet," in *Records Relating to United States Navy Fleet Problems I to XXII, 1923–1941* (1974), microfilm, roll 12, pp. 29, 36.

The torpedo-carrying aircraft was one of the earliest casualties. Torpedo planes were large, reducing the total number of aircraft that a carrier could hold. Furthermore, the requirement to maintain a straight and level approach when attacking made the aircraft vulnerable to fighter aircraft and shipboard antiaircraft fire. Dive bombing, however, offered a more promising alternative. The planes were smaller, so more could be jammed into a carrier. More dive-bombers meant more bombs. Planes at altitude were also more difficult to spot than low and slow torpedo planes. Finally, the dive-bomber in attack provided a more difficult targeting problem for ships' gunners. As a consequence, by 1929 only one of the Navy's three torpedo squadrons had the primary mission of conducting torpedo attacks. The other two were assigned the primary mission of dive bombing, a tactic that CINCUS Wiley characterized as the "most serious problem in anti-air defense."[7]

War Planning

During the 1920s and 1930s, naval officers used their planning machinery to resolve what they perceived as a paradox in national defense. Civilian policy makers argued that America could be protected through domestic economic strength, continental defense, and disarmament. Naval officers looked beyond the rhetoric to China and the Philippines and doubted the ability of an insular policy to support American interests abroad. The solution Navy planners came to was simple. Lacking any specific policy guidance, they largely ignored national policy in their war planning. The Versailles Treaty ending World War I eliminated the necessity for a war plan against Germany. While war with Britain was unlikely, planning for such a conflict resumed soon after the Washington Naval Conference in 1922. Army planners envisioned that the US Navy would concentrate in the western Atlantic in order to prevent a British reinforcement of Canada. The fact that the Navy stationed its newer battleships on the West Coast demonstrated that naval leaders believed it was Japan that posed the main threat to US inter-

ests. Studies at the Naval War College, planners in Washington, and professional commentary converged to form a consensus on the general outline of a war with Japan. It was believed that hostilities would begin with a Japanese advance against the resource-rich areas of the southwestern Pacific, after which offensives would be mounted against the Philippines and Guam to further consolidate Japanese control of the region. Following mobilization, the US Fleet would fight its way west across the Pacific. An advance base would be established either in the Philippines (assuming the Army held out) or on another island suitable for sustaining the fleet in the western Pacific until its decisive engagement with the Imperial Japanese Navy. Thereafter, a blockade would coerce Japan to sue for peace.

While the guiding principles of this plan ("War Plan Orange") remained consistent throughout its existence, two competing schools of thought vied for control of Pacific strategy. Edward Miller, a historian of War Plan Orange, characterized advocates of these two schools of thought as "thrusters" and "cautionaries." So-called "thrusters" envisioned the fleet massing quickly and immediately steaming across the Pacific along a north-central route that could take advantage of the US-held islands of Midway and Wake, leading to establishment of an advance base at Guam. From Guam, the fleet would rush to the Philippines to rescue its beleaguered defenders. If Manila had fallen, a base would be established in the southern islands of the archipelago. Interdiction of Japanese trade in the region would begin immediately, followed soon thereafter by a climactic fleet engagement that would seal the fate of Japan.

Arguing against the "through ticket" strategy were naval officers who advocated a slower pace. A direct thrust across the Pacific, they believed, would leave the fleet in such poor material condition that it might suffer the same fate that had befallen the Russians in the straits of Tsushima in 1905. Instead, "cautionaries" emphasized a progressive transpacific campaign. They argued that the fleet could best be supplied and protected by establishing a series of bases as it moved

---

[7] "Annual Report of the Commander-in-Chief, United States Fleet, Period 1 July, 1928 to 21 May, 1929," in *Annual Reports of Fleets and Task Forces of the US Navy, 1920–1941* (1974), microfilm, roll 7, p. 59.

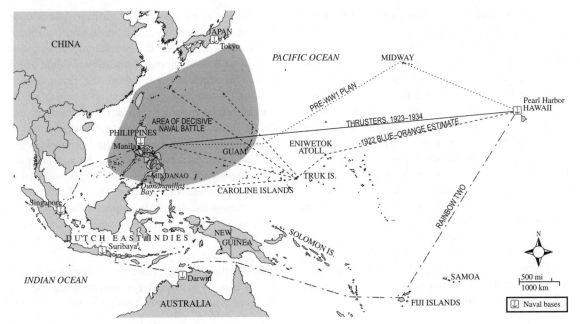

Map 13.2   Evolution of War Plan Orange.

westward (see Map 13.2). Cautionaries neither de-emphasized the importance of the Philippines nor rejected the notion of a decisive engagement with the Japanese fleet. A long war, they argued, while perhaps not palatable to the American public, was nevertheless essential to victory in the Pacific.

The international picture following World War I initially favored caution. The Versailles Treaty granted the Japanese a mandate to island chains that lay athwart the route the fleet would take to Guam or the Philippines. When the chief of naval operations and Secretary of the Navy approved an "Estimate of the Situation Blue-Orange" in September 1922, the US Navy held only a slight advantage over the Japanese in capital ships. Consequently, the Navy adopted the methodical approach advocated by the Cautionaries. Following mobilization, the fleet would steam west some 2,000 miles to the Marshall Islands, where an advance base would be established on the island of Eniwetok. From the Marshalls, the fleet would advance next to the Carolines and seize

Truk. The final contest for sea control in the western Pacific would not begin until Truk was made ready to support the fleet, some six months after initial mobilization.

The reign of the Cautionaries over war planning, though, proved short lived. The bone of contention was the Philippines. Criticism of the 1922 plan emanated from outside the service. Former army chief of staff and current governor-general of the Philippines Leonard Wood charged that the Navy plan would sacrifice the islands to caution. Wood's criticism resonated with the Thrusters. In May 1923, Admiral Samuel Robison, the director of the War Plans Division, submitted a memorandum modifying the Navy's standing War Plan Orange. The Mandates were to be ignored. The fleet would sail directly to the Philippines, a strategy that Chief of Naval Operations Robert Coontz admitted was bold but thought would be less costly than a deliberate war, which he believed would only give the Japanese time to "stiffen their resistance."[8] By the

---

[8] US Navy War Plans Division, "Estimate of the Situation Blue-Orange, September 1922," in *Records of the Strategic Plans Division*, roll 17, pp. 19–20.

summer of 1924, Thrusters were in control of War Plan Orange, and they remained so for the next 10 years.

Amphibious Warfare

The Navy's resurrection of war planning also created an opportunity for the Marine Corps. World War I had sidelined prior Corps efforts to develop an amphibious capability. That became the focus of Marine Commandant Major General John Lejeune when he assumed the office on June 30, 1920. Lejeune correctly surmised that the destiny of the Corps was closely intertwined with the fleet. Land operations in the Caribbean and China were important responsibilities, but building roads in Haiti and protecting the embassy in Peking also kept the Corps out of the Navy's sight. To Lejeune the future of the Marine Corps lay not in land warfare (such as on the Western Front in 1917 and 1918) or as a colonial constabulary but with the fleet, acting in support of the Navy's sea-control mission. Expeditionary forces would conduct "minor shore operations" to secure bases along the line of attack toward the enemy's homeland.[9] Once sea control was established, the Army could then invade and occupy the enemy's territory.

Integral to Lejeune's vision was the prospect of an Orange war (i.e., one of island hopping across the Pacific as called for in Plan Orange). Japan's acquisition of former German-held islands north of the equator fueled the imagination of Major Earl H. "Pete" Ellis, who served as the intelligence director of Lejeune's division of plans and training. In July 1921, Ellis prepared a report that emphasized the strategic relevance of the amphibious mission. Entitled "Advanced Base Operations in Micronesia," the document was a blueprint for Marine Corps participation in a Pacific war. Ellis hypothesized a worst-case scenario. Japan would initiate war but would conserve the bulk of its navy in the western Pacific. Its regional dominance would lead

to the loss of Guam and the Philippines. Hawaii would be left as the Navy's westernmost base. Any movement of the fleet west from Hawaii would be subject to attrition attacks from Japanese naval and air units operating from islands between Hawaii and the Philippines.

Ellis believed that the linchpin of any successful Pacific strategy lay in control of the Caroline, Mariana, and Marshall island chains. He was convinced that the threat they posed to the fleet made their reduction "practically imperative," to protect the battle fleet as it advanced to its western Pacific destiny. Ellis accompanied his strategic overview with a meticulous analysis of the requirements for successful amphibious operations. Included in his report was an extensive description of the geography of the region, including the physical characteristics of the coral and sand atolls and the volcanic islands. He described in great detail various aspects of the amphibious operations: reconnaissance of landing sites, use of feints and dawn landings, disembarkation, boat formations, the composition of the landing force, naval gunfire and air support, and even the use of poison gas.[10] Ellis provided the Marines legitimacy by identifying a viable role in a Navy war.

Lejeune also reformed the Marine Corps from within. He reorganized and expanded his headquarters to include a more formal staff system, establishing divisions of operations and training, personnel, education, and recruiting. Lejeune also transformed the Corps' educational infrastructure. The Marine Corps School of Application was expanded into a three-tiered education system incorporating an entry-level course for junior officers, a course for company-grade officers, and a course for field-grade officers. In 1923 Lejeune formalized the transformation when he directed that the Advanced Base Force be renamed the "Marine Expeditionary Force." In August 1933, Assistant Commandant John H. Russell recommended to the commandant that the Marine Expeditionary Force be renamed. On December 7, Navy

---

[9] John A. Lejeune, "The Marine Corps, 1926," US Naval Institute *Proceedings*, 52:10 (October 1926), 1964.

[10] Earl Ellis, *USMC 712H Operations Plan, Advanced Base Force Operations in Micronesia [1921]*, republished by Headquarters, Marine Corps, as *Fleet Marine Force Publication 12–46* (1992), 1–7.

Figure 13.2   Marine Corps amphibious exercises at Culebra, Puerto Rico, 1936. *Source:* National Archives.

Secretary Claude Swanson signed General Order 241, which officially established the Fleet Marine Force. The organization retained the same form as the Expeditionary Force. But the Fleet Marine Force was now specifically assigned to the fleet commander-in-chief, with a specific mission for landing operations. The commandant was directed as well to ensure that the Fleet Marine Force would be kept in readiness to support the fleet, and not detailed to support traditional Marine Corps responsibilities.

General Order 241 was followed by more significant developments. In October 1933 the commandant of the Marine Corps ordered staff and students at the Marine Corps Schools to focus their studies on the development of an amphibious warfare manual. The dominant themes of the *Tentative Manual for Landing Operations*, completed in January 1934, were the uniqueness of amphibious warfare and the integral role it would play in any naval campaign in the Pacific. Individual sections provided comprehensive requirements for successful amphibious operations. It approached naval gunfire support so as to ease the

inherent fear of sailors of engaging shore fortifications. Air support was emphasized to ensure adequate reconnaissance of landing sites, force protection, and coordination of activity between sea and shore. The manual proposed the creation of embarkation and debarkation teams to ensure that effective combat power was placed on beaches. Finally, the manual emphasized and articulated the concept of "combat loading," under the direction of a qualified transport quartermaster, to ensure that marines on beaches were adequately supplied (see Figure 13.2).

Interwar Problems and Weaknesses

Advances in naval aviation and amphibious warfare doctrine demonstrated the naval service's ability to adapt to the political and geopolitical environments. But that did not mean that all issues were resolved in the 1920s and 1930s. The submarine, for example, remained a work in progress. Throughout the Coolidge and Hoover administrations, the prospect of adding significant numbers of submarines to the fleet suffered along with the rest of the Navy's needs. Newer boats were built, but not in great numbers, and still without the speed and endurance for a transpacific campaign.

The corollary to employing submarines was defending against them. Naval officers envisioned that substantial resources would be available for antisubmarine operations. In a future war, convoys would be ringed by bands of armed escorts. Unfortunately, warship construction during the period failed to live up to service expectations.

Finally, even though the Marines had finally found a mission and developed a doctrine that made them distinct from their Army counterparts, they lacked the equipment and support needed to execute amphibious warfare. The Navy owned only two transports specifically designed to carry the Fleet Marine Force, and the Bureau of Construction and Repair stalled on development of suitable landing craft. Naval gunfire support was given only cursory attention. The fleet's commitment to prepping beaches was offset by its continued reliance on flat trajectories and armorpiercing shells, ordinance more suited to sinking battleships than destroying pillboxes.

War Clouds Gather

In 1922 many civilian policy makers scoffed when Captain Schofield expressed doubts concerning the notion that naval arms control alone could prevent another war, but by the end of the decade peace was unraveling. At least from one perspective the US Navy could be seen as prophetic, as events pointed to darkening skies in the western Pacific. The restoration of the emperor's power in Japan and the nation's modernization in the late nineteenth century fueled growing nationalism and imperial aspirations. War with China in 1894–1895 brought Japan the island of Taiwan. A decade later Japan defeated Russia and, in the Treaty of Portsmouth, an agreement brokered by President Theodore Roosevelt, Russia recognized Korea to be a Japanese sphere of influence (Japan annexed Korea in 1910) and ceded its naval base at Port Arthur on China's Shantung Peninsula and the southern half of Sakhalin Island to Japan. As favorable as the treaty was for Japan, militants there believed Japan deserved more and blamed Roosevelt for the terms. This added

to their resentment of America's Open Door policy in China, and bred an animosity that intensified when the United States forced Japan to moderate the "21 Demands" that it made on China during World War I. After that war American diplomats sought to curb Japanese ambitions at the Washington Naval Conference, but the Treaty System that emerged from the conference proved more of a band aid than a cure, and in some respects strengthened militants in Japan. Global depression further emboldened militarists and nationalists, who sought economic relief and great power status through expansion. In 1931, Japanese soldiers stationed in Manchuria staged an incident that provided justification for annexation. Japan attacked Shanghai the following year. In 1933 Japan left the League of Nations, yet it refused to relinquish control of the island mandates awarded it after World War I. By 1935, diplomacy had run its course. The strengthening "fleet faction" in Japan was by this time eager to embark upon a naval construction program that would guarantee both supremacy in the western Pacific and parity with the United States and Britain. When the United States and Britain refused to accommodate Japan's demands at the London Conference in 1935, the Japanese walked out. Two years later they invaded China.

Events in the Pacific had a profound effect on Navy plans. In July 1934, Chief of Naval Operations Admiral William Standley signed off on a revised Orange plan titled "the Royal Road." The plan assumed that the fleet would be incapable of mobilizing quickly enough to prevent Guam and the Philippines from falling into Japanese hands, and thus rejected the "through ticket" strategy, proposing instead a progressive movement through the islands of the central Pacific. Planners also believed that the Japanese would quickly fortify their island holdings in the central Pacific, if they had not done so already. The fleet would therefore advance as far as the Marshalls, taking as many islands as necessary to guarantee security. Having secured the Marshalls, it would continue westward to Truk in the Carolines, seizing various islands along the way to provide flank protection. Once established at Truk, the fleet would then select a target that would force a decisive battle with the Imperial Japanese Navy. By 1941, US war plans (codenamed "Rainbow") were based on assumptions that the Philippines would be forced to surrender to the Japanese before the fleet could reach Manila and provide support and that Britain and the United States would be fighting as allies. Thus, Rainbow 2 called for a joint campaign using British bases in Australia and Singapore (see Map 13.2).

Unfortunately, events in Europe and America conspired to complicate the Navy's strategic vision. The Versailles Treaty had been designed to prevent the resurgence of German militarism, but the treaty required signatories willing to enforce it over the long haul. In the late 1920s Germany's Weimar Republic fell victim to the global depression, instilling anger in the German people and opening the door for Adolf Hitler's emerging national socialist movement. By 1933 the Nazis were in control of the government and embarked on a program of rearmament. No less weakened by the depression, Britain and France chose a strategy of appeasement. German occupation of the Ruhr and Rhineland went unopposed. In 1935 Britain inked a treaty permitting the once defunct German navy to build up to 35 percent of the Royal Navy tonnage. Three years later Hitler annexed Austria and convinced Prime Minister Neville Chamberlain that Czech-Sudeten Germans would be safer if the region were under German control. Soon thereafter Hitler marched into Czechoslovakia.

Responding to an American public wary of being entangled in another war, Congress implemented a series of neutrality acts to prevent direct US engagement in European affairs. Recognizing that strict neutrality could no more contain fascism now than it had Germany in 1917, President Roosevelt embarked on a cautious program of convincing the American public of the impending menace while also convincing Congress to rearm. The strategy proved both beneficial and problematic for the Navy. In a series of bills shepherded by Representative Carl Vinson and Senator Park Trammel, Navy construction was methodically increased up to, then beyond, treaty limits. Congress would ultimately pass the Two-Ocean Navy Act in July 1940. The largest naval construction act in US history, it provided ships to increase the size of the fleet by 70 percent.

But the shipbuilding program came with a price. Franklin Roosevelt's strategic focus was not on a Pacific offensive against Japan. In 1940 he signed an agreement with Britain to exchange 50 old US destroyers for basing rights in the Caribbean, New-foundland, and Bermuda. One year later the president convinced Congress that neutrality alone could not keep the nation out of the war. America would have to help Britain and Russia by lending or leasing military equipment and supplies. Of course, ensuring that Lend-Lease support reached its destination intact meant that it would have to be protected against German submarines. And so Roosevelt directed the Navy to conduct neutrality patrols and escort of Lend-Lease convoys partway across the Atlantic.

Roosevelt's grand strategy could be condensed into two words: "Germany First." In his mind the fascist threat in Europe was far closer and more immediate to America than Japanese ambitions in the western Pacific. To check Japan, he ordered the US Fleet to remain in Hawaii following its 1941 strategic exercises, and sent several dozen B-17 bombers to the Philippines to buttress General Douglas MacArthur's forces. The Navy demurred, but it accepted the Germany First mantra and modified its vision to accommodate an initial defensive position in a war with Japan.

Conclusion

In the fall of 1941, the US Navy was conceptually prepared, albeit imperfectly, to wage a war at sea. It had a reasonable vision of war with Japan yet also supported America's policy of defeating Germany first. Officers had learned how to employ new weapons such as aircraft carriers and dive-bombers, and Marines the basics of amphibious warfare. And yet, issues remained. The ships authorized by the Vinson–Trammel Acts were months if not years away from completion. The fleet that would go to war in December was composed of ships dating back to World War I. The service still believed that a climactic engagement with the Japanese would settle the war in the Pacific. And few, if any, officers gave a thought to the possibility that German U-boats might take the fight to US shores. Concerns would become a reality in December 1941 and January 1942, when sailors on Pacific Fleet warships looked to the skies over Pearl Harbor and saw Japanese carrier planes, while their Atlantic shipmates watched in shock as Hitler's U-boats ravaged merchant shipping along the East Coast of the United States.

CHAPTER 14

World War II in the Atlantic and Mediterranean

The Battle of the Atlantic was the most important Allied victory of World War II. Winston Churchill described it as "the dominating factor all through the war, never for one moment could we forget that everything happening elsewhere on land, at sea, or in the air depended ultimately on its outcome."[1] It was the only campaign to persist, in varying degrees, from the war's very first day to its last. Without victory at sea, the major operations and victories of the western theater—including the flow of Lend-Lease and other material support, the Combined Bomber Offensive, and the invasion of the European continent—would have been far costlier and more difficult, if not impossible. By the time the war was over, Germany had sunk some 2,700 Allied and neutral merchant ships of 13.5 million gross tons, and a further 145 Allied warships and auxiliaries. Some 75,000–85,000 Allied seamen lost their lives. On the German side, 761 of 1,170 commissioned U-boats were lost, along with 28,000 of 40,900 crewmen, or 70 percent. In addition to the immense fortitude and sacrifices of its participants, the Battle of the Atlantic involved massive industrial mobilization, a sensitive dependence on sophisticated technologies and organizational innovation, and a decisive role for intelligence in its critical phases. As such it instantiates the most important and revealing aspects of modern mass warfare and offers crucial lessons to the contemporary observer of military affairs.

World War II began in Europe when Germany invaded Poland on September 1, 1939. Two days later Britain and France declared war on Germany. On September 4 President Franklin Roosevelt proclaimed American neutrality and ordered establishment of a Neutrality Patrol to enforce a ban on belligerent activities in US waters (see Figure 14.1). A month later the Congress of American States extended this "neutral zone" to include waters 200 miles from the coasts of the Americas south of Canada. Disappointed by the results of Allied and American victory in World War I, the United States sought to avoid involvement as the Axis powers swept across Europe and North Africa.

The fall of France on June 14, 1940, shocked Americans who had thought in terms of a repeat of World War I. In 1914 operations had settled into a stalemate on land, and the Allies ultimately defeated the Axis Central Powers in a war of attrition in which the Allies' access to resources outside Europe tipped the balance in their favor. Thirty-one years later, the surrender of France not only increased the area from which Germany and Italy could draw resources but also gave the German navy ports on the Bay of Biscay from which to deploy U-boats.

---

[1] Winston S. Churchill, *The Second World War* (2013), 676.

America, Sea Power, and the World, First Edition. Edited by James C. Bradford.
© 2016 John Wiley & Sons, Inc. Published 2016 by John Wiley & Sons, Inc.

Figure 14.1   Neutrality Patrol. A SB2U Vindicator scout bomber from USS *Ranger* flies anti-submarine patrol over Convoy WS-12 en route to Cape Town, November 1941.

The US Congress responded to the fall of France by passing the Two-Ocean Navy Act, which authorized construction to double the size of the Navy, and President Franklin Roosevelt signed the Destroyers-for-Bases Deal in which the United States traded 50 destroyers that had been mothballed at the end of World War I to Britain in exchange for leasing rights to bases throughout the northwestern hemisphere (see Map 14.1). The aged destroyers were hardly suited to engage modern surface warships but provided crucial reinforcement for British antisubmarine operations at a point of critical vulnerability.

During the summer of 1941 the US Navy assumed a more proactive stance in the Atlantic, partially in response to incidents that reflected a willingness by both German and American naval leaders to risk

direct confrontation. On June 2 the U-203 sighted the USS *Texas* west of Greenland and, assuming that the battleship had been transferred to the Royal Navy, submerged and attempted to attack. Only the speed and zigzag course of the battleship prevented a major international incident.

Over the next 18 months US participation in the Battle of the Atlantic continued to escalate. On July 7 Roosevelt ordered the Navy to protect all shipping of any nationality sailing between the United States and Iceland and dispatched a Marine brigade to defend the island. After an attack on the *Greer* by U-652 on September 4 (an incident provoked by the US destroyer), Roosevelt denounced German "piracy," moving the German naval leadership to beg Hitler for a declaration of war against the United States

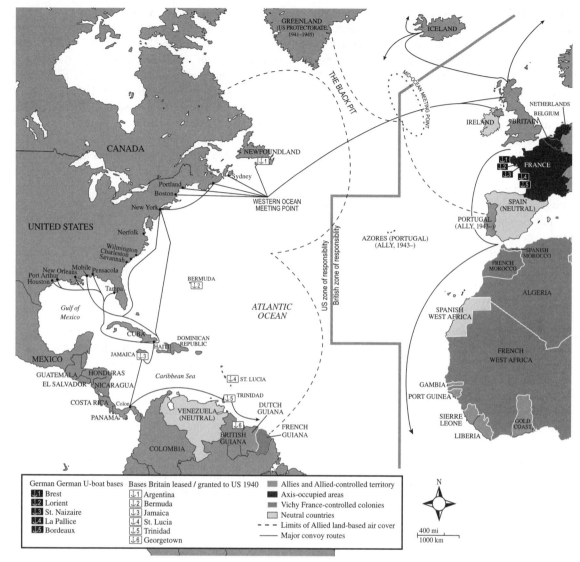

Map 14.1 Battle of the Atlantic.

(although it had conducted no serious assessment of the strategic implications of engaging the United States in a war). Matters nearly came to a head in mid-October 1941, when U-boat attacks killed 11 sailors on the USS *Kearny* and sank the *Reuben James*, killing 115 crewmen. Eager as they were for war, however, both navies were forced to wait to come to grips until Hitler's formal declaration of war on the United States on December 11.

Allied and German Strategy

Once in the war, Allied leaders quickly reaffirmed their previous agreement—despite Pearl Harbor—that defeat of Germany—which they considered the most dangerous enemy—should receive highest priority. The strategy they developed contained a series of steps, all of which depended on Allied control of the Atlantic to ensure safe passage of matériel and men from North America to Britain. The first phase of the strategy was aid to Britain and the Soviet Union, both of which were already at war with Nazi Germany; the next would be a strategic bombing campaign from British and other European bases; and finally a massive invasion of the European continent. In all, circumstances were propitious for a Germany First strategy. The War Department saw advantage in directing the bulk of American resources against one main front, instead of dispersing forces piecemeal against numerous smaller objectives. Geography favored Europe as the first target: distances from North America to Europe were much shorter than those to the Far East and thus less time was required to bring American resources and power to bear against an enemy in the European theater. The eastern regions of the United States were the most developed economically, and the eastern ports were the best from which to dispatch the huge amounts of military matériel and goods necessary to sustain American forces and their allies. From this overall strategic objective derived the primary mission of the US Navy in the Atlantic, which was to safeguard the sea lanes to Britain and protect the men and supplies necessary for the war against Germany. Britain was the ideal staging ground for such an invasion because forces could concentrate there relatively safely during the time required to build them up.

German strategic objectives in the Battle of the Atlantic were the obverse of the American objectives. Hitler's primary goal was to establish a German continental empire across Eurasia based on the German "master race," involving the ruthless subordination or annihilation of racial minorities. The empire would stretch west to east from the English Channel to the Ural Mountains and north to south from the Norwegian fjords to the Mediterranean. Recalling the terrible German experience of World War I, Hitler envisioned the new German empire to be economically self-sufficient and invulnerable to blockade or external suasion. He had served as an army corporal on the Western Front and saw little strategic value in challenging Anglo-American predominance on the high seas, and consequently had scant use for a battle fleet. The German navy assumed a comparatively minor significance in prewar and wartime strategic planning, and would be permanently subordinate in military production to Germany's air force and army.

On the basis of the Anglo-German naval treaty, Hitler and other senior Nazi leaders assumed until 1938 that France and the Soviet Union would be the main enemies of the Reich and constructed only a limited number of comparatively small and short-ranged U-boats to deal with them. The majority of naval officers, led by Grand Admiral Erich Raeder, made a case before the war for a large surface fleet that would tie the heavy units of the British Home Fleet to the North Sea and roam the high seas hunting enemy convoys, avoiding direct battle with the heavy units of the Royal Navy while chipping away at it from the margins. Initially, Hitler offered tentative support for this scheme and authorized the Z Plan, which envisioned a fleet of 23 battleships, four aircraft carriers, and dozens of lesser ships, including some 240 submarines. But the plan was unrealistic given Germany's priorities. Moreover, it soon became evident that the fuel requirements of such an armada far exceeded the production capacity of the Third Reich. Thus, Hitler canceled the Z Plan shortly after the war began, leaving the German fleet with one full-sized battleship and another half completed, as well as an unfinished aircraft carrier. With it disappeared Raeder's notion of a balanced fleet. Ultimately, the capital ships of the German navy hardly moved during the war. They had shown some early promise as surface raiders, mainly in distant seas, but suffered heavy losses in the North Atlantic. After declaring war on the United States, Hitler canceled all Atlantic surface sorties and ordered his heavy units to withdraw from Atlantic ports. Later, after the German surface fleet failed to break up a convoy off Norway, Hitler threatened to scrap all the big ships and Raeder resigned in January 1943.

Badly divided over what kind of war to fight, the German naval leadership did its submarine service few favors. Had it undertaken a serious strategic analysis, it may have recognized that the weakness of the German battle fleet dictated a reprisal of the German campaign of World War I and initiated a submarine war early on. But such an analysis was never undertaken, and at the outbreak of war Germany had only a few dozen operational submarines of varying sizes and capabilities under the direction of Karl Dönitz, an experienced submariner from World War I. Dönitz had spent the interwar years devising ways for the U-boat to be more effective in a future conflict through such innovations as short-range tactics, night operations, and wolf packs. Submarines at this time were not much more than temporarily submersible torpedo boats, operating on the surface as much as possible. Because of their very limited underwater speed and utility, they dove only to avoid counterattack or poor weather. Until the Allies began to make extensive use of airborne radar, surface operations also reduced the likelihood of sonar detection. But Dönitz's innovations could not solve the larger operational problems involved in a campaign against Allied commerce. With the exception of a handful of Type IX boats, German submarines were too small to operate effectively in the further reaches of the Atlantic shipping lanes, and were already technologically obsolete by the time of the war's outbreak. The Germans also lacked an effective naval intelligence service to support such a campaign, and would continually lack the air assets crucial to pinpointing the convoys on the high seas.

Dönitz's operational objective in the U-boat campaign was to sink the maximum number of Allied ships without regard for their location or destination, their cargoes, or even whether they had cargo on board at all. As he put it in a key policy statement, "the strategic task of the German navy was to wage war on trade; its objective was therefore to sink as many enemy merchant ships as it could. The sinking of ships was the only thing that mattered." The campaign to sink more cargo vessels than the Allies produced came to known as the "tonnage doctrine." According to this idea, merchant ships were functionally interchangeable. "The enemy's shipping comprises one great entity. It is therefore immaterial where a ship is sunk—it must in the final analysis be replaced by a new one."[2] Believing this, Dönitz sent his boats wherever targets were thought to be most plentiful. In principle it did not matter whether the ships were laden or empty, what they were carrying, or where they were, just that they were sunk and had to be replaced. To critics, Dönitz's decision to prioritize the concept of tonnage instead of specific targets of immediate military value was a failure of strategic prudence and overlooked British dependence on certain commodities and the Royal Navy's dependence on capital ships. In fact, anecdotal evidence suggests that U-boat captains tended to discriminate between targets of lesser and greater importance, and went after oilers in particular. A more serious criticism was that the strategy was simply wrong. Even if Britain could not replace the lost shipping tonnage, US shipyards probably could. Of course, such objections are often persuasive in retrospect. The brute fact was that, as he was considering his approach to the conflict, Dönitz had too few assets to prosecute the war in other ways and settled on commerce interdiction chiefly because it offered the best prospect of success with the limited means at his disposal.

The U-boat Ascendant

As it was, the U-boats never came close to success, even in 1940 and 1941, when Britain struggled alone against Nazi Germany and the U-boats ran amok against lightly defended shipping. After 10 months of war, Dönitz had 65 submarines to throw against the sea lanes, a total that had risen to 91 by January 1942. In March and April 1941 the Germans sank more than half a million tons of shipping, increasing their monthly total to 324,000 tons in May and 318,000 tons in June. Had Dönitz 300 boats at the outset of the war—the number he had argued was minimally necessary to wage a successful commerce war against the British Isles—then he might well have broken the British economy and turned the tide of the war in the West. Even against the few boats he had in the first months of the war, British prospects seemed dim. But the British rallied, American indirect support began to tell, and the convoy system and increasingly effective antisubmarine countermeasures undermined the effectiveness of Dönitz's boats. British society cut its consumption of certain key commodities to the bone. Most importantly, the British began to work out the crucial organizational requirements of a successful antisubmarine effort. Increasingly close coordination between the British Admiralty, the Royal Canadian Navy, and the British Royal Air Force centralized the direction of antisubmarine efforts and made more efficient use of resources.

But no single factor made a greater difference in this crucial period than British codebreaking success against

---

[2] Bundesarchiv-Militärarchiv (BA-MA), RM7/39, Kriegstagesbuch des B.d.U. 1–15.4.42, p. 32.

German communications. Its background is among the most interesting details of the military history of the twentieth century. In February 1918 a German engineer filed for a patent on a device to securely encrypt and decrypt messages between two parties who shared a common code key. Through a complex system of rotors and connectors, one party typed a message in plain text, which the so-called Enigma machine encoded and transmitted to a receiving Enigma machine. The latter decoded the message through the same rotor settings. The German armed forces made wide use of the Enigma system to send secure communications. Polish cryptanalysts broke the German ciphers in December 1932, leading the Germans to add additional layers of complexity to their communications in the years before the war. Just before the fall of their country in 1939, Polish cryptanalysts provided British intelligence with a full briefing on Enigma cipher systems, allowing the British to read German signals traffic with increasing frequency and accuracy by summer 1940.

The British called the resulting product "very special intelligence," or "Ultra." The process was far from simple. British codebreakers at Bletchley Park had to determine the required rotor settings each day, either through a captured German schedule or through analysis based on mistakes made by German operators, such as transmitting the same message heading each day and thereby revealing the day's settings. Luftwaffe operators were notoriously careless in this regard. German naval ciphers were largely secure until March 1941, when the British captured an armed German trawler and its Enigma enciphering tables. Subsequent captures of a German weather ship and especially the U-110, which produced a copy of the highly secret "officers only" cipher, allowed Bletchley Park to read German transmissions to and from the U-boats with great regularity. The British succeeded in establishing decryption procedures of such effectiveness that they could continue to read large numbers of messages even after the scheduled settings expired, making it possible to target and sink the entire German fleet of resupply ships by June 1940, among other victories. Most importantly, the information allowed them to penetrate German operational methods, especially how and where the U-boats were deployed and for what duration, how Dönitz concentrated his packs, and how his operational intentions developed over time. In specific cases, Ultra intelligence often allowed planners at Headquarters Western Approaches, responsible for protecting Atlantic convoy traffic, to steer major convoys around U-boat patrol lines. Alarmed that the sinkings were declining and suspecting the worst, German naval intelligence conducted two reviews of German encryption procedures in 1941 and 1942. The results of both reviews were inconclusive, primarily because they proceeded from the premise that Enigma encryption was unbreakable. The contribution of Ultra intelligence to the Battle of the Atlantic was one of the most significant Allied successes of the war, and the only one in which intelligence alone had a decisive impact on the outcome of major operations.

War in American Waters

The need to address strategic priorities other than the Atlantic sea lanes compromised the U-boat's prospects for success. British success against Erwin Rommel's Afrika Korps in late 1941 necessitated the diversion of 23 U-boats to the Mediterranean, while Hitler's concern for the security of his northern flank sent another 16 to Norway. Instead of biding his time and mounting a major sudden challenge with the 100 or so boats he thought minimally necessary, Dönitz went ahead and opened a new front against shipping in North American waters (Operation Paukenschlag, or Drumbeat) with only five boats. The U-boats were initially refueled and supplied with provisions and torpedoes by commercial tankers from Europe and then, after April 1942, by newly developed submarine tankers known as "milch cows." Fortunately for the Germans, the US Navy had learned all too little from World War I or the hard won experience of the British over the preceding two years. Even with only a few escort vessels to spare, US commanders—including Chief of Naval Operations Ernest King and Admiral Royal Ingersoll, commander-in-chief of the Atlantic Fleet—judged weakly defended convoys to be worse than no convoys at all, deemphasized joint antisubmarine operations by the Navy and Army Air Force, and persisted at patrolling on timetables so rigid that U-boat commanders could often predict their patterns virtually to the minute. The result was a slaughter of US coastal shipping and the US Navy failing to sink a single U-boat until April 1942. Paukenschlag eventually sank some 276,795 tons of shipping, but even more striking was the fact that the five U-boats sent to the US coast represented only 12 percent of those at sea but accounted for 70 percent of Allied shipping sunk in January 1942. Losses in February and March 1942 totaled nearly a million tons, making the latter month one of the worst of the war (see Figure 14.2).

King quickly came under enormous pressure from Secretary of War Henry Stimson and Army Chief of Staff George Marshall to defeat the U-boat menace. The latter went so far as to send King a letter in June 1942

admonishing him that the failure to protect shipping endangered the entire war effort. However, it is unclear whether an early and firm commitment to convoy escort would have averted the crisis. The basic problem was a lack of ships. The Navy had spent most of its money in the interwar period upgrading battleships and expected, in the event of war, to rely on destroyers left over from World War I until new escorts could be built. But the Destroyers-for-Bases Deal with Britain had cut into that

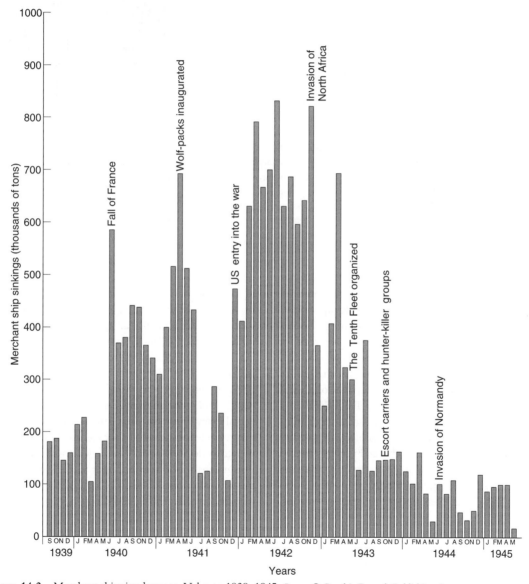

Figure 14.2 Merchant shipping losses to U-boats, 1939–1945. *Source:* © Cynthia Parzych Publishing, Inc.

Ernest J. King

A staunch supporter of the "Germany First" strategy even as he waged an unprecedentedly far-flung war against Japanese forces in the Pacific, Admiral Ernest Joseph King (1878–1956), a native of Ohio, graduated with distinction with the US Naval Academy Class of 1901, and served two years at sea—then required—before being commissioned ensign in 1903. After a series of progressively more senior sea duties in battleships and cruisers, and a two-year tour as an instructor at the Naval Academy, King commanded a destroyer. During World War I his service on the staff of Henry T. Mayo, commander-in-chief of the Atlantic Fleet—from whom he later said that he learned how to run a staff—brought him into contact with officers of the Royal Navy. After the war he commanded a submarine division and the submarine base at New London before transferring to naval aviation. He took command first of the aircraft tender *Wright* in 1926, then, after qualifying as a naval aviator, the carrier *Lexington*. King took the senior officers' course at the Naval War College and commanded the Navy's Aircraft Scouting and Battle Forces before his 1941 promotion to admiral as commander-in-chief of the Atlantic Fleet and later that same year commander-in-chief of the US Fleet. In March 1942 Admiral King assumed the combined duties of commander-in-chief and the chief of naval operations. His experience in submarines, aviation, and surface warfare gave King a breadth of experience

Ernest J. King. *Source:* US Navy, now in the collection of the National Archives. US Naval History and Heritage Command # 80-G-416886.

valuable to making maximum use of all Navy assets during World War II. In December 1944 King was advanced to the newly created rank of fleet admiral.

reserve, and new escorts had to compete in priority with large landing craft, which were also in short supply. Vice Admiral Adolphus Andrews, commander of the Eastern Sea Frontier, was left to cover a 3,000-mile stretch of coast with a handful of antiquated patrol craft manned by inexperienced crews. King understood the gravity of the escort deficit, even acknowledging at one point that "escort is not just one way of handling the submarine menace, it is the only way that gives any promise of success."[3] But he remained staunchly opposed to weakly defended convoys, which—in his view—served to do no more than mass poorly protected targets for the predators. Essentially, American doctrine conflated two different ends—the defense of ships and the destruction of U-boats—and conceived of convoys as bait to draw out U-boats, which an offensively oriented escort would stalk and destroy. If King can be faulted, it is for clinging obstinately to his conceptions of offensive antisubmarine warfare and reacting angrily against those who suggested otherwise. When confronted with the US Navy's obdurate refusal to learn from the Royal Navy's efforts, King's chief of staff, Admiral R. E. Edwards, growled to a Royal Navy envoy that "the Americans wished to learn their own lessons and that they had plenty of ships with which to do so."[4] The British tried to convince King that, no matter how gratifying it was to sink U-boats, the highest priority must be to get the cargoes to their destinations and that he could convoy with fewer and

---

[3] King to George C. Marshall, June 21, 1942, as quoted in Theodore Roscoe, *United States Destroyer Operations in World War I* (1953), 84.

[4] As quoted in Patrick Beesly, *Very Special Intelligence* (2006), 109.

weaker escorts if he used a strictly defensive strategy. The Royal Navy had wrestled with this conflict only a year earlier and issued Admiralty Instructions to that effect: "the safe and timely arrival of the convoy … is the primary object and nothing relieves the escort commander of his responsibility in this respect."[5] In view of the fact that U-boats were slow and difficult to operate effectively when submerged, only a small number of escort vessels were generally needed to force them to dive and permit the convoy to lumber along. A more efficient use of convoy escorts, oriented along the correct principles, stood to limit Allied losses and support the war effort more effectively. During 1942, the British sank 68 U-boats, the United States only 17. Eventually, the US Navy would adapt to the principles and practices of effective antisubmarine warfare and coordinate more closely with its allies, but the adaptation would take too long and prove costly in ships and lives.

When that adaptation came, radar and aircraft were key parts of it. Before U-boats were equipped with snorkels, allowing them to run submerged on their diesel engines, they were vulnerable to radar detection on the surface. Countermeasures initially lessened that possibility, but the British development of microwave radar was an enormous breakthrough that the Germans figured out too late. It afforded U-boats scant seconds to dive after detection. Between March and June 1942 the United States managed to double the number of aircraft available to cover convoys along the East Coast, pushing the Germans to redeploy U-boats to the Gulf and Caribbean. But, even as late as spring 1943, the Mid-Atlantic Air Gap, also known as the Black Pit, a swath of uncovered ocean some 300 miles wide, well beyond the range of land-based aircraft, provided the U-boats with ample room to hide (see Map 14.1). An Allied convoy conference at that time induced the chiefs in Washington to assign 140 long-range US aircraft to North Atlantic convoy duty—aircraft therefore unavailable to the strategic bombing offensive—and managed to reduce the air gap considerably. But the really decisive step came with the advent of hunter-killer groups, consisting of antisubmarine ships and small escort carriers with radar-equipped aircraft roving over the convoy routes.

As Allied patrol coverage extended to even marginal areas, submarines found progressively less empty space in which to hide (see Figure 14.3). U-boats had enjoyed good returns in the southern reaches of the US eastern seaboard until early 1943, sinking more than half a million tons of shipping in May alone. But, by the end of June, the US Navy implemented defensive measures for most of the shipping in those areas and sinkings fell off by a third in July, while the number of U-boats destroyed began to creep up (see Figure 14.4). Nonetheless, the first half of 1942 was an unmitigated disaster for the Allies. Despite the hard-earned gains and lessons of the British in 1941, the Germans succeeded in recovering the Happy Time of 1940 by shifting the battle to the other side of the ocean, against an ill-prepared and under-resourced enemy (see Figure 14.2).

More importantly than through antisubmarine warfare, the United States met the German challenge through a level of industrial ingenuity and productivity virtually without parallel in human history. In 1941 American shipyards produced about a million tons of oceangoing cargo vessels. In 1942 that number exploded to 8 million, and during 1943 industry pushed no fewer than 19 million tons of shipping tonnage down the ways. The bulk of the shipping tonnage was in the form of Liberty ships, an American derivative of a basic cargo carrier ordered by the British mission to the United States in December 1940. These were prefabricated, dependable vessels of 7,176 tons that could sail at a respectable 11 knots when loaded. The British had initially invested in two specialized US construction facilities; by 1943, 16 more had been added, all US funded. Dominating the program was Henry J. Kaiser, an organizational genius whose capacity for self-promotion was eclipsed only by his skill at building ships on a heroic scale. Between 1939 and 1945, US shipyards built 2,708 Liberty ships, along with 2,893 transports of other kinds, all operated under the aegis of the War Shipping Administration, created in February 1942 to operate the cargo fleets, while the US–British Combined Shipping Adjustment Board coordinated resources and allocated tonnage for cargo and troop

---

[5] *Admiralty Convoy Instructions*, as quoted in Stephen Roskill, *The Secret Capture* (2011 [1959]), 140.

Figure 14.3   Coast Guardsmen training for convoy duty practice gunnery. *Source:* US Coast Guard Historian's Office.

transport. Dönitz's tonnage strategy had no reasonable prospect of success against productivity on such a scale. Overall, U-boats sank 1,160 merchant ships, some 6.2 million tons of Allied merchant shipping, in 1942, but in August American shipyards, for the first time, constructed more merchant ship tonnage than the Axis destroyed (see Figure 14.5).

During the second half of 1942 the tide began to turn in favor of the Allies. German U-boat losses more than tripled from 20 during the first six months of the year to 65 in July through December (see Figure 14.4). In May the US Navy deployed its first strong coastal convoys backed by 300 antisubmarine patrol aircraft flying from 19 airfields along the coast. Rather than face these forces, Dönitz shifted his U-boats to areas with weaker coverage, first southward along the Atlantic coast and into the Gulf of Mexico, then, once convoys were instituted there, to off

Panama, Venezuela, and Trinidad, then finally to Brazil as far south as Rio de Janeiro. By August he was forced to virtually abandon operations in American waters and return to the Central Atlantic.

Invasion of North Africa

With the U-boats temporarily at bay the Allies felt confident enough to invade North Africa (codenamed Operation Torch). On October 24 the Western Naval Task Force under the command of Rear Admiral H. Kent Hewitt left Hampton Roads carrying 35,000 US troops with orders to put them ashore at Fedala, Port Lyautey, and Safi near Casablanca on the Atlantic coast of Morocco. The landings were coordinated with those by two groups that sailed from England to the Mediterranean; the Central Eastern Naval Task Force landed 39,000 American troops around Oran,

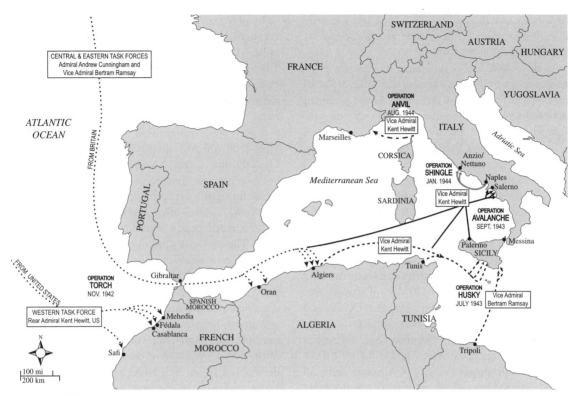

Map 14.2 The Mediterranean theater.

Algeria, and the Eastern Task Force put ashore 10,000 US and 33,000 British troops to the east at Algiers (see Map 14.2). The entire operation was a success, demonstrating the decline of the U-boat menace in the Atlantic.

Allied Ascendancy in the Atlantic, 1943

Given the time and cost associated with training new crews, Dönitz could ill-afford the losses of late 1942. Even if he could replace the U-boats, the need to crew the new boats inevitably led to a decline in the training and experience of U-boat commanders, in particular. Moreover, the Battle of the Atlantic was a technologically intensive effort, and the Germans could not adequately keep pace with key Allied advancements, such as long-range air cover to close the gap over the Central Atlantic, more efficient and numerous radars on escorts and aircraft, direction-finding and localizing equipment, and better weapons

and communications equipment. Most German U-boats still lacked radar in 1943, for example. The German surface fleet could not shoulder more of the burden. The Germans positioned the mighty battleship *Tirpitz* in northern Norway, where it and other heavy surface units posed a direct threat to Allied convoys making the hellish run to the Russian Arctic city of Murmansk. The northern route to the Soviet Union through raging, frigid seas was not the most important means of Allied reinforcement of Russia—the great bulk made its way to Siberia through the Sea of Japan or into southern Russia from the Persian Gulf—but U-boat attacks, significant German assets in Norway, and the threat of *Luftwaffe* attacks from land bases made it the worst. One convoy in May 1942 endured no fewer than 108 air attacks and lost more than a third of its ships. The saga of another, PQ 18, illustrates the immense challenges faced on the Murmansk run. The convoy of 40 ships had an escort of no fewer than 57 naval vessels—including an aircraft carrier, three battleships, and 30 destroyers—and still lost a quarter of its vessels, even as the escorts brought down 41 aircraft and sank three U-boats.

At the Casablanca Conference in January 1943, Roosevelt and Churchill agreed that "the defeat of the U-boats [is] our first objective." As the Germans mounted a final heroic effort to send shipping tonnage to the bottom, the month of March 1943 was so bad for the Allies that some advocated abandoning convoys (see Figure 14.2). The United States still lacked sufficient escorts to contribute more than minimally to the defense of the North Atlantic convoys. As of January, the British still furnished 50 percent of the escorts, the Canadians 46 percent, and the United States a scant 4 percent. A report of the British Admiralty stated that the U-boats were never closer to cutting the umbilical cord between North America and Britain than in the first 20 days of that month. The epic battles over convoys SC122, HX229, and HX229A—the largest of the war—underscored the immense damage that the Germans could still inflict in 1943. In a running battle lasting March 16–19, three wolf packs converged to sink 21 of 90 vessels and send nearly 150,000 tons of shipping to the bottom. By March 20, the German submarine force had managed to sink more than a half million tons of Allied shipping overall and brought the war effort to its most dangerous point. German codebreakers continued to read the British convoy codes, permitting Dönitz to direct attacks with occasionally disastrous results for the Allies. But most convoys made the trip safely. In an ongoing game of cat and mouse, Bletchley Park succeeded in burning through the encryption added by Enigma's fourth rotor, and Western Approaches Command steered a large number of convoys around U-boat patrol lines. In the year before May 1943—which saw long stretches without access to German signals—some 60 percent of the North Atlantic convoys were routed around wolf packs. In a major triumph for Allied planning, the invasion forces sent to North Africa in November 1942 arrived intact and without meaningful loss. By spring 1943, Allied air power covered ever greater swaths of ocean and made the daily routine of patrolling increasingly hazardous for U-boats. Escorts were more numerous, and their crews and commanders by now understood the job of antisubmarine warfare.

By this time the Allies were clearly winning the competition for technological supremacy. Shortwave radar, Huff-Duff, and Hedgehog entered service in 1942 and by mid-1943 enough escorts were equipped that most convoys benefited from them. Shortwave radar could penetrate water, thereby extending the range of radar beyond the curvature of the earth and preventing ocean swells from shielding U-boats. Huff-Duff (high-frequency/direction finding—i.e., HF/DF) units could almost instantaneously calculate the bearing and distance of a submarine by analyzing radio signals. Hedgehog fired a pattern of 24- to 32-pound contact-fused bombs ahead of a surface vessel as it advanced toward a U-boat tracking it with sonar. The projectiles did not explode unless they hit something so sonar contact was not lost with each salvo like it was with depth charges set to explode at a designated depth. As more and more of these weapons were deployed, advantage in the Atlantic tipped more and more in favor of the Allies. It is estimated, for example, that Huff-Duff contributed to 24 percent of the sinking of U-boats during the war and to the destruction of an even larger portion of milch cow supply submarines. German technological innovations—such as the *schnorchel* (snorkel, which allowed U-boats to run submerged on their diesel engines thereby rendering them harder to spot) and effective homing torpedoes—were deployed too late and in too few numbers to have a significant impact, plus the Allies were usually quick to develop countermeasures, such as Foxer, an acoustic decoy deployed to confuse German torpedoes that homed in on the sounds of a ship's propulsion system. In the years before 1943 the Allies had managed to sink 153 U-boats. In February and March 1943 they sank 49 U-boats and during "Black May" another 41, leading Dönitz to concede defeat and pull his U-boats from the Atlantic (see Figure 14.4). With this, the basic strategic asymmetry inherent in the effort became apparent. The Battle of the Atlantic, while crucial for Germany, paled in significance to the war on the Eastern Front or the air war over the homeland. There were limits to what Hitler would devote to the effort, and it is arguable whether Dönitz ever had the resources to fulfill the goal of the campaign. For the Allies, there was no alternative to the Atlantic shipping lanes to transfer across the great ocean spaces the great mass of men

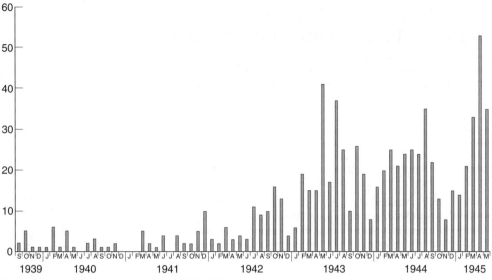

Figure 14.4   German U-boat losses, 1939–1945.

and material on which the entire war effort depended. As postwar analysts put it, "the most unstable element in the logistical process was not the capacity to produce, but the capacity to deliver fighting power to the firing line. [In] mid-1942 no great effort of the imagination was needed to foresee a day when German submarines might succeed in sealing off the eastward flow of American deployment altogether."[6] Fearing such a day, Britain and the United States devoted whatever resources were necessary to keeping the sea lanes open.

Invasion of Italy

The sea control established at bitterly high cost against the U-boat threat was the essential precondition for every other Allied success in the European theater. On January 14, 1943, the British and American leadership conducted 10 days of discussions on Allied strategy at a momentous conference at Casablanca. The Americans were still committed to invading northwest Europe in 1943, having no interest in

further Mediterranean operations after the defeat of Axis forces in North Africa. But the British prevailed in forestalling any major landing on the French coast in 1943 and Operation Husky, the Allied invasion of Sicily, on July 10, 1943, was approved with the stipulation that it be executed with forces already in North Africa so that it would not delay landings scheduled for northwestern Europe in 1944. The invasion was the largest amphibious operation of the war to date, at least on the first day, and was quickly followed up by the landings on the Italian mainland at Salerno in September and Anzio in January 1944 (see Map 14.2). The Navy's task was to provide secure transport for the troops and equipment and to support the landings, which the Germans opposed only somewhat less bitterly than they would those at Normandy later. American and Allied troops landed under a curtain of naval gunfire and air support, which enabled them to establish beachheads and push inland. After the initial landings, the Navy's role in each instance fell to maintaining the pipeline of supplies and support required to maintain the drive on land.

---

[6] Robert W. Coakley and Richard M. Leighton, *Global Logistics and Strategy: 1943–1945* (1968), 712.

High-Frequency Direction Finder

Success in the Battle of the Atlantic depended heavily on the advantages in several key technologies that the Allies built over time and used to great effect. High-frequency direction finding, usually abbreviated as HF/DF or "Huff-Duff," is a type of signal direction finding used extensively by the Allies during the Battle of the Atlantic to locate enemy radios while they transmitted. The system used a coordinated set of antennae to receive the signal in various slightly different locations or from different angles, interpreting the variations among the receivers to find the bearing of the transmitter on an oscilloscope display. HF/DF could locate the source of a signal much quicker than other systems, a significant advantage because German submarines used "burst transmissions,"

typically lasting less than 20 seconds, when radioing status and weather reports and Allied convoy sightings to U-boat headquarters in Brest, France. HF/DF could also detect the location of a transmitter at a greater distance than radar could detect the submarine carrying the transmitter. The US Navy began installing HF/DF on destroyers and destroyer escorts in 1942 and by mid-1943 all convoys were protected by escorts using HF/DF. The British (whose development of HF/DF was spurred for use against German aircraft during the Battle of Britain) and US HF/DF systems differed in various ways, but together contributed to the sinking of some 25 percent of U-boats destroyed during the war. Signals direction finders, along with microwave radar, sonar,

and Ultra signals decryptions, contributed significantly to the defeat of the U-boat threat.

High-Frequency Direction Finder in operation. *Source:* Destroyer Escort Historical Museum.

Victory in the Atlantic

May 1943 marked the turning point of the Atlantic War, and, while the conflict wore on, the imbalance of losses thereafter shifted decisively against the U-boats (see Figure 14.2). That month Admiral King set up the Tenth Fleet under his personal control, not to conduct the war as such (the command had no ships) but to unify all aspects of antisubmarine operations. The Tenth Fleet retained the authority to detach ships and airplanes as required from the different Atlantic commands and direct convoys and routing, and soon took over responsibility from the Army Air Force for shore-based aircraft patrols. Dönitz attempted to mount another offensive in

September, but it fizzled quickly in the face of overwhelming matériel superiority and determined and skilled Allied resistance. The Allies sank 141 U-boats in the final half of 1943, a terrible loss to Germany, which could not replace the experienced crews and commanders. After mid-1943 the British, Canadian, and US navies could claim reasonable security in their use of the sea. The Germans lost 237 U-boats in 1943 altogether and another 242 in 1944. Perhaps the best indication of how complete was American and British success was that the U-boat fleet was virtually helpless to contest the Normandy invasion in 1944.

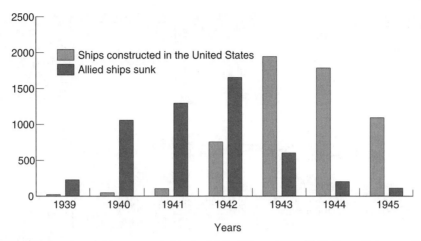

Figure 14.5 Allied ships sunk and ships constucted in the United States, 1939–1945. *Source:* Data compiled from American Merchant Marine at War, www.usmm.org.

Invasion of France

Before the Allied invasion of France, Germany still controlled the resources and industry of Western Europe and could throw the great bulk of its military power against Soviet forces on the Eastern Front. The successful invasion of France in June 1944 and the drive inland decisively altered Germany's strategic fortunes. Secure convoy routes across the Atlantic were fundamental to the success of the operation, and by late 1943 planning for the invasion had begun and large numbers of men and large amounts of equipment were being gathered in Britain. The Navy's role in Operation Neptune, the assault phase of Overlord, lay in ferrying the invasion force from England to Normandy and putting the troops ashore in landing craft; providing shore bombardment and gunfire support for the invading troops; and protecting the invasion corridor from mines, submarines, and aircraft (see Figure 14.6). To execute Neptune, the largest amphibious landing in history, the Allies employed 6,939 vessels (including 1,213 warships, 4,126 transport/landing craft, 736 ancillary craft, and 864 merchantmen). By the end of the day, 132,715 troops—including 52,889 Americans on Omaha and Utah beaches—were ashore, supported within five days by 54,186 vehicles and 104,428 tons of supplies.

Having largely won the Battle of the Atlantic by that point, the Allies could depend on superior firepower on the beaches—provided by the guns of the warships—and complete air superiority over all of northern France. The Germans lost 18 of the 43 U-boats that attempted to intercept the invasion force. During the first five days of the campaign 326,547 troops, 54,186 vehicles, and 104,428 tons of supplies were put ashore. Together Anglo-American naval forces enabled Allied troops to expand these initial landings rapidly inland; reinforce the front lines with fresh troops, munitions, and supplies; and then break out of Normandy and liberate most of France and Belgium by year's end.

In the four months of 1945 before the war in Europe ended, improved U-boats, heavier convoy traffic, and relaxed escort discipline led to the sinking of 122,729 tons of shipping, but, even then, the Germans lost 151 submarines. Dönitz never regained the initiative he had so tenuously held in late 1942, and the Allies commanded the seas for most of the final two years of the war.

The Final Year

Of course, few officers have ever conceded the strategic bankruptcy of their service, and Dönitz was convinced to the end that, with the proper tools, his campaign against the Atlantic lifeline could be

Figure 14.6 LST landing vehicles and equipment at Normandy, June 1944.

victorious yet. Late in the war Dönitz persuaded Hitler to redouble his bet on the U-boat campaign and fund the development of the Type XXI *Elecktroboote*, designed to wrest the final advantage from Allied anti-submarine crews. The XXI-class boats were the first serially built submarines designed to operate entirely submerged. They possessed the capabilities and weapon systems essential to effective undersea warfare: automatic depth-keeping equipment, improved passive listening arrays, active sonar, radar-search receivers, effective active radar, and a snorkel. Of course, Dönitz understood that a limited number of even superlative boats could not tip the balance in Germany's favor and that his only hope lay in building the Type XXI in large numbers. But the program came too late, never entirely overcame its considerable teething problems, and delivered too few operational boats to make a difference by the end of the war. Moreover, it offered no meaningful solution to the acquisition problem, which badly hobbled German efforts throughout the Battle of the Atlantic. In the frequently poor weather of the North Atlantic and on boats with low freeboard and limited visibility to the horizon, U-boats found it all too challenging to find even the largest convoys. Consistent air surveillance was the solution, and Dönitz had no prospect of achieving it. In the last two years of the war, Allied intelligence provided the information to divert almost every convoy around the few U-boats that could dodge the air patrols picking them off right from their pens on the French coast. The U-boat pens along the Atlantic coast themselves withstood punishing air raids but finished the war largely intact, ceasing operations only when Allied forces finally seized the territory around them.

Conclusion

Victory in the Battle of the Atlantic for the Allies came at a needlessly high cost in men and matériel and only after a period of painful adaptation. The failure to preserve the hard lessons of antisubmarine warfare in the interwar period and refusal to learn from the British experience in the war's first years reflected poorly on the strategic culture of the US Navy, even as eventual success demonstrated the competency and fortitude of that organization once it set itself to the task. US Navy leadership, especially Admiral King, thought initially more in terms of ship numbers than the advantages of improved coordination of the disparate commands responsible for different aspects of the antisubmarine and convoy problems. At the outset of the war, it also misjudged the types of ships and other assets required to address the U-boat menace most effectively. But, in the end, the leadership assessed the situation well enough, adapted its organization, and undertook the most remarkable shipbuilding campaign in history.

To place that shipbuilding campaign in context, the enormous expansion of output between 1942 and 1945 not only enabled the Allies to overcome Dönitz's campaign to cut off the British Isles but also provided for ultimate victory in the Pacific War and lay the groundwork for the projection of American military power during the Cold War. The outcome of World War II depended on resources and industrial production, and in this contest Soviet Admiral Sergei Gorshkov judged the Battle of the Atlantic differently:

Soon after Germany's attack on the Soviet Union, more than 2000 British and American ASW [antisubmarine warfare] combatants and specially-configured merchantmen and several thousand aircraft were in operation against German U-boats in the Atlantic theater. For each German U-boat there were 25 British and US warships and 100 aircraft, and for every German submariner at sea there were 100 British and American antisubmariners ... One can hardly find a similar ration of forces between attacking and defending forces among all other branches of the armed forces.[7]

---

[7] Sergei Gorshkov, "Navies in War and in Peace," *Morskoi Sbornik* [*Soviet Naval Digest*], 11 (1972), 26.

CHAPTER 15

Defense in the Pacific, 1937–1943

In 1937 Japan laid down the *Yamato*, the lead ship of a class of super-battleships. Displacing over 72,000 tons when fully loaded and mustering nine 18.1-inch main guns, the *Yamato* was the most powerful battleship in the world. The *Yamato* was not only the pride of the Imperial Japanese Navy; it also represented Japan's rising militarism and imperial aspirations, which would lead to its invasion of China in the summer of 1937 and war with the United States in 1941. The *Yamato* lay at the core of the Japanese naval strategy for war with the United States. Better protected and with longer-range guns than any US warship, the *Yamato* was designed for one purpose, to engage and destroy a numerically superior US Fleet in a climactic clash of battleships. That the *Yamato* was destined to play only a very small role in determining the outcome of the war in the Pacific illustrates how the instruments of war at sea had changed by the 1940s. The early stages of the war would demonstrate that the battleship had been superseded as the instrument of decision in naval warfare by the aircraft carrier and the submarine.

The Road to War

Japanese use of war as an instrument of expansion dated to the Sino-Japanese and Russo-Japanese wars, in which Japan had gained territory and commercial rights in Manchuria. By 1936 China was becoming economically stronger, and, with the support of the United States and Britain, the Nationalist Chinese under Chiang Kai-shek were determined and more capable of resisting continued Japanese expansion. The militarism and nationalism that contributed to rising anti-Japanese feelings in China were mirrored in Japan as Chinese opposition to Japanese dominance of Manchuria increased. Rising tensions between Japan and China resulted in shots being exchanged at the Marco Polo Bridge on July 7, 1937.

Ensuing mobilizations led to fighting around Shanghai that escalated into a full-scale invasion of China by Japan. As the fighting spread inland, Japanese aircraft attacked and sank the gunboat USS *Panay* outside the Chinese capital of Nanking. The Japanese claimed it was a case of mistaken identity and apologized to the United States, temporarily easing tensions. The Japanese offensive quickly captured Nanking and the occupying army forces graphically demonstrated the brutality of the war in China when they massacred over 300,000 Chinese civilians. However, Japan's invasion soon became bogged down, stymied by the sheer size of China and the stiffening of Chinese resistance.

The increasingly vicious nature of the war in China soon earned Japan worldwide condemnation. President Franklin Roosevelt denounced Japan's invasion but, limited by a strong isolationist movement, he was unable to put significant political, economic, or military pressure on Japan. War started in Europe when

America, Sea Power, and the World, First Edition. Edited by James C. Bradford.
© 2016 John Wiley & Sons, Inc. Published 2016 by John Wiley & Sons, Inc.

Germany invaded Poland in September 1939, drawing the attention of Britain and France to Europe and leaving the United States as the only political and military obstacle to Japanese expansion in the Pacific.

US Response

With aggressive German and Japanese expansion, war was on the horizon, and the United States began to prepare by expanding its armed forces. In 1934 Congress passed the Vinson–Trammell Act, which provided funding to bring the US Navy up to the Washington Naval Treaty limits. Successive Naval Expansions Acts in 1938–1940 authorized additional warship construction as political tensions continued to rise around the world. Japanese expansion in Asia combined with the defeat of France pushed Congress to pass the Two-Ocean Navy Act in July 1940. It was the largest naval expansion program to date, but those forces would not be operational until early 1943, and in response to relentless Japanese aggression the United States had only military deterrence and economic sanctions. President Roosevelt transferred the bulk of the US Fleet from the West Coast to Pearl Harbor in Hawaii in May 1940 as a show of force. Following Germany's defeat of France in June 1940, Japan pressured France's new Vichy government into granting Japan use of air and naval bases in French Indochina and into closing the vital Haiphong–Hanoi–Kunming path for Lend-Lease supplies flowing into China. Three months later—in an effort to deter further US support for China by raising the threat of a simultaneous conflict in the Atlantic and Pacific—Japan signed the Tripartite Pact with Germany and Italy. The United States responded economically by placing an embargo on the export of war matériel, aviation gas, and scrap iron to Japan. The following April, Japan entered a non-aggression pact with the Soviet Union to secure its rear as it prepared to expand southward. When Germany invaded Russia, tying Soviet troops down in Europe, Japan seized control of all of Vietnam and positioned 140,000 troops in the south ready to move into British Malaya and the Dutch East Indies. The United States reacted by placing an embargo on all oil shipments to Japan. With the United States supplying 80 percent of Japan's oil, Japan's strategic position began to deteriorate as a result of the embargo until it had only enough oil to last about a year and a half. Japan then had few options: withdraw from China, wait until lack of oil forced it to end the war in China, or seize control of another source of oil—the closest was in the Dutch East Indies. Japanese militarism and nationalism made the first two options politically impossible. That left no choice: Japan had to seize the Dutch East Indies and their oil and the US-controlled Philippines had to be taken to prevent interference with oil shipments to Japan's Home Islands. In the eyes of the Japanese military, war was inevitable and should be initiated as quickly as possible, before declining oil reserves forced the issue in China and before the US completed its rearmament programs.

Japanese Strategy

Recognizing the political impasse, the Japanese army and navy were developing a plan for war in the Pacific. With the Japanese army heavily engaged in China, the Japanese navy would bear the brunt of conflict with the United States and its ally Britain. The strategy adopted had three phases. During the first phase, the US Fleet at Pearl Harbor and the British fleet at Singapore would be neutralized; the Southern Resource Area (the Dutch East Indies and Malaya) with its oil, tin, rubber, and quinine would be captured; and a defensive perimeter would be established to defend Japan and its new possessions from counterattack. The second phase would establish bases and reinforce the defensive perimeter. The third phase would use submarines and air attacks operating from these bases to attrite US counterattacks, leading to a climactic Mahanian battle in which the Japanese fleet would destroy what remained of the US Navy.

Japan was better prepared for war than the Allies. The Japanese Combined Fleet, led by Admiral Isoroku Yamamoto, contained 10 aircraft carriers, 10 modern battleships, and over 3,000 carrier and land-based aircraft. The two super-battleships *Yamato* and *Musashi* would soon be added to the fleet (see Table 15.1). Japanese pilots, while limited in number, were highly trained, and most had gained combat experience in China. Japan's carrier-based fighter, the Mitsubishi A6M (dubbed the "Zero" by the Allies), was superior to any of the Allied planes it would encounter early

Table 15.1   Balance of naval forces in the Pacific, November 1941.

Warships	Japan	United States[a]	British Commonwealth	Dutch
Capital ships	10	9	2	0
Aircraft carriers	10	3	0	0
Cruisers	38	22	9	3
Destroyers	112	63	5	7
Submarines	65	50	0	15

[a]Includes the Pacific Fleet and the Asiatic Fleet.

in the war. Japanese torpedoes were also superior to those of the Allies, as were their night-fighting tactics. Japan's strategy for victory relied heavily on land-based airpower operating from island bases to destroy US forces while they were beyond the range of carrier aircraft.

US Counterstrategy

At the ABC-1 Conference, held in March 1941, Allied leaders agreed on a "Germany First" strategy, committing the United States to only defensive operations in the Pacific. The priority assigned to the Atlantic left the US Pacific Fleet numerically inferior to the Japanese Combined Fleet. Responsibility for developing and executing global naval strategy rested with Admiral Ernest King; Admiral Husband Kimmel commanded the Pacific Fleet, which contained three aircraft carriers and nine battleships based at Pearl Harbor; and General Douglas MacArthur commanded the forces in the Philippines and was supported by the small Asiatic Fleet, composed of cruisers, destroyers, and submarines. As the war started, the United States was in the process of replacing obsolete carrier aircraft with the F4F Wildcat fighter and the SBD Dauntless dive-bomber. However, many obsolete aircraft such as the TBD Devastator torpedo bomber were still in fleet use. With the exception of the Dauntless dive-bomber, which would serve very effectively as both an attack plane and a scout, US aircraft were generally inferior to their Japanese contemporaries.

Pearl Harbor

In October, Japanese and US diplomats began discussions aimed at averting war. The Japanese proposed that they would evacuate Indochina if, in return, the United States would reopen oil shipments and stop its support of China. American diplomats countered with an offer to lift the oil embargo in return for Japanese withdrawal from French Indochina and an end to Japan's war in China. With no compromise in sight, Japan set the date to begin hostilities in the event the negotiations failed and began positioning forces for simultaneous strikes against Malaya, the Dutch East Indies, the Philippines, and Pearl Harbor (see Map 15.1).

To prevent the interference of the US Fleet in Japanese operations, Admiral Yamamoto developed an innovative plan. All six Japanese fleet carriers were combined as the First Air Fleet and would launch a surprise attack on the US Fleet at its base in Pearl Harbor, destroying the battleships and carriers. Assembled and trained in complete secrecy, the First Air Fleet sailed from Japan on November 26, 1941, and headed east through the northern Pacific, well away from any islands or commercial shipping lanes. On December 2 its commander, Vice Admiral Chūicuhi Nagumo,[1] received news that negotiations had failed and was ordered to attack Pearl Harbor on December 7 (Hawaii time). A Sunday was chosen on the basis that most of the US Fleet would be in port and its readiness low.

---

[1] Japanese place family names first followed by given names, while English usage is inconsistent concerning the order for Japanese names. Thus Nagumo Chūichi (Japanese rendering) is commonly rendered Chūichi Nagumo in English-language publications. This work will adhere to common English usage.

Figure 15.1 Japanese photo of Pearl Harbor under attack, December 1941.

As the sun came up on December 7 the Japanese began launching aircraft. The first wave of attackers hit the eight US battleships with bombs and torpedoes while simultaneous attacks on Hawaiian airfields destroyed most US warplanes while they were still on the ground. A second wave destroyed the remaining US aircraft to prevent attacks on the Japanese carriers and finished the destruction of the US battleships. *Arizona, California, Nevada, Oklahoma*, and *West Virginia* were sunk in the attack and *Maryland, Pennsylvania*, and *Tennessee* severely damaged (see Figure 15.1). Having destroyed much of the US Fleet with almost no losses and the US carriers still unlocated—they were at sea delivering airplanes to Midway and Wake Islands—Vice Admiral Nagumo decided not to risk his carriers in a third assault on Pearl Harbor and returned to Japan. The attack succeeded in neutralizing the US Pacific Fleet; however, Pearl Harbor was left intact as a base, its critical submarine base, oil-storage facilities, and shipyards undamaged.

Japanese Advance Southward

The attack on Pearl Harbor was the first in a series of coordinated attacks on the US Philippines, British Malaya, and the Dutch East Indies. Hours after the Pearl Harbor attack, Japanese land-based aircraft surprised and destroyed most of the US aircraft in the Philippines while they were still on the ground. With air superiority, the Japanese launched an amphibious assault on the Philippines that pushed the US forces to a last stand on the Bataan Peninsula and the Island of Corregidor. The US forces would hold out under conditions of extreme duress until May 1942 before finally surrendering. By then Guam had been taken and Wake Island surrendered after a few weeks of determined resistance.

Simultaneously with the invasion of the Philippines, Japanese air and naval forces moved down Malaya toward the main British base at Singapore. With most of the British military resources defending

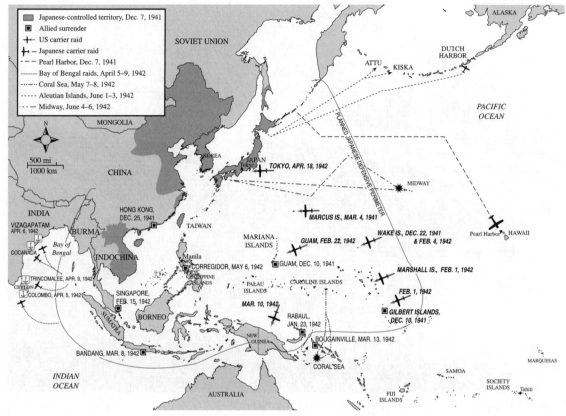

Map 15.1 Japanese offensives, 1941–1942.

Britain against Germany, there was only a weak task force built around the battleship *Prince of Wales* and the battle cruiser *Repulse* along with some obsolete fighter aircraft for defense of Malaya. On December 10, 1941, the two British ships sortied to engage a Japanese invasion fleet reported moving toward Singapore. Without fighter cover, *Prince of Wales* and *Repulse* were caught by Japanese land-based aircraft and sunk. Continued Japanese advances captured Singapore on February 15, 1942. Japanese occupation of northern Borneo in mid-December positioned them to attack Dutch Java from both the west and the east, securing the oil resources that were their main objective. The last remnants of the combined Allied fleets were destroyed at the Battle of Java Sea on February 27, and Java would fall in early March 1942. In only a few months the Japanese had captured Malaya, Singapore, the Philippines, and the Dutch East Indies and destroyed the main units of US and British Pacific fleets with no significant losses. The combination of surprise and Allied weakness enabled the Japanese to sweep the uncoordinated and mainly obsolete Allied forces completely out of the western Pacific (see Map 15.1).

US Reaction

The speed and ease of the Japanese victories stunned American leaders. Admiral King appointed Admiral Chester Nimitz to replace Admiral Kimmel as commander of the Pacific Fleet after the disaster at Pearl Harbor. King and Nimitz knew that, with most of the surface fleet out of commission, it would be impossible to execute War Plan Orange (see Chapter 13) in the immediate future. They agreed that the United States would have to remain on the defensive until warships under construction were completed and began joining the fleet in late 1942.

Chester W. Nimitz

Taking command of the US Pacific Fleet among the wreckage of Pearl Harbor, Admiral Chester Nimitz (1885–1966) quickly demonstrated his greatest qualities of leadership: the ability to calm and inspire those whom he led. Nimitz demonstrated this by retaining all of Admiral Husband Kimmel's staff. Rather than replace those officers, he turned them from a staff stung by their failure at Pearl Harbor into the confident and capable staff that would stop the Japanese and ultimately win the war in the Pacific. Blessed with a good eye for people, Nimitz trusted his subordinates and delegated responsibility to them, rarely interfering in the details of how they accomplished their assigned tasks. The result of his concern and support for his troops was the ability to get the best out of those who worked for him. When officers had to be replaced (e.g., Vice Admirals

Robert Ghormley and Frank Jack Fletcher), Nimitz assigned them billets that maintained their dignity and prevented divisions in the naval officer corps.

As the Japanese piled up success after success, Nimitz calmly steadied US forces, restored their confidence, and planned to counterattack. His previous experience in destroyers, submarines, and strategic planning gave him unique insights into the best means to employ the remnants of the fleet during the early months of 1942. An aggressive commander, Nimitz took calculated risks that paid off. The Battle of the Coral Sea stopped the Japanese advance for the first time and his decisive victory at Midway, against long odds, turned the tide of the war in the Pacific. Nimitz then directed the US offensive through the central Pacific, seizing island bases while bypassing Japanese strongholds. Nimitz was also able

Chester W. Nimitz. *Source:* US Navy, now in the collection of the National Archives. US Naval History and Heritage Command # 80-G-427844.

to work well with the notoriously difficult General Douglas MacArthur, coordinating forces and operations as they advanced along two fronts, finally uniting to recapture the Philippines.

During that time, the United States and its allies focused on holding Australia as a base for future operations, securing the sea lines of communication (SLOC) to Australia, and delaying Japanese expansion wherever possible. The only forces remaining to pursue those goals were the carrier task forces and submarines that had survived the Pearl Harbor attack. Once fear of a Japanese invasion of Hawaii subsided, US submarines were dispatched to attack Japanese warships and commercial shipping, but defective torpedoes limited their effectiveness throughout 1942.

In an effort to slow the enemy advance and keep the Japanese guessing as to US intentions, Nimitz launched a series of carrier raids in February and

March of 1942. The raids were designed to keep the Japanese off balance, provide operational experience, and build the morale of the Pacific Fleet. Using a combination of carrier planes and cruiser bombardments, US forces attacked Japanese positions in the Marshall and Gilbert Islands; on Marcus, Wake, and New Britain Island; and along the northern coast of New Guinea (see Map 15.1). These raids met their objectives but did not significantly impact or slow down Japanese operations in the South Pacific.

In the most important raid, Vice Admiral William Halsey led the *Enterprise* and the newly arrived carrier *Hornet* in a raid on the Japanese Home Islands. On April 18, 16 Army B-25 medium bombers took

off from the *Hornet*, under the command of Lieutenant Colonel James Doolittle (see Figure 15.2). After
bombing Tokyo, Yokohama, Kobe, and Nagoya, survivors crash-landed in China. While boosting US
morale at home, the Doolittle Raid would have an
impact on the Japanese strategy in the Pacific well
beyond the limited physical damage it caused (see
Map 15.1).

During this same period Allied leaders were
organizing for global war. On March 24 the US and
British Combined Chiefs of Staff assigned primary
responsibility for the war in the Pacific to the United
States. A week later the US Joint Chiefs of Staff established a command structure for the Pacific Theater
of Operations by dividing it between the South
West Pacific Area Command (SWPA), under the

command of General MacArthur (CINCSWPOA),
and the Pacific Ocean Area (POA), commanded by
Admiral Nimitz (CINCPOA). The huge POA was
subdivided into the North Pacific Area (NORPAC),
Central Pacific Area (CENPAC), and South Pacific
Area (SOPAC).

Battle of the Coral Sea

By early 1942 the initial Japanese strategic objectives
had been achieved without significant Allied resistance. The Japanese sensed an opportunity to further extend their defensive perimeter and to secure
their hold on the Southern Resource Area. From
their recently captured base at Rabaul, the Japanese
looked to seize Port Moresby, on the south coast of

Figure 15.2   Halsey–Doolittle Raid, April 1942. Army Air Force B-25 bombers on the deck of USS *Hornet* en route to
launch point. *Source:* US Naval History and Heritage Command # NH 53426.

New Guinea. The capture of Port Moresby would enhance the Japanese defensive perimeter by removing a major Allied air base within bomber range of Rabaul and threaten to cut SLOC vital to keeping reinforcements and supplies flowing to Australia and MacArthur's troops fighting in New Guinea.

Operation MO, the Japanese plan for the invasion of Port Moresby, was a complex operation using forces widely dispersed across the Coral Sea. Not expecting significant resistance from US forces, the Japanese planned simultaneous operations supported by two carrier groups. The first operation was to capture and establish a seaplane base on the small island of Tulagi in the Eastern Solomons. The second, primary operation was designed to seize Port Moresby. The invasion force of transports and their escorts, including the light carrier *Shoho*, was to proceed south through the Jomard Passage and turn west to attack Port Moresby. A covering force made up of the fleet carriers *Shokaku* and *Zuikaku* under Vice Admiral Takeo Takagi was to proceed around the eastern side of the Solomon Islands to intercept and destroy any US forces attempting to oppose either invasion.

Nimitz knew from decoded Japanese radio traffic that the enemy planned to move against Port Moresby in early May. With the *Enterprise* and *Hornet* returning from the Doolittle Raid and unavailable, Nimitz sent the *Yorktown* and its escorts under the command of Rear Admiral Frank Fletcher to the South Pacific to join the *Lexington* Task Group. The carrier groups would rendezvous in the Coral Sea on May 1 under Fletcher's overall command.

Learning that the Japanese had occupied Tulagi on May 3, Fletcher launched a series of air strikes against the ships supporting the Japanese landings. The attacks were moderately effective, sinking a Japanese destroyer and a few small craft, shooting down a few seaplanes, and driving the Japanese ships out of the harbor, but they ultimately did not stop the establishment of the seaplane base.

The Japanese Port Moresby Invasion Force was detected and unsuccessfully attacked by land-based aircraft while moving toward the Jomard Passage. On the morning of May 7, Fletcher launched a strike from the *Lexington* and *Yorktown* that found the *Shoho* and the support group. The strike commander radioed "scratch one flattop" as the *Shoho* took 13 bomb and seven torpedo hits in a well-executed attack. With the *Shoho* lost and the US carriers still unlocated, the Port Moresby Invasion Force turned back to Rabaul.

Meanwhile the Japanese carrier force had entered the Coral Sea from the east and was searching for the US carriers. When a scout plane reported sighting a US carrier, Takagi launched an air strike at about the same time the *Shoho* was being attacked. The reported carrier turned out to be the oiler *Neosho* accompanied by the destroyer *Sims*, both of which had detached from the fleet the night before. After a cursory search for the reported carriers, the Japanese sank the *Sims* and reduced the *Neosho* to a burned-out hulk. Both sides resumed searching for the enemy carriers, but a significant weather system in between the two fleets prevented their detection.

On the morning of May 8, US and Japanese search planes simultaneously located the opposing carriers and launched large strikes. When the US strike arrived over the Japanese fleet, the *Zuikaku* was concealed by a rainsquall, leaving only the *Shokaku* for the US planes to attack. US dive-bombers managed three hits on the *Shokaku*, damaging its flight deck and prevented the launching and recovering of aircraft, but did not threaten its seaworthiness. With excellent weather over the US Fleet, the Japanese attacked, hitting the *Lexington* with two torpedoes and five bombs that temporarily knocked it out of the battle. Extensive evasive maneuvers by the *Yorktown* enabled it to avoid all the torpedoes dropped and all but one minor bomb hit. Shortly after the Japanese attack, the *Lexington*'s damage-control efforts had brought fires under control and the ship was beginning to operate aircraft when gasoline vapors from ruptured fuel lines exploded. The crew was forced to abandon ship and the crippled carrier ultimately had to be sunk by US destroyers.

The unbroken string of Japanese successes early in the war had created a sense of overconfidence in the Japanese. Simultaneous operations with relatively small formations had succeeded due to surprise and the dispersion of Allied forces. But, against determined and prepared resistance, dividing their forces and launching complex operations requiring intricate timing proved a recipe for failure. Japanese division of their forces into multiple groups, each smaller than the combined US task force, allowed American

commanders to attack and defeat each Japanese formation in sequence. Rather than learn from their errors
in the Coral Sea, Japanese commanders repeated
them at the Battles of Midway and the Philippine Sea.

Coral Sea was a strategic defeat for the Japanese as
the Allies maintained control of Port Moresby, but it
cost the United States the carrier *Lexington*, the oiler
Neosho, and the destroyer *Sims*. The Japanese lost the
light carrier *Shoho*, a destroyer, and assorted smaller
ships at Tulagi. In addition, the *Shokaku* was severely
damaged and the *Yorktown* lightly damaged. The
real story, however, is in the loss of 65 US and 108
Japanese aircraft and pilots. The Battle of the Coral
Sea was the first naval battle where the opposing fleets
never saw each other; it was conducted entirely by
air attack. This new reality in naval combat clearly
demonstrated the importance of aircraft and aircraft
carriers. The *Shokaku* required extensive repairs and,
as a consequence, it missed the Battle of Midway.
In addition, the loss of 87 out of 126 carrier aircraft
and many experienced pilots meant the *Zuikaku* was
also unavailable for Midway. In contrast, the undamaged shipyards at Pearl Harbor were able to repair the
Yorktown in time to participate at Midway. The Battle
of the Coral Sea was the first setback for the Japanese
at the strategic level and demonstrated a stiffening of
Allied resistance.

Battle of Midway

Strategically, the unexpected speed and success of
Japan's initial plans and the neutralization of the
British navy by air raids against bases in Ceylon and
India created opportunities for follow-on operations.
Desiring to stay on the offensive, the overconfident
Japanese debated whether to attack westward in hopes
of sparking a rebellion in India, to attack southeast-
ward to cut SLOC between Hawaii and Australia,
or to extend their defensive perimeter further into
the central Pacific. The surprise and embarrassment of the Doolittle Raid led leaders to select the
third alternative and move against Midway and the
Aleutian Islands. By capturing the Western Aleutians
and Midway, the Japanese would acquire airbases that
could prevent further incursions like the Doolittle Raid. The capture of Midway would also enable
the Japanese to attack Pearl Harbor with long-range

bombers and deny its use to the United States as an
advanced operating base for air and submarine operations. Finally, the seizure of Midway would provide
an opportunity to lure out the remaining American
carriers and destroy them in a decisive battle.

Admiral Yamamoto's plan divided the Combined
Fleet into five units to execute precisely timed attacks
designed to capture first the Aleutian Islands and then
Midway, and finally to destroy the remaining US carriers as they tried to assist in the defense of Midway.
Part one of the plan would land Japanese troops on
Attu and Kiska in the Aleutian Islands. The Aleutian
operation was designed to attract US attention and
divert forces away from Midway. The Japanese Carrier Striking Force under Vice Admiral Nagumo, consisting of the carriers *Akagi, Hiryu, Kaga, and Soryu*,
would neutralize Midway's defenses for the Midway
Invasion Force, which was following close behind.
The Midway Invasion Force, supported by the light
carrier *Zuiho* and two battleships, would then assault
Midway. When the US Fleet responded, a picket line
of Japanese submarines deployed between Hawaii and
Midway would attack the US forces headed for Midway. Warned of the approach of the American fleet
by those submarines, the Carrier Striking Group and
planes from newly captured Midway would then
attack the US Fleet as it approached Midway. Finally,
the main Japanese battle fleet, including seven battleships, would arrive under the personal command
of Admiral Yamamoto to surprise the Americans and
destroy them in a decisive Mahanian-style battle. The
Japanese plan, however, was overly complicated, difficult to coordinate under radio silence, and completely
dependent on surprise for success.

The problem was that Japan did not have the
element of surprise. US naval intelligence had broken
the Japanese JN-25 naval code and learned that the
Aleutian operation was a diversionary ploy and that
Midway was the main target. Admiral Nimitz now
knew where, and approximately when, the Japanese
would strike, but was still heavily outnumbered.
Against Japan's 11 battleships and eight carriers, Nimitz had only the *Enterprise* and *Hornet* Task Forces. The
only chance for any reinforcement came from the
damaged *Yorktown*, limping back to Pearl Harbor after
the Battle of the Coral Sea. In addition to naval forces,
Nimitz heavily reinforced Midway with ground

troops and aircraft, sending Marine fighters and dive-bombers, Army B-17 heavy bombers, and Navy torpedo bombers and patrol seaplanes—119 warplanes in all—essentially turning Midway into an additional aircraft carrier for the battle.

Nimitz knew that, regardless of the balance of forces against him, it was critical to defend Midway. Indeed, armed with the information about the Japanese plans, Nimitz believed that Midway offered an opportunity to concentrate his forces and to ambush and destroy part of the Japanese fleet, ideally its carriers. Seizing the initiative, Nimitz merged the *Enterprise* and *Hornet* groups into Task Force 16 under the command of Rear Admiral Raymond A. Spruance and sent them to the north and east of Midway, the least likely place the Japanese would expect the US ships to be. After only three days in dry dock, the *Yorktown* put back to sea as the center of Task Force 17 under Rear Admiral Fletcher. Although not completely repaired, the *Yorktown* would be a critical addition to the US carrier strength at Midway. By massing his three carriers and the additional planes on Midway, Nimitz's fleet, while still numerically inferior, would outnumber the Japanese in the critical area of aircraft.

The battle opened on June 3 with Japanese airstrikes on Dutch Harbor, the main US base in the Aleutians. Knowing the Japanese thrust at the Aleutians was mainly a distraction, Nimitz chose to mass his forces on the critical objective at Midway. Nimitz established daily patrols by long-range PBY Catalina seaplanes from Midway, patrolling 700–800 miles to the north and west, while the US carriers waited in radio silence to the northeast of Midway, ready to strike when the Japanese carriers were located. On the morning of June 3, 1942, one of the PBYs discovered the Japanese invasion force approaching from the west; Midway-based aircraft attacked the transports that night but failed to inflict any significant damage.

On the morning of June 4 the still undetected Japanese Carrier Striking Force launched a heavy attack to soften up Midway for the invasion. Prudently, Nagumo held back half of his aircraft armed with torpedoes and armor-piercing bombs in case any US naval forces intervened. Not expecting any US forces and receiving no indication from his submarine pickets that there were any American ships in the area, Nagumo launched only a token scouting force of seven seaplanes from the escorting ships to look for US forces. As fate would have it, the plane assigned to search the area where the US carriers were located was delayed at launching. The initial Japanese attack on Midway severely damaged the airfield infrastructure but met heavy resistance from US fighters and antiaircraft fire that convinced the Japanese raid commander that another attack would be required before Midway could be invaded. Shortly after the first Japanese strike on Midway had launched, US reconnaissance planes located the Japanese carriers and Midway-based aircraft set out to attack. These attacks were uncoordinated and, attacking in small groups, the Americans suffered heavy losses while scoring no hits. The heavy air attacks from Midway and the recommendation of the strike commander persuaded Nagumo to order a second strike on Midway. With no US naval forces detected, he instructed the planes he had held in reserve to replace their anti-ship weapons with ground attack ordnance.

While the Japanese second strike was being rearmed, the delayed scout plane finally located the US carriers north of Midway. Nagumo now found himself in the nightmare scenario of a carrier commander. He had two choices: launch the planes that were ready, minus their fighter escort, in a weak but timely strike or wait until the entire strike was rearmed. He chose the latter. The returning Midway strike aircraft were low on fuel, so Nagumo had to further delay the launch of the second strike until those aircraft were recovered. After a significant delay, Nagumo had just turned into the wind to begin launching the strike against the US carriers when the first US carrier planes began their attack.

Admiral Spruance had launched the *Enterprise*'s and *Hornet*'s planes as soon as the Japanese carriers had been located, and these were followed shortly by the *Yorktown*'s strike. The US warplanes became separated and attacked the Japanese carriers piecemeal. First to arrive were the torpedo squadrons, which attacked without fighter cover. Torpedo Squadron Eight lost every aircraft and the other two squadrons suffered heavy losses, without scoring any hits. The sacrifice of the torpedo planes had the unintended, but critical, effect of pulling the Japanese fighter cover down to low altitude, leaving the Japanese fleet undefended when the US dive-bombers arrived overhead. The dive-bombers scored numerous hits on three Japanese carriers, which were destroyed when the fueled and armed aircraft on deck began exploding. The remaining Japanese carrier *Hiryu* avoided the US attack and its planes followed the American aircraft back to, and severely damaged, the *Yorktown* (see Figure 15.3). Later in the evening, US dive-bombers would locate and sink the *Hiryu*, but a submarine would sink the damaged *Yorktown* while it was en route to Pearl Harbor.

Midway was an even greater victory for the United States than Coral Sea as the Japanese lost four carriers, 275 aircraft, and most of their veteran pilots. Nimitz

had reacted decisively to the intelligence provided by cryptanalysis and, acting with speed of decision, aggressiveness, and a willingness to risk the bulk of his remaining forces, had the major US units in place and waiting to attack the Japanese. With the element of surprise, Admiral Yamamoto's plan may have succeeded. The critical fault of Yamamoto's plan was the assumption that the US would react as the Japanese expected (with the US carrier forces starting at Pearl Harbor) and that the United States would have a maximum of only two carriers available. Based on these assumptions, Yamamoto divided his vastly superior fleet into

Figure 15.3 USS *Yorktown* struck by dive-bombers at Midway, June 1942. *Source:* US Navy, now in the collection of the National Archives. US Naval History and Heritage Command # 80-G-312018.

multiple groups, each with separate objectives and not mutually supportive of each other. In fact, none of these critical assumptions proved valid. This enabled the far weaker US Fleet to mass and engage the isolated Japanese Carrier Striking Force with better than even odds in terms of aircraft and with the critical element of surprise on the US side. The destruction of the major striking arm of the Japanese navy would severely limit the offensive options of the Japanese in the campaigns to come.

The Guadalcanal Campaign

Japanese expansion had been blunted at the Coral Sea and Midway, but not in the Solomon Islands, where, during the Coral Sea operation, the Japanese navy had established a seaplane base on Tulagi. During the summer of 1942, Allied intelligence detected the Japanese had moved troops to the neighboring island of Guadalcanal and begun construction of an airfield. If completed, this airfield would threaten the SLOC to Australia. Its temporary superiority in carriers after Midway gave the United States an advantage and Admiral King sensed the opportunity to switch to the offensive. King directed Nimitz to seize Guadalcanal before the airfield was completed and establish a US airbase there. US control of Guadalcanal and its airfield would not only protect the SLOC to Australia but also threaten the Japanese stronghold at Rabaul.

Admiral King assigned the offensive, codenamed Operation Watchtower, to Vice Admiral Robert Ghormley, newly appointed Commander South Pacific Forces. His assets were limited, as the Guadalcanal Campaign would be fought primarily with the surviving elements of the prewar fleet. Major General Alexander Vandegrift led the ground forces consisting of 15,000 men of the 1st Marine Division augmented by the 1st Marine Raider battalion and the 2nd Marines. The units making up the assault force had never operated together and had departed from multiple locations before assembling in New Zealand. Shipping limitations and inadequate dock space delayed the arrival of the troops and further compressed an already tight timeline. After herculean efforts on the docks got the ships combat loaded, a quick rehearsal was conducted at the end of July. The incomplete rehearsal was a failure, but the time was

well spent as many of the problems exposed were corrected in time for the assault. Vice Admiral Fletcher would command the air support for the landing with the carriers *Enterprise*, *Saratoga*, and *Wasp* (newly arrived from the Atlantic). The amphibious forces that would land the Marines and provide logistics were under the command of Rear Admiral Richmond Kelly Turner. The US plan called for Marines to seize both the Japanese base at Tulagi and the airfield under construction on Guadalcanal. With the urgency of time, August 7 was set for the invasion.

Still reeling from the dramatic setback at Midway, Japanese commanders were surprised and unprepared for the sudden US offensive in the Solomons. The Japanese construction troops on Guadalcanal fled into the jungle and the initial US landings were unopposed. The Marines immediately set to work finishing the airfield, which they renamed Henderson Field. The Japanese surprise did not last long, however. Planes from Rabaul quickly responded and attacked the US forces, significantly delaying the unloading of supplies for the forces ashore. Realizing the weakness of the US position on Guadalcanal, the Japanese sortied a strong force of heavy cruisers to attack the US beachhead during the night of August 8. Three groups of Allied heavy cruisers patrolled around Savo Island to protect the transports unloading at the beachhead to the south. Under cover of darkness, the undetected Japanese attacked and, using their superior night-fighting and torpedo tactics, destroyed one Australian and three US heavy cruisers in the Battle of Savo Island, in waters that would become known as "Ironbottom Sound." The loss of the naval forces protecting the transports combined with heavy losses in carrier fighters prompted Fletcher to withdraw the US carriers and the transports before they were completely unloaded, leaving the marines ashore short on supplies and air support. Nevertheless, the marines worked quickly and aircraft began operating from Henderson Field on August 20, launching strikes against Japanese positions ashore and ships at sea (see Map 15.2).

After Savo Island the Japanese surface forces established control of the sea at night, and could bombard Henderson Field and transport reinforcements and supplies to Guadalcanal. These runs, nicknamed the "Tokyo Express" by the marines, would dash in

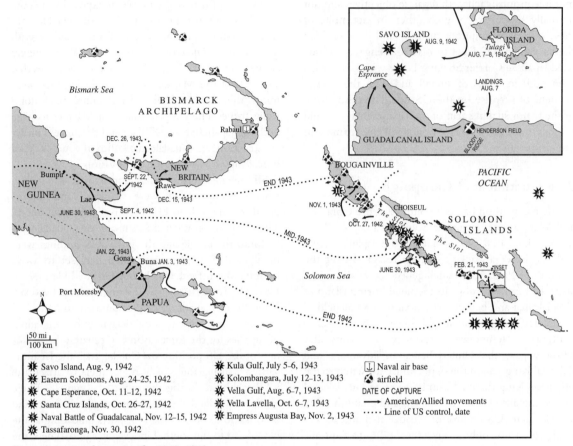

Map 15.2   Southwest Pacific, 1942–1943.

under the cover of darkness and retreat out of US air attack range by morning. However, Japanese transports proved too slow to avoid US air attacks, forcing the Japanese to use faster destroyers to transport troops to Guadalcanal. Use of destroyers significantly reduced the numbers of troops and heavy equipment that could be brought in at any one time. A stalemate quickly developed in the southern Solomons; US aircraft dominated the air over the islands during the day and Japanese surface ships controlled the waters around Guadalcanal at night. Consequently, Henderson Field, the "unsinkable aircraft carrier," became the focus of the whole campaign and a lifeline for the Marines. The Guadalcanal Campaign, a US offensive-for-defensive-purposes campaign, quickly became something the Japanese could not afford: a war of attrition.

In an effort to break the stalemate, the Japanese gathered 1,500 reinforcements and planned a convoy covered by three Japanese carriers. The three US carriers in the Solomons intercepted the Japanese convoy. In the Battle of the Eastern Solomons, the Japanese convoy was turned back and the Japanese lost the light carrier *Ryujo* and 60 irreplaceable carrier planes and pilots, while the *Enterprise* was damaged and forced to withdraw for repairs (see Map 15.2). Following the battle, US carrier strength would be further reduced with the damaging of the *Saratoga* and the sinking of the *Wasp* by Japanese submarines. The loss of carrier strength only increased the importance of Henderson Field.

Ashore, Vandegrift and the Marines, short of supplies and ammunition, dug in to defend Henderson Field. The Japanese had underestimated the strength

F4F Wildcat

In December 1941, the F4F Wildcat was the primary carrier-based fighter for the US Navy. Over the next six months the superior performance of the Japanese A6M "Zero" fighter shocked Allied airmen. Close comparison of the two aircraft revealed that the Zero's advantages were the result of substantial design compromises resulting from differing design philosophies. The Japanese conceived the Zero to take advantage of their well-trained carrier pilots and they emphasized speed and maneuverability over survivability. Reduction in weight achieved by the omission of cockpit armor and self-sealing fuel tanks made the Zero lighter, faster, more maneuverable, and able to out-climb the Wildcat, but the lack of protective armor and self-sealing fuel tanks also rendered the Zero vulnerable to the heavier firepower of the F4F. Wildcat pilots overcame these weaknesses by developing innovative tactics that maximized the strengths of their fighters. Lieutenant Commander Jimmy Thatch perfected a system for flying F4Fs two abreast to provide mutual support. When one of the aircraft was attacked, the pilots would immediately turn toward each other, cross paths, then repeat the maneuver with the target plane ("bait") leading the enemy in front of his wingman, the "hook," who would drive off or destroy the attacker. The second Wildcat would turn to cross behind the attacked aircraft and shoot the attacking aircraft off his tail. First employed in the Battle of Midway, the "Thatch Weave" enabled US pilots flying the Wildcat to successfully fight against the Japanese Zero and had become a standard American tactic by the time of Guadalcanal in August 1942.

F4F-3A Wildcats flown by Lieutenant Commander "Jimmy" Thatch and Lieutenant "Butch" O'Hare, April 1942. *Source:* US Navy, now in the collection of the National Archives. US Naval History and Heritage Command # 80-G-10613.

of the marines on Guadalcanal. On the night of August 20–21, the Japanese launched their first major counterattack against the marines, who destroyed the 800 men of the elite Ikke Unit in the Battle of Tenaru River. By September 13 the Japanese had built up 6,000 troops and launched another attack on the marine positions along the ridge south of Henderson Field. Led by Colonel Merritt Edson, the marines repulsed the Japanese attack on "Bloody Ridge" with machine guns and artillery and destroyed the Japanese force. Tenaru River and "Bloody Ridge"

established a pattern of ground combat in which the Japanese landed troops, built up and assaulted the marines' defensive perimeter, and suffered heavy losses. Throughout September and early October both the United States and Japan fed air and ground reinforcements into the continuing battle of attrition. The Japanese had amassed 20,000 troops on Guadalcanal by late October, but General Vandegrift had also been reinforced with supplies and fresh troops, bringing his strength to 23,000. Between October 22 and 26, the Japanese launched what proved to be their final attempt to retake Henderson Field. The marines met a series of piecemeal and uncoordinated Japanese attacks with machine-gun and artillery fire that decimated the enemy. Those Japanese who survived soon lost much of their effectiveness due to their lack of food and medical supplies.

Strong efforts to reinforce and resupply the respective forces would lead to a series of naval battles for sea control around the Solomons. As midnight neared on October 11–12, an American task force of four cruisers and five destroyers intercepted a Japanese troop convoy escorted by three cruisers and two destroyers off Cape Esperance. Using superior radar and improved night-fighting tactics, the Americans surprised the Japanese force, sinking a cruiser and two destroyers while losing one destroyer, but failed to prevent the troop convoy from delivering its reinforcements to Guadalcanal.

With victory in the Guadalcanal Campaign still in the balance, Nimitz relieved Ghormley as commander in the South Pacific and replaced him with the more aggressive Halsey, who immediately set his forces toward reinforcing Guadalcanal and defeating Japan's surface warships. The Japanese had also made a heavy push to land troops to capture Henderson Field. In late October, Admiral Yamamoto committed the Combined Fleet, with its four aircraft carriers, four battleships, and 14 cruisers, to the struggle. Halsey countered with two carriers, a battleship, and six cruisers. In the Battle of Santa Cruz (October 26–27) the Japanese suffered heavy damage to the carriers *Shokaku* and *Zuiho* and lost over 90 carrier planes and experienced pilots, and the United States lost the carrier *Hornet*, leaving the damaged *Enterprise* as the only operational US carrier in the Pacific. It was a tactical victory for the Japanese but a strategic victory for the United States because the Japanese fleet retreated, leaving the Marines in control of Henderson Field.

By early November the tide turned in favor of the United States. The Japanese air and ground units were being destroyed faster than they could be replaced in the meat grinder of Guadalcanal. In addition, new ships (e.g., the fast battleships *South Dakota* and *Washington*) began arriving to reinforce Halsey. The Naval Battle of Guadalcanal (November 12–15) would finally give the United States sea control in

the southern Solomons. On the night of November 12–13, Admiral Yamamoto sent two battleships, a cruiser, and 14 destroyers to bombard Henderson Field. This force was intercepted by a US task force of seven cruisers and eight destroyers. In an engagement lasting only 15 minutes, the US warships, in a line-ahead formation, steamed through the wedge-shaped Japanese formation crippling or sinking a battleship, a cruiser, two destroyers, and seven transports while losing only two cruisers and four destroyers. The next night the surviving Japanese battleship led a last-ditch effort to resupply Japanese troops, but that sortie was met by the battleships *South Dakota* and *Washington*, which in another night action sank the battleship *Kirishima*. While the fighting would continue, this series of battles effectively ended the campaign, as the Japanese, no longer able to send in reinforcements or adequately supply their troops on Guadalcanal, began to withdraw their troops in January 1943.

Conclusion

The Guadalcanal Campaign was the true turning point in the Pacific War. For the last time, Japan launched a strategic offensive. The long, evenly matched campaign demonstrated that Japan was far from beaten, but, by its end, Japan had lost more men, ships, warplanes, and experienced pilots than the United States. More importantly, Japan could not replace any of these losses at a time when US production was only beginning to hit its stride. The campaign also marked the first time that the United States took the offensive, albeit for defensive purposes. Their defeat at Guadalcanal forced the Japanese to fight a costly, defensive war of attrition from that point forward. At the same time, the Americans could move to the offensive in the Pacific. In the South Pacific Area, US forces advanced northwestward through the Solomon Islands to land on Bougainville in November. West of them in the South West Pacific Area, US and Australian Army troops (commanded by General Douglas MacArthur and supported by the newly formed US Seventh Fleet) slowly pushed Japanese defenders northwestward on New Guinea and crossed to land on New Britain in December (see Map 15.2). Meanwhile a lull settled over the central Pacific for the first 10 months of 1943 as both sides prepared for the next round of combat.

CHAPTER 16

Offensive in the Pacific, 1943–1944

On the morning of July 7, 1943, Admiral Chester W. Nimitz, commander-in-chief of the Pacific Fleet, broke his flag on the new fast carrier *Essex*, moored at Ford Island in Pearl Harbor. Only four months after the ship's commissioning, the *Essex*, skippered by Captain Donald B. ("Wu") Duncan, had just joined the Fifth Fleet, and Nimitz wanted to observe first-hand the progress the ship and its crew had made preparing for combat. At sea later that day, *Essex*'s air group, now flying the new Grumman F6F Hellcat, impressed Nimitz and the rest of the brass with an air show. Seven weeks later, after more exercises and training, the *Essex* was ready to go to war. At 1552 on August 22, the ship cleared Pearl, joined three escorting destroyers, and rendezvoused the next morning with Task Force 15. Under the command of Rear Admiral Charles Pownall, flying his flag in the new *Essex*-class *Yorktown*, Task Force 15 also included the speedy, light carrier *Independence*, the fast battleship *Indiana*, and a screen of light cruisers and destroyers. Once formed up, the task force settled onto a course northwest at 18 knots toward its objective, the Japanese-held Marcus atoll, 2,700 miles from Hawaii.

Marcus was an opportunity for Nimitz to see how well a multicarrier task force formation functioned under real-world combat conditions. After refueling, the task force closed on Marcus overnight on August 30–31, reaching a position north of the island before dawn. The *Yorktown* launched its first strike at 0422,

followed by the *Essex* a little more than an hour later, with the *Independence* providing search and combat air patrols. The carriers flew three more strikes that day, the last returning to the *Essex* at 1651, after which the task force retired to the northeast under the cover of rain squalls. The American planes had cratered the runway and destroyed radio and radar installations, hangars, fuel dumps, antiaircraft batteries, and at least seven aircraft on the ground. No enemy aircraft challenged the attackers, who lost five planes and six pilots and crew to antiaircraft fire and accidents.

The Marcus raid was a baptism of fire for the fast carrier task force. It also marked the beginning of a two-year American offensive in the Central Pacific Area that extended thousands of miles to the west and resulted in the destruction of the Imperial Japanese Navy and led ultimately to the defeat of Japan. The Guadalcanal Campaign, which ended in February 1943, had resulted in victory for the Americans but had left both adversaries exhausted from six months of attrition warfare. Meanwhile, the Allies in the South West Pacific Area, under the command of Army General Douglas MacArthur, had driven the Japanese out of southeastern New Guinea after a grueling and costly offensive that did not end until late January 1943.

Relative calm in the spring of 1943 allowed the Americans and Japanese time to assess their strategies. In the South Pacific, the primary objective was the

Japanese stronghold of Rabaul on the island of New Britain (see Map 15.2). South Pacific and Third Fleet commander Admiral William F. Halsey planned to hop from island to island in the Solomons, supported by land-based air power. At the same time, MacArthur's South West Pacific troops were to advance along the north coast of New Guinea to Lae, from which they could sever Japanese lines of communication to Rabaul and invade New Britain. On or about February 1, 1944, Halsey, with MacArthur's support, would either seize or neutralize Rabaul. At the Casablanca Conference in January 1943, Allied strategic planners agreed that there should also be an offensive in the Central Pacific. After subsequent Anglo-American meetings, the Joint Chiefs of Staff approved plans for the simultaneous offensives, with the Japanese-held Gilbert Islands to be assaulted in November 1943 and the Marshalls in January 1944.

For their part, the Japanese realigned their lines of defense to positions running on an axis through the Bismarcks to Salamaua in New Guinea while reinforcing Rabaul and their defenses in the Gilberts. To accomplish this, the Japanese bolstered their Third Fleet Striking Force with six old and new carriers, supported by battleships and cruisers. Admiral Yamamoto Isoroku used Third Fleet aircraft to augment land-based navy planes to attack American shipping and other targets in the central Solomons in a costly effort to slow Halsey's advance from Guadalcanal. At the same time, the Imperial Japanese Navy undertook a desperate building and conversion program to make up for the losses in 1942, with five carriers expected to join the fleet by the middle of 1944. But naval aircraft and aviators lost in the Solomons and New Guinea were more difficult to replace, and the death of Yamamoto, shot down over Bougainville in April, was a blow to Imperial Japanese Navy morale and leadership.

With the *Essex* and its sisters, along with the *Independence*-class carriers and a constellation of fast battleships, cruisers, and destroyers, Nimitz finally had the ships necessary to expedite the naval campaign in the Central Pacific and support the effort in the South West Pacific. He also had to make decisions about the command of the new fleets and carrier task forces. Only a handful of senior admirals were acceptable to both Nimitz and his boss, Admiral Ernest J. King, chief of naval operations and commander-in-chief of

the US Fleet. Halsey was one, respected for his experience and glorified by the public as a heroic fighting seadog. Another was Vice Admiral Raymond A. Spruance, who projected a modest, thoughtful, and deliberate presence. He had stood in for Halsey at the Battle of Midway, then joined Nimitz as his chief of staff, where he was instrumental in planning the Central Pacific offensive.

Gilbert Islands Campaign

More carrier raids in the fall of 1943 on Japanese-held islands kept the enemy off balance in the Central Pacific while planning and preparations went ahead for Operation Galvanic: the invasion of Makin and Tarawa in the Gilbert Islands (see Map 16.1). Nimitz chose Spruance to command both the Central Pacific Force and the Fifth Fleet for the assault. Under Spruance were the Fifth Amphibious Force, commanded by Rear Admiral Richmond Kelly Turner, and an Army and Marine assault team under Major General Holland M. Smith, supported by battleships, cruisers, and escort carriers. Eleven fast carriers in Pownall's Task Force 50 were to soften up the Japanese defenses on the islands, then provide tactical support for the landings and subsequent operations. Worried that the Japanese might intervene with a powerful carrier–battleship force from their bases at Truk and the Marshall Islands, Spruance and Turner decided to hold the carriers in defensive positions close to the beaches, despite objections from some of the aviators, who believed it was a blunder to deny carriers their chief asset of mobility. Spruance also determined that in order to achieve surprise there would be no surface-ship bombardment until the morning of the invasion.

Turner's amphibious force consisted of a Northern Attack Force of Army troops to invade Makin and a Southern Attack Force of marines to assault Tarawa (see Map 16.2). Two carrier groups from Hawaii joined two of Halsey's groups from the South Pacific, where they had just completed massive raids on Rabaul. On November 18, the carriers struck Tarawa, after which they annihilated the Japanese air defenses on Makin as well as positions in the Marshalls. Battleships, cruisers, and destroyers shelled Makin and Tarawa three hours before the landings on the 20th. On Butaritari, the largest of the islands in the Makin atoll, 6,500 soldiers

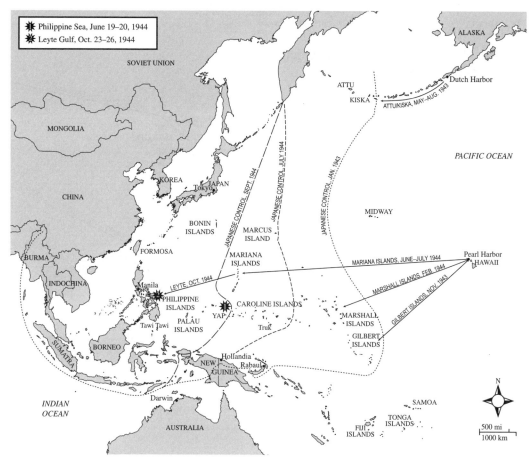

Map 16.1 US offensives, 1943–1944.

encountered surprisingly strong resistance from the relatively small number of Japanese defenders, who held out for three days before being subdued.

The Southern Force struck the heavily defended Betio in the Tarawa atoll at about the same time as the Northern Force landed on Makin. Two and a half hours of shore bombardment and a belated air strike from the carriers preceded the invasion, delayed due to communications and visibility problems and adverse winds. Not until 0900 did the first marines go ashore, negotiating a coral reef and tough beach defenses, while facing artillery and machine-gun fire. Unarmored LVT (landing vehicle tracked) amphibious tractors (or amphtracs) broke down or were hit by enemy fire, and conventional landing craft could not clear the reef due to the receding tide. Struggling to

maintain the beachhead, and suffering nearly 50 percent casualties, the marines held on and even advanced in one sector; not until the 23rd did they overcome Japanese resistance.

The Gilberts were a costly lesson. Of the 18,500 marines in the Tarawa assault, more than 3,000 were casualties, among whom more than 1,000 were dead. On the evening of the 20th, Japanese bombers torpedoed and badly damaged the *Independence*, and four days later the supporting force lost the escort carrier *Liscome Bay*, torpedoed and sunk by a Japanese submarine. It was clear that in the future surprise would have to give way to more intense and prolonged shore bombardment; close air support techniques needed to be refined; command and control needed to be rationalized; and fast carriers had to be

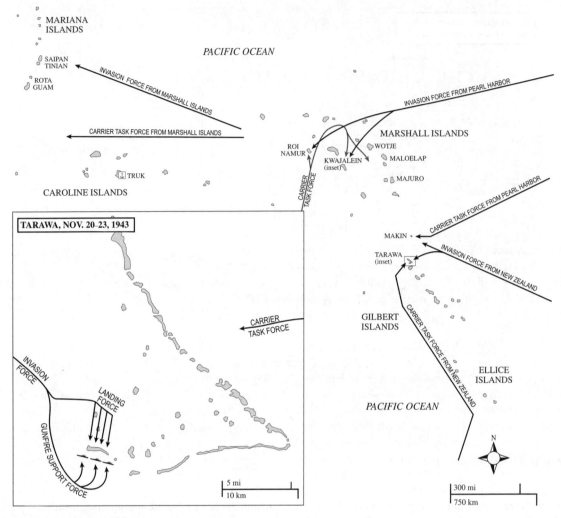

Map 16.2 Central Pacific drive, 1943–1944.

unleashed to strike Japanese sea and air forces at the source, especially in the Marshalls. On the other hand, the Japanese had lost nearly all of their air power in the Central Pacific, and their surface and carrier forces were in no position to mount an attack on the Fifth Fleet, as Spruance had expected.

Solomon Islands Campaign

In contrast to the attack on the Gilberts, the second prong of the Pacific offensive in the northern Solomons was practically a model of coordinated land, sea, and air power (see Map 15.2). Initially the plan was

to advance island by island up the chain to Rabaul, establishing base facilities and airfields and using carrier forces for support as needed. But, rather than invade those heavily defended islands northwest of Guadalcanal, Halsey decided that he could instead take more lightly held positions, thus bypassing (or "leapfrogging") major strongholds and saving time and lives. Under the command of Rear Admiral Theodore S. Wilkinson, the Third Amphibious Force easily took the island of Vella Lavella on August 15. In the confused naval Battle of Vella Lavella on the night of October 6–7, a Japanese destroyer group mauled an American destroyer force.

Bougainville, capping the top of the Solomons archipelago, was the next objective of Halsey's Third Fleet. The plan was to have Marines, led by General Alexander A. Vandegrift, a Guadalcanal veteran, go ashore at Cape Torokina, on the west coast of the island. Support came from a cruiser–destroyer task force and from Rear Admiral Frederick C. Sherman's carriers *Princeton* and *Saratoga*. In preparation for the November 1 landing, land-based and carrier aircraft struck Japanese airfields in Bougainville and pummeled Rabaul again. Wilkinson's 14,300 marines secured the beachhead within 24 hours of the landing and quickly moved inland against light resistance.

With Rabaul now threatened, the Japanese immediately took steps to disrupt the invasion force. Early on November 2, American cruisers and destroyers, aided by radar, defeated a Japanese cruiser–destroyer force in Empress Augusta Bay, not far from Torokina. Before the Japanese could regroup and reinforce their positions in and around Bougainville, Halsey's carriers launched strikes against Rabaul on November 4, damaging six cruisers and three destroyers. Over the next month and a half, marines on Bougainville fought against determined Japanese opposition to clear enough of the island to build airfields that brought land-based air power to within reach of Rabaul. Once major operations on Bougainville ended the following April, and the decision was made to leapfrog rather than reduce Rabaul, the long South Pacific campaign ended, and Halsey became available to Nimitz for fleet command in the Central Pacific.

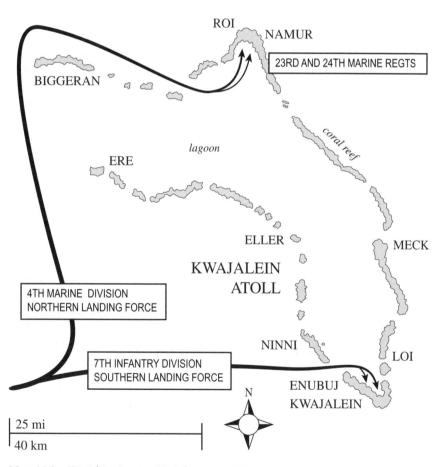

Map 16.3 Kwajalein, January 31–February 6, 1944.

The Marshall Islands Campaign

Nimitz and Vice Admiral John H. Towers, Commander Air Force Pacific Fleet, were displeased with Pownall's handling of the carriers in the Gilberts campaign. They agreed to replace him with Rear Admiral Marc A. ("Pete") Mitscher, a veteran naval aviator who had commanded the carrier *Hornet* in the Halsey–Doolittle Tokyo raid and at the Battle of Midway. There were doubts about Spruance's performance, too, but he retained command of the Fifth Fleet and was charged with developing plans for Operation Flintlock, the invasion of the Marshall Islands. Northwest of the Gilberts, the Marshalls were a crucial stepping stone to the Carolines and the big Japanese fleet base at Truk (see Map 16.1). Initially the islands of Kwajalein, Maloelap, and Wotje were to be invaded simultaneously, but Tarawa convinced planners that doing so was logistically unwise and was likely to incur heavy casualties. Spruance and Turner wanted to take Maloelap and Wotje first, then Kwajalein. Instead, Nimitz decided to bypass Maloelap and Wotje and go directly to Kwajalein, although he agreed to seize Majuro in the southern Marshalls as an advanced fleet anchorage.

In preparation for the February 1 assault, Mitscher's Task Force 58, operating in Spruance's Fifth Fleet, struck Maloelap and Wotje, as well as Eniwetok in the western Marshalls. The carriers also wiped out what remained of Japanese air power on Namur and Roi Islands at the northern extremity of the Kwajalein atoll and on Kwajalein itself at the southern end (see Map 16.3). Turner's Fifth Amphibious Force was split into Northern and Southern Attack Forces, totaling 53,000 soldiers and marines. Before sunrise on the 1st, carrier planes, Army Air Forces bombers, and ships offshore bombarded Kwajalein, Namur, and Roi. Marines met little resistance on Roi and quickly secured the island; Namur took another day before Japanese resistance ended. Kwajalein fell to two Army regimental combat teams on February 4. Total casualties in the operation were less than 2,000, including 372 dead.

In light of the relative ease of taking Kwajalein, Nimitz accelerated the Central Pacific offensive, with either the Marianas or Truk to be assaulted sometime in June. But, first, Nimitz decided to take Eniwetok, using reserve troops left over from Flintlock. Meanwhile, Task Force 58 attacked Truk on February 17–18, destroying or damaging more than 200 aircraft and sinking 200,000 tons of shipping, including 15 warships. Previously unassailable Truk, the "Gibraltar of the Pacific," ceased to exist as a fulcrum in the Japanese defense perimeter. Four days later, a Marine force secured Eniwetok after six days of tough fighting that cost more than 700 American casualties. Contemporaries and historians alike agree that the Marshalls and Truk operations allowed enemy strongholds in the Caroline Islands to be bypassed and expedited the offensive against Japanese defenses further to the west.

The Mariana Islands Campaign

Next in the drive through the Central Pacific were the Marianas, under Operation Forager. Over the objections of Douglas MacArthur, the Joint Chiefs of Staff—composed of Admiral King, Admiral William D. Leahy, General George C. Marshall, and General Henry H. Arnold, chief of the Army Air Forces—agreed that the Central Pacific forces would capture the Marianas in June. King wanted to continue the Central Pacific Drive; Arnold wanted to construct air bases in the islands from which long-range B-29s could strike Japan's Home Islands—earlier plans had called for basing the B-29s in China, but recent Japanese advances on the continent threatened the site where the B-29 bases were to be constructed (see Map 17.1). After capturing the Marianas, Central Pacific forces would seize the Palau Islands and then assist MacArthur's South West Pacific forces in taking Mindanao, in the Philippines, sometime in November. Thereafter the combined offensive would either assault Formosa or secure a lodgment on the Chinese mainland, leading to a partial blockade of Japan. Like Rabaul, Truk was to be bypassed. Nimitz and his planners correctly anticipated that the Japanese would fight hard to defend the Marianas, a vital artery through which ships and aircraft flowed south and east into the enemy's empire. They also knew that bases in the Marianas brought the Home Islands within reach of American long-range bombers. Moreover, the Japanese had done a remarkable job reconstituting their Mobile Fleet, with nine carriers under Vice Admiral Ozawa Jisaburō and 440 aircraft, flown by fresh, albeit not fully trained,

Daniel E. Barbey

On January 10, 1943, Rear Admiral Daniel E. Barbey (1889–1969) reported to General Douglas MacArthur as commanding officer of the South West Pacific Amphibious Forces, later designated as the Seventh Amphibious Force. Before Pearl Harbor, Barbey had been chief of staff to the commanding officer of the Training Force, Atlantic Fleet, where he was exposed to the latest developments in amphibious warfare. His orders from MacArthur were simple— build an amphibious force to allow MacArthur's forces to carry out an offensive to isolate the Japanese stronghold of Rabaul and to advance along the north coast of New Guinea toward the Philippines.

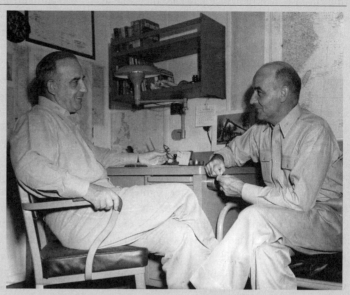

Daniel E. Barbey (left) on board his flagship, the USS *Blue Ridge*, c. October 1944. *Source:* US Navy, now in the collection of the National Archives. US Naval History and Heritage Command # 80-G-301530.

Although the assignment was straightforward, carrying it out was complex. In an era before jointness became gospel, Barbey's political instincts allowed him to work closely with the Army as well as with Marines and Australian forces. Virtually from scratch he acquired specialized amphibious warfare vessels (foremost being the ubiquitous landing ship tank or LST), assembled an experienced planning staff, and developed a training program, all while fighting a determined enemy and overcoming seemingly insurmountable problems of distance and tropical diseases. Within six months of taking command, Barbey launched assaults on Kiriwana and Woodlark Islands, seizing them as fighter bases needed to attack and bypass Rabaul. Nine major amphibious operations followed in New Guinea over the next year, including the landing at Hollandia in April 1944 with more than 200 ships and 84,000 troops. The climax came in January 1945, when Barbey commanded 420 ships and 50,000 men in the invasion at Lingayen Gulf on Luzon in the Philippines.

In 18 months, Barbey's Seventh Amphibious Force accomplished 21 major amphibious operations and another 31 minor landings, transporting over water nearly a million men and 1.2 million tons of supplies and equipment. Admiral Barbey and "MacArthur's Navy" were essential for the 1943–1944 South West Pacific offensive.

aircrew. Spruance believed—again correctly—that the Fifth Fleet would meet the Japanese in what both adversaries thought would be the long-awaited decisive fleet engagement of the Pacific War.

Nimitz counted on Halsey, Mitscher, and Spruance to prosecute this phase of the offensive, along with a newcomer to the carrier task forces—Vice Admiral John S. McCain, Deputy Chief of Naval Operations for Air in Washington. McCain was a favorite of Admiral King, who insisted that Nimitz offer him a major combat command. With McCain came a rotation scheme whereby Halsey and his Third Fleet staff would alternate command with Spruance and his Fifth Fleet staff. When Spruance completed an operation—in this instance Forager—he and his staff would plan the Navy's next moves in the Central Pacific; meanwhile, Halsey would take over command of the fleet, the constitution of which remained basically the same as far as ships and aircraft were concerned. Task Force 58 under Mitscher therefore became Task Force 38 under McCain as the fleets changed designation and commanders. This "two-platoon" system provided the command staff relief from the rigors of combat while hastening the Central Pacific offensive.

As Spruance planned for Forager, Task Force 58 supported MacArthur's April 22 invasion of Hollandia, on the north coast of New Guinea (see Map 15.2). Land-based air usually covered MacArthur's operations, but Hollandia was a 400-mile jump that stretched the limits of Fifth Air Force fighters and left the amphibious force vulnerable to air attacks from the Palaus and southern Philippines. To ensure that there was minimal interference with the landing, Mitscher's carriers struck Palau and Yap Islands and other enemy installations in New Guinea. Spruance's Fifth Fleet escort carriers protected the Seventh Amphibious Force, with its 84,000 troops. Once ashore, the soldiers rapidly secured an airfield for use by Army Air Forces fighters, and by the 26th had achieved victory. American casualties were relatively light—1,200, of whom 152 were dead. By the first week of June in the central Pacific, 535 warships and amphibious craft had assembled at Majuro to transport and support more than 127,000 marines and soldiers of the Marianas invasion force. Saipan was the first objective, to be followed by Tinian and Guam. The major units under Spruance were Mitscher's Task Force 58, the Joint Expeditionary Force (Task Force 51, under now Vice Admiral Turner), and land-based aircraft (Task Force 57) under Vice Admiral John H. Hoover. Task Force 58 alone comprised 93 ships and more than 900 aircraft. No fewer than 15 fast carriers were split into four task groups.

On June 6, as Task Force 58 cleared Majuro, the Japanese put in motion Operation A-Go to engage and defeat the American forces. Ozawa's Mobile Fleet,

with its nine carriers arranged in three divisions, sortied from the Philippines on June 13. That same day fast battleships attached to Task Force 58 struck Saipan and Tinian; on June 14, Turner's fire support units, centering on old battleships, helped to soften up the beachheads before the invasion. On the 15th, following four days of Task Force 58 strikes that decimated Japanese air strength in the Marianas, two Marine divisions landed on Saipan's west coast, where they met stiff Japanese resistance. Gunfire from battleships and cruisers and close air support from escort carriers covered the assault and the days of hard fighting that followed (see Figure 16.1).

Intelligence provided Spruance with a clear picture of the size and composition of the Japanese carrier forces but he remained mostly in the dark about their whereabouts and the timing of their operations. Not until June 14 did US submarines report that the Japanese Mobile Fleet, with six carriers, three battleships, and nearly 50 more warships, had sortied from Tawi-Tawi in the southwestern Philippines, and a day later that the carriers had entered the Philippine Sea. On the 16th Nimitz sent a dispatch to Spruance: "On the eve of a possible fleet action you and the officers and men under your command have the confidence of the naval service and the country. We count on you to make the victory decisive."[1]

Still unsure of the exact location of Ozawa's ships but now certain that there would be a major fleet action, Spruance planned to have Mitscher's carriers defeat their Japanese counterparts, then attack the enemy battleships and cruisers. Afterward, Vice Admiral Willis A. Lee's fast battleships, organized into a separate task force, would pursue and defeat any elements of Ozawa's force remaining after Task Force 58's aerial onslaught. Finally, late on June 17, the submarine *Cavalla* radioed that it had sighted and was trailing the Mobile Fleet about 350 miles east of the Philippines and more than 800 miles west of Task Force 58. Mitscher determined that, if the Japanese held course to the east and Task Force 58 steered west, it was possible that late in the afternoon of the 18th Ozawa

[1] Message 170314, Commander-in-Chief, Pacific Fleet (CinCPac) to Commander Fifth Fleet, June 17, 1944, roll 129, record group (RG) 313: CinCPac Dispatches and Message Traffic, Naval Operating Forces, National Archives and Records Administration, Archives II, College Park, MD (henceforth NARA).

Figure 16.1 USS *New York* delivering gunfire support. *Source:* US Navy, now in the collection of the National Archives. US Naval History and Heritage Command # 80-G-308952.

would be within the extreme range of the task force's aircraft. But no attack could be launched until Task Force 58 aircraft spotted the Mobile Fleet. Instead, using their range advantage over the Americans, Ozawa's searchers made the first contact, locating Task Force 58 on the afternoon of the 18th.

Now Spruance made a crucial and controversial decision based on the limited information he had available. He still did not know precisely where the Mobile Fleet was, but he did know that the Japanese had an advantage in range, enhanced by their ability to shuttle attackers from their carriers to airfields on Guam, attacking US ships en route, then refueling and rearming on Guam before flying back to the carriers while again striking the American ships. He further guessed that a separate element of their force

might attempt an "end run" or flanking maneuver to get behind Task Force 58 and disrupt the invasion forces; after all, the Japanese had a penchant for dividing their forces and using feints. As Turner withdrew most of the vulnerable transports east of Saipan, leaving behind his escort carriers to provide air support, Spruance determined to have Task Force 58 remain in position just west of the Marianas. Furious at the prospect of remaining immobile off Saipan, Mitscher asked Spruance for permission to speed westward during the night and strike the Japanese at first light on June 19. But Spruance would not budge, and Mitscher reluctantly conceded to his orders. Spruance had made his decision: Task Force 58 would stand off the Marianas and meet the full fury of the Japanese.

Service Force

Adhering to the maxim that no campaign was ever lost due to an excess of logistics support, the Service Force, Pacific Fleet, under the command of Vice Admiral William L. Calhoun, made possible the extraordinary mobility so critical to the offensive in the Central Pacific. Organized in March 1942, the Service Force consisted of more than 1,100 ships, divided into five squadrons by July 1944; at the end of the war it included 456,000 personnel. Service squadrons supplied the fleet and established advance bases extending from Tarawa in the Gilberts westward to Majuro and Eniwetok in the Marshalls and Ulithi in the Carolines. Sophisticated mobile repair and replenishment facilities and procedures supported the fleet as the offensive converged in the Philippines. At Ulithi, for example, two large maintenance ships effected major repairs to 20 ships, including rebuilding the storm-battered and combat-damaged flight decks of four fast carriers—work that previously would have sent the ships back to Pearl Harbor or California. Obsolete tankers provided a mobile "tank farm"

USS *Mount Hood*, an ammunition ship and part of the Service Force, blew up while moored off Manus, in the Admiralty Islands, November 10, 1944, leaving 45 dead, 327 missing, and 371 injured. *Source:* US Naval History and Heritage Command # NH 45735.

that moved from one advance base to another.

By the fall of 1944, the At Sea Logistics Service Group, centering on Service Squadrons 8 and 10, regularly accompanied the Third and Fifth Fleets. Thirty-four oilers and more than 50 destroyers and destroyer escorts, organized into task groups, rotated in support of the fast carrier forces. Eleven escort carriers provided air cover and antisubmarine defense for the force and brought in replacement

aircraft and personnel. Underway replenishment of fuel, dry stores, spare parts, and other supplies became routine by late 1943; by February 1945 the service group had perfected ammunition resupply at sea, which allowed the carrier and surface forces to operate in combat zones virtually indefinitely. Little known and underappreciated, the Service Force was the Navy's secret weapon that helped to ensure victory in the Pacific.

Ozawa launched his first strike early on June 19, when his carriers were beyond Mitscher's reach. With favorable prevailing winds, the Japanese carriers could remain on course to the east when launching and recovering aircraft, whereas the American carriers had to double back from a westerly heading to gain enough wind over the deck for takeoffs and landings. About 0950 Task Force 58 radar detected unidentified aircraft 130 miles out, and within less than an hour

200 F6Fs were in the air ready to intercept the Japanese planes. In the meantime, the submarine *Albacore*, shadowing the Japanese fleet, torpedoed Ozawa's flagship, the new carrier *Taiho*, which sank later in the day. Shortly after noon, the *Cavalla* torpedoed and sank the *Shokaku*. Three more air attacks followed, the last of which ended about 1500. Two battleships suffered bomb and torpedo hits, with little damage, and none of the carriers suffered a direct hit, although some

were damaged by near misses. The final accounting showed 261 Japanese aircraft downed by fighters and antiaircraft fire, the most ever in a single day of aerial combat; in return the Americans lost 31. More important were the irreplaceable Japanese carrier pilots and aircrew who perished that day. Likened to a "turkey shoot," the June 19 battle was a stunning American victory that for all intents and purposes marked the end of Japanese carrier-based air power.

Ozawa retired to the northwest, still determined to reenter the fray after his remaining ships refueled and regrouped. Spruance, continuing to fret that a detached element of the Japanese force might pounce from an unexpected direction, hesitated in granting Mitscher permission to pursue. More than 300 miles behind Ozawa, Mitscher's carriers would have to make good time to the west to bring the Japanese force within range, all while conducting air operations. Finally, Spruance authorized Task Force 58 to steam westward in hopes of contacting the Japanese, while he released one task group to refuel and stay close to Saipan. Mitscher's searchers did not sight Ozawa's carriers until after 1530 on June 20. Although he knew the Japanese were barely within range and that the strike would have to be recovered after dark, Mitscher ordered full deckload strikes to be launched.

By 1630, the first of 240 planes took off and headed west, their crews anxious about whether they would have enough fuel to get back home. A little more than two hours later and 30 minutes before sundown, they attacked Ozawa's force, scoring bomb hits on the big *Zuikaku* and the light carriers *Chiyoda* and *Junyo* and sinking the light carrier *Hiyo* with bombs and torpedoes. The statistics are unclear, but it is likely upwards of 60 more aircraft were lost defending the Mobile Fleet; Ozawa now had no choice other than to retreat to the northwest.

Task Force 58 aviators, low on fuel and enveloped by darkness, had to navigate back to their carriers, which fortunately had closed some of the distance in the interim. Gas-hungry Curtiss SB2C dive-bombers were among the first to ditch, but shot-up Grumman TBF Avenger torpedo bombers also went down

short of the carriers. On Mitscher's orders, the entire fleet lit up to guide the fliers to safety. In a frenzy to avoid going into the water, pilots brought their aircraft down on any carrier they could; when the chaos was over, 140 aircraft had been recovered, but 86 planes and their pilots and crews were missing. Search and rescue efforts picked up 138 survivors. With only a slim chance that Task Force 58 could catch the Mobile Fleet, Mitscher launched a strike shortly after dawn on June 21, but his aircraft failed to contact the Japanese, now more than 350 miles distant. Finally realizing that pursuit of the Japanese was a forlorn hope, Spruance abandoned offensive air operations that evening, and the weary ships and sailors turned back toward Saipan.

Critical assessment of what became known as the Battle of the Philippine Sea (see Map 16.1) began almost immediately. On June 21 Towers offered that he was frustrated by the outcome and after the war blamed Spruance for allowing the bulk of the Japanese carrier force to escape destruction. Mitscher's draft action report summarized much of the sentiment at the time that Spruance had made a mistake in not ordering Task Force 58 to pursue the Japanese on the night of June 19–20. It ended cryptically: "The enemy had escaped. He [Ozawa] had been badly hurt by one aggressive carrier air strike, at the one time he was within range. His fleet was not sunk."[2] In reply to those who believed that Spruance had been right to keep Mitscher close to Saipan to cover the invasion force, Rear Admiral Joseph J. Clark and other aviators responded that the best defense would have been to take the fight directly to the Japanese Mobile Fleet. In the final analysis, the Battle of the Philippine Sea was a decisive victory, the grand fleet engagement in the western Pacific that both antagonists had anticipated for nearly a half-century. No one at the time knew that they had witnessed the greatest carrier battle of all time, and few recognized that it—and not Midway two years before—was the pivotal battle of the Pacific War. No one knew, either, that in essence Japan's carriers were finished as a fighting force. They did know that the Japanese still had at least six operational

---

[2] Commander of Task Force 58 to Commander-in-Chief of the US Fleet (Cominch), Operations in Support of the Capture of the MARIANAS—Action Report, September 11, 1944, RG 38: World War II War Diaries, Other Operational Records and Histories, 01/01/1942 to 05/30/1946, NARA.

carriers, that their army and air forces had not been defeated, and that the US Navy and Marines still had much more to do as naval sea and air power carried the offensive beyond the Marianas.

Leyte Gulf and the Philippines

Based on the recommendations of Nimitz and MacArthur, the Joint Chiefs proposed that their forces converge on the southern Philippines, from which Allied forces could assault Formosa or Luzon, penetrate the Japanese inner defense perimeter by invading Okinawa in the Ryukyus, and advance from there to the Home Islands. The southern Philippine island of Mindanao was the first objective, with the invasion tentatively set for November 15, followed by Leyte, in the middle of the archipelago, which was attractive as a fleet anchorage and site for air bases. Airfields on Peleliu in the southern Palaus Islands and on Morotai in the Halmaheras, east of New Guinea, would have to be established first, and Ulithi and Yap in the western Carolines either occupied or neutralized (see Map 16.1). Halsey disagreed with planners that a forward position in the Palaus was necessary and believed the islands could be safely leapfrogged. Nimitz and MacArthur were in agreement about Mindanao and Leyte, but not about Luzon, the largest island and home of the capital Manila, which MacArthur had pledged to liberate. King and Nimitz wanted to bypass Luzon and attack Formosa, allowing Allied forces to link up with the Chinese on the mainland and augment Army Air Forces B-29 bases in the Marianas. After MacArthur and Nimitz met with President Roosevelt in Hawaii in late July, MacArthur seemed to have made his case for Luzon. The Joint Chiefs also favored Luzon but decided to wait until after the Leyte landings on December 20 before making a final decision.

Under the "two-platoon" rotation system, McCain was slated to relieve Mitscher in the fast carrier command after the Marianas operation. Yet Mitscher was adamant about staying on for the next phase of the offensive. King forged a compromise: Mitscher became the new Commander First Fast Carrier Task Force Pacific and McCain became Commander Second Fast Carrier Task Force Pacific, as well as commander of Task Group 58.1, under Mitscher. In

August, Halsey took over from Spruance, and Task Force 58 mutated into Task Force 38.

Reports of the weakness of Japanese air power in the southern and central Philippines led Halsey to suggest that Nimitz cancel Mindanao and invade Leyte. Other than Ulithi, it was not necessary to seize Yap or other islands in the western Carolines; unfortunately, it was too late to cancel Peleliu, which proved to be a costly and unnecessary operation that did nothing to expedite the advance into the Philippines (see Figure 16.2). Nimitz liked the idea of diverting forces assigned to taking Mindanao and Yap to Leyte. King broached the idea with the Joint Chiefs of Staff, who on September 15 authorized the Leyte operation (codenamed King-II) to begin on October 20, exactly two months sooner than previously anticipated.

Planning was urgent. Under MacArthur's South West Pacific command, Vice Admiral Thomas C. Kinkaid's Central Philippines Attack Force, organized as Task Force 77, had responsibility for the amphibious landing, support for which included escort carriers from Nimitz's Central Pacific forces. Because no land-based air support was within range, Mitscher's Task Force 38 would provide air cover. That in itself was a potential complication, but the big problem was that the divided command meant there was no direct line of communication between Halsey and Kinkaid and that all messages had to be routed through Nimitz and MacArthur. Unlike the Marianas, where Spruance had exercised unified command over both the amphibious forces and the fast carrier task force, Kinkaid had the amphibious operation and Halsey the carriers.

Nimitz's operation plan specified that, beginning nine days before the landings, Halsey's carriers were to neutralize enemy air and shipping in Formosa, Luzon, and Mindanao. Two days before the operation and continuing after the landings, Task Force 38 was to provide close air support for the ground forces. Thereafter escort carriers would take over that job, freeing the fast carriers to operate more widely against enemy objectives. Not wanting to see the Japanese fleet get away as it had after the Battle of the Philippine Sea, Nimitz directed Halsey that "in case opportunity for destruction of major portions of the enemy fleet offers or can be created, such destruction becomes

Figure 16.2   Landing craft assault Peleliu, 1944. LVTs (Landing Vehicle Tracked) move past LCI (Landing Craft Infantry) gunboats toward smoke and dust-shrouded landing beaches while battleships and cruisers bombard Peleliu from the distance. *Source:* US Naval History and Heritage Command # NH 80-G-283553.

the primary task."[3] Because his plans coincided with Nimitz's directive, Halsey welcomed the possibility of engaging enemy air and sea forces that might menace the amphibious forces at Leyte. Mitscher and McCain divided the carrier command, with McCain now in charge of Task Group 38.1. Admiral Lee's fast battleships constituted Task Force 34, an administrative unit that could be brought together as the tactical situation demanded. Task Force 38 now included four task groups and no fewer than 17 fast carriers with nearly 1,100 aircraft.

The Japanese navy's high command understood that losing the Philippines jeopardized Japan's inner defensive perimeter and the lines of communica-

tion south to the strategically vital Dutch East Indies. Combined Fleet commander Admiral Toyoda Soemu devised a complex multiphase plan, known as Sho-Go, that progressively included the defense of the Philippines, Formosa and the Ryukyus, and finally Kyushu and the Home Islands. Troops and aircraft in the southern Philippines would be reinforced from Formosa and Luzon, and Admiral Ozawa's Mobile Fleet carriers would engage the American carriers and any other covering air and surface forces. Underlying the strategy was the basic principle of interior lines of operation, which theoretically allowed the Japanese to shift forces as needed from one defensive position to another. The Japanese also believed that

---

[3] CinCPac to Cominch, May 31, 1945, Operations in Pacific Ocean Area—October 1944, Annex A, RG 38: World War II War Diaries, Other Operational Records and Histories, 01/01/1942 to 05/30/1946, NARA, 56.

they could concentrate their land, sea, and air forces sufficiently at a vital point—in this case the Philippines—to fight and win a decisive battle, even against a superior enemy at this late stage of the conflict.

Toyoda's scheme divided the Japanese forces. Constituting what the Americans called the "Northern Force," Ozawa's four carriers (*Chitose*, *Chiyoda*, *Zuiho*, and *Zuikaku*), augmented by two hybrid battleship-carriers (*Hyuga* and *Ise*), were to contact Task Force 38 and divert it from its covering mission. But Toyoda had stripped Ozawa's carriers of most of the air groups, using them up in the air defense of Formosa, and he had transferred many Mobile Fleet cruisers and destroyers to the other Japanese forces. Ozawa's component of the Mobile Fleet would thus sacrifice itself so that the First Striking Force and the battleships and cruisers commanded by Admiral Kurita Takeo (the so-called Center Force) could slice through the San Bernardino Strait in the central Philippines to attack the American transports and covering ships in Leyte Gulf. Meanwhile, old battleships and newer cruisers under Vice Admiral Nishimura Shoji (the "Southern Force") would advance from the south toward Leyte. It, too, would give itself up but in the process pull Kinkaid's heavy ships and escort carriers away from the beachhead, leaving the landing force uncovered and vulnerable to the superior firepower of Kurita's big ships. Another component of the plan, which Toyoda wanted to implement only if absolutely necessary, were the kamikaze suicide pilots assembled by Vice Admiral Ōnishi Takijirō, whose planes would in effect function as deadly guided missiles. For the Japanese the operation was a colossal, almost hopeless gamble that was likely to mean the end of their fleet and most, if not all, of their nation's air forces.

For three weeks leading up to Leyte, Mitscher's carriers blasted Japanese airfields in Formosa, northern Luzon, and Okinawa. Japanese aircraft losses from October 10 to 17 numbered more than 580. Then, on schedule, Mitscher's carrier aircraft launched fighter sweeps and strikes against Japanese defensive positions to provide direct cover for the Leyte landings on October 20. Following bombardment by old battleships, cruisers, and destroyers operating with Task Force 77, the first of four Army divisions went ashore at 1000 on the northwestern corner of Leyte Gulf, where they found little initial opposition. Lacking intelligence about the movement of major Japanese

units and convinced that there would not be a major fleet engagement, Halsey decided to rotate Task Force 38's groups one by one to Ulithi to rearm and replenish their stores. On the 22nd, McCain's five-carrier group was the first to break off action to return to Ulithi. At this juncture, no one in Pearl Harbor or the Third Fleet knew that Ozawa's carriers had slipped out of Japan's Inland Sea on the 20th, followed by Kurita's and Nishimura's heavy ships from Borneo on the 22nd, all three forces converging on the Philippines.

At about 0600 on October 23 the submarines *Dace* and *Darter* spied Kurita's force southwest of Palawan Island, radioed its location, then torpedoed and sank two cruisers and severely damaged another. When Mitscher's searches to the west early the next day found Kurita's ships just south of Mindoro, Halsey ordered Mitscher to attack (see Map 16.4). At the same time Halsey was worried about the possibility that a Japanese carrier force might surprise his three task groups from somewhere to the north. He therefore recalled McCain's group with orders to search to the north and northwest at daylight on the 25th.

Task Force 38's strikes on Kurita's Center Force as it threaded its way through the Sibuyan Sea resulted in the sinking of the super-battleship *Musashi* and severe damage to a heavy cruiser, but other ships were hurt hardly at all. In what became known as the Battle of the Sibuyan Sea (see Map 16.4), the Americans overestimated the damage they had inflicted, and when Kurita reversed course to the west it looked as if he were retreating. Meanwhile, Japanese land-based aircraft bombed and sank the light carrier *Princeton*.

The reported losses in the Sibuyan Sea and what appeared like Kurita's withdrawal gave every appearance of a Japanese defeat, thus ensuring no further threat from that quarter to Kinkaid's Seventh Fleet forces at Leyte. Even if the remaining Japanese ships did manage to get through the San Bernardino Strait, Halsey believed Lee's battleships were more than adequate to repel them. That afternoon he informed Lee that, if needed, four of his battleships, accompanied by cruisers and destroyers, would be formed by subsequent message as Task Force 34. Kinkaid picked up the signal, which he wrongly interpreted to mean that Task Force 34 had already been organized to cover San Bernardino.

For his part, Halsey assumed that Kinkaid's heavy ships and escort carriers were sufficient to handle

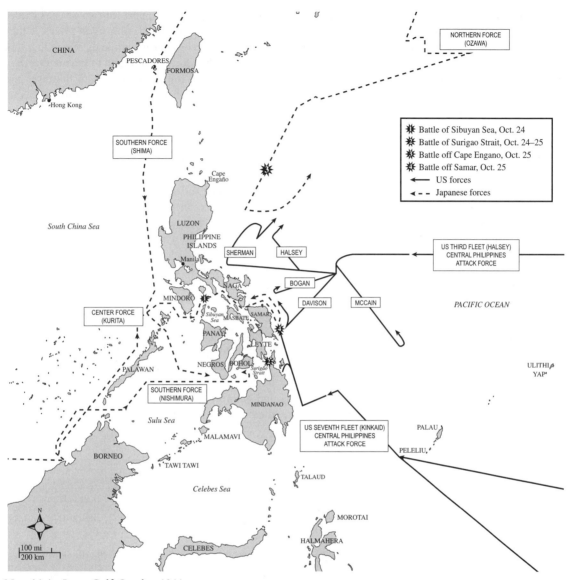

Map 16.4   Leyte Gulf, October 1944.

Nishimura's Southern Force, which entered Surigao Strait that evening. He was right. In a classic night gun duel that ended in the predawn darkness on October 25, Rear Admiral Jesse B. Oldendorf's battleships virtually wiped out the Japanese force, then pursued the stragglers out of the strait and away from the gulf. Halsey was also correct that Oldendorf's battleships could deal with the weakened Japanese Center Force, which according to reports had turned back east on the evening of the 24th. Determined to destroy Ozawa's carriers, Halsey made the critical decision to bring Task Force 38 together for a run north and a dawn strike, with all of Lee's battleships now assembled in Task Force 34. By daybreak, Kinkaid lacked any heavy ships or fast carriers to defend his amphibious force at just the moment when Kurita charged out of San Bernardino and down the coast of Samar.

At that point, events began to happen with star-tling—and confusing—rapidity. As Task Force 38 closed on Ozawa's carriers off Cape Engano and launched their first strikes, Kurita's big ships emerged from San Bernardino and fell on Kinkaid's Task Force 77 escort carrier groups off Samar, first target-ing Rear Admiral Clifton A. F. Sprague's task unit. Kinkaid radioed Halsey of the situation at 0707, but, due to communication delays, Halsey did not receive the message for more than an hour, at which point he assumed that Kinkaid had enough air power to deal with what he believed were only remnants of Kurita's force. He also thought that Oldendorf's bat-tleships were close to the gulf, when in fact they had moved far south into Surigao Strait. Minutes later Kinkaid urgently called for a strike from Mitscher's carriers on Kurita's force, which was not possible. However, McCain's group was better positioned to help. Monitoring the radio traffic, McCain, north-east of Samar, knew that Kinkaid was in trouble, and on his own initiative turned his carriers toward the action, reaching a launching point at extreme range by 1030. As Sprague's valiant little flattops launched aircraft and turned south to avoid certain destruction while his covering destroyers braved heavy shellfire to prosecute suicidal torpedo attacks on Kurita's ships, Kinkaid desperately radioed that "my situation is critical."[4] Still thinking that Kinkaid could deal with Kurita's depleted Center Force on his own, and that he, Halsey, had gone out of his way in committing McCain's carriers to assist Task Force 77, Halsey was mystified by reports of the dire situation off Samar. Halsey's puzzlement turned to consternation when at 1000 he received a communication from Nim-itz, who had been closely following developments. The message—"Where is Task Force 34? The world wonders"[5]—is one of the most famous dispatches in naval history. Halsey fumed at what he considered an unprofessional, gratuitous insult until he realized that the last sentence was superfluous cryptologic padding. At that point he ordered Rear Admiral Gerald Bogan's

task group to provide support for two of Lee's battle-ships (including Halsey's flagship *New Jersey*), as they broke off to succor Kinkaid, while the remaining Task Force 38 carrier forces continued to pursue Ozawa.

Kurita, having lost three cruisers to destroyer and air attacks and believing that more American car-riers were nearby, reversed course toward San Ber-nardino Strait at just the moment when he could have overwhelmed Kinkaid's defenders and fallen on the invasion force in the gulf. McCain's and Bogan's air groups hit Kurita's heavy ships as they retreated and sank a cruiser and destroyer before Halsey called off the strikes late on October 26. All four of Ozawa's carriers had gone down, and Kinkaid's vulnerable invasion force, by a combination of grit and good luck, was secure, at least from attacks from the sea, if not from Japanese land-based bombers and kamikazes. What was to be known as the Battle of Leyte Gulf, by some calculations the greatest naval engagement of all time, was finally over (see Table 16.1).

Like the Battle of the Philippine Sea, but for almost exactly the opposite reasons, the Battle of Leyte Gulf generated its own set of controversies. The major one, obvious in retrospect, but unavoidable as MacArthur's and Nimitz's forces converged in the Philippines, was the divided command. That there had been no direct

Table 16.1 Losses in the Battle of Leyte Gulf.

US Navy	Imperial Japanese Navy
1 light carrier	1 fleet carrier
2 escort carriers	3 light carriers
2 destroyers	3 battleships
2 destroyer escorts	10 cruisers
3 submarines	12 destroyers
1 torpedo boat	4 submarines
1 fleet tug	1 destroyer transport
	1 oiler
c. 200 aircraft	c. 300 aircraft

[4] Commander Third Fleet (Com3rdFleet), Action Report, October 23–26, 1944, enclosure A, RG 38: World War II War Diaries, Other Operational Records and Histories, 01/01/1942 to 05/30/1946, NARA, 33.

[5] Message 25044, CinCPac to Com3rdFleet, October 25, 1944, roll 173, CinCPac Dispatches and Message Traffic, Naval Operating Forces, RG 313, NARA. (The outgoing message in this file is Nimitz's original and lacks the extraneous phrase.)

line of communication between the Third and Seventh Fleets had created confusion and hindered cooperation, especially in the crisis facing Task Force 77 on the morning of October 25. Given the politics of command and the realities of inter-service rivalries, though, it is hard to see what, if any, alternatives might have been effected. If anyone were to be blamed, it would be MacArthur and Nimitz.

Halsey anticipated that he would be criticized for leaving Leyte to chase Ozawa's carriers. Late on the 25th, he had radioed a long message to Nimitz explaining that it made no sense to him to keep his carriers off Samar and outlining why he believed Ozawa's force and not Kurita's represented the main threat to Kinkaid. In his opinion the Japanese carriers were decidedly not a decoy or an inferior force, as some had implied. His only mistake was sending Bogan's carriers and Lee's battleships south and thus ending any chances of destroying Ozawa's remaining heavy ships—especially the hybrid carrier-battleships *Hyuga* and *Ise*. Where Nimitz was guarded in his criticism of Halsey, King was more open in his disapproval, even though after the war he moderated his tone and spread the blame between Halsey and Kinkaid.

Conclusion

For the most part historians have formed a balanced interpretation of the people and events of October 1944. Clark Reynolds, biographer of John Towers, acknowledges that mistakes resulted in an incomplete victory at Leyte. Willful as always, Halsey had failed to draw on the experience of his subordinates, especially Mitscher, who played virtually no role in the battle. With more efficient planning and coordination, Halsey might have split his forces, leaving some of Lee's battleships and one of his carrier groups behind to guard the exit of the strait while still having plenty left over to annihilate Ozawa. That, however, would have violated the sacred doctrine of concentration of force and Mahanian admonitions about dividing the fleet. Kinkaid, lacking adequate information about Halsey's actions and those of the Japanese, should have sought confirmation that Task Force 34 had indeed been formed to guard San Bernardino. For reasons not entirely his own fault, he never fully comprehended the tactical situation leading up to and through the crucial developments of October 24–25. Of the two—Halsey and Kinkaid—the latter was more focused on the mission; that is, Kinkaid understood his responsibility for getting forces ashore at Leyte and ensuring their protection. In going north after Ozawa and not ensuring that Kurita's Center Force had been neutralized or defeated, Halsey had not fulfilled his basic command obligation.

Nevertheless, amid the after-action analyses and the reality that some Japanese ships had escaped destruction, the Battle of Leyte Gulf marked the end of the Imperial Japanese Navy as an effective sea and air force and culminated the 1943–1944 offensives. The stage was now set for the final phases of the war: retaking Luzon; breaking through Japan's inner defense perimeter to either Formosa or the Ryukyus; opening the Home Islands to air and sea assault; and, in time, bringing victory in the Pacific.

CHAPTER 17

The Victory of Sea Power in the Pacific

The sea power of the United States reached a peak during the last eight months of World War II in the Pacific and was instrumental in destroying both Japan's physical capacity and its will to resist. Earlier in the conflict, the battles of Midway, the Philippine Sea, and Leyte Gulf had accomplished the goal of American naval strategists for the past half-century: the elimination of the Imperial Japanese Navy.

This success enabled Admiral Chester W. Nimitz to concentrate the power of his Pacific Fleet against enemy ground- and shore-based air forces, the merchant marine, and the Home Islands of Japan itself. On October 3, 1944, the Joint Chiefs of Staff decided that, following the landing of US forces at Leyte, the next major operation in the Philippines would be an amphibious assault on the large, strategically vital island of Luzon.

Before Nimitz and General Douglas MacArthur (supreme commander of the Allied forces in the South West Pacific) could launch that operation, the enemy inaugurated a new, deadly tactic. In a desperate attempt to stem the seemingly unstoppable US tide across the Pacific, Japanese airmen sacrificed their lives by crashing planes loaded with aviation gasoline and bombs into fleet warships. These kamikaze (Divine Wind Special Attack Corps) pilots registered their first success by sinking escort carrier *St. Lo* during the Battle of Leyte Gulf. In October and November 1944, kamikaze and other shore-based planes sank or heavily damaged scores of fleet carriers, escort carriers, and other warships.

Luzon

Understanding that a landing at Lingayen on Luzon would put the fleet at great risk from enemy aircraft based in the Philippines and nearby Formosa, Nimitz dispatched Vice Admiral William F. Halsey's Third Fleet on a wide-ranging operation to neutralize the threat. Halsey's carriers executed devastating air attacks against enemy airfields and ports in Formosa, Hong Kong, and southern China and merchant ships in the South China Sea. In the later months of 1944, naval air forces destroyed thousands of Japanese planes and sank over 600 oceangoing vessels.

On the second day of 1945, the Lingayen invasion force sortied from a staging area off Leyte. Vice Admiral Jesse B. Oldendorf, flying his flag in battleship *California*, led the fire support force of battleships, cruisers, destroyers, minesweepers, and escort carriers. Vice Admiral Thomas C. Kinkaid, Commander Seventh Fleet and Commander Luzon Attack Force, followed with the necessarily slower amphibious assault force.

Oldendorf's lead force took the brunt of the Japanese air attacks as it moved past Leyte and Negros and entered Mindoro Strait. A kamikaze crashed into the escort carrier *Ommaney Bay*, igniting a blaze that ultimately sank the ship. Several days

America, Sea Power, and the World, First Edition. Edited by James C. Bradford.
© 2016 John Wiley & Sons, Inc. Published 2016 by John Wiley & Sons, Inc.

later, the attackers got through the combat air patrol of 68 Navy and Army fighters to hit the US cruiser *Louisville* and Australian cruiser *Australia*, the escort carrier *Manila Bay*, and the destroyer escort *Stafford*. As Oldendorf's warships began their bombardment on the morning of January 6, the enemy unleashed a determined two-day effort to frustrate the landing. Kamikazes and conventional aircraft sank the destroyers *Hovey*, *Long*, and *Palmer* and inflicted additional damage on the cruisers *Australia* and *Louisville*. The kamikaze that slammed into the battleship *New Mexico* killed Rear Admiral Theodore E. Chandler, a task force commander and grandson of a nineteenth-century Secretary of the Navy. Kinkaid's element did not escape Japanese attention. Air attacks sank a landing ship tank, an Australian amphibious vessel, and a transport.

On January 9, 1945, Kinkaid gave the go-ahead for the assault on Luzon. Vice Admiral Daniel E. Barbey's Attack Force landed Army Major General Innis P. Swift's I Corps near San Fabian, while the Lingayen Attack Force, under Vice Admiral Theodore S. Wilkinson, deployed Lieutenant General Oscar W. Griswold's XIV Corps ashore near the towns of Lingayen and Dagupan. Oldendorf's armada of six battleships, nine heavy and light cruisers, and numerous destroyers bombarded the enemy-held shore. Escort carriers and submarines put up a protective shield around the assault force.

The enemy army did not contest the landing at Lingayen. Japanese General Tomoyuki Yamashita understood that the US Fleet's naval and air power could devastate his units positioned just inshore. Instead, he withdrew his troops to the mountainous interior to carry out a determined defense. Unsure of the enemy's intentions, the infantry divisions of Lieutenant General Walter Krueger's Sixth Army, reinforced by Lieutenant General Robert L. Eichelberger's Eighth Army, then advanced on Manila.

The Japanese commander in Manila, however, disobeyed Yamashita's withdrawal order. His fanatical defense of the capital resulted in the destruction of Manila, the death of 100,000 Filipinos, and the annihilation of his command. The Sixth Army also suffered thousands of casualties. Not until the end of the war in August 1945 did organized Japanese resistance cease in the Philippines.

The fight for Leyte and Luzon established once and for all that the United States could sustain major ground combat operations not only on the small islands of the Central Pacific and the Solomons but also in the 7,000-island Philippine archipelago, 8,000 miles from the US West Coast. In addition, an enormous establishment of advance bases and underway replenishment ships ensured that the fleet would not suffer from the lack of "beans, bullets, and black oil." By 1945, 3,000 oil, ammunition, stores, and repair ships along with floating drydocks and hospital ships fueled the fleet's unrelenting advance. Airfields opened by naval construction battalions (Seabees) and Army engineers on islands seized from the enemy guaranteed that the offensive would not be delayed or stalled for lack of air cover. The success of the seaborne logistic support of Philippine operations convinced American leaders that this key pillar of their war machine could sustain follow-on amphibious assaults and the invasion of Japan itself.

Iwo Jima

In the spring and summer of 1944, months before the Allied landings in the Philippines, Iwo Jima in the Bonin Islands drew American attention (see Map 17.1). Japanese bombers flying from this volcanic island 760 miles from Tokyo attacked US airfields on Saipan in the Marianas, destroying 15 B-29 Superfortress bombers and damaging another 40 aircraft. The Joint Chiefs of Staff decided not only to end the enemy's access to Iwo Jima but also to appropriate the island for Allied use. Possession of the Bonin Islands would deny the Japanese bases from which their fighters could attack US bombers en route to Japan from Tinian and Saipan and radar stations that provided the Home Islands with warnings of impending attacks. Admiral Nimitz and the planners on his Pacific Fleet staff also determined that the island could serve as an emergency landing base for Army Air Forces bombers operating from the Marianas on missions against Japan and provide an operating base for shorter-ranged US fighter planes.

Nimitz charged Admiral Raymond A. Spruance, Commander Fifth Fleet, with organizing and executing the seizure of Iwo Jima. Serving under Spruance

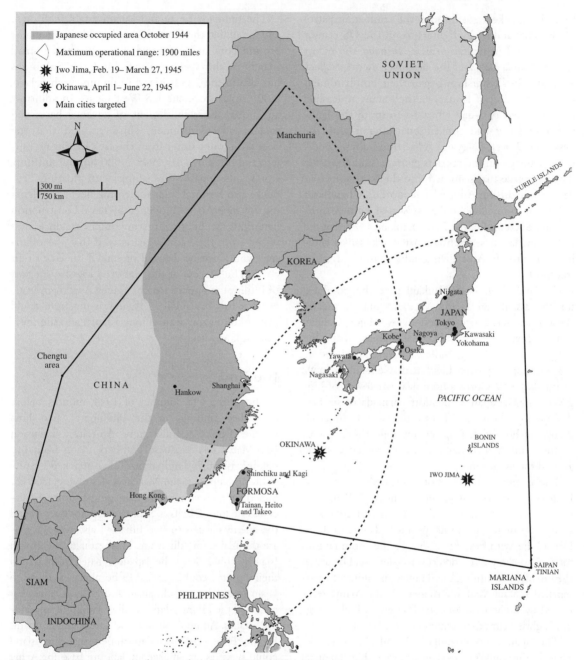

Map 17.1 Air campaign and approach to Japan, 1944–1945.

Japanese occupied area October 1944

Maximum operational range: 1900 miles

Iwo Jima, Feb. 19– March 27, 1945

Okinawa, April 1– June 22, 1945

Main cities targeted

N

300 mi
750 km

SOVIET
UNION

Manchuria

KURILE ISLANDS

KOREA

Chengtu
area

CHINA

Hankow   Shanghai

Niigata

JAPAN
Tokyo

Kobe   Nagoya   Kawasaki
Yokohama
Osaka

Yawata

Nagasaki

PACIFIC OCEAN

OKINAWA

BONIN
ISLANDS

IWO JIMA

Shinchiku and Kagi

FORMOSA

Hong Kong

Tainan, Heito
and Takeo

SAIPAN
TINIAN

MARIANA
ISLANDS

SIAM

INDOCHINA

PHILIPPINES

Richmond Kelly Turner

From Guadalcanal to Okinawa, no US naval leader was more responsible for the success of Allied amphibious operations in the Pacific than Admiral Richmond Kelly Turner (1885–1961). Graduating fifth in his 1908 class from the US Naval Academy, Turner demonstrated a professionalism and pursuit of excellence that would characterize his entire Navy career. His assignments in command of surface ships and aviation units and on planning staffs during the 1920s and 1930s exposed the fast-rising officer to many aspects of naval warfare. Turner enhanced that practical experience with an understanding of sea power theory gained during tours at the Naval War College, first as a student and then as head of the Strategy Department. While in the latter billet, Turner incorporated the Navy's history, the teachings of Alfred Thayer Mahan, and war game exercises to anticipate how a war with Japan would be fought. He honed that understanding during 1940–1941 as the chief strategic planner on the Navy staff. Recognizing Turner's superior qualities, the Navy sent him to the Solomon Islands to command amphibious forces in the Allies' first Pacific offensive.

The loss of four Allied cruisers in the Battle of Savo Island did not augur well for Turner's continued service, but naval leaders in Washington retained faith in the amphibious commander. As in every operation he planned and commanded, Turner gained insight not only from his successes but also from his failures. The hard lessons learned in the Solomons and at Tarawa significantly improved the performance of his amphibious forces during follow-on campaigns in the Marshall and Mariana Islands. Turner worked tirelessly to incorporate the advice of his Marine and Army counterparts and subordinates, to ensure essential logistical support for operations, and to refine battle plans. He was a deep thinker, but more importantly a doer.

The admiral was not an easy man to work with or for. Labeled "Terrible Turner" by the press, he rarely smiled, often spoke bluntly, and did not gladly suffer fools. He demanded excellence. Turner's staff did not express warm feelings for

Rear Admiral Richmond Kelly Turner (left) and Major General Alexander A. Vandegrift (right) on the flag bridge of USS *McCawley*, c. July–August 1942. *Source:* US Navy, now in the collection of the National Archives. US Naval History and Heritage Command # 80-CF-112-4-63.

the boss, but they did respect his genius for leadership.

Turner was never more valued than during the amphibious assaults on Iwo Jima and Okinawa. In the latter operation, he oversaw the movements of 1,213 ships and landing craft and the assault landing of 116,000 Marines and soldiers. In recognition of Turner's stellar accomplishments, on May 24, 1945, the Navy promoted him to full admiral. Turner retired from the Navy in 1947 and died in 1961.

---

was Vice Admiral Richmond Kelly Turner, commander of the Joint Expeditionary Force, and Marine Lieutenant General Holland M. Smith, commander of the Expeditionary Troops. Marine Major General Harry Schmidt would lead the fight ashore as commander of the V Amphibious Corps, composed of the 3rd, 4th, and 5th Marine Divisions.

The invasion plan entailed the latter two divisions landing abreast northeast of Mt. Suribachi, a 546-foot-high extinct volcano that loomed far above the southern reaches of the island. Once ashore, the 5th Marine Division's 28th Marines were to secure Suribachi. The other five regiments were charged with occupying Japanese Airfield No. 1 and reaching the island's far shore before pivoting to the right for a major assault on enemy positions to the north. The 3rd Marine Division was slated to come ashore in reinforcement. The plan was simple, but none of the naval leaders expected the job to be easy.

The Japanese command had anticipated an Allied amphibious assault on Iwo Jima and spent the latter half of 1944 preparing for the island's defense. Japanese

Prime Minister Hideki Tojo ordered Lieutenant General Tadamichi Kuribayashi[1] to lead the fight to hold the position. Kuribayashi was determined to turn the unpopulated, barren, eight-square-mile island into an impregnable fortress. Having served as an assistant naval attaché in Washington and traveled throughout America before the war, the general considered it unlikely that his garrison could survive the air, naval, and ground power of the United States. But he was determined to hold Iwo Jima as long as possible, thereby giving Japan a chance to delay an invasion of the Home Islands and perhaps prevent his country's defeat in the Pacific War.

US leaders came to appreciate that the enemy defenses on Iwo Jima would be formidable. Repeated flights by photoreconnaissance aircraft over the island documented the steady improvement of Kuribayashi's fortifications—at least those seen above ground. Consequently, long before the February 1945 amphibious assault, the Navy and the Army Air Forces did what they could to complicate his efforts. Two days after the Japanese general's arrival on the island, Fifth Fleet carrier aircraft destroyed 66 of the 100 aircraft in the aerial defense force. In following months, Army Air Forces B-29 and B-24 bombers repeatedly plastered the airfields and other sites.

The US ground commanders expected direct and sustained bombardment by Navy warships to be essential to the neutralization of Kuribayashi's defenses. The Marines called for 10 days of continuous shelling before any "Leatherneck" set foot on the island. The top Navy leaders did not concur. Spruance averred that it would interfere with his plans for a carrier strike on airfields in Japan, and Turner argued that he would not have enough ammunition on hand for such an extended mission. The Marines got three days of preliminary bombardment—it would not be enough.

During February 16 and 17, 1945, Spruance's battleships, cruisers, destroyers, and rocket vessels arrived off Iwo Jima and pummeled known defensive positions ashore. Behind smoke-screens, minesweepers and underwater demolition team "frogmen" ensured that approach lanes off the landing beaches were free of mines and underwater obstacles. These units accomplished their missions under heavy enemy fire that sank or damaged ships and craft and killed or wounded sailors. Coastal defense guns put six rounds into the heavy cruiser *Pensacola*, killing 17 men and wounding more than 100. Another round hit a destroyer, causing 40 casualties. Mortar fire plunged into landing craft rocket vessels, necessarily operating close to the shore, sinking one and wreaking havoc on others. The Japanese defenders were buoyed by their performance during these first days of the operation but their exultation would be short lived.

To improve the effectiveness of the bombardment, on February 18 Turner deployed his five battleships and other naval gunfire vessels within a mile and a half of the shore. From these close-in waters, the warships eliminated numerous targets identified by aerial and surface observation. So skillfully had Kuribayashi's troops fortified and concealed their coastal gun emplacements, machine-gun positions, and pillboxes, however, that the shelling hardly compromised the island's defenses.

As LVT (landing vehicle tracked) amphibian tractors and other landing craft headed for the beach on the morning of February 19, the warships opened up a 30-minute barrage that blanketed the shore with 8,000 rounds of naval gunfire (see Map 17.2). Just before 0900, the first wave of amphibian tractors hit the beach and within 15 minutes the next three waves followed suit. Loaded down with as much as 120 pounds of ammunition and gear per man, the marines debouched from their landing vehicles and struggled up the loose, gray-ash-covered beach. Dazed and disoriented by the ferocity of the naval bombardment and following Kuribayashi's orders to wait until the marines drew close, the defenders responded with only desultory fire for the first half-hour. After that, however, fire from Japanese artillery,

---

[1] Japanese place family names first followed by given names, while English usage is inconsistent concerning the order for Japanese names. In English-language publications Tojo Hideki (Japanese rendering) is commonly referred to as Hideki Tojo and Kuribayashi Tadamichi (Japanese rendering) as Tadamichi Kuribayashi. This work will adhere to common English usage.

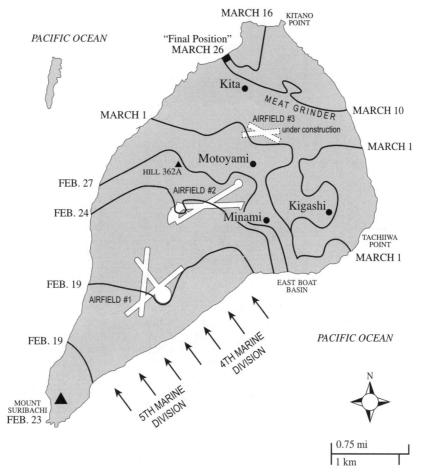

Map 17.2   Iwo Jima, February–March 1945.

mortars, automatic weapons, and rifles rained down on the assault platoons, several of which had managed to get close to the far shore. Behind them, incoming artillery, tanks, and supplies began to fill the beachhead, which was already teeming with marines, dead and alive. The enemy killed or wounded 2,500 American servicemen that first day, but by nightfall the 4th and 5th Marine Divisions had firmly established their beachhead.

The second day of the invasion witnessed the start of the planned assault on Suribachi. Fire from nine 16-inch and 20 5-inch guns of the battleship *Washington*, other warships, Marine artillery, and aircraft from "jeep" carriers offshore pounded the mountain, wiping out pillboxes and artillery posi-

tions. Working their way through the blasted and difficult terrain, Marine tanks managed to neutralize enemy fortifications at the foot of Suribachi, but only Marine riflemen were able to scale the mountain's steep slopes (see Figure 17.1). It took two more days of intense, bloody fighting before rifle- and flamethrower-wielding marines destroyed concrete bunkers and caves defended to the last by enemy soldiers.

Finally, on the morning of February 23, Lieutenant Harold G. Schrier led his patrol to the summit, where it raised the American flag on a section of pipe found nearby. Soon, horns and sirens on the ships of the fleet blasted out to mark this memorable occasion. Witnessing the action from the deck of a nearby ship, Secretary of the Navy James Forrestal exclaimed to

Figure 17.1   Marines fire on Japanese positions on Mount Suribachi, Iwo Jima. *Source:* US Marine Corps Archives.

the commander of the Expeditionary Troops, "Holland, the raising of that flag on Suribachi means a Marine Corps for the next 500 years."[2]

Several hours later, men from the regiment replaced the flag with a larger one obtained from the landing ship tank *LST 779*. The inspiring image of that event, taken by Associated Press photographer Joe Rosenthal, became the iconic representation of the Marine Corps' contribution to victory in World War II. It also made famous Marines Harlan Block, Rene Gagnon, Ira Hayes, Franklin Sousley, and Michael Strank and Navy Corpsman John H. Bradley. Attesting to the ferocity of the fighting on Iwo Jima, only Bradley, Gagnon, and Hayes survived the battle.

Hundreds of American sailors also made the ultimate sacrifice in the epic battle. As combat raged ashore, Japanese kamikazes flying from the Home Islands targeted the Fifth Fleet. On two separate occasions, suicide pilots guided their aircraft into the carrier *Saratoga*, killing or wounding more than 300 men, badly damaging the ship, and forcing it to withdraw from the operation. Other kamikazes sank the escort carrier *Bismarck Sea*, which suffered a heavy loss of life.

The conquest of Suribachi marked only the beginning of the long campaign ashore. Even as the 28th Marines struggled up its slopes, regiments of the 4th and 5th Marine Divisions clawed their way northward.

---

[2] Holland M. Smith and Percy Finch, *Coral and Brass* (1949), 261.

Soon after coming ashore, the fresh 3rd Marine Division relieved hard-hit units of the 4th Marine Division, enabling General Schmidt's V Amphibious Corps to continue the advance. On February 24, warships, naval aircraft, and Marine artillery unleashed a furious 75-minute barrage against the Japanese defenders, enabling a limited push northward until halted by enemy mines and anti-tank defenses. It took another three days of desperate fighting before marines were able to overrun Airfield No. 2 and move on Airfield No. 3. The men employed flamethrowers and dynamite to kill their enemies or seal them forever in their underground lairs (see Map 17.2).

Meanwhile, on the left flank the 5th Marine Division assaulted Japanese defenses centered on Hill 362A. Not until March 1, and at a cost of 224 casualties from enemy artillery and mortar fire, were divisional units able to seize the objective. The next targets of the Marine advance proved even more challenging. A series of hills, gullies, depressions, and shell holes defended by dug-in Japanese troops routinely fighting to the death came to be called the "Meat Grinder" for its deadly impact on the Americans.

On the night of March 8, some exhausted, hungry, isolated, and desperate Japanese troops, against Kuribayashi's earlier orders, opted to go on the offensive. These soldiers launched a banzai charge against the 4th Marine Division. It availed them little since the marines killed 650 soldiers and filled the vacuum in the line left by the dead attackers. By March 10, the Americans had overrun the Meat Grinder and put an end to organized enemy resistance. The fighting was far from over, however.

Between March 10 and 25, the three Marine divisions had to methodically reduce pockets of die-hard Japanese soldiers with flamethrowers, tanks, explosives, and small arms. The enemy fought bravely and fanatically for each and every position or executed fruitless banzai charges. During the last few days of resistance, as the Marines closed in on his headquarters at Kitano Point, General Kuribayashi radioed Tokyo his final farewell. He had accomplished his goal of delaying the American victory—but at great cost. Only 216 of the 20,000 defending Japanese soldiers surrendered.

The US victory was dearly bought. The fighting had killed 6,000 and wounded another 17,000 American fighting men. These marines, sailors, airmen, and soldiers accomplished the mission of securing the island and its airfields for use by the B-29 fleet. By the end of the war, 2,251 bombers (with 22,000 crewmen), low on fuel or damaged, were able to make emergency landings on the island rather than ditch at sea or try to make it back to the Marianas. Admiral Nimitz and many other observers appreciated the sacrifices made to secure Iwo Jima. He blessed future generations with the remembrance that "among the Americans who served on Iwo Jima, uncommon valor was a common virtue."[3]

Okinawa

Even before Allied forces secured Iwo Jima and the Philippines, strategists set their sights on an island that would be large enough to sustain the war's final amphibious assault—the invasion of Japan. Okinawa, a 60-mile-long island in the Ryukyu chain, boasted protected waters for naval vessels, several airfields, and abundant land space for the buildup of supplies. Equally important, the distance from Okinawa to Kyushu, the southernmost of Japan's Home Islands, was only 350 nautical miles. On October 3, 1944, the Joint Chiefs of Staff instructed Admiral Nimitz to begin serious planning for a spring 1945 seizure of an island in the Ryukyus, with Okinawa the likely candidate (see Map 17.1).

Nimitz assigned the job to Admiral Spruance, who would also be responsible for directing the February 1945 operation to capture Iwo Jima. As Commander Central Pacific Task Forces and Commander Task Force 50, Spruance would have available for the Okinawa mission (soon named Operation Iceberg) his own Fifth Fleet, Admiral Marc Mitscher's Fast Carrier Task Force, and a new entrant to the war in the Pacific, the British Carrier Task Force. Steaming offshore to protect and support the fight for Okinawa was Admiral Spruance's armada of 260 major US and British warships, including 40 aircraft carriers, 18 battleships, and 200 destroyer types.

---

[3] Nimitz as quoted in Karal Ann Marling and John Wetenhall, *Iwo Jima: Monuments, Memories and the American Hero* (1991), 1.

Vice Admiral Turner, already a veteran of numerous amphibious landings in the Pacific, would serve as Commander Joint Expeditionary Force and in that capacity control the landing phase. His resources included all the warships and landing ships and craft assigned to Operation Iceberg; these vessels would carry out the amphibious assault, naval bombardment, and close air support duties.

Once the Army and Marine divisions were firmly established ashore, Army Lieutenant General Simon Bolivar Buckner, Jr., commanding general of the Tenth Army, was charged with leading the campaign against the Japanese garrison. Slated to carry the fight to the enemy were the 1st, 2nd, and 6th Marine Divisions and the Army's 7th, 27th, 77th, and 96th Infantry Divisions, all veterans of previous island campaigns. Buckner's force consisted of more than 180,000 soldiers, sailors, airmen, and marines. A fleet of 1,213 ships and craft directly supported the ground campaign.

As the Allied juggernaut closed in on Japan, there was little doubt that the Ryukyus would be seized as a stepping stone to Japan. The garrison commander, Lieutenant General Mitsuru Ushijima, and his soldiers knew that this battle was their last chance to retard that advance. They also understood that, if they could delay the island's fall long enough, the Allied fleet would be compelled to remain offshore and be subject to destruction by kamikazes based in Japan. All but a few Japanese soldiers were prepared to sacrifice their lives to stave off the invasion of their homeland.

Manning concrete bunkers, fortified caves, and other fighting positions on Okinawa was the 100,000-strong 32nd Army. Included in this total were several thousand sailors organized into special fighting units. Like Kuribayashi on Iwo Jima, Ushijima knew that it would be fruitless for his forces to oppose the landing at the beaches; Allied air, naval, and ground power was just too overwhelming. Instead, he oversaw the development of a series of defensive lines in the rugged, southern reaches of the island. The invaders would face minefields, artillery, and mortar concentrations, and redoubts jammed with anti-tank and automatic weapons sited for interlocking fields of fire. With months to prepare for the invasion, the Japanese stowed in underground bunkers and tunnels a mountain of ammunition. Ushijima established his headquarters at Shuri, the site of an ancient castle on a ridge in southern Okinawa.

Seizing the initiative in the campaign, Spruance ordered a preemptive attack on the enemy's air fleet, which was gathering for the defense of Okinawa. On March 18 and 19, 1945, Mitcher's fast carriers struck airfields in the Home Islands, in the process destroying more than 500 enemy aircraft in the air and especially on the ground. As a foretaste of the air–sea battle that would soon take place off Okinawa, the Japanese exacted a heavy price for this early success. Conventional aircraft and kamikazes struck the carriers *Enterprise*, *Franklin*, *Intrepid*, *Wasp*, and *Yorktown*, causing significant damage and casualties. A pair of bombs caused a massive fire on *Franklin* that killed or wounded close to 1,000 of its 2,600-man crew, came close to sinking the carrier, and forced its retirement from the war. On March 26 and 27 the British Carrier Task Force neutralized enemy air strength on the Sakishima Islands.

The Army's 77th Infantry Division executed the next preliminary operation when elements occupied the Kerama Islands, just west of southern Okinawa, on March 26. These islands provided a protected anchorage for repair, supply, and other support ships throughout the campaign. Unexpectedly, the occupying forces discovered hundreds of small boats that the enemy intended to load with explosives and send against the invasion fleet. During the second half of March, Navy minesweepers cleared lanes through the Keramas and the approaches to Okinawa, enabling battleships and other naval gunfire ships to begin bombarding targets ashore. Meanwhile, fleet aircraft, radar picket ships, and other surface combatants deployed protective screens around the island. By the 29th, the Fifth Fleet had established air supremacy over the island—but it would not last.

At 0406 on April 1, Easter Sunday in 1945, Admiral Turner gave the traditional order to "land the landing force." As warships, rocket ships, and naval aircraft pounded the area around the Hagushi beaches, on the western coast of Okinawa, transports disgorged LVTs and landing craft, which headed for shore. At 0830 the first assault waves touched the beach.

To the surprise of veterans from many previous island fights, the enemy was almost nowhere to be seen. Marine Major General Roy S. Geiger's III Amphibious Corps and Army Major General John R. Hodge's

XXIV Corps quickly secured the Kadena and Yontan airfields and moved inland. Two days later, US troops reached the far shore. Thereafter, the Marines swung north and after a sharp, bloody fight on the Motobu Peninsula secured the northern reaches of the island. The 77th Infantry Division fought another hard battle to seize the airfield on Ie Shima, a small island off Okinawa's northwest coast.

On April 6, the Japanese launched their first major counterstroke in the battle for Okinawa. In the afternoon, 735 kamikazes and conventional aircraft based in Japan converged on Admiral Spruance's fleet. That day and the next, the enemy air assault sank six ships and damaged another 27, in the process killing or wounding 1,000 sailors. This operation was the opening salvo of an aerial campaign the Japanese labeled Kikusui (floating chrysanthemums), which would entail nine other major strikes and last until June 22.

Often unable to get through the fleet's protective air-defense ring to strike carriers and other large warships, the enemy pilots focused on the first ships they encountered—destroyers manning radar picket stations on the periphery. The experience of destroyer *Laffey* typified the ferocity of the Japanese air assault. In the course of one day on the radar picket line, the ship was attacked by kamikazes and other aircraft 22 times. Six kamikazes and four bombs smashed into the ship, killing 31 sailors and wounding another 72, one-third of the crew. Somehow, the ship miraculously survived this onslaught.

The Imperial Japanese Navy, almost negligible after the Battle of Leyte Gulf, also sortied against the naval forces off Okinawa. The battleship *Yamato*, armed with 18-inch naval rifles, departed Japan on April 6, accompanied by the cruiser *Yahagi* and seven destroyers, and headed for Okinawa. *Yamato* had only enough fuel for a one-way trip but the battleship, pride of the Imperial Japanese Navy, never got close to the invasion beaches. Spotted by US submarines and patrol planes, Admiral Mitcher's carrier aircraft pounced on the behemoth and sent it to the bottom with ten torpedo and five bombs. The Americans also sank the cruiser and four of the destroyers. The desperate suicidal attacks cost the lives of 3,400 Japanese sailors.

Defeating the Japanese air offensive off Okinawa proved to be the bloodiest battle in the US Navy's history. The enemy killed close to 5,000 sailors and

wounded another 4,874. Suicide planes and bombs dropped by conventional planes sank 34 naval vessels and damaged 368.

Despite these horrific losses, the Navy's object in Operation Iceberg was to protect the lodgment on Okinawa until the battle ashore had been won, and on that score it was mission accomplished. Moreover, in defeating the Kikusui assault, the fleet eviscerated what was left of Japan's air forces, destroying 7,800 kamikaze and conventional planes.

Meanwhile, the battle on the island had taken a more deadly turn. As Hodge's corps headed south, and in stark contrast to the early days of the invasion, the Japanese army arrayed along the first of three defensive lines resisted fiercely. By April 12, the attack of the 7th and 96th Infantry Divisions had become bogged down. Even when reinforced by the 27th Infantry Division and provided with massive air, naval, and artillery support, Hodge's troops made only short gains and only broke through the first line on the 24th. Buckner replaced two of the exhausted Army divisions with the 1st Marine Division, 77th Infantry Division, and 6th Marine Division. Japanese counterattacks also failed to change the situation on the ground and resulted in the death of 5,000 enemy soldiers. The Marines faced the same determined enemy resistance as the Army troops and made only limited progress while suffering heavy casualties. Fearing that his second line of defense would be flanked, in the third week of May General Ushijima withdrew his units to the last defensive line, only four miles from his headquarters at Shuri castle.

From June 10 to 17, the III Amphibious Corps and the XXIV Corps launched a simultaneous assault that breached the last defensive line and finally ended organized enemy resistance on the island. Some Japanese soldiers fought on until American troops killed them or they killed themselves. General Ushijima committed *seppuku*, or ritual suicide, and 110,000 Japanese soldiers and many Okinawan civilians died on Okinawa.

Despite the American success, the Tenth Army suffered almost 40,000 battle casualties and 26,000 nonbattle casualties on Okinawa, including the loss of General Buckner, killed on the front line by an enemy artillery round. On June 22, the Tenth Army formally raised the American flag over the tortured landscape

Gato-Class Fleet Submarine

The *Gato*-class submarine of World War II proved to be the US Navy's most effective weapon against the merchant marine of Japan. Benefiting from the design and construction experience of the interwar years, *Gato*—launched by the Electric Boat Company at Groton, Connecticut, on December 31, 1941—and the 76 other boats of the class entered service during the war. Shipyards at Portsmouth, New Hampshire; Mare Island, California; and Manitowoc, Wisconsin, also built *Gato* submarines.

Designed to work with the battle fleet in the vast expanse of the Pacific, and thus referred to as "fleet submarines," the *Gato* boats were ideally suited to operations against Japan. The boats' primary weapons were 24 standard Mark XIV and later in the war Mark XVIII electric torpedoes. The relatively large submarines (311-foot length, 27-foot beam) boasted a 5-inch or 3-inch deck gun and 40-mm and 20-mm antiaircraft weapons. To avoid enemy antisubmarine forces, the *Gato* submarines could safely submerge in less than a minute and

then dive to 300 feet and remain there for up to 48 hours.

Several engine types propelled the *Gato* boats but the most successful were Fairbanks-Morse 38D and GM-Winton 16-248 diesel-electrics, which enabled speeds of 21 knots on the surface and nine knots submerged. The submarines could accommodate enough fuel, stored in spaces between double hulls, and refrigerated food for a 75-day patrol to Japan and return to Hawaii. Habitability was critical for the long patrols, often in tropical waters, so each submarine had air conditioning for the comfort of the crew of six officers and 54 enlisted sailors but also for the effective operation of the machinery.

With the Pacific Fleet temporarily out of action after the Pearl

Harbor attack, the Navy ordered its submarines to engage in unrestricted warfare against Japan's merchant fleet. Though hampered initially by lackluster commanders and faulty torpedoes, the *Gato* and other Pacific submarines eventually became especially adept at sinking enemy merchantmen. By war's end, the entire US submarine force had sunk 1,113 Japanese merchant ships totaling 4.8 million tons. In addition, the *Gato* submarines took a toll of Imperial Japanese Navy warships, sinking aircraft carriers *Shokaku* and *Taiho*, cruisers, and destroyers.

Grunion (SS-216) bow view at rest, off Groton, Connecticut, March 20, 1942. *Source:* Electric Boat Corporation photo courtesy of ussubvetsofworldwarii.org via navsource.org.

of Okinawa. Work was already underway to develop the island as the major staging area for the invasion of Kyushu. Sobered by the heavy losses ashore and at sea in the titanic struggle for Okinawa, Allied leaders grimly prepared for what they believed would be an even bloodier final assault on Imperial Japan.

Japan Isolated and Under Siege

As the US Navy's carriers, battleships, and other surface warships swept the Imperial Japanese Navy from the Pacific Ocean, American submarines and mines severely reduced the merchant fleet of Japan. More

importantly, the submarine and mine campaigns were instrumental in starving the island nation of oil, iron ore, lead, tin, and other raw materials needed for its Asian war effort, making it impossible for Japan to avoid defeat in World War II.

Simultaneously with the Japanese December 7, 1941, attack on Pearl Harbor, Admiral Harold Stark, the Chief of Naval Operations, had ordered the execution of unrestricted air and submarine warfare against Japan. At the outbreak of war, America's 51-boat submarine fleet operated for the most part in Hawaiian waters and in the Philippines. The undersea force consisted of S-class submarines dating from the 1920s and so-called fleet submarines, completed in the mid-to-late 1930s. Built for defensive roles, the S-boats lacked the fuel capacity for long-range patrols and air conditioning, a critical requirement for operations in tropical waters. In contrast, the 271- to 381-foot fleet boats could hold 90,000 gallons of fuel, enabling 10,000-nautical-mile patrols.

The submarine campaign did not begin well. Many officers who had taken command during peacetime lacked the drive essential for successful undersea warriors. They routinely failed to adopt aggressive, adaptive tactics against their Japanese foes. The submarine force sank only 13 merchantmen during the first three months of the war. Faulty torpedoes posed an even greater problem. Having never been live-fire-tested, the magnetic exploder on the standard Mark XIV torpedo failed in its combat debut. Submarine crews grew exasperated when they heard a torpedo strike the hull of an enemy ship but not explode. Other torpedoes failed to run or explode at the proper depth. During 1942 the submarine fleet sank a little over 600,000 tons of Japanese shipping—a dismal record.

The situation began to change in late 1942 and in 1943. A total of 88 fleet boats joined the force and Vice Admiral Charles A. Lockwood, Commander Submarine Force, Pacific Fleet, consigned the less effective S-boats to training duties or retired them from service. He put younger, professionally skilled, and combat-proven officers in command. Lockwood also began using his boats in groups, rather than singly against enemy convoys. These three-to-four-boat groups, akin to the German navy's "wolf packs," worked together to infiltrate and decimate an enemy formation. Japanese antisubmarine destroyers and other escorts, plagued by poor detection equipment, weapons, and intelligence support, never matched the effectiveness of the Allied antisubmarine effort in either the Atlantic or the Pacific. The Navy's technical support establishment finally resolved the torpedo depth and exploder problems. In addition, the US scientific–industrial establishment turned out increasingly effective weapons, target-plotting, sonar, and navigational equipment.

Then, in early 1943, US intelligence presented the submarine force with an advantage of immense value. Fleet Radio Unit Pacific cryptanalysts broke the Japanese merchant shipping code, allowing them to gather very detailed information on the routing of enemy merchant convoys. Submarine commanders could then set up ambushes at specific locations rather than search the vast waters of the western Pacific on the off chance they might happen upon a target.

1943 and 1944 witnessed the flowering of the submarine campaign. American boats sank two times more enemy merchantmen in 1943 than they had the previous year and almost 2,390,000 tons of shipping in 1944. During this period, Japan lost 40 percent of the merchant fleet it had begun the war with (see Figure 17.2). The industrial economy of the island nation received less than half of the raw materials it needed to sustain wartime production.

In 1945, with Allied forces having occupied the Philippines and largely driven the Japanese merchant marine from the Asian littoral, Admiral Lockwood had his submarines zero in on the heavily defended Sea of Japan. In June, nine fleet boats equipped with mine-detecting sonars evaded enemy minefields in the Strait of Tsushima and safely entered the sea. Once inside, the boats wreaked havoc on their unsuspecting prey, sinking 44 merchant vessels in two weeks (see Map 17.3). The group accomplished its mission and exited the Sea of Japan through another mined strait, except for *Bonefish*, which was sunk by enemy action. In addition to that boat, the submarine fleet suffered the loss, often with all hands, of 48 submarines during World War II in the Pacific.

Their sacrifice helped to achieve victory for Allied arms. At war's end, less than one-quarter of Japan's prewar merchant fleet remained afloat. American submarines sank 1,113 Japanese merchant ships totaling 4.8 million tons—54.6 percent of the vessels destroyed by Allied naval forces.

Mines also took a toll on Japanese shipping, sinking 19 warships and 247 merchant vessels (see Table 17.1). Equally importantly they denied the enemy access to essential sea transportation routes, ports, and rivers. The Allies employed two basic mine types: magnetic mines that exploded when a ship—and its magnetic field—passed nearby or actually hit a mine; and acoustic mines, triggered by the propeller and other noises of a ship underway. The mine-laying forces often set up minefields in the path of unsuspecting convoys to ambush and sink as many ships as possible before the enemy chose alternative routes. Another tactic

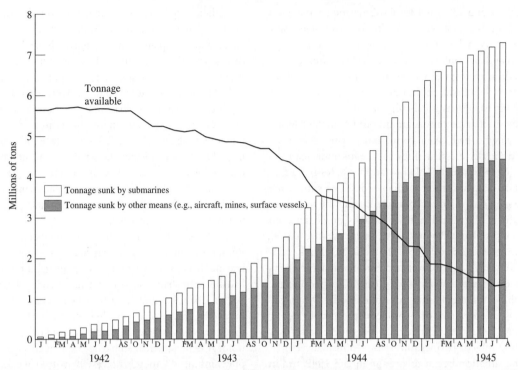

Figure 17.2   Total Japanese merchant ship tonnage sunk and remaining available, 1942–1945. *Source:* Government Printing Office, *The Campaigns of the Pacific War: United States Strategic Bombing Survey (Pacific) Naval Analysis Division* (1946), 384.

was to deploy minefields between Japanese rear areas and islands under Allied assault to deny the defending units reinforcements and supplies of food and ammunition. Finally, the Allies flooded narrow straits and the approaches to enemy ports with mines, compelling the Japanese either to accept the closure of these vital waterways or make the difficult and dangerous effort to clear them.

In the fall of 1942, US submarines based in Australia and Hawaii kicked off the first strategic mine-laying operations when they seeded shipping routes in Southeast Asia and along the coasts of China and Japan. In early 1943, US destroyer minesweepers successfully mined waters traversed by ships of the "Tokyo Express," attempting to aid Japanese soldiers fighting desperately to hold islands in the Solomons. Throughout the war, submarines and warships continued to sow minefields in enemy waters.

Aerial mine laying, however, came to be the most often employed and most effective means of sinking Japanese merchant ships and stifling oceangoing

movement. Beginning in February 1943, US Army Air Forces B-24 Liberators based in India essentially closed the Japanese-held port of Rangoon, Burma. Similar operations complicated life for the enemy at the ports of Haiphong in French Indochina and Shanghai in China. In 1944, US, British, and Australian planes aggressively mined waters throughout Southeast Asia, where the B-29 Superfortress made its debut as an aerial minelayer.

In November 1944, Admiral Nimitz suggested to General Henry H. "Hap" Arnold, chief of staff of the Army Air Forces, that an aerial mining campaign had the potential along with the submarine campaign to isolate Japan. Persuaded, Arnold directed Major General Curtis E. LeMay's XXI Bomber Command to begin the operation in conjunction with the invasion of Okinawa. The campaign's objectives were to isolate the Home Islands from external sources of raw materials and food, prevent the deployment of troops to Okinawa, and disrupt shipping on Japan's Inland Sea.

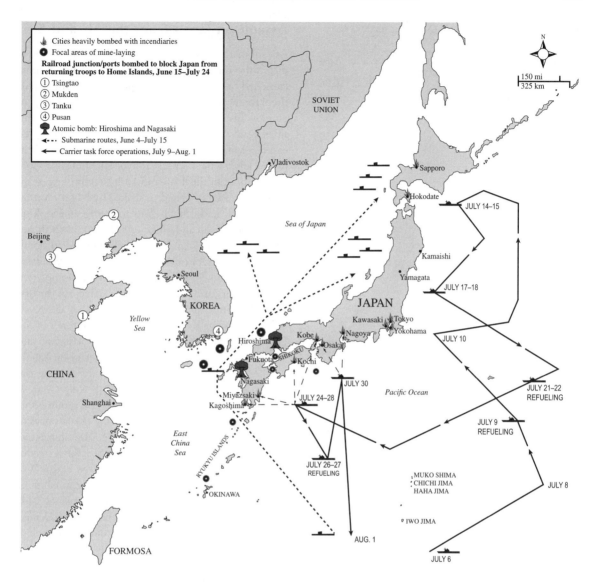

Map 17.3   Japan isolated and besieged, 1945.

From late March to August 5, 1945, LeMay's 313th Bomb Wing B-29s executed a five-phase aerial mine-laying assault that, with the submarine and strategic bombing campaigns, rapidly brought the war in its ferocity home to the Japanese people. In the initial two operations, the bombers dropped mines into the Inland Sea and across Shimonoseki Strait, between Honshu and Kyushu (see Table 17.2). Admiral Nimitz especially wanted to interdict the sea lanes between Japan and the Ryukyus so the remaining ships of the Imperial Japanese Navy could not join the fight for Okinawa. The operations closed the strait, disrupted traffic on the Inland Sea, and resulted in the sinking or damage of 35 vessels for the loss of five US bombers. In the next two phases, the B-29s focused their efforts on the ports of northwestern Honshu and Kyushu. The more than 5,000 mines they dropped heavily damaged or sent to the bottom another 75 to 100 Japanese vessels for the

Table 17.1 Japanese merchant shipping: method of destruction, 1941–1945.

Method	US	British	Other	Total
Submarine	1,113	29	10[a]	1,152
Surface warship	11	1	0[b]	12
Carrier aircraft	359	1	2	362
Land-based aircraft	354	3	18	375
Mines	247	13	0	260
Submarine and aircraft	9	0	0	9
Surface warship and aircraft	9	1	4	14
Mines and aircraft	1	0	0	1
Carrier and land-based aircraft	9	0	0	9
Mines and aircraft	1	0	0	1
Sabotage	1	2	0	3
Total	**2,114**	**50**	**34**	**2,198**

[a] Dutch.
[b] Remainder of column by a combination of aircraft, submarines, and warships of two nations.

loss of four planes. During the last phase of the campaign, the 313th lost six bombers, but the 3,700 mines deployed by the unit discouraged many of Japan's remaining vessels from operating on the Inland Sea. The four-and-a-half-month mining campaign, during which Army Air Forces bombers laid more than 12,000 magnetic and acoustic mines among the Home Islands, completed the effort begun years earlier to isolate Japan from its overseas sources of sustenance.

Table 17.2 Mining in the Shimonoseki Strait, 1945.

Month	Number of mines laid	Number of merchantmen sunk
March	1,006	0
April	155	11
May	957	36
June	1,139	42
July	650	37
August	0	2
Total	**3,907**	**128**

Assault on Japan from the Air and Sea

As submarines and mine-laying bombers interdicted the waters surrounding Japan, Admiral Nimitz launched one more of his sea power weapons against the Home Islands. He directed Admiral Halsey to employ his Third Fleet carriers and bombardment ships against airfields and industrial sites all along the east coast of Japan (see Map 17.3). On July 10, aircraft from Halsey's fleet struck Tokyo, encountering little opposition. On the 14th and 15th they hit targets on Hokkaido, then returned to strike targets on Honshu on the 17th and 18th before refueling and striking targets on Kyushu and Shikoku between the 24th and 28th (see Figure 17.3). They then returned to bomb Osaka and Nagoya on Honshu, and finally withdrew. At the same time, a task force of three battleships, two heavy cruisers, and nine destroyers carried out the first US naval bombardment of Japan when they destroyed the iron plant at Kamaishi. On the 16th, three of the US Navy's newest battleships—*Iowa*, *Missouri*, and *Wisconsin*—leveled steel and iron factories on Japan's northernmost large island of Hokkaido. During the same mission, the Royal Navy's HMS *King George V* and the other warships of the British task group bombarded a nearby defense plant. During the last days of July, Halsey's planes carried out especially destructive strikes against shipping in the Inland Sea. Reflective of Japan's parlous situation at this stage of the Pacific War, there was no refuge for the few surviving warships of the Imperial Japanese Navy. US carrier planes sank, capsized, or heavily damaged the battleships *Haruna*, *Hyuga*, and *Ise*—not far out to sea but moored close to the shore.

Adding to Japan's misery, in March 1945 General LeMay ordered his B-29 fleet to destroy the enemy's cities by fire. Previously, the big bombers had concentrated on hitting industrial and defense plants, but routinely foul weather over Japan, the lack of sufficient targeting precision, and other operational difficulties had stymied the effort. LeMay concluded that destruction of Japan's cities would not only eliminate targets of military importance but also convince the Japanese government and people that continued resistance would be especially costly and ultimately futile. From March to July, incendiary bombs dropped by B-29s flying more than 6,900 sorties caused

Figure 17.3 TBM Avengers and SB2C Helldivers bombing Hakodate, Japan, July 1945. *Source:* United States National Archives, 80-G-490232.

fire storms in Japan's six most important cities and hundreds of other population centers (see Table 17.3). Over half of Tokyo became a howling wilderness. There was little the Japanese could do to counter this assault, since few resources had been devoted in previous years to national air defense.

Both LeMay and Spruance argued that the naval blockade and air assault of the Home Islands had so devastated the enemy nation's war-making capacity and civilian morale that the Japanese government would soon have to capitulate. These leaders felt that time was on the side of the Allies and hence that there was no need for a ground invasion of Japan. They understood that the cost to the Allies in terms of killed, missing, and wounded during the Iwo Jima

Table 17.3 Destruction of Japan's six largest cities by incendiary bombing, mid-March to mid-June 1945.

City	Area (sq. miles)	Percent destroyed
Toyko	111	51
Nagoya	40	31
Kobe	16	56
Osaka	17	26
Yokohama	20	44
Kawasaki	11	33

Source: © Cynthia Parzych Publishing, Inc.

and Okinawa campaigns would pale in comparison to the anticipated losses from an invasion of Kyushu and subsequent occupation of all Japan.

The Joint Chiefs of Staff argued instead that an invasion was absolutely necessary. General George C. Marshall, the Army chief of staff, contended that, despite their weakened state, the Japanese government and military could be expected to fight to the last, as the war's previous battles had shown. Army leaders also highlighted the heavy price in casualties that air and naval forces would incur maintaining an extended blockade. A larger consideration was the understanding by the Washington-based Joint Chiefs of Staff that the American people were tiring of the long, bloody war and wanted to cap the defeat of Germany with a victory over Japan sooner rather than later. Even though Admiral Ernest J. King, the chief of naval operations and Commander-in-Chief, US Fleet, was a strong advocate of sea power, he shared the conclusion of his Joint Chiefs of Staff colleagues.

Accordingly, on June 18, 1945, the new president, Harry S. Truman, approved the planning and preparation for Operation Olympic, the invasion of Kyushu. Already, more than 600,000 US troops slated for the operation were headed to the Pacific from Europe and the United States. The Navy stockpiled mountains of ammunition, fuel, weapons, equipment, and food on board its logistics fleet and at more than 400 bases all over the Pacific. Spruance concentrated a mighty armada for Olympic, including 1,137 warships, almost 15,000 aircraft, 2,800 large landing ships, and thousands of smaller landing craft.

In August 1945, Japan was on the verge of collapse, as Spruance and LeMay sensed, but it took a shock of enormous ferocity and destructiveness to compel that nation's surrender. The leveling of Hiroshima on August 6 and Nagasaki three days later by US-dropped atomic bombs provided the catalyst that ended the war. But it was the more than three years of herculean effort by the US and Allied nations and their armed forces that brought down the Japanese Empire.

Conclusion

Sea power proved to be the war-winning tool of the Allied war effort in the Pacific. Carriers, battleships, destroyers, and other warships of the fleet swept the Imperial Japanese Navy from the sea; submarines and mine-laying ships and planes destroyed the enemy's merchant marine; and marines and soldiers deployed from the sea seized one stubbornly defended island after the other in the steady advance on Tokyo. As American strategist Alfred Thayer Mahan understood long before the titanic conflict of 1941–1945, the nation that effectively employed sea power would be the victor in a struggle for mastery of the vast Pacific.

CHAPTER 18

The Uneasy Transition, 1945–1953

With the signing of the Japanese unconditional surrender on board USS *Missouri*, anchored in Tokyo Bay, the US Navy stood at its greatest moment of prestige and power. Britain's was the only other navy with substantial forces. With no maritime enemy in sight for the foreseeable future, the US Navy nonetheless planned to operate in its new two-ocean posture as a powerful deterrent to hostilities and an insurance against the unthinkable prospect of global conflict. Navy leaders sensed that something new had been added to conventional notions of sea power. The exceptional nature of the Pacific War and its aeronaval amphibious campaigns combined with the conquest of polar skies wrought a unique unification of the Atlantic and Pacific theaters that rendered the United States as vulnerable as other nations—a change from the past, when vast oceans had insulated North America from Eurasia.

The Postwar Navy and Marine Corps

The last year of World War II saw the US Navy and Marine Corps preparing for the postwar era. On V-E Day, Chief of Naval Operations Ernest King published his "Basic Post-War Plan No. 1." It began with the observation that the United States had fought two world wars within 25 years, despite all peaceful

intentions, and predicted that a future major war would likely involve it and another world war might cost it dearly. Adequate military force would be the most effective means of defense and of preventing another world war.[1]

In Admiral King's view, the United States needed to be prepared to protect its territories, act against any threat of hostilities in concert with other powers or alone, and be prepared to join international peacekeeping efforts. His objectives required the maintenance of active fleets in the Atlantic and Pacific, supported by adequate bases and shore establishments, both backed by reserve fleets, a reserve aircraft pool, and a trained naval reserve.

The two oceanic fleets would operate five carrier task forces, each with at least two fleet carriers, escorted by battleships, cruisers, and destroyers. Two would operate in the Atlantic and three in the Pacific, the latter using bases on Hawaii, the Philippines, and the West Coast of the United States. Each fleet would include amphibious shipping capable of lifting a Marine Corps division stationed on each coast and its associated aircraft groups, plus antisubmarine, service, and minesweeping groups. The total force envisioned just for the active component was 10 fleet carriers, five battleships, 28 cruisers, and another 254 combatants, supported by 161 mine vessels, 161 patrol vessels,

---

[1] "OP-50B, Serial 004850-D, Subj: Basic Post-War Plan No. 1, 7 May 1945," Box 191, Strategic Plans Division Records, Post-War Naval Planning and Sea Frontier Section (Series XIV) Operational Archives, Naval History and Heritage Command, Washington, DC.

America, Sea Power, and the World, First Edition. Edited by James C. Bradford.
© 2016 John Wiley & Sons, Inc. Published 2016 by John Wiley & Sons, Inc.

and 252 amphibious ships. Backing this force would be a reserve of 785 combatants and 4,412 auxiliaries and support craft. Only 222 combatants of the wartime US Navy would be considered excess and disposable from this scheme.

Immediate postwar missions for the Navy and Marine Corps centered upon the occupation of Japan, supporting the Nationalist Chinese, and repatriating Japanese forces and Korean laborers to their homelands. Both the Atlantic and Pacific Fleets participated in Operation Magic Carpet (October 1945–September 1946), the return of demobilized US forces from overseas to the United States. Although the transport services initially carried the bulk of the troops, and in some cases dependents, the Navy augmented its own transports with aircraft carriers, battleships, and cruisers to return home over 2 million persons. At the same time the tedious but deadly business of sweeping mines scattered across the shipping lanes and coastlines would occupy all naval forces for another year.

Operation Blacklist, the occupation of Japan, was initially assigned to the Army; however, the rapid decision of Japan to surrender found only elements of the US Third Fleet and 6th Marine Division available for the immediate task of securing the Tokyo Bay area. The occupation soon changed into an all-Army mission, except for naval facilities taken over by the Navy, and the 2nd and 5th Marine Divisions departed Japan by mid-1946. Almost simultaneously with the occupation of Japan, the Seventh Fleet transported army troops of the XXIV Corps from Okinawa to Korea in order to secure and disarm the Japanese forces in the southern half of the peninsula.

More complex were the activities of the fleet with regard to China. The movements of Chinese troops to the north and Japanese troops to their homeland stalled because of the presence of the communist Chinese forces under Mao Zedong in Manchuria and parts of North China. Under Operation Beleaguer, units of the Seventh Fleet landed the 6th Marine Division at Shanghai and 1st Marine Division at Tientsin to secure Peking as well as other ports and the all-important rail lines. In contrast with the situation in Japan, where the Marine divisions quickly terminated their occupation duties, the deployments in China dragged on into early 1947, with a reprise into 1949 as the Chinese communists triumphed in the civil war. The last major Marine Corps combat units departed China by June 1947, and the remaining battalions and companies tasked with safeguarding ports and evacuating civilians operated under an ad hoc command, Fleet Marine Force, Western Pacific, initially operating out of Tsingtao and later Guam, where several battalions and aircraft squadrons remained as a reinforcement for the final evacuation operations of 1948. The Seventh Fleet departed Tsing-tao (now Qingdao), its homeport since 1946, on May 25, 1949.

Hopes of keeping a Navy and Marine Corps presence in Guam as a strategic bulwark continued with a robust naval base and a new 1st Provisional Marine Brigade headquarters. In the end, the budget could not support such a forward deployment, and on January 5, 1949, the chief of naval operations ordered a bare base structure for Guam; the brigade disbanded. Navy and Marine Corps combat forces thus ended their almost continuous presence in the western Pacific since 1927. Large stockpiles of ammunition remained, but much equipment from Guam also headed back to storage facilities in the United States.

Japan's surrender found most of the US Marine Corps, then some 458,000 strong, deployed in the western Pacific, but by the end of 1946 barely 15,000 Marines remained on the rolls of Fleet Marine Force, Pacific and an even smaller number in the fledgling Fleet Marine Force, Atlantic.

In early 1945, the US Navy began to stand down its activities in the Mediterranean as liberated ports reverted to sovereign states. The Eighth Fleet disbanded that September, leaving a small postwar collection of US Navy ships, known as Naval Forces, Mediterranean, based at Naples. The Navy's presence in the Mediterranean began to grow in 1946, in response to foreign policy decisions to resist Soviet influence in the region using the traditional naval presence mission of the fleet. Even before the Cold War was recognized as an accomplished fact, US concern with the aims of the Soviet Union in Europe and its ambitions to spread communism worldwide led US leaders to consider a sustained naval presence in the Mediterranean vital. Early efforts were limited, but separate cruises of the battleship *Missouri* and fleet carriers *Leyte*, *Randolph*, and *Roosevelt* received much publicity in 1946 and 1947. As the British Mediterranean fleet dwindled, port visits by these ships in support

Table 18.1 Demobilization, 1945–1950.

	1945	1950
Navy personnel	3,400,000	380,000
Marine Corps personnel	475,000	75,000
Major warships	1,200+	237

of the 1947 Truman Doctrine's commitment to the defense of anticommunist governments in Greece and Turkey influenced public opinion and political leaders throughout the eastern Mediterranean. Flyovers of cities by naval aviation were also organized to increase the visibility of America's naval power. The finalization of the peace treaty with Italy left borders in dispute, especially concerning Trieste, on the Adriatic Sea. US and Allied ships in port stymied any notion that an insurrection could be mounted by irredentist groups. By January 1948, the carrier *Midway* cruised the Mediterranean in the company of six cruisers and 10 destroyers. With the establishment of the Sixth Fleet in mid-1948, the US Navy became a permanent fixture in the Mediterranean.

In spite of the extended engagement of the Navy and Marine Corps in both the Far East and the Mediterranean, the force levels of both continued to decline under budget shortfalls far below the ambitious plans for a continued Two-Ocean Navy as a guarantor of postwar peace. The Secretary of the Navy's annual report to Congress showed about half the number of active ships and vessels of the December 1945 Plan 1A remained on duty, although most losses had been taken in mine, patrol, amphibious, and auxiliary ships. Nevertheless, the 12 fleet carriers and four battleships might have preserved a final basis of global sea power, but continuing budget cuts would force the decommissioning of all but one battleship and a decline of total combatant ships on active service to 271 (with 658 in reserve) by 1949 (see Table 18.1).

The US Defense Establishment

After two years of sometimes tense negotiations between the services and Congress, the unification of the American defense establishment took place in the form of the National Security Act of 1947. With a goal of simplifying strategic planning and achieving economies by avoiding duplication among the services, the act formed the cabinet-level National Defense Establishment, headed by the first secretary of defense, James V. Forrestal. Subsidiary secretaries of the Army, Navy, and (newly established independent) Air Force would administer those services. A quasi-unified intelligence community was also provided for in the form of the Central Intelligence Agency; the National Security Council was established to advise the president on military and diplomatic affairs; and the role of the wartime Joint Chiefs of Staff was codified to confirm its authority to direct the operating forces, which were organized into unified and specified commands.

Despite the fears of the Navy for its own aviation and ground-combat force—the Marine Corps, supposedly coveted by the Air Force and Army—there were few if any restrictions placed upon the three departments. The specific authority of the secretary of defense remained rather weak because the service secretaries reported to the president *via* the secretary of defense until a 1949 amendment to the National Security Act reduced their power by providing that they report *to* the secretary of defense, who was no longer required to forward the views. The services came to an agreement in advance of this legislation in a series of conferences resulting in the 1948 Key West Agreement on service roles and missions, which primarily delineated the roles of the aircraft to be operated by the three services. The Navy received authority to operate aviation in the process of naval campaigns, the Army would operate reconnaissance and medical airlift planes, and the Air Force garnered the lion's share, encompassing all strategic aircraft and most tactical and transport types as well.

Many Marine Corps leaders viewed the defense unification process with alarm, fearing that Army, Air Force, and some congressional leaders were striking secret deals that threatened the very existence of the Marine Corps. Corps Commandant Alexander Vandegrift stated that the 1947 legislation gave "the War Department a free hand in accomplishing its expressed desire to reduce the Marine Corps to a position of military insignificance."[2] A circle of advocates guided by

---

[2] ["Bended Knee Speech"], US Congress, Senate, Committee on Naval Affairs, Hearings, S 2044, 79th congress, 2d session (1946), 118–119.

World War II icons such as Brigadier General Gerald C. Thomas and Colonel Merrill B. Twining (leading members of the "Guadalcanal Gang," loosely mentored by Vandergrift, their commander on the island) worked feverishly to counter perceived attempts by the Army and Air Force to strip the ground and aviation elements from the Corps. Members secretly provided information deemed crucial to sympathetic congressmen and their staffers, perhaps earning the oft-quoted charge of President Truman (also judged by some an "enemy" of the Corps) that "the only propaganda machine that rivals that of Stalin is that of the United States Marine Corps."[3]

The problem with all this lore is that there is no smoking gun, and not a single document can be found in Army archives showing any intention to argue for the disbanding or absorption of the Marine Corps. One can further doubt that the Corps entered into the Air Force scheme, except perhaps to dismiss the few Marine squadrons as irrelevant. For example, one Marine Corps officer, then Major General Oliver P. Smith, opposed this perhaps hysterical reaction by Marine Corps officers in Washington, characterizing the key players as "wheels within wheels," and another, Commandant Clifton B. Cates, later remarked that Truman's statement was accurate.[4] The real story of the postwar period remained the defense reductions, not any perceived struggle to "save" the Corps by a number of self-important officers in 1946–1947.

If there was any "victim" of the now amended National Defense Act it was the Navy, which experienced heavy seas caused by Louis A. Johnson, who replaced Forrestal as secretary of defense in early 1949. Johnson heavily favored the Air Force in the defense budget, and continued to pare down all the other services, cutting the Marine Corps, for instance, in personnel by almost 20 percent in the 1949–1950 budgets. The Air Force, with its emphasis on winning wars through global nuclear bombardment, already planned that several of its 40 aircraft groups would operate B-29 strategic bombers, but it was not content with this evident superiority. Its next-generation intercontinental bomber, the 42-ton B-36, had first flown in 1946, with the first production aircraft delivered in 1948. Twice the size of the B-29 and eight times that of the World War II B-17, its 4,000-mile range would, according to the Air Force, mean that it would not require overseas bases. Thus, it was feared that a single aircraft program could negate the roles and missions of both the Army and Navy. The Navy, conscious of the changes to strategy augured by the atomic bomb, already planned to operate new twin-engine bombers from its three largest fleet carriers and planned a new class of "super-carriers" that would carry advanced twin-engine jet bombers, all for the delivery of the heavy and oversized atomic bombs then in production.

Secretary Johnson moved quickly to cut personnel in the other services and programs, including funding for the super-carrier *United States*, so he could procure an air force of 70 groups, initially including 16 with B-29 and five (later 11) with B-36 aircraft, which were capable of carrying atomic bombs.

Cancelation of the *United States* precipitated the now infamous "revolt of the admirals," during which Chief of Naval Operations Admiral Louis E. Denfield, Pacific Fleet commander Admiral Arthur Radford, and Vice Admiral Gerald Bogan (commander of carriers, Atlantic) all wrote public letters to Secretary of the Navy Francis P. Matthews criticizing defense policy and especially the B-36, citing evidence that it was already obsolete in the face of the newest jet fighters. During the resulting imbroglio Secretary Matthews forced the resignation of Admiral Denfield and several other officers suffered career limitations, but Secretary of Defense Johnson was also forced to resign after Congress criticized his unilateral cancellation of the

---

[3] "The only propaganda machine that rivals that of Stalin is that of the United States Marine Corps" has been widely quoted. It is based on Truman to Representative Gordon L. McDonough, August 29, 1950, in which the president wrote: "I read with a lot of interest your letter in regard to the Marine Corps. For your information the Marine Corps is the Navy's police force and as long as I am President that is what it will remain. They have a propaganda machine that is almost equal to Stalin's." Letters to the commandant of the Marine Corps League and to the commandant of the Marine Corps, Harry S. Truman Library and Museum, Independence, MO, printed in the *Congressional Record* (1950), 96:A6323.

[4] As quoted in Clifton La Bree, *The Gentle Warrior: General Oliver Prince Smith* (2001), 93–97.

USS *United States* (CVE-58)

The design of the first US super-carrier reflected strategic thinking in the Navy that carrier aviation should operate bombers for nuclear strikes against enemy targets on land. Funding for it was approved in 1948, and, although short lived because of inter-service rivalries and defense politics, the ship enabled progress in naval architecture and technology, and guided service and defense thinking that proved essential when the United States began its rearmament in the 1950s.

The new super-carrier showed the influence of World War II carrier task force commander Admiral Marc A. Mitscher, who considered a larger aircraft carrier as a necessity to accommodating aircraft capable of delivering the atomic bomb. Such an aircraft was already under development in 1945; thus, the new carrier would the first to have its design dictated by the aircraft it would operate. Mitscher and other aviators were anxious to go to a flush deck design that suppressed superstructure, stacks, and antennae for a clean and unobstructed landing deck.

USS *United States* (CVE-58). Artist's conception by Bruno Figallo.
Source: National Archives.

Although the design first envisioned carrying only atomic bombers, the new carrier eventually became more of a battle carrier, with fighters for air defense and escort akin to its predecessors. The 70,000-ton design had four elevators to service two fighter catapults amidships and two heavy bomber catapults on the bow for launching its 80 fighters and 18 heavy attack bombers. The ship would be large enough to accommodate the required fuel, ordnance spaces, and armor protection yet capable of speeds of 33 knots. The end result yielded a 1,090-foot-by-125-foot hull, with the flight deck extending to a beam of 190 feet. USS *United States* could not transit the Panama Canal and fit into only 10 US dry docks. Funding for the carrier was canceled only five days after the laying of its keel in April 1949.

United States and his policies were blamed for setbacks suffered at the outbreak of the Korean War.

The furor was only quelled by the dual shocks of the Russian atomic bomb test and the coming of the Korean War. The cancellation of the *United States* stood, but the actions of naval officers in keeping the next-generation aircraft carriers in the public and political limelight would prove justified in the US rearmament that ensued.

New Strategies, Doctrine, and Weapons

Although the postwar planning for the Navy and Marine Corps continued to emphasize concepts of operations in wartime practically identical with those at the end of World War II, the influence of three weapons would receive priority attention. These were the atomic bomb, the jet-propelled aircraft, and the high-underwater-endurance submarine. Many believed that atomic bombs rendered previous forms of warfare obsolete. How could ships concentrated in the usual carrier task force or amphibious landing operations succeed if a single bomb could destroy most men and matériel within several miles of its impact?

In 1946 US testing with nuclear weapons delivered by air against a target array of ships anchored in the Bikini Atoll (Operation Crossroads) demonstrated that modern warships could survive atomic attack. The two tests employed 21-kiloton fission bombs like those dropped on Nagasaki in 1945, the first an aerial burst, the second a shot positioned 90 feet underwater in the center of the 95-ship target array. While several ships sank, most survived relatively intact even at close range and the Navy took heart in the evidence that mobile and somewhat dispersed task forces could survive atomic munitions, provided personnel remained within the ships' hulls and structures. New self-washdown equipment would be required to decontaminate the ships' exteriors from radioactive fallout.

Marine Corps studies of the Crossroads testing convinced planners that amphibious landing forces could be effective in the face of atomic weapons if ships were dispersed at sea and anchored at a distance from the objective area and if helicopters were used to land troops and supplies at the site of the attack. An alternative concept called for developing a force of large seaplanes that would fly directly to the beach, nosing ashore like landing craft to offload over bow ramps. The R3Y-1 Tradewind, a transport seaplane, was tested in 1954–1958 but abandoned in favor of emerging helicopter capabilities.

In each case, the mainstay operations of naval forces were confirmed as viable in the atomic age. However, the new turbojet aircraft, the presumed delivery method for atomic ordnance, posed increased dangers for defending ships and would require new weapons and techniques to counter. Already in hand were new rapid-fire automatic cannon with radar-directed fire-control systems that had been developed to combat the kamikaze attacks of the latter part of the Pacific War, and these were first incorporated on board ships laid down in 1949. However, the real dynamic for coordinated antiaircraft warfare in the fleet would combine improved radars, jet fighters from aircraft carriers, and guided missiles, all under development

since 1945, and the Navy began converting cruisers to employ these missiles in 1952, the first entering service in 1955.

Thus the missile and the nuclear Navy emerged later in the 1950s, developed largely from the concepts and research of the late 1940s, despite the relative dearth of funds. Perhaps the capstone of this process would be the activities of then-Captain Hyman G. Rickover, who advocated and eventually supervised the design and construction of nuclear-powered ships and submarines through the end of his career, beginning with submarine USS *Nautilus*, ordered in 1951.

Offensive use of nuclear weapons by the Navy was initially vested in the aircraft carrier, which would have to grow in size in order to operate the larger and heavier aircraft required to carry the early generations of atomic bombs. The new US Air Force naturally laid claim to exclusive employment of atomic weapons, but in mid-1946 then-Assistant Secretary of the Navy John L. Sullivan urged President Truman to authorize the Navy to begin preparations for the delivery of atomic munitions by carrier aviation. Beginning in mid-1950, large carriers of the *Midway* class began carrying atomic bombs (but lacking their cores) for operations during North Atlantic and Mediterranean deployments.

The first heavy attack bomber capable of carrier operations, the AJ-1 Savage, first flew in July 1948. Production versions began to outfit Navy squadrons in late 1949, with six of these assigned to the first nuclear-capable squadron, VC-5. With a gross weight of almost 24 tons and a wingspan of 75 feet (unfolded), the Savage could carry the Mark III or IV atomic bomb to a range of 750 miles. The first Savages were not particularly welcomed by the carrier air groups, as just four of them displaced about 30 other aircraft.

Despite the setbacks to the Navy over the B-36 controversy, it remained fully in competition, with a successor turbojet heavy attack bomber already in development with an operational range double that of the AJ-1 (see Figure 18.1). The prototype version of that aircraft, the A3D Skywarrior, first flew in October 1952. Not content with the carrier-borne nuclear delivery system in the works, the Navy also placed high hopes in plans to develop the P6M SeaMaster, a turbojet seaplane designed to operate from remote bases and seaplane tenders, refueled if necessary

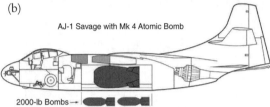

AJ-1 Savage with Mk 4 Atomic Bomb

2000-lb Bombs →

Figure 18.1 (a) AJ-1 Savage over Korea and (b) diagram showing potential bomb loads. *Source:* Navy Naval History Center.

from submarine tankers at forward operating bases, in order to carry out reconnaissance, nuclear strikes, and related missions such as mine laying to neutralize enemy naval bases. Two prototypes were followed by nine pre-production versions of the SeaMaster aircraft before the program was canceled in 1959 in favor of the naval ballistic missile program. These aircraft programs demonstrated the serious interest of the US Navy in developing a credible naval alternative to the exclusive claims of the Air Force to the strategic bombardment mission in the post–World War II period.

Social Progress

It remains to the credit of the armed forces of the United States that, in the midst of their institutional and political difficulties of the postwar period, they continued to make progress in their racial integration. The need for effective use of manpower in the war had assisted in breaking several barriers to service by American blacks in the enlisted and officer ranks of the force. The Navy, arguably more hidebound and traditional than the hugely expanded Army and Army Air Forces in World War II, had managed to officially open several enlisted specialties beyond the usual steward rating to blacks and had accepted its first black officer

candidates during 1943–1944. With the accession of James Forrestal as secretary in 1944, the Navy began to assign black sailors to auxiliaries and eventually all types of ships of the fleet, not to exceed 10 percent of the crews. The number of blacks in the Navy had doubled by the war's end, although some 40 percent of those on duty continued to serve in the steward rating. In the Marine Corps, a pair of defense battalions were formed and many service supply depot companies were established, in the main consisting of black troops led by white officers, but despite these actions the Corps fell far short of reaching the goal of 10 percent blacks of the Corps' overall strength set by 1943.

Unfortunately, the shrinking size of the postwar Navy resulted in the loss of many black sailors in the force and their proportion in the steward rating reached 62 percent in 1948. As Secretary Sullivan put it at the time, the Navy had reverted to its comfortable prewar ways, with black sailors waiting upon white officers. As the sole black midshipman at the Naval Academy was still two years from his epoch-making graduation, not a single black regular naval officer served.

In the midst of such doldrums, President Truman's Executive Order 9981, of July 1948, compelled action. With his avowed intention of ending segregation in the armed forces, the president appointed a committee to report on progress, and the Navy had to admit that there were no programs in place to recruit or commission blacks. The resulting changes brought some black reserve officers, such as Samuel Gravely, back on duty and coincided with the 1949 graduation and commissioning from the Naval Academy of Ensign Wesley A. Brown, the first black to complete the program since Reconstruction. The next black graduate did not emerge from the academy until 1953. As with so many other issues facing the armed forces in the postwar period, it would take the manifold pressures of the Korean War to provide sufficient impetus toward resolution.

Women made similar progress in the postwar Navy. Established in July 1942, the US Naval Reserve (Women's Reserve) became nicknamed the WAVES, for "Women Accepted for Volunteer Emergency Service"—an acronym whose inclusion of the word "emergency" implied that, as during World War I, women would leave the Navy at war's end, as had the Yeomen F after World War I. Wartime recruits entered either the V10 WAVE Enlisted Rating Volunteer

Samuel Lee Gravely, Jr.

One of the earliest black American commissioned officers in the US Navy, Samuel Lee Gravely, Jr. (1922–2004) became the first of his race to command a surface warship and the first to reach flag rank in the Navy. Born in Richmond, Virginia, the son of a postal worker and a housewife, Gravely attended Virginia Union University but left in 1942 to enlist in the Navy. After basic training, he attended the University of California, Los Angeles, under the Navy V-12 officer program, taking his commission as a line officer in late 1944. His first assignment was as the only black officer onboard the submarine chaser *PC-1264*, one of the two warships selected for evaluating all-black crews, but with white officers mostly in charge.

Gravely left active duty in 1946 but remained in the Navy Reserve, marrying and raising a family in Richmond, where he completed studies in history at Virginia Union and worked for the Postal Service. Recalled to active duty in 1949, Gravely helped to create an active recruiting policy in the Navy for blacks, who had declined in number since World War II. During the Korean War, he served in communications billets at sea and ashore before augmenting his commission from the reserves to the regular Navy in 1955. Gravely sought expanded opportunities as a surface line officer, and his qualifications led to the command of three destroyers between 1961 and 1967; he took the last one, USS *Taussig*, to the Vietnam War. In 1971, while a captain commanding the guided-missile frigate USS *Jouett*, he received a nomination to the grade of rear admiral. His flag officer duties included command of a cruiser–destroyer group and

the roles of director of naval communications, commander of the Third Fleet, and director of the Defense Communications Agency before he retired as a vice admiral in 1980. The destroyer USS *Gravely* honors his service.

Samuel Lee Gravely, Jr., 1970. *Source:* US Naval History and Heritage Command # NH 96775.

Program or the V9 WAVE Officer Candidate Volunteer Program, and graduates served at shore installations in the United States or its territories. Most were assigned to clerical duties, but some performed aviation, medical, intelligence, research and development, and logistical–supply duties. The Women's Armed Services Integration Act, passed in June 1948, made permanent women's service in the Navy and opened both enlisted ranks and the officer corps of the regular Navy to them.

New Strategic Shocks, 1949–1950

Though initially overshadowed by the debate concerning defense reorganization, National Security Council Report number 68 (NSC-68), issued in April 1950, proved a seminal document in Cold War strategy. Sparked by the Soviet Union's detonation of its first atomic bomb in August 1949 and the victory of Mao Zedong's communist forces in China, NSC-68 was based on the premise that the Soviet Union sought "to impose its absolute authority over the rest of the world," predicted that Soviet aggression would more likely be "piecemeal" than enacted through a major war, and warned that a failure to respond to such aggression could lead to "a descending spiral of … gradual withdrawals under pressure until we discover one day that we have sacrificed positions of vital interest." To make possible the countering of such threats the study recommended increasing the defense budget from the current $13 billion to $35 billion in order to build a balanced force.

War in Korea, 1950–1953

Ten weeks later the prediction of NSC-68 appeared to be confirmed when North Korean troops crossed the 38th parallel into the Republic of Korea on June 25, 1950. Whether this represented a local quarrel, piecemeal aggression backed by the Kremlin, or the precursor to World War III (perhaps even a stratagem to lure occidental attention and forces away from the real main effort, the invasion of Europe by the Soviet Army) remained unclear, but President Truman felt forced to respond. That evening, he ordered his commander-in-chief of the Far East Command in Tokyo, General of the Army Douglas MacArthur, to evacuate US citizens from Korea, to provide munitions and equipment to the Republic of Korea, and to report on the aid required to save that nation.

As the news went from bad to worse, Truman authorized the dispatch of combat troops to Korea to secure the seaport and air facilities at Pusan, in the southeast corner of the peninsula, and also ordered the air and naval bombardment of North Korea. At this early stage, no action in the vicinity of Seoul or the Han River by ground troops was considered, only the retention of an enclave on the peninsula.

The initial response of the Joint Chiefs of Staff to MacArthur's reports was to prepare reinforcements for East Asia. Chief of Naval Operations Admiral Forrest Sherman ordered ships and aircraft from both the Atlantic and Pacific Fleets to reinforce the Seventh Fleet, which at that moment could support MacArthur's command with only a single fleet carrier, a heavy cruiser, and eight destroyers. MacArthur's own Naval Forces, Japan, consisted of an antiaircraft cruiser, four amphibious ships, and a few minesweepers. Fortunately, the British Commonwealth Forces in the Far East included an aircraft carrier, two cruisers, and three destroyers. The combined forces joined off Okinawa on July 1 and sortied for Korean waters under the command of Vice Admiral Arthur D. Struble, who also commanded the Seventh Fleet. Commandant of the Marine Corps General Clifton B. Cates urged the chief of naval operations to offer a Marine Corps brigade. Cates' briefing included the manpower strength of the Fleet Marine Forces, Pacific (11,853) and Atlantic (15,803), showing that neither one could provide a complete Marine division right away.

The first great wave of naval, air, and ground reinforcements departed the United States in early July. Tensions remained high alongside the perception that the Korean conflict merely covered a larger outbreak of war, presumably with the Soviet Union. Admiral Sherman urged the greatest speed to his fleet commanders, but initially the Pacific Fleet units sailed in complete task groups or increments. The first sailings from San Diego came only after sweeping the channels for mines, and standing antisubmarine measures remained in effect for many weeks to come. Some message traffic included anti-sabotage alerts. Once arrived at Hawaii, some ships proceeded unescorted and others in groups, arriving at Japanese ports beginning July 18.

The sparse naval and air units in the Far East went into action against North Korean forces and lines of communications. UN warships blockaded Korea beginning July 5 and air strikes from the US–British task force began hitting North Korean targets, including the capital (Pyongyang), air bases, and bridges, with a second effort hitting rail yards and locomotives. With only two carriers in action, there was no chance of maintaining steady bombardment of the enemy, but by the end of the month more carriers had arrived and bombing missions increased. Flying from carriers offshore, naval aircraft could respond more quickly to calls for close air support and remain over the battlefield to provide cover longer than Air Force planes sortieing from the Japanese islands.

The command of the sea ensured by the growing strength of the US Seventh Fleet and UN reinforcements gave tremendous advantages to the land campaign. July witnessed a total of 309,314 tons of military supplies and equipment flowing into Pusan, with 230 ships arriving in the second half of the month alone. Three reinforcing ground units arrived by sea transport in the first week of August, with many more to follow. Though outnumbered at first, the UN ground forces reached a slight superiority on the ground by the time decisive actions at the Pusan Perimeter began on August 4.

Among the first arrivals was the 1st Provisional Marine Brigade, thrown together in July from the resources of the under-strength 1st Marine Division at California, which itself turned to rebuilding for its own deployment to the theater, in part by a call to

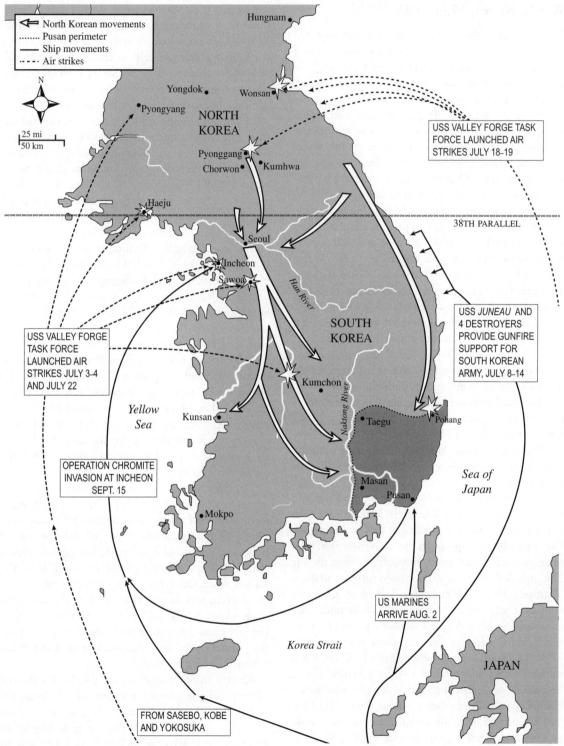

Map 18.1 Korea, June–September 1950.

active duty of the Marine Corps Reserve. The Provisional Marine Brigade was fed into the lines on three different counterattacks, each throwing back North Korean divisions that had pressed into the Pusan Perimeter defenses. The air group accompanying the brigade sent its two fighter-bomber squadrons aloft from two escort carriers of the Seventh Fleet, and these rendered outstanding close air support to Marine Corps and army units alike as the Pusan Perimeter fight reached its climactic end in early September.

As the ground and air fighting stabilized the Pusan Perimeter, MacArthur launched his planned amphibious riposte against the enemy-occupied coast near Seoul (see Map 18.1). Marshaling the 1st Marine Division at sea, with a late-to-arrive regiment replaced by the South Korean Marine Corps, the Navy swept mines and bombarded Incheon prior to landing a two-punch assault force in the face of narrow channels, fast currents, and a daunting 29-foot tidal range. Launched on September 15, the amphibious operation achieved complete surprise and the Marines cleared the port, advanced upon the main air base, and seized the capital of South Korea in just 10 days (see Figure 18.2).

The astounding success achieved at Incheon owed much to the veteran ships, staffs, troops, and sailors who had completed the Pacific Campaign in like fashion only five years earlier. Despite the postwar drawdown in critical weapons and combat forces, the acquired World War II skills resident in the Navy–Marine Corps team paid off handily at this moment.

The double shock of the Incheon landing and the Eighth Army offensive breakout from the Pusan Perimeter set the North Korean Army on a long retreat across the 38th Parallel with the UN forces in pursuit as the reunification of Korea replaced liberation of South Korea as the American war aim. Emboldened by victory on the west coast of Korea, MacArthur duplicated the success with landings at Wonsan and Iwon in late October and began a dual-pronged drive toward the Yalu River. Minefields protecting the landing sites held up operations, giving the enemy time to withdraw in good order. This event quickly revived Navy attention in mine-countermeasures vessels.

The North Korean invasion and the UN reinforcement and counterattack lasted barely six months before the UN forces' approach to the Yalu River and North

Figure 18.2   Lt. Baldomero Lopez, US Marine Corps, scaling a seawall at Incheon, September 15, 1950. *Source:* US Marine Corps photograph, from the collections of the Naval Historical Center. US Naval History and Heritage Command # NH 96876.

Korea's border with China led Communist China to send troops into Korea on November 25. With support from Chinese- and Russian-manned aircraft flying from Manchurian bases, Chinese intervention threw the war into another phase, forcing the United Nations to pull back its forces under great duress and refight the war to an eventual stalemate along the previous border of the two Koreas (see Map 18.2).

As the US Eighth Army and South Korean forces fell back on the west coast, the US X Corps, operating on the east coast of the peninsula north of its Hungnam supply port, suffered surprise attacks the night of November 27–28, 1950, from the Chinese Ninth Army. In the vicinity of the Chosin Reservoir, elements of the 7th Infantry Division were smashed and routed. The 1st Marine Division had two of its regiments west of Chosin (Changjin) at Yadam-ni, but these were better disposed for self-defense. The division's headquarters and supporting units to the south held the vital airfield at Hagaru-ri, with its third

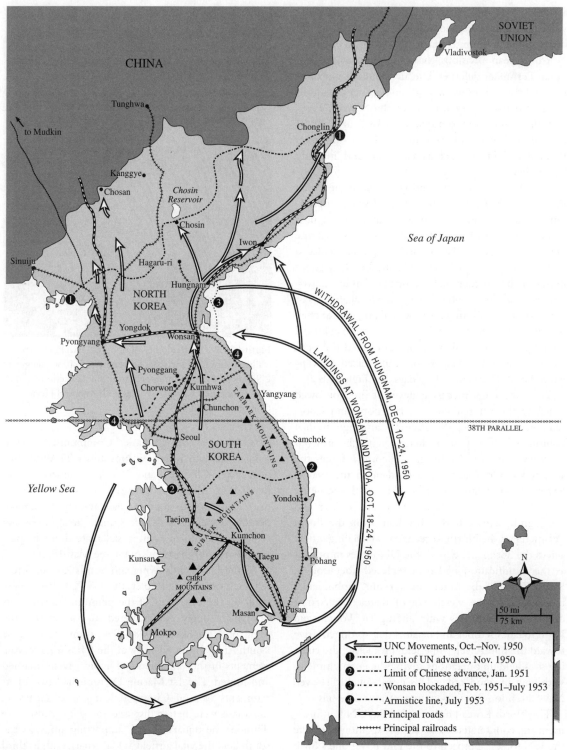

Map 18.2 Korea, October 1950–July 1953.

infantry regiment positioned halfway to Hungnam at Kot'o-ri.

Outnumbered by the Chinese, the X Corps had to withdraw to Hungnam, where the 3rd Infantry Division assembled after its arrival from the United States. The 1st Marine Division brought in its forward regiments and Army survivors from Chosin Reservoir and staged a fighting withdrawal to Hungnam. Air support from the 1st Marine Aircraft Wing and off-shore carriers and the supporting arms of the ground forces made it impossible for the Chinese to stop them and more Chinese died of exposure in the severe cold than from combat (see Map 18.3). Upon reaching Hungnam, the Navy organized and executed a large amphibious withdrawal of the three US divisions and other forces, destroying all supplies and equipment left in the port upon departure. In this final phase of the Korean War, naval forces had supported the ground troops with naval and air bombardments, evacuated forces trapped on the coastline, blockaded Wonsan to prevent its use as a port or naval base by North Korea, and contributed to the massive air campaign to secure air superiority over North Korea and interdict supplies and communications of the enemy troops.

The disappointing setback and end result of the Korean War came despite the massive expansion of the US Navy and Marine Corps from the doldrums of early 1950. The mobilization of the Navy and Marine Corps reserves and the reactivation of hundreds of aircraft, ships, and ground equipment had by 1951 brought much of the World War II-level force structure into active duty in both the Atlantic and Pacific major commands. The Navy continued to operate 1,129 ships for the rest of the war, including 14 fleet carriers, four battleships, 247 destroyers, and 233 amphibious ships. The Marine Corps had filled out its under-strength divisions and aircraft wings and added a third division and wing for duty in Japan as a strategic reserve while the war ensued. Total personnel strength reached 800,000 for the Navy and 250,000 officers and enlisted for the Marine Corps.

As in World War II, sea power weighed heavily in the favor of the UN forces. However, the rugged terrain of the Korean Peninsula and the primitive logistical "tail" of the Chinese and North Korean forces limited the effects of the overwhelming aerial and naval firepower that could be brought to bear.

Nor could the most destructive weapons used to end World War II be employed in bringing the victory that some leaders and the public expected.

Instead, the leadership and public of the United States learned that nuclear bombs provided no panacea in warfare, and that balanced forces of all arms had to be maintained in order to meet the uncertain threats of the present and future. The response to aggression in Korea had to be balanced against further moves by the Soviet Union and its bloc of collaborating nations. With nuclear weapons present on both sides, the substitute for victory had to be the quarantine of aggression, using flexible response and a strong alliance structure poised to contain the expansion of Soviet power. Thus the Korean War demonstrated the continued utility of carrier aviation, the enduring value of amphibious warfare, the need for sealift capacity, and the importance of the ability to defend sealines of communication.

Conclusion

The policy response to the Korean War reflected these points as well as the emerging technologies. The United States maintained peacetime conscription, expanded the defense budget from $13 billion to $60 billion, strengthened NATO (including rearming Germany), and expanded the Army and Navy, adding aircraft groups to both the Air Force and Navy, now equipped with both strategic bomber fleets and CVA-class aircraft carriers.

By 1953, the US Navy had received its last production piston-engine fighter and operated three different jet fighters. The second super-carrier of the *Forrestal* class was authorized as was the second nuclear-powered submarine. The first postwar destroyer class and a new class of destroyer escorts had begun, as well as an order for 350 new landing craft. The wartime fleet carriers were all slated for reconstruction with angled flight decks and steam catapults in order to operate the heaviest jet aircraft then under development. The Marine Corps operated three new tank models and was developing a new fleet of amphibious landing vehicles. It also operated new radars for night bombing against ground troops, and guided missiles were beginning to replace some field and antiaircraft artillery.

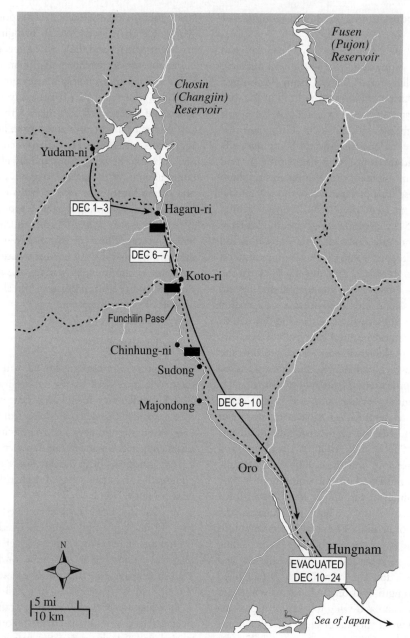

Map 18.3   Chosin Reservoir, December 1950.

Despite the swelling of the defense budgets, service rivalries would continue post-Korea and even increase in their intensity because of new wartime differences over the management of air power in a theater and the relative merits of sea- and land-based air and ground assault power. New technologies raised both the capabilities and expenses required by the forces. For the US Navy and Marine Corps, the nuclear and guided-missile ages had already begun and the shapes of new organizations, combat doctrines, and procedures remained to be developed in a world grown increasingly deadly at a time of full competition between rival blocs of superpowers.

The Korean War had equally important diplomatic repercussions. Most South Korean and many American leaders believed that the communists had been emboldened to cross the 38th Parallel by a speech that Secretary of State Dean Acheson delivered to the Washington Press Club on January 12, 1950. In it Acheson defined the American "defensive perimeter" in the Pacific as running from Alaska through Japan and the Ryukus to the Philippines.[5] Ranking members of the Eisenhower administration would seek to bolster the containment of communism and avoid future "Koreas" by signing a series of defensive alliances that would clearly delineate what areas lay within the area to be defended by the United States and its allies.

---

[5]"Secretary Acheson and the Defense of Korea," Korea File, Truman Library.

CHAPTER 19

Cold War Challenges, 1953–1963

During the Eisenhower and Kennedy administrations the United States enjoyed considerable economic, diplomatic, and military advantages over all other nations, which created an era of relative global peace, or Pax Americana, enforced by the nation's superiority in weapons of war. Pax Americana not only rested on the implied threat presented by the nation's nuclear stockpile but was also dependent on convincing prospective enemies of American unity (despite considerable social unrest at home) in the opposition to communism, no matter the cost. When Dwight Eisenhower became president in 1953 he appeared to have departed from the limited containment policy of his predecessor, Harry Truman, when he adopted a more aggressive stance toward the Soviets, threatening Moscow with possible nuclear war for any communist aggression in the world, no matter its source. When the Soviets had acquired enough ballistic missiles to assure that both superpowers faced total destruction in the event of a nuclear war, however, Eisenhower limited his military responses, even demonstrating a willingness to negotiate. John Kennedy began his presidency by abandoning his predecessor's "brinkmanship" diplomacy and "massive retaliation" military strategy. Believing the latter no longer viable given the ability of both the United States and the Soviet Union to strike the other's homeland with nuclear weapons, Kennedy replaced it with a "flexible response" strategy that entailed meeting any threat in

a like manner, with the application of "graduated pressure" that emphasized diplomacy, conventional weapons, and covert operations before threatening America's enemies with thermonuclear warfare. The young president demonstrated his willingness to use nuclear weapons, however, during the Cuban Missile Crisis after Khrushchev interpreted Kennedy's performance at the Vienna Summit (1961) as evidence of weakness. In the end neither Eisenhower nor Kennedy ever launched nuclear missiles. Despite their rhetoric, geopolitical circumstances drove both toward a modified version of Truman's containment—more global in scope than originally envisioned, and relying heavily on America's allies, the CIA, unconventional warfare, and anticommunism propaganda to undermine Soviet influence abroad and to strengthen American public will at home.

Throughout this era, the Navy played an important role in the nation's defense. The service skillfully maneuvered to develop nuclear capability while at the same time providing both presidents with the ability to respond quickly to hot spots around the world with conventional weapons. The Navy's future, though, looked bleak as Eisenhower assumed office in January 1953. The service had retained both naval aviation and the Marine Corps during the bitter unification battle of the late 1940s, and the Korean War demonstrated both the continued relevance of carrier aviation and amphibious warfare and the need for seaborne transportation of

America, Sea Power, and the World, First Edition. Edited by James C. Bradford.
© 2016 John Wiley & Sons, Inc. Published 2016 by John Wiley & Sons, Inc.

Polaris Missile

The linchpin of American nuclear deterrence during the 1960s was Polaris, an intermediate-range ballistic missile launched vertically from a submerged submarine. Carried to the surface in a bubble of compressed air, its booster rockets then ignited, propelling it toward its target. Polaris gave the United States a second-strike capability that was nearly impervious to Soviet countermeasures. Submarines armed with multiple Polaris (and later Poseidon) missiles could position themselves within reach of Soviet targets while remaining undetected.

The success of the Polaris missile program was a testament to Admiral Arleigh Burke's leadership and the ability of Rear Admiral William F. Raborn's Special Policy Office to fast-track the program. Raborn operated with considerable autonomy, selected the Navy's most gifted minds for his staff, and bypassed the service's

bureaucracy by reporting directly to the Secretary of the Navy. A new management system, PERT (Program Evaluation Review Technique), coordinated the efforts of the 3,000 contractors and agencies developing missile components. PERT created a sequence of events, predicted the time required to complete each task, and identified a "critical path," whose developments, if delayed, would prevent the project from moving forward.

Polaris submarines began to patrol by late 1960 well ahead of their 1963 deadline. Raborn achieved this, however, by rushing development and reducing the missile's capabilities. He cut the A-1 missile's desired range of 1,500 nautical miles to 1,200 and reduced the megatonnage of the nuclear warhead by half. The more dependable A-2, the second-generation Polaris missile (operational in 1962), corrected this shortfall. The subsequent A-3

Polaris Missile.

missiles, with precision gyroscopes and accelerometers, had a 2,500-nautical-mile range and carried three "multiple independently targetable reentry vehicles" that detonated in a triangular pattern. In 1972 Poseidon C-3 missiles armed with 10 or more individually guided reentry vehicles began to replace Polaris in America's nuclear arsenal.

men and supplies. Yet, when Eisenhower reduced military spending to balance the budget for the first time in a quarter-century, the Navy was alarmed by the deep cuts in its budget. By the time Kennedy restored the Navy's budget, the service was well on its way to acquiring nuclear propulsion and, with the Polaris missile, had become one leg of the Nuclear Triad (strategic bombers, intercontinental ballistic missiles, and submarine-launched ballistic missiles) designed to ensure America's ability to respond to, and thus to deter, an enemy from using nuclear weapons. In addition, Kennedy increased funding to the special forces including the Navy SEALs (Sea, Air, and Land Teams). During the Cuban Missile Crisis, the Navy's enforcement of the quarantine line

proved that conventional weapons could play a role in preventing a nuclear war, demonstrating that the Navy's traditional role as the nation's first line of defense remained relevant in the nuclear age.

Eisenhower Brinkmanship

Eisenhower designed his defense policies to both counter Soviet-backed communism and prevent internal economic decline. He and his advisors believed that Secretary of State Dean Acheson's January 1950 speech stating that the American "defensive perimeter [in the Pacific] runs along the Aleutians to Japan and then [through] the Ryukyu Islands [and on] to the

Philippine Islands" implied to North Korean leaders that the United States would not militarily oppose their invasion of the south.[1] To avoid future misunderstandings, Eisenhower signed a series of bilateral treaties and joined alliances that delineated the line behind which communism would be contained. These included the Southeast Asia Treaty Organization with Australia, Britain, France, New Zealand, Pakistan, and Thailand in 1954 and the Central Treaty Organization with Britain, Iran, Iraq, Pakistan, and Turkey in 1955.

Like Truman before him, Eisenhower was a fiscal conservative who feared that excessive defense spending could trigger another Great Depression. Once elected, he put together teams to study strategic policy and plan a major restructuring of the Department of Defense that would allow dramatic cuts to the defense budget while ensuring the containment of communism worldwide. His new secretary of state, John Foster Dulles, however, took center stage and urged Eisenhower to adopt a more aggressive foreign policy based on "brinkmanship" coupled with a cost-effective defense policy known as "massive retaliation." According to Dulles, Truman's costly containment policy of an equal and measured response to communist aggression had actually given the enemy an advantage. It allowed the Soviets to choose where and when to test American resolve. Over time, the Soviet Union would "divide and weaken the free nations by overextending them." Dulles urged the president to regain the initiative and deter Soviet aggression by targeting the Soviet Union with a retaliatory nuclear attack for any communist action in the world, no matter where it occurred or whether or not the Soviets were directly involved.[2] The Eisenhower administration was well aware that Moscow did not rule over a monolithic communist empire, and that the more doctrinaire Red Chinese resented Soviet willingness to compromise with the West for peaceful co-existence. Washington could pressure China and a number of independent and semi-independent regimes to behave by never acknowledging that the two communist powers differed and by refusing to clarify what actions would trigger a nuclear response. With the Soviets immobilized by fear, Dulles believed that the United States could take positive steps to "roll back" (or liberate) captive nations without fear of a Soviet response. Dulles played an important role in Eisenhower's so-called "hidden hand" style of leadership. The secretary of state made controversial defense and foreign policy statements while the president, who was fully in command behind the scenes, stood above the fray as a beloved and trusted war hero.

"New Look" Military Policy

With brinkmanship as the basis of US diplomacy, Eisenhower's "New Look" in military affairs (National Security Council report 162/2) favored the Air Force (especially its Strategic Air Command) and a greater dependence on nuclear weapons over the more costly conventional weapons and manpower levels requested by the Army and the Navy. In 1950 Truman's newly established National Security Council had called for the rapid buildup of conventional and non-conventional military forces in preparation for 1954, a year of "maximum danger" when experts predicted that the Soviets' technological and production capabilities would peak; in contrast, the New Look discounted any specific year for concern. Instead, America should plan for the long haul with steady, managed (nuclear) defenses. In other words, the other services would find their budgets slashed in order to fund the Air Force, which could, according to Secretary of Defense Charles Wilson, deliver a "bigger bang for the buck."[3] Further savings would come from relying on America's allies for ground forces and air bases as well as on the CIA to conduct covert operations in third-world nations threatened by indigenous communist movements. The heavy use of the CIA provided additional benefits. The agency operated in secrecy, giving the president "plausible deniability" as a way to conceal US involvement in foreign nations. Second, because the agency's expenses were classified, Eisenhower could send operatives to trouble spots around the world

---

[1] *Department of State Bulletin*, 20 (January 23, 1950), 115–116, as quoted in Dean Acheson, *Present at the Creation* (1969), 357.

[2] John Foster Dulles, "The Evolution of Foreign Policy" [January 12, 1954], *Department of State Bulletin*, 30 (January 25, 1954), 107.

[3] Sterling Michael Pavelec, *The Military-Industrial Complex and American Society* (2009), 325.

without any increase in the defense budget, which, consequently, could be slashed from over $50 billion in 1953 to a little over $40 billion in 1956.

The Navy and Army reacted differently to cuts in their budgets. Eisenhower appointed Admiral Arthur Radford, the Navy's leading advocate of air power, chairman of the Joint Chiefs of Staff (JCS) (1953–1957) because Radford was willing to state publicly that he agreed with the New Look's call for drastic cuts to the Army and, to a lesser extent, the Navy. The Army had understood during the election that the retired five-star general supported "universal military training," a large reserve, the National Guard, and the Marine Corps over the expensive ground forces of the regular Army. Generals were shocked, however, when they learned that the Navy and the Air Force were working with the new president to withdraw troops from bases in Europe and Asia and to cut overall manpower by half a million. Army Chief of Staff General Matthew Ridgway (1953–1955) warned that such a large reduction would make it impossible for the Army to rapidly mobilize in the event of another ground war. Despite new weapons, the basic nature of war and its objectives had not changed; according to Ridgway, they were to secure "control of land and of people living on land."[4] Eisenhower's next Army chief of staff, General Maxwell Taylor (1955–1959), had promised to support the president's defense policies before his selection, but once he was sworn in publicly he rejected the policy of massive retaliation, calling instead for "flexible response." Ground troops equipped with conventional weapons were needed, Taylor argued, in order to fight "brushfire" wars without setting off an exchange of missiles with the Soviets. The Army's public protests angered the president and led to further changes in the structure of the Department of Defense. The ensuing 1958 Reorganization Act placed the JCS in the operational chain of command and increased the power of its chair and the secretary of defense at the expense of the individual service chiefs who were Eisenhower's critics. It also set out to remove duplications in effort, especially in intelligence gathering.

Technological Revolution

With President Eisenhower and Congress intent on reducing military spending, the Navy's surface fleet (which lacked a peer competitor—the Soviet Navy focused on coastal defense during the 1950s) was a logical place to save money. As a result it was hit hard by the president's budget cuts. The rest of the Navy fared better—certainly better than the Army—under Eisenhower, who supported the service's acquisition of a nuclear mission. With the president's blessing, the Navy poured as many dollars as it could into the development of nuclear propulsion and ballistic missiles. A technological revolution had been underway in the Navy since the end of World War II and had produced, among other advances, automated ship-propulsion systems, self-correcting fire control, ordnance equipped with its own individual guidance system, and improvements in radar and sonar. In 1946, the Navy had streamlined and coordinated its research efforts with university scientists and defense contractors through the Office of Naval Research as it began in earnest to work on nuclear technology.

Hyman G. Rickover, the "father of the nuclear Navy," was the Navy's most knowledgeable nuclear specialist and a skilled bureaucrat. By virtue of his expertise and the sheer force of his personality, Rickover managed to corral the various civilian and military agencies working on nuclear power and weapons under his umbrella as the head of the Navy's Nuclear Power Branch of the Bureau of Ships, as well as from his leadership of the Division of Reactor Development of the civilian-based Atomic Energy Commission. From these key positions—and by securing allies in Congress—Rickover inserted himself into virtually every aspect of civilian and military nuclear development. Rickover championed nuclear propulsion and helped the Navy to secure tactical nuclear weapons and aircraft (e.g., A3D Skywarrior planes) for all deployed attack carriers by 1954. The Navy valued Rickover's achievements and admired his high standards, including a zero-tolerance policy for errors within the nuclear community. The top echelon, however, resented his open disdain for the chain

---

[4] "Ridgway Fears New Look Plan," *The Spokesman Review* (March 16, 1954), 2.

of command, as he positioned himself as the Navy's nuclear czar who answered to no one but his political friends in Congress.

On September 30, 1954, the first nuclear-powered submarine, *Nautilus* (SSN-571), entered service followed a year and a day later by the Navy's first super-carrier, *Forrestal* (CV-59). With angled flight decks and steam catapults, *Forrestal*-class carriers provided larger and more stable platforms to handle the aircraft needed to carry heavy nuclear payloads. *Nautilus*, designed to counter Soviet submarines, proved the superiority of nuclear propulsion over diesel for endurance, speed, and stealth when, nearly silently, it traversed the Arctic Ocean from the Pacific to the Atlantic Oceans in 1958, becoming the first submarine to reach the North Pole. Two years later *Triton* (SSN-586) became the first submarine to circumnavigate the globe while submerged.

In 1955 Admiral Arleigh Burke began the first of his three terms as chief of naval operations (1955–1961). Arguably the most important naval development during the Burke years was the Polaris missile. Beginning in 1956 Burke diverted money, although reluctantly, from nuclear-powered surface vessels to the Special Projects Office of Rear Admiral William F. Raborn to develop a 1,200-mile range, submarine-launched nuclear weapon system. The Navy had worked closely with the Army on surface, liquid-fueled rockets (Regulus) but could not launch a missile underwater until it acquired a lighter warhead and developed a less flammable, solid fuel. After these two issues had been resolved, Burke converted a nuclear-powered submarine already under construction into an underwater launching platform by cutting it in two and fitting it with a missile compartment. In the summer of 1960, the newly commissioned *George Washington* (SSBN-598) successfully fired its first Polaris missile, leading Congress to authorize 41 ballistic missile submarines over the next two years. The following November saw the first patrol by a nuclear-powered submarine carrying multiple Polaris missiles, thereby giving America a reliable second-strike capability.

Eisenhower Doctrine

At the beginning of his presidency, Dwight Eisenhower set out to reverse communist advances. In what became known as the Eisenhower Doctrine, America promised economic and military aid to any nation—specifically in the Middle East but applied to other regions as well—threatened by communist subversion or attack. Most Cold War conflicts occurred in third-world countries, where the Soviets were having great success increasing their influence. Moscow championed anticolonialism and support of indigenous social reform movements while Washington, more often than not, found itself backing corrupt anticommunist regimes in order to appease NATO allies. Eisenhower, who preferred using unconventional forces and covert actions in third-world nations, sent CIA operatives to Iran in 1953, Guatemala the next year, and Tibet in 1959.

When a military presence was needed, however, Eisenhower turned to the Navy and the Marine Corps. The Navy had gained the president's trust by publicly supporting brinkmanship and cuts to its budget outlined by the New Look, and by making the development of the Polaris missile a priority. Behind the scenes, however, the service continued to promote the Navy's ability to respond rapidly to a crisis with conventional weapons. According to a 1953–1954 JCS study the Navy was "ready to cope with limited aggression and at the same time be prepared for general war."[5] The Navy was mobile and versatile and could arrive in a trouble spot without tipping the president's hand on how much force (conventional or nuclear) he was willing to use. The mere presence of naval forces could stabilize regions and influence world events by projecting the nation's military power and allowing a variety of diplomatic and humanitarian missions to be performed.

Vietnam was a prime example of the Navy's versatility. When the Viet Minh laid siege to the French at Dien Bien Phu in 1954, Congress refused to back US airstrikes by land-based bombers and Navy carrier planes to rescue the French. Senator Lyndon B. John-

---

[5] JCS 2101/112, December 7, 1953, CCS 381 US (1–31–50) sec. 32, JCS, quoted in David Alan Rosenberg, "American Postwar Air Doctrine and Organization: The Navy Experience," in Alfred F. Hurley and Robert C. Ehrhart, eds., *Air Power and Warfare: The Proceedings of the 8th Military History Symposium* (1979), 267–268.

son of Texas opposed sending "American GI's into the mud and muck of Indochina on a bloodletting spree,"[6] and Senator John F. Kennedy of Massachusetts argued against American involvement in the region because it would be "dangerously futile and self-destructive."[7] The 1954 peace accords, which divided Vietnam at the 17th parallel, created a humanitarian crisis as over 600,000 noncommunist refugees attempted to escape south before the borders closed. Under the command of Rear Admiral Lorenzo Sabin, the Navy dispatched medical teams and transported around 310,000 refugees from North to South Vietnam in a relatively short time. While "Operation Passage to Freedom" was a humanitarian success, it also was an example of Eisenhower's unwillingness to accept a communist takeover of a country. He not only blocked the promised reunification elections for fear of a communist political victory but also hand-picked Ngo Dinh Diem to rule over the newly created South Vietnam and sent General J. Lawton Collins to Saigon to begin training the Army of the Republic of South Vietnam. In addition, the president authorized CIA operatives to round up and, at times, eliminate Viet Minh in the South with loyalty to Ho Chi Minh, who was solidifying his communist regime in the North.

Taiwan Straits Crisis

The Navy played an important role during the Taiwan Straits Crisis, the closest Eisenhower came to using an atomic weapon. In 1954 the Mainland Chinese began to shell the tiny islands of Matsu (Mazu) and Quemoy (Jinmen), garrisoned by 85,000 Nationalist soldiers from noncommunist Taiwan; in addition to killing numerous Taiwanese personnel, the constant barrage killed two American soldiers. While the president rejected JCS advice to bomb the mainland, he did send the Seventh Fleet to create a defense zone between Nationalist and communist forces, and to protect supply lines to the besieged Nationalists. While Eisenhower forced the Nationalists to sign a pact that placed their nation under US protection and prevented them

from invading the mainland on their own, the crisis only deepened. The next year the communists attacked the Tachen (Dachen) Islands, 200 miles distant from Taiwan. The president did not believe the Tachens were vital to US interests but viewed the new aggression as a precursor to an attack on Taiwan. Eisenhower drew a line in the dirt by using the Navy and Marine Corps to strengthen defenses on Matsu and Quemoy and by asking Congress for permission to use force if needed to protect Taiwan and "closely related localities." While he abandoned the Tachens to the communists, the president did send the Navy to evacuate the 29,000 civilians and troops living there (see Figure 19.1).

Conditions in the Taiwan Straits worsened during the next month (see Map 19.1). Eisenhower, as

Map 19.1   Taiwan Straits, 1954–1955.

---

[6] Congressional Record, 100:5281, as quoted in Howard Jones, *Crucible of Power: A History of US Foreign Relations since 1897* (2001), 295.

[7] *Congressional Record*, 83rd congress, 2nd session, 4672, as quoted in Hugh Brogan, *Kennedy* (1996), 188.

Figure 19.1   Evacuation of Tachen Islands, February 1955. Chinese civilians board Seventh Fleet landing craft during the evacuation of the Tachen Islands.

prescribed by brinkmanship, threatened to use tactical nuclear weapons if the Communists attacked Matsu and Quemoy or threatened Taiwan (the CIA estimated that 12 to 14 million Chinese civilians would die in the attack). When asked at a press conference about the crisis, Eisenhower responded that nuclear weapons could be used against "strictly military targets." "I see no reason why," he continued, "they shouldn't be used just exactly as you would use a bullet or anything else."[8] The Chinese, however, backed down and the president's resolve to use nuclear weapons was not tested. The fact that Nikita Khrushchev had issued his own warning, threatening a retaliatory nuclear strike if the United States attacked the Chinese mainland, indicates that Eisenhower might have set off a nuclear holocaust over the fate of the Taiwanese. When the communists again bombarded Quemoy in 1958, the Navy provided the Nationalists with Sidewinder air-to-air missiles and the Marine Corps supplied ground troops with artillery, giving the noncommunist military superiority until a diplomatic resolution was reached.

The Nuclear Balance

It is difficult to assess how determined either Eisenhower or Khrushchev was about using nuclear weapons, but it appears that the showdown over Matsu and Quemoy tempered Eisenhower's hardline brinkmanship. A number of policymakers were convinced that the United States would win a nuclear war against the Soviets; during the 1950s America's nuclear stockpile was always greater than the enemy's and the nation had developed superior delivery systems. In addition, by the end of Eisenhower's presidency the Navy had become an important component of the nuclear triad that included Air Force strategic bombers, land-based intercontinental ballistic missiles (ICBMs), and the Navy's Polaris sea-based submarine-launched ballistic missiles. While the United States could not prevent Moscow from launching a nuclear attack, Polaris missiles would ensure that the Soviets would never win a nuclear war. With each submarine armed with 16 Polaris missiles, the United States had the ability to strike every major military and urban center in the Soviet Union and inflict devastating losses.

---

[8] [President's News Conference], March 16, 1955, as quoted in Stephen E. Ambrose, *Eisenhower: Soldier and President* (1990), 383.

By the early 1960s, however, America's missile superiority no longer provided an adequate deterrent to a nuclear war. Russia's nuclear arsenal had grown rapidly during Eisenhower's presidency and Khrushchev, like the American president, took steps to convince the world that the Soviets were ready and willing to fight a nuclear war. Both superpowers published the number of bomb shelters built each year and produced propaganda to convince their publics that they could survive a nuclear attack. Scientists from around the world, however, had verified that any exchange of nuclear missiles would trigger "mutual assured destruction," with whole cities leveled, mass casualties (perhaps in the millions), and widespread nuclear fallout. The 1954 hydrogen bomb test at Eniwetok Atoll demonstrated what would happen if even one Soviet missile were to reach the United States. The test detonation created a mile-wide crater with a fallout territory large enough to cover the distance from Washington, DC, to the Canadian border. In 1960 Herman Kahn captured the dangerous mood of the day in *On Thermonuclear War* (parodied in the 1964 Hollywood film *Dr. Strangelove*), a novel about a fictitious doomsday machine that set off a nuclear exchange, ending the world.

Mediterranean Crises

Although neither Eisenhower nor his successors ever publicly rejected a possible nuclear response, the sobering realization within the United States following the Taiwan Straits Crisis that the country might provoke a nuclear war over a minor crisis led Eisenhower to rely even more heavily on the Navy and the Marine Corps. The president's response to communist aggression in Egypt and Lebanon demonstrates his more cautious approach and use of naval assets. During the Suez Crisis of 1956, Egyptian president Gamal Abdel Nasser, who had strong ties to the Soviet Union, seized the Suez Canal as a first step in creating a pan-Arab bloc. When British and French troops landed to reassert ownership of the canal, Eisenhower ordered

the Sixth Fleet to "prepare for imminent hostilities." Vice Admiral Charles R. Brown replied, "Am prepared for imminent hostilities, but which side are we on?"[9] The exchange reflected the ambiguity of the American position in the Mediterranean. The United Nations and American diplomacy ultimately resolved the conflict, but not before the Navy evacuated 1,680 American citizens by sea and 533 by air. In 1958, Lebanese president Camille Chamoun invoked the Eisenhower Doctrine, calling for US military assistance to thwart a potential communist insurrection. Chamoun believed that Nasser had worked with the Soviets to provoke an army revolt in Iraq. Eisenhower wasted no time ordering military action after Chamoun claimed that communist operatives from Syria had arrived in Lebanon and were organizing an insurrection. The Sixth Fleet, under the command of Admiral James L. Holloway, Jr., reached Lebanon within a day of the request and landed 5,000 marines, who were followed by the arrival of a reinforced Army brigade flown in from Europe and an Air Force strike group from the United States. Despite the fact that the US forces found no rebels, only vacationers, the Navy's rapid deployment sent a message to the Soviet Union and its satellite nations that America could and would respond with force if the communists ever took action in the Middle East.

Despite Eisenhower's foreign policy successes, by the end of his administration geopolitical stability seemed uncertain. In 1957, the Soviets scored a propaganda coup by using a ballistic missile to lift Sputnik, an artificial satellite, into orbit. A month later they launched Sputnik II and put a dog into space. By the end of 1959, the United States had successfully launched 15 satellites, including the Navy's Vanguard, but Sputnik seemed to support claims by the Democrats that Eisenhower had allowed the development of a three-to-one missile gap favoring the Soviet Union. Because the information was classified, Eisenhower was unable to report to the public that CIA-directed U-2 spy flights over Soviet territory had proved that America had the advantage in ballistic missiles. The

---

[9] As quoted in Robert W. Love, Jr., ed., *Chiefs of Naval Operations* (1980), 283.

president capitalized on the false report to increase science and technology in public education, to fund the interstate highway system, and to pass legislation creating the National Aeronautics and Space Administration (NASA). The reported missile gap and the embarrassment that followed the U-2 incident (when the Soviets shot down a U-2 spy plane deep in Soviet territory and captured its CIA pilot, Gary Powers), however, were two of the factors that brought Democrat John F. Kennedy to the White House.

Throughout his presidency Eisenhower had hoped to prevent militarization of American society by reducing the size and expenses of the regular armed forces in favor of a nuclear deterrent. Geopolitical conditions and a prolonged struggle with the Soviets, however, had fostered a scientific–technological elite and a permanent and powerful arms industry. The American people must keep a watchful eye over their traditional freedoms, Eisenhower urged in his Farewell Address. "Only an alert and knowledgeable citizenry can compel the proper meshing of the huge industrial and military machinery of defense with our peaceful methods and goals, so that security and liberty may prosper together."[10]

John F. Kennedy Takes the Helm

The country was focused, however, on its new, dynamic president, John F. Kennedy, and the "Age of Camelot," as the style and glamour surrounding his administration would later be known. Kennedy fired America's imagination in his acceptance speech for the Democratic nomination by claiming that the nation stood on the edge of a new frontier, ready to find answers to "unsolved problems of peace and war, unconquered problems of ignorance and prejudice, unanswered questions of property and surplus."[11] During the campaign, Kennedy criticized the Eisenhower administration for its lackadaisical response to Soviet technological superiority, as demonstrated by Sputnik. Kennedy

also capitalized on leaks from the top-secret 1957 *Deterrence & Survival in the Nuclear Age* (the Gaither Report) to warn voters that Soviets would soon have a strategic advantage in the number of ballistic missiles, making it possible for the enemy to launch a successful attack on American territory. Once in office, however, Kennedy announced that the Gaither Report was inaccurate. It had greatly overestimated the number of Soviet ICBMs and that the so-called "missile gap" actually favored the United States 8:1. At the same time, he seized the lead in space exploration by dramatically increasing appropriations for NASA's Apollo Program to land a man on the moon by the end of the decade.

Kennedy's main obstacle as commander-in-chief was the perception, held by the Soviet Union as well as the JCS, that the new president was a weak, inexperienced military leader. The president's steely resolve during the Cuban Missile Crisis convinced Khrushchev that Kennedy would order a nuclear strike if pushed. Kennedy's strained relationship with his military chiefs, however, persisted throughout his administration. His service as a PT (patrol torpedo) boat commander in the Pacific during World War II had given him an understanding of the needs of the common sailor and soldier, and perhaps a certain disdain for admirals and generals, leading him to turn to his secretary of defense, Robert S. McNamara (1961–1968), to communicate with the JCS. Unfortunately, McNamara quickly alienated the military brass. While he had little experience in national security affairs, the new secretary of defense often rejected the counsel of seasoned military officers and turned instead to his staff of young, aggressive academics (Whiz Kids) and civilian experts, as well as the RAND Corporation and other think tanks, for advice. In addition, McNamara managed the armed forces with the same modern business theories that had made him a success as a Ford Motor Co. executive, without making allowances for the traditional command culture of the military.

[10] Eisenhower, "Farewell Address," January 17, 1961, in *Public Papers of the Presidents of the United States: Dwight D. Eisenhower, 1960–61* (1999), 1035–1040.

[11] As quoted in Arthur M. Schlesinger, *A Thousand Days: John F. Kennedy in the White House* (1993), 61.

Alan B. Shepard, Jr.

Astronaut Alan B. Shepard, Jr. (1923–1998) became the first American to reach outer space on May 5, 1961. While Soviet cosmonaut Yuri Gagarin had orbited the earth the previous month, NASA pronounced Shepard's 15-minute, 116-mile-high *Freedom 7* suborbital mission a triumph and the astronaut a hero. President Kennedy built off the positive publicity surrounding Shepard and called on Congress to fund his goal to land a man on the moon and return him safely to earth by the end of the decade.

After graduating from the Naval Academy in 1944, Shepard had fought kamikazes from the deck of a destroyer. Following the war he became a Navy test pilot known for his fierce competitiveness and defiance of rules; he was nearly court martialed for "flat-hatting" (i.e., flying in a reckless manner) around the Chesapeake Bay Bridge. He was chosen for the historic flight, however, because he was the most capable aviator of the

pioneer astronauts (Shepard, Scott Carpenter, Gordon Cooper, John Glenn, Gus Grissom, Wally Schirra, and Deke Slayton). NASA had recruited Shepard and the other astronauts, together known as the "Mercury Seven," after a series of grueling physical and psychological tests. Their all-American image helped to increase NASA's funding as the public closely followed their dangerous missions.

Only two years after his historic flight, Shepard was sidelined by an inner-ear disorder, becoming NASA's first chief astronaut. Known as the "Icy Commander," Shepard directed all aspects of training and flight selection, until a 1969 operation restored his flight status. He missed *Apollo 11* and the first lunar landing, but commanded *Apollo 14* in 1971. Shepard spent over 33 hours on the moon gathering rocks before hitting a golf ball across the lunar surface, to the delight of television viewers back on earth. In 1974 Shepard retired from the Navy as

a rear admiral, becoming a wealthy businessman before his death in 1998.

Alan B. Shepard, Jr. *Source:* NASA.

Kennedy and Flexible Response

While the service chiefs had qualms about Kennedy and McNamara's leadership, the Army and the Navy generally approved of the re-emphasis on conventional weapons in the administration's new "flexible response" defense policy. Flexible response largely reflected the ideas of General Maxwell Taylor and political scientist William W. Kaufmann. Taylor had retired from the Army at the end of his term as chair of the JCS to publish *The Uncertain Trumpet* (1960), a

manifesto against New Look cuts to the Army that urged a greater reliance on conventional weapons to prevent escalating a small crisis into a nuclear show-down. Kaufmann of RAND recommended replacing the threat of brinkmanship with a controlled escalation or "graduated pressure" to induce the enemy "to accept limitations of geography, weapons, and possibly time."[12] Kennedy and McNamara believed that they could achieve diplomatic and military objectives by gradually increasing pressure on the enemy with conventional and unconventional forces

---

[12] Kaufmann, *Military Policy and National Security* (1956), 113.

as well as limited nuclear strikes if necessary. To the dismay of the Air Force, which had overshadowed the other services under the New Look, Kennedy championed a major upswing in appropriations to the Army and the Navy for conventional weapons and counterinsurgency operations. Making matters worse, Air Force General Curtis LeMay stubbornly refused to acknowledge the president's sole authority to order a nuclear strike.

The president maintained cordial relations with the Navy, however. When ballistic missiles replaced aircraft carriers as the center of the Navy's strategic defense—it was safer to launch a nuclear attack from the ground or from submarines—carrier doctrine shifted back to conventional war at sea and power projection ashore. The Navy readily accepted the change. McNamara and Kennedy relied on the Navy's ability to quickly arrive and depart from a hot zone with the air power needed to gather intelligence and provide cover for the landings, evacuations, interdictions, and combat missions called for in limited wars. At the same time the Navy still could arm planes with nuclear bombs for attacks on a variety of sea-control targets. In effect, the heart of the president's "flexible response" was the Navy and the Marine Corps.

Bay of Pigs

The 1961 Bay of Pigs incident, however, momentarily sidetracked Kennedy's defense plans as the failed invasion of Cuba increased tensions between the new president and the JCS. Before Kennedy's inauguration, the CIA had briefed him about a clandestine plan in the works since March 1960 to remove Fidel Castro from power using Cuban exiles and a handful of disguised CIA and US military assets. Inadequate security had alerted Castro to the planned invasion, making it necessary to revise the scope of the operation to include an antisubmarine squadron of seven destroyers and one aircraft carrier (Task Group 81.8) disguised as Central American vessels. Because of the service's flexibility and the proximity of the US naval base at Guantanamo Bay on the eastern end of Cuba, the CIA had relied heavily on the Navy in its plans.

The Bay of Pigs was a complete disaster. A series of CIA blunders and intelligence failures plagued the operation. The president complicated matters by changing the landing site to the more remote Bahía de Cochinos (Bay of Pigs), which contributed to the confusion. The JCS was not blameless—it had approved "Operation Bumpy Road," the planned invasion. Its members were furious, however, when the president refused to respond to the pleas of Chief of Naval Operations Arleigh Burke to commit additional naval resources when Castro's forces overwhelmed the exiles. The JCS, however, had assured Kennedy that no Americans would directly participate in the landing. Destroyers could escort the old freighters purchased by the CIA to carry the Cuban exiles, weapons, and supplies from Guatemala but were ordered not to fire on the enemy unless they were directly attacked. After a mere two days of fighting (April 16–17, 1961), Castro's forces had killed or captured nearly the entire invasion force of 1,400 exiles while the Navy looked on with frustration, only allowed to rescue those invaders who had escaped to the sea.

While the president publicly took responsibility for mismanaging the invasion, privately he faulted the CIA and the JCS for poor planning and bad advice. The president fired CIA head Allen Dulles (brother of Eisenhower's secretary of state) but continued to value the agency's skill in gathering information and running clandestine missions. The president's relationship with the JCS, however, never recovered. He further isolated himself from the top brass by handpicking officers as his military advisors and by calling Maxwell Taylor, a strong proponent of flexible response, out of retirement as his chief liaison to the military. In the future, the president instructed in a memo, the JCS should consider the overall context of a conflict and not just the immediate military objective before sending him their "direct and unfiltered" advice.[13] He would decide how to proceed after he had considered all relevant information. Never again, he vowed, would he defer to the military's judgment over his own.

[13] National Security Action Memorandum 55, June 28, 1961, as quoted in Steven L. Rearden, *Council of War: A History of the Joint Chiefs of Staff, 1942–1991* (2012), 216.

The most serious consequence of the Bay of Pigs, however, was on US foreign policy. Castro became a hero to regimes hoping to resist the so-called "Yankee imperialists," strengthening communism not only in Cuba but also throughout Latin America. In addition, Kennedy's handling of the crisis, followed by his lackluster performance when he met the Soviet leader in Vienna two months later (June 1961), convinced Khrushchev that Kennedy was a weak leader who would not seriously contest Soviet advances. The Kremlin was eager, therefore, to provide weapons and supplies when Castro sought Soviet protection from future American invasions and from ongoing CIA assassination attempts (Operation Mongoose) ordered by the president.

Returning home from the Vienna Summit, Kennedy set out to demonstrate to Khrushchev his resolve to resist international communism. The president immediately mobilized two National Guard divisions of 75,000 men and strengthened NATO defenses with air guard fighter squadrons and additional armored cavalry and infantry units. In addition, the president signed the Foreign Assistance Act (September 1961), which created the US Agency for International Development to administer non-military assistance. In what became known as the Kennedy Doctrine, the president targeted Central and South America as well as Southeast Asia and Africa with economic aid, health care, democratic reforms, and military assistance. For example, Kennedy bought votes in the Congo and funded UN peacekeeping forces, hoping to create a stable, noncommunist regime and prevent the Soviet Union from expanding its influence in Africa. The president also dispatched unconventional forces, along with CIA operatives, to fight brush wars and undermine unfriendly regimes in the Dominican Republic, Ecuador, Laos, Vietnam, and Zaire. In addition, the Pentagon authorized the Navy SEALs to conduct intelligence operations and covert missions in December 1961. The SEALs' first missions were in Vietnam, where they provided support to the South Vietnamese and conducted covert raids on North Vietnamese transportation routes.

In June 1961 Kennedy's flexible response and graduated pressure were ready to be tested in his administration's first open confrontation with the Soviet Union—the Berlin Crisis. Encouraged by the president's weak performance during the Bay of Pigs and the Vienna Summit, Khrushchev took steps to force the Western Allies from the divided city. Adhering to his graduated pressure strategy, the president first ordered significant increases to the defense budget and military manpower levels, and deployed a number of army units to bases in Europe. Tensions rose further after Kennedy ordered fighter pilots to keep the Berlin air corridors open and sent a platoon to probe the situation on the ground. If the Soviets fired on American forces, the next step in Kennedy's plan was to fight back in the air and to go on the offensive by sending armed troops into East Berlin, followed, if necessary, by selective nuclear attacks. Before the crisis escalated, however, the president accepted a less than satisfactory resolution acquiescing to East Germany's building the Berlin Wall (first with barbed wire, then followed by a more permanent barrier) to divide the city.

Kennedy's "graduated pressure" was designed to prevent tensions from reaching the nuclear threshold. Yet, the success of the policy rested on the deterrence provided by the nation's rapidly increasing number of strategic bombers, land-based ICBMs, and nuclear-powered Polaris submarines, now roaming the world's oceans armed with A-3 Polaris missiles. At the end of the Eisenhower administration, the Navy had outmaneuvered the Air Force's attempt to take control of its Polaris missile, and, with completion of the *Lafayette*, *James Madison*, and *Benjamin Franklin* classes of fleet ballistic missile submarines, the service reached its goal of 41 nuclear-powered ballistic missile submarines in 1967.

Cuban Missile Crisis

The closest the two superpowers came to an exchange of nuclear weapons was the Cuban Missile Crisis of October 1962. With the United States distracted by the Berlin Crisis, Khrushchev had launched Operation Anadyr (the codename for the Soviet movements of strategic missiles and military forces to Cuba). Khrushchev had planned and commenced Anadyr without consulting his intelligence experts, who would undoubtedly have warned him that the Soviet Union lacked the naval resources required for such an operation and that Washington would not

Map 19.2   Cuban Missile Crisis, 1962. IRBM: intermediate-range ballistic missiles; MRBM: medium-range ballistic missiles.

tolerate the installation of first-strike nuclear-tipped missiles 90 nautical miles from its shores. Although Kennedy learned of the Soviet arms buildup in late summer, he was unaware of the magnitude of the crisis until September 4, 1962. At that time, a CIA U-2 mission photographed a missile launch pad under construction. Using low-level photography, further U-2 flights revealed eight separate missile installations capable of launching medium-range and intermediate-range ballistic nuclear missiles. Using low-level photography, Navy and Marine air patrols charted the movements of Soviet and Eastern Bloc transport ships riding low in the water, with suspicious cargo on the decks, headed toward Cuba. Specialists who studied the photos reassured the president that the missile launch pads were not yet operational, allowing Kennedy to act before the work was completed. Scholars now know, however, that the situation was far more dangerous than was first believed. Despite reports to the contrary, several silos were operational. In addition, Soviet submarines patrolling the area had permission to fire their nuclear torpedoes on

American ships and submarines without first contacting the Kremlin.

To find a solution to the escalating crisis, the president assembled EXCOM (the Executive Committee of the National Security Council and additional advisors) to consider his options. A number of civilian advisors argued for a diplomatic response—that is, giving the Soviets and Cubans a strongly worded warning and then negotiating a resolution that included, perhaps, the withdrawal of US Jupiter missiles in Turkey. On the opposite end of the policy spectrum, the JCS and a handful of civilian advisors called for an immediate military response: a strategic airstrike against the missile sites followed by an invasion of the island. Fearing this might provoke nuclear retaliation by the Soviets, a third group advocated establishing a naval blockade. After a frustrating meeting with Soviet Ambassador Anatoly Dobrynin and Foreign Minister Andrei Gromyko on October 18, Kennedy adopted the third option, ordered a strict naval "quarantine" of Cuba, and issued a letter to the Kremlin demanding removal of the missile sites. Khrushchev responded that the word "quarantine" did not mask America's blockade, which was an illegal act of war, and vowed that he would not recall the transport ships en route to Cuba.

When the crisis first began to unfold, the Navy called the aircraft carrier *Enterprise* home to Norfolk, and sent the antisubmarine hunter-killer group assigned to USS *Essex* to Guantanamo Bay. As the situation became more confrontational, Admiral Robert Dennison took command of Task Force 136 with orders to establish a blockade line 500 nautical miles off Cuba and to stop and search any vessel that approached (see Map 19.2). Task Force 135, built around the aircraft carriers *Enterprise* and *Independence*, was positioned south of Jamaica in position to launch strikes in support of Guantanamo, if necessary. Further parameters detailed that Soviet submarines were to be detected and followed, but no shots were to be fired without Kennedy's prior approval, and Kennedy himself would communicate directly with commanders as events unfolded. At the end of the EXCOM meeting on October 21, the president told Admiral George W. Anderson, "Well, Admiral it looks as though this is up to the Navy," and the chief of naval operations reportedly replied, "Mr. President, the Navy will not let you down."[14] The next day Kennedy announced on television that the quarantine would take effect on October 24, but also warned the United States would launch a "full retaliatory" attack on the Soviet Union if Moscow launched missiles on any target in the Western Hemisphere.

Within two days of Kennedy's televised appearance, most Soviet and Eastern Bloc cargo ships carrying missile parts turned around. The crisis, however, had reached its most crucial stage (see Figure 19.2). A handful of suspicious vessels were still proceeding, and additional U-2 flights revealed that the missile launchers were almost operational. The president put US forces on DEFCON 2 (nuclear war imminent) alert and increased his efforts to reach a diplomatic resolution. Khrushchev's hope that the United States would not effectively respond to missiles in Cuba was dashed. The Soviet premier, who was well aware that his naval forces were overwhelmingly outclassed

and was unwilling to engage in a nuclear exchange, reached out to Washington for a face-saving resolution. In one diplomatic note Khrushchev promised to remove the missiles from Cuba if the United States promised not to invade. In another, he added the requirement that Kennedy remove American missiles in Turkey. The president publicly accepted the first proposal, ending the confrontation. Privately, however, Kennedy also agreed to eventually remove the Jupiter missiles in Turkey. The Navy continued to monitor events until the Soviets dismantled all their equipment and returned home and the last enemy submarine left the area.

While Castro continued to rule Cuba, Kennedy's success during the Cuban Missile Crisis was a significant victory against the Soviets, demonstrating the merits of a flexible response and graduated pressure. Moreover, Khrushchev's willingness to accede to American demands had infuriated Castro and China's Mao Zedong, further dividing the communist world. In addition, the crisis led the United States and the Soviet Union, both frightened by how close the world had come to nuclear holocaust, to work together to begin arms-limitation negotiations, leading to the Limited Test Ban Treaty (September 1963) as well as an agreement to install a "hotline" between Moscow and Washington for direct communications during a possible future crisis.

But all was not peaceful. The two superpowers still competed for hearts and minds in third-world nations, especially in Vietnam. While the Soviets wanted to avoid an open confrontation with the United States over Indochina, an area Moscow considered to be outside the Soviet Union's national security interests, the Kremlin increased arms and economic assistance to Ho Chi Minh's North Vietnamese communist regime. In 1961 the North Vietnamese reorganized their allies in the South to form the People's Liberation Armed Force, which by late 1962 could mount battalion-sized attacks. Kennedy viewed the conflict in Vietnam to be part of a worldwide communist testing of his and America's will. The president agreed with an advisor who said that "it is on this spot [Vietnam] that we have to break

---

[14] As quoted in Sheldon Stern, *The Week the World Stood Still* (2005), 75.

Figure 19.2   P-2 Neptune flying over a Soviet freighter with crated II-28 "Beagle" bombers on deck.

the liberation war … If we do not break it here we shall have to face it again in Thailand, Venezuela, and elsewhere. Vietnam is a clear testing ground for our policy in the world."[15] To meet the challenge, Kennedy increased the number of US advisors in Vietnam from 1,500 when he took office to 16,000 by 1963. Secretary of Defense Robert McNamara acknowledged in 1962 that the advisors, as well as US Air Force pilots flying support missions for the

noncommunist regime, "participate in combat-type training activities which can be considered combat missions."[16] By 1963 Kennedy had begun to question the American commitment to South Vietnam, and he discussed withdrawing American troops following his 1964 presidential reelection. Whether or not he would have done so is unknown, for on November 22, 1963, Lee Harvey Oswald assassinated the president in Dallas, Texas, leaving the nation in mourning.

---

[15] Walt Rostow as quoted in Walter A. McDougall, *Promised Land, Crusader State* (1997), 187.

[16] "McNamara Confirms US Pilots Bombing," *Wilmington Morning Star*, March 16, 1962.

CHAPTER 20

The Test of Vietnam

On April 30, 1975, images showing the fall of Saigon were transmitted from South Vietnam's war-torn capital to every point on the globe. The photographs and film footage depicted chaotic scenes of South Vietnamese soldiers and civilians scrambling to escape the besieged city by any means possible. Overcrowded patrol boats and other military vessels choked the Saigon River as the terrified and the desperate sought to escape the final acts of bloodletting in this long and brutal conflict. The most arresting of the day's images shows the men of the 9th Marine Amphibious Brigade escorting evacuees from the roof of an American apartment complex to a waiting Air America helicopter perched atop a tiny makeshift landing platform. The helicopter would carry these fleeing officials, military personnel, and their dependents to US warships waiting offshore in the South China Sea. In the photographs, the marines are calm and focused despite the precarious circumstances and location. They manage the crush of panicked humanity with a resolute professionalism that defies the danger of their situation. Photographs of the ships awaiting the refugees show American naval commanders and crews improvising landing protocols and rearranging deck configurations to accommodate the surge of refugees that turned up that day in every flying and floating vessel imaginable. In 18 hours, these marines and sailors would evacuate approximately 1,000 American and 7,000 Vietnamese personnel from Saigon while pulling many thousands more out of the South China Sea.

These acts of courage and innovation during the final day of the war stand as symbols of the US Navy's and Marine Corps' involvement in the Vietnam War. They show that the Navy was everywhere—on the ground, in the air, up the rivers, and on the sea—and they illustrate the remarkable professionalism of the people in uniform as they searched for a means to prevail. They also show the stark reality of the result: failure. Despite the awesome power of its military, despite its almost limitless financial and material resources, and despite the steadfast commitment of its military men and women, the United States did not win in Vietnam. Its forces fought to a stalemate on the battlefield before withdrawing under pressure from an unsupportive public. In the aftermath of this failure, the US Navy would use its experiences in Vietnam to transform its fleet and personnel and to apply the costly-but-valuable lessons in ways that would improve operations for decades to come.

Origins of War

The roots of the Vietnam War lie in the late nineteenth century, when French imperialists seized control of Indochina and forced its people to toil in remote locations—coal mines, rubber plantations, and road-building sites—that were dangerous and unhealthy.

America, Sea Power, and the World, First Edition. Edited by James C. Bradford.
© 2016 John Wiley & Sons, Inc. Published 2016 by John Wiley & Sons, Inc.

Vietnamese who resisted were imprisoned, exiled, and, in many cases, executed. Among the strongest and best organized of those who resisted French colonialism were the communists, who looked to the Soviet Union for support.

Ho Chi Minh, Vo Nguyen Giap, and Pham Van Dong found each other among the anticolonial groups operating clandestinely within Vietnam and in southern China. Ho had spent decades traveling the world in search of the means to liberate his people. But, for all his tenacity and grit, he had achieved few successes prior to World War II. That conflict proved critical to Ho's rise to power, especially after the Japanese detained all French officials in March 1945. Rushing to Hanoi from the forests of northern Vietnam, Ho's communist-dominated Viet Minh claimed control of all of Vietnam in the days immediately following Japan's surrender. A year later, French colonial forces reoccupied the cities and ports, crushed Ho's fledgling government, and forced his military forces to abandon the cities for the forests and farms of the countryside, first as guerrillas and later in increasingly larger regular units. The United States initially opposed France's reoccupation of Indochina, but the victory of Mao Zedong's communists in China drove American leaders to support the French in their war against the Viet Minh. In 1950, the United States sent a 35-man Military Assistance Advisory Group to work with the French and began giving France what would eventually become $2.5 billion to support its war. Four years later, in May 1954, General Vo Nguyen Giap's troops overran the French outpost at Dien Bien Phu to win the war, though the peace terms agreed to in Geneva two months later denied Ho the total victory his forces had secured on the battlefield.

Although the Geneva Accords of 1954 were never formalized, the practical result was to leave Vietnam divided at the 17th parallel with a demilitarized zone separating two states. The communists took the north while the noncommunists and remaining French forces regrouped in the south. The plan hammered out in Geneva by the world's powers called for nationwide elections within two years to determine the government of a unified Vietnam. Washington and the nascent regime in Saigon had not signed these accords, and, aware of Ho Chi Minh's likely election as president if elections were held, they chose to ignore

them. US psychological warfare teams encouraged fearful northerners—especially Roman Catholics—to flee the north and settle in the south during the regrouping phase. Their efforts were helped by communist-led attacks on landlords and those perceived to be pro-French, and by the disastrous economic policies imposed by Hanoi in the aftermath of Dien Bien Phu. US Navy transport vessels ferried the frightened émigrés who had jammed the ports seeking a way out. Almost a million refugees found their way to South Vietnam during this period, most traveling on American ships.

The United States placed its support behind Ngo Dinh Diem, an ascetic Roman Catholic anticommunist from an elite family who had emerged as the strongest and most capable political figure among those vying to control South Vietnam. Taking power following a strongly manipulated presidential election in 1955, Diem built a relatively stable regime from the shakiest of foundations. With help from American advisors, he set about developing a national army, police force, and government administration to support an independent South Vietnamese nation known as the Republic of Vietnam. Using oppressive laws and a ruthless security network, he ferreted out the enemies of his regime, killing many innocent suspects along the way. For a while, Diem appeared to be on his way to wiping out the communist-dominated anti-Diem coalition that called itself the National Liberation Front and its military wing the People's Liberation Armed Forces, which was better known as the Viet Cong, a derisive label created from a contraction of the term "Vietnamese communist traitor," which Diem's regime had applied to them. With these pro-communist southern guerrillas on the verge of extinction, their leaders appealed to Hanoi for assistance. Beset by economic and social problems in the north, Hanoi's leaders were initially reluctant to restart the war in the south. But, with the southern cadres teetering on destruction, North Vietnam acquiesced to reigniting the armed struggle in January 1959.

Advisory Period

President John F. Kennedy was convinced that the resumption of guerrilla activity was part of a worldwide communist offensive. Invoking his military strategy of flexible response, he increased the number of American military advisors to more than 3,000 and raised military and economic aid to the Saigon regime. The Military Assistance Advisory Group became the Military Assistance Command, Vietnam (MACV), and its US Navy component would become known as the Naval Advisory Group. The US Navy's earliest job in South Vietnam was to build up the Republic of Vietnam's navy and to advise on its operations. At the time, the South Vietnamese were relying on some 600 junks, the traditional eastern Asian sailing vessel, to patrol their coast. In its effort to build an effective sea force, the United States donated additional seagoing vessels and trained South Vietnamese sailors in surveillance and control of the coast. Using converted World War II landing craft, American naval advisors trained their Vietnamese counterparts on the inland waterways to create what was to be called the River Assault Group. The Naval Advisory Group also trained the South Vietnamese sailors in mine sweeping, escorting, and river transportation. In the five years after the guerrilla war erupted, the South Vietnamese navy ballooned to 8,000 officers and men and doubled its fleet to 44 seagoing vessels and more than 200 smaller patrol and transport craft.

Throughout this early advisory phase, US Navy personnel were bedeviled by challenges beyond their comprehension and abilities. The Americans lacked the language skills to communicate effectively with their counterparts—English became the principal means of communication despite the setting and the limited English skills of Vietnamese sailors—and they did not possess the cultural knowledge necessary to understand Vietnamese military ways. These American advisors were frustrated by what they took to be the South Vietnamese officers' inclination for petty intrigues, bitter rivalries, and careerism. While plenty of meaningful friendships were forged between the members of these two navies, the culture gap would remain a hindrance to successful cooperation to the end of the war.

On a broader level, official American advice failed to persuade Diem to make changes that would expand democratic participation in his government. Beset by protests from Buddhists and political rivals, Diem turned away from his American advisors. On November 1, 1963, Diem was overthrown and, later,

executed by a group of ambitious Vietnamese military officers who had received tacit approval for their coup d'etat from the Kennedy administration. Three weeks later, Kennedy himself was dead. And, in the aftermath of these profound changes in South Vietnam, the US Navy's role deepened.

The Gulf of Tonkin Incident

An encounter between US Navy destroyers and North Vietnamese PT (patrol torpedo) boats proved to be the catalyst for America's direct military involvement in the Vietnam War. To this day events in the Gulf of Tonkin remain a matter of controversy. On August 2, 1964, the destroyer *Maddox* was patrolling in international waters outside the three-mile limit to territorial waters recognized by the United States, when it intercepted a North Vietnamese message ordering an attack on an unspecified offshore enemy. Believing his ship to be the intended target of the attack, Captain John J. Herrick contacted the commander of the US Seventh Fleet and a nearby carrier task group to request air support. Herrick increased speed and altered course to take the *Maddox* away from North Vietnam's coast. The carrier *Ticonderoga* launched four F-8E Crusaders, and another destroyer, the *Turner Joy*, sped toward the *Maddox* to provide support. Around 1600 hours, the *Maddox*'s radar showed three North Vietnamese PT boats about five miles out and closing rapidly. As the boats zeroed in on the *Maddox*, its crew opened fire with five- and three-inch guns.

Why had North Vietnam targeted the American ships? What was the source of this escalation? Two days before the *Maddox* entered the gulf, four South Vietnamese fast patrol boats had shelled installations on North Vietnam's Hon Me and Hon Nieu Islands then raced back to their base at Danang. It is likely that North Vietnam's military analysts believed the *Maddox* to be a participant in the raids on the islands. Under heavy fire from the American ships, the North Vietnamese attackers launched four torpedoes against the *Maddox*, only two of which came within a few hundred yards of the destroyer. The Americans fired 280 rounds at the enemy boats and inflicted heavy damage on one with a single 5-inch shell. The *Maddox* itself sustained only one hit when a 14.5-mm round smashed into the base of its fire-control system. After the short exchange of fire, the PT boats turned back toward the coast and sped away just as the Crusaders launched from the *Ticonderoga* were arriving on the scene. Led by Commander James B. Stockdale, the fighter jets attacked the fleeing boats. Despite hitting the North Vietnamese craft and killing some of their crew members, the jets did not sink any of the boats. All three PT boats survived the encounter and went on to attack US Navy vessels later in the war.

President Lyndon B. Johnson chose not to retaliate further against the attacks militarily but warned the North Vietnamese publicly against future attacks. The *Maddox* and *Ticonderoga*—their crews tense from the engagement—resumed their patrols further away from North Vietnam's coast. On August 4, *Maddox* and *Turner Joy* each detected fast-moving surface objects closing on them and opened fire on their suspected attackers. Sonar operators reported incoming torpedoes. Some sailors perceived torpedo wakes and machine-gun flashes in the darkness, and sailors on the *Turner Joy* were certain they had seen the outline of a PT boat by the light of a flare. Jets from two nearby aircraft carriers were scrambled and arrived at the scene. But, on this dark night of low cloud cover and poor visibility, the pilots could not identify with certainty any enemy boats or torpedoes. The two destroyers maneuvered sharply, their guns blasting into the darkness. By 0100 on August 5, all suspicious radar detections had vanished. In the initial reports sent by the destroyers, the crews claimed to have sunk six North Vietnamese PT boats. But, failing to locate any debris in the water, Captain Herrick of the *Maddox* grew uncertain. "Freak weather and overeager sonarmen [not enemy boats] may have accounted for many reports," he reflected.[1] After a day of pressing investigations, interviews, and discussions up and down the chain of command, the doubts about the incident grew. It is now known that this second "attack" almost certainly did not occur. But President Johnson, who had not been informed by Secretary of Defense Robert McNamara about the growing skepticism, announced that the United States was launching retaliatory raids against North Vietnam for the attacks over the previous days. A few days later the US Congress passed the Gulf of Tonkin Resolution, authorizing military action without a formal declaration of war. Johnson told aides "it [the Resolution] was like grandma's nightshirt, it covered everything."[2]

America's military response to the seaborne attacks came almost immediately as the US Navy staged Operation Pierce Arrow against North Vietnamese naval targets. On August 5, 1964, aircraft from the *Constellation* and *Ticonderoga* struck North Vietnamese PT boat bases and other coastal installations. They also destroyed some 90 percent of the massive oil-storage facilities in the coastal city of Vinh. History would record the day as the first of many thousands of sorties against North Vietnam. The strike was a sharp blow to North Vietnam's naval facilities. But the US Navy would also pay a heavy price for its success. Of the 67 Navy planes involved in the raids, two were shot down. Lieutenant (junior grade) Everett Alvarez, Jr., became the US Navy's first prisoner of war when his A-4 Skyhawk was brought down. On the same day, Lieutenant (junior grade) Richard C. Sather became the Navy's first pilot killed in action when his A-1 Skyraider was hit. He was the first of nearly 15,000 US Navy and Marine Corps personnel killed in the Vietnam War.

In February 1965 the death of eight American advisors and the wounding of 126 more at Pleiku led Johnson to order the 3,500-man 9th Marine Expeditionary Brigade to land at Danang. This was the first commitment of American ground troops to Vietnam. Initially ordered only to provide security for air and naval facilities in the immediate area, their mission soon expanded to cover the areas surrounding the bases in the northernmost tactical zone, called I Corps. And by the summer they were joined in South Vietnam by US Army infantry units deployed to the south. The US military presence grew steadily for the next few years as successive MACV commanders requested more troops to counter the growing numbers and capabilities of the insurgents. With American forces

---

[1] Message CTG72 [Herrick] 0417272 August 1964, Operational Archives, Naval History and Heritage Command, Washington, DC, as quoted in Edward J. Marolda, "Grand Delusion: US Strategy and the Tonkin Gulf Incident," *Naval History*, 28:4 (2014), 30.

[2] As quoted in Stanley Karnow, *Vietnam: A History* (1983), 374.

James B. Stockdale

Few Navy officers have enjoyed the historical perspective that Vice Admiral James B. Stockdale (1923–2005) gained during the Vietnam War. And few have endured the enormous suffering that came with that vantage point. From the cockpit of an F-8 Crusader, he had a bird's eye view of both Tonkin Gulf incidents. He was the first pilot on the scene when North Vietnamese PT boats attacked the USS *Maddox* on August 2, 1964. That day he helped to drive off the attackers, disabled one of the fleeing boats, and accompanied a damaged jet to safety. After flying over the scene of the second "attack," he was among the few to voice strong skepticism about the incident. The next day he fired the first shots of the Vietnam War when he led a raid that destroyed oil facilities at Vinh. Four hundred days later—after flying nearly 200 missions—he became a prisoner of war after his A-4E Skyhawk was shot down. Denied medical care for weeks after capture, Stockdale suffered through a dislocated shoulder, a broken leg, and multiple other injuries—yet he never stopped resisting the abuse of his Hanoi jailers. A graduate of the US Naval Academy, he had also earned a master's degree in international relations from Stanford University. By his own account it was his studies at both schools–especially of the works of the Greek philosopher Epictetus–that gave him the intellectual and spiritual strength to impose "civilization" among the American prisoners of war as they were tortured and mistreated. It also helped him to maintain his physical and mental integrity during seven and a half years of imprisonment, four of them in solitary confinement. Released in February 1973, Stockdale returned to the United States to resume his stellar naval and academic career. A larger-than-life statue of Stockdale at the US Naval Academy reminds passing midshipmen of the sacrifices that sometimes accompany a brilliant career.

James B. Stockdale.

now cleared for combat, Navy and Marine units cooperated in what were called "amphibious ready group/special landing force" operations throughout the coastal areas of I Corps. They used amphibious vessels and landing craft to move Marine infantry battalions quickly wherever enemy movement was detected. Marine helicopter squadrons provided additional support for these operations.

The Navy was quickly called upon to support Marine and Army operations ashore. Its warships shelled suspected enemy positions and supported Marine and Army offensives, especially in I Corps. The Naval Gunfire Support Unit, consisting of cruisers, destroyers, and even a battleship, blasted North Vietnam's shipping and port installations. During 1968, the peak year of shelling, the US Navy fired more than a million rounds from offshore. To aid this ongoing effort it reactivated the World War II-era battleship *New Jersey*, whose 16-inch guns shelled enemy locations over the demilitarized zone in North Vietnam and struck troop concentrations along the coast in the south (see Figure 20.1). The *New Jersey* was one of many World War II-era vessels recommissioned or kept in service because of the demands that the war in Southeast Asia placed on the American fleet.

Figure 20.1   USS *New Jersey* bombarding targets in South Vietnam's central coast, March 1969.

Multiple Strategies

US strategy for fighting the Vietnam War was a study in conflicts. The US military that went into combat in 1965 had been assembled during the 1950s, when the Eisenhower administration was emphasizing the defense of American interests around the globe through "massive retaliation." But, by the early 1960s, some American military leaders had embraced the notion of "flexible response" being promoted by Kennedy's civilian advisors.

The expanded role of US forces in 1965 was accompanied by debates concerning the appropriate strategy for prosecuting what was rapidly becoming a conventional rather a counterinsurgency war. President Johnson, his advisors, and military leaders soon expanded the American role in Vietnam from advisory and support to one that encompassed command and the conduct of operations. US commanders

did not halt all irregular warfare operations, but they relied far more heavily on a conventional strategy than they did a counterinsurgency approach. MACV commander General William C. Westmoreland in particular was unable to imagine any strategic approach beyond a conventional one. Like the other top brass of his day, he had learned soldiering in conventional battles in World War II and the Korean War. Likewise, the force he deployed had been organized, equipped, and trained to fight a conventional war.

Westmoreland's strategy had two phases. In the first, the United States would build a logistical base from which it would take the battle to the enemy in the Central Highlands of Vietnam, where the US Army would deploy large-scale conventional units to hilltop firebases armed with artillery. The Army units would then conduct sweep-and-destroy operations in remote and thinly populated areas where superior American firepower could be employed to

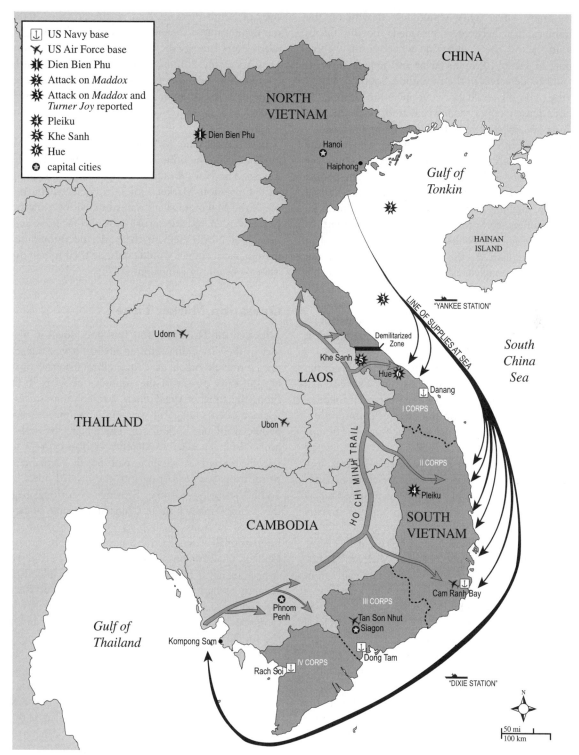

Map 20.1 Vietnam.

maximum effect. They would rely heavily on the mobility that helicopters provided, moving troops swiftly across the countryside wherever main-force units of Hanoi's People's Army of Vietnam (PAVN) could be detected. In the meantime, South Vietnam's army (ARVN) would carry out operations among the more densely populated lowland areas where the Viet Cong was most active. The United States would try to stop North Vietnam from providing support to the southern insurgents by destroying Hanoi's military infrastructure and the pipeline that brought people and matériel south. It relied on aerial bombing and offshore shelling to achieve this objective. American war planners strove to achieve a "crossover point" at which the enemy would be losing more troops than it could replace. As the war continued, this point became increasingly elusive. The enemy appeared able to replace losses without difficulty through 1967. By then the US military had been obliged to add hundreds of thousands more troops and to expand its areas of operation into parts of the Mekong Delta that it had initially entrusted to the ARVN.

The Marine Corps did things differently. From the start it rejected Westmoreland's big-unit conventional approach and, instead, pursued a "spreading inkblot" strategy based, in part, on the ideas of counterinsurgency theorists such as Britain's Sir Robert Thompson. The plan called for focusing on winning the support of the civilian population of a limited area, excluding enemy operatives in that area, then expanding the area by repeating the process nearby. One of the most successful means of executing the strategy involved the "combined action program" (CAP). Each CAP unit included 13 Marine riflemen, a Navy corpsman, and 35 members of South Vietnam's Popular Forces. The Popular Forces militiamen came from the villages that CAP platoons patrolled. These men—usually older men and youths whose age disqualified them from serving in the ARVN—gave the units local knowledge, language skills, and kinship ties in areas contested by the guerrillas. The Marines provided combat skills and leadership. Together they pacified and secured villages and hamlets that had formerly been bases of support for the Viet Cong. Although the CAP has sometimes been romanticized as the formula that could have won the war, it is not clear that such an approach could have been extended to all tactical

areas of South Vietnam. And, as the progress of the war demonstrated, the enemy was adept at adapting to nearly every strategy the US military tried. Either way, MACV's Army-dominated command showed little interest in abandoning its big-unit search-and-destroy methods to try something the Marines had pioneered. Instead, MACV addressed its failures by adding more troops.

In the meantime, MACV put the Navy to work implementing the other important components of its strategy. The Navy would interdict coastal smuggling with Operation Market Time, deny the enemy the use of the Mekong Delta's waterways with Operation Game Warden, provide security for port facilities, and, later, mine North Vietnam's harbors. And, throughout the war, naval aircraft would continue their role in the strategic bombing campaigns.

Operation Market Time

Although the Ho Chi Minh Trail goes down in history as the Viet Cong's storied lifeline, it was the sea that conveyed much of communists' matériel during the early phases of the conflict (see Map 20.1). From the time of the French War, communist vessels had been smuggling weapons, ammunition, and people from north to south. Their ragtag vessels—junks, fishing trawlers, and other civilian craft—had become expert at slipping past South Vietnamese patrol boats before darting into the myriad inlets of South Vietnam's coastline. Bearing no national flag, these ships—many built in China and capable of carrying several tons of supplies—would sail through international waters in the South China Sea or the Gulf of Thailand until they appeared to be free of American naval surveillance. Then they would turn abruptly toward South Vietnam's coast and head for a river entrance, beach, or mangrove where guerrillas or sympathizers awaited. The smugglers would transfer the supplies to smaller vessels that would then carry them through the natural and man-made mazes of South Vietnam's interior waterways, especially those of the Mekong Delta. South Vietnam's navy was inadequate to halt the flow of arms during the first few years of the war. US military advisors bristled at the enemy's ability to convey great quantities of matériel to the waiting guerrilla forces in the South.

To combat the seaborne smuggling, the US Navy set up an elaborate anti-infiltration program known as Operation Market Time (Task Force 115) in early 1965. Market Time divided South Vietnam's coastal waters into nine sectors that extended 40 miles out to sea. The operation was coordinated from five surveillance centers on shore. Initially, the US Navy used 14 ships, including seaplane tenders, destroyers, and ocean minesweepers, to patrol South Vietnam's territorial waters. Closer to land, the US Navy deployed 84 "Swift Boats" (patrol craft fast, or PCFs) in coordinated patrols with 26 US Coast Guard cutters. Aided by P2 Neptunes and P3 Orions, Market Time air patrols sought to interdict the weapons-laden trawlers before they could sprint to the coast.

With the addition of American combat soldiers to South Vietnam, Market Time grew rapidly. Using some 600 vessels and surveillance aircraft, the forces of Market Time wove a floating-and-flying dragnet designed to catch the smugglers. They intercepted, boarded, and searched any suspicious boat. For the American crews, the work was boring, uncomfortable, and dangerous. Laboring under the blazing sun or in the surprisingly chilly darkness, they searched every conceivable type of vessel in their effort to find contraband. On occasion they would capture an enemy boat without a fight, but most of the time the smugglers refused to surrender peacefully and the Americans faced fierce resistance from the heavily armed crews. Firefights at close range involved both sides blasting powerful automatic weapons into the sides of each other's crafts. The Americans' .50-caliber machine guns, rockets, cannon fire, and grenades—as well as their superior training—almost always guaranteed a swift triumph for the US Navy. The smugglers' boats were frequently sunk in torrents of American firepower that ripped apart hulls and engine works. But the enemy's tenacity and courage in these chaotic encounters generated American casualties even in brief exchanges.

To this day the effectiveness of Market Time remains contested. Although US commanders never had reliable statistics to confirm their assumptions of its efficaciousness, they declared Market Time a success. As material proof they pointed to the amount of supplies intercepted. They strongly asserted that the extensive sea and air patrols shut down seaborne smuggling and drove the communists to rely more heavily on the Ho Chi Minh Trail as their main conduit of arms. But the amount of captured matériel was miniscule compared to the cost and scope of the operation. And, because it is impossible to determine how many enemy boats slipped in undetected among the thousands of coastal vessels plying the waters each day, it is difficult to determine the precise degree of success. Just as important as the material considerations were human costs. The disruptive nature of these operations—the stopping and searching of innocent fisher folk—often antagonized precisely the same people from whom the Americans and the South Vietnamese sought support.

The Air War

The other communist supply route, the Ho Chi Minh Trail through Laos and Cambodia, was impossible to seal with ground forces, so the United States attempted to slow the flow of supplies from the north through massive bombing of the area. To halt aid to the southern guerrillas, to cripple Hanoi's war-making capacities, and, most importantly, to break the will of the North Vietnamese to continue the war, the United States instituted a bombing campaign called Operation Rolling Thunder. From March 1965 to October 1968 the Navy participated in the operation by launching hundreds of thousands of sorties from the decks of the carrier group known as Yankee Station. North Vietnam was divided into six zones ("Route Packages"). The Air Force had primary responsibility for zones I, V, and the northwestern section of VI; the Navy for II, III, IV, and the remainder of VI (see Map 20.2). Aiding in the missions over the south was a single aircraft carrier at Dixie Station, situated off the coast of the Mekong Delta between May 1965 and August 1966. The US bombing campaign began small and grew gradually over the course of the war. At first targets were limited to the southern portion of North Vietnam, but by July 1966 only areas along the border with China, the capital at Hanoi, and the main port at Haiphong were off limits to the A-1 Skyraiders, A-3 Skywarriors, A-4 Skyhawks, A-5 Vigilantes, A-6 Intruders, F-4 Phantoms, F-8 Crusaders, and other supporting aircraft that flew round-the-clock sorties against North Vietnam. During the first years of

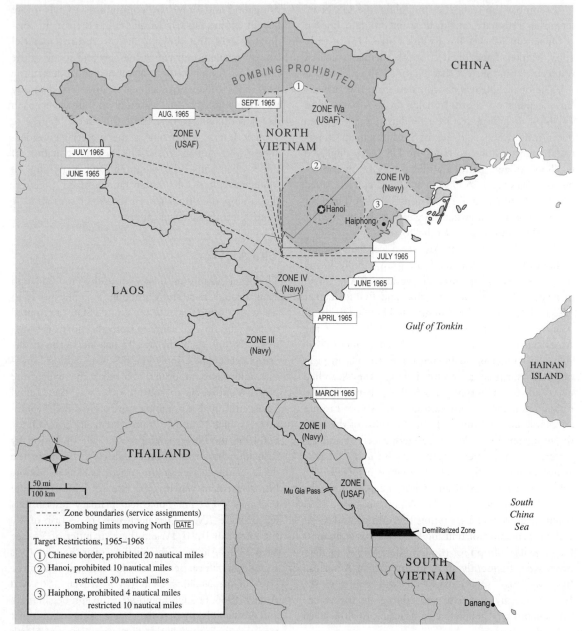

Map 20.2   The air war over North Vietnam.

Rolling Thunder, American aircraft focused on strategically vital targets such as bridges, ferries, truck parks, oil facilities, radar installations, and barracks. The Air Force launched ground-based bombers from Thailand, and these were joined in 1966 by B-52s from Guam that struck jungle locations adjacent to the Mu Gia Pass, near Laos, and later expanded to targets elsewhere (see Map 20.1). The bombing was intense, but so was the resistance. American aircraft contended with lethal fusillades of surface-to-air missiles, antiaircraft fire, and automatic weapons whenever they entered North Vietnamese airspace. A sophisticated early-alert system coordinated North Vietnam's defenses and made every bombing mission perilous for the pilots who braved it. The Navy lost 382 aircraft in the treacherous skies over North Vietnam. And yet the 1 million tons of bombs dropped on North Vietnam paled in comparison to the 4 million tons dropped on South Vietnam. Targets for missions from Yankee Station were selected in Washington, while those from Dixie Station in the south were flown in response to requests from commanders ashore in support of American units operating in South Vietnam.

Yankee Station was the site of one of the most tragic mishaps for the US Navy during the war. On June 29, 1967, while preparing to launch strikes, the USS *Forrestal* erupted in flames after an F-4 errantly fired one of its Zuni rockets while on deck. The rocket struck a waiting A-4 Skyhawk, spilling hundreds of gallons of burning fuel onto the carrier's deck. For hours the *Forrestal*'s crew struggled to extinguish the inferno that had spread below decks before finally bringing it under control. The conflagration killed 134, injured several dozen, and destroyed 21 aircraft.

On March 31, 1968, President Lyndon Johnson suspended bombing above the 20th parallel and in November announced an end to Rolling Thunder. By then Navy and Marine Corps pilots had flown 152,399 sorties against North Vietnam, and the Air Force pilots another 153,784.

Johnson's successor, Richard M. Nixon responded to a North Vietnamese offensive in the south by ordering a continuous air campaign against the North codenamed Linebacker I (May 9–October 22, 1972). Nixon halted the campaign when the communist offensive in the south stalled and peace talks being held in Paris appeared to be making progress, but he ordered the bombing resumed when those talks hit another impasse. During Linebacker II (December 18–29, 1972) Hanoi was targeted and mines were sown in Haiphong Harbor (see Table 20.1). Four decades later, the impact of the air campaign against North Vietnam remains controversial.

Despite the awesome power of the world's most technologically advanced military, the bombing campaign failed to defeat North Vietnam. Some of the reasons were political. US civilian leaders imposed

Table 20.1 Tons of bombs dropped on North Vietnam, 1969–1972.

Year	Tons of bombs
1969	659
1970	892
1971	1,842
1972	218,561[a]
1973	15,347

[a] Dropped during Linebacker I and Linebacker II.

severely restrictive rules of engagement on the bombers, a policy that military leaders would criticize as overly cautious and contrary to objectives. But, as the progress of the war would demonstrate, the subsequent lifting of these restrictions did not force North Vietnam to back down. Instead, Hanoi always found the means to continue its effort while maintaining the morale of its beleaguered populace.

Game Warden

The Navy's brown-water operations provide a study of adaptation under fire. The Navy had had little experience with riverine warfare in the previous century, and during the post-World War II era it had concentrated heavily on developing a blue-water force capable of checking the global reach of the Soviet Union. Learning to fight in the narrow passes and shallow depths of remote Southeast Asian rivers would be difficult under any circumstances, but, faced with a determined and imaginative guerrilla foe, the mission was extremely perilous. American sailors had to devise new and untested tactics under deadly conditions. Like their enemy, they survived by becoming flexible and adaptable—and sometimes they paid dearly with their lives for this education in the midst of war. Even the vessels that became the mainstays of their operations—Swift Boats, PBRs (patrol boats, river), and monitors (modified landing craft)—were conceived and constructed within the first years of the war.

When Market Time patrols endangered coastal smuggling, the communists compensated by expanding their inland smuggling routes coming out of

PBR (Patrol Boat, River)

The fiberglass-hulled PBRs of Operation Game Warden became symbols of the US Navy's new brown-water mission. They embodied the Navy's adaptation to guerrilla warfare in a newly built and sleekly high-tech package. Propelled by two 220-horsepower diesel engines that drove Jacuzzi pumps, and with a draft of only two feet, the 31-foot highly maneuverable craft could zip along extremely narrow waterways at 25 knots. Their twin .50-caliber machine guns on the bow, M-60 machine guns port and starboard amidships, and a .30-caliber machine gun and grenade launcher at the aft gave PBRs extremely lethal firepower. Aided by pathfinder surface radar and twin radios, two-boat PBR patrols proved effective in anti-smuggling operations from their introduction in 1966. The following year, with improved pumps and strengthened armor, the stealthy PBR Mark II acquired greater speed as its crews introduced increasingly innovative tactics. In one effective maneuver, crews would cut one boat's engines upriver at dusk and then drift until concealed within a reedy riverbank, where they awaited the Viet Cong. "If anything moved on the river at night," one PBR gunner's mate recalled, "we shot it."[3] The enemy sought, with only limited success, to disrupt PBR patrols by ambushing them with sniper fire, grenades, or underwater mines. Led by a first class petty officer, the four-men crews generated an esprit-de-corps that was reflected in their slogan "Proud, Brave, Reliable." In popular culture, the PBR became famous as the transport vessel of the fated Navy crew in Francis Ford Coppola's 1979 Vietnam War film *Apocalypse Now*.

PBR (Patrol Boat, River).

Laos and Cambodia. To slow the flow of supplies via this route, the Navy set up a special task force (Task Force 116) dubbed Game Warden in December 1965. Concentrating on the Mekong Delta region and the Rung Sat Special Zone near Saigon, Game Warden initially deployed 100 PBRs to hunt for contraband and the people who moved it. The fiberglass-hulled PBRs of Game Warden became symbols of the US Navy's new brown-water mission. Supported by 20 LCPLs (landing craft personnel, large), an LST (landing ship, tank), and an LSD (landing ship, dock), all of which acted like docking stations for smaller river patrol boats, the PBRs swarmed through southern waterways operating in conjunction with UH-1B helicopter gunships called Seawolves. A similar program, Task Force Clearwater, operated on the Cua Viet and Huong Giang (Perfume) Rivers between Tan My and Hue in I Corps.

[3] David Larsen, interview by Kelly Crager, July 1, 2009, The Vietnam Archive Oral History Project, The Vietnam Archive, Texas Tech University, Lubbock, Texas.

Mobile Riverine Force

While Game Warden concentrated on intercepting inland contraband, the purpose of the Mobile Riverine Force (MRF) was to locate and destroy Viet Cong units through force of arms. The plan called for the movement of ground troops and heavy weapons as far up the river systems as possible. With the US Marines tied up in I Corps, MACV transferred the US Army's 9th Infantry Division into the Mekong Delta to participate in this joint Army–Navy effort.

Topography complicated operations from the start. The watery environment of the delta meant that there was little solid ground on which to station these troops. To solve this, the MRF base was composed of a series of floating barracks—most of them repurposed World War II-era LSTs—and repair stations that could be moved about the river system depending on operations and weather. The MRF also had a fixed base called Dong Tam (see Map 20.1), whose foundation had literally been dredged up from the Mekong's sandy bottom by Navy Seabees (construction battalions). The approximately 180 vessels of the MRF included armored troop carriers, command and control boats, assault support patrol boats, monitors, and refuelers—an armada with a jumble of capacities, functions, and firepower that struck at Viet Cong units when it could find them.

The attack force was divided into several riverine assault squadrons, each built around an armored troop carrier, a boxy vessel that in some models carried a helicopter landing pad on its bow. Armed with 20-mm cannons, .50-caliber machine guns, automatic grenade launchers, and a host of other small arms, an armored troop carrier could carry an entire infantry platoon into battle, providing close fire support. Armor-clad monitors bearing an arsenal of lethal force that included a .50-caliber machine gun, 40- and 20-mm guns, two 40-mm grenade launchers, and an 81-mm mortar provided the main punch of the MRF. Some of the monitors were outfitted with flamethrowers capable of shooting napalm. Photographs of these "Zippo boats" spewing flaming arcs of napalm onto a riverbank became another iconic image of the Navy's time in the Vietnam War.

During their first year of operation MRF units located, trapped, and killed more than 1,000 Viet Cong soldiers. Staging joint-action sweeps alongside South Vietnamese naval units, the MRF also located large caches of enemy weapons and supplies. Enemy insurgents would ambush MRF units, but rarely with success. In one enemy attack in September 1967, the guerrillas suffered at least 213 killed with a few dozen more probably dead while killing only three Americans and wounding 77 others. But, as awesome in function and appearance as these armored vessels were, the MRF search-and-destroy missions were only partially successful. The enemy adjusted to the new American tactics, and the guerrillas were capable of avoiding the MRF patrols that were hunting them by hiding among the people and the landscape.

SEALORDS

With the MRF's search-and-destroy missions becoming less effective in stopping enemy operations, the Navy searched for a better way to deny the insurgents the supplies and personnel they needed to launch attacks. The solution came with the arrival of Rear Admiral Elmo R. "Bud" Zumwalt, Jr. as chief of the Naval Advisory Group in September 1968. Zumwalt masterminded and implemented a broad and highly integrated program designed to interdict swiftly enemy supplies as they made their way in from the ocean or over the border into the Mekong Delta. The plan was called SEALORDS, for "Southeast Asia, Lake, Ocean, River, and Delta Strategy." From a logistical base at Rach Soi, SEALORDS commanders coordinated elements from Game Warden, Market Time, and the MRF on operations deep into South Vietnam. SEALORD sailors were joined in the air by an attack squadron of fixed-wing OV-10 Broncos known as the "Black Ponies." Relying mostly on Swift Boats, PBRs, and SEAL teams, the SEALORDS units raced along the trans-delta waterways to strike wherever electronic sensors or aerial spotters detected enemy logistical movement. Supported by air cavalry and by slower-but-more-powerful riverine assault vessels, the group would hit enemy positions with all available firepower before sending in SEALs to wipe up the last of the holdouts. In the aftermath of an engagement, South Vietnam's naval forces would occupy the site to prevent the enemy from resuming operations there.

After a slow start, these well-orchestrated multi-unit operations proved effective in disrupting the Viet Cong's supply system throughout the Delta. In their first year of operation, the barrier patrols set up along the western waterways of the Mekong severely hampered the enemy's ability to move supplies and replacement troops, killed more than 3,000 guerrillas, and captured another 300 at a cost of 186 Allied deaths and more than 1,000 wounded. With SEALORDS established, Admiral Zumwalt then set up a defensive barrier called Giant Slingshot on the rivers to the west of the Parrot's Beak, a salient jutting into South Vietnam from Cambodia that the enemy used to supply its troops around Saigon, only 30 miles away.

Khe Sanh

By the end of 1967, some 6,000 US marines had been deployed to a remote cluster of villages around the town of Khe Sanh in the western corner of I Corps in Quang Tri province (see Map 20.1). Their mission was to conduct reconnaissance and search-and-destroy missions in this strategic area adjacent to important infiltration routes of the Ho Chi Minh Trail some 14 miles below the demilitarized zone and six miles from the Laotian border. In January 1968, some 20,000 PAVN troops from North Vietnam struck the Marine encampments in the hills around Khe Sanh, overrunning some of the outposts before concentrating their fire on the largest remaining Marine camp. Many observers believed that the PAVN attack on Khe Sanh was designed to deliver "an American Dien Bien Phu"—a disastrous defeat of trapped soldiers that would strike a psychologically fatal blow to the US effort in South Vietnam. To counter the two PAVN divisions, the United States moved some forces from the south to Khe Sanh, and soon the number of Americans defending Khe Sanh swelled to 50,000. For the next two months the marines staved off countless enemy attacks while hunkered down in a chaotic and garbage-strewn environment in which enemy fire competed with vicious rats to harm the American defenders. The remote location and bad weather conditions compounded the difficulties that the marines faced. US aircraft struggled to supply the besieged base and remove the wounded as planes landed and took off under fire, with most never stopping unless they were hit by artillery. Michael Herr, a journalist who stayed with the marines during the siege, wrote, "Khe Sanh was a very bad place then, but the airstrip there was the worst place in the world."[4] The US Air Force staged a massive aerial bombardment called Operation Niagara against the attacking North Vietnamese soldiers that included B-52 strikes dangerously close to the marines they were defending. In total the United States dropped more than 100,000 tons of explosives on the enemy during the siege. More than half of the PAVN forces sent there were casualties. By the end of March, the unsuccessful North Vietnamese attackers withdrew, and a couple months later the marines abandoned Khe Sanh, its tactical importance having vanished with the PAVN.

Tet Offensive

On January 30, 1968, war came to the cities and towns of South Vietnam. Taking advantage of a truce during the Lunar New Year festival called Tet (Tet Nguyen Dan in Vietnamese), the southern insurgents sprang a surprise attack on five municipalities, 36 provincial capitals, and 72 district towns throughout the country. With war on the battlefield at a stalemate and US President Johnson seeking to open peace talks with the north, hardliners in Hanoi pressed the Viet Cong to carry out a military offensive that they hoped would spark a general uprising among South Vietnam's urban population. The hardliners feared that the intensifying Sino-Soviet split could lead to a drop in external support for the war if one of Hanoi's patrons tried to outflank the other by reaching out to Washington for détente. The hardliners believed that a surprise attack would stun the Americans, dishearten the ARVN, and encourage the war-weary populace to withdraw support for the Saigon regime. Although the Viet Cong's meticulous planning and derring-do resulted in huge caches of arms and ammunition being

---

[4] Michael Herr, *Dispatches* (1978), 94.

smuggled ingeniously into urban centers, the guerrillas were unable to move enough fighters into position
to make the attacks more than volatile flashes. American and ARVN units, despite missing many troops on
holiday leave, quickly cut down the commandos at
their attack sites. Of the 86,000 insurgents who took
part in the battle, 32,000 were killed and nearly 6,000
captured. The US military lost 1,001 in the battles,
while the South Vietnamese military and other Free
World Forces saw 2,082 killed.

The only place where the Tet Offensive showed
any signs of success was at Hue (see Map 20.1). There,
in the city that had served as the imperial center for
the Nguyen dynasty for two centuries, three under-
staffed Marine battalions fought alongside two US
Army battalions and 11 ARVN battalions in the most
intense urban battles of the war. The brutal fighting
lasted 26 days as the marines, denied much of the
available air cover because of foul weather, fought
building to building to root out the occupiers. Most
of the city lay in ruins by the time the marines overcame the last enemy positions. Thousands of civilians
were slain in the fighting.

The Tet Offensive was a military disaster for the
southern guerrillas. The fighting so devastated their
military infrastructure that they would cease to
be a major factor in the war as PAVN forces from
the North took over much of the fighting. Yet the
communists secured a political victory from the Tet
Offensive. In light of MACV's continuous claims
of progress, the Viet Cong's audacious attack made
the American generals' claims to have the enemy
nearly beaten appear unrealistic and untruthful. The
American press' surprise at the offensive and its erro-
neous reports about the guerrillas' success in several
key battles contributed to the growing weariness
regarding the conflict among the American public.
After President Johnson announced in March 1968
that he would not seek another term in office, the
war gradually but steadily lost support in the United
States. In November, Richard M. Nixon was elected
president on a platform constructed in part around
disengaging the United States from the war in Southeast Asia. Nixon's plan was to turn over the fighting
to the South Vietnamese while the American military provided economic and logistical support. He
called the plan "Vietnamization." And yet, even after

Figure 20.2   Lieutenant Commander Dorothy Ryan,
a Navy nurse on board the hospital ship USS *Repose*, off
South Vietnam, checks a wounded soldier's medical chart,
April 4, 1966. *Source:* © Everett Collection Historical /
Alamy.

Nixon's electoral victory, the US military in South
Vietnam would fight for four more years, suffering
half of its casualties during this period of withdrawal
(see Figure 20.2).

Vietnamization

Before leaving South Vietnam in April 1970 to
become chief of naval operations, Zumwalt began
overseeing the transfer of US Navy assets and duties
to South Vietnam's navy. Nixon's plan for the "Vietnamization" of the war put pressure on the US
Navy to rapidly transfer its well-functioning system
to a fledgling South Vietnamese navy. Ultimately,

the transfer plans were shown to have been predicated on unrealistic assumptions. The men of South Vietnam's navy were in no shape to assume the monumental tasks formerly performed by their US Navy counterparts. Underpaid and ignored by their commanding officers, many of the Vietnamese sailors and junior officers spent more time trying to secure food for themselves and their families than training for their added responsibilities. These distractions plagued the South Vietnamese sailors during this critical phase and prevented them from becoming competent in time to replace the Americans. But the Americans continued to rotate out. In the final years, the US Navy's role was limited. It provided offshore fire support for South Vietnamese troops, notably during the Easter Offensive of 1971. It increased the number of attack carriers at Yankee Station to five as Nixon sought to pressure Hanoi's negotiators with resumed bombing campaigns against North Vietnam and the mining of its harbors, including Haiphong, in mid-1972.

The Paris Peace Agreement, forged by Nixon's National Security Advisor Henry Kissinger and Hanoi's representative Le Duc Tho, marked the end of American direct involvement. By March 1973 all US combat personnel had left South Vietnam, but some military advisors and Marine security units remained. The fighting raged on for two more years as North Vietnam's forces and remnants of the Viet Cong campaigned against South Vietnam's military. Despite the bravery and competence of many of the South Vietnamese sailors trained by the Americans, South Vietnam's navy withered under the intense attacks.

Conclusion

Communist forces captured Saigon on April 30, 1975. With the utter defeat of South Vietnam it is understandable that some would see the US Navy's Vietnam War adventure as a complete and terrible waste. But history shows that the operational doctrine developed by the US Navy and the Marine Corps based on their experiences in Southeast Asia was enormously valuable in later conflicts. A decade of war had taught Navy leaders much about how to effectively conduct carrier-based operations, naval gunfire support, amphibious landings, coastal patrols, port security, and embargoes. The Top Gun program, established in 1968 to teach lessons in aerial combat, raised carrier aircraft to a 12:1 margin of victory in dogfights. Similarly, the SEALs, created in 1961–1962, cite the Vietnam War as the most important learning environment for their new unit. All of the doctrine written and refined on the water, in the air, and on the ground in Vietnam would be deployed to great impact in the decades to come in Libya, the Persian Gulf, the Balkans, and other spots around the world.

CHAPTER 21

Twilight of the Cold War

Contraction, Reform, and Revival

The US Navy faced daunting challenges and underwent unprecedented change during the final decades of the Cold War—years that spanned America's drawdown in Vietnam and its huge buildup for Operation Desert Storm. The demands of wartime operations in Southeast Asia diminished the strength and readiness of the fleet, thereby facilitating the Soviet navy's emergence as a global rival. Coinciding with America's withdrawal from Vietnam, Admiral Elmo R. "Bud" Zumwalt, Jr. (chief of naval operations (CNO), 1970–1974) implemented reforms designed to make the service more reflective of American society, while naval strategists debated how best to meet the Soviet challenge. From the late 1970s through the 1980s, a series of foreign crises influenced that debate, led to expansion of the fleet, and tested the Navy's capabilities. By 1990 the United States possessed a fleet of nearly 600 ships and a naval strategy to fight any war between the two superpowers on a worldwide basis, including operations against the Soviet homeland. Incredibly, just as the Navy's strength crested, the Soviet Union collapsed, and by 1991 the Cold War had ended, leaving the United States the world's only major military power.

Vietnam's Impact on the US Navy and the Rise of the Soviet Navy

America's long war in Vietnam profoundly affected the US Navy, as Presidents Lyndon Johnson and Richard Nixon slashed naval construction, modern-ization, and maintenance funds to pay for combat operations, resulting in an aged fleet manned by combat-weary officers and sailors whose morale was further eroded by their concern over the emerging power of the Soviet fleet. Competition within the Navy for scarce resources intensified contention between the nuclear propulsion and surface warfare branches. Led by Admiral Hyman G. Rickover, members of the nuclear community considered themselves an elite within the Navy. On the other hand, the surface officers and sailors viewed themselves as true warriors. They engaged the enemy and endured uninhabitable conditions on antiquated ships in the tropical environment of Vietnam, while nuclear-trained sailors, mostly submariners, lived and worked in relatively luxurious conditions. During the 1970s, competition between the communities would intensify as naval officers debated the size and composition of the fleet during a period of high inflation and shrinking defense budgets.

During World War II, the Soviet navy played a relatively small role in the huge conflict, primarily conducting coastal operations in support of the Red Army, but Admiral Sergei Gorshkov, commander-in-chief of the Soviet navy from 1956 to 1985, understood the strategic importance of sea power and steadily expanded his fleet, which by the time of the Cuban Missile Crisis was larger than the US fleet but not yet a serious rival, since the latter had 28 aircraft carriers and the Soviets had none.

America, Sea Power, and the World, First Edition. Edited by James C. Bradford.
© 2016 John Wiley & Sons, Inc. Published 2016 by John Wiley & Sons, Inc.

Gorshkov used the hard lessons from Cuba to obtain support for the construction of a large force of submarines, missile-firing surface combatants, and long-range naval aircraft that could challenge the US Navy's ability to exercise its power worldwide. During the 1967 Arab–Israeli War and the 1970 Jordanian Civil War, the Soviet navy was sufficiently strong to deter US military intervention. When the Arab–Israeli War of October 1973 erupted, the United States reinforced the Sixth Fleet from 43 to 65 warships; the Soviets increased their Fifth Eskadra (flotilla) from 55 to 98 ships. For the first time, the Soviet navy could compete on par with the US Navy. The war began when Egyptian and Syrian forces attacked Israeli-held territories along the Suez Canal and in the Golan Heights, respectively. Within two weeks, Israeli forces counterattacked, first halting the Syrian offensive and then crossing the canal into Egypt and trapping more than 30,000 Egyptian soldiers in the Sinai. At this critical moment, both the United States and the Soviet Union called for a ceasefire. The crisis came at the height of the Watergate scandal, which severely hobbled Nixon's ability to exercise power. The numerical superiority of the Soviet fleet, coupled with Nixon's diminished leadership, blocked the United States from supporting Israel's further prosecution of the war.

During the 1970s, the Soviets established bases in South Yemen and Vietnam. By the end of the decade, the Soviet navy outnumbered the US Navy in every class of warship except aircraft carriers, and it enjoyed a wide lead in anti-ship missiles (see Table 21.1). For the first time in three decades, Americans faced an adversary able to challenge its use of the seas. "The flag of the Soviet Navy flies over the oceans of the world," declared Gorshkov. "Sooner or later, the United States will have to understand it no longer has mastery of the seas."[1]

Gorshkov demonstrated growing Soviet power by directing two huge naval exercises: Okean (Ocean) I in 1970 and Okean II in 1975. In the first exercise, the Soviets deployed 206 warships, executing coordinated maneuvers in the Baltic, Black, and Mediterranean Seas and in the Arctic, Atlantic, Indian, and Pacific Oceans. During Okean II, the Soviet navy deployed 220 ships worldwide, attacked a simulated US carrier force entering the Norwegian Sea, and then moved south to practice disrupting NATO convoys transiting the Atlantic. The scope and offensive character of the Okean exercises and the Soviet navy's ability to deploy more ships than the US Navy during the 1973 Middle East conflict generated concern and undermined confidence among American naval officers and sailors. Reinforcing their apprehension were the writings of Gorshkov, collected in the book *Red Star Rising at Sea* (1974), in which he advocated an aggressive, expansive naval policy. By the 1980s, the Soviets were constructing their first large-deck carrier and were capable of sustained long-range naval deployments.

To counter the Soviet naval expansion of the 1970s, NATO strategy called for the US Navy to keep open the "sea lines of communication" (SLOC) between North America and Europe, while Allied land and air forces conducted a conventional war against the Soviet Union and its Warsaw Pact allies along the central front in Germany. Admiral Zumwalt doubted the Navy's ability to carry out this role, commenting that "the odds are that we would be unable" to protect both the Atlantic SLOC and NATO's flanks.[2] Planners began speaking of "sea denial," a strategy that involved preventing an enemy from using the sea but not necessarily being able to use it for one's own purpose, rather than Mahan's "command of the sea," in which a nation could use the sea as it wished while denying its use to an enemy. In 1978, the Soviet navy had 740 major warships (ships longer than 250 feet) while the US Navy possessed only 289. This disparity was the result of years of Soviet naval construction unmatched by the United States. From 1966 to 1970, the US Navy commissioned 88 warships, the Soviets 209. Every warship category in the US Fleet was affected by the slow rate of new construction. In 1968, the US Navy had 31 aircraft carriers; by 1978, only 21. The inventory of cruisers declined from 34 to 26; amphibious ships from 77 to 36; destroyers from 227 to 62; and conventional submarines from 72 to 10.

---

[1] Sergei G. Gorshkov, *Red Star Rising at Sea* (1974), 141.

[2] As quoted in Malcolm Muir, Jr., *Black Shoes and Blue Water: Surface Warfare in the United States Navy, 1945–1975* (1996), 202.

The only gain in the American inventory was nuclear submarines, which increased in number from 40 in 1964 to 109 in 1978. The American fleet was also aging. By 1970, nearly 60 percent of US ships were more than 20 years old, while only 1 percent of Soviet warships had seen service that long. Zumwalt readily acknowledged the "accelerating obsolescence of the US Navy … as opposed to the impressive growth and modernization of the Soviet Navy."[3] Fortunately, during Zumwalt's term as CNO (1970–1974), the Nixon administration implemented a "Vietnamization" policy, which reduced US combat operations in Southeast Asia, making it possible to retire more World War II-era ships and free up additional funds for new construction.

As the number of warships shrank, the Navy grappled with an increasingly voluble debate over the structure of the fleet. Since World War II, the service had been dominated by carrier admirals, who sought the construction of ever larger flattops. Furthermore, in 1974, Admiral Rickover won passage of a law—later repealed—mandating nuclear propulsion for combatants over 8,000 tons. A significant number of officers questioned Rickover's views and were concerned that decades of emphasis on Cold War power projection had pushed aside another important mission: sea control. They argued that the emphasis on large-deck carriers had created a Navy as unbalanced as the one dominated by the big-gun battleship prior to World War II.

Zumwalt agreed and proposed a fleet comprised of a "high–low" mix of ships that could effectively stretch scarce construction funds while enabling the Navy to meet its global responsibilities.[4] At the high end would be carriers, cruisers, ballistic missile submarines, and new *Spruance*-class destroyers; at the low end would be sea-control ships of approximately 17,000 tons carrying helicopters and vertical and/or short takeoff and landing (V/STOL) aircraft, frigates, hydrofoils, and ocean-skimming surface effect ships. Zumwalt argued that several ships of moderate capability could contribute more to the mission of sea control than one large carrier. His critics questioned how a less powerful ship could secure an area in which a super-carrier could not survive.

Zumwalt oversaw the decommissioning of older cruisers and destroyers, reducing the number of those ships from 261 in 1968 to 88 in 1978. Funds generated by ship retirements were used to pay for new warship classes, aircraft, and weapon systems. Between 1968 and 1978, the inventory of frigates increased from 50 to 64, and the number of nuclear attack submarines more than doubled from 33 to 68. *Spruance*-class destroyers (31 commissioned between 1975 and 1983) embarked Light Airborne Multi-Purpose System (LAMPS) helicopters to conduct their primary mission of antisubmarine warfare. *Ticonderoga*-class guided-missile cruisers (27 commissioned between 1983 and 1994) incorporated the Aegis Combat System, built around the SPY-1 phased-array radar, to provide advanced air defense. Both of these gas-turbine-powered warships were included in the high end of the mix. Most numerous among low-end combatants were the gas-turbine-driven *Oliver Hazard Perry*-class guided-missile frigates (51 commissioned between 1977 and 1989), designed as ocean escort ships. In the air, the F-14 Tomcat replaced the F-4 Phantom II as the Navy's premier fighter plane, and F/A-18 Hornets succeeded F-4s, A-4 Skyhawks, and A-7 Corsair IIs, providing the fleet with fighter-attack versatility in a single aircraft. Finally, Harpoon and Tomahawk cruise missiles, which could be launched by a variety of platforms, added a strike capability against enemy warships and land targets.

In 1978, Admiral James L. Holloway III, Zumwalt's successor as CNO (1974–1978), argued that the US Navy was still superior to the Soviet fleet. The Navy's sizable lead in aircraft carriers permitted it to project air power against an enemy fleet or targets ashore. Similarly, although the Soviet Union possessed 294 submarines to the US Navy's 119, the Soviet submarine fleet included 172 non-nuclear submarines, while only 10 American boats were conventionally powered. Admiral Rickover was not impressed with these statistics, and he surprised members of Congress when he informed them that, if he had the choice, he

[3] Elmo R. Zumwalt, Jr., *On Watch* (1976), 59.
[4] Ibid., 72.

would prefer to command the Soviet submarine fleet, if war broke out between the superpowers, believing that it had a better chance of winning. Zumwalt agreed that the US Navy would probably lose a shooting war with the Soviet fleet. From retirement, he reflected: "The odds are that we would have lost a war with the Soviet Union if we had had to fight it any year since 1970; the navy dropped to about a 35 percent probability of victory."[5]

Z-Grams: Zumwalt's Reforms

The end of conscription in 1973, another major consequence of the Vietnam War, meant that the Navy would have to rely on an all-volunteer personnel base to operate its increasingly sophisticated ships and weaponry. Zumwalt, who became CNO at age 49, the youngest man to hold the post, was convinced that the Navy could not remain isolated from the cultural revolution and changes in race relations that swept American society in the 1960s. He believed the service had to change in order to recruit sailors for the volunteer military and retain experienced service members.

To foster the needed changes, Zumwalt issued a series of directives, or "Z-grams," that eliminated many "Mickey Mouse" rules and regulations that had been intended to maintain good order and discipline but, in the words of one senior naval officer, had only managed "to piss people off."[6] Zumwalt also took steps to extend shore tours and to permanently base ships overseas to decrease the length of time that sailors served away from their families. Finally, he directed efforts to make the Navy—a service long dominated by white males—more open to minorities and women.

Two Z-grams were so controversial and far-reaching that they defined his term as CNO. Z-57 ("Demeaning and Abrasive Regulations, Elimination of"), released in November 1970, delighted sailors and junior officers but alarmed traditionalists, who believed it would breed permissiveness in the fleet. Aimed at ridding the service of trivial restrictions and

unnecessary inconveniences, it required, for example, that every naval base provide check-cashing services; permitted sailors to wear working uniforms to meals on board ship and on base, and civilian clothes while on liberty; and allowed sailors to drive motorcycles on naval installations. Famously, it allowed sailors to grow beards, mustaches, and sideburns. Later, junior sailors adopted the same dress uniform and cover worn by officers and chief petty officers, thus retiring the iconic "Cracker Jack" uniform.

Z-66 ("Equal Opportunity in the Navy"), announced five weeks after Z-57, addressed the long-neglected needs of minority sailors, especially African Americans, stating emphatically: "Ours must be a Navy family that recognizes no artificial barriers of race, color, or religion. There is no black Navy, no white Navy—just one Navy—the United States Navy."[7] It directed commanding officers to appoint an officer or petty officer as special assistant for minority affairs and to ensure the serving of ethnic foods, appropriate training for barbers and beauticians, and acquisition of books, magazines, and recordings of interest to black sailors.

A third groundbreaking directive, Z-116 ("Equal Rights and Opportunities for Women in the Navy"), did not elicit the same reaction as the other two directives when it was issued in August 1972. It opened a "full spectrum of challenging billets" to female personnel, including service as aides, briefers, detailers, service college instructors, attachés, chaplains, civil engineers, senior enlisted advisors, and commanders of major shore installations.[8] In 1976, women were admitted to the US Naval Academy, and by 2014 the Navy had opened all warfare branches to women except special warfare.

Less than two years after Zumwalt issued Z-66, riots and disturbances on three ships dramatically illustrated how poorly prepared Navy leaders were for the generation of sailors who had been shaped by the societal changes wrought by the tumultuous 1960s. The first outburst took place on the carrier *Kitty Hawk*. In

---

[5] As quoted in Stephen Howarth, *To Shining Sea: A History of the United States Navy, 1775–1998* (1999), 531.
[6] As quoted in ibid., 526.
[7] Zumwalt, *On Watch,* 204.
[8] Ibid., 264.

Elmo R. Zumwalt, Jr.

Regarded by many as a visionary naval leader and by others as a radical assailant on naval tradition, Admiral "Bud" Zumwalt's (1920–2000) efforts to improve morale, increase reenlistments, and end institutional racism and sexism stood the Navy establishment on its head in the early 1970s. As commander of the naval forces in Vietnam and later CNO, Zumwalt knew full well how long combat deployments and anti-war protests, followed by the postwar drawdown, encouraged many experienced sailors to leave the service. Navy leaders seemed out of touch with changing social norms regarding young Americans, in general, and with women and minorities, in particular. Pride and professionalism declined, and reenlistments dwindled to an alarmingly low level. For a service dependent on a large pool of experienced, tech-savvy sailors, this was—in Zumwalt's words—a "catastrophic situation."[9]

One measure of the success of Zumwalt's innovative reforms was that reenlistments skyrocketed by 70 percent in one year. Guiding the service during a time of social turmoil, political crisis, and anti-

military sentiment, he never backed down from his efforts to improve Navy life. In retirement, Zumwalt stood by his decision to use the defoliant Agent Orange as a means to save American lives in Vietnam, even though his son, Elmo III, a Swift Boat skipper, died of cancer caused by the chemical, whose long-

term health effects were unknown during the war. At Zumwalt's funeral in 2000, President Bill Clinton hailed him as "the conscience of the Navy."[10] In 2014, the Navy honored the reforming CNO by christening the *Zumwalt* (DDG-1000), the lead vessel of a class of revolutionary stealth warships.

Elmo R. Zumwalt, Jr. (seated, center left in white uniform) meeting with sailors in Yokosuka, Japan, in 1971. *Source:* Photographed by PH2 Edward C. Mucma. Official US Navy photograph. US Naval History and Heritage Command # NH 97204.

October 1972, the strains of eight months of combat had reached a boiling point, and sailors from the ship were involved in a brawl while on liberty in Subic Bay, the Philippines. The cause of the fight and the identity of those involved are not fully known, but a few days later a black sailor refused to answer questions regard-

ing the fight, inciting a nine-hour shipboard rampage that involved at least 100 black crewmembers and that injured approximately 60 sailors. The Navy charged several sailors, all black, with rioting and assault and ordered they be court martialed. A few days later, another violent altercation occurred between white

---

[9] As quoted in Frederick H. Hartmann, *Naval Renaissance: The US Navy in the 1980s* (1990), 18.

[10] William J. Clinton, *Public Papers of the Presidents of the United States: William J. Clinton, 2000–2001* (2001), 1:23.

and black sailors on the oiler *Hassayampa*, while the ship was docked in Subic Bay. Six black sailors were charged with rioting and assault. In early November, several sailors, mostly black, refused to carry out their duties on board the carrier *Constellation*, while it was operating off the coast of California. After the ship's return to San Diego, more than 100 crewmembers, a few of them white, resumed the protest on the pier at North Island. They displayed clenched fists, used inflammatory rhetoric, and succeeded in attracting the attention of the media. A few sailors received dishonorable discharges, and several others received nonjudicial punishment for being absent without leave.

In the early 1970s, drug abuse was widespread in the fleet, reenlistments of first-term sailors stood at 10 percent, and the desertion rate reached an alarming level. Many officers and senior enlisted personnel blamed the problems on the Z-grams, which they claimed had undermined their authority and eroded discipline in the fleet. The press reported that a number of congressional leaders and active-duty and retired admirals were trying to oust Zumwalt. The CNO survived the wave of opposition, asserted that the Navy's problems reflected changes ongoing in American society, and pledged to continue fighting for equal opportunities for all personnel. He saw the disturbances as "an opportunity to nail equal treatment for minorities and women so firmly into the Navy that anyone would have trouble removing it."[11] He succeeded: his policies on race and gender could not be ignored and were woven into the fabric of the naval service.

The Rickover Effect and the Advent of the Surface Warfare Community

Another problem affecting the Navy in the 1970s was the continuing acrimony between the Navy's warfare communities. In his memoirs, *On Watch* (1976), Zumwalt wrote: "For the last quarter-century ...

there have been three powerful 'unions' ... in the Navy—the aviators, the submariners, and the surface sailors—and their rivalry has played a large part in the way the Navy has been directed."[12] An important factor determining the degree to which competition is either healthy or harmful to a service is how camaraderie is nurtured within a community and how members of one community interact with members of the others. Rickover convinced Congress of the virtues of nuclear propulsion, which he regarded as a special "vocation" within the service; imposed a requirement on the US Naval Academy that 80 percent of its graduates major in math, science, and engineering to prepare them for entry into his nuclear training pipeline; and personally interviewed and approved all officer candidates for his exclusive program—and by extension the submarine service. Rickover opposed many of Zumwalt's reforms, such as acceptance of facial hair, and often denigrated the Navy's other communities.

Rickover's methods were particularly detrimental during the Vietnam War, when manpower and material resources were scarce and the competition for them was especially keen. By the late 1970s, naval officers were going public with their disdain for the nuclear community, in general, and Rickover, in particular. Writing in the US Naval Institute's *Proceedings* in 1978, one author argued that a majority of naval officers "generally sense that the submariner is not a 'team player.' He expects the rest of the service to bend to his requirements ... No outsider must be allowed to criticize or even scrutinize the nucs' [officers in the nuclear power community] actions or programs."[13] John F. Lehman, Jr., President Ronald Reagan's first Secretary of the Navy (1981–1987), a reserve naval flight officer and leading Rickover critic, charged that "the ultimate allegiance of all nuclear-trained officers was conditioned ... to lie with [Rickover's command, the Division of Naval Reactors,] rather than the operational navy."[14]

The office of Deputy CNO for Air had been established in 1943, but no similar billet for the surface

[11] Ibid., 265.

[12] Ibid., 63.

[13] K. W. Estes, [Commentary on] "'Some Thoughts from an Unrepentant Nuc' (see J. D. Jones, *Proceedings* (November 1977), pp. 86–87); 'Run Deep? Yea. Run Silent? Nay' (see E. R. Callahan, *Proceedings* (January 1978), p. 90)," Naval Institute *Proceedings*, 104:2 (February 1978), 21.

[14] John F. Lehman, Jr., *Command of the Seas* (1988), 22.

Aegis Combat System

Development of the Aegis combat system, a vital component of the US combat fleet of the twenty-first century, began in the early 1960s. At the heart of Aegis—hailed as "the Shield of the Fleet"—is the SPY-1 phased-array radar, which can trace hundreds of air contacts at distances reaching hundreds of miles. Employing powerful computers, highly capable sensors, and sophisticated weapons, the system can engage and destroy several targets simultaneously. Aegis entered service in 1983 in *Ticonderoga*, the first of 27 guided-missile cruisers, and remains the principal weapons system of the *Arleigh Burke* class of guided-missile destroyers, more than 60 of which have joined the fleet since 1991.

USS *Ticonderoga*, the first warship equipped with the Aegis Combat System, test fires a standard surface-to-air missile. *Source:* Photo Robert M. Cieri.

Old salts would be amazed if they entered the combat information center of an Aegis-equipped warship; it is a dark, air-conditioned room filled with four large screens and numerous smaller radar consoles displaying tactical information obtained by air, surface, and satellite assets and shared in a real-time, global, computer-linked network.

The surface-to-air missile system associated with Aegis is the very effective, yet simply named, "standard missile" (SM). The single-stage, medium-range SM-2 MR missile and two-stage, extended-range SM-2 ER missile entered service in the early 1980s, intended specifically for use on Aegis warships. Both missiles use mid-flight guidance information uplinked from the SPY-1 radar and contain advanced features to defeat sea-skimming cruise missiles and frustrate enemy electronic countermeasures. In the early 2000s, the three-stage SM-3 was introduced to the fleet. Capable of low outer-space altitude, the missile has intercepted numerous test ballistic missiles. In 2008, the cruiser *Lake Eire* destroyed a crippled satellite prior to its atmospheric reentry. More than a shield for the US Fleet, Aegis—specifically the Aegis Ballistic Missile Defense System—provides vital protection for the United States and its allies, five of whom (Australia, Japan, Norway, South Korea, and Spain) operate their own Aegis warships.

community existed, and this omission disturbed surface warfare officers, who recognized that submariners had Rickover as their advocate and aviators had a representative in the CNO's office. Furthermore, submariners were promoted to fleet and higher-level commands during the Vietnam War, although none had commanded a submarine crew exceeding 150 men, and aviators achieved flag rank at a very high rate. Many surface officers concluded that these results were due largely to the other communities having agents in the highest echelons of the Department of the Navy. The status of the surface community improved in 1971, when the office of Deputy CNO for Surface Warfare was established, giving surface officers a strong organizational base and greater clout, and in 1975, when they earned recognition as a separate warfare community, with their own distinctive badge—swords crossed behind the bow of a warship cutting through the water—comparable to the dolphins worn by submariners and the wings of aviators.

President Carter and the SLOC Strategy

The Watergate scandal forced Nixon from office in August 1974, and his successor, Gerald Ford, lost the presidency in 1976 to former Georgia governor Jimmy Carter. A 1946 graduate of the US Naval Academy, Carter had joined the nuclear submarine service and served on active duty until 1953, when he left the Navy to run his family's businesses.

The Navy of the mid-1970s was a force of increasingly fewer and older combatants, and there was hope within the service that Carter would reverse its declining fortunes, but he did not. The new president initially emphasized human rights over the containment of international communism. He believed that, since World War II, the United States had focused too little on slowing the arms race and that the United States could induce the Soviet Union to limit its defense budget, if it did so first.

In 1978, a third nuclear-powered *Nimitz*-class carrier was under construction. Despite the high cost—$2 billion each—the Navy planned a fourth carrier, but in 1977 Congress refused to fund the ship, and, to the Navy's disappointment, Carter accepted its decision. The following year, Carter proposed cutting Ford's naval construction plan for 1979–1984 from more than 150 new ships to only 70. Taken aback by Carter's building program, Congress authorized the fourth *Nimitz*-class carrier, but Carter vetoed the bill.

By 1978, the disparity in the number of ships in the US and Soviet navies was dramatic. Only in aircraft carriers did the US Navy enjoy an absolute superiority over the Soviet Navy: 21 to three. In all other

classes of major surface warships, the Soviet Union outnumbered the United States 443 to 196. The gap between the two submarine fleets was also huge: 294 Soviet submarines to 119 for the United States. US submariners were encouraged by the commissioning in 1976 of the first of 62 *Los Angeles*-class nuclear attack submarines and by plans for 18 new *Ohio*-class ballistic missile submarines, which would begin entering service in 1981 (see Table 21.1). Aviators and surface warfare officers were less sanguine. Carter was not the Navy's savior, and there was very little agreement within the government over the Navy's principal missions and how to structure the fleet to meet them.

Carter subscribed to the NATO strategy that called for employing most of America's military resources to support the Allied front in Germany. The Navy's primary role would be the defense of Atlantic SLOC, a task that would not require many large-deck carriers. Carter's SLOC strategy prompted Admiral Holloway and a number of naval analysts to warn that, if the Navy implemented this policy, it would be unable to perform other vital wartime tasks. Since a large portion of the US Pacific Fleet would sprint to the Atlantic at the onset of war, the strategy essentially ceded the Pacific theater to the Soviets. In effect, the United States was replacing a global maritime strategy with a continental one. In 1977, Holloway published *Sea Plan 2000*, a report in which he challenged Carter's focus on Europe. He argued for a fleet of at least 12 carrier battle groups, which would permit the Navy to carry out the twin missions of sea control (meaning the reinforcement of NATO's central front) and power projection (which would enable the fleet to confront the Soviets on NATO's northern and southern flanks and in the Pacific). In the end, Carter agreed to retain a dozen carriers, but he did not support the CNO's call for a new class of strike cruiser, which would have combined nuclear power and the Aegis air defense system in the same warship.

The new CNO, Admiral Thomas B. Hayward (1978–1982) also challenged Carter's SLOC strategy. Testifying before a congressional subcommittee in February 1979, he argued that the United States must maintain "maritime superiority" over the Soviets in order "to protect its interests worldwide, and to deter actions which could lead to a major war."[15] If deterrence failed, the Navy would aggressively deploy its carrier forces to take the fight to the enemy. No region of the globe would be handed to the Soviet Union. Soviet forces based at the extreme ends of the Russian land mass would be pinned down, forcing the transfer of Soviet troops from the European front.

Crises in Iran and Afghanistan

Hayward's view of the importance of global naval power was validated by crises in the Middle East during Carter's presidency. After Britain withdrew the Royal Navy from the Persian Gulf in 1968, the United States took steps to fill the void. To protect the flow of oil from the Gulf to the United States, Europe, and Japan, the US Navy established a permanent logistical base on Diego Garcia, a British possession in the Indian Ocean, and crafted a strategy to keep the United States from becoming directly involved militarily in the region.

Beginning with the Nixon administration, the United States had relied on Iran to maintain stability in the Gulf and provided its ruler, Mohammad Reza Shah Pahlavi, with a huge arsenal of modern weapons. Carter dangled more arms as an incentive for the shah to expand liberal reforms begun in the 1960s, but Carter's policy backfired when the shah's efforts at liberalization tore the lid off decades of Iranian resentment against both him and the West. In early 1979, Carter watched helplessly as anti-Western militants, led by the Shi'ite cleric Ayatollah Ruhollah Khomeini, swept the shah from power and established an Islamic republic. In November, student revolutionaries seized the US embassy and took 66 American hostages; the Iranian government supported their actions. The students demanded that Carter, who had admitted the shah to the United States for cancer treatment, return him to Iran to stand trial. Four days after the embassy takeover, Congress authorized the fourth *Nimitz*-class carrier; this time, Carter concurred.

Less than two months after the embassy takeover, Carter was alerted that a Soviet invasion of Afghanistan was imminent. He warned the Kremlin against such a move, but Soviet leaders ignored him, and in late December the Soviet military rolled into Afghanistan to prop up a Marxist dictator under assault from Muslim insurgents.

The turmoil in the region raised fears in the West that the Soviet Union was intent on seizing control of the Gulf and its oil reserves. Carter recognized the threat and adopted a hard line toward the Soviets. Grain sales and high-technology transfers were halted, and a new strategic arms-limitation treaty was withdrawn from the Senate. In January 1980, Carter issued a policy statement, subsequently known as the "Carter Doctrine," that declared: "An attempt by any outside force to gain control of the Persian Gulf region will be regarded as an assault on the vital interests of the United States … and such an assault will be repelled by any means necessary, including military force."[16]

The crises marked a turning point for both the president and the Navy. Carter authorized the creation of a rapid-deployment joint task force—composed of three US Marine brigades and their logistical components—that later became the US Central Command. Putting teeth into the Carter Doctrine, the Navy maintained two carrier battle groups and an amphibious task force in the Arabian Sea and positioned seven supply ships at Diego Garcia. These deployments buttressed the Navy's arguments for a fleet capable of meeting the nation's global commitments. The Arabian Sea and adjoining Gulf of Oman were exceptionally challenging waters in which to sustain high-tempo operations. It took weeks for ships to reach station from US bases, vessels were completely dependent on underway replenishment, and warships operating in the constrained waters of the Strait of Hormuz and the Gulf of Oman were vulnerable to mines and land-based cruise missiles.

By the spring of 1980, nearly 30 US warships were operating in the region, but the hostages were still held by their Iranian captors. Unable to gain their freedom through diplomacy and military pressure or by economic and political sanctions, Carter author-

---

[15] Hayward, Opening Statement in Testimony before the Subcommittee on Seapower and Strategic and Critical Materials of the House Armed Services Committee, reprinted as "The Future of US Sea Power," Naval Institute *Proceedings*, 105:5 (May 1979), 66.

[16] Jimmy Carter, *Public Papers of the Presidents of the United States: Jimmy Carter, 1980–81* (1981), 1:197.

Table 21.1 US and Soviet fleets, 1981.

	United States	Soviet Union
Aircraft carriers		
Large deck, attack	13	0
VSTOL	0	2
Helicopter	7	2
Submarines		
Nuclear ballistic missile	35	69
Nuclear cruise missile	0	50
Nuclear scout/attack	78	60
Diesel-electric ballistic missile	0	18
Diesel-electric cruise missile	0	20
Diesel-electric scout/attack	5	160
Cruisers	27	36
Destroyers	89	68
Frigates	74	168
Minesweepers	25	395
Patrol	3	395
Patrol missile craft	0	145
Amphibious warfare ships	65	86
Auxiliaries and misc.	122	756

Source: Stephen S. Roberts, *The US Navy in the 1980s* (1981), 13; Department of Defense, *Soviet Military Power* (1981), 40.

ized a daring rescue mission, codenamed Operation Eagle Claw. In late April, eight RH-53D helicopters launched from the *Nimitz* and joined six US Air Force C-130 transports flying out of Oman, but the mission was aborted after three helicopters reported mechanical failures. At a staging area in the Iranian desert, dubbed "Desert One," the operable helicopters and transport planes were preparing for takeoff when a fourth helicopter collided with a transport, causing a huge inferno that claimed the lives of eight servicemen.

The Desert One tragedy tarnished America's international prestige and, combined with high inflation and unemployment at home, undermined Carter's campaign for reelection. In November, Ronald Reagan won the presidency in a landslide, but for Carter the Iranian hostage affair had one final insult: the Americans, who had been held captive for 444 days, were not released until the precise moment that his term expired.

Reagan, Lehman, and the 600-Ship Navy

Reagan's inauguration signaled a major shift in America's foreign and defense policies. He promised that the United States would never again be humiliated by another country, vowed to contain the power of the Soviet Union, asserted America's right to intervene around the globe to defend American citizens and interests, and initiated the largest peacetime military expansion in US history.

His Secretary of the Navy, John Lehman, embraced Admiral Hayward's principles of maritime superiority, which became known as the "Maritime Strategy." While endorsed by the new administration, it never officially became part of the national military strategy, largely because of its central assumption that a global conflict with the Soviet Union would not escalate to nuclear war. To achieve naval superiority, Lehman promoted a three-ocean, 600-ship fleet composed of 15 aircraft carrier battle groups; four surface action groups built around modernized World War II-era battleships; over 200 cruisers, destroyers, and frigates; over 100 auxiliaries; enough amphibious warfare vessels to simultaneously deploy a Marine Amphibious Force of over 50,000 troops and a Marine Amphibious Brigade of nearly 16,000 marines; and 100 nuclear attack submarines. Aviators would receive upgraded versions of all aircraft, including a new LAMPS helicopter. Harpoon anti-ship cruise missiles would be installed on a variety of ships, submarines, and aircraft, and Tomahawk anti-ship and land-attack cruise missiles would be deployed on both surface ships and submarines.

Backed by Reagan's steadfast commitment to rebuild America's military, Lehman guided the huge naval expansion. In fiscal year 1982, the Navy received an increase of $5 billion over Carter's budget, but before long journalists reported that the Navy was spending hundreds of dollars for such ordinary items as hammers, ash trays, and toilet seats. Lehman met the allegations head on and overhauled the Navy's contracting process. He was determined that the new fleet would be good value for American taxpayers. For example, by promoting competition in the shipbuilding industry, the price of an Aegis cruiser dropped from $1.2 billion per ship to $900 million.

Lehman did not shrink from making controversial changes. For example, he overturned a number of Zumwalt's reforms. Sailors could no longer wear beards, and they returned to the traditional "Cracker Jack" uniform. Significantly, he pushed Rickover into retirement in 1982, eliminating his extraordinary influence over the composition of the fleet. On the other hand, Lehman sometimes resisted reform, as, for instance, when Congress, in the aftermath of the trouble-plagued 1983 Grenada operation, took steps to improve inter-service operability by increasing the power of the chairman of the Joint Chiefs of Staff, strengthening the chain of command between the president and regional or specified commanders, and requiring all colonels and Navy captains to serve in a joint-duty assignment to be eligible for promotion to flag rank. Dedicated to the Navy's culture, Lehman unsuccessfully fought these reforms, which were incorporated in the Goldwater–Nichols Department of Defense Reorganization Act of 1986. Upon leaving office in 1987, he could validly assert that a "few battles were lost, but in the main we succeeded in what we set out to do. We left the navy better than we found it."[17] Nevertheless, despite his strenuous efforts, the fleet never reached his goal of 600 ships.

Debate over the Maritime Strategy

Over the course of the 1980s, critics disparaged the Maritime Strategy as being more a rationalization for 600 ships than a serious plan for deploying the fleet in wartime. They regarded the "forward operations" against distant Soviet bases that the strategy called for to be suicidal and considered the plan to destroy Soviet ballistic missile submarines at the onset of hostilities as a move guaranteed to trigger a nuclear conflict. Retired Admiral Stansfield Turner knew of no admiral who would carry out the daring tactics required by the strategy. "Our carrier forces would clearly not survive a thrust against Murmansk," Zumwalt added. "The Soviet Union in that kind of war would use tactical nuclear weapons against them."[18]

Lehman disagreed. As he saw it, the most effective way to support the NATO front was not "vertical escalation" (employing ever more destructive weapons, moving from the use of conventional weapons first to tactical and then to theater nuclear weapons). The threat of "horizontal escalation" promised to be a more effective deterrent. The Maritime Strategy called for the United States and its allies to respond to any Soviet aggression in Central Europe with carrier raids and amphibious assaults against the Soviet flanks in the Black, Mediterranean, and Norwegian Seas and the Pacific. These

---

[17] Lehman, *Command of the Seas*, 430.

[18] As quoted in Howarth, *To Shining Sea*, 541–542.

assaults would be launched from bases encircling Soviet Russia and would include Marines stationed in Okinawa and serving afloat in the Mediterranean. This would compel the Soviets to pull forces from the central front, thus weakening their European offensive. According to the strategy's main tenet, the Navy would seize the initiative from the Soviets and, rather than defend SLOC between the United States and its allies, would block Soviet submarines from passing Greenland, Iceland, and Norway to enter the Atlantic and would attack the Soviet navy in its homeports. This would turn the war into a prolonged, global, conventional conflict that the West, with its superior resources, would win. According to Lehman's strategic vision, the United States must be prepared to win the war, not merely contain it. This offensive strategy, he believed, would prove to be a powerful deterrent against Soviet aggression.

Global Operations under Reagan

Reagan's use of naval power differed markedly from Carter's, and during his presidency the Navy operated under increasingly challenging and more dangerous circumstances. In August 1981, the US Sixth Fleet demonstrated America's renewed resolve when two F-14 Tomcats from the *Nimitz* downed two Libyan jets that had fired on them over the Gulf of Sidra. Since 1973, the Libyan dictator Muammar al-Gaddafi had claimed the Gulf as Libyan territorial waters. The United States rejected his illegal claim, and the Sixth Fleet conducted annual exercises in the Gulf until 1980, when Carter halted them out of concern that they might provoke a new international crisis; Reagan resumed them. Gaddafi suffered a humiliating defeat, and the freedom to operate ships in international waters was upheld.

The tragedy in Lebanon and the invasion of Grenada were the most significant military events of 1982–1983. In August 1982, the Sixth Fleet landed 800 US Marines in Beirut to supervise, along with French and Italian troops, the evacuation of 12,000 Palestine Liberation Organization (PLO) fighters, who were trapped by Israeli forces that had invaded

Lebanon intent on destroying the PLO. The marines left Beirut following the evacuation of the PLO fighters but returned a few weeks later, as part of a multinational peacekeeping force, following the assassination of Lebanon's president-elect. Despite their heroic efforts, Lebanon disintegrated into civil war. Some belligerents turned their wrath on the peacekeepers, namely the 1,500 marines of the 24th Marine Amphibious Unit, hunkered down at the Beirut airport, where they became targets for snipers and mortar attacks (see Figure 21.1). Naval gunfire directed at Muslim militia positions near the airport brought the Marines little relief. On October 23, a suicide bomber from the Shi'ite organization Islamic Jihad detonated a huge truck bomb at the Marines' barracks, killing 241 servicemen (see Map 21.1).

Reagan remained committed to the Marine deployment, but by year's end Lebanon had ceased to exist as a viable state, and in February 1984 he ordered the beleaguered marines to redeploy to ships offshore. The Lebanese debacle, like the Vietnam experience, spoke to the inadvisability of sending troops into danger without an articulated mission.

Two days after the Beirut bombing, US forces invaded the Caribbean island of Grenada, a former British colony, "to restore order and democracy" and evacuate approximately 1,000 Americans, many of them medical students at a hospital near the capital at St. George's.[19] Radical Marxists had recently overthrown the government and murdered the prime minister. Furthermore, the Soviet Union had built a naval base, barracks, supply depots, and training facilities on the island, and Cubans were working on a 10,000-foot runway at Point Salines Airport that clearly had military applications. Refusing to let Granada become a Soviet bastion, Reagan ordered the invasion (see Map 21.2). Vice Admiral Joseph Metcalf III, commander of the US Second Fleet, directed Operation Urgent Fury, which was an invasion spearheaded by 1,900 marines of the 22nd Marine Amphibious Unit, who seized Pearls Airport and the harbor at Grenville before dawn on October 25. Shortly thereafter troops of the US Army's 82nd Airborne Division parachuted onto the new runway at Port Salines. Navy SEALs

---

[19] Ronald Reagan, *Public Papers of the Presidents of the United States: Ronald Reagan, 1983* (1985), 2:1520–1521.

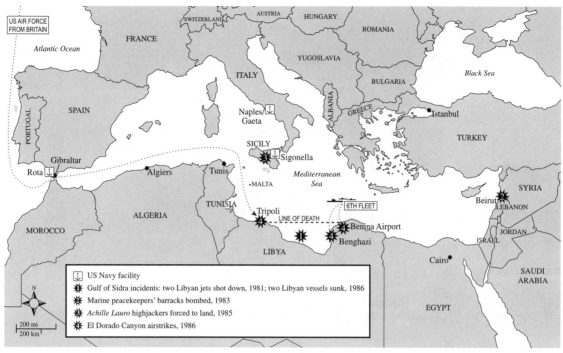

Map 21.1   Mediterranean Sea, 1975–1990.

and Army Rangers secured other strategic areas, as a dozen warships—led by the carrier *Independence* and the amphibious assault ship *Guam*—provided support from off shore. Although a rapid success—there were only 18 US fatalities—Urgent Fury was plagued by inadequate intelligence and poor communications and coordination, and the outcome prompted calls to improve joint-service planning and operations.

By 1985, terrorism was a major global concern. That year, the US State Department recorded nearly 700 terrorist incidents. In June, gunmen from the Shi'ite organization Hezbollah seized an American airliner, killed a Navy petty officer, and held the other passengers hostage for nearly two weeks. The administration won their freedom through lengthy negotiations, not military force. In October, four terrorists from the Palestine Liberation Front seized the Italian cruise ship *Achille Lauro* and murdered an elderly, wheelchair-bound American. Soon afterward, F-14s from the carrier *Saratoga* intercepted an Egyptian airliner flying the perpetrators to Tunisia and forced the plane

to land at Sigonella naval air station in Sicily, where Italian authorities arrested the hijackers and charged them with kidnapping and murder. But the victory was short lived. In late December, Palestinian terrorists attacked the Rome and Vienna airports, leaving 20 travelers dead, including five Americans. Investigators discovered that Gaddafi, a major proponent of terrorism, had supported the attacks. American military power was soon brought to bear on the Libyan dictator.

In March 1986, a battle force composed of the carriers *America*, *Coral Sea*, and *Saratoga* and 23 other warships conducted a huge freedom-of-navigation operation in the Gulf of Sidra (see Map 21.1). When the Libyans fired missiles at American fighter aircraft and threatened the force with missile boats, the Sixth Fleet commander, Vice Admiral Frank B. Kelso II, retaliated with a precision airstrike against a land-based missile battery (see Figure 21.2). A-6E Intruders armed with Harpoons and cluster bombs subsequently destroyed a Libyan fast missile boat and missile corvette.

Figure 21.1   Marine checkpoint in Beirut, August 1982. *Source:* US Marine Corps Archives.

To avenge his humiliating defeat, Gaddafi ordered Libyan agents based in East Berlin to bomb a West Berlin discotheque popular with US servicemen. The explosion killed two American soldiers and a Turkish woman. When US and British intelligence services intercepted messages between Tripoli and East Berlin that proved Tripoli's involvement in the attack, Reagan authorized Operation El Dorado Canyon, a mid-April strike on Libya. With approval from British Prime Minister Margaret Thatcher, US Air Force F-111F fighter-bombers, based in England, joined A-6Es flying from the carriers *America* and *Coral Sea* in attacking terrorist facilities and airfields in and around Benghazi and Tripoli. A stunned Gaddafi—who went into hiding for a month after

the strike—received the unmistakable message that he could no longer attack Americans without paying a huge penalty.

If the Mediterranean was the focus of American naval power in 1986, over the next two years the focus shifted to the Persian Gulf, where the Iran–Iraq War had raged since 1980. Begun when Iraqi dictator Saddam Hussein invaded his unstable neighbor, by mid-decade, the conflict had become a war of attrition, both along the front and in the waters of the Gulf, where each side sought to thwart the other's ability to export petroleum. When Iran installed Silkworm cruise missiles along the Strait of Hormuz, Reagan deployed additional warships to the Gulf to safeguard American interests. In March 1987, he

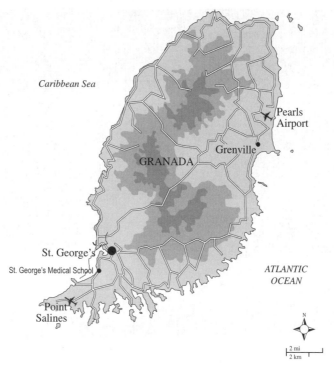

Caribbean Sea

Pearls Airport

Grenville

GRANADA

St. George's

St. George's Medical School

Point Salines

ATLANTIC OCEAN

N

2 mi
2 km

Map 21.2   Grenada, 1983.

announced that 11 tankers from Kuwait, a staunch supporter of Iraq, would be reflagged as US vessels and afforded the protection of the US Navy, a mission named Operation Earnest Will. Before long, the guardians became targets. In May, the frigate *Stark*, on radar picket duty in the central Gulf, was struck by two Exocet missiles fired from an Iraqi F-1 Mirage, whose pilot thought the blip on his radar screen was an Iranian tanker (see Map 21.3). Thirty-seven crewmen were killed, and it took heroic firefighting efforts to save the ship. Questions were raised about the ship's combat readiness, its crew's defensive actions, and the rules of engagement under which it operated. Inevitably, the *Stark*'s captain was relieved of his command, and, henceforth, commanders were encouraged to act in self-defense before being fired upon by a contact exhibiting hostile intent.

Two months later, while steaming in the Navy's first convoy of reflagged vessels, the supertanker *Bridgeton* hit a contact mine, which blasted a huge hole in its hull. No one was injured, but the Navy was embarrassed, since Iranian mines were known to be present. To deal with the threat, the Navy dispatched six minesweepers and eight minesweeping helicopters to the Gulf.

On April 14, 1988, the frigate *Samuel B. Roberts* struck a mine, suffering a gaping hole in its hull. Fortunately, no crewmember was killed, and magnificent damage-control efforts kept the ship afloat. Four days later, the US Navy carried out a retaliatory attack that evolved into the largest naval battle since World War II. The action, codenamed Operation Praying Mantis, began when destroyers *Lynde McCormick* and *Merrill* and marines and a Navy Explosive Ordinance Disposal detachment from the amphibious ship *Trenton* destroyed oil platforms being used by the Iranians as command and surveillance posts. Later, an Iranian missile corvette fired a Harpoon at the cruiser *Wainwright* but missed. *Wainwright* and the frigate *Simpson* responded with four SM-1 missiles that hit

Figure 21.2   USS *America* prepares to launch an F-14 Tomcat, an A-7E Corsair II, and an EA-6B Prowler during Operation El Dorado Canyon, April 1986.

the corvette, which exploded in flames. A few hours later, an Iranian frigate steamed toward the destroyers *Joseph Strauss* and *O'Brien* and frigate *Jack Williams* and opened fire on an A-6E Intruder attempting to identify it. The Intruder and other carrier-based aircraft dropped several laser-guided bombs and fired missiles that destroyed the frigate. The day-long battle ended when an A-6E crippled a second frigate with a perfectly placed bomb.

America's sailors and airmen demonstrated extraordinary bravery and skill during the lopsided battle, and their sensors and weapons performed superbly. Nevertheless, despite its exceptional quality, sophisticated equipment is still operated by humans,

who can misread a tactical situation, especially during the extraordinary confusion generated by combat.

On July 3, Iranian speedboats fired on a helicopter operating from the Aegis cruiser *Vincennes*, which retaliated with its five-inch guns. During the skirmish, the cruiser's SPY-1 radar detected an aircraft approaching from Bandar Abbas, Iran (see Map 21.3). The crew designated the contact as hostile, since it appeared to be descending toward the ship, would not identify itself, and was transmitting an electronic signal conforming to a military aircraft. When the aircraft closed to nine miles, the captain, mindful of the near loss of the *Stark*, fired two missiles. The plane was

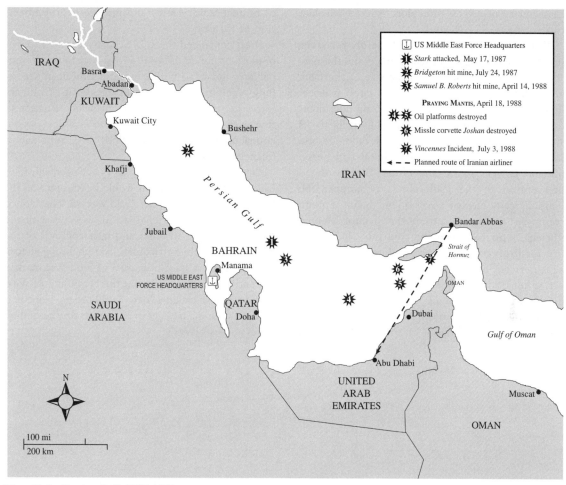

Map 21.3 Persian Gulf, 1987–1988.

destroyed, but it was soon discovered that it had been an Iranian airliner bound for Dubai. All 290 passengers and crew were lost. A Navy inquiry concluded that the ship's crew had misinterpreted the actions of the airliner—the plane was not descending—and that the emission may have come from a military aircraft parked at an airfield.

In late August, Iran and Iraq agreed to a UN-sponsored ceasefire that left them near the positions they had held when the war began. The US Navy played a key role in ending the conflict. It kept oil flowing from the Gulf by escorting 270 tankers in 135 convoys and thwarted Iran's efforts to intimidate Iraq's Arab supporters.

The End of the Cold War

As Ronald Reagan handed the presidency over to George H. W. Bush in 1989, the world was being transformed. The Soviet Union was imploding, and democracy was spreading through the once-Soviet-dominated states of Eastern Europe at a pace that stunned the world. Unable to match the American arms buildup, Soviet leader Mikhail Gorbachev chose to pursue a less confrontational foreign policy. Believing that Gorbachev was sincere, Reagan retreated from his commitment to build a huge fleet. Lehman's successor, James H. Webb, still fought for a 600-ship fleet and resigned as Navy secretary in 1988 to protest the secretary of defense's decision to retire 16 older frigates.

With the Soviet military threat rapidly receding, the Maritime Strategy lost its rationale, and the new administration set out to trim the size of the fleet, but it did not reduce the United States' overseas obligations. Its 1990 *Base Force* planning document proposed to reduce the number of carriers to 12 and total warships to 451 by mid-decade. Despite the shrinking force, the United States still flexed military power around the globe. Bush ordered intervention in the Philippines to support the democratically elected government during a coup attempt; in Panama to capture the dictator Manuel Noriega, who had been indicted by a US grand jury for drug trafficking; and in Liberia to evacuate Americans caught in the country's bloody civil war. When Saddam Hussein stunned the world by invading Kuwait on August 2, 1990, Bush immediately reinforced US naval forces in the region, then skillfully assembled a large international coalition to protect Saudi Arabia and prepare for the liberation of Kuwait.

Bush convinced the UN Security Council to pass resolutions condemning the Iraqi invasion and compelling Saddam to withdraw from Kuwait under stifling economic sanctions and the threat of military force. The Soviets and China made no attempt to thwart the American initiative, and coalition nations contributed troops, planes, ships, fuel, supplies, or financial support.

Operation Desert Storm, as the US-led effort to evict Saddam from Kuwait would be known, was the last military episode of the Cold War era. The United States put its great arsenal to full use and with the direct support of its allies and tacit approval of the Soviet Union achieved a quick, overwhelming victory over the hapless Iraqi military. The Gulf War marked the end of the Cold War and the beginning of what President Bush called a "new world order"—one that brought with it a new set of challenges for the United States and its Navy.

CHAPTER 22

Contours of Conflict

Worldwide War on Terrorism, 1990–2015

The 1990s began with events that would shape the next quarter-century for the US Navy: the end of the Cold War, the collapse of the Soviet Union, the dismantling of the Warsaw Pact, and the First Gulf War. In the wake of these, many small-scale conflicts broke out in areas with failed or weak states, parallel with a rise in terrorism and irregular warfare. For the US Navy this posed a new set of challenges. The buildup of the 1980s brought it close to 600 ships, creating a force ready to fight a large-scale encounter against the Soviets. The precipitous downfall of the Soviet Union left the US Navy without a serious rival, but not without serious challenges. Maintaining freedom of the seas and defending American security remained central to the Navy's mission as always. Added to these traditional challenges were the obligation to work with the Army and Air Force in new land conflicts against adversaries employing techniques of irregular warfare as well as the responsibility to counter a large number of small but lethal challenges to maritime security in the form of pirates and marine terrorists. The experiences of the 1990s and 2000s helped to reshape the Navy and Marine Corps as they evolved from the Cold War-era "Maritime Strategy" of the late 1970s to the 2007 "A Cooperative Strategy for 21st Century Seapower."

Gulf War I (1990–1991)

The conflict that presaged the end of the Cold War struck in August 1990 when Iraq, which the United States had intermittently assisted in its war with Iran during the 1980s, suddenly invaded its neighbor Kuwait. This assault had been precipitated in part by the accusations of Iraq's leader, Saddam Hussein, that the Kuwaitis were overproducing oil and slant-drilling across the border into Iraqi oil fields. Within a few days, Iraqi forces had taken the country and were poised on the border ready to invade Saudi Arabia. Responding to an official Saudi request for help, the United States launched Operation Desert Shield by sending aircraft and troops to Saudi Arabia and two carrier battle groups to the region. Built around the *Dwight D. Eisenhower* and the *Independence*, these were soon joined by surface action groups led by the battleships *Missouri* and *Wisconsin*. Various US ships commenced a maritime interception program that quickly weakened Iraq's war efforts. The Military Sealift Command, expanded in the 1980s, transported over 12 million tons of supplies in support of efforts to contain Iraq.

In January 1991, Operation Desert Shield morphed into Operation Desert Storm when US and coalition forces commenced airstrikes to put pressure on Saddam to withdraw from Kuwait. By this time,

America, Sea Power, and the World, First Edition. Edited by James C. Bradford.
© 2016 John Wiley & Sons, Inc. Published 2016 by John Wiley & Sons, Inc.

Carrier Battle Groups

Carrier battle groups have been made up of an aircraft carrier and its escort ships since World War II. During the Cold War, the United States had responsibility for blue-water naval operations while its NATO allies focused on coastal and riverine operations, so this was an important time for these units.

Since the end of the Cold War, there has been vigorous debate about the role of carrier battle groups. Supporters maintain that they provide unique force-projection capabilities, while detractors note that they are ever more vulnerable to cruise missiles. Such debates notwithstanding, carrier groups were called upon in the 1990s and 2000s as first responders even in conflicts where conventional land-based aircraft were also employed. The US Navy deployed six carriers for Operation Desert Storm. These ships arrived with full magazines and support vessels, allowing them to conduct strikes indefinitely.

The endurance of carrier groups was again demonstrated after September 11, 2001, when two steamed to the Arabian Sea to support Operation Enduring Freedom. During the months that followed the group headed by the *Theodore Roosevelt* spent 159 days underway without visiting a port, their location being closer to targets in Afghanistan than any land-based assets. The versatility of such groups was demonstrated when the *Kitty Hawk* was adapted to be a support base for special operations helicopters.

By the early twenty-first century, "carrier strike group" had become the more common term for these units. By then the Navy maintained 11 such groups, each usually consisting of one aircraft carrier, three multi-mission surface combatants (usually one cruiser and two destroyers equipped with missiles for attack on land targets and for anti-air and antisubmarine warfare), an attack submarine, and a combined ammunition and oiler supply ship.

A new generation of carriers began with development of the *Gerald R. Ford* class of carriers. The hull of the first in the class was laid down in 2009 and launched in 2013 with plans to commission the *Ford* in 2016 followed by the *John F. Kennedy* in 2020. *Ford*-class carriers are designed to be very adaptable as technology and equipment needed on board change.

USS *Abraham Lincoln* carrier battle group in the Pacific, 2000.

Eisenhower and *Independence* had rotated out and been replaced by six other carriers from which Navy and Marine Corps pilots flew about one-third of all sorties in this operation. American cruisers, destroyers, battleships, and submarines fired more than 280 Tomahawk cruise missiles at Iraqi targets, devastating Iraq's infrastructure in the first combat use of this new weapon.

More than 100 Iraqi naval vessels were destroyed during Desert Storm, which also saw the first combat use of several new types of aircraft, such as the F-14A+, F/A-18C and F/A-18D night-attack planes.

Navy surface forces conducted a dramatic operation on the first day of Desert Storm when helicopters from the frigate *Nicholas* attacked Iraqi positions on plat-

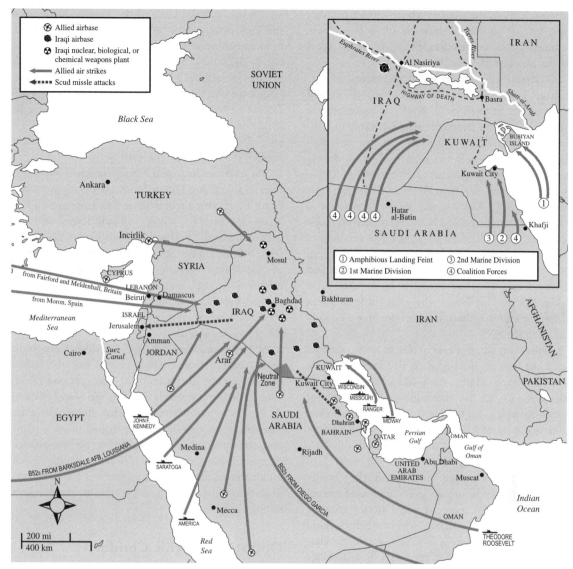

Map 22.1   Gulf War, 1991.

forms in a major oilfield 40 miles from Kuwait's coast. Their missiles forced the Iraqi garrison to surrender quickly as US boarding teams destroyed fortifications on the rest of the platforms. The battleships *Missouri* and *Wisconsin* fired their 16-inch guns in combat for the first time since the early 1950s, against Iraqi targets along Kuwait's coast. Over the next few days, US and allied Marine units and ships conducted operations offshore to give the impression that an amphibious landing in Kuwait was imminent, keeping thousands of Iraqi troops tied down on the coast.

US ships were able to avoid Silkworm missiles fired at them soon after the ground offensive began on February 24, yet both the amphibious assault ship *Tripoli* and the cruiser *Princeton* soon ended up striking mines. Nevertheless, the two ships quickly returned to service. This incident revealed the Navy's lack of minesweeping capabilities, although this conflict saw the first use of the *Avenger*-class countermeasures ships, the first introduced since the 1950s. Regardless, the burden of mine detection fell largely on the Royal Navy and other allied forces.

US Marine Corps units performed several important roles in the Gulf War. Marines secured the coastal salient of the Saudi–Kuwaiti border in collaboration with Arab coalition forces, allowing US Army units to attack from behind Iraqi frontlines in the west. Key Marine operations near the coast took place during the Battle of Khafji (January 29–February 1, 1991). This began when elite Iraqi Republican Guards suddenly crossed the Saudi border to seize the town of Khafji after Iraqi forces had been relentlessly pounded with airstrikes for about two weeks. The retaking of Khafji was spearheaded by Saudi and Qatari forces, aided by air cover from US Air Force bombers and Marine Corps Harriers attacking Iraqi convoys, as well as Marine land forces who engaged Iraqi forces further west to stop them from reinforcing their colleagues in Khafji.

Marines also played a crucial role in the actual land assault on Kuwait that began on February 24. There were two prongs to this attack, one consisting of US, British, and French forces crossing into Iraq from just west of Kuwait to hit the Iraqis from behind, and the other made up of US Marines, Saudis, and Qataris advancing along the coast directly into Kuwait City (see Map 22.1).

As the Marines pushed into Kuwait, they swiftly disarmed minefields, moved over large sand berms, and dodged booby traps, all while under sporadic Iraqi artillery fire. General Norman Schwarzkopf described the operation as "a classic, absolutely classic military breaching of a very, very tough minefield, barbed wire, fire trench-type barrier. They went through the first barrier like it was water. Then they brought both divisions streaming through that breach. Absolutely superb operation—a textbook, and I think it will be studied for many, many years to come as the way to do it."[1] Startled by the huge amount of air and artillery support provided for the advancing coalition troops, Iraqi soldiers began to surrender at

a pace that actually blocked the forward progress of the Marine units. On the second day of the invasion, numerous Marine units got into fairly intense battles, but, by the time a ceasefire was declared on the fourth day, the 1st and 2nd Marine Divisions had defeated an Iraqi force of 11 divisions. During this offensive, Iraqi forces had been relentlessly pounded by coalition air strikes, in particular from the USS *Ranger*, creating a line of destroyed vehicles on the road to Iraq later dubbed the "Highway of Death."

The Marine Corps and Navy performed important roles in Operation Desert Storm, but these were different from what their training had emphasized. The Navy supported the advance of land forces with airstrikes and artillery as well as interdicting Iraqi shipping. Marine units distracted the enemy with threats of amphibious invasion while launching a ground offensive on the coast. All the while, Saddam was warned that US warships had the capacity to attack Iran with nuclear weapons should he employ chemical or biological warfare.

All operations were conducted in close cooperation with coalition forces. It was crucial that the public face of Kuwait's liberation be as "Arab" as possible, to counter Iraqi propaganda that this was merely part of an American campaign to control the Middle East. The speedy success of this war shaped military planning in important ways, highlighting the importance of coordinating operations within a multi-service, multinational force as well as opening planners' eyes to ways for units to be more effective in urban civilian settings.

Operation Provide Comfort

The question of how to deal with civilian refugees emerged after the Gulf War. Although the ground war and liberation of Kuwait ended after only 100 hours of combat, the official cessation of hostilities was deceptive. Just days after the ceasefire, uprisings against Saddam broke out, first among Shi'i Arabs in southern Iraq and then in the Kurdish population of the north. Half of Iraq's military equipment had escaped

[1] Norman Schwarzkopf, Briefing, February 27, 1991, as quoted in Department of the Navy, *The United States Navy in "Desert Shield" "Desert Storm"* (1991), 46.

destruction and was still usable by Saddam's forces. In addition, although the ceasefire terms prohibited the Iraqis from flying airplanes, it placed no restrictions on their use of helicopters. The Iraqi armed forces thus retained enough firepower to crush both revolts by April 1991.

By this time, two million Iraqi refugees (of whom 1.5 million were Kurds) had fled north into the mountains of the Kurdish area, south into the marshes of southern Iraq, or over the borders into Iran, Syria, or Turkey. To manage this sudden humanitarian crisis, the United States set up refugee camps close to Iraq's northern border and established "no-fly zones" in northern and southern Iraq, in which US Navy and Marine Corps pilots played important enforcement roles. As this humanitarian mission was launched, on April 20, 1991 the 24th US Marine Expeditionary Unit was the first ground force to reach the town of Zakho, in northern Iraq. After supervising the construction of refugee camps and stabilizing the security situation there, the unit left in mid-July. In total, 20,000 personnel from 10 countries led by US Marines helped to provide security and humanitarian relief to refugees in Zakho.

Operations Provide Comfort II, Southern Watch, and Northern Watch

After the departure of most coalition ground forces from Iraq in 1991, Operation Provide Comfort II was set up to deter Iraqi aggression against the Kurds, who became organized into their own semi-autonomous governing authority. Iraqi forces were forced to withdraw altogether from northern Iraq. Security there was enforced by coalition air units, which included many US Navy and Marine Corps pilots. From April to October 1991 the carrier *Theodore Roosevelt* steamed off the Turkish coast to support Operation Provide Comfort II. This northern no-fly zone was complemented by a southern Iraqi no-fly zone that began with Operation Southern Watch in August 1992 as a response to Saddam's attacks on Shi'is in the south.

In October 1994, two divisions of Iraqi Republican Guards suddenly began advancing toward Kuwait. The United States quickly moved Army and

Marine units there in Operation Vigilant Warrior, which prompted the Iraqis to retreat. A more serious situation developed when Iraq suddenly launched a large ground offensive with 40,000 troops on August 31, 1996. It attacked one of the two main Kurdish political groups (the Patriotic Union of Kurdistan) in order to help its main rival Kurdish political group (the Kurdistan Democratic Party). This threat was quickly stopped by Operation Desert Strike on September 3, when Tomahawk missiles were launched from the *Carl Vinson* and *Enterprise* carrier battle groups simultaneously with US Air Force cruise missiles from B-52 bombers (see Figure 22.1). This attack was followed the next day by a second wave of strikes, which deterred Iraq's plans to break out of its containment and also helped to avert a Kurdish civil war.

At the beginning of 1997, Operation Provide Comfort II transitioned into Operation Northern Watch, which mirrored the ongoing Southern Watch. Both operations were components of the "dual containment" strategy, which aimed to restrain both Iran and Iraq in the aftermath of the 1991 Gulf War. By 1998, political pressure in the United States was building for President Bill Clinton to go beyond containment of Iraq, to overthrow Saddam, and to permanently deter Iraq from ever acquiring weapons of mass destruction (WMDs).

Operation Desert Fox

The result was Operation Desert Fox, a joint US–British bombing campaign against Iraqi targets in December 1998 designed to degrade Iraq's ability to produce WMDs. It was brought on by Iraq's failure to cooperate with UN weapons inspectors. Aircraft from the *Carl Vinson* and the *Enterprise* flew missions that marked the first time women flew combat sorties as strike fighter pilots. On the second night of the operation, Air Force B-52s launched cruise missiles. This pattern was repeated over the next several evenings, resulting in significant degradation of Iraq's missile program. Operation Desert Fox became the largest-scale attack on Iraq between the 1991 Gulf War and the launch of Operation Iraqi Freedom in March 2003.

Figure 22.1   USS *Shiloh* launches a Tomahawk cruise missile against Iraq, 1996. *Source:* Photo courtesy of the US Department of Defense.

At a strategic level, Operation Desert Fox set the stage for Operation Iraqi Freedom, but it also broke up the coalition that the United States had brought together for the 1991 Gulf War, because by 1998 some nations were skeptical that Iraq posed a real military threat anymore. Another negative outcome of Desert Fox was that Iraq barred UN inspectors for the next four years, so the United States received much less current intelligence about Iraqi WMD activities. In such an information vacuum, analysts soon began to focus on worst-case scenarios for Iraq's purported WMD research. Although Iraq appears to have accelerated its missile development program after Desert Fox, this operation effectively squelched any plans at all that Iraq may have had for WMD development.

The Middle East was not the only area where Navy and Marine Corps pilots conducted air interdiction in the 1990s. Overlapping with operations against Iraq, Operation Deny Flight between 1993 and 1995 as well as its follow-on Operation Deliberate Force in 1995 were important NATO no-fly zones over Bosnia-Herzegovina during key phases of the conflict there as the former Yugoslavia was unraveling. After Bosnian Serbs killed 37 people in a mortar attack on Sarajevo in 1995, NATO commander Admiral Leighton Smith directed 3,515 air strikes against the Serbs in Operation Deliberate Force, including sorties flown from the carriers *America* and *Theodore Roosevelt* on station in the Adriatic Sea (see Map 22.2).

Maritime Interdiction Operations in the 1990s

Another key component of the Iraq containment strategy was the continuous maritime interdiction operations of the US Navy and its allies in the Persian Gulf in the 1990s and early 2000s. The US Navy joined similar missions in the Adriatic: Operation Sharp Guard was set up to seize weapons bound for the former Yugoslavia between 1992 and 1996,

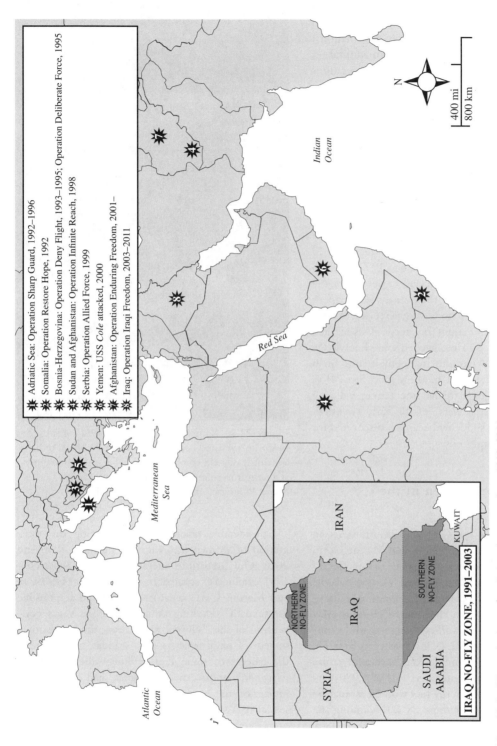

Adriatic Sea: Operation Sharp Guard, 1992–1996
Somalia: Operation Restore Hope, 1992
Bosnia-Herzegovina: Operation Deny Flight, 1993–1995; Operation Deliberate Force, 1995
Sudan and Afghanistan: Operation Infinite Reach, 1998
Serbia: Operation Allied Force, 1999
Yemen: USS *Cole* attacked, 2000
Afghanistan: Operation Enduring Freedom, 2001–
Iraq: Operation Iraqi Freedom, 2003–2011

IRAQ NO-FLY ZONE, 1991–2003

SYRIA

NORTHERN
NO-FLY ZONE

IRAN

IRAQ

SOUTHERN
NO-FLY ZONE

KUWAIT

SAUDI
ARABIA

Atlantic
Ocean

Mediterranean
Sea

Red Sea

Indian
Ocean

N

400 mi
800 km

Map 22.2 Humanitarian and anti-terrorism operations, 1992–2014.

and Operation Allied Force was an air campaign designed to reduce the military power of Serbia and Yugoslavia in 1999. This embargo's multinational enforcement group was led by an Italian admiral—a harbinger of multinational naval security operations to come. Another sort of maritime interdiction long performed by the US Navy continued in the 1990s as well: drug interdiction by joint task forces in the Caribbean.

Return of the "Small Wars"

Alongside interdiction missions, the Navy and the Marine Corps were tasked with helping in numerous humanitarian and peacekeeping activities (see Map 22.2). One was Operation Restore Hope in Somalia, which began in December 1992 to keep thousands of Somalis from starving to death. For the Marine Corps in particular, the Somalia deployment was one in which civic actions were perceived to be as important as military actions for success. This recalled an earlier era when Marines needed some knowledge of local norms and customs to do their jobs. Such topics had been discussed in the classic *Small Wars Manual* (1940), a guide for Marine activities during the so-called "Banana Wars" of the early twentieth century. This book suddenly became rediscovered for these new Marine missions.

A New Era for Women in the Naval Service

With the lifting of the Combat Exclusion Act in 1993, more positions in the Navy and Marine Corps became open for women than ever before. Secretary of Defense Les Aspin allowed women aviators to fly combat aircraft. One of the pioneers, Lieutenant Commander Kathryn Hire, joined VP-62 in May 1993 as the first female officer assigned to a combat aircrew (see Figure 22.2). Just two years later, the *Dwight D. Eisenhower* completed a successful cruise with 400 women crew members out of 6,280 personnel on board. In 2012, the first women submarine officers reported to their ships. By 2015, among the very few units not open to women were SEAL (Sea, Air, and Land) special operations teams.

Figure 22.2   Kathryn Hire, a naval reservist, joined NASA in 1989 and became the first female officer to be a member of a US combat aircrew when she was assigned as a navigator/communicator in a P-3 in May 1993. *Source:* Photo by Matt Stroshane / Getty Images.

Considerable challenges arose during the integration of women into the fleet between 1990 and 2016. One notorious incident was the September 1991 "Tailhook" scandal. In it, around 100 US Navy and Marine Corps aviators were found responsible for sexually assaulting women at a Las Vegas convention of the Tailhook Association, the professional society of naval aviators. This scandal, which ended the careers of some high-ranking officers and has remained controversial ever since, had a substantial impact on the Navy's corporate culture: problems of sexual harassment were taken seriously and handled with much greater care thereafter. The proportion of women in senior positions rose steadily during the decades before and after 2010 until, by August 2015, there were 35 female admirals out of approximately 279 flag officers.

The Marine Corps made its own pioneering strides in this realm when it chose its first female drill instructor in 1992 and gradually opened more military occupational specialties to women. In January 2013, Defense Secretary Leon Panetta announced a decision to eliminate *all* combat exclusions for women in the armed services, except in specific cases. One key test of this was the Marine Corps Infantry Officer Course: the only gateway to becoming a Marine Infantry Officer. As of mid-2015, all female officers who have begun this course have failed to pass it (although 34 percent of the women who took the equivalent course for enlisted soldiers did pass).

"Don't Ask, Don't Tell" in the Navy and Marine Corps

The integration of women into most parts of the naval service was not the only major social change affecting the Navy and Marine Corps in the 1990s and 2000s. Another big issue was the question of whether to allow gay, lesbian, and bisexual (GLB) personnel into the naval service. The long-standing policy of the armed forces had been not to admit GLB personnel. By the late 1980s, gay rights groups had begun to challenge this position and in 1989 an official Pentagon study observed that "having a same-gender or an opposite-gender orientation is unrelated to job performance in the same way as is being left- or right-handed."[2] This shift in position coincided with several lawsuits fighting military discharges on the basis of sexual orientation.

In 1992, General Carl Mundy, commandant of the Marine Corps, praised a paper written by a Marine Corps chaplain stating that "the DOD [Department of Defense] homosexual-exclusion policy is designed to preserve, promote, and protect legitimate military interests, including the personal privacy rights of ser-

vice members."[3] The murder that fall of Allen Schindler, a gay petty officer, prompted a renewed push by activists for the newly elected Clinton administration to allow GLB personnel to serve openly in the military.

After much public debate, in its 1994 budget Congress required the military to abide by earlier regulations barring GLB personnel from military service. Nevertheless, on December 21, 1993, President Bill Clinton issued Defense Directive 1304.26, which stated that people seeking to join the military were not to be asked about their sexual orientation. This instruction set the basis for the policy known as "Don't Ask, Don't Tell" (DADT).

Over the next decade, this policy evolved functionally into "Don't Ask, Don't Tell, Don't Pursue." "Don't Ask" required military officials not to ask about or require members to reveal their sexual orientation. "Don't Tell" meant that a sailor or an officer could be expelled from the service for claiming to be gay, lesbian, or bisexual, or even saying things to show his or her sexual orientation. "Don't Pursue" established *what* was minimally required for an investigation to take place about an individual's sexual preferences.

Between 1996 and 2008, five federal courts of appeal upheld the legality of DADT, clearing the way for the acceptance of openly GLB personnel in the armed forces. By November 2007, more than 25 retired generals and admirals had urged Congress to repeal DADT entirely, noting that 65,000 GLB men and women were presently serving in the military. The directive was formally repealed by legislation in December 2010. The Palm Center, a policy institute focusing on issues of sexuality and the military, released a study in September 2012 showing that there had been no negative effects on military readiness and effectiveness resulting from the repeal of DADT. The idea of homosexuals openly serving in the Navy and Marine Corps had gone from being an anathema in the 1980s to becoming officially permitted and more socially accepted by the second decade of the twenty-first century.

---

[2] Defense Personnel Security and Education Center, "Nonconforming Sexual Orientations and Military Suitability," PERS-TR-89-002 (December 1988), 29.

[3] Eugene T. Gomulka, Deputy Chaplain, USMC, "Why No Gays?" Naval Institute *Proceedings*, 118:12 (1992), 45. For Mundy's reaction, see "Marine Corps Chaplain Says Homosexuals Threaten Military," *New York Times* (August 26, 1992).

Stanley R. Arthur

Stanley R. Arthur (b. 1935) flew 513 A-4 Skyhawk missions in Vietnam to become one of the most highly decorated aviators of the war. Through the 1970s and 1980s, he advanced steadily through the ranks of naval aviation. Soon after Saddam Hussein's invasion of Kuwait, the US Seventh Fleet commander, normally based in Japan, moved to the Persian Gulf to lead naval operations there. Arthur became Seventh Fleet commander in December 1990. When Operation Desert Storm commenced in January 1991, he was in command of 96,000 sailors and Marines along with 130 US Navy ships and allied vessels: the largest US naval armada since World War II. Arthur oversaw this remarkable force (including six carriers) until April 1991, when he returned to Yokosuka, the Seventh Fleet's normal homeport.

Admiral Arthur became vice chief of naval operations on July 6, 1992. In that job, he also happened to be the Navy's most senior naval aviator just after the Tailhook incident of September 1991. In 1994, when President Bill Clinton nominated Admiral Arthur to become the next commander of the US Pacific Command, Senator Dave Durenberger (R-Minnesota) questioned how Arthur had dealt with a sexual harassment case brought by Rebecca Hansen, one of his constituents. Hansen, a Navy student pilot, charged that her failure to pass flight training was in retaliation for a sexual harassment charge that she had successfully pursued against her instructor, but the Navy inspector general rejected her accusation. Admiral Arthur agreed with the inspector general's report. When Durenberger blocked Arthur's nomination, Chief of Naval Operations Michael Boorda asked Arthur to withdraw his name from consideration, effectively ending Arthur's career. Admiral Arthur retired in 1995 and his defenders

charged that Boorda had sacrificed him to improve the Navy's image regarding its handling of cases of sexual harassment. Two years later the Admiral Stan Arthur Award for Logistics Excellence was established in his honor.

Stanley R. Arthur, Commander Seventh Fleet, 1991.

The New Global Military Threat of Religious Extremism in the 1990s

Beginning in the 1990s, the rise of non-state religious extremist groups ready to carry out terrorist attacks across the globe presented military and security challenges radically different from anything experienced during the Cold War.

The first such attacks were carried out by bands of zealots led by devout militants who had fought as Muslim *mujahideen* guerrillas against the Soviets after the latter invaded Afghanistan in 1979. When the Soviets left that country in 1989, some of these highly religious warriors organized insurgent groups

and shifted their hostility to the West, particularly the United States. Just after returning to Saudi Arabia from Afghanistan in the spring of 1990, Osama bin Laden, one of the most radical Saudi *mujahideen*, angrily denounced the Saudi leadership for relying on foreigners to defend them in the Gulf War of 1990–1991, for which he was exiled to Sudan.

There he found a willing host in the Islamic radical leader Hassan al-Turabi, who had recently seized control of Sudan in a coup. For a while, Turabi gave bin Laden a refuge for the anti-Western movement that he was creating. When bin Laden and his followers were finally expelled from Sudan under pressure from the Saudis and Egyptians, they fled to Afghanistan. There, bin Laden was welcomed back by the radical Taliban government that had just taken power. Within a few years, he and his disciples evolved into "al-Qaeda," a full-fledged Islamic extremist group. In February 1998, bin Laden, as al-Qaeda's leader, issued a declaration of war against the United States and Israel.

In August 1998, two weeks after al-Qaeda bombers struck American embassies in Kenya and Tanzania (in each of which US marines were killed), the United States retaliated with Operation Infinite Reach, a bombing campaign of cruise missiles from the *Abraham Lincoln* carrier battle group against al-Qaeda targets in Afghanistan and Sudan. The inconclusive results of this operation led to accelerated development of unmanned aerial vehicle drones with potentially greater accuracy. Just over one year later, al-Qaeda launched a new round of terrorist actions. One of them was a failed attack on the Navy destroyer *The Sullivans*, then moored in the harbor of Aden, Yemen. This went awry because the ship carrying the explosives was overloaded and sank.

Attack on the USS *Cole*

A similar type of al-Qaeda maritime plot did succeed in October 2000, when the USS *Cole* was docked in Aden for routine refueling (see Map 22.2). It was suddenly approached by a small craft that blew up as it drew alongside, carving a 40-by-40-foot gash in the ship's hull. Analysis suggests that approximately 400 to 700 pounds of explosive were detonated. The blast struck just as the crew was gathering for lunch. Seventeen sailors were killed and 39 injured, with the cost of the damage estimated to be around $250 million. Considerable evidence soon pointed to al-Qaeda's responsibility for the attack. A few months later, an al-Qaeda video circulated depicting bin Laden boasting about this action and encouraging people to copy it.

Just as the ship was struck, the US defense attaché in Yemen, Lieutenant Colonel Robert Newman, happened to be in the town of Aden, heard the explosion, and made his way to the harbor. Despite the breakdown of the ship's communications, Newman was able to alert Fifth Fleet headquarters in Bahrain via cellphone, leading to the dispatch of a Marine Corps FAST (Fleet Antiterrorism Security Team) company

based in Bahrain. FAST units were first organized in 1987 as special quick-reaction anti-terrorism forces and have served globally as first responders to incidents such as the *Cole* bombing ever since. This company quickly set up a temporary protection zone around the *Cole* and secured a nearby hotel to serve as a command center for rescue and clean-up operations.

In March 2007, a US federal court held the Sudanese government liable for the bombing. While many figures associated with al-Qaeda have been tangentially linked to this action, no definitive proof of who really planned and supervised it has ever been produced. The incident, though, did expose flaws in the Navy's ship security rules. Later investigations noted that the *Cole*'s rules of engagement had focused much more on protecting the ship from terrorist threats emanating from land than from waterborne attacks. Ship guards had in fact been prohibited from firing on small boats not confirmed to be carrying explosives without explicit permission from the ship's captain or another officer.

The *Cole* bombing forced the Navy to reassess its whole anti-terrorism and force-protection plan, and a Navy judge advocate general's report on the incident recommended significant changes in procedure. The Navy immediately stepped up "random anti-terrorism measures," designed to make patterns in ship activities harder to detect. To develop such practices, an Antiterrorism and Force Protection Warfare Center was opened in Virginia Beach, Virginia. By 2004, several Navy anti-terrorism and force-protection units had been brought under a single command, the Maritime Force Protection Command. The *Cole* bombing also became an important part of training in damage control for new sailors. This now took place in boot camp with a pre-graduation "Battle Stations" exercise on board a destroyer mock-up.

Bringing the perpetrators of the *Cole* attack to justice has remained elusive. In September 2004, a Yemeni judge sentenced Abd al-Rahim al-Nashiri and Jamal al-Badawi to death for their roles in the bombing. Nashiri, believed to be the operation's mastermind, then had his death sentence dropped but later reinstated. He ended up in US custody at the Guantanamo Bay detention camp without there being any further plans to prosecute him formally.

While in Yemeni custody, Badawi denounced the verdict against him as "an American one." He later escaped, was recaptured, then ultimately was released by Yemeni authorities and remains at large. Based on the March 2007 US federal court decision that held Sudan responsible for the attack, US courts by 2014 had awarded millions of dollars in frozen Sudanese assets to survivors of sailors killed. However, no money has been disbursed because the case still remains under appeal.

The Navy and Marine Corps in Operation Enduring Freedom

The first wave of al-Qaeda terrorist operations culminated on September 11, 2001, when suicide teams hijacked four American passenger jetliners and flew them into the twin towers of the New York World Trade Center as well as the Pentagon. Blame for this attack was soon fixed on bin Laden and his followers, who had earlier settled in Afghanistan. After the Taliban government refused to surrender bin Laden, the United States and Britain commenced Operation Enduring Freedom on October 7, 2001, to force the Taliban to give him up. It began with airstrikes and Tomahawks launched from the *Carl Vinson* and *Enterprise* battle groups, in coordination with airstrikes by US Air Force bombers from Diego Garcia. A few days later, Navy SEALs were part of a force that secured the first US base in Afghanistan: Forward Operating Base Rhino, 120 miles southwest of Kandahar. On November 25, Camp Rhino became the main staging location for the 15th and 26th Marine Expeditionary Units. These Marine units went on to secure the Kandahar International Airport by December 2001, which marked the end of Taliban rule over Afghanistan (see Map 22.3).

Navy SEALs took part in two other important special operations early in the war: the Battle of Tora Bora in December 2001 and Operation Anaconda in the Shah-i-Kot Valley in February 2002. Both were designed to root out the last remnants of Taliban forces and possibly capture senior al-Qaeda leaders,

including bin Laden. Although neither operation achieved this, they forced the remaining Taliban and al-Qaeda leadership to flee to Pakistan.

By 2003, US Marines and Navy forces were being called to assist in Operation Iraqi Freedom, the US–British operation to end Saddam's threat of chemical and biological weapons. Iraq thus became a new focus of combat activities, although sailors and Marines continued to serve in Afghanistan. By 2008, after Taliban forces had conducted several years of insurgency, US Marine forces were sent into the Helmand River Valley in southern Afghanistan to clear out Taliban strongholds and centers of opium production there. Over the next six years, the Marines worked very hard to secure that area. They made considerable progress in stabilizing the situation despite continuing to face major challenges. By December 2014, US forces had withdrawn from Helmand and in other regions of Afghanistan, ending major American involvement in Afghanistan.

Operation "Iraqi Freedom"

Following the end of Taliban rule in Afghanistan in late 2001 and the establishment of a new government there, political pressure increased in the United States for a campaign to go after Saddam Hussein. Based on accusations that Saddam might have helped al-Qaeda and was hiding WMD development programs, US and British forces invaded Iraq on March 20, 2003, to begin Operation Iraqi Freedom. In September 2003, the US government stated that it had "defeated a regime that developed and used weapons of mass destruction, that harbored and supported terrorists, committed outrageous human rights abuses, and defied the just demands of the United Nations and the world."[4] From March 2003 until the end of Operation Iraqi Freedom in December 2011, strategic and tactical challenges in Iraq took on many different shapes for Marine Corps and Navy units as the struggle to secure that nation's future unfolded (see Map 22.4).

---

[4] US Department of State, Bureau of Public Affairs, "Winning the War on Terror," September 11, 2003, http://2001-2009.state.gov/documents/organization/24172.pdf.

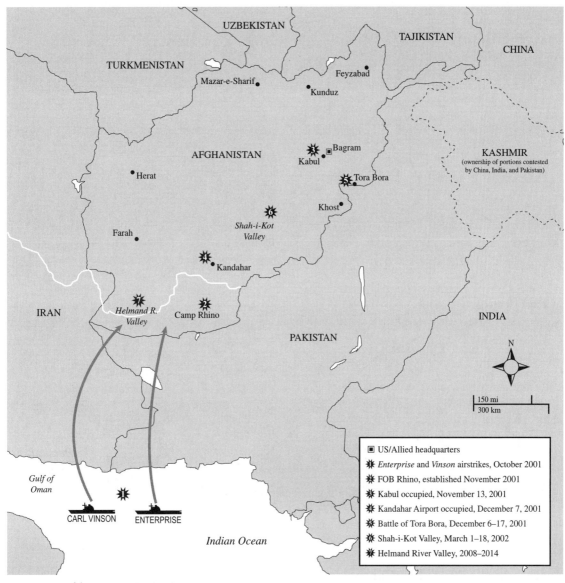

Map 22.3 Afghanistan, 2001–2014.

Marine Corps units were an important part of the initial invasion force. The 15th Marine Expeditionary Unit became one of the main units to secure the port of Umm Qasr, after four days of intense urban combat. This port's harbor was soon demined by the US Navy's Helicopter Mine Countermeasures Squadron 14 and Naval Special Clearance Team ONE, which rapidly made it available as a transit point for humanitarian supplies.

At approximately the same time, the 2nd Marine Expeditionary Brigade fought the Battle of Nasiriyah (March 23–April 2, 2003), a key action to secure this important city on the Euphrates River, 200 miles southeast of Baghdad. The bloodiest day of combat for this unit was March 23, when 18 men were killed in heavy fighting near the Saddam Canal.

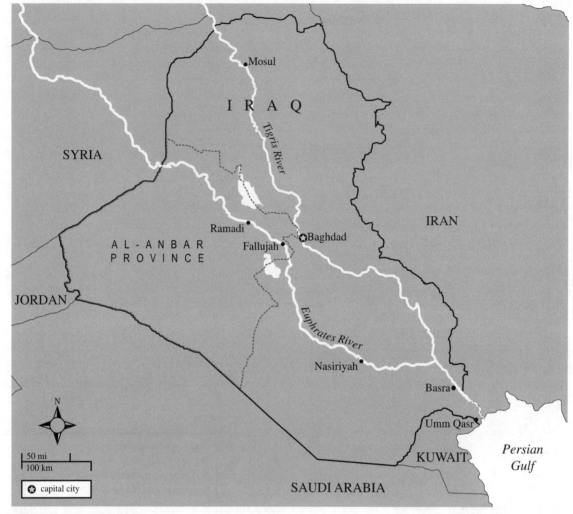

Map 22.4   Iraq, 2003–2011.

Marines in the Al-Anbar Campaign (2004–2010)

The biggest conflict of the Iraq War involving marines was a counterinsurgency battle between April 2004 and September 2007 to quell a Sunni uprising that had gradually arisen in the province of al-Anbar in western Iraq. It became one of the major actions of Operation Iraqi Freedom. Centered in the so-called "Sunni Triangle" around the cities of Fallujah and Ramadi, it was defined by heavy urban combat and the extensive use of improvised explosive devices,

and claimed the lives of nearly 9,000 Iraqis and 1,335 Americans. Many Marine units were involved in this campaign, including parts of both the 1st and 2nd Marine Divisions.

Al-Anbar, the most heavily Sunni province in Iraq, had remained peaceful during the initial invasion of Iraq but fell into revolt by April 2004. Some of the fiercest combat experienced by American troops since the Vietnam War took place during the Second Battle of Fallujah (November–December 2004). Over the next 18 months, violence increased in the struggle to secure the Euphrates River Valley, which runs through the eastern part of the province. The extremist group al-Qaeda in Iraq emerged at this time as the main Sunni insurgent group in the area. In August 2006, several Sunni tribes in al-Anbar revolted against al-Qaeda in Iraq in the "Anbar Awakening." This turned the tide against the insurgents, so that fighting to secure the province was mostly finished by September 2007. Marine units there were replaced by US Army forces in January 2010.

Naval Forces at Sea and Ashore

The US Navy saw no big confrontations against naval opponents in Operations Enduring Freedom and Iraqi Freedom. Instead, it focused on its traditional role of safeguarding maritime security and freedom of the seas while augmenting ground forces in numerous nontraditional ways. Some of the Navy's tasks were well-known duties, such as construction projects performed by Seabees (construction battalions) and medical care given by Navy corpsmen stationed with Marine units. Other Navy units found themselves performing unfamiliar missions such as customs inspections, administering civil affairs, and supervising detention facilities. In Afghanistan, several hundred sailors worked on provincial reconstruction teams helping to build stable, viable local governments. Many Navy personnel who deployed to Iraq and Afghanistan also worked as "individual augmentees," placed in non-Navy ground units as needed to support the war effort. Several thousand in number, they were mainly involved in a diverse range of non-combat activities such as base security and logistics, but the group also included a significant force of US Navy medics who did serve in combat zones.

The wars in both Afghanistan and Iraq also demonstrated the continuing value of naval forces, which can operate free of fixed land bases. Sea-basing offered strategic and tactical independence in an era when guaranteed use of land bases often became problematic. One very important part of this aspect of naval warfare continued to be the submarine forces, which still provided a unique level of strategic deterrence not matched by any other nation since the diminution of the Soviet submarine fleet. Submarines also took on important new roles as cruise missile platforms, starting with the use of submarines to fire Tomahawks at the beginning of the Gulf War (the first submarine combat action since the end of World War II). With these new weapons, submarines gave naval commanders a vastly expanded range of possibilities from where missiles could be launched, and they took advantage of this during the next few conflicts. As the "silent service," submarines had an important role to play in supporting special operations through their ability to insert SEAL and explosive ordnance disposal teams in secret landings or using mini-submersibles.

The power of fleet special operations was shown in Operation Neptune Spear, conducted by the Naval Special Warfare Development Group (formerly SEAL Team Six). Moving in covertly from Afghanistan by helicopter, the team found and killed Osama bin Laden, who had eluded conventional forces for many years, in Pakistan on May 2, 2011. Bin Laden was first taken to Afghanistan for identification, then buried at sea within 24 hours of his death, ending this chapter of the al-Qaeda story.

"A Cooperative Strategy for 21st Century Seapower" (2007)

By the end of the first decade of the twenty-first century, there was a sense among the commanders of the US Navy and Marine Corps that maritime strategy needed to be rethought, partly as a result of the many lessons learned since the end of the Cold War. Thus, in October 2007, the chief of naval operations, the commandant of the Marine Corps, and the commandant of the Coast Guard jointly issued "A Cooperative Strategy for 21st Century Seapower." This new maritime strategy, the first comprehensive one presented since 1986, describes the roles and functions of the naval services in a post-Cold War era of globalization and increased international connections and communications. The document presents the case for how sea power helps to defend American prosperity through its pivotal role in maintaining safe commerce across the globe as well as freedom of navigation and safety on the sea. It recognizes how much the global economic system relies on freedom of movement across the maritime "commons": still the main way that 90 percent of the world's commercial goods are moved. The document makes the case that vital American interests rely on the Navy keeping "forward-positioned" forces around the globe, deployed in a such a way as to deter and contain conflicts and disruptions to the global system. It also notes the great importance of developing partnerships with other nations to establish a resilient peace.[5]

During the two years prior to the publication of the new strategy, Admiral Mike Mullen (chief of naval operations, 2005–2007, and chairman of the Joint Chiefs of Staff, 2007–2011) spoke often of a "1,000 ship Navy—a fleet-in-being, if you will—comprised of all freedom-loving nations, standing watch over the seas, standing watch over each other."[6] This concept of the US and other navies forming regional partnerships—later renamed the "Global Maritime Partnership"—was a fundamental component of the new strategy. The concept incorporated the Cooperation Afloat Readiness and Training series of exercises conducted with the Bruneian, Malaysian, Philippine, Singapore, and Thailand navies since 1995, to which the navies of Cambodia and Bangladesh were added in 2010, and other similar exercises.

The "Cooperative Strategy" has guided Navy and Marine Corps activities in two particular areas: combating piracy and managing disaster relief. To fight piracy and promote general maritime security in the Arabian Gulf and Indian Ocean, the US Navy has partnered with 29 other navies to create the Combined Maritime Forces, whose tasks are to thwart terrorism, defeat piracy, encourage international cooperation, and promote safety at sea.

Over their histories, the Navy and Marine Corps have continually been involved in providing humanitarian assistance. The new maritime strategy document builds on this heritage by arguing that humanitarian assistance missions are an integral part of promoting national security. There has been a substantial expansion of humanitarian missions in the past few years, notably in Operation Unified Assistance (the response to the 2004 Indian Ocean tsunami in Indonesia), Operation Tomodachi (the US Navy's participation in the 2011 Fukushima nuclear reactor disaster clean-up in Japan), and Operation Damayan (the US Navy and Marines' help in the Philippines after super-typhoon Hainan in 2013).

Although the 2007 "Cooperative Strategy" document, and its March 2015 follow-on edition "Forward, Engaged, Ready: A Cooperative Strategy for 21st Century Seapower," recognized the need for the Navy and Marine Corps to adapt to new and very different realities in pursuing their roles in defending American strategic interests, many of the themes they address recall timeless duties performed by the naval service such as combating piracy and providing humanitarian relief around the globe. Nevertheless, the strategic climate in which it was issued had undergone extraordinary changes since the standoff of the Cold War against the Soviet Navy.

Conclusion

In 2003, the US Fleet was reduced to below 300 ships for the first time since 1916, yet no other naval power could challenge its global maritime primacy. New contenders such as the Chinese had begun to build fleets designed to catch up with the American navy someday. American leaders will continue to be forced to make hard choices about balancing the benefits of maintaining the capabilities of the US Fleet against the costs, but essential Navy and Marine Corps missions have persisted despite vast geopolitical changes.

---

[5] [US Marine Corps, US Navy, and US Coast Guard], *A Cooperative Strategy for 21st Century Seapower* (2007).

[6] Mullen, Speech at US Naval War College, Newport, Rhode Island, August 31, 2005, http://www.navy.mil/navydata/leadership/quotes.asp?q=11&c=2.

CHAPTER 23

Quo Vadis?

The exercise of sea power, like all human activities, is influenced by a variety of factors that render it subject to constant change. Two centuries of American sea power provide the context within which to ponder the future of sea power in general and American sea power in particular. To offer predictions about the future is a risky undertaking, for contingency has a habit of creating surprise. As history demonstrates, the future can diverge widely from present realities and anticipated futures. The sudden realignment of alliances, of which there exist numerous historical examples, can fundamentally change a balance of sea power, as demonstrated when the French entered the American Revolutionary War and brought ships-of-the-line to challenge the Royal Navy. Similarly, in the highly variable realm of the "human factor," the decisions of individual commanders can exert a powerful effect on the outcomes of military operations, as evidenced by decisions made by Thomas Macdonough prior to the Battle of Plattsburg. Even more variable is the factor of luck, as exemplified in American aircraft catching Japanese carriers in the midst of changing ordnance at Midway.

Despite the profound role of chance and contingency, some persistent patterns relating to sea power, national interests, naval missions, and a trajectory of technological development can be discerned. Based on past experience, these two key themes, the roles of sea power in protecting America's national interests

and the trajectory in technological innovation, provide the focus for projecting the course of American sea power deeper into the twenty-first century.

Since World War II, leaders have directed American sea power to a set of purposes, or "ends," which have exhibited remarkable continuity. In general, American sea power has been deployed to promote American national interests and protect American citizens at sea and on land; to preserve the freedom of navigation in the maritime commons for purposes of commerce and communications; and to assist allies or other nations in need. Many of these purposes can be accomplished through the peaceful "presence" of naval power. But, periodically, American sea power has been called on to confront determined opponents. The Cuban Missile Crisis, which risked global annihilation, and the Vietnam and Gulf Wars illustrate how American sea power has been used to deter conflict but also, when deterrence fails, to fight.

The broad pattern of technological change must be considered because the execution of modern sea power is dependent on advanced technology, and it is virtually certain that naval power will continue to evolve to increasing levels of complexity, into a combination of human operators and smart machine sensors, platforms, and weapons, tied together by artificially intelligent control and decision aids. These increasingly "smart" technologies will reach into multiple geo-spatial environments, and "sense-think-act"

America, Sea Power, and the World, First Edition. Edited by James C. Bradford.
© 2016 John Wiley & Sons, Inc. Published 2016 by John Wiley & Sons, Inc.

in these environments at higher speeds of operation. A potential renewed naval arms race looms, and the "race" will be won by new types of sailors who more quickly and efficiently solve the problem of the human and machine nexus at sea. But it is also possible, with the rise of cyber computer warfare, that machines will fight machines, and humans will be on the margins of the most decisive encounters. While the "goals" pursued by leaders exercising American sea power have shown a remarkable constancy, the exact "ways and means" of sea power have varied widely. Successive generations of naval leaders have had to solve a four-part variable equation. First, the leaders have had to understand the socio-geographic environment in which the fleet would operate; second, to develop the ideas, theories, relationships, and operational and tactical doctrine to guide the fleet; third, to build the appropriate mix of ships, planes, submarines, weapons, sensors, and decision aids; and, fourth, to adapt or rebuild the Navy's personnel, who form the human core of the navy, educated and trained for the new challenges posed by a changed environment and technology

Recurring Patterns of Missions and Trends of Technological Change

The modern US Navy was formed in the crucible of World War II through accelerated parallel processes of combat adaptation at the front line and massive transformation in the rear areas. The later was wrought through re-equipping, reorganization, and scientific–technological revolutions at both research and industrial facilities. This war, more clearly than any previous conflict, witnessed the proliferation of increasingly fast and "smarter" machines, from navigation systems and Huff-Duff to proximity fuses, Hedgehog, and the creation of the first human–machine decision nexus at sea, the combat information centers—developments that led Winston Churchill to call World War II the "Wizard War."[1]

War began on December 7, 1941, with a Japanese attack on a handful of bases. In the ensuing weeks, Navy leaders had to solve four problems. The first problem was to understand the scope of the socio-geographical environment in which the war would be fought. Very quickly, the environment became transoceanic and three dimensional as US naval operations rapidly expanded to both the Atlantic and the Pacific Oceans, and the pace of combat operations sped up as faster and "smarter" weapon systems were deployed. The second problem, the development of a transoceanic strategy and tactics to guide the fleet in battle, became an ongoing process that evolved up to the last battles, when the Japanese unleashed a surprise suicide tactic, the kamikazes.

Defeating the technologically advanced Japanese armed forces, entrenched on island fortresses, required a continuous flow of new or upgraded technologies. The creation and integration of these technologies posed the third problem to be solved by Navy leaders, from senior commanders to senior enlisted sailors. Almost monthly, new or improved weapons poured out of America's laboratories and factories; the range and speed of aircraft increased; new warships, notably the 24 *Essex*-class "fast carriers" and myriad landing craft, entered service; and new tactics, from the "Thatch Weave" to sector fire, were developed. Innovations in science and technology to speed up and improve naval combat gathered coherence, with new inventions in the field of electrical–mechanical engineered technology, electro-mechanical computation devices, and technologies to better control radio waves for communications and sensing (e.g., low-frequency radar and improved analog fire-control computers). The ancient requirement of a leader to "know the enemy" took on new meaning through the maturation of signals intercept technology and cryptography, which arguably provided the margin of victory in the Battle of the Atlantic. The development of hybrid human–machine decision centers named combat information centers established an entirely new trajectory of command and control of warfare, from the exclusive purview of the human commander to a nexus of human and machine.

The challenge to personnel managers, the fourth problem, was to provide the human capital for a two-ocean war. This proved to be such a gargantuan task

[1] Winston Churchill, *The Second World War*, vol. 2: *Their Finest Hour* (1949), 337.

that the prewar personnel plans crumbled before the realities of the Navy's manpower challenge. Hundreds of thousands of naval aviators and support personnel would be required, as well as a different kind of officer such that entirely new programs were developed to train these officers "of the line." In addition, the demands of transoceanic, unrestricted submarine warfare challenged the traditional model of a submarine officer, and a high percentage of prewar-trained officers would be replaced by a younger, more aggressive type of officer. In the last months of the war, the threat of accurate kamikaze planes revealed the limits of the manual control of air defense and accelerated warfare to such speeds that human decision making would increasingly integrate with electronic machines, a trajectory that gained further coherence in the Cold War. The new kind of warfare required new kinds of sailors with increasing understanding of advanced technology, electronic devices, and rudimentary electro-mechanical computers.

The process of building sea power on a global scale during World War II helped to establish a trajectory that continues today: increasingly "smart" machines that speed up and extend the range of action, and the integration of human tactical decision making with machines in order to control other machines operating at higher speeds and longer ranges.

During the Cold War, the geo-security environment in which American sea power operated remained global and expanded to include outer space. In parallel, the continual increases in speed and reach of weapons systems required ever closer integration of human and machine in decision-making processes. From this period emerged the first exemplars of artificial specialized intelligence and semi-autonomous weapons systems that operated beyond human speed—for example, the Aegis weapon system.

With the advent of nuclear weapons, the creation of strategies, doctrines, and tactics posed a particularly challenging task. Political strategists in Washington crafted an overarching "containment strategy" while a combination of scientists and military strategists created strategic nuclear doctrines, such as mutual assured destruction. The Navy played a significant role in stabilizing the nuclear arms race with the development of the ballistic missile submarine, the only platform essentially immune to a destabilizing nuclear first strike.

If anything, the pace of technological change increased during the Cold War as the Navy deployed waves of smarter, faster, longer-range weapons that benefited from the computer and electronic revolutions. During the 1950s Admiral Rickover created his "different kind of man," a technocrat in command of a growing fleet of nuclear submarines and nuclear surface ships.[2] During the same decade the aviation community created a cadre of new jet aviators, the "Jet Jocks," who could fly at faster speeds while in command of an ever more complex array of weapons and sensors. The new systems required reliable global communications links, including data links for the tactical control of increasingly fast and dispersed ships and aircraft. Developed during the 1950s and first deployed during the 1960s, the Naval Tactical Data System was succeeded in the 1980s and 1990s by the Joint Tactical Information Distribution System, with its greater capacity and faster speed. The range of aircraft and missiles continued to extend in the form of surface-to-air Standard missiles, air-to-air Phoenix missiles, and anti-ship Harpoon missiles.

These trends of speeding up engagement times and extending weapon ranges continued, even as the Cold War began to thaw. The Navy continued to test and then deploy increasingly "smart," long-range, lethal weapon systems directed against land targets. The Tomahawk missile would almost become a household word during the Middle East wars of the late twentieth and early twenty-first centuries (see Figure 23.1). The Tomahawk and other smart munitions, when seen in context, were another step in the evolution and proliferation of machine intelligence, the early phases of a robotic revolution that may grow from the first decades of the twenty-first century to become a potentially dominant factor in the sea battles of the future. In response to rapid technological advances, human capital programs were pushed to create new models for officers and sailor education and training.

---

[2] Hyman Rickover, *Education and Freedom* (1959), 19.

Figure 23.1 Tomahawk cruise missile launch by the USS *Florida*, 2003.

Rear Admiral Wayne Meyer headed a group that developed the Aegis system and trained the first sailors to operate it (see Aegis Combat System vignette in Chapter 21). The Aegis system was designed to defend against incoming high-speed anti-ship missiles. In barrage situations, the system possesses a fully automatic mode, which, if activated, can sense threats, make decisions, and actuate weapons systems to engage incoming missiles, all of which transpires at decision speeds beyond the human operator's ability. The narrow functionality of Aegis is an example of a form of artificial specialized intelligence that acts independent of human operators, but only for a limited range of tasks.

During the period following the Cold War, the Navy continued to defend American national interests at sea and on land, but in a changed geopolitical environment. For two decades both China and Russia were quiescent, leaving the US Navy dominant in the Atlantic and western Pacific.

Meanwhile, the weight of US Navy operations shifted perceptibly to the Middle East. Almost simultaneously with the collapse of the Soviet Union in 1990–1991, the United States came to the aid of its ally Kuwait. The intervention resulted in Operations Desert Shield and Desert Storm, both enabled by American sea power. The relative quiet of the mid-1990s was punctuated by periodic Tomahawk strikes against Baathist military targets and terrorist havens in Iraq, but the relative quiet was shattered with the attacks of September 11, 2001. In the months that followed, a large share of the combined US fleets was called upon to project two land armies ashore, first in Operation Enduring Freedom and then in Operation Iraqi Freedom. A surprisingly small number of special forces (launched in great part from the sea and supported from the air) displaced the Taliban in the highlands of Afghanistan in 2001–2002, though a larger occupation force would eventually follow. America once again went to war against Iraq, and in 2003 a fleet of aircraft carriers and missile-firing surface and submarine combatants deployed to the crowded waters of the Middle East and quickly toppled the Baathist government of Saddam Hussein.

During the ensuing years, however, the stabilization of these countries did not proceed smoothly, and as a consequence additional land forces were deployed to these two countries and remained there conducting counterinsurgency operations. Perhaps for the first time in the history of the US Navy, more Navy personnel were deployed ashore in combat zones than were forward-deployed on ships. Indeed, this historically anomalous situation is a reminder that there always remains the possibility of radical divergence, however temporary, from the expected patterns and trajectories of sea power.

During this period, new technologies came into wider use, including two with potential to profoundly influence the future of sea power: qualitatively "smarter" unmanned systems and what became known as cyber warfare technologies. Unmanned systems evolved rapidly during the land campaigns in Afghanistan and Iraq, especially for surveillance, precision targeting, and detecting or destroying mines and improvised explosive devices. Cyber warfare technologies had been growing in prior years but remained largely classified and thus out of the public eye. But, in this period of rapid change, the full implications of these revolutionary new technologies for sea power remained to be seen.

A Future of Continuity and Change

In what environment will American fleets operate in the future? What policies and doctrines seem likely to guide the fleet? What types of technology will the US Navy build and employ? And, finally, what types of sailors will command and control sea power in the future? The security environment will be dynamic, and a complex interaction of social, technical, economic, and military factors will redefine power relationships. Of particular concern to Navy planners is the eroding stability of nations in the Middle East and the increasingly assertive power of China in East Asian waters.

Middle East

The US Navy has committed major forces to the Middle East on an almost continuous basis since the Royal Navy began withdrawing from "East of Suez" (i.e., from Malaysia and Singapore, the Maldives, and the Persian Gulf during the 1960s). In 1971 US naval forces occupied facilities formerly used by the Royal Navy in Bahrain, and Seabees (construction battalions) began constructing facilities on British-owned Diego Garcia. The narrow and congested waters of this region present a complex problem, and the requirement for American sea power appears to be expanding. Iran has been a security concern for the United States since the fall of the shah in January 1979. But the volatility of the larger Middle East and North Africa continues to surprise policy makers and naval strategists in the second decade of the twenty-first century. Beginning in Tunisia in 2010, the "Arab Spring" of popular movements destabilized Tunisia, Egypt, and Libya along the southern Mediterranean coastline, and, most recently, Syria. In 2011 naval forces played a major role in the removal of the Gaddafi regime in Libya.

Contributing to the instability of the region was the premature withdrawal of all US ground forces from Iraq in 2011. In 2014, an insurgent group, the so-called Islamic State of Iraq and Syria, invaded Iraq and took control of several major urban areas. To provide aid to the Iraqi government, American sea power was rapidly redeployed to the Arabian Gulf, small numbers of Marines and special forces (including SEALs) were deployed ashore, and naval aircraft conducted strikes against Islamic State forces in both Iraq and Syria. For the foreseeable future, US naval forces will continue to deploy in force to this region.

South China Sea and East China Sea

The Navy's "traditional" mission of maintaining freedom of navigation has re-emerged as a key challenge for American sea power in the South and East China Seas, waters that had been relatively quiet since the end of the Vietnam War. The proximate cause for this renewed mission was the rise of China as a major world and sea power.

The US Navy has exercised a near constant presence in this region since the establishment of the East India Squadron in 1835. During the 30 years after the defeat of Nationalist China by communist forces, periods of tension sometimes required demonstrations of US sea power in support of Taiwan to deter communist China. But, with the death of Mao Zedong in 1976, tensions abated for the most part, and many observers hoped for a peaceful advancement of China to superpower status.

The likelihood of such a rise, however, appeared increasingly doubtful by the mid-2010s. The maritime flash points moved beyond Taiwan as China began to aggressively assert claims to islands in the East and South China Seas, bringing it into conflict with Japan, the Philippines, and Vietnam (see Map 23.1). The region witnessed a steady increase in Chinese maritime activity, leading to a collision between a Chinese fighter and a US Navy surveillance/patrol plane over the South China Sea in 2001 and to violent clashes with neighboring countries, including the sinking of a Vietnamese fishing boat and naval vessel in a dispute over oil drilling in 2014. In February of that year Chief of Naval Operations Jonathan Greenert assured students at the Philippine National Defense College that "of course [the United States] would help you" if China occupied one of the Spratly Islands claimed by both nations and announced hopes to increase the number of US warships deployed in the western Pacific from 45–50 to 60.[3]

To achieve its goals, China has adopted a dual-prong strategy consisting of both a legal–political component and a sea-power component. China has attempted to build a legal case for claims to waters in the South and East China Seas. The Chinese claims, based on a "legal rights protection chain," appear highly problematic when viewed through the lens of established maritime legal precedent.[4] In some cases, Chinese claims overlap those previously established by neighboring nations—for example, China, Japan, and Taiwan all claim the Senkaku Islands and various portions of the Spratlys are claimed by China and another six nations.

In other cases, China has attempted to establish territorial claims employing arguably unethical and illegal tactics, some of which involve depositing concrete and other building materials in shoal waters or atop submerged reefs to establish "islands" above sea level, a tactic China employed more aggressively in 2015.

In 2014, China claimed an air defense identification zone (ADIZ) in waters that overlap territorial claims by neighboring countries. In addition, China adopted a novel interpretation of what constituted an ADIZ, one that required any foreign military aircraft merely passing through the air space to check in with Chinese controllers, which is a contravention of the accepted use of ADIZs. To neighboring nations this ADIZ claim was unprecedented in terms of its geographic reach, the questionable legal basis for the claims, and the methods employed to enforce it. In 2014, for example, the Chinese appeared to openly harass Japanese aircraft that were flying in the vicinity of a newly designated ADIZ.

In parallel with its legal strategy, China has sought to increase its influence with a steady expansion of Chinese maritime capabilities, a product of two decades of uninterruptedly increasing defense budgets. China crossed a symbolic threshold when its People's Liberation Army Navy (PLAN) commissioned the nation's first aircraft carrier, the Liaoning (see Figure 23.2). The operations of the Chinese carrier, bought from Ukraine in 2008 and deployed to the South China Sea in 2013, have not been without controversy, especially when PLAN forces violated well-established international navigation norms of conduct and one of the carrier's escorts nearly collided with the USS Cowpens in December 2013. In another sign of China's naval expansion, the PLAN has, since 2008, conducted continuous anti-piracy operations in the Gulf of Aden.

In addition to growing the numbers and types of its ships, China has continued to expand its arsenal of surface-to-surface missiles, the most capable of which seem to be directed at countering the movement of US aircraft carrier battle groups into waters off the

---

[3] Manuel Mogato, "US Admiral Assures Philippines of Help in Disputed Sea," *Reuters News Service* (February 13, 2014), http://www .reuters.com/article/2014/02/13/us-philippines-usa-southchinasea-idUSBREA1C0LV20140213.

[4] Peter A. Dutton, "China's Maritime Disputes in the East and South China Seas: Testimony before a Hearing of the House Foreign Affairs Committee, January 14, 2014," *Naval War College Review*, 67:3 (2014), 7–18.

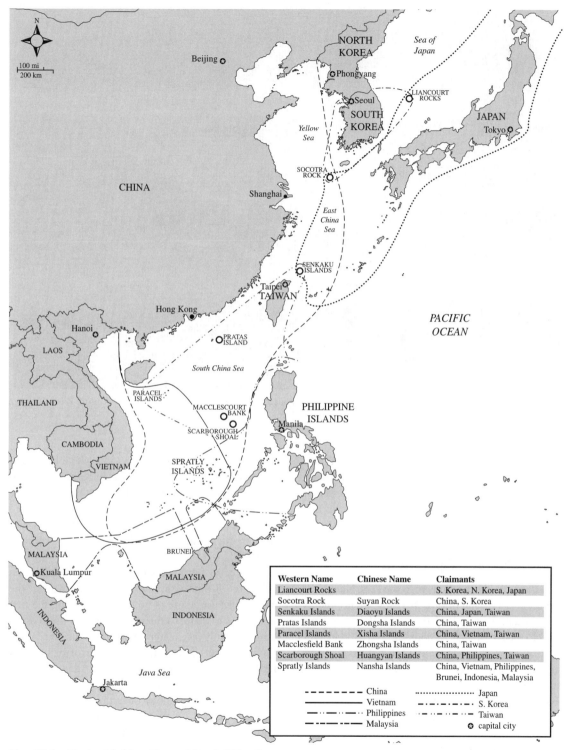

Map 23.1   Territorial claims, East and South China Seas.

Figure 23.2   China's PLAN aircraft carrier *Liaoning*, commissioned 2012. *Source:* © Zha Chunming / Xinhua Press / Corbis.

Chinese coast. The expansion of the Chinese fleet and the deployment of new missiles challenge established US Navy deployment patterns and the presumed freedom of movement of American sea power in this region.

Future US Navy Operations

Proceeding on the premise that the US Navy will continue to face contentious operating environments in the Middle East and off the coast of China, how might the fleet operate differently? What role will allies play? And, if tensions between powers did boil over into open conflict, how might sea power be manifest in such a future battle?

Recent history—exemplified by the unanticipated Russian–Ukraine crisis of 2014—suggests that unpredictability will characterize future challenges to the standing international order. In response,

the US Navy has adopted a more flexible, adaptable deployment policy that has become known as the "Fleet Response Plan." Under this system the ships and aircraft of the US Fleet have experienced shorter stays at home port, longer deployments, and more frequent "turnarounds" to the trouble spots of the world.

In an echo from the past, piracy on the high seas and in the littoral continue to plague areas from the Straits of Malacca, site of 56 incidents during the first six months of 2015, to the transit lanes off the coast of Africa, placing yet greater demands on limited American naval assets. The October 2000 terrorist attack on the USS *Cole* during a port visit to Aden in Yemen demonstrated that, while the Navy must prepare for complex, high-technology operations against emerging superpowers, it must also maintain the capability to counter explosive-laden speedboats or man-portable anti-tank and air-defense systems.

To meet these challenges, Chief of Naval Operations Michael Mullen presented the "1,000 Ship Navy" concept, through which the US Navy would join in a series of regional partnerships with other navies to deal with a spectrum of interests, including natural-disaster relief and operations to counter piracy, drug-smuggling operations, and human trafficking. The ideas underlying the new strategy were enunciated in the publication "Cooperative Strategy 21," jointly signed by Mullen's successor, Admiral Gary Roughhead, and the other sea service chiefs in 2007.[5]

Confronting a Peer Competitor

As the twenty-first century progresses, one of the most difficult "thought problems" confronting US Navy leaders involves how to continue to meet national goals of maintaining freedom of navigation, support of allies, and the ability to project power into a region from which a rising high-tech superpower seeks to exclude US operations. It might be tempting to view the Navy's success in projecting power from the sea into Afghanistan and Iraq between 2001 and 2003 as a validation of the health and vigor of traditional US sea power capabilities, but these operations faced no substantive maritime opposition. Such a fortuitous imbalance of power, which was favorable to the American sea services, is unlikely to recur in the future, especially in the South China Sea and East China Sea.

In the face of a peer competitor, the Navy would seek to project power or fight, if necessary, as a joint partner, in particular with the Air Force, unless base access from neighboring allies proved unavailable and Air Force space assets were neutralized. In 2014, the Department of Defense reported to Congress that for the past decade China had made "sustained investments in strategic forces modernization, as well as

[in] key anti-access/area-denial (A2/AD) capabilities such as advanced intermediate and medium-range conventional ballistic missiles, long-range land-attack and anti-ship cruise missiles, counter-space weapons, and offensive cyber capabilities."[6] As other regional powers begin to deploy such A2/AD systems it will become increasingly dangerous for US forces to operate on, above, and below contested waters.

In response to these developments, US naval and air force strategists began to develop a countervailing doctrine built upon advanced air and naval technologies. This 2010 Navy–Air Force initiative, initially known as "Air Sea Battle," was broadened to include the Army and the name changed to "Joint Concept for Access and Maneuver in the Global Commons" (JAM-GC) in January 2015. Though partially a marketing campaign to explain the need for a long-term reinvestment plans to Congress, JAM-GC was nonetheless successful in focusing American thinking on the growing challenge and, at the same time, in building support for the tools needed to counter what might be seen as a classic challenge of "sea denial."[7] But the question of how to fulfill traditional sea power missions in the twenty-first century is made increasingly complex due to rapid technological change. What kind of technology is needed to combat a peer competitor's new, more capable sea denial technologies?

Technology in a Future War at Sea

The incremental "speeding up" of naval warfare technologies—of reconnaissance, the speed of decision, the speed of movement, and the speed and accuracy of "fires"—will continue in the future. Looking forward into the twenty-first century, should American sea power confront a peer competitor, the environment will be contested in all physical domains of air, surface, subsurface, and space by faster and smarter

---

[5] Chief of Naval Operations, Commandant of the Marine Corps, Commandant of the Coast Guard, *A Cooperative Strategy for 21st Century Sea Power (CS 21)* (2007).

[6] Office of the Secretary of Defense, *Annual Report to Congress, Military and Security Developments Involving the People's Republic of China 2014* (2014).

[7] US Department of Defense, "Air Sea Battle Office," in *Air-Sea Battle: Service Collaboration to Address Anti-Access and Area Denial Challenges* (2013); Joint Staff Memorandum 0009-15, January 8, 2015, "Document: Air Sea Battle Name Change Memo," http://news.usni .org/2015/01/20/document-air-sea-battle-name-change-memo.

technologies. Based on the American order of battle in the 2010s, the US Navy will likely seek to dominate in all domains and will still deploy predominantly manned systems in the near to medium term. As of late 2015, the US Navy continues to plan for large, manned machines, to include additional P-8 maritime surveillance aircraft, *Gerald R. Ford*-class carriers equipped with an Electromagnetic Aircraft Launch System, and two new classes of manned submarines. One, a "Block V" variant of current *Virginia*-class submarines, will have four vertical tubes capable of launching robots or divers; the other, an "Ohio Replacement Submarine," will have a significantly quieter propulsion system. Similarly, the F-18 attack and fighter variants will be followed by the manned Joint Strike Fighter.

The surface navy building plans of the early century remain in considerable debate. The venerable *Burke*-class destroyers—the first was commissioned in 1991—continue in production, albeit with considerable modifications for helicopter hangars and enhanced radar and weapons systems capabilities. The *Zumwalt*-class destroyer, though few in number, may prove to be a game changer in its role as a technology exemplar, including its integrated all-UNIX ship's network. In an effort to lower the cost of the surface fleet, the Navy also produced a new class of frigates, initially named the Littoral Combat Ship and reclassified as frigates in 2015. While smaller, cheaper, and faster, these warships have been criticized as less survivable than more traditional and larger ships. In terms of the surface ships of the future, the advent of directed energy systems and the long-range rail gun may increase the survivability of large platforms in increasingly inhospitable maritime environments. Though the future of surface-ship construction is uncertain, innovative acquisition strategies, to include co-production with allies, may help lower unit costs and thereby contribute to stability in the size of the surface force.

Alternative Future: A Robotic Battlefield?

The maritime environments of the future may be so lethal that manned platforms become non-survivable. In such a future, swarms of smart, unmanned subsurface, surface, and air systems may be deployed to establish sea control to allow the follow-on entry of traditional manned warships and aircraft. Such a development would not come as a total surprise, as evidence since World War II reveals a trajectory wherein the Navy has come to rely on progressively "smarter," more accurate, more automatic, and faster machines; the Aegis system can be seen in hindsight as an evolutionary step in this direction. What may be different this time is that cumulative advances in artificial intelligence could produce a qualitatively new level of reliance on autonomous machines that challenges fundamental theories of war as a human and machine endeavor. Some influential Department of Defense officials have predicted the proliferation of automated, smart fleets of robots in the early twenty-first century.

Evidence of such a possible future may be accumulating. In the second decade of the twenty-first century, the first fully autonomous takeoff and landing of an unmanned aircraft, catapulted and retrieved from an aircraft carrier, was demonstrated by the X47B. The surveillance fleet of the P3 and P8 tradition will be augmented with MQ-4C Triton, a long-endurance, unmanned air vehicle. A multitude of smaller scale unmanned aerial vehicle drones also entered production and were deployed in the early 2010s, most capable of launching and retrieval from small ships. In the field of mine warfare, unmanned systems have shown particular promise, with numerous programs and technologies in development in the early twenty-first century. Other platform communities, such as submarine and surface warfare, continue to research and develop their own unmanned undersea vehicles and unmanned surface vehicles. As traditional ships and aircraft remain in production alongside growing numbers of unmanned systems, the question of the human operator remains: what kind of officer and sailor is needed to operate the traditional platform alongside a robotic fleet?

In the past century, the naval officer was in many ways challenged to become something of a "machine operator"—that is, required to spend vast amounts of time mastering the mechanical aspects of machine platform operation. In the future, a human operator will need to maintain a minimum of operational–mechanical proficiency, especially in a cyber contested environment that may threaten the autopilot,

Triton

Machines have always been integral to sea power. With breakthroughs in artificial intelligence, electronics, and control systems, sea power may enter a new age wherein the human is replaced entirely across all fields of naval operations. The MQ-4C Triton, an unmanned aircraft system, first flew in 2013 with plans for its deployment in 2017 as a companion to manned surveillance platforms such as the P-8 Poseidon. Triton promises to provide real-time intelligence, surveillance, and reconnaissance over vast ocean and coastal regions. Triton will be equipped with a sensor suite that provides a 360-degree view of its surroundings and allows ships to be tracked over time by gathering information on their speed, location, and classification. Triton will support a wide range of missions including maritime patrol and search and rescue. The aircraft can fly up to 24 hours at a time, at altitudes higher than 10 miles, giving it an operational range of 8,200 nautical miles. The Navy's program of record in 2015 calls for 68 aircraft to be fielded.

Numerous additional unmanned, semi-autonomous systems are in various stages of development. While current doctrine envisions unmanned systems as a complement to manned platforms, there remains the possibility unmanned systems will assume greater operational roles. The historical tendency of new technologies to exceed the man-made bounds of their creators is well documented, as the first naval aircraft were envisioned as the "eyes of the fleet," not as a revolutionary combat system. Yet, within months of the beginning of World War II, naval attack aircraft had transformed the nature of sea power. It remains to be seen whether these new, semi-autonomous technologies will remain complements to manned platforms or will instead come to dominate one or more sea power domains under sea, on the sea surface, or in the air.

MQ-4C Triton.

navigation, and control functions of modern platforms (i.e., the officer may need to reassume more manual control of his/her platform). But, with the proliferation of smart machines, natural language processors, and highly efficient training simulators, it is plausible that the officer of the future may be required to spend less time honing machine operational skills than in the past. If such time savings materialize, where will officers of the future refocus their energies? One possibility is that the future officer will have to become more computer-electronic proficient, a variant of "cyber officer" discussed below, in order to defend his/her network and platform from cyber attacks. Another possibility is that automation may free the human to focus on a different mix of challenges. The human may have to become an even better integrator, becoming a repository of knowledge and judgment that weaves together the myriad factors of sea power—the technical as well as the non-technical. To most effectively wield a military force requires the integration of multiple knowledge sets, to include political, ethical, social, software, hardware, and environmental, as well as knowing the human enemy. Perhaps as the Navy relies more heavily on allies of different cultures there could be a renewed emphasis on cultural education and foreign languages for future officers and enlisted personnel.

Since the early nuclear age the US Navy has fulfilled a global strategic mission: the defense of the homeland as a component of the nuclear deterrence triad. It is expected that this mission will continue, and budget projections in the mid-2010s assume that the Navy will continue to maintain a submarine ballistic missile fleet of 18. While the Navy continues to fulfill the nuclear deterrent mission, a new strategic mission has emerged: ballistic missile defense. After decades of development, such a capability is taking physical form in a sea-based ballistic missile defense capability built around the Navy's Aegis fleet. In 2014, Israel's Iron Dome, a system similar to the Navy ballistic missile defense technology, demonstrated the value of such a system when it intercepted several hundred incoming munitions fired by Hamas in neighboring Gaza.

Alternative Future: The Rise of Electromagnetic-Cyber Warfare

Nuclear deterrence and missile defense against nuclear weapons may not be the only strategic mission demanded of the Navy of the future. In the early twenty-first century, a new form of warfare emerged that made it possible for an enemy to mount a direct attack against computer and information networks, a form of conflict that coalesced around the term "cyber warfare" or the combined term "electromagnetic-cyber warfare." An entirely new security environment appears to be emerging in the form of cyber space, and with it concomitant requirements for new technology; novel ideas about doctrine, tactics, and strategy; and new sailor skill sets.

The possibility of computer warfare began to be taken seriously by forward-thinking naval officers in the mid-1990s when a former combat aviator, battle group commander, and War College president, Vice Admiral Arthur Cebrowski, and his team predicted the coming of conflict termed "network-centric warfare." While Cebrowski's vision of war still rested on physical platforms, the decisiveness in war shifted to those who could integrate the platforms across networks of computers. In contrast, more traditional officers were not convinced that the computer network would offer a decisive advantage in war, arguing instead for the continued primacy of the independent platform, which would carry and direct the missiles, torpedoes, and other launched weapons. The quiet debate between a loose collection of traditionalists and reformers led by Cebrowski persisted out of the public eye for almost a decade. The network-centric visionaries began to gain advantage when Cebrowski was promoted to head of the Office of Force Transformation, located in close proximity to other reformers inside the Office of the Secretary of Defense in 2001. However, Cebrowski did not live to see his speculations validated a few years later, when a cyber conflict erupted between nation states.

In 2007 Estonia experienced a rudimentary cyber conflict when one of the largest ever "denial of service" attacks was perpetrated against this small country. The attacks were traced to a distributed network of computers controlled by hackers sympathetic to Russia, but the Kremlin claimed innocence. A year later, in 2008, a brief Russian incursion into neighboring Georgia was accompanied by cyber attacks on Georgian government and commercial sites, and, in this case, the Russian government made few claims of innocence.

Cyber warfare became manifest among weapon systems when Israeli fighter-bombers penetrated Syrian airspace, undetected, in a bombing raid on a suspected nuclear research site in 2007. Though the exact details remain classified by the countries involved, it appears that Syrian air defense radars never "saw" the bombers, because a computer virus, inserted by Israeli special forces, had "blinded" the air defense computers. While these cyber attacks demonstrated the capacity of an aggressor to degrade computers' performance, either to slow essential government services in the Estonian case or to blind sensors in the Syrian case, in neither case was physical damage caused by the cyber attacks. However, such a threshold, that of cyber induced physical damage, was crossed in 2010 when unknown countries deployed malware, later known as Stuxnet, against Iranian uranium centrifuges. Destructive computer code destroyed a multitude of the uranium-processing machines and set back Iranian nuclear weapons development by several years. Perhaps in retaliation, Iranian cyber attackers targeted thousands of Aramco (Saudi Arabia's national oil

Arthur Cebrowski

Arthur Cebrowski (1942–2005), a 1964 graduate of Villanova University, held a master's degree in computer systems management from the Naval Postgraduate School and was a federal executive fellow in the Council on Foreign Relations. A naval aviator, he commanded at all levels, from attack squadron to aircraft carrier, culminating in command at sea of the USS *America* battle group. A veteran of multiple conflicts, he served in combat in both the Vietnam War and Desert Storm and in UN operations off Bosnia and Somalia in 1993. Despite what appeared to be a traditional career path in aviation, Cebrowski took an early interest in how to apply his knowledge of computers, communications, and networks to naval warfare. His thinking began to influence naval doctrine when he served as Commander Carrier Group Six, where he exercised

command of a distributed US–NATO task force, operating across the Mediterranean Sea and off the coasts of Bosnia and Somalia in 1993. He continued groundbreaking work in the field of networks and information systems when he was assigned as director of Command, Control, Communications, and Computers (J-6), Joint Staff, during the mid-1990s. It was during this time that he assembled a team of like-minded reformers and began to develop his concepts of what would become network-centric warfare—concepts that helped to shape early thinking on what became known as electromagnetic-cyber warfare. His influence on both the study of war and the future officer corps grew when he served as president of the Naval War College between 1998 and 2001. After retirement from the Navy, Cebrowski continued his

work as a military reformer and early thinker on network-centric and cyber warfare when he assumed duties as Director of the Office of Force Transformation, a division in the Office of the Secretary of Defense, a position he held until forced to retire anew due to health reasons.

Arthur Cebrowski.

company) corporate computers in an attack known as Shamoon, which erased the hard drives of the targeted machines and disrupted company operations.

In the United States the portent of cyber attack became evident following a major penetration of US government and military systems in 2008, one that required a subsequent clean-up operation dubbed Buckshot Yankee. The cause proved to be a careless government employee who picked up what appeared to be a discarded flash drive and inserted the infected device into a classified computer. The result was one of the largest government computer network compromises in US history, a security disaster that prompted the Department of Defense and the US Navy to accelerate the creation of a credible cyber defense force. In 2014 the computer system of

Sony Pictures, a US subsidiary of a Japanese corporation, was penetrated—probably by North Korean agents—and internal documents posted on the internet, much to the embarrassment of corporate officials. The three reprisals that followed interrupted internet and 3G network services for varying periods. In 2015 it remains unclear what this new environment may mean for American sea power and security, but, nevertheless, the cyber domain has been officially recognized by the Navy as a fifth domain of conflict.

The Department of Defense established US Cyber Command (CyberCom), a subunified command subordinate to the US Strategic Command, in 2009, and the Navy established a shore-based Tenth Fleet command, which focused not on any particular physical security environment (such as land or sea) but

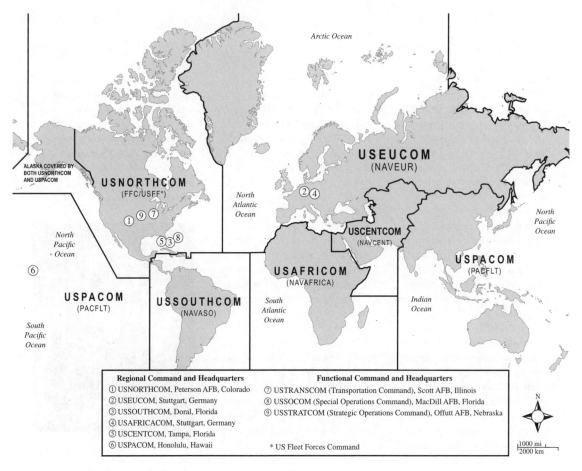

Map 23.2   Unified commands (Navy component commands).

on cyber space (see Map 23.2). In response to the recognition of this fifth domain, in the early 2010s the Navy began the process of creating new cyber strategies, technology investment plans, command structures, and career paths. At the service academies and war colleges, new curricula were developed and a new hybrid corps, the Information Dominance Corps, a community of professionals focused on intelligence and information warfare in cyber space, began to take shape. These investments in ideas, money, and people came none too soon. In the mid-2010s problems relating to the "cyber" show no signs of abating and may be growing in complexity as the "internet of things" proliferates and the deployment of increasingly intelligent, netted machines leaves open the possibility of

even wider cyber conflict than Cebrowski envisioned just a decade ago.

Despite the establishment of CyberCom and the US Tenth Fleet, cyber attacks continued against American targets. US Navy networks were compromised again in 2013, a penetration so deep that it required months of cyber forensics and defensive operations to clear out the enemy cyber bots and malware. American defense forces will not only face Iranian, Russian, or Syrian cyber challenges in the future. The greatest threat may again arise in the Far East. China is perhaps the largest purveyor of cyber malware in the world, and is known to have penetrated American defense contractors, government sites, and utility systems. The scale of the Chinese cyber effort was revealed with the publication of the Mandiant Corporation's *APT1: Exposing One of China's Cyber Espionage Units* (2013), which resulted in the first ever indictment of a foreign country's cyber intelligence officers.[8]

Does this all mean that it is possible that the next conflict will play out in the new environment of a cyber space? In contemplation of such a possibility, countries around the world are rapidly expanding their cyber commands and capabilities. For the foreseeable future, Navy leaders will grapple with perhaps the most complex, murky questions in a generation: what kind of navy do we need to win a cyber war? What strategic concept or doctrine best applies in this situation? What kind of technology should be built and what types of officers are needed to lead at the nexus of the human and machine? The struggle to create strategic, operational, and tactical concepts for cyber conflict may be one of the greatest intellectual challenges of a generation.

Some Speculations: Discontinuous Change and the Future of Sea Power

Despite the emergence of new challenges and technology, deployment patterns and strategic uses of the Navy will exhibit continuity with many practices of the past several decades. New technologies will continue to advance on a trajectory to increasingly fast and more automated systems but will still operate in close proximity to the human operator. Even in the case of cyber war, it seems likely humans will remain in overall control of sea power technologies in the future.

Yet it is possible that the future may more radically diverge from the trajectories discussed thus far. If cyber space becomes the dominant, strategically vital environment and overshadows the physical realms, traditional concepts of sea power could radically change. It is possible that cyber war may accelerate to such speeds that only autonomous artificial general intelligence machines will be able to master the complexity of war, leaving human "commanders" more as spectators than participants, perhaps only in "control" of an internet kill switch. Conversely, if a cyber battle

should be fought to a draw, where no side can gain an electronic victory, the advantage could shift back to the Navy, which will likely have preserved a modicum of analog systems controlled by more skilled human operators.

Another alternative future, not without historical precedent, may lie on the horizon: there could be significantly more restrictive arms control measures that limit the technical advance of the American and rival navies. In the 1920s the United States promoted major cuts to naval building programs via the Washington Naval Treaties. In the 1980s, President Reagan championed the Strategic Arms Reductions Talks, which resulted in previously unimaginable cuts to nuclear arsenals. Might such an arms control alternative future await naval leaders, one that places strict limits on both unmanned systems and cyber technologies? If such a future lies ahead, traditional naval capabilities may continue to dominate calculations of sea power for decades to come.

Finally, an alternate future driven by socio-economic disruption ashore may await strategists and shipbuilders of the future. Even if the United States is never "beaten" at sea, tight budgets may result in a much smaller, less capable fleet. An economic shock could severely limit the ability of the United States to fund the building of a state-of-the-art navy. There have been precedents for such a radical reduction of major sea powers: the American post-Civil War period, when an austere federal budget was directed to internal investments, leaving a once highly advanced navy rusting pier side; the collapse in the Royal Navy building programs as a result of economic decline in the post–World War II period; and the eclipse of the once global Soviet navy in the 1990s due to economic collapse. Such an economic-driven reduction in US sea power would not be out of the question, especially for a nation so indebted to overseas creditors. But, even if the United States does not itself experience economic crisis, should the world system of states become increasingly pressed by non-state or terrorist organizations—the very concept of "great powers" could be rendered obsolete—there may be a major reapportionment of scarce defense dollars into

---

[8] Mandiant Corporation, *APT1: Exposing one of China's Cyber Espionage Units* (2013), http://intelreport.mandiant.com.

counter-terrorist, special operations, or intelligence organizations, which could result in a much smaller Navy.

Conclusion

It seems probable the Navy will continue in traditions of sea power not radically different from those dating from the mid-twentieth century. The US Navy will deploy to regions similar to those in which the fleet operates today. The missions will be a continuation, in many ways, of what sailors do today. However, the proliferation of ever smarter machines may result in a type of warfare increasingly dominated by unmanned systems. If cyber space becomes the dominant domain

of warfare, sea power may change even more radically. But these possible futures remain uncertain speculations. The fundamental challenges ahead will require steady leadership and thoughtful discernment, but can the military and political leaders of this new century anticipate the future trajectory of sea power and rise above special interests and inertia to build and deploy a navy fit for these new times? The answers to these questions are unknown. What can be said with complete certainty is that American sea power will be dynamic in the decades ahead. For those who go down to the sea in ships, the twenty-first century will witness neither fair winds nor following seas, but perhaps the most challenging era in the history of American sea power.

Further Reading

General Works

Baer, George W. *One Hundred Years of Sea Power: The US Navy, 1890–1990* (1993).

Borneman, Walter R. *The Admirals: Nimitz, Halsey, Leahy, and King—The Five-Star Admirals Who Won the War at Sea* (2012).

Bradford, James C., ed. *Quarterdeck and Bridge: Two Centuries of Naval Leaders* (1997).

Chisholm, Donald. *Waiting for Dead Men's Shoes: Origins and Development of the US Navy's Officer Personnel System, 1793–1941* (2001).

Coletta, Paolo E., ed. *American Secretaries of the Navy*, 2 vols. (1980).

George, James L. *History of Warships: From Ancient Times to the Twenty-First Century* (1998).

Hagan, Kenneth J. *This People's Navy* (1991).

Harding, Richard. *Modern Naval History: Debates and Prospects* (2015).

Herring, George. *From Colony to Superpower: US Foreign Relations since 1776* (2011).

Howarth, Stephen. *To Shining Sea: A History of the United States Navy, 1775–1991* (1991).

Love Robert W., Jr., ed. *The Chiefs of Naval Operations* (1980).

Love Robert W., Jr. *A History of the US Navy*, 2 vols. (1992).

Mahan, Alfred Thayer. *The Influence of Sea Power upon History, 1660–1783* (1890).

Millett, Allan R. *Semper Fidelis: The History of the United States Marine Corps* (1980).

Moskin, J. Robert. *The US Marine Corps Story*, 3rd ed. (1992).

Rose, Lisle A. *Power at Sea: A Violent Peace, 1946–2006* (2007).

Ryan, Paul B. *First Line of Defense: The US Navy since 1945* (1981).

Sweetman, Jack, ed. *Great American Naval Battles* (1998).

Symonds, Craig L. *The Naval Institute Historical Atlas of the US Navy* (2001).

1 Sea Power and the Modern State System

Brewer, John. *The Sinews of Power: War, Money and the English State, 1688–1783* (1988).

Davies, J. D. *Pepy's Navy: The Ships, Men and Organization, 1649–1689* (2008).

Dull, Jonathan. *The Age of the Ship of the Line: The British and French Navies, 1650–1815* (2009).

Harding, Richard. *Seapower and Naval Warfare, 1650–1830* (1999).

Kennedy, Paul. *The Rise and Fall of British Naval Mastery* (1976, 1983).

Lavery, Brian. *The Ship of the Line: Design, Construction, and Fittings*, 2 vols. (1983).

Lewis, Archibald, and Timothy Runyan. *European Naval and Maritime History, 300–1500* (1985).

Padfield, Peter. *Maritime Supremacy and the Opening of the Western Mind: Naval Campaigns that Shaped the Modern World, 1588–1782* (1999).

Starr, Chester G. *The Influence of Sea Power on Ancient History* (1989).

Wilson, Ben. *Empire of the Deep: The Rise and Fall of the British Navy* (2013)

2 The American War for Independence at Sea

Bell, William Clark. *George Washington's Navy: Being an Account of His Excellency's Fleet in New England Waters* (1960).

Buker, George E. *The Penobscot Expedition: Commodore Saltonstall and the Massachusetts Conspiracy of 1779* (2002).

America, Sea Power, and the World, First Edition. Edited by James C. Bradford.
© 2016 John Wiley & Sons, Inc. Published 2016 by John Wiley & Sons, Inc.

Dull, Jonathan R. *The French Navy and American Independence: A Study of Arms and Diplomacy, 1774–1787* (1975).

McGrath, Tim. *Give Me a Fast Ship: The Continental Navy and America's Revolution at Sea* (2014).

Miller, Nathan. *Sea of Glory: A Naval History of the American Revolution* (1974).

Morgan, William James. *Captains to the Northward: The New England Captains in the Continental Navy* (1959).

Morison, Samuel Eliot. *John Paul Jones: A Sailor's Biography* (1959).

Nelson, James L. *Benedict Arnold's Navy: The Ragtag Fleet that Lost the Battle of Lake Champlain but Won the American Revolution* (2006).

Patton, Robert H. *Patriot Pirates: The Privateer War for Freedom and Fortune in the American Revolution* (2008).

Smith, Charles R. *Marines in the Revolution: A History of the Continental Marines in the American Revolution, 1775–1783* (1975).

Syrett, David. *The Royal Navy in American Waters, 1775–1783* (1989).

Syrett, David. *The Royal Navy in European Waters during the American Revolution* (1998).

3 Genesis of the US Navy, 1785–1806

Fowler, William M. *Jack Tars and Commodores: The American Navy, 1783–1815* (1984).

Hayes, Frederic H. "John Adams and American Sea Power," *American Neptune*, 25:1 (January 1965), 35–45.

Kohn, Richard. *Eagle and Sword: The Federalists and the Creation of the Military Establishment in America, 1783–1802* (1975).

Lambert, Frank. *The Barbary Wars: American Independence in the Atlantic World* (2005).

Leiner, Frederick. *Millions for Defense: The Subscription Warships of 1798* (2000).

London, Joshua. *Victory in Tripoli: How America's War with the Barbary Pirates Established the US Navy and Shaped a Nation* (2005).

McKee, Christopher. *A Gentlemanly and Honorable Profession: The Creation of the US Naval Officer Corps, 1794–1815* (1991).

Palmer, Michael. *Stoddert's War: Naval Operations during the Quasi-War with France, 1798–1801* (1987).

Smelser, Marshall. *The Congress Founds the Navy, 1787–1798* (1959).

Symonds, Craig L. *Navalists and Antinavalists: The Naval Policy Debate in the United States, 1785–1827* (1980).

Toll, Ian W. *Six Frigates: The Epic History of the Founding of the US Navy* (2006).

4 The Naval War of 1812 and the Confirmation of Independence, 1807–1815

Daughan, George. *The Shining Sea: David Porter and the Epic Voyage of the USS* Essex *during the War of 1812* (2013).

Dudley, Wade G. *Splintering the Wooden Wall: The British Blockade of the United States, 1812–1815* (2002).

McCranie, Kevin D. *Utmost Gallantry: The US and Royal Navies at Sea in the War of 1812* (2011).

Morriss, Roger. *Cockburn and the British Navy in Transition: Admiral Sir George Cockburn 1752–1853* (1998).

Roosevelt, Theodore. *The Naval War of 1812* (1882).

Schroeder, John H. *The Battle of Lake Champlain: A "Brilliant and Extraordinary Victory"* (2015).

Skaggs, David Curtis. *A Signal Victory: The Lake Erie Campaign, 1812–13* (1997).

Skaggs, David Curtis. *Thomas Macdonough: Master of Command in the Early US Navy* (2003).

Smith, Gene A. *"For the Purposes of Defense": The Politics of the Jeffersonian Gunboat Program* (1995).

Smith, Gene A. *Thomas ap Catesby Jones: Commodore of Manifest Destiny* (2000).

Stagg, J. C. A. *The War of 1812* (2012).

Tucker, Spencer C., and Frank T. Reuter. *Injured Honor: The Chesapeake–Leopard Affair, June 22, 1807* (1996).

5 The Squadron Navy: Agent of a Commercial Empire, 1815–1890

Bain, David Haward. *Bitter Waters: America's Forgotten Naval Mission to the Dead Sea* (2011).

Canney, Donald L. *Africa Squadron: The US Navy and the Slave Trade, 1842–1861* (2006).

Drake, Frederick C. *The Empire of the Seas: A Biography of Rear Admiral Robert Wilson Shufeldt, USN* (1984).

Henson, Curtis, Jr. *Commissioners and Commodores: The East India Squadron and American Diplomacy* (1982).

Johnson, Robert E. *Thence Round Cape Horn: The Story of United States Naval Forces on Pacific Station, 1818–1923* (1963).

Leiner, Frederick C. *The End of Barbary Terror: America's 1815 War against the Pirates of North Africa* (2006).

Long, David F. *Gold Braid and Foreign Relations: Diplomatic Activities of US Naval Officers, 1798–1883* (1988).

Philbrick, Nathaniel. *Sea of Glory: America's Voyage of Discovery, The US Exploring Expedition, 1838–1842* (2003).

Schroeder, John H. *Shaping a Maritime Empire: The Commercial and Diplomatic Role of the American Navy, 1829–1861* (1985).

Still, William N., Jr. *American Sea Power in the Old World: The United States Navy in European and Near Eastern Waters, 1865–1917* (1980).

Wiley, Peter Booth. *Yankees in the Land of the Gods: Commodore Perry and the Opening of Japan* (1991).

Williams, Frances L. *Matthew Fontaine Maury, Scientist of the Sea* (1963).

6 Technological Revolution at Sea

Brown, Wesley A. *Analysis of the Relationship between Technology and Strategy and How They Shaped the Confederate States Navy* (1999).

Canney, Donald L. *The Old Steam Navy*, vol. 2: *The Ironclads, 1842–1885* (1993).

Coletta, Paolo E. *Admiral Bradley Fiske and the American Navy* (1979).

Cooling, Benjamin Franklin, III. *Gray Steel and Blue Water Navy* (1979).

McBride, William M. "From Measuring Progress to Technological Innovation: The Prewar Annapolis Engineering Experimental Station," in Steven A. Walton, ed., *Instrumental in War: Scientific Research and Instrumentation Between Knowledge and the World* (2005).

McBride, William M. *Technological Change and the United States Navy, 1865–1945* (2000).

Mindell, David A. *War, Technology, and Experience Aboard the USS* Monitor (2000).

Morison, Elting E. *Admiral Sims and the Modern American Navy* (1942).

Reilly, John C., Jr., and Robert L. Scheina. *American Battleships, 1886–1923: Predreadnought Design and Construction* (1980).

Roland, Alex. *Underwater Warfare in the Age of Sail* (1978).

Schneller, Robert J. *A Quest for Glory: A Biography of Rear Admiral John A. Dahlgren* (1996).

Sloan, Edward William, III. *Benjamin Franklin Isherwood, Naval Engineer: The Years as Engineer in Chief, 1861–1869* (1965).

7 The Civil War: Blockade and Counter-Blockade

Bennett, Michael J. *Union Jacks: Yankee Sailors in the Civil War* (2004).

Browning, Robert M. *From Cape Charles to Cape Fear: The North Atlantic Blockading Squadron during the Civil War* (1993).

Browning, Robert M. *Success Is All that Was Expected: The South Atlantic Blockading Squadron during the Civil War* (2002).

Davis, William C. *Duel between the First Ironclads* (1975).

Hearn, Chester G. *Gray Raiders of the Sea: How Eight Confederate Warships Destroyed the Union's High Seas Commerce* (1991).

McPherson, James M. *War on the Waters: The Union and Confederate Navies, 1861–1865* (2012).

Roberts, William H. *Civil War Ironclads: The US Navy and Industrial Mobilization* (2002).

Symonds, Craig L. *Lincoln and His Admirals: Abraham Lincoln, the US Navy, and the Civil War* (2008).

Symonds, Craig L. *The Civil War at Sea* (2009).

Taaffe, Stephen R. *Commanding Lincoln's Navy: Union Naval Leadership during the Civil War* (2009).

Wise, Stephen R. *Lifeline of the Confederacy: Blockade Running during the Civil War* (1988).

8 The Civil War on Rivers and Coastal Waters

Canfield, Daniel T. "Opportunity Lost: Combined Operations and the Development of Union Military Strategy, April 1861–April 1862," *Journal of Military History*, 79:3 (2015), 657–690.

Cornish, Dudley Taylor, and Virginia Jeans Laas. *Lincoln's Lee: The Life of Samuel Phillips Lee, United States Navy, 1812–1897* (1986).

Hearn, Chester. *Admiral David Dixon Porter: The Civil War Years* (1996).

Johnson, Ludwell H. *Red River Campaign: Politics and Cotton in the Civil War* (1999).

Joiner, Gary. *Mr. Lincoln's Brown Water Navy: The Mississippi Squadron* (2007).

McPherson, James M. *War on the Waters: The Union and Confederate Navies, 1861–1865* (2012).

Milligan, John D. *Gunboats Down the Mississippi* (1965).

Pratt, Fletcher. *Civil War on Western Waters* (1956).

Reed, Rowena. *Combined Operations in the Civil War* (1978).

Roberts, William H. *Now for the Contest: Coastal and Oceanic Naval Operations in the Civil War* (2004).

Tucker, Spencer C. *Andrew Foote: Civil War Admiral on Western Waters* (2000).

9 The New Navy, 1865–1895

Cooling, B. Franklin. *Gray Steel and Blue Water* (1979).

Dorwart, Jeffery M. *The Office of Naval Intelligence: The Birth of America's First Intelligence Agency, 1865–1918* (1979).

Goldberg, Joyce S. *The Baltimore Affair* (1986).

Harrod, Frederick. *Manning the New Navy: The Development of a Modern Naval Enlisted Force, 1899–1940* (1978).

Healy, David. *US Expansionism: The Imperialist Urge in the 1890s* (1970).

Herrick, Walter R., Jr. *The American Revolution* (1966).

Karsten, Peter. *The Naval Aristocracy: The Golden Age of Annapolis and the Emergence of Modern American Navalism* (1972).

Rentfrow, James C. *Home Squadron: The US Navy on the North Atlantic Squadron* (2014).

Seager, Robert, II. *Alfred Thayer Mahan: The Man and His Letters* (1977).

Shulman, Mark R. *Navalism and the Emergence of American Sea Power, 1882–1893* (1995).

Still, William N., Jr. *American Sea Power in the Old World: The United States Navy in European Waters, 1865–1917* (1980).

Swann, Leonard Alexander, Jr. *John Roach: Maritime Entrepreneur, the Years as Naval Contractor, 1862–1886* (1985).

Thiesen, William H. *Industrializing American Shipbuilding* (2006).

Karnow, Stanley. *In Our Image: America's Empire in the Philippines* (1990).

Langley, Lester D. *The Banana Wars: United States Intervention in the Caribbean, 1898–1934* (2001).

Noble, Dennis L. *The Eagle and the Dragon: The United States Military in China, 1901–1937* (1990).

Rosenberg, Emily. *Spreading the American Dream: American Economic and Cultural Expansion, 1898–1945* (1982).

Schmidt, Hans. *Maverick Marine: General Smedley D. Butler and the Contradictions of American Military History* (1987).

Schmidt, Hans. *The Occupation of Haiti* (1971).

Stephanson, Anders. *Manifest Destiny: American Expansionism and the Empire of Right* (1995).

Sweetman, Jack. *The Landing at Veracruz: 1914* (1968).

Tolley, Kemp. *Yangtze Patrol: The US Navy in China* (1971).

10 War with Spain and the Revolution in Naval Affairs, 1895–1910

Alden, John D. *The American Steel Navy: A Photographic History of the US Navy from the Introduction of the Steel Hull in 1883 to the Cruise of the Great White Fleet, 1907–1909* (1989).

Bradford, James C., ed. *Crucible of Empire: The Spanish–American War and Its Aftermath* (1993).

Braisted, William R. (1958). *The United States Navy in the Pacific, 1897–1909* (1958).

Cooling, Benjamin Franklin. *USS Olympia: Herald of Empire* (2000).

Dowart, Jeffery M. *ONI: The Office of Naval Intelligence* (1979).

Hill, Richard. *War at Sea in the Ironclad Age* (2000).

Leek, Jim. *Manila and Santiago: The New Steel Navy in the Spanish–American War* (2009).

Morgan, H. Wayne. *America's Road to Empire: The War with Spain and Overseas Expansion* (1965).

Reckner, James. *Teddy Roosevelt's Great White Fleet* (1988).

Spector, Ronald H. *Admiral of the New Empire: The Life and Career of George Dewey* (1974).

Spector, Ronald H. *Professors of War: The Naval War College and the Development of the Naval Profession* (1977).

Trask, David F. *The War with Spain in 1898* (1981).

11 Defending Imperial Interests in Asia and the Caribbean, 1898–1941

Benjamin, Jules R. *The United States and Cuba: Hegemony and Dependent Development, 1880–1934* (1977).

Boot, Max. *The Savage Wars of Peace: Small Wars and the Rise of American Power* (2002).

Clark, George B. *Treading Softly: US Marines in China, 1819–1949* (2001).

12 Naval Rivalry and World War I at Sea, 1900–1920

Feuer, A. B. *The United States Navy in World War I: Combat at Sea and in the Air* (1999).

Jones, Jerry W. *US Battleship Operations in World War I* (1998).

Kennedy, Paul. *The Rise of the Anglo-German Antagonism* (1987).

Klachko, Mary, with David F. Trask. *Admiral William Shepherd Benson: First Chief of Naval Operations* (1987).

Morison, Elting E. *Admiral Sims and the Modern American Navy* (1942).

Rossano, Geoffrey L. *Stalking the U-Boat: US Naval Aviation in Europe during World War I* (2010).

Sims, William S. *The Victory at Sea* (1920).

Sondhaus, Lawrence. *The Great War at Sea* (2014).

Spector, Ronald H. *Admiral of the New Empire: the Life and Career of George Dewey* (1974).

Stein, Stephen K. *From Torpedoes to Aviation: Washington Irving Chambers and Innovation in the New Navy, 1876–1913* (2007).

Still, William N. *Crisis at Sea: The United States Navy in European Waters in World War I* (2007).

Wimmel, Kenneth. *Theodore Roosevelt and the Great White Fleet* (2000).

13 Finding Certainty in Uncertain Times: The Navy in the Interwar Years

Buckley, Thomas H. *The United States and the Washington Conference, 1921–1922* (1970).

Davis, Vincent. *The Admirals' Lobby* (1976).

Felker, Craig C. *Testing American Sea Power: US Navy Strategic Exercises, 1923–1940* (2004).

Kuehn, John T. *Agents of Innovation: The General Board and the Design of the Fleet that Defeated the Japanese Navy* (2008).

McBride, William. *Technological Change and the United States Navy, 1865–1945* (2000).

Melhorn, Charles. *Two-Block Fox: The Rise of the Aircraft Carrier, 1911–1929* (2001).

Miller, Edward S. *War Plan Orange: The US Strategy to Defeat Japan, 1897–1945* (1993).

Reynolds, Clark G. *Fast Carriers: The Forging of an Air Navy* (1968).

Spector, Ronald H. *At War at Sea: Sailors and Naval Combat in the Twentieth Century* (2001).

Trimble, William F. *Admiral William A. Moffett: Architect of Naval Aviation* (1994).

Vlahos, Michael. *The Blue Sword: The Naval War College and the American Mission, 1919–1941* (1980).

Weir, Gary E. *Building American Submarines, 1914–1940* (1991).

Wheeler, Gerald E. *Prelude to Pearl Harbor: The United States Navy and the Far East, 1921–1931* (1963).

14 World War II in the Atlantic and Mediterranean

Bailey, Thomas A., and Paul B. Ryan. *Hitler vs. Roosevelt: The Undeclared Naval War* (1979).

Blair, Clay. *Hitler's U-Boat War*, 2 vols. (1996–1998).

Bunker, John. *Liberty Ships: The Ugly Ducklings of World War II* (1972).

Gannon, Michael. *Operation Drumbeat: The Dramatic True Story of Germany's First U-Boat Attacks along the American Coast in World War II* (1990).

Gardner, W. J. R. *Decoding History: The Battle of the Atlantic and Ultra* (2000).

Kahn, David. *Seizing the Enigma: The Race to Break the German U-Boat Codes, 1939–1943* (1991).

Morison, Samuel Eliot. *History of United States Naval Operations in World War II*, vol. 9: *Sicily-Salerno-Anzio, January 1943–June 1944* (1954).

Rohwer, Jurgen. *The Critical Convoy Battles of March 1943: The Battle for HX.229/SC122* (1977).

Symonds, Craig L. *Neptune: The Allied Invasion of Europe and the D-Day Landings* (2014).

Syrett, David. *The Defeat of the German U-Boats: The Battle of the Atlantic* (1994).

Van der Vat, Dan. *The Atlantic Campaign: World War II's Great Struggle at Sea* (1988).

Williams, Kathleen Broome. *Secret Weapon: US High-Frequency Direction Finding in the Battle of the Atlantic* (1996).

15 Defense in the Pacific, 1937–1943

Borneman, Walter. *The Admirals* (2012).

Buell, Thomas B. *Master of Sea Power: A Biography of Fleet Admiral Ernest J. King* (1980).

Frank, Richard B. *Guadalcanal: The Definitive Account of the Landmark Battle* (1990).

Garfield, Brian. *The Thousand-Mile War: World War II in Alaska and the Aleutians* (1969).

Henry, Chris. *The Battle of the Coral Sea* (2003).

King, Ernest. *First Report to the Secretary of the Navy Covering Our Peacetime Navy and Our Wartime Navy and Including Combat Operations up to 1 March 1944* (1944).

Lundstrom, John. *The First South Pacific Campaign* (1976).

Reynolds, Clark. *The Fast Carriers: The Forging of an Air Navy* (1968).

Symonds, Craig L. *The Battle of Midway* (2011).

Toland, John. *But Not in Shame: The Six Months after Pearl Harbor* (1961).

Winslow, W. G. *The Fleet the Gods Forgot: The US Asiatic Fleet in World War II* (1982).

Wukovits, John. *Pacific Alamo: The Battle for Wake Island* (2005).

16 Offensive in the Pacific, 1943–1944

Buell, Thomas B. *The Quiet Warrior: A Biography of Admiral Raymond A. Spruance* (1974).

Goldberg, Harold J. *D-Day in the Pacific: The Battle of Saipan* (2007).

Morison, Samuel Eliot. *History of United States Naval Operations in World War II*, vol. 6: *Breaking the Bismarcks Barrier, 22 July 1942–1 May 1944* (1950).

Morison, Samuel Eliot. *History of United States Naval Operations in World War II*, vol. 8: *New Guinea and the Marianas, March 1944–August 1944* (1953).

Morison, Samuel Eliot. *History of United States Naval Operations in World War II*, vol. 12: *Leyte, June 1944–January 1945* (1961).

Potter, E. B. *Bull Halsey* (1985).

Potter, E. B. *Nimitz* (1976).

Thomas, Evan. *Sea of Thunder: Four Commanders and the Last Great Naval Campaign, 1941–1945* (2006).

Tillman, Barrett. *Clash of the Carriers: The True Story of the Marianas Turkey Shoot of World War II* (2005).

United States Marine Corps. *History of US Marine Corps Operations in World War II*, 5 vols. (1958–1971).

Willmott, H. P. *The Battle of Leyte Gulf: The Last Fleet Action* (2005).

Wukovits, John. *One Square Mile of Hell: The Battle for Tarawa.* (2006).

17 The Victory of Sea Power in the Pacific

Belote, James, and William Belote. *Typhoon of Steel: The Battle of Okinawa* (1970).

Blair, Clay, Jr. *Silent Victory: The US Submarine War against Japan* (1975).

Frank, Bemis M. *Okinawa: The Great Island Battle* (1978).

Frank, Richard B. *Downfall: The End of the Imperial Japanese Empire* (1999).

Holmes, W. J. *Undersea Victory: The Influence of Submarine Operations on the War in the Pacific* (1966).

Johnson, Ellis A., and David A. Katcher. *Mines against Japan* (1973).

Morison, Samuel Eliot. *The Two Ocean War: A Short History of the United States Navy in the Second World War* (1963).

Nalty, Bernard C., ed. *War in the Pacific: Pearl Harbor to Tokyo Bay* (1991).

Newcomb, Richard F. *Iwo Jima* (2002).

Ross, Bill D. *Iwo Jima: Legacy of Valor* (1985).

Sledge, E. B. *With the Old Breed: At Peleliu and Okinawa* (1981).

Spector, Ronald H. *Eagle against the Sun: The American War with Japan* (1985).

18 The Uneasy Transition, 1945–1953

Barlow, Jeffrey G. *Revolt of the Admirals: The Fight for Naval Aviation, 1945–1950* (1998).

Cagle, Malcom W., and Frank A. Manson. *The Sea War in Korea* (2000).

Estes, Kenneth W. *Into the Breach at Pusan: The 1st Provisional Marine Brigade in the Korean War* (2012).

Field, James A., Jr. *History of United States Naval Operations: Korea* (1962).

Keiser, Gordon W. *The US Marine Corps and Defense Unification 1944–47: The Politics of Survival* (1982).

La Bree, Clifton. *The Gentle Warrior: General Oliver Prince Smith, USMC* (2001).

Marolda, Edward J. *Ready Sea Power: A History of the US Seventh Fleet* (2012).

Millett, Allan R. *The War for Korea, 1950–1951: They Came from the North* (2010).

Nalty, Bernard C. *Long Passage to Korea: Black Sailors and the Integration of the US Navy* (2003).

Polmar, Norman. *Aircraft Carriers: A History of Carrier Aviation and Its influence on World Events*, vol. 2: *1946–2006* (2008).

Shaw, Henry I., Jr. *The United States Marines in North China 1945—1949* (1960).

Sheehy, Edward J. *The US Navy, the Mediterranean, and the Cold War, 1945–1947* (1992).

Winkler, David F. *Cold War at Sea: High-Seas Confrontation between the United States and the Soviet Union* (2000).

19 Cold War Challenges, 1953–1963

Bouchard, Joseph F. *Command in Crisis* (1991).

Bury, Helen. *Eisenhower and the Cold War Arms Race: "Open Skies" and the Military–Industrial Complex* (2014).

Divine, Robert A. *The Sputnik Challenge* (1993).

Gaddis, John Lewis. *The Cold War: A New History* (2005).

House, Jonathan M. *A Military History of the Cold War, 1944–1962* (2012).

Poole, Walter S. *Adapting to Flexible Response, 1960–1968* (2013).

Rockwell, Theodore. *The Rickover Effect: The Inside Story of How Adm. Hyman Rickover Built the Nuclear Navy* (1995).

Spinardi, Graham. *From Polaris to Trident: The Development of US Fleet Ballistic Missile Technology* (1994).

Szonyi, Michael. *Cold War Island: Quemoy on the Front Line* (2008).

Thompson, Neal. *Light This Candle: The Life and Times of Alan Shepard, America's First Spaceman* (2004).

Utz, Curtis A. *Cordon of Steel: The US Navy and the Cuban Missile Crisis* (1993).

20 The Test of Vietnam

Bradford, James C. "The Effects of the Vietnam War on the US Navy," in Malcolm Muir, Jr. and Mark F. Wilkinson, eds., *From Quagmire to Détente: The Cold War from 1963 to 1975* (2005).

Croizat, Victor J. *The Brown Water Navy: The River and Coastal War in Indo-China and Vietnam* (1984).

Cutler, Thomas J. *Brown Water, Black Berets: Coastal and Riverine Warfare in Vietnam* (1988).

Goldsmith, Wynn. *Papa Bravo Romeo: US Navy Patrol Boats at War in Vietnam* (2001).

Larzelere, Alex. *The Coast Guard at War: Vietnam, 1965–1975* (1997).

Marolda, Edward J. *By Sea, Air, and Land: An Illustrated History of the US Navy and the War in Southeast Asia* (1994).

Mersky, Peter. *The Naval Air War in Vietnam* (1981).

Schreadley, R. L. *From the Rivers to the Sea: The United States Navy in Vietnam* (1992).

Turley, William S. *The Second Indochina War: A Concise Political and Military History* (2009).

Uhlig, Frank, ed. *Vietnam: The Naval Story* (1986).

21 Twilight of the Cold War: Contraction, Reform, and Revival

Berman, Larry. *Zumwalt: The Life and Times of Admiral Elmo Russell "Bud" Zumwalt, Jr.* (2012).

Bolger, Daniel P. *Americans at War: 1975–1986, An Era of Violent Peace* (1988).

Duncan, Francis. *Rickover: The Struggle for Excellence* (2001).

Frank, Benis M. *US Marines in Lebanon, 1982–1984* (1987).

Gorshkov, Sergei G. *Red Star Rising at Sea* (1974).

Lehman, John R., Jr. *Command of the Seas* (1988).

Martin, David C., and John Walcott. *Best Laid Plans: The Inside Story of America's War against Terrorism* (1988).

Muir, Malcolm, Jr. *Black Shoes and Blue Water: Surface Warfare in the United States Navy, 1945–1975* (1996).

Palmer, Michael A. *Guardians of the Gulf: A History of America's Expanding Role in the Persian Gulf, 1833–1992* (1992).

Sheehy, Edward J. *The US Navy, the Mediterranean, and the Cold War* (1992).

Stanik, Joseph T. *El Dorado Canyon: Reagan's Undeclared War with Qaddafi* (2003).

Zumwalt, Elmo R., Jr. *On Watch: A Memoir* (1976).

22 Contours of Conflict: Worldwide War on Terrorism, 1990–2015

Estes, Kenneth W. *US Marine Corps Operations in Iraq, 2003–2006* (2009).

Estes, Kenneth W. *US Marines in Iraq, 2004–2005: Into the Fray* (2011).

Halley, Janet. *Don't: A Reader's Guide to the Military's Anti-Gay Policy* (1999).

Haynes, Peter D. *Toward a New Maritime Strategy: American Naval Thinking in the Post-Cold War Era* (2015).

Lehrack, Otto. *America's Battalion: Marines in the First Gulf War* (2005).

Lippold, Kirk S. *Front Burner: Al Qaeda's Attack on the USS Cole* (2012).

Lowry, Richard. *Marines in the Garden of Eden* (2006).

Pokrant, Marvin. *Desert Storm at Sea: What the Navy Really Did* (1999).

Schultz, Richard. *The Marines Take Anbar* (2013).

Williams, Scott. *The Battle of Al-Khafji* (2002).

Winkler, David F. *Amirs, Admirals & Desert Sailors: Bahrain, the US Navy, and the Arabian Gulf* (2007).

Wright, Lawrence. *The Looming Tower* (2006).

23 Quo Vadis?

Bousquet, Antoine J. *The Scientific Way of Warfare: Order and Chaos on the Battlefields of Modernity* (2009).

Clarke, Richard, and Robert K. Kanake. *Cyber War: The Next Threat to National Security and What to Do about It* (2010).

Cole, Bernard D. *The Great Wall at Sea: China's Navy in the 21st Century* (2010).

Danzig, Richard. *Surviving on a Diet of Poisoned Fruit: Reducing the National Security Risks of America's Cyber Dependencies* (2014).

Demchak, Chris, and Peter Dombrowski. "Cyber War, Cybered-Conflict and the Maritime Domain," *Naval War College Review*, 67:2 (Spring 2014), 71–96.

Hagerott, Mark R. "Robots, Cyber, History, and War," in Gérard de Boisboissel, Jean Paul Hanon, and Didier Danet, eds., *Robots on the Battlefield: Contemporary Issues and Implications for the Future* (2014).

Macris, Jeffrey, and Saul Kelly, eds. *Imperial Crossroads: The Great Powers and the Persian Gulf* (2012).

Rubel, Robert C. "National Policy and the Post Systemic Navy," *Naval War College Review*, 66:4 (Autumn 2013), 11–29.

Rushkoff, Douglas. *Present Shock: When Everything Happens Now* (2013).

Schmidt, Eric, and Jarod Cohen. *The New Digital Age: Reshaping the Future of People, Nations, and Businesses* (2013).

Singer, Peter W. *Wired for War: The Robotics Revolution and Conflict in the 21st Century* (2009).

Work, Robert O., and Shawn Brimley. *20YY: Preparing for War in the Robotic Age* (2014).

Index

Entries for figures and illustrations are in italics. "HMS" (His/Her Majesty's Navy) entered usage during the 1790s; warships prior to that time are denoted "Royal Navy" before their rating in guns — for example, *Serapis* (Royal Navy, 50). Continental Navy warships include their rating in guns. "USS" indicates a ship of the US Navy, "CSS" indicates a ship of the Confederate States Navy, and "HMAS" indicates a ship of the Royal Australian Navy.

America, Sea Power, and the World, First Edition. Edited by James C. Bradford.
© 2016 John Wiley & Sons, Inc. Published 2016 by John Wiley & Sons, Inc.